T0134769

Communications in Computer and Information Science   1752

More information about this series at https://link.springer.com/bookseries/7899

Irena Koprinska · Paolo Mignone ·
Riccardo Guidotti · Szymon Jaroszewicz ·
Holger Fröning · Francesco Gullo ·
Pedro M. Ferreira · Damian Roqueiro et al. (Eds.)

Machine Learning and Principles and Practice of Knowledge Discovery in Databases

International Workshops of ECML PKDD 2022
Grenoble, France, September 19–23, 2022
Proceedings, Part I

 Springer

For the full list of editors *see next page*

ISSN 1865-0929   ISSN 1865-0937 (electronic)
Communications in Computer and Information Science
ISBN 978-3-031-23617-4   ISBN 978-3-031-23618-1 (eBook)
https://doi.org/10.1007/978-3-031-23618-1

This Springer imprint is published by the registered company Springer Nature Switzerland AG
The registered company address is: Gewerbestrasse 11, 6330 Cham, Switzerland

Editors

Irena Koprinska (iD)
University of Sydney
Sydney, Australia

Paolo Mignone
University of Bari Aldo Moro
Bari, Italy

Riccardo Guidotti (iD)
University of Pisa
Pisa, Italy

Szymon Jaroszewicz
Warsaw University of Technology
Warsaw, Poland

Holger Fröning (iD)
Heidelberg University
Heidelberg, Germany

Francesco Gullo
UniCredit
Rome, Italy

Pedro M. Ferreira (iD)
University of Lisbon
Lisbon, Portugal

Damian Roqueiro
Roche
Basel, Switzerland

Gaia Ceddia
Barcelona Supercomputing Center
Barcelona, Spain

Slawomir Nowaczyk (iD)
Halmstad University
Halmstad, Sweden

João Gama (iD)
University of Porto
Porto, Portugal

Rita Ribeiro (iD)
University of Porto
Porto, Portugal

Ricard Gavaldà (iD)
UPC BarcelonaTech
Barcelona, Spain

Elio Masciari (iD)
University of Naples Federico II
Naples, Italy

Zbigniew Ras (iD)
University of North Carolina
Charlotte, USA

Ettore Ritacco
ICAR-CNR
Rende, Italy

Francesca Naretto
University of Pisa
Pisa, Italy

Andreas Theissler
Aalen University of Applied Sciences
Aalen, Germany

Przemyslaw Biecek (iD)
Warsaw University of Technology
Warszaw, Poland

Wouter Verbeke
KU Leuven
Leuven, Belgium

Gregor Schiele (iD)
University of Duisburg-Essen
Essen, Germany

Franz Pernkopf (iD)
Graz University of Technology
Graz, Austria

Michaela Blott
AMD
Dublin, Ireland

Ilaria Bordino
UniCredit
Rome, Italy

Ivan Luciano Danesi
UniCredit
Milan, Italy

Giovanni Ponti
National Agency for New Technologies
Rome, Italy

Lorenzo Severini
Unicredit
Rome, Italy

Giuseppina Andresini
University of Bari Aldo Moro
Bari, Italy

Guilherme Graça
University of Lisbon
Lisbon, Portugal

Naghmeh Ghazaleh
Roche
Basel, Switzerland

Diego Saldana
Novartis
Basel, Switzerland

Arif Canakoglu
Fondazione IRCCS Ca' Granda Ospedale
Maggiore Policlinico
Milan, Italy

Pietro Pinoli
Politecnico di Milano
Milan, Italy

Sepideh Pashami
Halmstad University
Halmstad, Sweden

Annalisa Appice
University of Bari Aldo Moro
Bari, Italy

Ibéria Medeiros
University of Lisbon
Lisbon, Portugal

Lee Cooper
Northwestern University
Chicago, USA

Jonas Richiardi
University of Lausanne
Lausanne, Switzerland

Konstantinos Sechidis
Novartis
Basel, Switzerland

Sara Pido
Politecnico di Milano
Milan, Italy

Albert Bifet
University of Waikato
Hamilton, New Zealand

Preface

The European Conference on Machine Learning and Principles and Practice of Knowledge Discovery in Databases (ECML PKDD) is the premier European conference on machine learning and data mining. In 2022, ECML PKDD took place in Grenoble, France during September 19–23.

The program included workshops on specialized topics held during the first and last day of the conference. This two-volume set includes the proceedings of the following workshops:

1. 7th Workshop on Data Science for Social Good (SoGood 2022)
2. 10th Workshop on New Frontiers in Mining Complex Patterns (NFMCP 2022)
3. 4th Workshop on eXplainable Knowledge Discovery in Data Mining (XKDD 2022)
4. 1st Workshop on Uplift Modeling (UMOD 2022)
5. 3rd Workshop on IoT, Edge and Mobile for Embedded Machine Learning (ITEM 2022)
6. 7th Workshop on Mining Data for Financial Application (MIDAS 2022)
7. 4th Workshop on Machine Learning for Cybersecurity (MLCS 2022)
8. 2nd Workshop on Machine Learning for Buildings Energy Management (MLBEM 2022)
9. 3rd Workshop on Machine Learning for Pharma and Healthcare Applications (PharML 2022)
10. 1st Workshop on Data Analysis in Life Science (DALS 2022)
11. 3rd Workshop on IoT Streams for Predictive Maintenance (IoT-PdM 2022)

Each workshop section contains the papers from the workshop and a preface from the organizers.

We would like to thank all participants and invited speakers, the Program Committees and reviewers, and the ECML PKDD conference and workshop chairs – thank you for making the workshops successful events. We are also grateful to Springer for their help in publishing the proceedings.

October 2022

Irena Koprinska
on behalf of the volume editors

Organization

ECML PKDD 2022 Workshop Chairs

Bruno Crémilleux   Université de Caen Normandie, France
Charlotte Laclau   Télécom Paris, France

SoGood 2022 Chairs

João Gama   University of Porto, Portugal
Irena Koprinska   University of Sydney, Australia
Rita P. Ribeiro   University of Porto, Portugal
Ricard Gavaldà   BarcelonaTech, Spain

NFMCP 2022 Chairs

Elio Masciari   University Federico II of Naples, Italy
Paolo Mignone   University of Bari Aldo Moro, Italy
Zbigniew W. Ras   University of North Carolina, USA
Ettore Ritacco   ICAR-CNR, Italy

XKDD 2022 Chairs

Riccardo Guidotti   University of Pisa, Italy
Francesca Naretto   Scuola Normale Superiore, Italy
Andreas Theissler   Aalen University of Applied Sciences, Germany
Przemysław Biecek   Warsaw University of Technology, Poland

UMOD 2022 Chairs

Szymon Jaroszewicz   Polish Academy of Sciences and Warsaw University of Technology, Poland
Wouter Verbeke   KU Leuven, Belgium

ITEM 2022 Chairs

Holger Fröning   Heidelberg University, Germany
Gregor Schiele   University of Duisburg-Essen, Germany
Franz Pernkopf   Graz University of Technology, Austria
Michaela Blott   AMD, Dublin, Ireland

MIDAS 2022 Chairs

Ilaria Bordino	UniCredit, Italy
Ivan Luciano Danesi	UniCredit, Italy
Francesco Gullo	UniCredit, Italy
Giovanni Ponti	ENEA, Italy
Lorenzo Severini	UniCredit, Italy

MLCS 2022 Chairs

Pedro M. Ferreira	University of Lisbon, Portugal
Annalisa Appice	University of Bari, Italy
Giuseppina Andresini	University of Bari, Italy
Ibéria Medeiros	University of Lisbon, Portugal

MLBEM 2022 Chairs

Pedro M. Ferreira	University of Lisbon, Portugal
Guilherme Graça	University of Lisbon, Portugal

PharML 2022 Chairs

Damian Roqueiro	Roche, Basel, Switzerland
Lee Cooper	Northwestern University, USA
Naghmeh Ghazaleh	Roche, Basel, Switzerland
Jonas Richiardi	Lausanne University Hospital and University of Lausanne, Switzerland
Diego Saldana	Novartis, Basel, Switzerland
Konstantinos Sechidis	Novartis, Basel, Switzerland

DALS 2022 Chairs

Gaia Ceddia	Barcelona Supercomputing Center, Spain
Arif Canakoglu	Fondazione IRCCS Ca' Granda Ospedale Maggiore Policlinico, Milan, Italy
Sara Pido	Massachusetts Institute of Technology, USA, and Politecnico di Milano, Italy
Pietro Pinoli	Politecnico di Milano, Italy

IoT-PdM 2022 Chairs

Joao Gama	University of Porto, Portugal
Albert Bifet	Telecom-Paris, Paris, France, and University of Waikato, New Zealand
Sławomir Nowaczyk	Halmstad University, Sweden
Sepideh Pashami	Halmstad University, Sweden

Contents – Part I

Workshop on eXplainable Knowledge Discovery in Data Mining (XKDD 2022)

Workshop on Uplift Modeling (UMOD 2022)

**Workshop on IoT, Edge and Mobile for Embedded Machine Learning
(ITEM 2022)**

Contents – Part II

Workshop on Data Analysis in Life Science (DALS 2022)

**3rd Workshop and Tutorial on Streams for Predictive Maintenance
(IoT-PdM 2022)**

Workshop on Data Science for Social Good (SoGood 2022)

Workshop on Data Science for Social Good (SoGood 2022)

The Seventh Workshop on Data Science for Social Good (SoGood 2022) was held in conjunction with the European Conference on Machine Learning and Principles and Practice of Knowledge Discovery in Databases (ECML PKDD 2022) on September 23, 2022, in Grenoble, France. The previous six editions of the workshop were also held jointly with ECML PKDD in 2016–2021.

The possibilities of using data science for contributing to social, common, or public good are often not sufficiently perceived by the public at large. Data science applications are already helping people at the bottom of the economic pyramid or people with special needs, improving healthcare systems, reinforcing international cooperation, and dealing with environmental problems, disasters, and climate change. In regular conferences and journals, papers on these topics are often scattered among sessions with names that hide their common nature (such as "Social Networks", "Predictive Models", or the catch-all term "Applications"). Additionally, such forums tend to have a strong bias for papers that are novel in the strictly technical sense (new algorithms, new kinds of data analysis, new technologies) rather than novel in terms of the social impact of the application.

This workshop aims to attract papers presenting applications of data science for social good (which may or may not require new methods), or applications that consider social aspects of data science methods and techniques. It also aims to bring together researchers, students, and practitioners to share their experience and foster discussion about possible applications, challenges, and open research problems, and to continue building a research community in the area of data science for social good.

There are numerous application domains; the call for papers included the following non-exclusive list of topics:

- Government transparency and IT against corruption
- Public safety and disaster relief
- Access to food, water, sanitation, and utilities
- Efficiency and sustainability
- Climate change
- Data journalism
- Social and personal development
- Economic growth and improved infrastructure
- Transportation
- Energy
- Smart city services
- Education
- Social services, unemployment, and homelessness
- Healthcare and well-being
- Support for people living with disabilities
- Responsible consumption and production

- Gender and racial equality
- Ethical issues, fairness, and accountability
- Trustability and interpretability
- Topics aligned with the UN development goals

The workshop papers were selected through a XX blind peer-review process in which each submitted paper was assigned to three members of the Program Committee. The main selection criteria were the novelty of the application and its social impact. Out of the XX submission received for SoGood 2022, 13 papers were accepted – eight for oral presentation and five for poster presentation.

The SoGood 2022 Best Paper Award was awarded to Tito Griné and Carla Teixeira Lopes for their paper "A Social Media Tool for Domain-Specific Information Retrieval - A Case Study in Human Trafficking". The award selection committee included Anne Laurent (University of Montpellier, France), Rafael Morales-Bueno (University of Malaga, Spain), and André de Carvalho (University of São Paulo, Brazil).

The program included a keynote talk by Virginia Dignum (Umeå University, Sweden) on "Responsible AI: From Principles to Action". More information about the workshop can be found on the workshop website: https://sites.google.com/view/ecmlpkddsogood2022/.

Many people contributed to making this workshop a successful event. We would like to thank Virginia Dignum for her excellent talk, the Program Committee members for their detailed and constructive reviews, the authors for their well-prepared presentations, and all workshop attendees for their engagement and participation.

October 2022

João Gama
Irena Koprinska
Rita P. Ribeiro
Ricard Gavaldà

Organization

Workshop Co-chairs

João Gama   University of Porto, Portugal
Irena Koprinska   University of Sydney, Australia
Rita P. Ribeiro   University of Porto, Portugal
Ricard Gavaldà   BarcelonaTech, Spain

Publicity Chair

Carlos Ferreira   INESC TEC, Portugal

Program Committee

Thiago Andrade	INESC TEC, Portugal
Cédric Bhihé	Barcelona Supercomputing Center, Spain
José Del Campo-Ávila	University of Málaga, Spain
André de Carvalho	University of São Paulo, Brazil
Elaine Faria	Federal University of Uberlandia, Brazil
Carlos Ferreira	University of Porto, Portugal
Cèsar Ferri	Technical University of Valencia, Spain
Sérgio Jesus	Feedzai, Portugal
Konstantin Kutzkov	Amalfi Analytics, Spain
Ana Lorena	Technological Institute of Aeronautics, Brazil
Anne Laurent	University of Montpellier, France
Rafael Morales-Bueno	University of Malaga, Spain
Ana Nogueira	INESC TEC, Portugal
Slawomir Nowaczyk	Halmstad University, Sweden
Maria Pedroto	INESC TEC, Portugal
Bernhard Pfahringer	University of Waikato, New Zealand
Solange Rezende	University of São Paulo, Brazil
Nirbhaya Shaji	INESC TEC, Portugal
Sónia Teixeira	INESC TEC, Portugal
Emma Tonkin	University of Bristol, UK
Alicia Troncoso	Pablo de Olavide University, Spain
Aleix Ruiz de Villa	Freelance Data Scientist
Kristina Yordanova	University of Rostock, Germany
Martí Zamora	BarcelonaTech, Spain

SoGood 2022 Keynote Talk

Responsible AI: From Principles to Action

Virginia Dignum

Department of Computer Science, Umeå University, Sweden

Abstract. Every day we see news about advances and the societal impact of AI. AI is changing the way we work, live and solve challenges but concerns about fairness, transparency or privacy are also growing. Ensuring AI ethics is more than designing systems whose result can be trusted. It is about the way we design them, why we design them, and who is involved in designing them. In order to develop and use AI responsibly, we need to work towards technical, societal, institutional and legal methods and tools which provide concrete support to AI practitioners, as well as awareness and training to enable participation of all, to ensure the alignment of AI systems with our societies' principles and values.

Biography

Virginia Dignum is Professor of Responsible Artificial Intelligence at Umeå University, Sweden and associated with the TU Delft in the Netherlands. She is the director of WASP-HS, the Wallenberg Program on Humanities and Society for AI, Autonomous Systems and Software, the largest Swedish national research program on fundamental multidisciplinary research on the societal and human impact of AI.

She is a member of the Royal Swedish Academy of Engineering Sciences, and a Fellow of the European Artificial Intelligence Association (EURAI). Her current research focus is on the specification, verification and monitoring of ethical and societal principles for intelligent autonomous systems. She is committed to policy and awareness efforts towards the responsible development and use of AI, as member of the European Commission High Level Expert Group on Artificial Intelligence, the Global Partnership on AI (GPAI), the World Economic Forum's Global Artificial Intelligence Council, lead for UNICEF's guidance for AI and children, the Executive Committee of the IEEE Initiative on Ethically Aligned Design, and as founding member of ALLAI, the Dutch AI Alliance.

Her book "Responsible Artificial Intelligence: developing and using AI in a responsible way" was published by Springer Nature in 2019. She studied at the University of Lisbon and the Free University of Amsterdam and obtained a PhD in Artificial Intelligence from Utrecht University in 2004.

Gender Stereotyping Impact in Facial Expression Recognition

Iris Dominguez-Catena$^{(\boxtimes)}$ (iD), Daniel Paternain (iD), and Mikel Galar (iD)

Institute of Smart Cities (ISC), Department of Statistics,
Computer Science and Mathematics, Public University of Navarre (UPNA),
Arrosadia Campus, 31006 Pamplona, Spain
{iris.dominguez,mikel.galar,daniel.paternain}@unavarra.es

Abstract. Facial Expression Recognition (FER) uses images of faces to identify the emotional state of users, allowing for a closer interaction between humans and autonomous systems. Unfortunately, as the images naturally integrate some demographic information, such as apparent age, gender, and race of the subject, these systems are prone to demographic bias issues. In recent years, machine learning-based models have become the most popular approach to FER. These models require training on large datasets of facial expression images, and their generalization capabilities are strongly related to the characteristics of the dataset. In publicly available FER datasets, apparent gender representation is usually mostly balanced, but their representation in the individual label is not, embedding social stereotypes into the datasets and generating a potential for harm. Although this type of bias has been overlooked so far, it is important to understand the impact it may have in the context of FER. To do so, we use a popular FER dataset, FER+, to generate derivative datasets with different amounts of stereotypical bias by altering the gender proportions of certain labels. We then proceed to measure the discrepancy between the performance of the models trained on these datasets for the apparent gender groups. We observe a discrepancy in the recognition of certain emotions between genders of up to 29% under the worst bias conditions. Our results also suggest a safety range for stereotypical bias in a dataset that does not appear to produce stereotypical bias in the resulting model. Our findings support the need for a thorough bias analysis of public datasets in problems like FER, where a global balance of demographic representation can still hide other types of bias that harm certain demographic groups.

1 Introduction

The development of technology in the last decades, especially in Machine Learning (ML) and Artificial Intelligence (AI), has exposed an ever-growing portion of the population to autonomous systems. These systems, from the mundane autocorrector in mobile devices to the critical autopilot in self-driving cars, impact the lives of people around the world. Despite their continuous improvement in

© The Author(s), under exclusive license to Springer Nature Switzerland AG 2023
I. Koprinska et al. (Eds.): ECML PKDD 2022 Workshops, CCIS 1752, pp. 9–22, 2023.
https://doi.org/10.1007/978-3-031-23618-1_1

all respects, this impact is not always positive. A point of particular concern is when the mistakes our AI systems make systematically harm certain demographic groups. We call this behavior an unwanted bias. Unwanted biases can be based on several demographic characteristics, the most common being age, sex, and race [10,19,25].

These biases have been studied and classified into many types according to the stage of the ML life cycle from which they originate [29]. Although all sources of bias must be taken into account to develop fair systems, dataset bias has gained special relevance in the last decade. For many ML applications, Deep Learning algorithms that use large amounts of data have become the standard approach [6]. This has led to the creation of large public datasets and to the decoupling of the dataset creation and model training phases. These datasets, despite their usefulness, many times exhibit heavy biases [25] that are easy to overlook for the teams using them. These dataset biases can be found in the demographic proportions of the datasets [18], in the relationships between data of multimodal datasets [8,33], in the sample labeling and the label themselves [25], and even in the images of the dataset [31]. A specific type of bias, the topic of this work, is stereotypical bias [1], where demographic groups can be equally represented but over or underrepresented in certain categories.

The impact of these biases on the predictions of the final model is highly variable, depending on both the severity and nature of the biases and the context of the application itself. For applications that involve human users, especially when the implementation of the system regulates access to resources or involves the representation of people, unfair predictions can directly lead to harm to population groups [5,19] (allocative and representational harms).

A current area of interest in AI is Facial Expression Recognition (FER) [22]. FER refers to a modality of automatic emotion recognition in which, from a picture of a face, the system predicts the emotional state of the subject. The readiness for implementation, possible with minimal hardware, combined with the nature of the data involved, makes FER an application where biases are easily developed and could potentially lead to representational harms. Furthermore, the face images have some demographic information naturally integrated into them, such as apparent age, gender, or race. With most datasets lacking explicit external demographic labels, bias mitigation techniques are hard to apply, and even bias detection poses a challenge. Regarding gender in particular, although public FER datasets are usually globally balanced, with similar proportions of male and female presenting people, they often hide stereotypical biases. That is, they are unbalanced for certain categories, despite the global balance, which can systematically skew the final model predictions depending on the subject's apparent gender.

In this work, we analyze stereotypical gender bias in the context of FER. In particular, we focus on the FER+ dataset [6], a refined version of the popular FER2013 dataset [16]. With this dataset as the base, in our experiments we generate derivative datasets with different amounts of stereotypical bias by altering the gender proportions of certain labels and measuring the variations in the final model predictions. These induced biases allow us to quantify the limits of the variations under extreme stereotypical bias conditions in FER problems. Although previous work [2,12–14,32] has also studied and revealed biases in general and gender biases in particular in FER, no other work has focused on the problem of stereotypical biases in this context. We hope that our contribution will help establish the importance of this type of bias and understand the extent of its impact in this context.

From our results, we observe a discrepancy in the recognition of certain emotions between genders of up to 29% under the worst bias conditions. Our results also suggest a safety range for stereotypical bias in the dataset that does not appear to produce bias in the final model. These findings can help future implementations avoid some potential harms in FER due to misrepresentation of groups.

The remainder of this work is organized as follows. Section 2 describes the related work and some background information for our proposal. Next, Sect. 3 describes the proposed experiments and the relevant implementation details. In Sect. 4 presents and analyzes the results of the experiments. Finally, Sect. 5 concludes this work and proposes future work.

2 Related Work

2.1 Facial Expression Recognition

FER is one of the simplest and most widespread modalities of the more general automatic emotion recognition. In automatic emotion recognition, the system tries to identify the emotional state of a person from their expressions and physiology. Several modalities are possible, depending on both the input data required by the system and the output codification of the emotional state [3]. FER, in particular, uses as input data a static image or a video of a human face, making it relatively easy to deploy with minimal hardware.

Regarding the emotion codification, the classical approaches are continuous [23] and discrete models of emotion [15]. The continuous model separates emotion into several independent dimensions, such as *valence* and *arousal*. Instead, the discrete model assimilates emotions into several prototypes, with the most common categorization being the six basic emotions of Ekman [15]: angry, disgust, fear, happiness, sadness, and surprise. Although the continuous codification is more expressive, the labeling of samples is more subjective and complex. Thus, most FER datasets are based on the discrete approach. In this work, we will focus on the same discrete approach.

2.2 Bias

Most definitions of fairness are based on the idea of absence of unwanted bias [30]. This unwanted bias, understood as a systematic variation in the treatment of a demographic group that can potentially lead to harm.

Although most definitions of bias as a proxy for fairness are designed around the predictions of a model, the general concept of bias can be linked to different sources of bias at different points of the ML life cycle [29]. In particular, for applications in ML where public datasets are common, bias present in the source data is particularly relevant [24]. Large datasets, in particular, have been subject to extensive analysis, finding different types of bias [11,25].

While data bias is predominantly studied in the form of representational bias, where certain demographic groups are overly prevalent in a dataset, another common bias in some types of datasets is *stereotypical bias* [1,9]. In classification tasks, this kind of bias is modeled as a correlation between the demographic attributes of a subject and the problem classes, and can easily leak into the datasets as different demographic profiles for certain classes.

Some works have already analyzed FER systems, finding demographic bias in general [17,20], including several instances of gender biases [2,12–14]. In particular, Ahmad et al. [2] analyzes the prediction of commercial systems, without working with the bias in the original datasets. Domnich and Anbarjafari [14] study the gender bias exhibited by six different neural networks trained for FER. Deuschel et al. [12] employ intentionally biased datasets, composed only of male or female subjects, to study the impact of these biases on the detection of action units, a problem closely related to FER. Finally, Dominguez et al. [13] also uses intentionally biased and balanced datasets to validate a set of metrics for bias detection, using FER as a case study and showing inherent representational and stereotypical biases in some FER datasets.

Unlike the previous work, we will focus on the stereotypical bias in FER. We will employ progressively biased datasets to measure the impact of this type of bias on the trained model. Bias is often measured with specific bias metrics, which helps quantify its impact. Despite this, it is important to notice that any application of a specific metric still requires a proper qualitative discussion of its context, or it can easily lose its usefulness [26]. For this reason, in this work, we will employ a qualitative and intuitive approach without employing a specific metric. Nonetheless, we will look for deviations in recalls (accuracy constrained to the examples of a certain class) between demographic groups, with an underlying notion of fairness consistent with the *conditional use accuracy equality* [7]. To the best of our knowledge, no other work on FER has focused on this type of bias, and most have only focused on representational bias.

3   Methodology

3.1   Datasets

In this work, we employ the FER+ dataset [16], based on FER2013 [16]. FER2013 [16] is one of the most popular publicly available *in the wild* FER datasets, with more than $32,000$ labeled images obtained from Internet searches. The images in the original dataset were automatically annotated, leading to systematic inaccuracies, which were later corrected by FER+ [6], a relabeling of the same image set. The images in FER+ are grayscale and have a small resolution of 48 × 48 pixels. This small image size supports fast and resource-light model training, one of the main reasons for its popularity.

3.2   Demographic Relabeling

As FER2013 is not gender labelled, we use an external model, FairFace [18] to obtain an apparent gender prediction for each image. The FairFace model was trained on the homonymous dataset, composed of 108, 501 images labeled for apparent gender, apparent race, and apparent age. In the original experiments, the model achieved an accuracy greater than 92% for gender recognition in FairFace and three other demographic datasets. The model is publicly available[1].

It is important to note that FairFace comes with some serious limitations. Although this is particularly evident in the race categories, limited to six stereotypical groups, namely White, Black, East Asian, Southeast Asian, Latino, Indian, and Middle Eastern, it is also present in the gender category. For the creation of FairFace, as is still common for most gender-labeled datasets, external annotators manually labeled gender into a binary classification of *Male* and *Female*. This classification correlates with how many societies identify gender, but can easily misrepresent people, as is the case for binary and non-binary transgender people and other gender non-conforming individuals [19]. Nevertheless, as almost no datasets have the required demographic information, proxy labels such as the ones provided by FairFace give us a reasonable overview of the population of the datasets, even if they could be unreliable for the individual subjects. Additionally, as the real demographic information is also unknown to the trained FER models, if bias is present in them it must be based only on the physical appearance. Thus, we perform our analysis on these labels, as they can help uncover biases based on these apparent demographic characteristics, even if they do not always correlate with the true self-reported characteristics. Any bias based on the apparent characteristics predicted by the auxiliary model must be considered under these limitations, and further work must be done to test if the bias is still present when we consider the real demographic characteristics.

3.3   Generation of Derivative Datasets

To study the impact of stereotypical bias, we generate three types of datasets, namely, stratified, balanced, and biased. All of these are created as subsets from the original FER+ dataset.

Stratified Subsets. To enable the comparison between different datasets, we implement a method to generate stratified subsets from a source dataset with a given target size, expressed as a ratio $r \in [0, 1]$ of the number of examples in the original dataset. To generate a stratified version, we consider both the set of target classification labels $L = \{angry, disgust, fear, happy, sad, surprise, neutral\}$,

---

[1] https://github.com/joojs/fairface.

and the demographic groups of interest, in our case $S = \{male, female\}$ and their combinations defined by the Cartesian product $L \times S$. For each of these combinations independently, we perform a random subsample with target ratio r. This process guarantees that the relative proportions between each label in L, the demographic group in S, or the combination of both in $L \times S$ are kept, while the overall size is reduced by the desired ratio r (plus or minus some rounding error). Thus, the stratified datasets maintain the same stereotypical deviations and general demographic proportions as the source data set.

Balanced Subsets. As the original FER+ dataset already contains some stereotypical bias [13], we generate a balanced version of it to serve as a general baseline. This dataset has the same proportions of each label in L as the original FER+, but for each of them, the proportions of the demographic groups in S are equalized. To generate this balanced dataset, we first calculate the most underrepresented group $(l, s) \in L \times S$ by calculating the imbalance ratio of each one in their respective label l:

$$\text{imb}(l, s) = \frac{|\{x | x \in D_l \text{ and } x \in D_s\}|}{|\{x | x \in D_l\}|} , \tag{1}$$

where D_l denotes the subset of the dataset samples labeled with l and D_s the subset identified as part of the demographic group s.

After this, we subsample each of the groups independently according to:

$$\text{ratio}(l, s) = \frac{\min_{l' \in L, s' \in S} \text{imb}(l', s')}{\text{imb}(l, s)} . \tag{2}$$

The resulting dataset keeps the distribution of the target labels while making the demographic groups in each label and in the whole dataset equally represented.

Biased Subsets. Finally, we also generate intentionally stereotypically biased datasets. These datasets are built from the balanced datasets, but inducing a certain amount of bias into one of the labels l with respect to a target demographic group s. The amount of induced bias $b \in [-1, 1]$ is applied as:

- If $b < 0$, a negative bias is introduced, that is, the target demographic group $\{x | x \in D_l \text{ and } x \in D_s\}$ is reduced by the ratio $1 + b$. The examples labeled as l belonging to the other demographic groups are kept intact.
- If $b > 0$, a positive bias is introduced, that is, the target demographic group is left intact, reducing the representation of the rest of the samples $\{x | x \in D_l \text{ and } x \notin D_s\}$ by the ratio $1 - b$.
- If $b = 0$, the balanced dataset is not modified, and no bias is introduced.

After biasing the target label l, the resulting number of examples of that label is $1 - \frac{|b|}{2}$ of the original label support. To compensate for this effect, the other labels are also subsampled by the ratio $1 - \frac{|b|}{2}$. This reduces the final dataset size, but keeps the label distribution equal to the original dataset.

The resulting dataset has, for $b = -1$ a total absence of the target demographic group in the label (underrepresentation), for $b = 1$ only samples of the target demographic group in the label (overrepresentation), and for $b = 0$ is balanced. The intermediate values allow for fine control of the amount of bias. In all cases, the label distribution is kept identical to the original dataset.

3.4 Experiments

In our experiments, we aim to generate biased datasets in the extremes of the stereotypical bias possibilities and then measure the final model accuracy imbalances for the relevant demographic groups and labels. For this, we first obtain the demographic profile of FER+ in the gender category. With this information, we chose some of the more heavily biased labels and generate datasets that exaggerate those same biases. The biased datasets are generated with different degrees of bias, from a negative bias of -1 to a positive one of 1 in steps of 0.2, all of them with respect to the "female" class as recognized by FairFace. The balanced datasets will serve as a baseline, showing the behavior expected in the absence of stereotypical bias for a certain dataset size.

To analyze the influence of the datasets on the performance of the model, we train a model for each generated dataset and obtain the predictions over the whole FER+ test partition. We then obtain the recall for each combination of dataset, label, and gender group, that is, the accuracy of the classifier for the examples belonging to the specific gender group and with a certain true label. In particular, we expect to obtain the maximum difference in recall between the demographic categories *male* and *female* in the extreme biased datasets for the biased labels, as a measure of the maximum impact of stereotypical bias on the recognition of the affected labels.

3.5 Experimental Setup

We employ a simple VGG11 [27] network with no pretraining as the base test model. This is a classical convolutional architecture often used as a baseline for machine learning applications. The experiments are developed on PyTorch 1.10.0 and Fastai 2.6.3. The hardware used is a machine equipped with a GeForce RTX 2060 Super GPU, 20 GB of RAM, an Intel® Xeon® i5-8500 CPU, and running Ubuntu Linux 20.04.

All the models are trained under the same conditions and hyperparameters, namely, a maximum learning rate of $1e^{-2}$ with a 1cycle policy (as described in [28] and implemented in Fastai) for 20 iterations. This parameter was decided using the *lr_finder* tool in Fastai. The batch size is set to 256, the maximum allowed by the hardware setup. For each dataset, we train the model 10 times and average the results over them. We have also applied the basic data augmentation provided by Fastai through the *aug_transforms* method, including left-right flipping, warping, rotation, zoom, brightness, and contrast alterations.

For each dataset configuration to be tested, we perform ten individual training processes, for each one regenerating a new resampled dataset to ensure that the sampling process does not affect the final results.

4 Results and Discussion

4.1 Dataset Initial Bias

We perform the demographic relabeling of FER+ with the FairFace public model, as described in Sect. 3.2. The proportions of the gender category in the whole dataset and for each label are shown in Fig. 1, together with the label supports. The global gender proportions are almost uniform, at 50.1% for the *Female* group and 49.9% for the *Male* group, showing very little direct representational bias. For stereotypical bias, the individual labels show a much greater disparity. The two extremes are the label *angry*, with an underrepresentation of the *Female* group (36.27% of the label support) and the label *happy*, with an underrepresentation of the *Male* group (38.7% of the label support). The rest of the labels in the dataset lie in between, with slightly lower imbalances.

Interestingly, the biases found in the labels *happy* and *angry* are consistent with the classical *angry-men-happy-women* bias, a psychological bias pattern well researched in the expression and recognition of human emotions [4, 21].

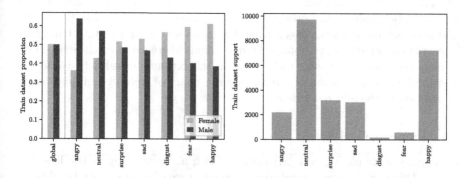

Fig. 1. FER+ gender distribution and support by label.

4.2 Induced Bias Impact

The recall results obtained by the models are shown in Table 1. For brevity, only the results for the four most extremely biased datasets and the size-equivalent stratified balanced dataset are reported in the Table, with the complete results being graphically presented in Fig. 2. The difference between gender recalls is highest for the biased datasets in all cases, with the largest absolute difference found in the labels *angry*, *disgust*, and *happy*. In particular, for the *angry* label, biasing against the *Female* group maximizes the recall difference at 29.36% in favor of the *Male* group, while for the *happy* label it is the positive bias in favor of the *Female* group that maximizes the difference at 15.03%. Biasing the *angry* label generates a total range of disparity of 49.53% between its extremes, while biasing the *happy* label of 26.17%.

The label *disgust* seems to be a particular case, with the largest recall differences between the gender groups overall. Difference values range from a 8.33% difference to a 23.92% difference, always in favor of the *Male* group. Recall that none of the biased datasets are designed to bias in this label, that is kept balanced in all the derivative datasets, and even in the original dataset exhibits only a mild stereotypical bias against the *Male* group, which constitutes a 43.25% of the original support. However, this label also has the lowest support in the original FER+ dataset, with the lowest general recalls of all labels for all configurations. The label *disgust* also shows the highest standard deviation, between ±10.22 and ±16.83, making the results for this label unreliable.

The rest of the labels show some variations in general, but generally seem unaffected by the bias induced in *angry* and *happy*. An exception seems to be in the application of the positive bias in the *happy* label, overrepresenting the *female* group for that label, which seems to decrease the recall for the *angry* label of the same group.

Table 1. Recall by label and gender for the key datasets analyzed. For the difference between gender recalls, the highest absolute value is in bold.

		Happy			Angry		
		Female −1.00	Female 0.00	Female +1.00	Female −1.00	Female 0.00	Female +1.00
	Size	9475	9476	9475	9477	9476	9477
angry	Male	74.40 ± 1.47	76.30 ± 3.40	74.24 ± 4.73	**81.25 ± 2.61**	76.30 ± 3.40	55.87 ± 2.24
	Female	74.53 ± 3.45	73.21 ± 3.33	67.74 ± 3.34	51.89 ± 3.77	73.21 ± 3.33	**76.04 ± 1.99**
	Diff	0.13 ± 3.75	−3.10 ± 4.76	−6.50 ± 5.79	**−29.36 ± 4.59**	−3.10 ± 4.76	20.17 ± 2.99
neutral	Male	66.45 ± 3.10	71.52 ± 2.71	67.24 ± 4.66	70.72 ± 1.84	71.52 ± 2.71	**74.91 ± 1.66**
	Female	66.33 ± 2.77	67.29 ± 3.00	64.86 ± 3.79	67.99 ± 2.48	67.29 ± 3.00	**68.85 ± 1.26**
	Diff	−0.12 ± 4.15	−4.22 ± 4.04	−2.38 ± 6.01	−2.73 ± 3.09	−4.22 ± 4.04	**−6.06 ± 2.09**
surprise	Male	80.50 ± 3.91	83.71 ± 2.58	81.93 ± 3.16	82.77 ± 2.32	83.71 ± 2.58	**84.16 ± 1.71**
	Female	83.46 ± 3.06	84.88 ± 2.67	84.83 ± 2.51	**87.22 ± 2.75**	84.88 ± 2.67	86.29 ± 1.87
	Diff	2.97 ± 4.97	1.17 ± 3.71	2.90 ± 4.03	**4.45 ± 3.60**	1.17 ± 3.71	2.13 ± 2.54
sad	Male	62.22 ± 3.71	66.82 ± 1.53	66.88 ± 3.90	**69.66 ± 2.53**	66.82 ± 1.53	69.55 ± 2.69
	Female	67.88 ± 2.71	70.33 ± 2.30	68.91 ± 3.26	**74.29 ± 2.25**	70.33 ± 2.30	68.59 ± 2.72
	Diff	**5.66 ± 4.60**	3.51 ± 2.76	2.04 ± 5.09	4.63 ± 3.39	3.51 ± 2.76	−0.96 ± 3.82
disgust	Male	51.25 ± 16.01	45.00 ± 9.19	**61.25 ± 11.46**	56.88 ± 9.86	45.00 ± 9.19	56.25 ± 12.18
	Female	35.33 ± 5.21	36.67 ± 4.47	37.33 ± 6.11	**44.67 ± 7.33**	36.67 ± 4.47	40.00 ± 7.30
	Diff	−15.92 ± 16.83	−8.33 ± 10.22	**−23.92 ± 12.98**	−12.21 ± 12.29	−8.33 ± 10.22	−16.25 ± 14.20
fear	Male	66.25 ± 5.73	65.83 ± 4.86	**68.75 ± 4.66**	56.67 ± 7.73	65.83 ± 4.86	59.58 ± 7.23
	Female	59.76 ± 3.76	58.33 ± 4.16	57.14 ± 5.11	**60.95 ± 5.02**	58.33 ± 4.16	55.48 ± 6.21
	Diff	−6.49 ± 6.85	−7.50 ± 6.40	**−11.61 ± 6.91**	4.29 ± 9.21	−7.50 ± 6.40	−4.11 ± 9.53
happy	Male	89.10 ± 2.46	87.66 ± 2.23	72.91 ± 3.47	87.90 ± 2.11	87.66 ± 2.23	**89.79 ± 1.71**
	Female	77.96 ± 1.86	87.75 ± 2.14	87.94 ± 1.87	**88.42 ± 1.89**	87.75 ± 2.14	88.02 ± 1.48
	Diff	−11.14 ± 3.09	0.09 ± 3.09	**15.03 ± 3.94**	0.52 ± 2.83	0.09 ± 3.09	−1.77 ± 2.26

The difference between the recalls of the *male* and *female* groups for each degree of induced bias is shown in Fig. 2. In the Figure, the vertical axis corresponds to the difference in recall from the *female* group to the *male* group, and the horizontal axis corresponds to the amount of induced bias. The difference of recall obtained in the balanced datasets is included as the comparison baseline.

For all labels, if no bias is introduced on that particular label, the recall differences are close to the baseline levels. When observing the differences in the recall of the affected label for the biased datasets, the effect of the dataset bias becomes apparent. For both the *angry* and *happy* labels, the negative biases, which correspond to an under-representation of the *female* group on the label, show a difference in recall in favor of the *male* group, and the opposite is observed for positive amounts of bias. For the datasets biased in the *angry* label with a

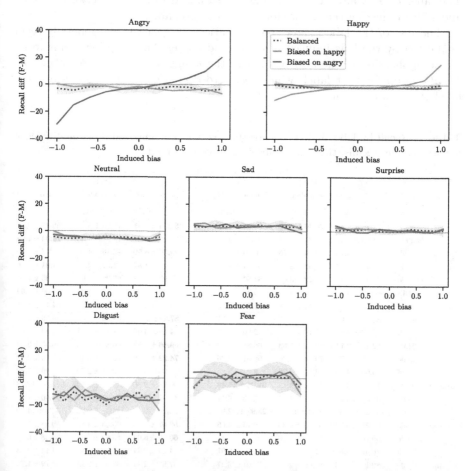

Fig. 2. Recall difference Male-Female in the different emotion labels. Positive numbers mean a higher recall for the *Female* group than for the *Male* one. The baseline balanced datasets are plotted according to size, aligned with the corresponding biased datasets.

negative or positive bias for the *female* group, the difference in recalls of the *angry* label quickly deviates from baseline levels when exposed to a bias of ± 0.2 or greater, exceeding $\pm 20\%$ of difference under extreme bias conditions. For the label *happy*, the effect is not as pronounced and only when trained on datasets with bias of ± 0.4 or higher does the difference in recalls deviate from the baseline behavior.

For both the labels *angry* and *happy*, a safe zone can be observed where bias in the dataset does not significantly affect the difference in recalls. The behavior of the biased model when trained under this limited amount of bias seems to be similar to the baseline dataset. In the case of the label *happy*, this safe zone includes the datasets with a stereotypical bias of ± 0.4 and lower, while on *angry* it is more restricted, including only those with a stereotypical bias of ± 0.2 and lower.

5   Conclusion

In this work, we have studied the impact of stereotypical bias in FER datasets and their resulting models through the induction of controlled bias in the dataset. In particular, for the FER problem, we have observed up to a 29% disparity in the recognition of certain emotions, namely *angry*, when the dataset lacks representation of a gender category for the label. We have shown that this kind of bias is already present in publicly available datasets, in particular in FER+, but our experiments suggest that a small amount of stereotypical bias in the gender category seems acceptable, not impacting the final performance for the underrepresented group. Nevertheless, it is important to notice that the acceptable amount of stereotypical bias seems to be context-dependent, varying at least between labels. Our findings support the importance of a thorough bias analysis of public datasets in problems like FER, where a global balance of demographic representation in the dataset can still hide other types of bias that harm certain demographic groups.

In light of our findings, we highly recommend that future datasets, especially those created from Internet searches and intended for public release, are tested for stereotypical bias and corrected accordingly by down-sampling the overrepresented demographic groups. Although other mitigation techniques could be performed later in the training phases, this type of bias is easy to overlook and can leak into bias in the trained models if left untreated. Furthermore, we strongly advise dataset creators to include the relevant demographic information of the subjects when possible, to allow the future study of new forms of demographic bias in their datasets.

A problem that requires further analysis is the large differences in the gender recall of certain labels, such as *disgust*. This difference is present even for the balanced versions of the dataset, suggesting a measurement bias or an inherent representation problem in this label. The label *disgust*, in particular, has low support, which could imply that stereotypical bias problems have a greater impact in smaller datasets. Further work is also required to replicate these results for other datasets, models and different applications. The development of properly labeled datasets that include demographic information of the represented subjects would also solidify this analysis, currently limited by the demographic relabeling model employed.

Acknowledgments. This work was funded by a predoctoral fellowship of the Research Service of Universidad Publica de Navarra, the Spanish MICIN (PID2019-108392GB-I00 and PID2020-118014RB-I00 / AEI / 10.13039/501100011033), and the Government of Navarre (0011-1411-2020-000079 - Emotional Films).

References

1. Abbasi, T.M., Friedler, S.A., Scheidegger, C., Venkatasubramanian, S.: Fairness in representation: quantifying stereotyping as a representational harm. In: Proceedings of the 2019 SIAM International Conference on Data Mining (SDM), pp. 801–809 (2019). https://doi.org/10.1137/1.9781611975673
2. Ahmad, Khurshid, Wang, Shirui, Vogel, Carl, Jain, Pranav, O'Neill, Oscar, Sufi, Basit Hamid: Comparing the performance of facial emotion recognition systems on real-life videos: gender, ethnicity and age. In: Arai, Kohei (ed.) FTC 2021. LNNS, vol. 358, pp. 193–210. Springer, Cham (2022). https://doi.org/10.1007/978-3-030-89906-6_14
3. Assuncao, G., Patrao, B., Castelo-Branco, M., Menezes, P.: An overview of emotion in artificial intelligence. In: IEEE Transactions on Artificial Intelligence, p. 1 (2022). https://doi.org/10.1109/TAI.2022.3159614
4. Atkinson, A.P., Tipples, J., Burt, D.M., Young, A.W.: Asymmetric interference between sex and emotion in face perception. Percept. Psychophys. **67**(7), 1199–1213 (2005). https://doi.org/10.3758/BF03193553
5. Avella, M.D.P.R.: Crime prediction artificial intelligence and the impact on human rights. Telecommun. Syst. Manage. **9**(3), 2 (2020)
6. Barsoum, E., Zhang, C., Ferrer, C.C., Zhang, Z.: training deep networks for facial expression recognition with crowd-sourced label distribution. arXiv:1608.01041 (2016)
7. Berk, R., Heidari, H., Jabbari, S., Kearns, M., Roth, A.: Fairness in criminal justice risk assessments: the state of the art. Sociolog. Methods Res. **50**(1), 3–44 (2018). https://doi.org/10.1177/0049124118782533
8. Birhane, A., Prabhu, V.U., Kahembwe, E.: Multimodal datasets: misogyny, pornography, and malignant stereotypes (2021)
9. Bordalo, P., Coffman, K., Gennaioli, N., Shleifer, A.: Stereotypes*. Quart. J. Econ. **131**(4), 1753–1794 (2016). https://doi.org/10.1093/qje/qjw029
10. Buolamwini, J., Gebru, T.: Gender shades: intersectional accuracy disparities in commercial gender classification. In: Friedler, S.A., Wilson, C. (eds.) Proceedings of the 1st Conference on Fairness, Accountability and Transparency. Proceedings of Machine Learning Research, vol. 81, pp. 77–91. PMLR (2018)
11. Denton, E., Hanna, A., Amironesei, R., Smart, A., Nicole, H.: On the genealogy of machine learning datasets: a critical history of imageNet. Big Data Society **8**(2), 205395172110359 (2021). https://doi.org/10.1177/20539517211035955
12. Deuschel, J., Finzel, B., Rieger, I.: Uncovering the bias in facial expressions. arXiv:2011.11311 (2021). https://doi.org/10.20378/irb-50304

13. Dominguez-Catena, I., Paternain, D., Galar, M.: Assessing demographic bias transfer from dataset to model: a case study in facial expression recognition (2022). https://doi.org/10.48550/arXiv.2205.10049
14. Domnich, A., Anbarjafari, G.: Responsible AI: gender bias assessment in emotion recognition. arXiv:2103.11436 (2021)
15. Ekman, P., Friesen, W.V.: Constants across cultures in the face and emotion. J. Personal. Soc. Psychol. **17**(2), 124–129 (1971). https://doi.org/10.1037/h0030377
16. Goodfellow, I.J., et al.: Challenges in representation learning: a report on three machine learning contests. arXiv:1307.0414 (2013)
17. Jannat, S.R., Canavan, S.: Expression recognition across age. In: 2021 16th IEEE International Conference on Automatic Face and Gesture Recognition (FG 2021), pp. 1–5 (2021). https://doi.org/10.1109/FG52635.2021.9667062
18. Karkkainen, K., Joo, J.: FairFace: Face attribute dataset for balanced race, gender, and age for bias measurement and mitigation. In: 2021 IEEE Winter Conference on Applications of Computer Vision (WACV), pp. 1547–1557. IEEE, Waikoloa, HI, USA (2021). https://doi.org/10.1109/WACV48630.2021.00159
19. Keyes, O.: The misgendering machines: trans/HCI implications of automatic gender recognition. In: Proceedings of the ACM on Human-Computer Interaction 2(CSCW), pp. 1–22 (2018). https://doi.org/10.1145/3274357
20. Kim, E., Bryant, D., Srikanth, D., Howard, A.: Age bias in emotion detection: an analysis of facial emotion recognition performance on young, middle-aged, and older adults. In: Proceedings of the 2021 AAAI/ACM Conference on AI, Ethics, and Society, pp. 638–644. Association for Computing Machinery, New York, NY, USA (2021)
21. Kring, A.M., Gordon, A.H.: Sex differences in emotion: expression, experience, and physiology. J. Pers. Soc. Psychol. **74**(3), 686–703 (1998)
22. Li, S., Deng, W.: deep facial expression recognition: a survey. In: IEEE Transactions on Affective Computing. p. 1 (2020). https://doi.org/10/gkk8dv
23. Mehrabian, A.: Pleasure-arousal-dominance: a general framework for describing and measuring individual differences in temperament. Current Psychol. **14**(4), 261–292 (1996). https://doi.org/10.1007/BF02686918
24. Ntoutsi, E., et al.: Bias in data-driven AI systems - an introductory survey. arXiv:2001.09762 (2020)
25. Prabhu, V.U., Birhane, A.: Large image datasets: a pyrrhic win for computer vision? arXiv:2006.16923 (2020)
26. Schwartz, R., Vassilev, A., Greene, K., Perine, L., Burt, A., Hall, P.: Towards a standard for identifying and managing bias in artificial intelligence. Tech. rep., National Institute of Standards and Technology (2022). https://doi.org/10.6028/NIST.SP.1270
27. Simonyan, K., Zisserman, A.: Very deep convolutional networks for large-scale image recognition (2015)
28. Smith, L.N.: A disciplined approach to neural network hyper-parameters: Part 1 - learning rate, batch size, momentum, and weight decay. arXiv:1803.09820 (2018)
29. Suresh, H., Guttag, J.V.: A framework for understanding sources of harm throughout the machine learning life cycle. arXiv:1901.10002 (2021)
30. Verma, S., Rubin, J.: Fairness definitions explained. In: Proceedings of the International Workshop on Software Fairness, pp. 1–7. ACM, Gothenburg Sweden (2018). https://doi.org/10.1145/3194770.3194776
31. Wang, T., Zhao, J., Yatskar, M., Chang, K.W., Ordonez, V.: Balanced datasets are not enough: estimating and mitigating gender bias in deep image representations (2019)

32. Xu, Tian, White, Jennifer, Kalkan, Sinan, Gunes, Hatice: Investigating bias and fairness in facial expression recognition. In: Bartoli, Adrien, Fusiello, Andrea (eds.) ECCV 2020. LNCS, vol. 12540, pp. 506–523. Springer, Cham (2020). https://doi. org/10.1007/978-3-030-65414-6_35

33. Zhao, J., Wang, T., Yatskar, M., Ordonez, V., Chang, K.W.: Men also like shopping: reducing gender bias amplification using corpus-level constraints. In: Proceedings of the 2017 Conference on Empirical Methods in Natural Language Processing, pp. 2979–2989. Association for Computational Linguistics, Copenhagen, Denmark (2017). https://doi.org/10.18653/v1/D17-1323

A Social Media Tool for Domain-Specific Information Retrieval - A Case Study in Human Trafficking

Tito Griné[1,2]([✉]) [iD] and Carla Teixeira Lopes[1,2] [iD]

[1] Faculty of Engineering of the University of Porto, Porto, Portugal
{up201706732,ctl}@fe.up.pt
[2] INESCT TEC, Porto, Portugal

Abstract. In a world increasingly present online, people are leaving a digital footprint, with valuable information scattered on the Web, in an unstructured manner, beholden to the websites that keep it. While there are potential harms in being able to access this information readily, such as enabling corporate surveillance, there are also significant benefits when used, for example, in journalism or investigations into Human Trafficking. This paper presents an approach for retrieving domain-specific information present on the Web using Social Media platforms as a gateway to other content existing on any website. It begins by identifying relevant profiles, then collecting links shared in posts to webpages related to them, and lastly, extracting and indexing the information gathered. The tool developed based on this approach was tested for a case study in the domain of Human Trafficking, more specifically in sexual exploitation, showing promising results and potential to be applied in a real-world scenario.

Keywords: Social media · Open-source intelligence · Information retrieval · Human trafficking

1 Introduction

The Web has been growing steadily in the last few years, meaning there is an ever-increasing number of users and information present on it [9]. With more people using the Internet, seemingly in more diverse ways, the more information they create and share, primarily through Social Media platforms. This results in every person having a meaningful and more descriptive digital footprint every day [6].

Accessing this information and subsequently using it in productive ways can help answer important questions about our world. Although there is a risk of using this information in harmful ways, it is also possible to leverage it for social good. However, given that this data is generated on multiple platforms, structure and consistency are regularly absent. Additionally, for most of the data created, accessing it is contingent on the website.

I. Koprinska et al. (Eds.): ECML PKDD 2022 Workshops, CCIS 1752, pp. 23–38, 2023.
https://doi.org/10.1007/978-3-031-23618-1_2

For example, websites that have search functionalities tailored to a specific use case and, as such, do not cover all potentially helpful scenarios. To exemplify this, we can consider a website like GitHub with an excellent search engine for finding code and repositories. This covers the most prominent use case of the platform, storing and sharing code. Nevertheless, we can imagine a company interested in looking up profiles from users interested or experts in a particular field. If using the native search functionalities, there is no clear and effective way of doing this.

A more extreme case is when websites and platforms do not offer any search options over the data they keep, or these are of significantly low quality. This could be not having a publicly available API to access its data or not supporting manual searching. Such could be the case for applications that do not have the resources or technical scale to offer good search capabilities or do not want bots to be able to query their system. A modern example of this is the social network platform OnlyFans. OnlyFans is a platform to share and directly monetize user-created content that has risen to popularity in the past few years as a means to offer sexually explicit content. Due to its minimal regulation and bear to entry, it has been increasingly tied to cases of sexual exploitation of minors and instances of human trafficking [10]. Perhaps intentionally, OnlyFans has poor search functionalities since they do not expose a public API, and manually searching returns only a handful of low-quality results.

One of the areas where this information is most valuable is in Human Trafficking investigations. Authorities and non-governmental organizations (NGOs) can leverage the information scattered on the Web to gain additional insights or discover new cases. Albeit helpful, readily accessing this information is a complex problem for the reasons mentioned above. In the above example of OnlyFans, to conduct investigations on this platform to prevent its use for human trafficking and sexually exploitative purposes requires searching for profiles, which is made extremely difficult by the available search options.

In this paper, we present an open-source intelligence (OSINT) tool utilizing a novel approach to circumvent these issues that authorities can use to aid in accessing and efficiently using data scattered on the Web. The approach relies on two key assumptions: (1) that people who actively use the Web will tend to reveal their presence online through Social Media platforms; (2) the more a person is involved or experienced in a given domain, the more likely they are to share content and information related to that domain. Under these two presuppositions, the tool retrieves information regarding a specific domain by identifying Social Media profiles related to the desired domain. Once a set of profiles is identified, its posts are analyzed in search of links to other web pages. The corresponding websites are crawled and, if classified as related to the profile in question, are kept for additional data extraction. With the profiles and their corresponding related web pages gathered, data is collected and structured so it can be visualized and queried to provide the user with insights into the results. The tool was tested in a mock scenario related to Human Trafficking, specifically, sexual exploitation.

2   Forensic Technology for Human Trafficking

The most relevant research field this work touches upon is Forensic Technology in the Human Trafficking domain. In general, this area focuses on ways to improve and even automate the access and analysis of information on the Web to aid the identification and collection of evidence of Human Trafficking. The approaches found in the literature can, with some overlap, be divided into three types: (1) extensive data extraction and linking; (2) tagging data with human trafficking indicators; (3) classification of data as suspicious human trafficking activity.

The first type and the most prevalent approach, with a greater real-world adoption in criminal investigations, concerns the collection of large quantities of data available on the Internet and creating strategies to efficiently and effectively analyze this information. Many of the tools developed under this approach were within the DARPA MEMEX [1], a program developing search technologies for better discovery, organization, and presentation of domain-specific content. One of the most meaningful works, built upon earlier systems from DARPA, was a system architecture called DIG (Domain-specific Insight Graphs) proposed by Szekely et al. [11] capable of building domain-specific Knowledge Graphs. In the study, the authors were able to create a Knowledge Graph with around 1.4 billion nodes from a starting collection of 50 million crawled web pages. This system was then integrated into an investigative search engine by Kejriwal et al. [8], specific to the Human Trafficking domain, helping investigators answer *entity-centric* questions regarding the data present on millions of crawled web pages from websites known to be associated with Human Trafficking activity. Their engine not only had to be concerned with extracting and structuring only the most relevant information but, to be used by authorities in a practical setting, also had to be scalable.

The second type attempts to tag data with previously defined indicators of Human Trafficking. These indicators can be set by authorities or NGOs like the United Nations Office on Drugs and Crime (UNODC) that are meant to reflect common patterns found in Human Trafficking activity and, if appropriately assigned to data segments, can automate part of the investigators' work. One of the projects following this technique is presented by Kejriwal et al. [7] as FlagIt (Flexible and adaptive generation of Indicators for text), an end-to-end indicator mining system with the principle goal of reducing the burden and potential bias stemming from manual supervision of suspicious text, like sex ads, that can contain signs of Human Trafficking activity. As part of the European ePOOLICE (early Pursuit against Organized crime using environmental scanning, the Law and Intelligence systems) project, Andrews et al. [2] took the framework described by Brewster et al. [3] and developed an Organized Crime taxonomy, combining it with entity extraction tools to filter social data that had more than a pre-defined number of signals of organized crime. It could later be manually reviewed by authorities, facilitating the access and use of social media as a new data source for investigations. The effectiveness of these systems relies heavily on the indicators defined, which can be highly subjective.

The third and final type includes works that attempt to classify meaningful blocks of data as containing or not suspicious signs of Human Trafficking activity. It is arguably a more difficult task since defining a threshold for what is considered enough evidence to classify as suspicious is challenging even among investigators. To simplify this problem, Hernández-Àlvarez [4] turned to Twitter and focused on Spanish data to identify signs of Human Trafficking of underage victims. Focusing on just underage victims made it easier to define an indicator of possible Human Trafficking since any minor attempting to provide sexual services is already a strong warning sign.

3   Architectural Overview

Considering the three approach types mentioned in the previous section, the tool we propose fits best in the first approach type. The key distinction from other works found in the literature is that, instead of relying on prior knowledge of platforms and websites known to house criminal activity, the proposed approach relies only on widely used Social Media platforms. Additionally, all the information that is gathered from other tools necessarily comes from the pages crawled of websites previously chosen. On the other hand, our proposal allows the extraction of relevant information from websites unrelated to criminal activity while still collecting information on other websites that can indicate such activity. Lastly, the websites selected in other works often have search engines that allow for quickly collecting a large number of links to existing profiles or forums, which can then be used to begin crawling. When a website does not provide this, like in the case of the aforementioned social platform OnlyFans, these proposed tools are harder to incorporate in investigations since it is difficult to get an initial batch of links to profiles and, moreover, the profile pages do not link to other ones. By relying on the searching capabilities of well-established Social Media platforms, the technology described in this paper can bypass these limitations, even if partially, and still provide valuable insights to authorities.

The tool's overall architecture is illustrated in Fig. 1. Currently, the tool relies only on the Twitter social media platform. Thus, the modules are targeted for this particular platform. Nevertheless, the proposed approach's underlying ideas and stages can be easily adapted to other social media.

The user first uses the interface to provide the search's configuration parameters, which include the search and domain keywords, and then triggers a search. Since the terms are provided by the user and no assumptions are made about the domain they reflect, the tool is domain-agnostic. The tool begins by using the Twitter API [1] to look for tweets containing the search terms, keeping the respective profiles until the desired number has been collected.

After having a set of profiles, the program initializes the Apache Spark engine [2] to parallelize the operations from the following modules by profile. It begins with the Profile Selection module, responsible for taking in the profiles

---

[1] Twitter API - https://developer.twitter.com/en/products/twitter-api.
[2] Apache Spark - https://spark.apache.org.

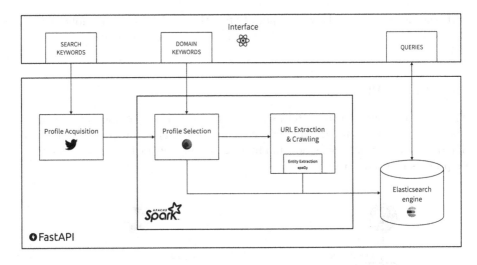

Fig. 1. Diagram of the application's overall architecture.

collected from the previous search, gather profile data, tweets and retweets and then use it to identify which ones are related to the desired domain, a process explained in Sect. 4.

The URL Extraction & Crawling module follows by taking the URLs extracted from the tweets of each selected profile and crawling the corresponding websites while collecting data from them. Part of this data is then used to filter the websites which are related to the profile and the ones that are not. How this is achieved is explained in Sect. 5.

In tandem with the processing that each module performs, for each profile, a JSON is kept saving all the information that is gathered from both Twitter and the related websites. When the previous module ends, all documents from profiles that have been selected are sent to an Elasticsearch engine [3]. It will index the data following a provided schema and allow the full-text search over the gathered information.

Lastly, once the search is finished, the user can analyze the results using the provided interface, filter the results, and query for specific terms, emails, phone numbers, or links.

4   Profile Selection Module

The Profile Selection module is responsible for discerning social media profiles related to a given topic, using only the publicly available information on the profile, such as posts or replies, and a user-given set of keywords. It can be seen as a binary classifier since, for a set of keywords, it will classify profiles as either related or not related to the underlying topic. This section begins

---

[3] Elasticsearch - https://www.elastic.co.

with the description of how the module functions in Subsect. 4.1 followed by the evaluation performed to validate and assess its performance, detailed in Subsect. 4.2.

4.1 Process Flow

This module requires a set of terms provided by the user, the domain keywords, that closely relate to and distinguish the domain of interest. A simplified activity diagram of the Profile Selection module can be viewed in Fig. 2 to accompany its process flow's description.

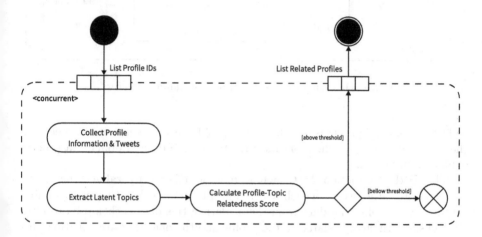

Fig. 2. Activity diagram of the profile selection module.

The module can be divided into four stages: (1) Extraction; (2) Processing; (3) Topic Discovery; (4) Classification. The *Extraction* and *Processing* stages happen together. The first involves going through each of the profile's tweets (up to a maximum defined by the user) and extracting necessary information such as the text, URLs contained in the tweets, and entities identified by Twitter. The second processes the text from the tweets to turn it more suitable for topic modeling. This includes operations like removing tags, punctuation, and stopwords and converting the text to lowercase.

In the *Topic Discovery* stage, the text extracted previously, which is divided into two corpora, one for the profile's tweets and another for its retweets, is tokenized and lemmatized using the WordNet lemmatizer[4]. The tweets are then aggregated in groups of five, by the order they were collected, to form documents instead of having each tweet be a document. The reason is that tweets have a character limit and tend to be short, making it harder for topic models to use them effectively. In topic modeling of Twitter profiles, a profile is understood to

---

[4] WordNet lemmatizer - https://www.nltk.org/_modules/nltk/stem/wordnet.html.

be drawing primarily from a limited pool of topics, where each tweet is of a topic following that same pool. Thus aggregating tweets is a common and inexpensive approach found to improve topic modeling results with tweets without incurring the risk of obfuscating topics [5].

For topic extraction, each corpus is converted to its Bag of Words representation and then fed into Gensim's Ensemble LDA model [5]. Since LDA is non-deterministic, the topics identified may vary with each run. In an attempt to single out only the most stable topics, the Ensemble LDA approach effectively trains multiple LDA models and considers only those that emerge multiple times. This makes it less likely that a topic distribution results from the model's natural variance. If stable topics are found, these are returned as an array of terms and their corresponding probabilities. The ten most probable terms of appearing from each of the top-5 identified topics are saved.

Finally, the *Classification* stage begins by converting both the user-submitted domain keywords and the topic terms previously identified to a vector representation that preserves semantic meaning. This is done through a word2vec word embedding model trained on text taken from Google News. Using a model that conveys semantic meaning, operations on the resulting vectors preserve this property. Two operations are essential for this classifier. The first is addition, which allows the user to submit composite domain keywords that can be interpreted as one term by adding them. For example, if the keyword is *"information integration"*, using the terms separately dilutes the desired domain since both *"information"* and *"integration"* are words widely used in other situations. By adding both terms, the resulting vector should point to a coordinate in the embedding space related to *"information integration"* and not just one or the other.

The second operation is the distance between vectors, or its inverse, the cosine similarity between two vectors. Once again, since the vectors preserve semantic meaning, the closer two vectors are in the embedding space, the more similar the corresponding terms are. Consequently, by calculating the cosine similarity between each domain keyword and the profile's identified topic words, we measure how similar the profile's identified topics are to the desired domain. This score is improved by applying some heuristics, namely, only keeping the best similarity score for each keyword and then removing the 30% worse keyword scores. This process happens for the profile's description, understood as the terms of a single topic, the tweets' and retweets' topics, ending with three different scores. The average of these scores is taken and used as the profile's overall score. If it is above a threshold, that is defined by the experiments described in the following subsection, the profile is kept and understood to be related to the desired topic.

---

[5] Ensemble LDA - https://radimrehurek.com/gensim/models/ensemblelda.html.

4.2   Evaluation and Comparison of Different Configurations

To evaluate different alternatives in the development of this module, a custom-built dataset of Twitter profiles and one closely associated topic. In order to create the dataset, topics were chosen beforehand, like *"ambient music"* and *"information retrieval"*, and lists of people known within these fields were searched for on the Web, most coming from Wikipedia. Each person's name was then searched for on Twitter, and the first returned profile was manually analyzed to assess the profile's actual relatedness to the topic. The resulting dataset, publicly available at rdm.inesctec.pt/dataset/cs-2022-007, contains 271 profiles belonging to one of six topics.

The dataset was used to evaluate the classifier's performance with different configurations. The evaluation was based on plotting and subsequently analyzing the resulting Receiver Operating Characteristic (ROC) curves and the corresponding Area Under the Curve (AUC) values. The ROC curve is a standard graphical plot to gauge the diagnostic ability of a binary classifier as its discrimination threshold varies.

Word Embedding Model. The first test was done to select a word embedding model for the classification phase. Four pre-trained models were tested, a Fast-Text model trained with text from Wikipedia, two GloVe models, one trained with text taken from Twitter and another from Wikipedia, and lastly a word2vec model trained with a corpus obtained from Google News. The ROC curves were plotted, see Fig. 3, as well as the resulting AUC values, which can be seen in Table 1. The word2vec model was ultimately chosen and used for the subsequent tests based on the results obtained.

Table 1. Area Under the Curve (AUC) values for the tested word embedding models.

Model	fasttext-wiki-news-subwords	glove-twitter	glove-wiki-gigaword	word2vec-google-news
Area Under the Curve (AUC)	0.901	0.743	0.863	0.983

Topic Sources and Heuristics. Another test was conducted to understand which topic sources were best to use. This required plotting the ROC curves for the classifier using just the score obtained from the description, the topics from the tweets, and the topics from the retweets. Additionally, the average of the three was also plotted. It was found that the highest diagnostic ability from a single source was with the classifier using the retweets' topics, having an AUC value of 0.967, and the lowest with the description, with an AUC value of 0.873. Moreover, the best performing classifier came from the average of the scores from all three sources, resulting in an AUC of 0.983. Consequently, the average of the three scores was chosen for the final classifier.

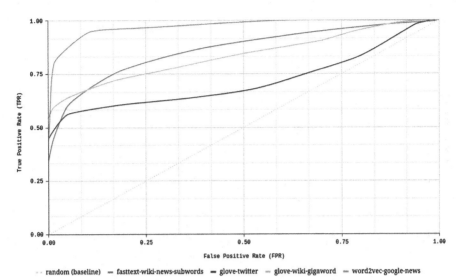

Fig. 3. ROC curves obtained with various word embedding models.

The classifier's heuristics described in the previous section were also validated to confirm that the performance did, in fact, improve when they were applied. These included keeping just the top-4 most related topic terms for each keyword and discarding the 30% worse scoring keywords. Although the improvement is not substantial, going from an AUC of 0.977 without any heuristics to 0.983 with both, it was still found valuable and worth keeping in the final classifier.

Threshold Definition. Most importantly, the dataset was used to define the classifier's threshold empirically. To do this, the dataset was divided into test and validation sets, with an 80/20 split, respectively. This split was performed to keep the proportion of topics roughly the same on each set. The ROC curves were plotted for both sets, which can be viewed in Fig. 4. Since both follow roughly the same shape, a threshold based on the test dataset will give similar results in the validation dataset.

Since the profile's score is correlated with the frequency with which that profile engages with the desired topic, a higher score means that the profile is more likely to be useful. With this in mind, the threshold was set to 0.275, which should result in about an 80% TPR. Although it may seem that not being able to identify 20% of cases is high, it is likely that the 20% of related profiles that are not identified do not engage with the topic enough on Twitter, so the quality and quantity of the data that would be able to be retrieved is expected to be low.

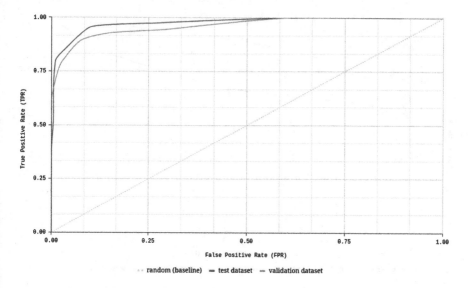

Fig. 4. ROC curves for threshold setting using the profile selection classifier.

5   URL Extraction and Crawling Module

The URL Extraction & Crawling module works with the profiles that have been selected from the previous module. It is responsible for taking the links collected for each profile, crawling the corresponding websites, identifying which ones are related to the profile in question, and, if it is the case, collecting and structuring information available on the websites.

5.1   Process Flow

Since hundreds of links can be collected from a profile's tweets, and web crawling is an expensive process, even with parallelized operations, it is impractical to crawl every URL from every profile selected. As such, the module only crawls up to a maximum number of websites defined by the user in the configuration, excluding the webpages crawled in depth. To guide the description of this module's process flow, a simplified activity diagram can be seen in Fig. 5.

This module can also be divided into three stages: (1) Crawling; (2) Classification; (3) Entity Extraction.

The *Crawling* stage is a specialized web crawler tailored to the application's specific needs. It crawls each link up to a specified depth, currently set to five, while remaining within the same hostname (internal crawling), and gathers data from each one. Besides keeping the entire webpage content stripped of $<script>$ and $<style>$ tags, it attempts to extract data like emails and phone numbers found in $<a>$ tags, links to external websites, images, and metadata from each page. It also attempts to identify *"link-tree"* websites, like linktr.ee and

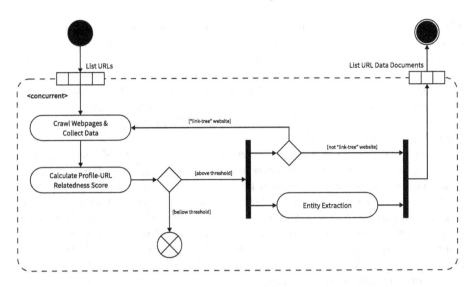

Fig. 5. Activity diagram of the URL Extraction and Crawling module.

linkgenie.co. These are websites dedicated to aggregating links to a person's presence online. Usually used by influencers, artists, and public figures in general, it is a practical way to easily share all relevant links to social media platforms, personal websites, and other relevant pages using a single link. These types of websites are useful for this tool since if it is determined that a particular *"link-tree"* website is related to the profile, then it can be presumed that all external links found on it also belong to that profile.

Upon some testing, it was found that the most significant bottleneck from this module was the requests made to retrieve a webpage's content. However, since the bottleneck is principally I/O bound, the module spawns a series of threads, each performing the stages for each URL. The use of threads is adequate in this case since while one is waiting for a request to return, another can advance with some other computation. Additionally, creating threads does not have the significant processing overhead as it does when in the case of multi-processing.

The *Classification* stage is where a relationship between the Twitter profile and the website is searched for to determine whether the extracted data should be kept or discarded. Since the crawled web pages can be from any arbitrary website on the Web, the classifier cannot make many assumptions regarding the structure or contents of the data found.

As such, the algorithm for classifying websites relies on searching the contents retrieved using regular expressions with fuzzy matching created from the Twitter profile's name and username. In order to achieve this, the name and username are first processed to convert characters that serve as word delimiters to whitespace. Then, a regular expression is formed by taking each word in the string and allowing a match with up to a given number of errors, defined as the Levenshtein distance, which depends on the length of the word. Additionally, the regular expression allows for up to two words and any word delimiter character to be between each name's word. For example, if the username was *"*John_Doe*"*, it starts by being converted to ``john doe``. Afterward, the fuzzy matching encoding for Python regular expressions is added to each word, resulting in ``(?b)(john){e<=1} (?b)(doe){e<=1}``. Lastly, the encoding for additional words in between each name generates the final regular expression, ``(?b)(john){e<=1}(\w){0,2}((\W|_)|(\W|_)(\w)*(\W|_)){0,2} (\w){0,2}(?b)(doe){e<=1}``.

Besides the regular expressions searching for the entirety of the name and username, additional ones are created from the individual words found in them. This increases the scope of the search but also allows for a greater chance of false positives. For this reason, each regular expression is weighted. The ones created from the full name have a weight of 1, and ones created from individual words have a weight which is inversely proportional to their Zipf frequency, calculated using wordfreq [6], up to a maximum of 0.25. This means that words that often appear in text will have a marginal impact on the website's score. These regular expressions are then searched among the corpus and metadata gathered from the website. If no match is found, the score for a particular search is 0. Otherwise, that search's score is given by the following formula:

$$score = \frac{L_{original}}{L_{original} + |L_{original} - L_{match}| + 2 \times n_{errors}} \tag{1}$$

where $L_{original}$ is the length of the original string, L_{match} is the length of the match string, and n_{errors} is the number of errors, *i.e.*, the Levenshtein distance.

The scores from all searches are multiplied by their weight, then averaged and normalized to a value between 0 and 1. If the score is above a given threshold, the website is considered related to the profile, and its data is kept.

Furthermore, if related, the *Extraction* stage follows, which takes the website's contents and uses Spacy's [7] pre-trained named-entity recognizer to extract named entities from the categories selected by the user in the configuration. These categories are the ones made available by Spacy (*e.g.*, people, dates, quantities) and can be selected by the user through a checkbox list when inputting a search's configuration in the tool's interface.

5.2   Evaluation and Comparison of Different Configurations

Like the Profile Selection module, this module was also tuned by testing multiple configurations with a custom dataset. It was created using the profiles gathered from the previous dataset, collecting the URLs that were in each profile's description and then manually analyzing them to determine if they were related or not to the entity behind the profile. The resulting dataset, also publicly available at rdm.inesctec.pt/dataset/cs-2022-007, contains 325 distinct pairs of Twitter profiles and related URLs, with some profiles having more than one link associated.

---

[6] wordfreq - https://github.com/rspeer/wordfreq.

[7] Spacy - https://spacy.io.

Search Expression. The dataset then served to validate the use of both the Twitter name and username for creating regular expressions. It was found that using just the Twitter name resulted in a slight performance improvement when compared to using both. However, the Twitter name, unlike the username, is not permanent, meaning users can change it when they please. As such, we believe using it as the single source for regular expressions would result in a more inconsistent classifier, highly dependent on the current profile's name, which commonly changes with, for example, culture shifts such as the inclusion of a person's pronouns at the end of the name. Hence, given that the difference was not substantial, the final classifier uses both the Twitter name and username.

Tokenization. Another choice that was analyzed was using the tokenization of the Twitter name and username to obtain additional search expressions from each individual token. The results show a minimal improvement with a classifier using individual tokens, which can best be perceived by the corresponding AUC values, which are 0.9849 and 0.9812 for the classifier with and without tokens, respectively. Albeit minimal, the choice to use individual tokens was kept. We believe that, in more complex cases, for example, when individual names from the Twitter name appear on a website multiple times but in inverse order, although the regular expression with the full name will not be able to match these instances, the individual tokens will, increasing the chance of it being detected.

Threshold Definition. As in the previous module, the dataset was split into a test and validation to determine an adequate threshold for the classifier. Analyzing the ROC curves, see Fig. 6, together with graphs of the classifier's F1-score and Accuracy for the various thresholds, it was found that a slight maximum was hit for threshold values between 0.025 and 0.075. We believe that the dataset does not accurately represent the variety of cases of website relatedness the classifier would commonly find since all websites were taken from the profiles' descriptions. This probably results in a selection of websites disproportionately highly related to their corresponding profiles. Hence, the final threshold was set to 0.06, a low value that serves mostly to rule out single matches, probably with a few errors, coming from words similar to a name token but unrelated. With it, the validation dataset predicts a TPR of around 87% with a 6% FPR.

6 Case Study

The tool was tested in a mock scenario of a possible use by law enforcement to detect suspicious cases of sex work. The goal was to assess the tool's ability to find Twitter profiles of sex workers and the type of information it can gather from them. Additionally, there was a focus on evaluating the tool's detection of OnlyFans accounts from sex workers, which could be useful for detecting suspicious accounts on this platform.

Due to limitations in the virtual machine where the application ran, the search had to be split into multiple instances. Although the application uses the

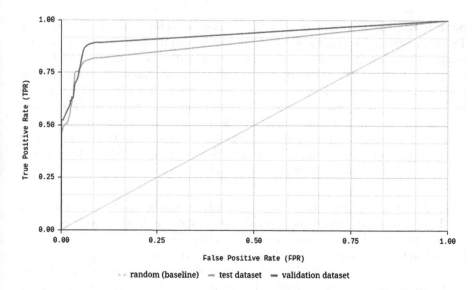

Fig. 6. ROC curves for threshold setting using the URL Extraction and Crawling classifier.

Apache Spark engine, it does so in local mode with only two cores available, thus not achieving any actual parallelization.

Ten searches were performed, each requesting an initial batch of 100 profiles for a total of 1,000 starting profiles that were active between the 6th and 12th of June 2022. The profiles were gathered from tweets that contained terms like *"escort"* and *"onlyfans"*, while discarding those with terms such as *"traffic"*. The combined time for all ten searches was 8 h and 13 min, without parallelization.

Of the 1,000 profiles analyzed, the tool identified 31 unique ones that it believed were related to the sex work domain. Since the searches were separate, the number of unique profiles analyzed was likely slightly less, between 700 and 800. Given the relatively low number of identified profiles, it was possible to examine each manually. In the end, it was found that, from the 31 identified profiles, 20 appeared to be from people actively performing some type of sex work. From the remaining 11, 6 were from accounts that frequently shared explicit adult content, albeit not involved in its production, and 1 from a person actively engaging with news from caught sex offenders. Only 4 accounts did not appear to have a significant relation to the domain and can therefore be considered false positives, resulting in a precision of about 87%.

Regarding the information gathered from the profiles, a total of 137 links were classified as related to their respective profile. However, not all profiles had related links, with 13 out of the 31 having no associated link. From the analysis of the links, more specifically their websites, only three did not appear to have any relation to the profile, considered therefore to be wrongfully classified. Furthermore, of the 20 profiles of sex workers, 7 had an OnlyFans account link correctly associated. Lastly, the tool collected 4950 images from the crawled web pages, nine emails, and three phone numbers. These can constitute valuable information in investigations to get leads or identify known potential victims. The breakdown of all the data collected from the searches can be found in Table 2.

Table 2. Distribution of profiles and extracted data from the searches performed.

Type	Profile Count	Related Links	Misidentified Links	Emails	Phone Numbers	Images
Sex Workers	20	132	1	9	3	4824
Non-Sex Workers but related to domain	7	1	0	0	0	3
Not related to domain	4	4	2	0	0	123
Total:	31	137	3	9	3	4950

An important outcome to mention is that, while working on this case study, a particular tweet drew attention to a profile that, upon closer inspection, appeared to be an underage person offering sexual services, and the account was subsequently reported to Twitter. Albeit an unfortunate occurrence, it is perhaps a testament to the potential of this tool.

7   Conclusions and Future Work

This paper presents a tool developed based on a novel approach to gathering domain-specific information from the Web. The approach relies on people's proclivity to share content they create and their overall presence online through Social Media platforms. The approach also introduces new strategies for problems not yet extensively tackled in the literature. This includes identifying profiles and, in general, text corpora that relate to a particular domain while remaining agnostic of the domain. An additional problem is detecting relationships between Social Media profiles, or the entities behind them, and arbitrary websites.

Nevertheless, it is imperative to thoroughly test the tool with a proper setup that allows for actual parallelization with Apache Spark and perhaps in coordination with authorities in a real-world scenario. Other enhancements have been conceived to improve and extend the tool's capabilities. An approach to the classifier for profile-website relatedness would be to use a named-entity recognition and entity linking model to find aliases of the Twitter name or username and then use them to create new regular expressions. Another improvement would be to link the gathered information with Linked Data from the Semantic Web.

From the evaluation of the individual modules and the case study performed, we consider that the application shows potential to be incorporated into the arsenal of OSINT tools available for authorities and investigators to aid in the fight against Human Trafficking and sexual exploitation. Moreover, by keeping the tool agnostic of the domain, we believe its use can be extended to other fields like investigative journalism.

References

1. Agency, D.A.R.P.: Memex. Available at https://www.darpa.mil/program/memex. Accessed Dec 2021
2. Andrews, S., Brewster, B., Day, T.: Organised crime and social media: detecting and corroborating weak signals of human trafficking online. Lect. Notes Comput. Sci. (including subseries Lecture Notes in Artificial Intelligence and Lecture Notes in Bioinformatics) **9717**, 137–150 (2016). https://doi.org/10.1007/978-3-319-40985-6_11
3. Brewster, B., Ingle, T., Rankin, G.: Crawling open-source data for indicators of human trafficking. Proceedings - 2014 IEEE/ACM 7th International Conference on Utility and Cloud Computing, UCC 2014, pp. 714–719 (2014). https://doi.org/10.1109/UCC.2014.116
4. Hernandez-Alvarez, M.: Detection of possible human trafficking in twitter. In: Proceedings - 2019 International Conference on Information Systems and Software Technologies, ICI2ST 2019, pp. 187–191 (2019). https://doi.org/10.1109/ICI2ST.2019.00034
5. Hong, L., Davison, B.D.: Empirical study of topic modeling in twitter. In: SOMA 2010 - Proceedings of the 1st Workshop on Social Media Analytics, pp. 80–88 (2010). https://doi.org/10.1145/1964858.1964870. http://www.bit.ly
6. Kapustina, L.V.: Digital footprint analysis to develop a personal digital competency-based profile. Lect. Notes Netw. Syst. **133**, 591–596 (2021). https://doi.org/10.1007/978-3-030-47458-4_68
7. Kejriwal, M., Ding, J., Shao, R., Kumar, A., Szekely, P.: Flagit: a system for minimally supervised human trafficking indicator mining. In: Workshop on Learning with Limited Labeled Data (2017)
8. Kejriwal, M., Szekely, P.: An investigative search engine for the human trafficking domain. Lect. Notes Comput. Sci. (Including subseries Lecture Notes in Artificial Intelligence and Lecture Notes in Bioinformatics) **10588 LNCS**, 247–262 (2017). https://doi.org/10.1007/978-3-319-68204-4_25
9. Roser, M., Ritchie, H., Ortiz-Ospina, E.: Internet. Our World in Data (2015). https://ourworldindata.org/internet
10. On Sexual Exploitation (NCOSE), N.C.: A look into onlyfans: child sexual abuse material and trafficking (2021). Available at https://endsexualexploitation.org/articles/a-look-into-onlyfans/. Accessed Dec 2021
11. Szekely, P., et al.: Building and using a knowledge graph to combat human trafficking. Lect. Notes Comput. Sci. (including subseries Lecture Notes in Artificial Intelligence and Lecture Notes in Bioinformatics) **9367**, 205–221 (2015). https://doi.org/10.1007/978-3-319-25010-6_12

A Unified Framework for Assessing Energy Efficiency of Machine Learning

Raphael Fischer$^{(\boxtimes)}$ (ID), Matthias Jakobs (ID), Sascha Mücke (ID),
and Katharina Morik (ID)

AI Group, TU Dortmund University, 44227 Dortmund, Germany
{raphael.fischer,matthias.jakobs,sascha.muecke,
katharina.morik}@tu-dortmund.de
https://www-ai.cs.tu-dortmund.de

Abstract. State-of-the-art machine learning (ML) systems show exceptional qualitative performance, but can also have a negative impact on society. With regard to global climate change, the question of resource consumption and sustainability becomes more and more urgent. The enormous energy footprint of single ML applications and experiments was recently investigated. However, environment-aware users require a unified framework to assess, compare, and report the efficiency and performance trade-off of different methods and models. In this work we propose novel efficiency aggregation, indexing, and rating procedures for ML applications. To this end, we devise a set of metrics that allow for a holistic view, taking both task type, abstract model, software, and hardware into account. As a result, ML systems become comparable even across different execution environments. Inspired by the EU's energy label system, we also introduce a concept for visually communicating efficiency information to the public in a comprehensible way. We apply our methods to over 20 SOTA models on a range of hardware architectures, giving an overview of the modern ML efficiency landscape.

Keywords: Energy efficiency · Sustainability · Resource-aware ML · Green AI · Trustworthy AI

1 Introduction

Machine learning (ML) solutions are successfully deployed in diverse application areas and thus affect more and more people, including but not limited to experts from science, less informed developers from industry, or end-users that only face model decisions. However, the energy required for deploying highly complex models has become a concern as the world strives towards reducing carbon emissions in all sectors of society [26]. When discussing novel methods in literature, authors tend to focus on predictive performance metrics, but often fail to discuss resource consumption in similar depth [32]. This is due to a lack of concise specification of ML model *energy efficiency* [29]. With the diversity of ML target groups, and in order to be truly beneficial for social good, such efficiency information also needs to be communicable at different levels of comprehension.

I. Koprinska et al. (Eds.): ECML PKDD 2022 Workshops, CCIS 1752, pp. 39–54, 2023.
https://doi.org/10.1007/978-3-031-23618-1_3

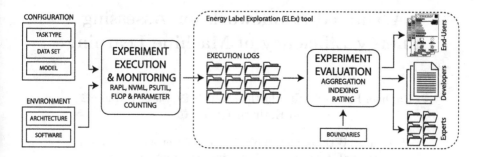

Fig. 1. Framework for assessing the energy efficiency of ML experiments.

In this work, we propose a general framework for assessing the efficiency of learning tasks. Besides power draw, we also take other important metrics like model size, computational runtime, and predictive performance into account. In order to make model performance comparable across diverse environments, we introduce novel routines that project those metrics onto rateable index scales. Wanting to benefit the whole society, we additionally show how results can be reported to varyingly informed audiences, like scientists from our field, developers in industry, or non-experts facing established ML systems. Here we draw inspiration from the way the European Union communicates energy efficiency of household appliances via *energy labels* [13]. With our proposed framework, the omnipresent trade-offs between predictive quality and resource consumption of ML systems becomes assessable for the public.

1.1   Contribution

The main contributions of this paper can be summarized as follows:

- We conceptualize an *energy efficiency framework* (schematically displayed in Fig. 1) for ML tasks and their respective metrics
- Our procedures for *indexing and rating* makes those metrics and models in general comparable, even across highly different execution environments
- Inspired by EU *energy labels*, we propose a method to communicate information on efficiency to a variety of target groups
- An *extensive experimental evaluation* on the most popular and widely-used models for image classification demonstrates our method's practicability, and provides a wide overview over the current energy efficiency landscape
- To make our framework as accessible as possible, we publish a software suite[1] that executes experiments, calculates metrics, and provides insight via an interactive *energy label exploration* (ELEx) tool

---

[1] www.github.com/raphischer/imagenet-energy-efficiency.

1.2   Related Work

We understand sustainability to be a core component of ongoing research on trustworthy AI [6,10]. The field discusses societal demands in a general scope [9,12], which also includes environmental aspects [29,32]. Computational cost and resource usage considerations have been discussed in the past [5], and directly correlate with energy consumption. Indeed, this correlation and resulting carbon emissions have been explicitly investigated for computer vision [14,29], data stream mining [14], and language models [4,26,31]. As expected, explicitly trading costly training for obtaining lightweight models with low energy demand has become a frequent phenomenon [18,33].

While these works identify the necessity for discussion on ML sustainability, they themselves only present exemplary results and do not provide a concise framework for assessing ML efficiency. This mission is especially hard, because a specific experiment's resource consumption depends strongly on the execution environment at hand (e.g., consumer PCs, micro-controllers [8,24,35], data centers [26], or quantum annealers [11]). Some works [1,16,28] introduce ways to directly measure and report the power draw of code execution on certain architectures. They utilize Python bindings of NVIDIA's Management Library (NVML)[2], Intel's RAPL[3] and Power Gadget[4], or just compute a rough estimate of power draw from the hardware's thermal design power (TDP) specification. However, these works neglect other metrics like predictive quality or number of model parameters, which are also important for assessing resource efficiency [29]. Recently, some important best practices for reducing the carbon emissions of ML experiments were presented [25].

The field also lacks methodology for combining all metrics into a concise report on ML efficiency, which ideally informs the affected target groups at their own level of understanding. Established frameworks for documenting ML experiments all have certain shortcomings for this task. OpenML [34] took an important step towards making ML research and results accessible to the greater public. However, they clearly did not consider sustainability to be important, as one can hardly find published results with measures on resource consumption. Fact Sheets [2] and Model Cards [22] document important practical properties of ML pipelines, but they do not provide a publicly available framework or database. Moreover, reporting on computational costs is also only optional. The aforementioned works have another significant drawback: They are too complicated and inaccessible for non-experts. For communicating the efficiency of electronic devices, the EU has successfully established the *energy label* system. It informs users about sustainability and resource demand in an easy-to-understand way [13]. Allowing more comprehensible communication about ML properties via "consumer" or "care" labels has recently been put forward [9,23,30]. However, the idea has not yet been thoroughly conceptualized for resource efficiency, or deployed practically for state-of-the-art (SOTA) models.

---

[2] www.pypi.org/project/pynvml/.

[3] www.pypi.org/project/pyRAPL/.

[4] www.intel.com/content/www/us/en/developer/articles/tool/power-gadget.html.

2   Assessing Energy Efficiency of Machine Learning

Better documentation and reporting of ML efficiency requires to first establish a coherent framework, which is this paper's main contribution (cf. Fig. 1). We start our methodology in Sect. 2.1 by defining the inputs to our framework, namely the execution environment and ML task configuration. To later assess efficiency, we closely monitor compute utilization and performance during task execution, as discussed in Sect. 2.2. As the resulting log files are verbose and hard to grasp, we propose a three-staged evaluation that is explained in detail in Sect. 2.3: First the task-specific metrics are *aggregated* from their bulky logs. To make them comparable, we project all metrics onto their *index scale*. We then *rate* the index scores per metric, and derive a compound model rating. As final step, Sect. 2.4 introduces energy labels that allow for communication of efficiency information at different levels of technical understanding.

2.1   Task Configurations and Their Environment

We argue that in order to reproduce SOTA experiments or estimate their environmental impact [29], we first have to thoroughly conceptualize and document both the *configuration* and *environment* of any ML system.

Definition 1. *A configuration C is a 3-tuple (T, D, M), which consists of the following components: (i) A task type T, i.e. a single action performed by means of an ML system, (ii) a data set D, and (iii) a model M including hyperparameter settings. The set of all possible configurations is denoted by $C = T \times D \times M$.*

A configuration, as defined above, can be seen as the abstract ML task a user wants to perform given a data set and an abstract model. Possible task types include but are not limited to: inference on data with a pre-trained model, training a model from scratch, fine-tuning a trained model on custom data, or testing a model for certain properties (e.g., explainability [7], robustness [27], verification [19]). It is important to differentiate between these tasks, because the performance of ML systems varies widely depending on the way they are used. This makes a fair comparison of models independently from the solved task nearly impossible. To give an example, a Nearest-Neighbor classifier can be trained instantly by just saving data to disk. Performing inference, on the other hand, is costly because it requires to calculate distances to all training data points. Conversely, training a high quality computer vision model requires a tremendous amount of energy, but performing inference is relatively cheap. Indeed, trading costly training for fast inference has been the explicit target of some works [18,33]. In this work we limit our methodology and discussion to the most prominent tasks, inference and training.

Executing a chosen task requires to also select among different data sets and models. This includes respective hyperparameters (e.g., model architecture, data augmentation, ...), while identifying optimal hyperparameters can be understood as a separate task type. Note that the definition of models in Definition 1 refers to abstract objects (a specific neural network, SVM, etc.), whose software or hardware implementations are mere instances. Due to computational imprecision or human error, these instances may fail to possess all theoretical properties of the underlying abstract model. By viewing models separately from their realization in software and hardware, we take into account all effects that may deteriorate (or, possibly, enhance) an ML system's efficacy for solving tasks.

For executing a given task and configuration, one is faced with a variety of options. Implementations can become arbitrarily complex, as libraries may be assembled from a multitude of more low-level libraries (e.g., ONNX, TensorFlow, scikit-learn). Furthermore, software can be run on different computing architectures, including embedded [35] or distributed systems. This leads to our definition of *environment*, which together with a configuration forms an *experiment*.

Definition 2. *An environment E is a tuple (A, S), consisting of (i) a computing architecture A, which is defined by the combination of hardware components, and (ii) software S which provides implementations of abstract ML models and tasks. We denote the set of all possible environments as $\mathcal{E} = \mathcal{A} \times \mathcal{S}$.*

Definition 3. *Given $(T, D, M) \in \mathcal{C}$ and $(S, A) \in \mathcal{E}$, an experiment X is the 5-tuple (T, D, M, S, A). We denote the set of all possible experiments as $\mathcal{X} \simeq \mathcal{C} \times \mathcal{E}$.*

Naturally, E and C depend on each other: $S \in E$ may not include implementations of some model $M \in C$, or conversely, M might require special hardware, which A does not provide (e.g., quantum annealing [20] requires quantum processors). Not only $\mathcal{C}$ and $\mathcal{E}$ influence each other, but also some $C \in \mathcal{T} \times \mathcal{D} \times \mathcal{M}$ or $E \in \mathcal{A} \times \mathcal{S}$ may be inadmissible in itself: The computing architecture limits the runable software (e.g., certain library versions may not be compatible with certain processors); conversely, certain software may require special hardware (e.g., specialized hardware-accelerated binaries [8] or integer-only networks [3]). The model choice might also restrict the options of usable data sets. Lastly, the task T may restrict which models are suitable, e.g., not all ML models allow for generating data, or probabilistic inference. Therefore we define the set of feasible combinations of configurations and environments as $\mathcal{X}_f := \{X : X \in \mathcal{X}, X \text{ is feasible}\} \subseteq \mathcal{X}$.

To exemplify our introduced terminology, we analyze how "training a TensorFlow implementation of ResNet101 on ImageNet" can be understood: The task T is "training" the abstract model M ResNet101 on the ImageNet data set D, along with certain hyperparameters (e.g., stop criteria, data preprocessing). S represents the TensorFlow software installation, which provides a compatible version of ResNet101 for the computing architecture A at hand.

2.2 Monitoring for Assessing Efficiency

An experiment $X \in \mathcal{X}_f$ is executable, and during execution should be closely monitored to later assess its efficiency. As already outlined in Sect. 1.2, monitoring is highly dependent on the environment E [14]. Certain tools (e.g., RAPL,

NVML) allow to inspect the hardware components' current power utilization. If no such tool is available, the power draw can be estimated from the hardware's TDP specification [28]. We propose an enhancement by also monitoring the compute utilization via tools like psutil, instead of just assuming constant utilization. For specialized hardware like field programmable gate arrays (FPGAs) or micro-controllers, on-board monitoring is challenging to implement [21]. In this case, one can fall back to measuring energy draw via external power meters. Note that the popularity of cloud-computing and virtualization (e.g., via Docker, AWS, Azure ML) can introduce more levels of complexity and thus complicate the monitoring. Assessing efficiency might also require specific code calls and libraries in addition to the task execution itself, for example to quantify the model's number of parameters or FLOPS.

2.3   Evaluation of Efficiency

We identified a range of important efficiency metrics (partly proposed in [29]):

- *Runtime* m_T in seconds, either aggregated per sample (m_{Ts}) (for inference), or per epoch (m_{Te}) and total (m_{Tt}) (for training)
- *Power Draw* m_P in watt-seconds, either aggregated per sample (m_{Ps}) (for inference), or per epoch (m_{Pe}) and total (m_{Pt}) (for training)
- *Predictive Quality* m_{Q1} and m_{Q5} as top-1 and top-5 accuracy on unseen validation data
- *Model Size* m_S in number of parameters
- *Model File Size* m_F in bytes
- *Model Complexity* m_C in number of GFLOPS

Only a subset $M_X \subseteq \{m_{Ts}, m_{Te}, m_{Tt}, m_{Ps}, m_{Pe} m_{Pt}, m_{Q1}, m_{Q5}, m_S, m_F, m_C\}$ of above metrics is used for a specific experiment. Whether a metric is applicable can be derived from the experiment's task type as provided in the configuration. Note that the list we give here is not exhaustive, as further metrics might be relevant for other tasks than training and inference. We later present how the impact of correlated metrics (e.g., different measures for predictive quality) can be lowered for a final efficiency rating. We purposefully leave out carbon emissions as the product of power draw and (static) local energy mix, as the latter is hard to determine from code [28].

Metric Aggregation. When an experiment is executed, it produces some output $O(X) \in \mathcal{O}$, containing task results (predictions, class labels, probabilities, etc.) as well as log files and collected statistics. The metrics need to be aggregated from this complex output. Running ML tasks is, in general, not deterministic under real-world conditions [36], due to environment factors such as different operating system loads, warm or cold caches, or non-deterministic algorithms. We therefore define the metric values $V(X)$ as a random variable, from which samples are drawn:

$$V(X) := (m(O(X)))_{m \in M_X} \tag{1}$$

To this end, we interpret all metrics as functions $m(\cdot) : \mathcal{O} \to \mathbb{R}^+$ that extract measurement values from the experiment's output. The measurements vary from being completely deterministic (e.g., number of parameters) to being quite random (e.g., power draw). The aggregation is straightforward for metrics such as accuracy, for which values can be directly extracted from log files. For runtime it makes sense to normalize the elapsed time during execution with the configured number of samples or epochs, making models more readily comparable for different configurations. Power draw is more difficult to aggregate, because monitoring tools take snapshots of power utilization in watt $P(t_i)$ at discrete time points t_i. A number of snapshots thus provides a time series, with the sum over watt-seconds approximating the overall power draw [16,28]. As different hardware components $a \in A' \subseteq A$ like CPU and GPU need to be monitored separately, the total power draw is provided by

$$m_P(O) = \sum_{a \in A'} \sum_i P_a(t_i) \cdot (t_i - t_{i-1}), \tag{2}$$

where A', t and P_a are extracted from O, which itself is a sample of $\boldsymbol{O}(X)$. Obviously, instead of computing the estimated total power draw, one could also adapt Eq. (2) to compute the maximum or average power draw.

Enabling Metric Comparability via Index Scales. After aggregating the experiment output, we obtain a sample $V(X)$ of $\boldsymbol{V}(X)$ containing measurements $\mu_i := m_i(O) \in V(X)$ for all $m_i \in M_X$. However, these measurements are incomparable among each other due to their different units. Even for a single metric like power draw, the unit magnitude might scale dramatically across different configurations and environments. Investigating trade-offs between different aspects of energy efficiency requires a unified scale. For this reason, we draw inspiration from the EU energy label system that makes use of an efficiency index [13], which replaces absolute with relative values. Using a relative error scale instead of absolute values is also common practice when testing neural networks for robustness [17].

Assume that task type T°, data set D°, and environment E° are fixed. We want to investigate the effect of choosing among models M w.r.t. to various metrics. To this end, we project all metric values $\mu_i \in V(X)$ onto relative index values $\iota_i \in I(X)$, which put all values in relation to *reference values* μ_i^*. These reference values are measurements V^* of $\boldsymbol{V}(X^*)$ such that $T^* = T^\circ$, $D^* = D^\circ$ and $E^* = E^\circ$. Ideally, V^* is stored in a database of reference measurements for different task/data set/environment combinations. These references are accessed when other experiments $\tilde{X}^\circ \in \{T^\circ\} \times \{D^\circ\} \times \mathcal{M} \times \{E^\circ\}$ with $\tilde{X}^\circ \in \mathcal{X}_f$ are executed. For all i, we set $\iota_i(X^*) = 1$ and assign

$$\iota_i(\tilde{X}^\circ) = \left(\frac{\mu_i(\tilde{X}^\circ)}{\mu_i(X^*)} \right)^{\sigma_i}, \tag{3}$$

Chiefly, we "plug in" different models M, keeping the task type, data set and environment fixed, take a measurement, and divide it by the reference measurement. The value σ_i is constant for each metric $m \in M$ and indicates whether the metric should be maximized ($\sigma_i = +1$) or minimized ($\sigma_i = -1$) to improve efficiency. If the metric should indeed be minimized (e.g., power consumption), the fraction is inverted. Thus ι_i indicates how much better or worse a respective combination of configuration and environment is with respect to the reference. As an example, assume we want to compare the metric m_S (model size). If the reference setup X^* measures $\mu_S(X^*) = 1000$ model parameters, and another setup $\tilde{X}^\circ$ measures $\mu_S(\tilde{X}^\circ) = 500$, then $\tilde{X}^\circ$ achieves an index score of $(500/1000)^{-1} = 2$ (as model size should be minimized). This value tells us that $\tilde{X}^\circ$ is "twice as good" as the reference w.r.t. model size.

Naturally, any combination of components T, D, M, S, A can be kept fixed, leading to analogous definitions of ι, but taking into account a wider scope of choices (e.g., how energy efficiency changes when changing the underlying hardware architecture, or when using different software packages). We find it sensible to keep at least the task type T fixed for any comparison.

Rating Model Efficiency. In order to make model efficiency even easier to assess and compare, we propose to determine discrete *ratings*. Based on the set of index values $I_i := \{\iota_i(X^\ell)\}_{\ell \in \{1,\dots,L\}}$ for L different experiments X^ℓ, we can assign ratings by partitioning I_i into a fixed number B of bins for each metric. To this end, we need to determine $B - 1$ boundary values $b_1, \dots, b_{B-1}$, with the rating $r_i(X^\ell)$ equaling the smallest j such that $\iota_i(X^\ell) \in [b_j, b_{j+1}]$. We define $b_0 = -\infty$ and $b_B = +\infty$ and assume $\forall j \in \{0, \dots, B-1\} : b_j < b_{j+1}$.

For our framework, we chose to use five bins which correspond to five ratings from **0** / A (best) to **4** / E (worst). Multiple strategies exist to determine boundaries: For their Energy Labels, the European Commission uses values that were hand-picked by experts [13]. A more mathematical approach would be to calculate specific q-quantiles of I_i (e.g., $q \in \{0.2, 0.4, 0.6, 0.8\}$).

Finally, we wish to assign a *compound* efficiency rating $R(X^\ell)$ that unifies all single-metric ratings. We propose to take a weighted median (WM) over all metrics,

$$R(X^\ell) := \mathrm{WM}\{w_i \cdot r_i(X^\ell) : i \in \{1, \dots, |M_{X^\ell}|\}\}, \tag{4}$$

such that $\sum_i w_i = 1$. By lowering weights, we can prevent highly correlated metrics like different accuracies from dominating the final rating. In addition to the choice of reference model and rating boundaries, the weights also allow for additional customization, if so desired. It enables users to precisely control which aspects of efficiency as represented by metrics are most important to them, allowing for adaption to their specific use cases. The introduced indexing and rating procedures also allow to easily follow the SOTA, as choosing newer and better reference models lowers all index values, and thus, ratings.

2.4   Communicating Machine Learning Efficiency

The aforementioned procedures allow us to specify an ML experiment, compute different metrics, and compare and combine them to investigate the given configuration's efficiency for the underlying environment. However, we argue that in order to benefit society as a whole, results from this assessment need to be conveyable at different stages of technical understanding. As shown in Fig. 1, we propose *three levels of communication* for results from a single experiment:

1. End-users without any understanding of ML should be provided a highly condensed energy label as visual summary, containing only the metric values $V(X)$ and respective ratings $r_i(X)$ and $R(X)$ represented via color codes
2. Developers and users of ML should be provided a log summary in form of a report, containing the metric values $V(X)$, their index scores $I(X)$, as well as the metric and compound ratings $r_i(X)$ and $R(X)$
3. Full output and log files $O(X)$ should be provided to ML experts, who might want to fully comprehend, reproduce, or build upon presented results

Besides efficiency metrics, general information on the configuration and environment at hand should also be provided to different extent (e.g. only the most important libraries for level 1, all ML-specific libraries and versions at level 2, or full list of installed software at level 3). The highest level of communication puts the idea of ML care labels [23] into effect, which in analogy to the EU's energy labels [13] enable less informed users to learn about efficiency aspects. The meaning of different metrics can be expressed in a more comprehensible way by depicting them as pictograms. Referring back to in-depth scientific results or implementations is possible via QR codes or similar links. Besides various other results we also show our own drafts of ML energy labels in the following section.

3   Experiments

To demonstrate practicability of our concept, we put it into effect and provide an in-depth experimental analysis. It investigates the efficiency of popular `ImageNet` models for two of the most prominent ML tasks, namely inference and training. Before discussing findings for both tasks, we provide some general information on the practical setup.

3.1   Experimental Setup

We chose two tasks T to investigate in terms of efficiency: (1) inference with pre-trained models on `ImageNet` (validation) data (D) and (2) fully training models from scratch (on train data). To underline the significance of index scaling, those tasks were performed in different execution environments E, as summarized in Table 1. We combined two hardware architectures A (full `NVIDIA DGX A100` node and consumer-level PC with a `Quadro RTX 5000` GPU) with different software installations S (`TensorFlow`, `PyTorch`, `ONNX`), optionally running code in CPU-only mode. The `ONNX` implementation first loads models from the other two libraries and then exports it for usage with `onnxruntime`. Training was only performed with GPUs due to time constraints, and is not supported by `ONNX`. We tested all `ImageNet` models M available with the standard installations of `torchvision` and `keras`, as well as `QuickNet`, a SOTA binarized

Table 1. Execution environments used for experimental evaluation

Environment Name	CPU Model	GPU Model	Libraries	Versions	# Experiments	
					Inference	Training
A100 x8 TensorFlow	AMD EPYC 7742	8 × NVIDIA A100-SXM4	tensorflow	2.8.0	26	21
			larq	0.12.2		
A100 x8 PyTorch	AMD EPYC 7742	8 × NVIDIA A100-SXM4	torch	1.10.2+cu113	22	13
			torchvision	0.11.3+cu113		
RTX 5000 TensorFlow	Intel Xeon W-2155	Quadro RTX 5000	tensorflow	2.4.1	26	10
			larq	0.12.2		
RTX 5000 PyTorch	Intel Xeon W-2155	Quadro RTX 5000	torch	1.10.2+cu113	22	12
			torchvision	0.11.3+cu113		
Xeon W-2155 TensorFlow	Intel Xeon W-2155	n.a.	tensorflow	2.4.1	26	0
			larq	0.12.2		
Xeon W-2155 PyTorch	Intel Xeon W-2155	n.a.	torch	1.10.2+cu113	22	0
			torchvision	0.11.3+cu113		
Xeon W-2155 ONNX TF	Intel Xeon W-2155	n.a.	onnxruntime	1.10.0	17	0
			onnx	1.11.0		
			tensorflow	2.4.1		
			larq	0.12.2		
Xeon W-2155 ONNX PT	Intel Xeon W-2155	n.a.	onnxruntime	1.10.0	15	0
			onnx	1.11.0		
			torch	1.10.2+cu113		
			torchvision	0.11.3+cu113		

network provided by `Larq` [3]. The exact number of experiments vary because the environment limits the repertory of runable models. We chose `ResNet101` as reference model V^*, due to its popularity and widespread availability [15]. All experiments were conducted with a batch size of 32. We implemented monitoring with the help of `RAPL`, `NVML`, and `psutil`, while `ptflops` and `onnx-opcounter` enable us to estimate the number of GFLOPS. Our software also uses `PyMuPDF` and `reportlab` to automatically generate hybrid energy labels.

Deploying our indexing and rating routines requires to determine rating boundaries $b_1, \ldots, b_{B-1}$ and metrics weights w_i, as explained in Sect. 2.3. The former were calculated as equidistant quantiles over all index values per metrics. Metric weights for the compound rating were chosen by the authors with justification as listed in Table 2, during rating calculation normalized to $\sum_i w_i = 1$. The full implementation of our methods as well as all results are publicly available at www.github.com/raphischer/imagenet-energy-efficiency. In this paper we only discuss selected results, but we invite readers to also take a deeper dive with our interactive *ELEx* tool.

3.2 Efficiency Results for Image Classification

We start our exploration of `ImageNet` classification efficiency by putting different metrics in relation to each other. The comparison of four important metrics $(m_{Ps}, m_{Q1}, m_S, m_{Ts})$ for the `A100 x8 - TensorFlow 2.8.0` environment is provided in Fig. 2. While measurement values occur with different units and magnitudes, our indexing procedure makes all metrics comparable. We always find `ResNet101` at $(1, 1)$, while other models are positioned in relative distance

Table 2. Determined metric weights and their justification

Metric(s)	Weight	Justification
m_{Ps}, m_{Pt} m_{Ts}, m_{Tt}	0.7 0.3	Highly correlated and important, power draw slightly more important, together shouldn't dominate too much
m_{Te}, m_{Pe}	0.2	Slight impact, as number of epochs might change with stop criteria
m_S, m_F	0.4	Highly correlated and rather important, should have the same impact without dominating too much
m_{Q1} m_{Q5}	0.8 0.2	Highly correlated and important, top-1 slightly more important, together shouldn't dominate too much
m_C	0.2	Smaller impact, because there is no unified implementation available for counting or estimating the number of FLOPS

to the reference model. One can clearly see how considering multiple metrics provides us with a Pareto frontier of optimal model choices. In the plots, rating boundaries of each metric are indicated by colored grid cells. Note that the scatter point color represents the compound model rating over all metrics, which thus remains equal for both comparisons. As only two of the seven metrics are shown in each plot, the point color can diverge from the cell color (e.g., for the VGG19 model).

Furthermore, computing index scores makes models comparable across different environments, as depicted in Table 3. It lists real numbers and corresponding index values of the four metrics for ResNet101 and EfficientNetB0. As expected, values for accuracy (m_{Q1}) and number of parameters (m_S) remain similar across environments, but power draw (m_{Ps}) and inference time (m_{Ts}) change drastically. The relative (index) performance however remains similar, resulting in mostly equal ratings as indicated by cell colors. Interestingly, only a single environment results in EfficientNetB0 running slower but more energy efficient and accurate than ResNet101. This demonstrates the unpredictable implications when deploying the very same model in different environments.

The comparability across environments can also be seen when looking at the frequencies of compound ratings, as depicted in Fig. 3. The sum of frequencies corresponds to the number of models tested on a specific environment, or in other words, the number of inference experiments in Table 1. Because models might perform differently when changing the hardware or software setup, the distributions differ but remain comparable. Each environment brings forth their own respective landscape to explore for efficiency, bringing us back to Fig. 2. Interestingly, the powerful A100 node provides slightly more narrow distributions of ratings for both software installations. As the rating boundaries and metric weights are fixed for all experiments, this indicates that models behave more similarly, having less relative distance to the reference model. We also see that our weighted median approach (cf. Sect. 2.3) provides few A and E compound ratings, even though the boundaries were chosen to evenly distribute the individual metric ratings. An exemplary energy label as generated by our software is also depicted in Fig. 3, allowing non-experts to understand efficiency aspects of deploying MobileNetV2 on A100 x8 - TensorFlow at a glance.

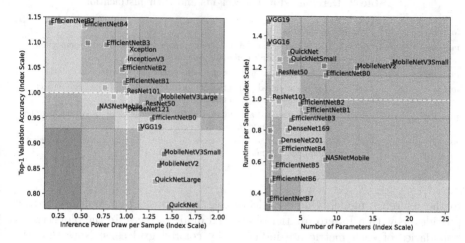

Fig. 2. Choosing among different models trades off different efficiency metrics, with accuracy, power draw, number of model parameters and runtime being shown here. Our introduced index scales make them compare- and rateable, as indicated by the background color grid. Point colors denote the compound model rating across all seven metrics, from which two are being shown per plot.

Table 3. Aggregated metrics and their index scores for different models and environments. While numeric measurements are hard to compare, their relative index scores allow for useful comparison and rating (displayed by color).

Environment	Model Name	Power m_{P_s}		Time m_{T_s}		Size m_S		Quality m_{Q1}	
		Value [Ws]	Index	Value [ms]	Index	Value	Index	Value [%]	Index
A100 x8 TensorFlow	ResNet101	0.859	1.00	1.579	1.00	44.7e6	1.00	0.718	1.00
	EfficientNetB0	0.673	1.28	1.369	1.15	5.3e6	8.39	0.681	0.95
A100 x8 PyTorch	ResNet101	0.897	1.00	1.664	1.00	44.5e6	1.00	0.770	1.00
	EfficientNetB0	0.877	1.02	1.870	0.89	5.3e6	8.42	0.777	1.01
RTX 5000 TensorFlow	ResNet101	0.680	1.00	2.653	1.00	44.7e6	1.00	0.718	1.00
	EfficientNetB0	0.260	2.62	1.180	2.25	5.3e6	8.39	0.681	0.95
RTX 5000 PyTorch	ResNet101	0.740	1.00	2.643	1.00	44.5e6	1.00	0.770	1.00
	EfficientNetB0	0.288	2.57	1.143	2.31	5.3e6	8.42	0.777	1.01
Xeon W-2155 TensorFlow	ResNet101	3.115	1.00	25.305	1.00	44.7e6	1.00	0.718	1.00
	EfficientNetB0	1.706	1.83	13.911	1.82	5.3e6	8.39	0.681	0.95
Xeon W-2155 PyTorch	ResNet101	4.121	1.00	33.532	1.00	44.5e6	1.00	0.770	1.00
	EfficientNetB0	1.330	3.10	11.909	2.82	5.3e6	8.42	0.777	1.01
Xeon W-2155 ONNX TF	ResNet101	2.188	1.00	15.947	1.00	44.7e6	1.00	0.720	1.00
	EfficientNetB0	1.059	2.07	9.309	1.71	5.3e6	8.39	0.683	0.95
Xeon W-2155 ONNX PT	ResNet101	2.110	1.00	15.101	1.00	44.5e6	1.00	0.770	1.00
	EfficientNetB0	0.745	2.83	6.388	2.36	5.3e6	8.42	0.777	1.01

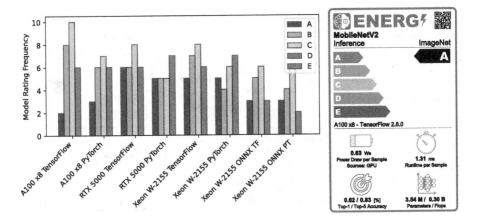

Fig. 3. With our indexing and rating procedures, each environment has its own meaningful distribution of compound ratings for different models. On the right, the energy label for `MobileNetV2` is displayed, one of the two `A`-rated models on the `A100 x8 – TensorFlow` environment.

3.3 Efficiency Results for Training Classification Models

Let us now discuss insights for training `ImageNet` models from scratch. Unfortunately, we found SOTA performances impossible to reproduce, because unambiguous information on hyperparameters is hard to find (e.g., learning rates, data augmentation, stop criteria). We therefore fell back to training for 10 epochs, aggregating metrics per epoch, and estimating the full expense based on training duration as found in literature. We also report the accuracy obtained with pre-trained weights, as we were unable to achieve comparable quality.

The comparison of total power draw m_{Pt} versus model accuracy m_{Q1} on the `A100 x8 – TensorFlow` setup is displayed in Fig. 4. Note that some models obtained index scores 0 for power draw, because information on total number of training epochs could not be retrieved [33]. Thus, we assigned `E` ratings and display *n. a.* in the corresponding energy label (shown for `EfficientNetB2`). Overall the efficiency landscape indicates that `DenseNets` and `ResNets` provide a reasonable trade-off between power demand and predictive performance. More recent models appear to sacrifice affordable energy costs for better accuracy. `MobileNetV3Small` [18] receives the best compound rating, and was also performing exceptionally well during inference experiments. Compared to Fig. 2, the x axis distribution of models is completely different, showing that models' relative power draw can be very different between inference and training.

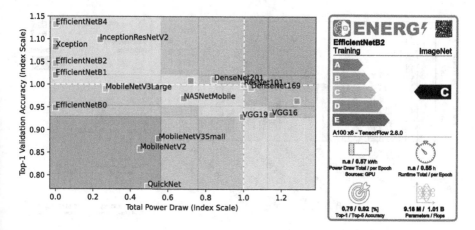

Fig. 4. Power draw versus accuracy trade-off for fully training models on the A100 x8 – TensorFlow setup. DenseNets and ResNets appear to make a reasonable trade for these metrics. If the number of training epochs is unknown, models (e.g. EfficientNetB2) receive an exceptionally bad rating.

4   Conclusion and Future Work

While others have identified the importance of assessing ML efficiency, we presented a concise framework for this endeavour. Firstly, we thoroughly formalized ML experiments and identified different efficiency metrics. With the introduced indexing approach, those metrics become comparable both among each other, and across various kinds of environments. The assessment step rates each index score and derives the compound experiment rating. Finally, we presented how information on efficiency can be communicated to different audiences at their respective level of understanding, thus truly contributing to social good.

We also successfully implemented our methodology, and were able to provide an extensive overview over the efficiency of SOTA ImageNet models. As expected, the ones with highest predictive quality tend to have alarming resource consumption during training and inference. Even though being a bit outdated, MobileNet models [18] still appear to make the most reasonable trade-off across all metrics. The shown energy labels are first drafts for a novel communication form, which allows even non-experts to learn about ML sustainability. Our concepts as well as implementations are also highly customizable and expandable.

For the future, we will extend our proposed methods for assessing other aspects of trustworthiness, such as model robustness. Additionally, we would like to also inform stakeholders about theoretical guarantees of investigated methods, and possibly test whether or not they hold for given environments. Serving as motivation for our presented energy labels, we argue that in order to improve the societal trust in ML, any communication of practical measurements and theoretical properties must take place at more diverse levels of comprehension.

Acknowledgement. This research has been funded by the Federal Ministry of Education and Research of Germany and the state of North-Rhine Westphalia as part of the Lamarr-Institute for Machine Learning and Artificial Intelligence, LAMARR22B.

References

1. Anthony, L.F.W., Kanding, B., Selvan, R.: Carbontracker: tracking and predicting the carbon footprint of training deep learning models. In: ICML Workshop on Challenges in Deploying and monitoring Machine Learning Systems (2020). arXiv:2007.03051
2. Arnold, M., et al.: FactSheets: increasing trust in AI services through supplier's declarations of conformity. IBM J. Res. Develop. **63**, 6:1-6:13 (2019)
3. Bannink, T., et al.: Larq compute engine: Design, benchmark, and deploy state-of-the-art binarized neural networks (2020). https://arxiv.org/abs/2011.09398
4. Bender, E.M., Gebru, T., McMillan-Major, A., Shmitchell, S.: On the dangers of stochastic parrots: can language models be too big? In: Conference on Fairness, Accountability, and Transparency, pp. 610–623 (2021). https://doi.org/10.1145/3442188.3445922
5. Birhane, A., Kalluri, P., Card, D., Agnew, W., Dotan, R., Bao, M.: The values encoded in machine learning research (2021). https://arxiv.org/abs/2106.15590
6. Brundage, M., et al.: Toward trustworthy AI development: mechanisms for supporting verifiable claims (2020). https://arxiv.org/abs/2004.07213
7. Burkart, N., Huber, M.F.: A survey on the explainability of supervised machine learning. J. Artif. Intell. Res. (JAIR) **70**, 245–317 (2021). https://doi.org/10.1613/jair.1.12228
8. Buschjäger, S., Pfahler, L., Buss, J., Morik, K., Rhode, W.: On-site Gamma-Hadron separation with deep learning on FPGAs. In: Dong, Y., Mladenić, D., Saunders, C. (eds.) ECML PKDD 2020. LNCS (LNAI), vol. 12460, pp. 478–493. Springer, Cham (2021). https://doi.org/10.1007/978-3-030-67667-4_29
9. Chatila, R., et al.: Trustworthy AI, pp. 13–39 (2021). https://doi.org/10.1007/978-3-030-69128-8_2
10. Cremers, A., et al.: Trustworthy use of artificial intelligence - priorities from a philosophical, ethical, legal, and technological viewpoint as a basis for certification of artificial intelligence (2019)
11. Elsayed, N., Maida, A.S., Bayoumi, M.: A review of quantum computer energy efficiency. In: Green Technologies Conference, pp. 1–3 (2019)
12. EU Ai HLEG: Assessment list for trustworthy artificial intelligence (ALTAI) for self-assessment (2020). https://futurium.ec.europa.eu/en/european-ai-alliance/pages/altai-assessment-list-trustworthy-artificial-intelligence
13. European Commission: Commission delegated regulation (eu) 2019/2014 with regard to energy labelling of household washing machines and household washer-dryers (2019). https://eur-lex.europa.eu/legal-content/EN/ALL/?uri=CELEX:32019R2014
14. García-Martín, E., Rodrigues, C.F., Riley, G., Grahn, H.: Estimation of energy consumption in machine learning. J. Parallel Distrib. Comput. **134**, 75–88 (2019)
15. He, K., Zhang, X., Ren, S., Sun, J.: Deep residual learning for image recognition (2015). http://arxiv.org/abs/1512.03385
16. Henderson, P., et al.: Towards the systematic reporting of the energy and carbon footprints of machine learning (2020). https://arxiv.org/abs/2002.05651

17. Hendrycks, D., Dietterich, T.G.: Benchmarking neural network robustness to common corruptions and perturbations (2019). http://arxiv.org/abs/1903.12261
18. Howard, A.G., et al.: MobileNets: efficient convolutional neural networks for mobile vision applications (2017). http://arxiv.org/abs/1704.04861
19. Huang, X., et al.: A survey of safety and trustworthiness of deep neural networks: verification, testing, adversarial attack and defence, and interpretability. Comput. Sci. Rev. **37**, 100270 (2020). https://doi.org/10.1016/j.cosrev.2020.100270
20. Kadowaki, T., Nishimori, H.: Quantum annealing in the transverse Ising model. Phys. Rev. E **58**(5), 5355 (1998)
21. Kourfali, A., Stroobandt, D.: In-circuit debugging with dynamic reconfiguration of FPGA interconnects. Trans. Reconfigurable Technol. Syst. **13**(1), 1–29 (2020)
22. Mitchell, M., et al.: Model cards for model reporting. In: Conference on Fairness, Accountability, and Transparency, pp. 220–229 (2019). https://dl.acm.org/doi/abs/10.1145/3287560.3287596
23. Morik, K., et al.: Yes we care! - certification for machine learning methods through the care label framework (2021). https://arxiv.org/abs/2105.10197
24. Mücke, S., Piatkowski, N., Morik, K.: Hardware acceleration of machine learning beyond linear algebra. In: Cellier, P., Driessens, K. (eds.) ECML PKDD 2019. CCIS, vol. 1167, pp. 342–347. Springer, Cham (2020). https://doi.org/10.1007/978-3-030-43823-4_29
25. Patterson, D., et al.: The carbon footprint of machine learning training will plateau, then shrink (2022). https://arxiv.org/abs/2204.05149
26. Patterson, D.A., et al.: Carbon emissions and large neural network training (2021). https://arxiv.org/abs/2104.10350
27. Rauber, J., Brendel, W., Bethge, M.: Foolbox: A Python toolbox to benchmark the robustness of machine learning models (2017). https://arxiv.org/abs/1707.04131
28. Schmidt, V., et al.: CodeCarbon: estimate and track carbon emissions from machine learning computing (2021). https://github.com/mlco2/codecarbon
29. Schwartz, R., Dodge, J., Smith, N.A., Etzioni, O.: Green AI. Commun. ACM **63**(12), 54–63 (2020). https://doi.org/10.1145/3381831
30. Seifert, C., Scherzinger, S., Wiese, L.: Towards generating consumer labels for machine learning models. In: International Conference on Cognitive Machine Intelligence, pp. 173–179 (2019). https://doi.org/10.1109/CogMI48466.2019.00033
31. Strubell, E., Ganesh, A., McCallum, A.: Energy and policy considerations for deep learning in NLP (2019). http://arxiv.org/abs/1906.02243
32. Strubell, E., Ganesh, A., McCallum, A.: Energy and policy considerations for modern deep learning research. In: AAAI Conference on Artificial Intelligence, pp. 13693–13696 (2020)
33. Tan, M., Le, Q.: EfficientNet: rethinking model scaling for convolutional neural networks. In: 36th International Conference on Machine Learning, pp. 6105–6114 (2019). https://proceedings.mlr.press/v97/tan19a.html
34. Vanschoren, J., Van Rijn, J.N., Bischl, B., Torgo, L.: OpenML: networked science in machine learning. SIGKDD Explor. Newsl. **15**(2), 49–60 (2014)
35. Warden, P., Situnayake, D.: Tiny ML: Machine Learning with Tensorflow Lite on Arduino and Ultra-Low-Power Microcontrollers. O'Reilly Media, Sebastopol (2019)
36. Zhuang, D., Zhang, X., Song, S.L., Hooker, S.: Randomness in neural network training: characterizing the impact of tooling (2021). https://arxiv.org/abs/2106.11872

Fault Detection in Wastewater Treatment Plants: Application of Autoencoders Models with Streaming Data

Rodrigo Salles[1,2]($\boxtimes$), Jérôme Mendes[2]🔘, Rita P. Ribeiro[1,3]🔘, and João Gama[3,4]🔘

[1] Faculty of Sciences, University of Porto, 4169-007 Porto, Portugal
engenharia.salles@gmail.com
[2] Institute of Systems and Robotics, University of Coimbra,
3030-290 Coimbra, Portugal
[3] INESC TEC, 4200-465 Porto, Portugal
[4] Faculty of Economics, University of Porto, 4200-464 Porto, Portugal

Abstract. Water is a fundamental human resource and its scarcity is reflected in social, economic and environmental problems. Water used in human activities must be treated before reusing or returning to nature. This treatment takes place in wastewater treatment plants (WWTPs), which need to perform their functions with high quality, low cost, and reduced environmental impact. This paper aims to identify failures in real-time, using streaming data to provide the necessary preventive actions to minimize damage to WWTPs, heavy fines and, ultimately, environmental hazards. Convolutional and Long short-term memory (LSTM) autoencoders (AEs) were used to identify failures in the functioning of the dissolved oxygen sensor used in WWTPs. Five faults were considered (drift, bias, precision degradation, spike and stuck) in three different scenarios with variations in the appearance order, intensity and duration of the faults. The best performance, considering different model configurations, was achieved by Convolutional-AE.

Keywords: Wastewater treatment plant · Fault detection · Autoencoder · BSM2

1 Introduction

Water is a strategic and fundamental resource for human beings. Activities carried out in the industry, agriculture, and services depend directly on access to water resources. And access to water is limited. Most of the water on the planet is in the seas and oceans (97%) [1]. There is only 3% of fresh water, but more than two-thirds is frozen in glaciers and polar ice [2]. The small fraction of fresh water remaining needs to serve more and more people. It is estimated that two-thirds of the world's population, 4 billion people, face water scarcity conditions at least one month a year, and approximately 500 million people live with water

I. Koprinska et al. (Eds.): ECML PKDD 2022 Workshops, CCIS 1752, pp. 55–70, 2023.
https://doi.org/10.1007/978-3-031-23618-1_4

shortages throughout the year [3]. Water is a strategic resource and must be managed consciously. The used water must be treated so that we can reused it. Wastewater may contain pollutants that pose risks to the environment and consequently to humans and need to be treated in appropriate places. Wastewater treatment plants (WWTPs) are structures that accelerate the treatment process in nature. The water used in human activities is sent to the WWTPs, which carry out the treatment in several stages, using chemical and physical processes. These structures are present in various parts of the world. In the United States of America, there are more than 16000 public administration WWTPs. Europe has more than 24000 treatment units. Brazil, Mexico, and China have 2820, 2540, and 1486 WWTPs, respectively [4].

WWTPs are important in dealing with water scarcity, but they must carry out their functions sustainably, with high quality and low cost. A monitoring system is needed to provide information from all stages of the treatment process so the necessary actions can be taken at the right time. With technological advances, new techniques were used to improve the functioning of WWTPs. The massive use of sensors in the monitoring of treatment plants generated a large amount of information and enabled the use of new control and optimization techniques. But the use of sensors also poses new problems. The actions taken by the control and optimization methods depend on the quality of the information provided by the sensors, and the quality of this information must be ensured. It is common for sensors to be exposed to extreme conditions at the monitoring site, as for example, temperature, vibrations, dust, chemical reagents, etc. It is of great importance that failures in these sensors are indicated as soon as possible, where undetected failures can represent damage to the structure of WWTPs, heavy fines, and environmental damage.

One of the main wastewater treatment phases occurs in the biological reactor. This reactor is composed of anoxic and oxygenated tanks, and it is the site of action of microorganisms that have the function of removing dangerous pollutants from wastewater. Oxygenated tanks need to maintain minimum oxygen levels. Lack of oxygen can result in the death of microorganisms, and excess oxygen represents a waste of energy spent on pumping. Considering that aeration is the most energy-intensive operation in wastewater treatment, amounting to 45–75% of plant energy costs [5], that of all the energy consumed in the world, approximately 3% is consumed in WWTPs [6], and that the energy spent on pumping depends on the information of the dissolved oxygen (DO) levels provided by the sensor, an efficient fault detection system is essential for the DO sensor. The main objective of this paper is to use autoencoder (AE) models to detect DO sensor failures in WWTPs. Early failure detection is important as it allows the necessary actions to be taken, benefiting higher safety, economy and quality of wastewater treatment. This work aims to assess the potential of AE in detecting failures in DO sensors, in WWTPs, in real-time, with streaming data. The simulator Benchmark Simulation Model n№2 (BSM2), which reproduces all phases of the treatment performed in a WWTP, was used to test the fault detection methodologies on the DO sensor in the biological reactor. This work analyzes the strengths and weaknesses of the Convolution-AE and LSTM-AE models, used to detect failures on DO sensors presented in WWTPs. The models are evaluated for the detection of five types of failures: bias, drift, precision degradation, spike and stuck. These faults were injected into the dataset, obtained with the help of BSM2, in three scenarios, with changes in the order of appearance, duration and intensity of the faults.

The rest of the paper is organized as follows: Sect. 2 brings a review of literature related to fault detection in WWTPs. Section 3 describes the simulator used and the case studies. Section 4 presents the structure of AE-based methodologies used to identify faults on DO sensors. Section 5 presents the experimental results, and compares the performance of Convolution-AE and LSTM-AE models in identifying the failures. Finally, in Sect. 6, the conclusion of the work is elaborated.

2   Related Work

Many works have already been proposed with the objective of detecting failures in sensors in WWTPs. The works can be divided into two large groups: failure detection using statistical methods, and failure detection using machine learning techniques. In [7], the use of artificial neural networks (ANNs) is proposed to identify six types of faults, one of which is the DO concentration sensor. The results proved a good ability of the ANN to recognize the faults, identifying 97% of case study failures. In [8], the authors use a Long short-term memory (LSTM) networks to identify collective failures in the sensors. The results obtained by the LSTM were compared to the results of the autoregressive integrated moving average (ARIMA), principal component analysis (PCA) and support-vector machines (SVM) models, and achieved the best performance, with a fault detection rate of over 92%. In [9], a radial basis function (RBF) neural network is used to identify faults in DO sensors by calculating the error limits. The proposed method obtained 0% false alarm, and a delay of 0.22 days in detection. In fault detection, unsupervised ANN can be trained to model a process by estimating the values of inputs and comparing the estimation to the actual values, also known as autoencoder. In [10], the authors used an AE, and the proposed model was used for detection of abrupt changes and drift in the sensor signal. The results showed that AE is capable of detecting sensor faults with good accuracy under different scenarios. In [11], a variational AE is used for fault detection. The proposed model takes into account the temporal evolution of the treatment process. The slow feature variational AE (SFAVAE) model is used to monitor processes and tries to identify faults such as sludge expansion fault and small magnitude variable step. Among the statistical methods the most used is the PCA. The PCA has many applications in WWTP, from direct fault detection [12] to data reconstruction [13]. In [14], the Incremental Principal Component Analysis (IPCA) method was used to identify several types of failures in WWTPs, one of them being failures in the DO sensor. The failures were injected into the dataset, and IPCA proved to be able to detect the failures and isolate the variable that originated the failure, with false alarm rate and missed detection rate of 0.07% and 18.53% respectively. A probabilistic PCA approach in process monitoring and fault diagnosis with application in WWTP is proposed in [15]. The probabilistic PCA is compared to PCA, PPCA (probabilistic interpretation of the PCA), GPLVM (version of the PPCA for nonlinear situations) and Bayesian GPLVM (uses the Bayesian theory for training). The GPLVM and GPLVM models showed better performance in detecting failures in relation to the other models analyzed in the paper, in relation to the considered metrics. The major drawback of PCA for WWTP, is the assumption that process variables are linearly related to each other [16]. In the present work, models based on AE will be used. The case studies in which the models will be evaluated will be explained in the following section.

3 Case Studies

The water resulting from human activities, which carry pollutants, cannot be returned to the environment without undergoing treatment. This treatment occurs in WWTPs and is done in several stages: primary treatment (removes floatable and settleable solids), secondary treatment (secondary decantation and activated sludge), tertiary treatment (reuse of treated water), and sludge treatment (mechanical and biological treatments) [17]. Before implementing and evaluating new techniques in real treatment plants, simulators are commonly used. A widely used simulator of WWTPs is BSM2 [14,18]. Section 3.1 provides a brief description of the BSM2, and Sect. 3.2 presents the case studies with the description of the injected failures.

3.1 Benchmark Simulation Model No 2 - BSM2

The BSM2 is a simulation environment in which the plant layout, the simulation model, influence loads, test procedures and evaluation criteria are defined. For each of these items, compromises were pursued to combine plainness with realism and accepted standards [19]. BSM2 allows the implementation of several techniques and the manipulation of many parameters related to WWTPs [20,21]. The influent dynamics are defined for 609 days, which takes into account rainfall effect, and temperature [19], with the data sampled every 15 min. The structure of BSM2 can be seen in the Fig. 1. The BSM2 was used to test the failure detection methods used in this work.

3.2 Faults in Dissolved Oxygen Sensor

BSM2 simulates the various stages of WWTPs. The biological reactor or activated sludge reactor can be seen in Fig. 1. Figure 2 shows the biological reactor in more detail. It consists of five tanks, the first two being anoxic and the next three oxygenated. In oxygenated tanks, the DO level must be kept at 2 [mg/L],

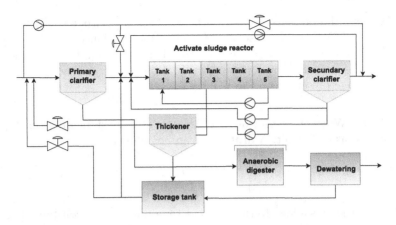

Fig. 1. Layout of Benchmark simulation model no 2 - BSM2.

by a proportional-integral (PI) controller, which receives the DO values measured in Tank 4, compares it with the reference value, and drives the pumps responsible for maintaining the DO at the correct levels.

The aeration system depends on the value measured by the DO sensor. A failure in this signal leads the system to malfunction. Through BSM2, we injected several faults. The objective is to identify the faults as early as possible. Also, in Fig. 2, it can be seen that the DO sensor performs its measurement in Tank 4 and it is used by the PI controller, and that the AE, represented in yellow, was positioned between the DO sensor and the PI controller, and has the function of detecting anomalous behavior in the measurement signal coming from the DO sensor.

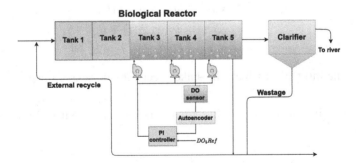

Fig. 2. Biological reactor details and case studies framework.

To evaluate the performance of the fault detection system, some faults were injected into the signal from the sensor. Deviations from expected behavior in the sensor output are considered faults, and they are classified according to the deviation from normal behavior. Let $s(t) = h(t) + \eta$ be the expected output of a sensor without the presence of faults, where $h(t)$ is the output of the sensor at time t, and $\eta \sim N(0, \delta_n^2)$ is noise, and δ_n^2 is the noise variance [22]. The failures considered in the present work are presented below [23,24]. They are common failures in sensors caused by corrosion, calibration errors, presence of noise and physical damage presented on the WWTPs.

Drift Fault. When the sensor output increases at a constant rate, this type of fault is called as drift fault. A drift fault can be defined as

$$s(t) = h(t) + \eta + b(t), \tag{1}$$
$$b(t) = b(t-1) + v,$$

where $b(t)$ is the bias added to the signal at time t, and v is a constant. The $s(t)$ value increases linearly from the normal value over time.

Bias Fault. In a bias fault, a constant value v is added to the sensor output and, as a consequence, a shift from the normal value is observed:

$$s(t) = h(t) + \eta + v. \tag{2}$$

Precision Degradation (PD) Fault. This type of fault adds noise with a zero mean and high variance (δ_v^2) to the output of a sensor:

$$s(t) = h(t) + \eta + v, \ v \sim N(0, \delta_v^2), \ \delta_v^2 \gg \delta_n^2. \tag{3}$$

Spike Fault. In spike faults, large amplitude peaks are observed at constant time intervals at the sensor output:

$$s(t) = h(t) + \eta + v(t), \tag{4}$$
$$\forall t = v \times \tau, \ h(t) + \eta,$$
$$\text{otherwise}, \ v = \{1, 2, ...\}, \ \tau \geq 2,$$

where τ is the interval in which the spikes occur in the sensor output.

Stuck Fault. It is a complete failure, with the sensor output being locked at a fixed value v:

$$s(t) = v. \tag{5}$$

4   Fault Detection Using Autoencoders

WWTPs exhibit marked nonlinear characteristics due to biochemical reactions and nitrification processes [25]. Thus, traditional statistical methods present difficulties in correctly identifying changes in the variables involved in the wastewater treatment process. In order to have a good performance in identifying the changes that may occur in WWTPs, the method used must be able to deal with non-linearities. The AE present, among other characteristics, the ability to deal with non-linear processes.

AE is an unsupervised machine learning algorithm that aims to reconstruct its input signal. The generic AE model consists of three parts: encoder (responsible for reducing the dimensionality of the data), code (reduced representation of the encoder input data), and decoder (responsible for expanding the dimensionality represented in the code, and reconstructing the input signal). A representation of the AE can be seen in the Fig. 3.

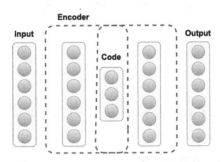

Fig. 3. Illustration of a generic AE model.

AE can have a simple structure, with only the code as the hidden layer, or can have several hidden layers. The representation of the input data, made by the code layer, can be classified as undercomplete or overcomplete. In undercomplete representation, the dimension of the representation of the input data by the code is smaller than the dimension of the input data, which forces the model to learn the most important characteristics of the input data. If the dimension of the code's input data representation is equal to the input dimension, the overcomplete representation, the model will just copy the input signal to the output without learning the most important characteristics of the input signal. The AE can be implemented as fully connected, convolution based or recurrent based units [26]. In this work, two models of AE will be used: LSTM-AE and Convolutional-AE. These models will be described in the next subsections.

4.1 LSTM Autoencoder

LSTM is a recurrent neural network that takes into account the historical context of events to make its predictions, with the help of memory cells. In an LSTM cell there are input, forget, memory and output gates.

In [27], the LSTM-AE is described as an extension to RNN based AE for learning the representation of time series sequential data. In this model, encoder and decoder are built using LSTM. The encoder LSTM receives a sequence of vectors that represents the signal from the DO sensor, and the decoder has the function of recreating the target sequence of input vectors in the reverse order. This is the model used in the present work. The generic structure of a LSTM-AE can be seen in Fig. 4

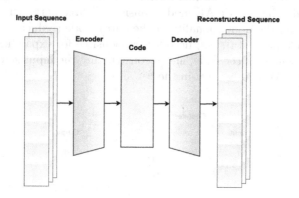

Fig. 4. Generic structure of the LSTM-AE.

4.2 Convolutional Autoencoder

Fully connected AEs ignore the spatial structure of the input signal, and this spatial structure can represent important information for the final reconstruction. To solve this problem, in [28] is proposed a model known as Convolutional-AE. Instead of using fully connected layers, Convolutional-AE use convolutional operators.

The Convolutional-AE is trained to reproduce the input signal from the DO sensor to the output layer. The signal passes through the encoder, composed of a convolution layer, which reduces the dimension of the representation of the input signal. In the decoder, composed of deconvolution layers, the compressed signal is reconstructed to obtain the original input signal, the DO sensor signal. The generic structure of a Convolutional-AE can be seen in Fig. 5.

The LSTM-AE and Convolutional-AE will be used to identify failures in these case studies. The experimental results will be described in Sect. 5.

5 Experimental Results

This section presents the results obtained by Convolutional-AE and LSTM-AE presented in Sect. 4, in detecting the faults described in Sect. 3.2. This section also describes the characteristics of injected faults and the evaluation metrics.

The dataset from the DO sensor, was separated into two equal parts, each part being equivalent to 100 days (9600 samples), keeping the temporal order. The first part was used to inject the faults described in Table 1 and represented in the graphs of Fig. 6. From the second part, without failures, 70% of the data was used for training the Convolutional-AE and LSTM-AE, and the remaining 30%

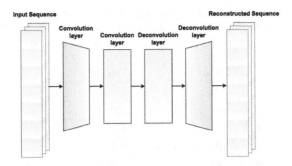

Fig. 5. Generic structure a Convolutional-AE.

was used for evaluating the models, according to the input signal reconstruction error. In order to obtain the best model for each algorithm, a grid search were performed, with the evaluation of the combination of hyperparameters. All the work was developed in Python programming language, version 3.7, with the help of the Keras neural network package, version 2.8.0. The following combinations of hyperparameters were analyzed:

- Convolutional-AE: Epochs = $[10, 20, 30, 40, 50]$; Batch size = $[32, 64, 128]$;
  AE layout : $[16, 32, 64, 128]$.
- LSTM-AE: Epochs = $[10, 20, 30, 40, 50]$; Batch size = $[32, 64, 128]$;
  LSTM cells (AE layout) = $[16, 32, 64, 128]$.

The best model was the one with the lowest mean absolute error (MAE):

$$\text{MAE} = \frac{1}{n} \sum_{i=1}^{n} |s_t - \hat{s}_t|, \tag{6}$$

where s_t and $\hat{s}_t$ are the real and estimated DO values at the instant of time t, and n is the number of samples used to validation.

The best models found, according to the MAE, were:

- Convolutional-AE: Epochs = 20; Batch size = 128;
  AE layout = [32, 16, 16, 32]
- LSTM-AE: Epochs = 20; Batch size = 64; cells (AE layout) = [128, 64, 32, 32, 64, 128]

Table 1 presents the types of faults injected into the dataset, as well as their duration. To better evaluate the performance of the AE three scenarios were considered with variations in the order of appearance, duration and intensity of failures. Figure 6 depicts the signal from the DO sensor, after the faults described in Table 1. The objective of Convolutional-AE and LSTM-AE is to identify the faults that can be seen in Fig. 6. The process of training AEs and choosing the best models will be described below.

Table 1. Three scenarios of faults injected in the signal obtained by the DO sensor: drift (Eq. 1), bias (Eq. 2), PD (Eq. 3), spike (Eq. 4) and stuck (Eq. 5). The faults in the scenarios have different order of appearance, duration and intensity.

Fault	Start [day]	Duration [hours]
Drift	10	120
Bias	30	120
PD	50	120
Spike	70, 72, 74, 76, 78	0.25
Stuck	90	120

(a) Scenario I

Fault	Start [day]	Duration [hours]
Drift	40	72
Bias	92	48
PD	18	96
Spike	60, 62, 64, 66, 68	0.25
Stuck	30	72

(b) Scenario II

Fault	Start [day]	Duration [hours]
Drift	58	96
Bias	45	72
PD	90	72
Spike	26, 30, 31, 33, 38	0.25
Stuck	15	48

(c) Scenario III

The purpose of the AE is to reconstruct the input signal. During its training, with the DO sensor data, the maximum value for the reconstruction error is adopted as a threshold. In tests, a failure is identified if the difference between the real and estimated DO values is greater than the determined threshold.

The fault identification methods were evaluated as follows:

– if a sample is identified as faulty, within the fault duration period, it is classified as true positive (TP);
– if a sample is identified as a failure, outside the fault duration period, is classified as a false positive (FP);
– if a sample, within the failure duration time, is classified as normal, we have a false negative (FN);
– if a sample outside the fault duration period is identified as normal, it is classified as true negative (TN).

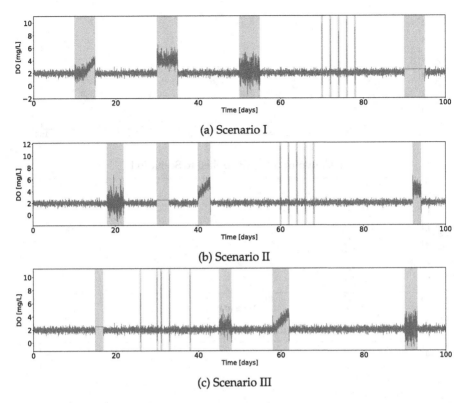

(a) Scenario I

(b) Scenario II

(c) Scenario III

Fig. 6. Faults implemented in the signal obtained from the DO sensor. Variations in the order of appearance, duration and intensity of faults.

The evaluation metrics used was for this study are TP rate (TP_r), FP rate (FP_r) and FN rate (FN_r) - cf. Eq. 7 and 9. The use of these metrics makes it possible to assess the reliability of the implemented error detection system.

$$TP_r = TP/(TP + FN) \tag{7}$$
$$FP_r = FP/(FP + TN) \tag{8}$$
$$FN_r = FN/(FN + TP) \tag{9}$$

The results obtained by the models are graphically represented in Figs. 7 and 8. Table 2 presents the performance of LSTM-AE and Convolutional-AE in identifying the present faults, where the values represent the arithmetic average of the algorithms' performance, for each fault implemented, in the three scenarios.

It is noticed that the two models are efficient in identifying the failures according to the evaluation metrics. The bias, drift and PD faults were correctly identified by Convolutional-AE, with TP_r of 95.6%, 95.15% and 97.8%, respectively. The LSTM-AE model presented a little lower performance with TP_r of 95%, 94% and 94.1% for the same failures, respectively. Both algorithms presented greater difficulties with the spike failure. The Convolutional-AE and LSTM-AE

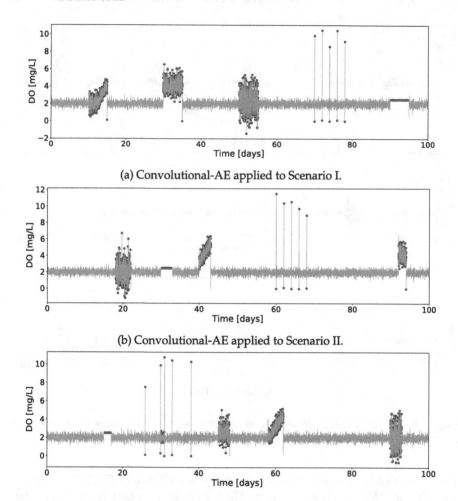

(a) Convolutional-AE applied to Scenario I.

(b) Convolutional-AE applied to Scenario II.

Fig. 7. Faults identified in the three scenarios by the Convolutional-AE.

showed correct identification of faults in 88.23% and 84.61%, and considerable FN_r, with values of 11.76% and 15.38%, respectively. Both models performed well on the Stuck fault. The Convolutional-AE presented 88%, and the LSTM-AE 86.39% for TP_r. But these two models showed considerable value for FN_r, with 12% for the Convolutional-AE, and 13.61% for the LSTM-AE model. There was an identification problem near the spike faults, in the third scenario considered. Outside the evaluation area, between the second and third spikes, the models identified 99 normal samples as faults.

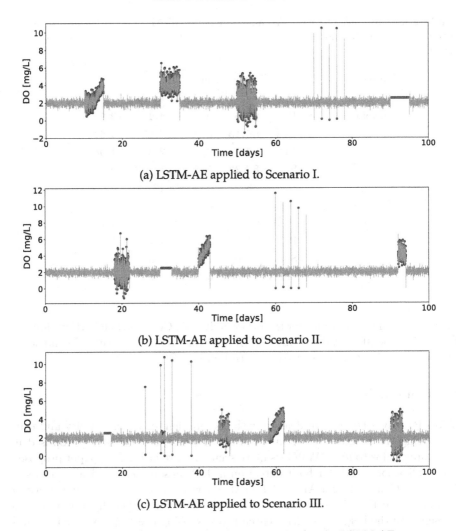

(a) LSTM-AE applied to Scenario I.

(b) LSTM-AE applied to Scenario II.

(c) LSTM-AE applied to Scenario III.

Fig. 8. Faults identified in the three scenarios by the LSTM-AE.

The treatment process carried out by WWTPs presents a characteristic of slow changes. In the BSM2 simulator, the water retention time in the activated sludge tank (where the DO sensor takes its measurements) is 14 h. Taking water retention time into account, both models had satisfactory results. The delay for fault detection, for each fault was calculated, as in the previous cases, by the arithmetic average of the delay detection times in the three proposed scenarios. The time that each algorithm took to identify the failures can be seen in Table 2. Related to the delay, it is observed that the Convolutional-AE obtained better results than the LSTM-AE, with the lowest average delay for fault detection. Only when detecting the bias fault, LSTM-AE obtain a better result, with 13.6% less delay in fault identification, in relation to Convolutional-AE. Both models readily identify the

Table 2. Performance of LSTM-AE and Convolutional-AE. The values are the arithmetic average of the models' performance in the three scenarios. In bold the best results.

Autoencoder	Fault	Assessment metrics			
		$TP_r[\%]$	$FP_r[\%]$	$FN_r[\%]$	Delay [h]
Convolutional-AE	Bias	**95.6**	0	**4.4**	**2.5**
	Drift	**95.15**	0	**4.85**	4.41
	PD	**97.8**	0	**2.2**	1.08
	Spike	**88.23**	12.5	**11.76**	0
	Stuck	**88**	0	**12**	5.25
LSTM-AE	Bias	95	0	5	2.16
	Drift	94	0	6	5.33
	PD	94.1	0	4	1.83
	Spike	84.61	12.5	15.38	0
	Stuck	86.39	0	13.61	6.03

first peak of the skipe fault. For the other faults, the Convolutional-AE performed better. It took 20.86%, 69.4% and 14.8% less time to identify drift, PD and stuck faults, respectively, when compared with LSTM-AE.

6 Conclusions

WWTPs play a key role in dealing with the problem of water scarcity and thus alleviating the resulting economic and social problems. The work proposed in this paper helps to make WWTPs more secure and reliable. This paper proposed the application of AE for fault detection in DO sensors in biological reactors of WWTPs. Convolutional-AE and LSTM-AE were used to detect five types of faults: bias, drift, PD, spike and stuck. The models had their hyperparameters chosen with the help of the grid search process, using the MAE metric to evaluate the input signal reconstruction error. Three scenarios were considered, with variations in the order of appearance, duration and intensity of faults injected into the dataset. The best performance was obtained by the Convolutional-AE, with better detection values, according to the considered metrics, and less delay time when identifying faults. The analysis of other combinations for hyperparameters or the use in conjunction with other methods that allow less delay in fault detection would make the Convolutional-AE a good option to detect faults such as bias and drift in real WWTPs, representing an important contribution to its safety and sustainability.

Acknowledgments. This research was supported by the ERDF and national funds through the project SYNAPPS (CENTRO-01-0247-FEDER-046978). We also acknowledge the support of the EC project CHIST-ERA-19-XAI-012, and project CHIST-ERA/0004/2019 funded by FCT.

References

1. Haglund, W.D., Sorg, M.H.: Human remains in water environments. In: Advances in Forensic Taphonomy: Method, Theory, and Archaeological Perspectives, pp. 201–218 (2002)
2. Cassardo, C., Jones, J.A.A.: Managing water in a changing world. Water **3**(2), 618–628 (2011)
3. Mekonnen, M.M., Hoekstra, A.Y.: Four billion people facing severe water scarcity. Sci. Adv. **2**(2), e1500323 (2016)
4. Macedo, H.E., et al.: Distribution and characteristics of wastewater treatment plants within the global river network. Earth Syst. Sci. Data **14**(2), 559–577 (2022)
5. Rosso, D., Stenstrom, M.K., Larson, L.E.: Aeration of large-scale municipal wastewater treatment plants: state of the art. Water Sci. Technol. **57**(7), 973–978 (2008)
6. Nakkasunchi, S., Hewitt, N.J., Zoppi, C., Brandoni, C.: A review of energy optimization modelling tools for the decarbonisation of wastewater treatment plants. J. Clean. Prod. **279**, 123811 (2021)
7. Miron, M., Frangu, L., Caraman, S., Luca, L.: Artificial neural network approach for fault recognition in a wastewater treatment process. In: 2018 22nd International Conference on System Theory, Control and Computing (ICSTCC), pp. 634–639 (2018)
8. Mamandipoor, B., Majd, M., Sheikhalishahi, S., Modena, C., Osmani, V.: Monitoring and detecting faults in wastewater treatment plants using deep learning. Environ. Monit. Assess. **192**(2), 1–12 (2020). https://doi.org/10.1007/s10661-020-8064-1
9. Li, X., Chai, W., Liu, T., Qiao, J.: Fault detection of dissolved oxygen sensor in wastewater treatment plants. In: IECON 2020 the 46th Annual Conference of the IEEE Industrial Electronics Society, pp. 225–230 (2020)
10. Xiao, H., Huang, D., Pan, Y., Liu, Y., Song, K.: Fault diagnosis and prognosis of wastewater processes with incomplete data by the auto-associative neural networks and ARMA model. Chemom. Intell. Lab. Syst. **161**, 96–107 (2017)
11. Wang, K., Chang, P., Meng, F.: Monitoring of wastewater treatment process based on slow feature analysis variational autoencoder. In: 2021 IEEE 10th Data Driven Control and Learning Systems Conference (DDCLS), pp. 495–502. IEEE (2021)
12. King, K.L., Wang, Z., Kroll, D.J.: Classification of deviations in a process, 14 February 2006. US Patent 6,999,898
13. Schraa, O., Tole, B., Copp, J.B.: Fault detection for control of wastewater treatment plants. Water Sci. Technol. **53**(4–5), 375–382 (2006)
14. Kazemi, P., Giralt, J., Bengoa, C., Masoumian, A., Steyer, J.-P.: Fault detection and diagnosis in water resource recovery facilities using incremental PCA. Water Sci. Technol. **82**(12), 2711–2724 (2020)
15. Wang, B., Li, Z., Dai, Z., Lawrence, N., Yan, X.: A probabilistic principal component analysis-based approach in process monitoring and fault diagnosis with application in wastewater treatment plant. Appl. Soft Comput. **82**, 105527 (2019)
16. Newhart, K.B., Holloway, R.W., Hering, A.S., Cath, T.Y.: Data-driven performance analyses of wastewater treatment plants: A review. Water Res. **157**, 498–513 (2019)
17. Spellman, F.R.: Handbook of Water and Wastewater Treatment Plant Operations. CRC Press (2003)

18. Mendes, J., Araújo, R., Matias, T., Seco, R., Belchior, C.: Automatic extraction of the fuzzy control system by a hierarchical genetic algorithm. Eng. Appl. Artif. Intell. **29**, 70–78 (2014)

19. Jeppsson, U., et al.: Benchmark simulation model no 2: general protocol and exploratory case studies. Water Sci. Technol. **56**(8), 67–78 (2007)

20. Mendes, J., Sousa, N., Araújo, R.: Adaptive predictive control with recurrent fuzzy neural network for industrial processes. In: Proceedings of the 16th IEEE International Conference on Emerging Technologies and Factory Automation, ETFA 2011, Toulouse, France, 5–9 September 2011, pp. 1–8. IEEE (2011)

21. Mendes, J., Araújo, R., Matias, T., Seco, R., Belchior, C.: Evolutionary learning of a fuzzy controller for industrial processes. In: Proceedings of the 40th Annual Conference of the IEEE Industrial Electronics Society, IECON 2014, Dallas, TX, USA, 29 October–1 November 2014, pp. 139–145. IEEE (2014)

22. Jan, S.U., Lee, Y.D., Koo, I.S.: A distributed sensor-fault detection and diagnosis framework using machine learning. Inf. Sci. **547**, 777–796 (2021)

23. Jan, S.U., Koo, I.: A novel feature selection scheme and a diversified-input SVM-based classifier for sensor fault classification. J. Sensors. **2018** (2018)

24. Zidi, S., Moulahi, T., Alaya, B.: Fault detection in wireless sensor networks through SVM classifier. IEEE Sens. J. **18**(1), 340–347 (2017)

25. Li, F., Su, Z., Wang, G.: An effective dynamic immune optimization control for the wastewater treatment process. Environ. Sci. Pollut. Res. **29**, 1–16 (2021). https://doi.org/10.1007/s11356-021-17505-3

26. Pedrycz, W., Chen, S.-M. (eds.): Deep Learning: Concepts and Architectures. SCI, vol. 866. Springer, Cham (2020). https://doi.org/10.1007/978-3-030-31756-0

27. Srivastava, N., Mansimov, E., Salakhudinov, R.: Unsupervised learning of video representations using LSTM. In: International Conference on Machine Learning, pp. 843–852. PMLR (2015)

28. Masci, J., Meier, U., Cireşan, D., Schmidhuber, J.: Stacked convolutional auto-encoders for hierarchical feature extraction. In: Honkela, T., Duch, W., Girolami, M., Kaski, S. (eds.) ICANN 2011. LNCS, vol. 6791, pp. 52–59. Springer, Heidelberg (2011). https://doi.org/10.1007/978-3-642-21735-7_7

A Temporal Fusion Transformer for Long-Term Explainable Prediction of Emergency Department Overcrowding

Francisco M. Caldas$^{(\boxtimes)}$ ⓘ and Cláudia Soares ⓘ

NOVA School of Science and Technology, Caparica, Portugal
f.caldas@campus.fct.unl.pt, claudia.soares@fct.unl.pt

Abstract. Emergency Departments (EDs) are a fundamental element of the Portuguese National Health Service, serving as an entry point for users with diverse and very serious medical problems. Due to the inherent characteristics of the ED, forecasting the number of patients using the services is particularly challenging. And a mismatch between the affluence and the number of medical professionals can lead to a decrease in the quality of the services provided and create problems that have repercussions for the entire hospital, with the requisition of health care workers from other departments and the postponement of surgeries. ED overcrowding is driven, in part, by non-urgent patients, that resort to emergency services despite not having a medical emergency and which represent almost half of the total number of daily patients. This paper describes a novel deep learning architecture, the Temporal Fusion Transformer, that uses calendar and time-series covariates to forecast prediction intervals and point predictions for a 4 week period. We have concluded that patient volume can be forecasted with a Mean Absolute Percentage Error (MAPE) of 5.91% for Portugal's Health Regional Areas (HRA) and a Root Mean Squared Error (RMSE) of 84.4102 people/day. The paper shows empirical evidence supporting the use of a multivariate approach with static and time-series covariates while surpassing other models commonly found in the literature.

Keywords: Time series · Emergency department · Machine learning · Temporal fusion transformer · Forecasting · Manchester triage system · Neural network · Explainable ML · National Health Service

1 Introduction

The forecast of the number of patients who use emergency services daily is essential to determine in advance the human resources needed at hospital Emergency Departments (ED). Multi-step ahead predictions allow hospital managers

This work was partially supported by the strategic project NOVA LINCS (UIDB/04516/2020), the FCT project DSAIPA/AI/0087/2018 and the Carnegie Mellon University - Portugal FCT project CMU/TIC/0016/2021.

to organise rotation schedules and diminish waiting times in urgent care facilities [21,39]. When not accounted for, overcrowding can lead to a decrease in the quality of patient care and worse clinical outcomes [5,20]. From a macro point of view, the influx in the emergency department combines an expected number of people who are taken to the emergency room with a very serious illness, for example, heart attack, with people that use the emergency hospital to deal with non urgent problems, such as common cold, strained muscles, or to deal with problems associated with chronic illness [20,42]. The most serious cases are reasonably constant over time, and, predominantly, people in life threatening conditions have no choice but to go to emergency care, thus the indicators of a rise in patients with serious illnesses might not be the same for non urgent users. A large number of patients that resort to urgent care are not, however, urgent, according to the Manchester Triage system, used in the Portuguese National Healthcare System. Roughly 40% of the patients are classified during triage at the green/blue level, which means not urgent. Unlike more urgent patients, the influx of green/blue patients has several factors that follow well-defined cycles. For example, it is easy to identify that the day with the most influx of non-urgent patients is Monday, with a smaller number of patients pursuing emergency care during the weekend [4,19,32]. To combine the predictive power of Deep Neural Networks with the explainability usually reserved for simpler algorithms, we will use a recently developed machine learning model to predict the influx of non-urgent patients: the Temporal Fusion Transformer (TFT)[26]; and study which variables, time-series or not, had the most impact on the model, and thus which are most relevant to predict daily patient volume.

In the following section, we will perform a brief literature review of the work done to tackle this problem, followed by a section in which we display the data and offer some exploratory analysis to obtain a better understanding of the dataset. In Sect. 4, the methodology of the experiment will be displayed, presenting the goals, the forecast horizon, and the forecast model. In the results section, we perform a comparison of the TFT model with other known models in the literature, followed by an analysis of covariate importance and attention weights. Finally, the conclusions of this study are drawn, acknowledging the strengths and limitations of the TFT model, and proposing future work.

2   Literature Review

Previous studies have examined the multi-step forecasting of daily patient volumes [10,21]. Most focus is on the use of classical statistical tools for temporal linear regression such as moving averages [28], and their many extensions, namely ARIMA, SARIMA or VARIMA [3,7,34,40]. In recent years, with the advent of machine learning, newer studies have been conducted that use neural networks [21,43], or otherwise other machine learning techniques to tackle the same problem [29,33,37]. From the use of Feed-forward Neural Networks [21,29], to Recurrent Neural Networks [15,22], 1-D Convolution Neural Networks [35], and later to Long Short-Term Unit (LSTM) [15,36], there has been a constant advance in the field, from linear models to deep neural network models. In most studies using ARIMA and its variants, it was found that calendar variables (day, day of the week, holidays) have a significant contribution to model results [6,17,21,39]. Weather data, such as temperature and rain, have shown predictive power for ED arrivals with respiratory problems [29], but in others studies that analysed the whole spectrum of ED visitors, it is either not a significant variable, or it could be replaced by calendar variables, e.g. month of the year [17,39]. This level of covariate interpretability is one of the frequent drawbacks of Neural Networks, alongside the failure to recognize long-term dependencies in time-series. One specific device that addresses both problems is the Attention Mechanism [38]: simply put, it evaluates long-term dependencies and also represents how each time-step impacts the model's prediction. Attention has been used as part of a specific Neural Network family of architectures called Transformers, that has shown impressive results in the Natural Language Processing field [9,41]. In the literature, we found only one example that used a Temporal Fusion Transformer model to predict Emergency Department (ED) volume in one hospital for one day ahead [31]. While not being the only work that performed only daily predictions [33,37], we find that a longer forecasting window produces increased value for hospital management and poses a different challenge from a machine learning perspective, as seasonal fluctuation needs to be fully represented, and common forecasting models tend to decrease in predictive quality as the forecast period becomes wider.

3   Data Analysis

In this section, we will present the database used in this work. The data was obtained from the public database "Transparência SNS"[1] and refers to daily data of care in primary health centres together with daily data of consultations and waiting times in hospitals' emergency departments (ED) across Portugal, divided by Regional Health Area (RHA). The time analyzed covers the time period from November 1st, 2016 to February 20th, 2022; with 6353 individual observations and 16 variables per observation that define, among other things, the Regional Health Area (RHA), Área Regional de Saúde (ARS) in Portuguese, of the observation. In total, the dataset contains information regarding the daily volume of patients in emergency care, the number of scheduled and unscheduled consultations in primary health facilities, the daily number of patients arriving at the Emergency Department (ED) with respiratory issues, the waiting times between triage and the first medical evaluation and categorical variables pertaining to calendar information, such as weekend, day of week or national holidays.

   In Fig. 1 we can observe the weekly variation in the number of non-urgent patients, as well as the volume shift according to RHA. It is visible that despite having different levels of affluence, the different RHA follow the same trend, with peaks of affluence occurring on Monday, and reduced volume on weekends

---

[1] https://transparencia.sns.gov.pt/explore/dataset/atividade-sindrome-gripal-csh
https://transparencia.sns.gov.pt/explore/dataset/atendimentos-nos-csp-gripe.

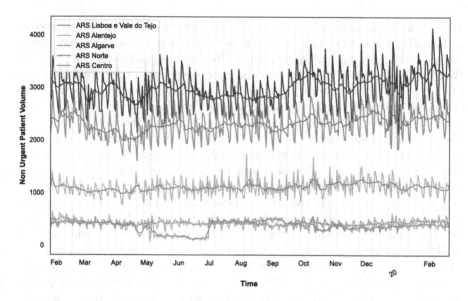

Fig. 1. Time series from January, 2019 to February 20, 2020. We can observe the weekly cycle, as well as annual trends and volume variation according to Regional Heath Area. The weekends are marked with grey lines, corresponding with diminishing number of non urgent patients searching for emergency care.

and during the Summer months, usually associated with vacations. This aspect of the data served as motivation for the application of a non-linear model over multiple time series, unlike well-established models such as ARIMA.

Another interesting feature of the data is the observation of the period in which Portugal was affected by the COVID-19 disease and took containment measures that reduced travel and in person work: in this period (10/03/2020–1/08/2021) the percentage of non urgent visits in the RHA of *Lisboa e Vale do Tejo* dropped from the normal value of 48% of the total to 40%, with more dramatic drops for example in the *Algarve* RHA from 45% to 30% at the beginning of the pandemic. This dramatic period influenced the way people used emergency services, and it can demonstrate how external factors influence people going to the emergency room. This shift, associated with the general decline in the number of people in urgent care, urgent or not, represents a distribution change in the time series, therefore making it exceedingly difficult to predict the COVID period using only pre-COVID information. In the same way, we can conclude that this COVID period does not have useful information about the post-COVID future, and, in fact, we have experimentally verified that the quality of the models decreased with the introduction of the COVID period, thus leading to the decision to exclude this temporal section from the training set.

It is, in a certain way, clear that the prediction of the influx in emergency rooms can be useful for a more efficient management of hospital services, but there is visible value added at user level, in the sense that they will get better and faster care [30]. To sustain this claim, we can observe the impact that the number of non-urgent patients has on the waiting time before being treated in the Emergency Department. In Fig. 2, for the RHAs with the highest daily affluence, we observe a positive, moderate to strong correlation between the number of non-urgent patients and the waiting time. This is an indicator, not entirely unexpected, that ED overcrowding of non urgent patients can lead to a substantial increase in the average waiting time for all patients, urgent or non urgent.

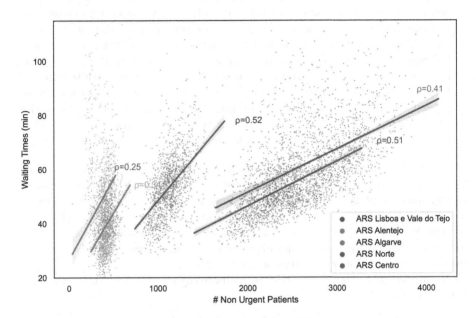

Fig. 2. Correlation between waiting times and non urgent patient volume. A strong to moderate correlation exist between these two variables, therefore implying that overcrowding increases waiting times.

4   Methods

4.1   Study Setting and Metrics

Now that we have presented the data used in this paper, let us define, and expose, the reasoning behind the rules by which we will create and evaluate the model.

- **Multivariate forecasting:** we want a model that leverages data and forecasts across different Regional Health Areas. In most research in the area, models are usually restricted to certain geographic areas, and a more general model, capable of working across different regions, might be able to uncover new interactions in data and increase robustness.

- **Long-time forecast:** In order to add value at the hospital management level, the forecast of the number of patients should not be limited to the following day or week. In this paper, we have chosen a 4-week (28-day) forecast, considering that it allows breathing room for management and personnel decisions. To the best of our knowledge, few works have worked on such an extended forecast horizon [6,7], with only partial success.
- **Probability prediction:** besides obtaining an estimate of the most likely value in the future, a model that presents a probability density function on the prediction conveys much more information. Of special value is, for example, the definition of confidence intervals, which can transmit to those who use the model an idea of the confidence, or precision, of the model in its estimation. Almost all classical linear methods, such as ARIMA or Exponential Smoothing, are able to deliver confidence intervals over the predictions. However, the same is not true for common Neural Networks architectures.
- **Explanatory variables:** Importantly, we want to evaluate the predictive capacity of different variables, determining up to which passed time-step the model finds predictive value or which covariates, categorical or numerical, have a significant impact on the prediction.

The covariates that we intend to evaluate as explanatory variables are: day of the year, month and weekend, holidays, total number of patients in emergency rooms, number of unscheduled consultations in health centres, waiting time, patients with respiratory problems and total number of consultations in health centres. We do not expect that all these variables are relevant or necessary to solve the problem we present, however, they were used precisely to assess how the models would deal with redundant variables.

In this paper, we use four metrics to evaluate the models. The Mean Absolute Error (MAE):

$$\text{MAE} = \frac{1}{5} \sum_{k=1}^{5} \frac{1}{n} \sum_{i=1}^{n} |y_i^k - \hat{y}_i^k| \tag{1}$$

the Root Mean Squared Error (RMSE),

$$\text{RMSE} = \frac{1}{5} \sum_{k=1}^{5} \sqrt{\frac{1}{n} \sum_{i=1}^{n} (y_i^k - \hat{y}_i^k)^2} \tag{2}$$

the Mean Absolute Percentage Error (MAPE),

$$\text{MAPE} = \frac{1}{5} \sum_{k=1}^{5} \frac{1}{n} \sum_{i=1}^{n} \frac{|y_i^k - \hat{y}_i^k|}{|y_i^k|} \tag{3}$$

and the Mean Squared Error (MSE)

$$\text{MSE} = \frac{1}{5} \sum_{k=1}^{5} \frac{1}{n} \sum_{i=1}^{n} (y_i^k - \hat{y}_i^k)^2. \tag{4}$$

Since we are evaluating the predictions over several groups (RHAs), the total error will be the average across RHAs. The most common metric across the literature for ED forecasting is the Mean Absolute Percentage Error (MAPE) [7, 11], however, when the true value is close to zero, this metric becomes unreliable. It also places a heavier penalty on negative errors (when the predicted value is higher than the true value) [27]. To overcome that, outliers values very close to zero are removed for this particular metric. To correctly evaluate the out-of-sample predictive capacity of the model, the dataset is divided into three subsets: train, validation, and test. The training set represents roughly 3.5 years, while the validation set and the test set have 10 weeks of data, each. The validation set is used to optimise hyper parameters and to identify overfitting during training, while the test set is unseen until the end and is only used to produce the final results. It contains the last 10 weeks available, from December 2021 to February 2022.

4.2   Models

The first and simpler method used for forecasting is the replication of the last k time-steps. This technique, which is used as Baseline in this paper, is also referred to as the naïve algorithm. By evaluating this model on the validation, the optimal value for k was estimated to be 7, thus representing the weekly periodicity in the data.

For comparison, other models commonly used in this area were also applied, namely AutoRegressive Integrated Moving Average (ARIMA) with a seasonal component [1, 12, 21, 23, 34], and its multivariate variant Vector AutoRegressive Integrated Moving Average (VARIMA) [23].

Also used was the exponential Smoothing algorithm, a simple method that has also shown good results in the literature [8]. Finally, to gauge the performance of common machine learning models, the XGBoost model was used. Out of these models, the XGBoost [24] (a Decision Tree Boosting algorithm), is the only model capable of using past and future covariates, with the disadvantage of not being specifically tailored for time-series data.

The model used in this paper, however, is the Temporal Fusion Transformer (TFT). We chose this model because it achieves all the goals mentioned previously. To define the model input, we first need to separate variables into static, target and time dependent. Static covariates, such as time-series variance or mean, are specific to each group, i.e. RHA, and are defined as s_i with $i = 0, ..., 4$. $y_{i,t}$ is the target for group i at time-step t and $x_{i,t} = [p_{i,t}^T, f_{i,t}^T]^T$ the time dependent covariates, with p representing past covariates, meaning covariates that are only known until the present, as f future covariates, that can be assumed to be known in the past and the future, in our case, holidays and weekends.

Table 1. Hyperparameters for TFT model after tuning.

Hyperparameter	Value
Encoder length	42
Batch size	40
Prediction length	28
Gradient clipping	0.022730
Learning rate	0.0011149
Hidden size	33
Number of attention heads	8
Dropout	0.19230
Hidden continuous size	19

The prediction function is defined as [26]:

$$\hat{y}_i(q, t, \tau) = f_q(\tau, y_{i,t-k:t}, x_{i,t-k:t}, s_i) \tag{5}$$

where $\hat{y}_i(q, t, \tau)$ is the predicted qth quantile for the $\tau \in \{1, ..., \tau_{max}\}$ value in group i, at time t. For the specific case of this work, $\tau_{max} = 28$, as we want to forecast simultaneously 28 days ahead. By predicting quantiles, we obtain a quasi-distribution of the expected value, and gain the capacity to define confidence intervals.

Initially introduced by [26], this model instantiated a novel architecture, combining a few mechanisms previously only used separately, in a single model. The key features of the TFT are:

- Variable Selection Network: three independent Selection Networks, one for each variable set, to select only relevant variables at each time-step. This module removes noisy variables that do not add predictive value, while giving some level of insight into the variables that are more significant to the prediction;
- A Gating Mechanism to skip any other element of the architecture. For specific cases where exogenous variables are not useful or there is no need for non-linear processing (e.g. in very simple forecasts) the Gating Mechanism, also referred to as Gated Residual Network [16], allows the model to only use non-linear processing when needed;
- Static Variables encoding to combine static information with time-series data;
- Temporal Dependency Processing to capture short-term dependency, with an LSTM encoder-decoder [13,18], and long-term dependency using a Multi-Head Attention mechanism [38]. By an additive aggregation of the different heads, this mechanism gains explainability, as the weights in the aggregated Multi-head represent time-step importance;
- Confidence Intervals: the output of the models are quantiles, that define prediction intervals, at each forecast time-step.

To obtain the quantile predictions, a specific loss, the Quantile Loss, is defined as [25]:

$$QL(y, \hat{y}, q) = \max\{q(y - \hat{y}), (q - 1)(y - \hat{y})\} \qquad (6)$$

for each quantile q. The final Loss is the average QL across quantiles and for the entire prediction horizon $[0, \tau_{max}]$. In this work, the quantiles used were [0.02,0.1,0.25,0.5, 0.75,0.9,0.98]. When $q = 0.5$ the Loss is equal to MAE divided by 2, and $q = 0.5$ (the median) is the value used for the point-wise prediction of the model.

The overall architecture of the TFT can be seen in Fig. 3 and the hyperparameters are defined in Table 1.

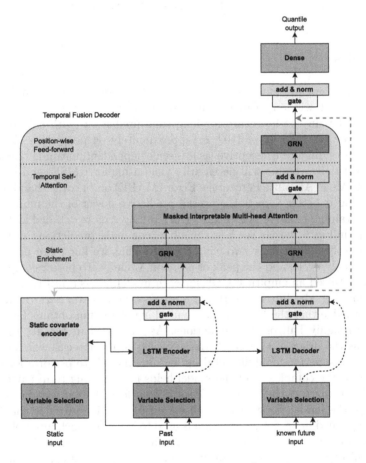

Fig. 3. TFT architecture. The inputs are static metadata, time-varying past inputs (including past target values) and known future information. The Variable selection unit selects the most relevant features, while the Gated Residual Network allows to skip over unused sections of the architecture. The interpretable multi-head attention is used to evaluate the most relevant time-steps. Image adapted from [26].

Table 2. Prediction accuracy for various models in the period 24/01/2022–20/02/2022. To evaluate the models, four metrics are used: Mean Absolute Error (MAE), Root Mean Squared Error (RMSE), Mean Absolute Percentage Error (MAPE) and Mean Squared Error (MSE). Bold indicates the best result; TFT is consistently more accurate than the baselines.

Models	MAE	RMSE	MAPE	MSE
Baseline	95.1643	116.5850	7.3483	20245.0643
Exp. Smoothing	112.5885	135.6158	7.3135	29888.6468
ARIMA	104.9886	129.6084	7.8484	22949.7471
VARIMA	94.6441	120.6674	7.9250	18407.9554
XGBoost	92.0307	112.3295	7.7027	16178.5531
TFT	**66.7551**	**84.4102**	**5.9084**	**8379.7340**

5   Results

In this section, we present the results of the TFT and the other models for a 4 week forecast window. Table 2 illustrates how the TFT outperforms other common models in the literature for long time prediction, with a Root Mean Squared Error (RMSE) of 84.4102, or approximately 84 people per day. This metric, however, might be deceptive, as it is scale dependent, meaning that RHAs with a larger daily volume will necessarily yield a higher RMSE, and skew the results. The Mean Absolute Percentage Error (MAPE) on the other hand, is scale invariant, and it better depicts the overall predictive power of the models, with the TFT obtaining a 5.91% percentage error. Taking a more detailed look at the predictions, in Fig. 6, we can see how the model can make predictions at different scales, correctly representing two characteristics that we know are part of the data, the weekly cycle, and the peak of users on Monday. To better compare the models, we utilised an empirical CDF for each model, as seen in Fig. 4a. In this Figure, depicting Absolute Error, the TFT shows overall better performance. We also acknowledge that the Exponential Smoothing algorithm obtains favourable results for roughly half of the predictions. As suggested in Fig. 4b, the TFT outperforms the other models in the last 2 weeks of the forecast window. This illustrates the superior capability of deep learning models to perform long term prediction, as the complexity of the model helps identify long term patterns.

But the strength of the Temporal Fusion Transformer used goes beyond the precision of the model. First, we can observe the attention given to each time-step. As explained in Sect. 4.2, attention is used to identify which input elements, containing up to 6 weeks of data, are most useful during forecast. In Fig. 5, it can be distinguished how the model values the most recent time-steps with a higher weight, which is intuitively expected and shows that old information has less value to the model. This validates a common assumption in linear models, that ascribe more weight to more recent observations, as is the case of the Exponential Smoothing model. In Fig. 6 we can also verify this effect, with the grey line over

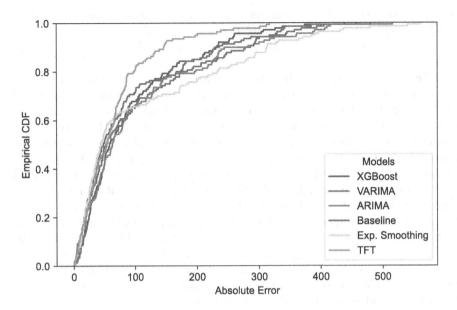

(a) Empirical Cumulative Distribution function for the absolute difference between the true value and the predicted value, for all RHA.

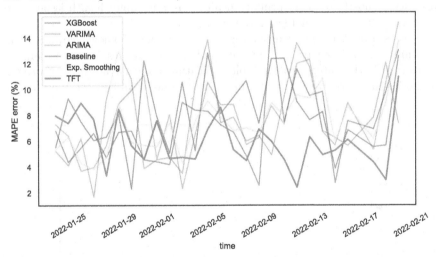

(b) Mean Absolute Percentage Error (MAPE) over time. Most models have increased error in the last two weeks, with the exception of the TFT model.

Fig. 4. Comparative analysis of model prediction.

the input period representing attention. In the forecasting figures, we can observe that different RHAs have different attention weights depending on the input vector of the model. In addition, we observe another more intriguing feature, which are spikes in attention during the weekend, this may happen because particular attention is given to one or two previous weekends to define patient volume in future weekends.

After having determined that the model attributes higher attention to more recent time-steps, we will now observe the importance attributed by the model to the covariates. We can categorise covariates into three categories: static, past, and future. In Fig. 7, it is possible to observe the importance attributed to each past or future covariate. In the left side figure, we see that the variable with the most weight is the percentage of patients in the emergency room with respiratory problems. For this period, excess affluence in hospital emergency rooms could be attributed to peaks in influenza/COVID-19 transmission, it therefore makes sense that this variable can be a predictive indicator of future positive trends in the number of non-urgent cases. The second most important variable is patient waiting time, which is in line with the positive relationship presented at the beginning of this article between the increase in waiting time and the increase in non-urgent patients. However, we should not focus our attention solely on the variables relevant to the model. There is interest in observing the variables that did not add value to the model; here we can observe that the information regarding health care centres ($n\_cons\_total, prog$) did not add value to the model, meaning that there is no clear interaction between patient volume in health care centres, mostly used for primary health care and minor health issues, and non-urgent patients in Emergency Departments.

As we see on the right side of Fig. 7, the number of known covariates in the future is a smaller part of the total number of covariates. The most important feature is the categorical variable indicating public holidays in Portugal. The model has attributed such an importance to holidays because they have a

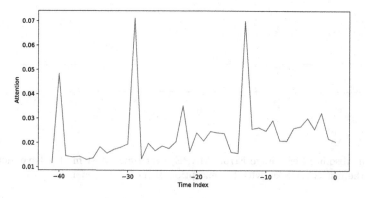

Fig. 5. Average attention attributed over the input vector. More recent time-steps are given more value than older time-steps.

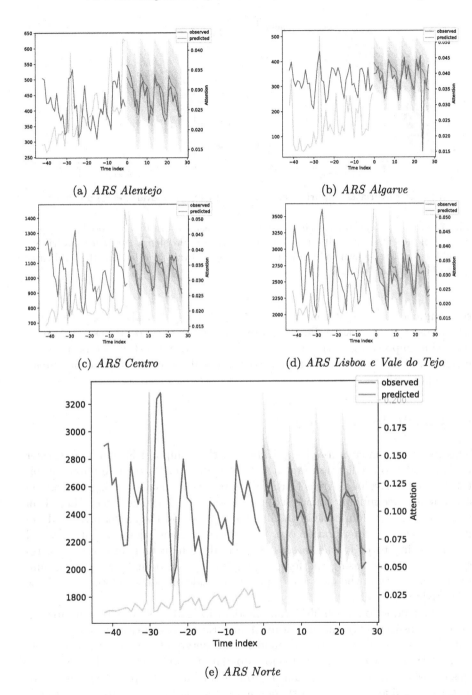

(a) *ARS Alentejo*

(b) *ARS Algarve*

(c) *ARS Centro*

(d) *ARS Lisboa e Vale do Tejo*

(e) *ARS Norte*

Fig. 6. Predictions over the test set. Over the input vector, we can see the grey line representing attention. In orange is the median predictive value (q = 0.5), with different quantiles shown as shaded area (Color figure online).

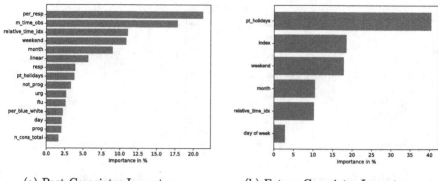

(a) Past Covariates Importance.   (b) Future Covariates Importance.

Fig. 7. Variable Importance. The most relevant past feature to the model is the percentage of patients in ED with indication of respiratory problems. For future covariates, variables that are known in the future, the most relevant is a feature that indicates public holidays in Portugal.

severe impact on patient volume, not only on the day, but also on the next day, when close to the weekend. Furthermore, the other future covariates have a non-negligible importance both as past and future covariates, thus supporting the claim found in the literature that calendar variables have a significant impact on the prediction.

6   Conclusion

This paper presented a novel application of the Temporal Fusion Transformer (TFT) model to predict non-urgent patient volume in Portuguese public hospitals by Health Regional Areas (HRA). The results were encouraging, surpassing other models commonly found in the literature [21,23]. The forecasting of an entire month is seldom done in the literature [2,7], and the model presented did not show signs of deterioration over the forecast window; despite that, it would be interesting to drive the forecasting period even further, either by autoregression or by increasing the forecast window, so as to analyse the maximum prediction length of the model, or a potential trade-off between forecast window and predictive quality.

The introduction of a multivariate model with good results across groups is a positive prospect, since one limitation of univariate time-series is the natural low-data regimen, while multivariate models can merge information from multiple sources, thus increasing the total amount of data fed to the models. In the future, this model can increase in granularity, forecasting at the hospital level instead of aggregated values by HRAs. Although a greater challenge, due to the increased noise and randomness that comes from the decrease in the study population, we expect that the combination of a large number of time-series could improve the robustness and global quality of the model, specifically if we add more relevant static variables. For this paper, only HRA and time-series statistics were used as static covariates, but as noted in [14], across different regions there is distinct demand for emergency care, thus impacting the scale and variance of the time-series. In future work, we plan to introduce other factors that might contribute to encode region-specific information as static covariates, such as demographics, modes of transport available, socio-economic characterisation of the patient population and number and capacity of private health care providers in the region. All these elements might help to represent each class, and ultimately be used for a generalisation of the model to unseen hospitals, where these variables might help to represent how similar a new unseen hospital/RHA is to hospitals/RHAs in the training data.

References

1. Abdel-Aal, R., Mangoud, A.: Modeling and forecasting monthly patient volume at a primary health care clinic using univariate time-series analysis. Comput. Meth. Programs Biomed. **56**(3), 235–247 (1998). https://doi.org/10.1016/s0169-2607(98)00032-7
2. Aboagye-Sarfo, P., Mai, Q., Sanfilippo, F.M., Preen, D.B., Stewart, L.M., Fatovich, D.M.: A comparison of multivariate and univariate time series approaches to modelling and forecasting emergency department demand in Western Australia. J. Biomed. Inform. **57**, 62–73 (2015). https://doi.org/10.1016/j.jbi.2015.06.022
3. Afilal, M., Yalaoui, F., Dugardin, F., Amodeo, L., Laplanche, D., Blua, P.: Forecasting the emergency department patients flow. J. Med. Syst. **40**(7), 1–18 (2016). https://doi.org/10.1007/s10916-016-0527-0
4. Batal, H., Tench, J., McMillan, S., Adams, J., Mehler, P.S.: Predicting patient visits to an urgent care clinic using calendar variables. Acad. Emerg. Med. **8**(1), 48–53 (2001). https://doi.org/10.1111/j.1553-2712.2001.tb00550.x
5. Bernstein, S.L., et al.: The effect of emergency department crowding on clinically oriented outcomes. Acad. Emerg. Med. **16**(1), 1–10 (2009). https://doi.org/10.1111/j.1553-2712.2008.00295.x
6. Boyle, J., et al.: Predicting emergency department admissions. Emerg. Med. J. **29**(5), 358–365 (2012). https://doi.org/10.1136/emj.2010.103531
7. Carvalho-Silva, M., Monteiro, M.T.T., de Sá-Soares, F., Dória-Nóbrega, S.: Assessment of forecasting models for patients arrival at emergency department. Oper. Res. Health Care **18**, 112–118 (2018). https://doi.org/10.1016/j.orhc.2017.05.001
8. Champion, R., et al.: Forecasting emergency department presentations. Aust. Health Rev. **31**(1), 83–90 (2007). https://doi.org/10.1071/AH070083
9. Devlin, J., Chang, M.W., Lee, K., Toutanova, K.: BERT: pre-training of deep bidirectional transformers for language understanding. In: Proceedings of the 2019 Conference of the North American Chapter of the Association for Computational Linguistics: Human Language Technologies, Volume 1 (Long and Short Papers), pp. 4171–4186. Association for Computational Linguistics, Minneapolis, Minnesota (2019). https://doi.org/10.18653/v1/N19-1423
10. Diehl, A.K., Morris, M.D., Mannis, S.A.: Use of calendar and weather data to predict walk-in attendance. South. Med. J. **74**(6), 709–712 (1981). https://doi.org/10.1097/00007611-198106000-00020

11. Ekström, A., Kurland, L., Farrokhnia, N., Castrén, M., Nordberg, M.: Forecasting emergency department visits using internet data. Ann. Emerg. Med. **65**(4), 436-442.e1 (2015). https://doi.org/10.1016/j.annemergmed.2014.10.008
12. Eyles, E., Redaniel, M.T., Jones, T., Prat, M., Keen, T.: Can we accurately forecast non-elective bed occupancy and admissions in the NHS? A time-series MSARIMA analysis of longitudinal data from an NHS trust. BMJ Open **12**(4) (2022). https://doi.org/10.1136/bmjopen-2021-056523
13. Fan, C., et al.: Multi-horizon time series forecasting with temporal attention learning. In: Proceedings of the 25th ACM SIGKDD International Conference on Knowledge Discovery and Data Mining, KDD 2019, pp. 2527-2535. Association for Computing Machinery, New York (2019). https://doi.org/10.1145/3292500.3330662
14. Farmer, R.D., Emami, J.: Models for forecasting hospital bed requirements in the acute sector. J. Epidemiol. Commun. Health **44**(4), 307-312 (1990). https://doi.org/10.1136/jech.44.4.307
15. Harrou, F., Dairi, A., Kadri, F., Sun, Y.: Forecasting emergency department overcrowding: a deep learning framework. Chaos, Solitons Fractals **139**, 110247 (2020). https://doi.org/10.1016/j.chaos.2020.110247
16. He, K., Zhang, X., Ren, S., Sun, J.: Deep residual learning for image recognition. In: 2016 IEEE Conference on Computer Vision and Pattern Recognition (CVPR), pp. 770-778 (2016). https://doi.org/10.1109/CVPR.2016.90
17. Hertzum, M.: Forecasting hourly patient visits in the emergency department to counteract crowding. Ergon. Open J. **10**(1) (2017). https://doi.org/10.2174/1875934301710010001
18. Hochreiter, S., Schmidhuber, J.: Long short-term memory. Neural Comput. **9**(8), 1735-1780 (1997). https://doi.org/10.1162/neco.1997.9.8.1735
19. Holleman, D.R., Bowling, R.L., Gathy, C.: Predicting daily visits to a walk-in clinic and emergency department using calendar and weather data. J. Gen. Intern. Med. **11**(4), 237-239 (1996)
20. Hurwitz, J.E., Lee, J.A., Lopiano, K.K., McKinley, S.A., Keesling, J., Tyndall, J.A.: A flexible simulation platform to quantify and manage emergency department crowding. BMC Med. Inform. Decis. Mak. **14**(1), 50 (2014). https://doi.org/10.1186/1472-6947-14-50
21. Jones, S.S., Thomas, A., Evans, R.S., Welch, S.J., Haug, P.J., Snow, G.L.: Forecasting daily patient volumes in the emergency department. Acad. Emerg. Med. **15**(2), 159-170 (2008). https://doi.org/10.1111/j.1553-2712.2007.00032.x
22. Kadri, F., Abdennbi, K.: RNN-based deep-learning approach to forecasting hospital system demands: application to an emergency department. Int. J. Data Sci. **5**, 1-25 (2020). https://doi.org/10.1504/IJDS.2020.10031621
23. Kadri, F., Harrou, F., Chaabane, S., Tahon, C.: Time series modelling and forecasting of emergency department overcrowding. J. Med. Syst. **38**(9), 1-20 (2014). https://doi.org/10.1007/s10916-014-0107-0
24. Ke, G., et al.: LightGBM: a highly efficient gradient boosting decision tree. In: Advances in Neural Information Processing Systems, NIPS 2017, vol. 30, pp. 3149-3157. Curran Associates Inc., Red Hook, NY, USA (2017). https://proceedings.neurips.cc/paper/2017/file/6449f44a102fde848669bdd9eb6b76fa-Paper.pdf
25. Koenker, R., Hallock, K.F.: Quantile regression. J. Econ. Perspect. **15**(4), 143-156 (2001). https://doi.org/10.1257/jep.15.4.143
26. Lim, B., Arık, S.O., Loeff, N., Pfister, T.: Temporal fusion transformers for interpretable multi-horizon time series forecasting. Int. J. Forecast. **37**(4), 1748-1764 (2021). https://doi.org/10.1016/j.ijforecast.2021.03.012

27. Makridakis, S.: Accuracy measures: theoretical and practical concerns. Int. J. Forecast. **9**(4), 527–529 (1993). https://doi.org/10.1016/0169-2070(93)90079-3

28. Milner, P.: Forecasting the demand on accident and emergency departments in health districts in the trent region. Stat. Med. **7**(10), 1061–1072 (1988). https://doi.org/10.1002/sim.4780071007

29. Navares, R., Díaz, J., Linares, C., Aznarte, J.L.: Comparing ARIMA and computational intelligence methods to forecast daily hospital admissions due to circulatory and respiratory causes in Madrid. Stoch. Env. Res. Risk Assess. **32**(10), 2849–2859 (2018). https://doi.org/10.1007/s00477-018-1519-z

30. Pines, J.M., Hollander, J.E.: Emergency department crowding is associated with poor care for patients with severe pain. Ann. Emerg. Med. **51**(1), 1–5 (2008). https://doi.org/10.1016/j.annemergmed.2007.07.008

31. Pulkkinen, E.: forecasting emergency department arrivals with neural networks. Bachelor's thesis, Tampere University, Tampere, Finland (2020)

32. Rathlev, N.K., et al.: Time series analysis of variables associated with daily mean emergency department length of stay. Ann. Emerg. Med. **49**(3), 265–271 (2007). https://doi.org/10.1016/j.annemergmed.2006.11.007

33. Rocha, C.N., Rodrigues, F.: Forecasting emergency department admissions. J. Intell. Inf. Syst. **56**(3), 509–528 (2021). https://doi.org/10.1007/s10844-021-00638-9

34. Schweigler, L.M., Desmond, J.S., McCarthy, M.L., Bukowski, K.J., Ionides, E.L., Younger, J.G.: Forecasting models of emergency department crowding. Acad. Emerg. Med. **16**(4), 301–308 (2009). https://doi.org/10.1111/j.1553-2712.2009.00356.x

35. Sharafat, A.R., Bayati, M.: PatientFlowNet: a deep learning approach to patient flow prediction in emergency departments. IEEE Access **9**, 45552–45561 (2021). https://doi.org/10.1109/ACCESS.2021.3066164

36. Sudarshan, V.K., Brabrand, M., Range, T.M., Wiil, U.K.: Performance evaluation of emergency department patient arrivals forecasting models by including meteorological and calendar information: a comparative study. Comput. Biol. Med. **135**, 104541 (2021). https://doi.org/10.1016/j.compbiomed.2021.104541

37. Tuominen, J., et al.: Forecasting daily emergency department arrivals using high-dimensional multivariate data: a feature selection approach. BMC Med. Inform. Decis. Mak. **22**, 134 (2022). https://doi.org/10.1186/s12911-022-01878-7

38. Vaswani, A., et al.: Attention is all you need. In: Guyon, I., et al. (eds.) Advances in Neural Information Processing Systems, vol. 30. Curran Associates, Inc. (2017). https://proceedings.neurips.cc/paper/2017/file/3f5ee243547dee91fbd053c1c4a845aa-Paper.pdf

39. Wargon, M., Guidet, B., Hoang, T.D., Hejblum, G.: A systematic review of models for forecasting the number of emergency department visits. Emerg. Med. J. **26**(6), 395–399 (2009). https://doi.org/10.1136/emj.2008.062380

40. Whitt, W., Zhang, X.: Forecasting arrivals and occupancy levels in an emergency department. Oper. Res. Health Care **21**, 1–18 (2019). https://doi.org/10.1016/j.orhc.2019.01.002

41. Wolf, T., et al.: Transformers: state-of-the-art natural language processing. In: Proceedings of the 2020 Conference on Empirical Methods in Natural Language Processing: System Demonstrations, pp. 38–45. Association for Computational Linguistics (2020). https://doi.org/10.18653/v1/2020.emnlp-demos.6

42. Zachariasse, J.M., van der Hagen, V., Seiger, N., Mackway-Jones, K., van Veen, M., Moll, H.A.: Performance of triage systems in emergency care: a systematic review and meta-analysis. Br. Med. J. Open 9(5) (2019). https://doi.org/10.1136/bmjopen-2018-026471
43. Zhou, L., Zhao, P., Wu, D., Cheng, C., Huang, H.: Time series model for forecasting the number of new admission inpatients. BMC Med. Inform. Decis. Mak. 18(1), 39 (2018). https://doi.org/10.1186/s12911-018-0616-8

Exploitation and Merge of Information Sources for Public Procurement Improvement

Roberto Nai$^{(\boxtimes)}$ ⓘ, Emilio Sulis ⓘ, Paolo Pasteris ⓘ, Mirko Giunta, and Rosa Meo ⓘ

Computer Science Department, University of Turin, Turin, Italy
{roberto.nai,emilio.sulis,paolo.pasteris,mirko.giunta,rosa.meo}@unito.it
https://www.cs.unito.it/do/home.pl

Abstract. The analysis of big data on public procurement can improve the process of carrying out public tenders. The goal is to increase the quality and the correctness of the process, the efficiency of administrations, and reduce the time spent by economic operators and the costs of the public administrations. As a consequence, being able to recognize as early as possible if a public tender might contain some flaws, can enable a better relationship between the public organizations and the privates, and improve the economic conditions through the correct use of public funds. With the proliferation of e-procurement systems in the public sector, valuable and open information sources are available and can be accessed jointly. In particular, we consider the sentences published on the Italian Administrative Justice website and the Italian Anti-Corruption Authority database on public procurement. In this paper, we describe how to find connections between the procurement data and the appeals and how to exploit the resulting data for the measurement of litigation and clustering into communities the nodes representing entities having similar interests.

Keywords: Public procurement · Open data · Information retrieval · Government transparency

1 Introduction

In the Internet age, the extraction of information from texts is of concern [15], as well as the use of search-based applications for the information sources integration [14,25]. This work investigates the automatic knowledge extraction from a set of public law archives. In particular, we focus on two legal datasets: first, the complete archive of the (Italian) National Anti-Corruption Authority (ANAC), which includes public procurement; and second, the vast online dataset of the appeals submitted to the Italian Administrative Justice (IAJ). Our work aims to find connections between the data on procurement in ANAC and the judges' sentences on appeals in IAJ that refer to the public contracts stipulated for procurement. The goal is to integrate the two information sources and gather the cases of procurement tenders whose execution leads to appeal to the administrative justice or controversies between a public authority and a private company on the procurement contracts execution. Being able to extract this information automatically makes it possible to suggest possible ameliorative solutions to decision-makers and anticipate or prevent problematic cases for the governance. Our research

I. Koprinska et al. (Eds.): ECML PKDD 2022 Workshops, CCIS 1752, pp. 89–102, 2023.
https://doi.org/10.1007/978-3-031-23618-1_6

question is: *(RQ) How can we automatically extract information from legal archives to identify the entities involved in a public procurement?* To address the issue, we propose a methodological framework that employs both information retrieval and graph analysis. Graph analysis allows us to connect the related business entities in a graph and then identify the communities or "clusters" as the graph components that share something. The remainder of the paper is organised as follows: Sect. 2 introduces the background with related works. In Sect. 3 we describe the case study, in Sect. 4 we describe the proposed methodology while Sect. 5 provides insights about the results of the research. Finally, Sect. 6 concludes the paper.

2 Related Work

Web-based archives are growing steadily, following the Internet expansion in recent times, as evidenced by the importance of the non-profit online libraries [1]. Online archives facilitate the dissemination of information for professionals, citizens, and researchers [5]. Digital documents, as in the case of legal texts, allow ample opportunity to apply automatic information extraction techniques [23]. The Information Retrieval (IR) community has developed many systems to support research [22]. Some recent examples include the cases of knowledge extraction from a collection of legal documents [9], the summarization algorithms applied to legal case judgments [6], the co-occurrence network on European Directives [24], the shift towards Open Science [17]. Recently, researchers benefited from new tools, such as the IR software Apache Lucene [3]. Lucene is nowadays a well-known platform for building and deploying search-based applications [26]. In [8], starting from the Portuguese Public Procurement portal, a graph-oriented user interface is proposed to support decision-making, using Cypher queries [10]. Besides this, supervised machine learning methods are used to find suspicious procurement. The authors of [20] propose the SALER software prototype. Inside SALER, several internal and external data sources are analyzed and assessed to explore possible irregularities in budget and cash management, public service accounts, salaries, disbursement, grants, subsidies, etc. SALER employs graph databases, too. Unlike the previous works, our research is based on the merge of two separate legal datasets. Their joint use enables some key elements useful to solve some tasks. One is the determination of possible exemplars of inefficiency or irregularity in tenders. Our ultimate aim is to train machine learning models on the tenders data in ANAC with the labels provided by the presence of judges' sentences in IAJ on those tenders. This paper shows the work to find a possible connection between a tender in ANAC and a sentence in IAJ necessary to gather the labels for training. The second task is the recognition of sets of agents, like the public entities or the economic operators that show strong connections that make them a community that forms a "cluster".

3 Case Study

The National Anti-Corruption Authority, abbreviated to ANAC, is an independent Italian administrative authority whose task is to prevent corruption in the Italian public administration, implement transparency and supervise public contracts. ANAC collects data on calls for procurement from the public contract authorities and provides a catalog of Open Data describing public procurement, contract authority, and contractors (interchangeably named economic operators). Currently, the ANAC website provides data on approximately 7.2 million of public tenders for procurement collected from the first of January 2007 to the end of March 2022 within a dataset collecting procurement whose cost is above 40 thousand euros. The Open Data is available on the ANAC website[1]. On the other side, the Italian Administrative Justice (IAJ) collects the judges' sentences related to the public procurement appeals. Currently, about 80,360 sentences on tenders are available on the website[2].

3.1 Data Overview

The ANAC dataset contains a table `Procurement` of 7,189,462 rows, a table `Contractors` of 42,393 rows that stores the public authorities, a table `Economic operators` of 265,039 rows about the successful bidders (also named economic operators), and finally a table `Awards` of 1.635.609 rows that reports the winner of the tenders. Unfortunately there are data quality problems in this table because it does not contain the winners for all the procurement. Each procurement is identified by an alphanumerical value called CIG (the key value). A procurement can be of three types: "supplies of goods", "public works", "services". Figure 1 shows that about 51% of contract types are for goods/supplies, followed by services (35.9%) and lastly for public works (13.1%) (Table 1).

4 Methodology

4.1 Problem Definition

Our methodological framework is grounded both in IR and in structured databases. They are complementary because the first one allows the efficient search in large corpora and the second to store large amounts of data and perform analytic. We applied IR to combine the two sources: procurement dataset (ANAC) and court rulings (IAJ). Following [27], the process of the full-text search is: build a texts database, create indexing, search and filter the results. Figure 2 resumes the applied workflow.

4.2 Data Gathering

Regarding the ANAC dataset, we imported the Open Data on the procurement (in CSV format) into an InnoDB table of a MySQL database (whose size is 5.5 GB). We chose a relational database to maintain the relationship between a procurement, the contractor, and the successful bidders via the shared key of the CIG (the ID of each procurement). We obtained the IAJ judgments via web scraping. Since these are text files in HTML, Doc/Docx, and PDF format, they were indexed using Lucene. In addition, we imported

---

[1] https://www.anticorruzione.it.

[2] https://www.giustizia-amministrativa.it.

Table 1. Quantitative description of ANAC (tables `Procurement, Contractors, Economic operators` and `Awards`) and IAJ datasets

Topic	Value
Total number of procurement	7,189,462
Temporal range of procurement	January 2007 - March 2022
Identifier (key) value for every procurement	CIG (alphanumerical value)
Total number of contractors (public authority)	42,393
Total number of successful bidders (economic operators)	265,039
Total number of awarded procurement	1.635.577
Total number of bids for all the procurement	8.199.059
Average number of bids received per procurement	4.113
Procurement contract type	goods/supplies: 51% services: 35.9% public works: 13.1%
Number of procurement by area	ordinary: 86.202% special: 13.798%
Total number of appeals in IAJ	80, 360
Identifier (key) value for every appeal	ECLI
Text file types in IAJ	html: 60,284 doc/docx: 20050/26 pdf: 12

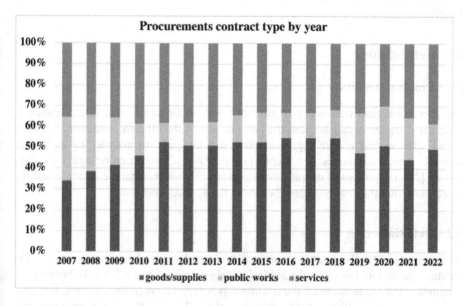

Fig. 1. Distribution of contract type from 2007 to 2022: from 2011 the main contract type concerns goods/supplies (blue bars), followed by services (grey) and public works (orange) (Color figure online)

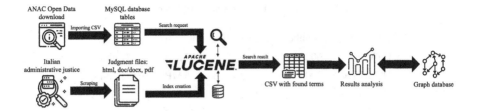

Fig. 2. Workflow of the research approach from data gathering to results analysis

the ANAC Open Data on the procurement between a public entity and a private company into the Neo4j[3] graph NoSQL database [2]. It permits the efficient navigation of the graphs formed by connection between two related business entities (a public authority and an economic operator) where a connection represents a stipulated contract. It permits also the application of sophisticated analysis algorithms of the graphs.

4.3 Technologies

We employed web scraping of the online archives from ANAC and the IAJ websites: we used the Python libraries with MechanicalSoup[4] and BeautifulSoup[5]. We opted for a relational database (MySQL) for the storage of the ANAC database, as the downloaded Open Data is organized in tabular form and referenced by key values. For IAJ, since the downloaded files are textual, we developed a Java application for textual search with Lucene (a native library in Java). We analyzed the results with the Pandas libraries in Python and plotted them with Matplotlib. We performed the computations on a 2.8 GHz Intel Core i5 quad-core with 8 GB of RAM with SSD drive, without GPU support. The source code in Java of this work is publicly available on GitHub[6].

5 Results

5.1 Data Indexing

Table 2 describes the results for each type of file of the 80,360 documents from the IAJ archive. Interestingly, Lucene indexed all the terms (614,696) in about 5 min. We excluded from indexing PDF files as well as image scans of old judgments (a negligible subset of only 12 files out of 80,360).

---

[3] https://neo4j.com.
[4] https://mechanicalsoup.readthedocs.io/en/stable.
[5] https://beautiful-soup-4.readthedocs.io/en/latest.
[6] https://github.com/roberto-nai-unito/ANACLucene.

Table 2. Indexing performance of Lucene

File type	Number of indexed files	Index size	Index time
HTML	60284	407 MB	2.577 min
DOC/DOCX	20050/26	135 MB	1.551 min

5.2 Search by Procurement

The connection between the two information sources occurred by searching for the procurement ID (CIG) in the IAJ sentences archive; it yielded the results shown in Table 3. It is worth mentioning that the search for 7,189,462 terms in about 80,000 files took 24 h. The total number of CIG found is 8,062: this means that the probability that a sentence in our archive refers to a CIG is 10% only. We continued the integration of the two datasets by performing a search via Lucene that is described in detail in Sect. 5.3. Thus we obtained further information on the procurement with sentences. As a result we computed the bar chart shown in Fig. 3 and show which courts deliberated most on procurement. In preparation for this bar chart, we exploited the ECLI code (the key of an appeal). Moreover, following the procurement types of Sect. 3.1, the highest number of judgments is related to the "services" procurement type (about 61%). Instead, the "supplies of goods" and "public works" have a lower ratio. The "ordinary" area has the highest percent of procurement (about 89%). Finally, the procurement in the "special" area rarely has an appeal. This result leads to a transparency gain in the search for courts with a high number of appeals and the identification of the most problematic kind of procurement.

Table 3. Quantitative description of ANAC procurement by application of Lucene on the procurement ID (CIG) inside sentences

Topic	Value
Procurement type	services: 61.634% public works: 22.163% goods/supplies: 16.248%
Procurement area	ordinary: 88.714% special: 11.331%

5.3 Search by Contract Authority and Economic Operators' Denomination

The search by contract authority and economic operators' denominations yielded the results shown in the first row of Table 4. The search for 42,393 contracting authorities' names in about 80,000 files took 23 min. The search for 265,039 economic operators' names in about 80,000 files took about 2 h and 15 min. This second result may be useful in bringing transparency to the contracting authority most affected by appeals from the economic operators: a higher presence may indicate greater "aggressiveness" toward an administration resulting in inefficiency in the implementation of the intended public tenders (Sect. 6).

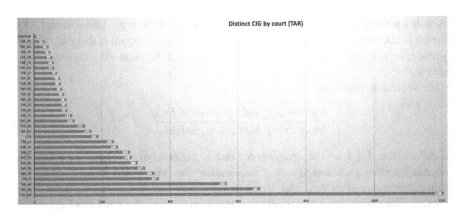

Fig. 3. Bar chart on the distribution by court of procurement with an ID (CIG): at the top there are the courts with the lowest number of judgements; in the bottom, the courts with a higher number

Table 4. Search result of the contracting authorities and economic operators in sentences by Lucene

Type	Names found (total)	Names found (percent)	Time
Contracting authorities	37,890	6.164%	23 min
Economic operators	152,934	24.880%	2 h:15 min

5.4 Definition of the Litigation Measure with Estimation of Participation in Public Tenders

In both ANAC and IAJ datasets, it is not easy to infer the identity of the companies that participated in tenders in case they did not win. Table *Awards* contains only the total number of participants for each tender and includes only the winner's identity. However, the knowledge about an economic operators' participation is useful to estimate the relative amount of administrative litigation to the participation amount: this is of particular interest because much litigation occurs when participants do not win.

One of the goals of our work is to define a way to measure the tendency to litigation of the economic operators. With reference to the generic economic operator i the first measure is:

$$\frac{Number\_appeals\_generated\_by\_i}{Number\_of\_bids\_won\_by\_i} \tag{1}$$

where the numerator is obtained by collecting the sentences in which the economic operator i is the generator of the appeal and the denominator is obtained by table *Awards*. We computed the numerator by means of the identification of the economic operators who started the appeal. This is not an immediate task. To this aim we first applied BeautifulSoup in the identification of the initial section of the judge's sentence that contains the denomination of the economic operator who started the appeal. In the second step, we applied Lucene to unify the multiple possible denominations for each economic operator into a single one stored in an internal dictionary. Unfortunately this equation is not suitable to estimate the litigation for those companies that did not win any tender or won just a few because the little number at the denomination inflates the evaluation.

The second measure is:

$$\frac{Number\_appeals\_generated\_by\_i}{Number\_of\_bids\_attempted\_by\_i} \tag{2}$$

that differs from Eq. 1 on the denominator that is the number of tenders in which the economic operator participated by not necessarily won. We would prefer to use Eq. 2 because appeals are often generated by participants who only attempted but did not win the tender. We show how we estimate the denominator, i.e., the number of economic operators' attempts to award a contract.

We assumed the number of attempts done by economic operators to win a public contract is similarly distributed as the number of awarded tenders per company, i.e., as a power-law distribution function, but differing from it by a constant factor that corresponds to the probability that a company, participating a tender awards the contract. We now try to estimate this probability that we call p_awd (probability of award).

We start from the table *Awards* of the awarded procurement. We calculated the probability a company awards a tender as the proportion of the number of success cases over the total number of cases. The number of success cases is the number of tenders for which we know there is a winner economic operator. The total number of cases is the total number of received bids in those tenders. In some cases (corresponding to 628,703 tenders, approximately 8.3% of the cases) this number was not specified, and we assumed it was one (presuming the public authority deemed it useless to communicate in case there was a single participant). Even if p_awd might differ from company to company (the most successful ones will have a higher probability of winning a contract than others) we assumed this probability is approximately constant over the population of the economic operators. As said, p_awd was computed as:

$$p\_awd = \frac{Total\_number\_of\_tenders\_awarded}{Total\_number\_of\_bids} = 0.199 \tag{3}$$

that corresponds to estimating that an economic operator wins a contract for every five participation to tenders. Equation 3 is useful to determine the litigation measure of Eq. 2 and in particular the denominator by application of the scaling factor obtained by Eq. 3. Thus, we obtain the litigation measure of Eq. 2 from the litigation measure of Eq. 1 multiplied by the scaling factor of 0.199. This result is important in the analysis of tenders participants to determine the ones with a high probability of litigation - an essential issue for the reduction of the overload on the justice.

As it is possible to see in Fig. 4, the plot of the cumulative distribution of the litigation measure in the logarithmic scale computed by Eq. 1 assumes an approximate linear form that corresponds to the power-law distribution. We fitted it by application of the Maximum Likelihood Estimation [12] and obtained the parameter of the exponential distribution equal to 3, corresponding to a strongly skewed distribution. On this distribution, we can rank the companies according to the litigation measure and find a threshold x_crit. x_crit is a critical value above which the probability to find a company with a litigation measure higher than this value is bounded by the confidence level α. α can be set to an arbitrarily low value (customarily set to 5% or 1%). In the case of Fig. 4 the threshold of the litigation measure is 19 for an $\alpha = 5\%$ (and of 85 for an $\alpha = 1\%$). This corresponds to saying that for every contract awarded to the companies with an extremely high tendency to litigation, the administrative justice expects to receive as many (and more) than 85 appeals. If we consider Eq. 2, the threshold is 16.9 for an $\alpha = 5\%$. It corresponds to saying that for every company with an extremely high tendency to litigation that participates in a tender, the administrative justice expects to receive almost 17 appeals. This occurs with a probability of $\alpha = 5\%$.

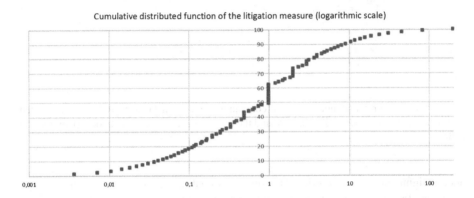

Cumulative distributed function of the litigation measure (logarithmic scale)

Fig. 4. Cumulative distribution function of the litigation measure obtained using Eq. 1

5.5   Analysis on the Graph

Following the Sect. 4.2, the graph database in Neo4j was constructed using a contract authority and an economic operator as nodes, while an edge represents a CIG that identifies the procurement won by the economic operator with the specific contract authority. An exemplary part of the obtained graph database is shown in Fig. 5.

Following [4], we decided to use Neo4j due its powerful visualization tools. We also exploited the fact that Neo4j contains the software library "Graph Data Science" (GDS) [13]. GDS was used because the algorithms of interest for this research are built into the tool, thus avoiding the need to use other external applications. We applied two main graph algorithms to analyze the graph: community detection and *betweenness centrality* detection. This latter one is a measure of importance of each node in the graph that is discussed in Sect. 5.5. Although we have extracted the communities at the structural level, we have extracted the community data noting that the community is homogeneous in supplies and contracts.

Community Detection. The Neo4j GDS library contains the Louvain method: it is an algorithm for the detection of communities in large networks [19]. It maximizes the modularity score for each community, where the modularity quantifies the quality of a

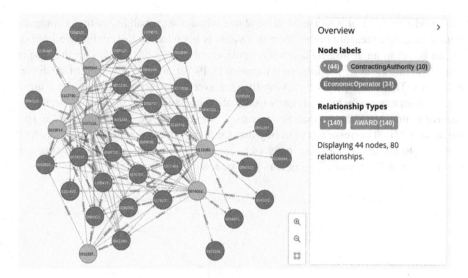

Fig. 5. Part of the graph obtained in Neo4j containing the relationship AWARD (edges) between the contracting authorities (yellow nodes) and the economic operators (pink nodes) (Color figure online)

node assignment to communities. This means evaluating how much more densely connected are the nodes within a community, compared to how connected they would be in a random network [16]. The Louvain algorithm is a hierarchical clustering algorithm, that recursively merges communities into a single node and executes the modularity clustering on the condensed graphs [11]. Figure 6 shows the first five communities detected by the algorithm. It is possible to see that the first community is composed by two sub-communities and contains 38 nodes (4 contracting authorities and 34 eco-

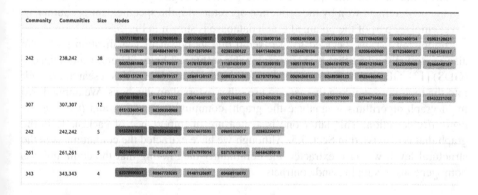

Fig. 6. First five communities detected by the Louvain algorithm: green nodes are contracting authorities; orange nodes are economic operators. The communities are in descending order according to their "Size" (number of nodes) (Color figure online)

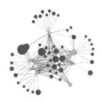

Fig. 7. Graphical representation of the community detection: light blue nodes are the contracting authorities; economic operators are the blue nodes (Color figure online)

nomic operators) while the second community is composed by 12 nodes (1 contracting authority and 11 economic operators). These clusters or communities can be used for various transparency analysis. For example, anomaly detection can be carried out by asking how likely a particular entity (contracting authority or economic operator) in a given cluster is likely to make a transaction (winning a procurement) with an arbitrarily selected cluster; the less likely that transaction takes place, the higher the assigned anomaly score (Fig. 7).

Betweenness Centrality. Betweenness centrality is often used to find the nodes that serve as a bridge from one part of a graph to another. The algorithm calculates unweighted shortest paths between all pairs of nodes in a graph. Each node receives a score, based on the number of shortest paths that pass through the node. Nodes that more frequently lie on shortest paths between other nodes will have higher betweenness centrality scores [19]. The Neo4j GDS library implementation is based on Brandes' approximate algorithm for unweighted graphs [7]. Figure 8 shows the first ten nodes with higher centrality score; these measures can help shed light on the accounts (eco-

ContractingAuthority Economic operator	
Node	**Score**
91120628057	491.34968585445193
09740180014	378.59719740952676
1977f180014	317.1539379367135
01127900049	173.06494422738956
62190148047	114.95825993792151
09053548019	101.4450803250535
00891180157	29.715850097064582
00832408104	29.715850097064582
92801709122	29.715850097064582
00017261404	29.715850097064582

Fig. 8. First ten nodes with higher centrality score: yellow nodes are contracting authorities; orange nodes are economic operators. The "Score" on the right side indicates how central the node is; nodes are sorted in descending order according to this value (Color figure online)

Fig. 9. Graphical representation of the betweenness centrality: light blue are contracting authorities; blue nodes are economic operators (Color figure online)

nomic operators) which are the most central to the entire transactions network and help to identify suspiciously well-connected accounts (Fig. 9).

6   Conclusions and Future Work

In this paper, we explored the possibility of the integration by IR of two information sources (ANAC and IAJ) about procurement using common data in both datasets. By fitting models on observed data applying the principle of MLE, we estimated the probability that a company awards a tender and the number of participation. These are the ingredients for the identification of the companies that cause the highest number of litigation whose elimination could drastically improve the justice overload. We applied also graph analytic to identify the communities formed by the public contractors and economic operators with recurrent procurement. As future work, we plan to study the use of Legal BERT [21] to search within the judgments for named entities [18] such as the names of the economic operators that were excluded from the tender selection (thus not tracked in the ANAC dataset) in order to create a graph database of the economic operators that may appear in the appeals despite an unsuccessful bid.

References

1. AlNoamany, Y., Alsum, A., Weigle, M.C., Nelson, M.L.: Who and what links to the internet archive. Int. J. Digit. Libr. **14**(3–4), 101–115 (2014). https://doi.org/10.1007/s00799-014-0111-5
2. Angles, R., Gutierrez, C.: Survey of graph database models. ACM Comput. Surv. (CSUR) **40**(1), 1–39 (2008)
3. Azzopardi, L., et al.: Lucene4IR: Developing information retrieval evaluation resources using Lucene. In: ACM SIGIR Forum, vol. 50, pp. 58–75. ACM New York, NY, USA (2017)
4. Baton, J., Van Bruggen, R.: Learning Neo4j 3.x: Effective Data Modeling, Performance Tuning and Data Visualization Techniques in Neo4j. Packt Publishing Ltd. (2017)
5. Berget, G., Hall, M.M., Brenn, D., Kumpulainen, S. (eds.): TPDL 2021. LNCS, vol. 12866. Springer, Cham (2021). https://doi.org/10.1007/978-3-030-86324-1

6. Bhattacharya, P., Hiware, K., Rajgaria, S., Pochhi, N., Ghosh, K., Ghosh, S.: A comparative study of summarization algorithms applied to legal case judgments. In: Azzopardi, L., Stein, B., Fuhr, N., Mayr, P., Hauff, C., Hiemstra, D. (eds.) ECIR 2019. LNCS, vol. 11437, pp. 413–428. Springer, Cham (2019). https://doi.org/10.1007/978-3-030-15712-8_27

7. Brandes, U., Pich, C.: Centrality estimation in large networks. Int. J. Bifurcat. Chaos **17**(07), 2303–2318 (2007)

8. Carneiro, D., Veloso, P., Ventura, A., Palumbo, G., Costa, J.: Network analysis for fraud detection in Portuguese public procurement. In: Analide, C., Novais, P., Camacho, D., Yin, H. (eds.) IDEAL 2020. LNCS, vol. 12490, pp. 390–401. Springer, Cham (2020). https://doi.org/10.1007/978-3-030-62365-4_37

9. Castano, S., Falduti, M., Ferrara, A., Montanelli, S.: A knowledge-centered framework for exploration and retrieval of legal documents. Inf. Syst. **106**, 101842 (2022). https://doi.org/10.1016/j.is.2021.101842

10. Francis, N., et al.: Cypher: an evolving query language for property graphs. In: Proceedings of the 2018 International Conference on Management of Data, pp. 1433–1445 (2018)

11. Ghosh, S., et al.: Distributed Louvain algorithm for graph community detection. In: 2018 IEEE International Parallel and Distributed Processing Symposium (IPDPS), pp. 885–895. IEEE (2018)

12. Goldstein, M.L., Morris, S.A., Yen, G.G.: Problems with fitting to the power-law distribution. Eur. Phys. J. B Condens. Matter Complex Syst. **41**(2), 255–258 (2004)

13. Hodler, A.E., Needham, M.: Graph data science using Neo4j. In: Massive Graph Analytics, pp. 433–457. Chapman and Hall/CRC

14. Konchady, M.: Building Search Applications: Lucene, LingPipe, and Gate. Lulu.com (2008)

15. Lakhara, S., Mishra, N.: Desktop full-text searching based on Lucene: a review. In: 2017 IEEE International Conference on Power, Control, Signals and Instrumentation Engineering (ICPCSI), pp. 2434–2438 (2017). https://doi.org/10.1109/ICPCSI.2017.8392154

16. Lu, H., Halappanavar, M., Kalyanaraman, A.: Parallel heuristics for scalable community detection. Parallel Comput. **47**, 19–37 (2015)

17. Manghi, P., Candela, L., Lazzeri, E., Silvello, G.: Digital libraries: supporting open science. SIGMOD Rec. **48**(4), 54–57 (2019). https://doi.org/10.1145/3385658.3385669

18. Nadeau, D., Sekine, S.: A survey of named entity recognition and classification. Lingvisticae Investigationes **30**(1), 3–26 (2007)

19. Needham, M., Hodler, A.E.: A comprehensive guide to graph algorithms in Neo4j. Neo4j.com (2018)

20. Martínez-Plumed, F., Casamayor, J.C., Ferri, C., Gómez, J.A., Vendrell Vidal, E.: SALER: a data science solution to detect and prevent corruption in public administration. In: Alzate, C. (ed.) ECML PKDD 2018. LNCS (LNAI), vol. 11329, pp. 103–117. Springer, Cham (2019). https://doi.org/10.1007/978-3-030-13453-2_9

21. Ravichandiran, S.: Getting Started with Google BERT: Build and Train State-of-the-Art Natural Language Processing Models using BERT. Packt Publishing Ltd. (2021)

22. Sansone, C., Sperlí, G.: Legal information retrieval systems: state-of-the-art and open issues. Inf. Syst. **106**, 101967 (2022). https://doi.org/10.1016/j.is.2021.101967

23. Solihin, F., Budi, I., Aji, R.F., Makarim, E.: Advancement of information extraction use in legal documents. Int. Rev. Law Comput. Technol. **35**(3), 322–351 (2021). https://doi.org/10.1080/13600869.2021.1964225

24. Sulis, E., Humphreys, L., Vernero, F., Amantea, I.A., Audrito, D., Caro, L.D.: Exploiting co-occurrence networks for classification of implicit inter-relationships in legal texts. Inf. Syst. **106**, 101821 (2022). https://doi.org/10.1016/j.is.2021.101821

25. Wikipedia: Search-based application, June 2022. https://en.wikipedia.org/wiki/Search-based_application

26. Yang, P., Fang, H., Lin, J.: Anserini: enabling the use of lucene for information retrieval research. In: Proceedings of the 40th International ACM SIGIR Conference on Research and Development in Information Retrieval, SIGIR 2017, pp. 1253–1256. Association for Computing Machinery, New York (2017). https://doi.org/10.1145/3077136.3080721
27. Zhang, Y., Li, J.: Research and improvement of search engine based on Lucene. In: 2009 International Conference on Intelligent Human-Machine Systems and Cybernetics, vol. 2, pp. 270–273. IEEE (2009)

Geovisualisation Tools for Reporting and Monitoring Transthyretin-Associated Familial Amyloid Polyneuropathy Disease

Rúben X. Lôpo[1,2]([✉]), Alípio M. Jorge[1,2][iD], and Maria Pedroto[1,2][iD]

[1] Faculty of Sciences of University of Porto,
Rua do Campo Alegre, s/n, 4169-007 Porto, Portugal
{up201709326,amjorge}@up.pt
[2] INESC-TEC LIAAD - Laboratório de Inteligência Artificial e Apoio à Decisão,
Campus da Faculdade de Engenharia da Universidade do Porto,
Rua Dr. Roberto Frias, 4200-465 Porto, Portugal
{ruben.x.lopo,alipio.jorge,maria.j.pedroto}@inesctec.pt

Abstract. Transthyretin-associated Familial Amyloid Polyneuropathy (TTR-FAP) is a chronic fatal disease with a high incidence in Portugal. It is therefore relevant to provide professionals and citizens with a tool that enables a detailed geographical and territorial study. For this reason, we have developed an web based application that brings together techniques applied to spatial data that allow the study of the historical progression and growth of cases in patients' residential areas and areas of origin as well as an epidemic forecast. The tool enables the exploration of geographical longitudinal data at national, district and county levels. High density regions and periods can be visually identified according to parameters selected by the user. The visual evaluation of the data and its comparison across different time spans of the disease era can have an impact on more informed decision making by those working with patients to improve their quality of life, treatment or follow-up. The tool is available online for data exploration and its code is available on GitHub for adaptation to other geospatial scenarios.

Keywords: Geovisualisation · Spatial data · Imputation

1 Introduction

The application of data science and data mining concepts can be beneficial in various domains and can lead to an advancement in the quality of life of people who are directly and indirectly affected by these applications. When it comes to the implementation of these concepts related to health care and well-being of the population, the construction of tools that focus on the study of the emergence, spread and prediction of diseases as endemic foci become indispensable to the community. The geographical trends of diseases can lead to assumptions and impact the quality of life of those who interact with them.

I. Koprinska et al. (Eds.): ECML PKDD 2022 Workshops, CCIS 1752, pp. 103–118, 2023.
https://doi.org/10.1007/978-3-031-23618-1_7

Transthyretin-associated Familial Amyloid Polyneuropathy (TTR-FAP) is an example of one of the many chronic diseases that affect communities in several countries as showed by Schmidt et al. in [1]. It is a rare, hereditary and neurodegenerative disease, with serious consequences that greatly affect the routine of those concerned, as well as being a disease that can lead to a fatal outcome. Carriers have abnormal deposits of a protein called amyloid that disable, with great emphasis, the body's extremities and sensory capacity and, due to the progression of the disease, eventually vital organs are also at risk as shown in [2] and by Coelho in [3]. This disease has been studied for the last century and has an evident research background that try to mitigate, as far as possible, some of the consequences of being a carrier.

Portugal is one of the countries with one of the most considerable incidences of the disease showed by Schmidt et al. [1] and whose first case was discovered more than 80 years ago as Corino states in [4]. There is a wide medical research of the disease but there is little detail in the geographical and territorial exploration of this information across Europe stated by Parman et al. in [5] that can help doctors and health professionals draw conclusions about their patients. It also shows that the average age of onset of the disease is 33.5 years and that 87% of patients develop symptoms before the age of 40. Portugal is one of the countries with a faster diagnosis (with a shorter delay) where each patient only needs to consult 2 specialists. Thus, by analysing values about past patients, it may be possible to improve the decisions made about the current patients and to those in years to come, regarding the delivery of medical care in correct areas.

In Sect. 1 we talk about the aim of the project and the paper as well as our contributions. In Sect. 2 we mention related work that is connected to spatial data, disease data and TTR-FAP. In Sect. 3 we talk about the data preparation, the techniques applied and the imputation done in more detail. In the Sect. 4 we show some of the results of simple Geovisualisation tools applied to the data. In Sect. 5 we show how AmiVis works as a tool for healthcare professionals. In Sect. 6 we talk about ongoing work with forecasting and incidence studies. We end with Sect. 7 with conclusions and future work.

1.1   Contributions

This paper describes a web based platform that is able to explore the geographical distribution and resulting combination of residencies and origins of cases in a national context of cases in mainland Portugal (excluding the Azores and Madeira archipelagos). As previously mentioned, Portugal is a cluster of TTR-FAP disease cases and a considerable part of this data is registered in the health unit of Santo António Hospital in the city of Porto. Through the application of data science and data mining concepts, and using an anonymized dataset that records, in part, the origin and residence by county of patients in the Portuguese geographic area by year, it is expected that knowledge and conclusions about the numbers, progression and concentration of the disease can be drawn.

Our contribution is to make this type of Geovisualisation exploration easily accessible to those who directly work with these patients. For this reason, the main goal is the creation of an interactive application which is usable by health professionals and other interested types of users. The application can also be adapted to other similarly geo temporal structured datasets.

Finally, this project's main objective is to put together medical and data science so that one half can give the necessary working data and information so the other half can return it with more complete tools that allow new possible theories. Thereby, those who will benefit are people who have this medical condition and healthcare professionals that work with these individuals and who need this sort of tools to justify how the disease behaves in the country, empowering them to make data-driven decisions.

2   Related Work

A literature review was conducted on three main components: analysis of the disease and its word wide geographical distribution, how Geovisualisation theory is currently and how other diseases with similar epidemiological behaviour are represented geographically.

Regarding disease representations, Mazzeo et al. studied the endemic area of Sicily in Italy from 1995 to 2015 in [6] just as Choi et al. regarding the South Korean territory in almost the same time period in [7]. Similarly, Motozaki et al. demonstrated the annual evolution, from 2003 to 2005, in Japan in [8], and Sousa et al. showed a clear territorial visualisation of Portugal regarding the origin and residence of patients in [9] with a clear focus in the north of the mainland. Still, the focus on the territorial progression of the disease is scarce and left somewhat open to interpretation.

Concepts of Geovisualisation theory such as the use of Map Visualisation and the use of small multiples for ease in visualisation of spatial data are extensively discussed. On the one hand, the sovereignty of visualisation of multiple dimensions, such as 2D and 3D, as a tool that achieves knowledge of spatial variables is reiterated since it allows drawing conclusions about economic, social and political problems, as stated by Nollenburg through the proportional spatial subdivision of the data in [10]. Some of the most commonly used types of visualisation include Choropleth and Cartogram maps or space-time cube. On the other hand, this data visualisation may be multiple, allowing the distinct visualisation of small portions of information that guarantee a temporal dimensionality, a concept present with great notoriety in the work of MacEachren et al. in [11].

Other authors directly touched on the geographical exploration of other diseases with epidemiological properties of geographical distribution and share some of the concepts already mentioned. Among the various publications reviewed, works done by Gaudart et al. and Jing et al. that present Geovisualisation conclusions in small multiples from France on cases of COVID-19 in relation to various possibly correlated themes such as climate in [12] and other statistics such as small multiples from Chongqing in China on Acute Hemorrhagic Conjuctivitis stand out in [13]. Overlapping time curves, case diagrams and various mutations of Choropleth maps are also common tools to the vast majority of similar works. Work on diseases that do not share hereditary characteristics like TTR-FAP is still valuable since the tools and types of visualisations are based on the same type of spatial data structure based on the location of people. Therefore, conclusions have to be drawn from the visualisations taking into account the type of disease.

3   Data Preparation and Subgroup Methodology

First of all, we must be aware that the data we are working with is relative to a medical unit, so the introduction of the values is endowed with noise because, sometimes, it is introduced in the day-to-day routine without guarantees that it is completely correct by human action. These records were registered from different healthcare professionals for decades with different medical backgrounds which may also explain its inconsistencies.

The data we have includes, for each individual record, the family to which they belong, which identifies the family group of cases, the dates of birth and death by year, the sex of the registered patient, the genetic symbol of the patient which identifies their last known state (such as affected, clear or heterozygous), as well as the asymptomatic or non-symptomatic situation of the patient and the year of onset of symptoms, the record of the county and district of residence and of origin. Besides these, there are other data that were not relevant for this work but have a medical and clinical relevance.

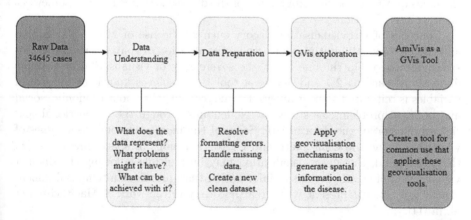

Fig. 1. Simplified version of the pipeline used during the geo-visualisation work of the TTR-FAP data.

The work performed followed a work pipeline that is simplified in Fig. 1, since this process is not merely iterative and involves moving forward and backwards through the phases according to the findings in the data and the work to be performed over time. Regarding the Data Understanding phase and answering these three important questions, the medical and clinical data represented suffer from a considerable lack of values in each record and this is notoriously something common in this type of area. Even so, each record, with the values of each variable described above, can be studied in detail since it is possible to create subgroups of quite heterogeneous values and this leads to a panoply of directions to follow. The presence of textually, numerically and spatially represented values lead to the possibility of finding hypothesis about sets of patients.

It should be noted that one of the biggest problems with this data is the lack of depth because, for example, the dates provided have a granulation reserved only for years when it could be advantageous to obtain statistics and conclusions about periods throughout the year such as months or weeks and this data is not available. Furthermore, since one of the main goals of this work is the geographical and territorial exploration of the data, when a new patient from a family already registered with the disease is introduced, usually the location of the new patient is not entered in the dataset and he/she inherits the location of his/her family members in terms of internal medical processes. Unsurprisingly, this significantly limits what could be the actual veracity of the data and was one of the problems to overcome.

Regarding data preparation, and without clarifying too much what the data cleaning work of the raw dataset was, tools were applied to remove noise from the attribute values and feature engineering was applied in which some attributes were created from other existing attributes, as is the case of the creation of counties and districts. In addition, a discretisation was applied to the data in order to transform numerical values into intervals or conceptual labels so as to simplify the data and reach new conclusions.

One of the issues involved in data preparation that received special attention and that has already been mentioned involves the lack of spatial values in the patient records. Although not all present records identify patients, every record has a connection to an affected patient that can result in some data to be retrieved (a family can have connections between grandparents, parents and sons despite not all of them being a carrier). For this reason, imputation methods were applied to this attribute. This process involves solving the problem of missing values by substituting them for estimates of the same missing value.

There are a total of 117 locations of origin of patients and a total of 159 locations of residence which culminate in a total of 174 unique district-county pairs in this dataset out of a total of 278 pairs at the national level. Since we have information about the patient's family subgroup, it makes sense to use all records that have residential location and origin values when we are imputing a value for a patient.

To perform the imputation, 2 different techniques were applied: family mode and future generation parenting. While the mode is auto explicit since patients inherit the family mode, the parenting of future generations considers the origin and residence locations of the parents and grandparents (previous generations) to assign the location to the patient in question. This type of imputation imposed the use of patients' age of birth so that when newer generations were evaluated, they would have their relatives available with the location value already previously recorded by the raw dataset or recorded by the algorithm. This procedure used the id values of the fathers and mothers that were provided. Table 1 shows the results taken from a performance study done in order to understand what would be the most accurate method to use on the data, the family mode or the future generation parenting.

Table 1. Evaluation values for mode and parenting of future generations plus mode for origin and residence, using a K-Fold = 10 and using up to 2 generations in the parenting values. The first half are values taken from applying Parenting and the second half are those in comparison with and against Mode.

K – F = 10, P = 2	Origin	Residence
Available	6472	6098
Train 0.7	4590	4343
Test 0.3	1882	1755
Avg Irresolvable records	1092,8	1046,9
Avg Correctly Predicted records	780,6	473,4
Avg Wrong Predicted records	8,6	234,7
Precision (Parenting) for Correctly Predicted records	0,989	0,669
Avg Parenting + Mode Irresolvable records	58,1	70,3
Avg Different values Parenting vs mode (for predicted by Parenting)	3,8	140,5
Avg Wrong predicted Parenting (for predicted by Parenting)	8,6	234,7
Avg Wrong predicted mode (for predicted by Parenting)	6,4	167,3
Precision (Mode) for predicted values by Parenting	0,992	0,764

Although there were 34654 records registered in the dataset, only those with existing data regarding the location of origin and residence were considered, creating two distinct datasets, the first with 6472 for existing records with origin and the second with 6098 records with available residence information. It is important to note that the primary dataset available that contains all data, includes records of affected, clean, unaffected, carrier, heterozygous (carrier who received the gene from both parents) and possibly affected individuals. Since records are organised by families and this information is key to this study but their medical condition is not relevant for the imputation of values, the performance study considers individuals that did not develop any form of the disease yet but have valuable geographical data that we can use because they are related to patients that in fact have TTR-FAP.

The values result from an application of imputation to a training and test by random splitting the data in 70/30. There are irresolvable records that result from the data split itself, since entire families can be entirely both in the training and the test meaning that they are impossible to predict. It is also important to mention that since only records that have location values are considered, the families will be smaller than they were actually recorded in the original dataset. Even so, as it is possible to verify in Table 2, the number of families that it is not possible to predict at least 1 record is about 1/20 of the existing total. Here it is possible to verify that the numbers of families evaluated are quite similar for both locations and that a considerable number are used in Train and Test splits (more than 90% of families in Train 773 out of 821 for origin and 770 out of 824 for residence a and almost 70% of families in Test 580 out of 821 for origin and 564 out of 824 for residence).

Table 2. Unique families in the origin and residence study.

K − F = 10, P = 2	Origin	Residence
All unique families	821	824
Avg train unique families	773,3	770,1
Avg test unique families	579,7	564,3
Avg unique families test parenting w/at least 1 NA record	444,8	438,4
Avg unique families test parenting+mode w/at least 1 NA record	47,7	53,9

In terms of conclusions to be drawn from Table 1, it can be seen that Parenting successfully predicts most of the values it tried to predict (Avg Correctly Predicted vs Avg Wrong Predicted) when it comes to the origin of the patients but, when it comes to residence, these values are one third lower (0.99 vs 0.67). These values show that patients of more recent generations tend to have the same origin as their relatives but live in different locations. When comparing the Parenting values with the mode, regarding the values that Parenting was able to predict, both correctly and incorrectly, in both cases the mode is the procedure with better results, and although it is not very different in origin, in residence these values are 10% more accurate.

With these results, it was possible to apply the mode of the household locations to the data, which resulted in two distinct datasets that will be used in the remaining visualisation work. Considering only affected, carrier, heterozygous and possibly affected patients, the final datasets encompassing all data entries containing origin and residence locations each have 5782 and 5762 records.

4   Applying Geovisualisation Techniques

In this section, we show results of applying Geovisualisation techniques in most of the work to ensure that a territorial representation of the disease in Portugal was obtained and correctly displayed. These Geovisualisations include patients registered with known date of birth since 1871 and date of symptoms detected since 1907 and have spatial information.

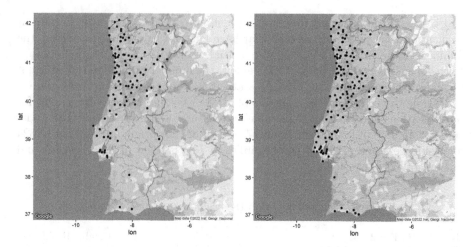

Fig. 2. Unique locations of TTR-FAP cases by origin (left) and by residence (right) in Portugal.

Despite the first case being discovered by Corino in 1939 in [4], there are people called hearsays that are given the TTR-Condition because a family member that is followed in the Medical Unit believes that this other member has the same condition and healthcare professionals have enough data to recognize it to some degree. This is why there are cases before this year in the data and even after despite not being patients at the Unit.

In order to obtain the longitude and latitude of the plain text locations that exist in the dataset automatically, the ggmap package was used, which accessed a key on the Google Cloud Platform and allowed access to the stored Google Maps coordinates for all the cities in the dataset using the ggmap package [14].

This type of information alone makes it possible to represent the totality of the cases with respect to the uniqueness of the locations, which can be demonstrated in Fig. 2 and Fig. 3. Only with these visualisations, it is possible to verify that there are no cases registered in the medical unit in the district of Beja and Portalegre regarding the residential zone of the patients. It is also possible to see that there are many more cases in the Centre/South region and in the Lisbon area in terms of the patients' residence than in terms of their origin. We can also see that there are differences in the Alentejo area (bottom of the country) and in the North area in Bragança and Guarda.

Although single locations alone are relevant information, this does not express the number of cases per location which by themselves form clusters of patients with the same origin and residence. For this reason, when assessing the national panorama in terms of locations with the highest incidence (new cases of disease in a population over a specified period of time) of cases, we obtain figures like 4 and 5, with data for all cases. With this information it is possible to see that with regard to origin, there are more cases in the counties with the highest incidence than when considering residence (percentile 90 with values of 87 vs 67 cases per county).

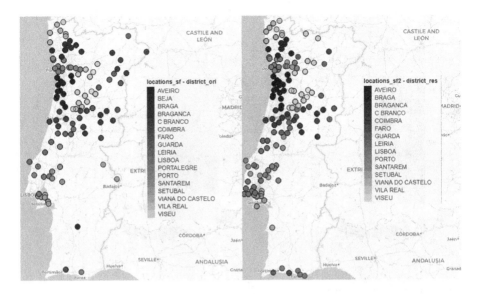

Fig. 3. Unique locations of TTR-FAP cases by origin (left) and by residence (right) in Portugal, by district.

There are several counties in common which are considered to be the areas of highest incidence of cases by origin and residence: Braga, Vila do Conde, Matosinhos, Porto and a few others. The county of Pampilhosa da Serra appears as the only locality, of the most affected, that does not have an equal residential concern. On the other hand, in addition to more counties of Porto and Braga, the municipality of Lisbon emerges as a residential area of much greater concern than originally.

It is also important to note that the quantity of counties with a represented incidence relative to residence is greater in number than the origin in what concerns the proximity to the coastline of the country which has been considered, for some years now, the preferred area of quality of life for the availability of national services.

Since the total number of cases since 2000 has already exceeded more than half of the cases recorded from 1950 to 1999, would make sense to study the incidence and progression of cases temporally or even considering other factors such as a subset of spatial data in particular localities in order to draw conclusions. While this is possible with these types of tools, they will certainly not be customised to the extent of allowing health professionals to choose the parameters themselves.

5   AmiVis as a Geovisualisation Tool

As this project aims to provide health professionals with a visualisation tool, an application has been developed that allows doctors and health entities to choose

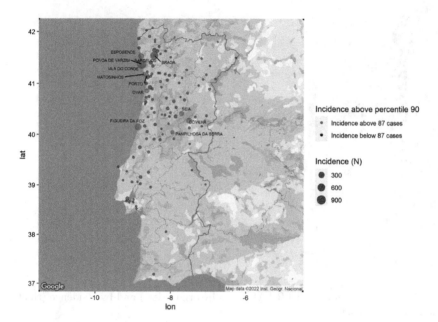

Fig. 4. Incidence of affected and possibly affected individuals, carriers and heterozygous for TTR-FAP, by county and origin, in Portugal.

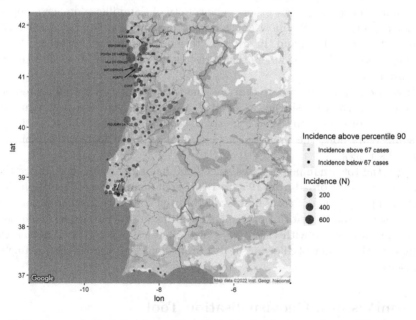

Fig. 5. Incidence of affected and possibly affected individuals, carriers and heterozygous for TTR-FAP, by county and residence, in Portugal.

the parameters and to decide themselves what to visualise. Parameters include the choice of district and county to consider, the range of years of symptoms, the choice of visualisation of origin and residence, and whether or not to consider records with no date of symptom origin but which have spatial data. The direct comparison of all cases to the cases filtered by the parameters is something that exists in this tool in order to allow the differences between the two views to be evaluated, as seen in Fig. 6.

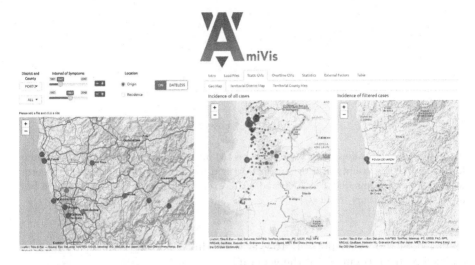

Fig. 6. Overview of AmiVis app Geo Map comparison between all cases and filtered cases regarding TTR-FAP patients in Porto, by origin, between 1942 and 1982 not considering Dateless records (with no onset of symptoms). Parameters are at the top left, unique locations at the bottom left, the menu of different Geovisualisations at the top right and the comparison of maps at the bottom right.

Initially, users are given the opportunity to upload their own dataset, which can be pre-processed as long as it meets the standards of the application.

Using the package leaflet [15], it is possible to represent the incidence of the total and filtered cases side by side. This type of Geovisualisation allows it to be possible, for example, to compare the incidence in a specific period of years as in Fig. 7. In this example, by selecting the parameters Origin, Range of symptoms between 2006 and 2016, considering all districts and counties and discarding records with no temporal data regarding the date of symptoms, we obtain two distinct images especially regarding Northern Portugal.

A different path to follow would be the representation of cases by the territorial level. GADM, the Global Administrative Areas Database, provides level information on the national divisions of each country in various formats and, using the R packages GADMTools [16], which allows this type of data to be

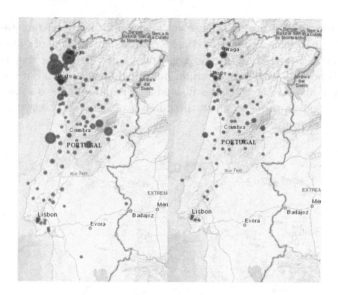

Fig. 7. Incidence of affected and possibly affected individuals, carriers and heterozygous for TTR-FAP, by county and origin, in Portugal for all records (left) and for records with onset symptoms between 2006 and 2016, excluding records with spatial data but no onset of symptoms (right).

managed, it has been possible to construct differentiating visualisations that enable greater recognition of the geographical area.

It is important to note that, at least in Portugal, there are more detailed levels of municipalities but the dataset does not contain information about parishes, so it is only possible to use level 2 of this type of data. Figure 8 shows one of the filtering applications in AmiVis that allows filtered results to be split at district and municipality level, in order to be compared to the general picture of the disease. In this case, in the first 50 years of disease registration, the central coast of Portugal did not have such a high incidence of cases, which increased over the years.

6 Ongoing Work

Currently the work involves creating models that have a prediction of the incidence of the disease over time and that can be adapted to the location chosen in the application. To do this, firstly, a symptom year prediction model needs to be adapted so that more patients with recent years of symptom onset can be correctly used. In this way, it will be possible to apply the model to the recent globality of the data and predict future years.

Still, there is already work being done on these strands with past data that have some consistency. It is important to note that the more recent data suffer from a paucity of recorded cases perhaps due to, maybe, the delay in diagnosis

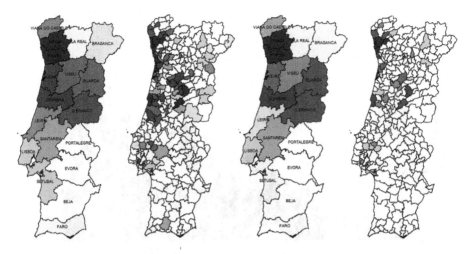

Fig. 8. Incidence of affected and possibly affected individuals, carriers and heterozygous for TTR-FAP, by district, county and origin, in Portugal for all records (first and second) and for records with onset symptoms between 1907 and 1957, excluding records with spatial data but no onset of symptoms (third and fourth).

or Medically Assisted Procreation. It is also relevant to note most of the new cases are from new recently found families and these will start to shrink overtime as there are a limited number of families in the country. Examples like the Fig. 9 using the package forecast [17] for forecasting with ARIMA modelling for the years after 2010, considering the worsening of cases while the Fig. 10 shows what

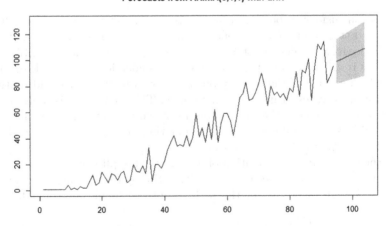

Fig. 9. Example of forecasting for the number of affected and possibly affected individuals, carriers and heterozygous for TTR-FAP in Portugal for each year with onset symptoms for 2011–2015

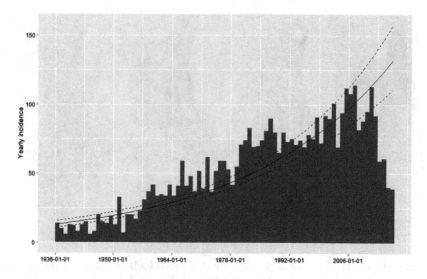

Fig. 10. Incidence of affected and possibly affected individuals, carriers and heterozygous for TTR-FAP, by district, county and origin, in Portugal for each year with onset symptoms between 1936 and 2006 with curve by early fitting.

would be an incidence growth curve with the incidence package [18]. Although these methods work relatively well for value estimation and even prediction for a 95% confidence interval, more detailed individual forecasting is still needed to ensure higher data quality over the last decade.

7   Conclusions and Future Work

As far as conclusions to be drawn from this work are concerned, these fall into two important strands. On the one hand, the creation of visualisation tools shows, noticeably, the current state of the country and how the concentration of the disease is different in distinct regions. This endemic disease is clearly more incident in the north of the country but has moved to the centre and south the concentration of cases in more recent periods. This movement is more notable with regard to residence than to the origin of the patients, showing that there is a clear differentiation between cases originating in the centre-south and cases of residents coming from other locations.

On the other hand, the creation of a web based application allows its applicability in the national ecosystem of patients through health professionals who may have at their disposal a platform that controls the visualisations based on the time and space they want.

Finally, it will also be an objective to frame the resulting data and conclusions with other external data in order to verify correlations. Examples such as the number of specialists per geographical area, the annual migration rate per residential area or even the difference in quality of life may be determining factors in the movement and progression of the disease in certain regions.

In summary, we have demonstrated some of the techniques for applying Geovisualisation to TTR-FAP data which, together with an application, will give the opportunity for health professionals themselves to control what they want to see. This way, it will be possible to support patients because the understanding of the disease will be increased and differentiating measures can be taken such as the decision to allocate professionals, treatment equipment or even previous indications in the health centres where patients are expected, without ever forgetting to raise awareness in highlighted areas. The GitHub repository is available in [19] and it is also available online at shinyapps in [20].

Acknowledgements. This work is financed by National Funds through the Portuguese funding agency, FCT - Fundação para a Ciência e a Tecnologia, within project LA/P/0063/2020.

References

1. Schmidt, H.H., Waddington-Cruz, M., Botteman, M.F., Carter, J.A., Chopra, A.S., Hopps, M., Stewart, M., Fallet, S., Amass, L.: Estimating the global prevalence of transthyretin familial amyloid polyneuropathy. Muscle Nerve **57**(5), 829–837 (2018)
2. Medlineplus, National Library of Medicine: "Transthyretin amyloidosis". https://medlineplus.gov/genetics/condition/transthyretin-amyloidosis/. Accessed 6 Jun 2022
3. Coelho, T.: Disease modifying therapies for ATTR amyloidoses: clinical development of new drugs and impact on the natural history of the disease, ICBAS - Thesis (2019)
4. Corino, A.: A peculiar form of peripheral neuropathy, familiar atypical generalized amyloidosis with special involvement of the peripheral nerves. Brain **75**(3), 408–27 (1952)
5. Parman, Y., et al.: Sixty years of transthyretin familial amyloid polyneuropathy (TTR-FAP) in Europe: where are we now? A European network approach to defining the epidemiology and management patterns for TTR-FAP. Current Opin. Neurol. **29**(Suppl. 1), S3–S13 (2016)
6. Mazzeo, A., et al.: Transthyretin-related familial amyloid polyneuropathy (TTR-FAP): a single-center experience in Sicily, an Italian endemic area. J. Neuromuscul. Dis. **2**(s2), S39–S48 (2015)
7. Choi, K., et al.: Characteristics of South Korean patients with hereditary transthyretin amyloidosis. J. Clin. Neurol. (Korea) **14**, 537–541 (2018)
8. Kato-Motozaki, K., et al.: Epidemiology of familial amyloid polyneuropathy in Japan: identification of a novel endemic focus. J. Neurol. Sci. **270**(1–2), 133–140 (2008)
9. Sousa, A., Coelho, T., Barros, J., Sequeiros, J.: Genetic epidemiology of familial amyloidotic polyneuropathy (FAP)-type I in Povoa do Varzim and Vila do Conde (north of Portugal). Am. J. Med. Genet. (Neuropsychiatr. Genet.) **60**, 512–521 (1995)

10. Nöllenburg, M.: Geographic visualization. In: Kerren, A., Ebert, A., Meyer, J. (eds.) Human-Centered Visualization Environments. LNCS, vol. 4417, pp. 257–294. Springer, Heidelberg (2007). https://doi.org/10.1007/978-3-540-71949-6_6
11. MacEachren, A., Boscoe, F., Haug, D., Pickle, L.: Geographic visualization: designing manipulable maps for exploring temporally varying georeferenced statistics, pp. 87–94 (1998)
12. Gaudart, J., et al.: Factors associated with the spatial heterogeneity of the first wave of Covid-19 in France: a nationwide geo-epidemiological study. Lancet Public Health 6(4), e222–e231 (2021)
13. Jing, D., Zhao, H., Ou, R.: Epidemiological characteristics and spatiotemporal analysis of acute hemorrhagic conjunctivitis from 2004 to 2018 in Chongqing, China. Sci. Rep. 10, 9286 (2020)
14. ggmap   3.0.0.   https://cran.r-project.org/web/packages/ggmap/index.html. Accessed 30 Jun 2022
15. leaflet   2.1.1.   https://cran.r-project.org/web/packages/leaflet/index.html. Accessed 30 Jun 2022
16. GADMTools 3.9-1. https://cran.r-project.org/web/packages/GADMTools/index. html. Accessed 30 Jun 2022
17. forecast   8.16.   https://cran.r-project.org/web/packages/forecast/index.html. Accessed 30 Jun 2022
18. incidence   1.7.3.   https://cran.r-project.org/web/packages/incidence/index.html. Accessed 30 Jun 2022
19. AmiVis - GitHub. https://github.com/raluxu/AmiVis_Demo_Paper. Accessed 30 Jun 2022
20. AmiVis Demo - shinyapps. https://raluxu.shinyapps.io/amivis-r-demo/. Accessed 30 Jun 2022

Evaluation of Group Fairness Measures in Student Performance Prediction Problems

Tai Le Quy[1](✉)(iD), Thi Huyen Nguyen[1](iD), Gunnar Friege[2](iD),
and Eirini Ntoutsi[3](iD)

[1] L3S Research Center, Leibniz University Hannover, Hanover, Germany
{tai,nguyen}@l3s.de
[2] Institute for Didactics of Mathematics and Physics, Leibniz University Hannover,
Hanover, Germany
friege@idmp.uni-hannover.de
[3] Institute of Computer Science, Free University Berlin, Berlin, Germany
eirini.ntoutsi@fu-berlin.de

Abstract. Predicting students' academic performance is one of the key tasks of educational data mining (EDM). Traditionally, the high forecasting quality of such models was deemed critical. More recently, the issues of fairness and discrimination w.r.t. protected attributes, such as gender or race, have gained attention. Although there are several fairness-aware learning approaches in EDM, a comparative evaluation of these measures is still missing. In this paper, we evaluate different group fairness measures for student performance prediction problems on various educational datasets and fairness-aware learning models. Our study shows that the choice of the fairness measure is important, likewise for the choice of the grade threshold.

Keywords: Fairness · Fairness measures · Student performance prediction · Machine learning · Educational data mining

1 Introduction

Educational data mining (EDM) applies data mining, artificial intelligence (AI), and machine learning (ML) to improve academic experiences. In recent years, AI-infused technologies have been widely studied and deployed by many educational institutions [3,19]. One of the most important tasks in EDM that attracts great attention is student performance prediction. The early estimation of student learning outcomes can help detect and notify students at risk of academic failure. Besides, it supports institutional administrators in identifying key factors affecting students' grades and providing suitable interventions for outcome improvement. The performance prediction process relies on historical academic records and trains ML algorithms on labeled data to predict students' performance. Various datasets [11,26,37] and approaches [16,24,41] have been proposed for the purpose. With the widespread use and benefits of AI systems, fairness has become a crucial criterion in designing such systems.

I. Koprinska et al. (Eds.): ECML PKDD 2022 Workshops, CCIS 1752, pp. 119–136, 2023.
https://doi.org/10.1007/978-3-031-23618-1_8

Non-discriminative ML models have been a topic of increasing importance and growing momentum in education. Despite advances and superior accuracy of recent ML models, some studies have shown that ML-based decisions can be biased to protected attributes such as gender or race due to historical discrimination embedded in the data [28,32]. Endeavoring to reduce biases is important and decisive in the applicability of an ML model in education. As an example, a recent study has proposed approaches that aim at predicting calculated grades of students in England as a replacement for actual grades due to the cancellation of exams during COVID-19 [5]. However, the proposal could not be applied as a consequence of some exposed historical biases.

A large variety of fairness measures have been introduced in ML area. However, choosing proper measures can be cumbersome due to the dependence of fairness on context. There are more than 20 different fairness measures introduced in the computer science research area [28,36]. In fact, no metric is universal and fits all circumstances [15,28,36]. Model developers should explore various fairness measures to decide the most appropriate notions for the context. Fairness is a fundamental concept of education, whereby all students must have an equal opportunity in study or be treated fairly regardless of their household income, assets, gender, or race [29]. Fairness definitions in education, hiring, and ML in the 50-year history have been discussed in the research of [20]. However, no previous work exists on the efficiency of different fairness metrics and how to choose them in educational settings.

In this paper, we provide a comprehensive study to evaluate the sufficiency of various fairness metrics in student performance prediction. We consider a group of the most prevalent fairness notions in ML. Various experiments are conducted on diverse educational datasets and evaluated using different fairness metrics. Our experiments provide users a broad view of unfairness from diverse aspects in an educational context. Besides, the results also guide the selection of suitable fairness measures to evaluate students' grade predictive models. We believe our contributions are crucial to alleviate the burden of choosing fairness measures for consideration and motivate further studies to improve the accuracy and fairness of student performance prediction models.

The rest of the paper is organized as follows. In Sect. 2, we present some closely related work on fairness-aware ML and student performance prediction. Section 3 describes the most popular group fairness measures in ML. Next, we conduct quantitative evaluations of predictive models on educational datasets and discuss the choice of suitable fairness metrics in Sect. 4. Finally, we conclude the paper in Sect. 5.

2   Related Work

Extensive research efforts have been conducted to provide useful insights into students' performance analysis and prediction [38]. Various ML models were tested on different problem settings. Cortez et al. [11] presented an early study to predict the grades of secondary students in Portuguese and Mathematics classes. Their results showed that good predictive accuracy could be achieved when previous school period grades are available. Similarly, Berhanu et al. [7] employed Decision Tree to predict students' performance using the agriculture college dataset. Some studies [25,41] proposed diverse approaches to forecast students' grades in higher education. Besides, many other studies were reviewed in multiple surveys [1,31,33,34]. They pointed out the most common techniques such as Decision Tree, Naive Bayes, Support Vector Machines, and neural networks and dominant factors impacting predictive outcomes (i.e., Cumulative Grade Point Average, previous grades, classroom attendance, etc.).

There are more than 20 fairness notions introduced for classification [28, 36]. One of the most well-known fairness measure is *demographic parity*, so-called *statistical parity*. It requires an equal probability of positive predictions in protected and non-protected groups. However, Dwork et al. [13] argued that the metric fails to ensure individual fairness. To avoid this, Hardt et al. [18] proposed *equalized odds* metric. It measures whether a classifier predicts labels equally well for all values of attributes. Besides, many other popular metrics were introduced and used in fairness ML studies such as *predictive parity*, *predictive equality* [9], *treatment equality* [8], etc. Despite a substantial number of fairness measures, there is no metric that fits all circumstances [28,36].

Following the evolution of fairness measures, recent studies have attempted to evaluate fairness in an educational context [17,22,39]. Anderson et al. [6] conducted two post-hoc fairness assessments for existing student graduation prediction models. Renzhe et al. [39] studied different combinations of student data sources for building highly predictive and fair models for predictions of college success. Jiang et al. [23] proposed several strategies to mitigate bias in the LSTM grade prediction model. They report experimental results on the true positive rate (TPR), true negative rate (TNR), and accuracy.

3   Fairness Measures

Table 1. An overview of group fairness measures

Measures	Proposed by	Published year	#Citations
Statistical parity	[13]	2012	2,367
Equal opportunity	[18]	2016	2,575
Equalized odds	[18]	2016	2,575
Predictive parity	[9]	2017	1,430
Predictive equality	[10]	2017	878
Treatment equality	[8]	2018	626
Absolute Between-ROC Area	[17]	2019	84

This section presents the most prevalent group fairness notions used in ML. The list of notions[1] is summarized in Table 1. To simplify, we consider the student

---

[1] The number of citations is reported by Google Scholar on 1st August 2022.

performance prediction problem as a binary classification task, which is formalized as below:

Let $\mathcal{D}$ be a binary classification dataset with class attribute $Y = \{+, -\}$, e.g., $Y = \{pass, fail\}$. S is a binary protected attribute, $S \in \{s, \overline{s}\}$, e.g., S = "gender", $S \in \{female, male\}$. In which, s is the discriminated group (protected group), e.g., "female", and $\overline{s}$ is the non-discriminated group (non-protected group), e.g., "male". The predicted outcome is denoted as $\hat{Y} = \{+, -\}$. The notions s_+ (s_-), $\overline{s}_+$ ($\overline{s}_-$) are used to denote the protected and non-protected groups for the positive (negative, respectively) class.

We use a confusion matrix (Fig. 1) to demonstrate the group fairness measures with an example of a dataset with 100 instances, class $Y = \{pass, fail\}$. The protected attribute is "gender", and the protected group is "female"; the distribution of "female":"male" is 46:54. Examples of fairness measures in the following sub-sections are computed based on this confusion matrix.

Predicted class

		Positive +	Negative -
	Positive +	True Positive (TP) $TP_{prot} + TP_{non-prot}$ **70 (32:38)**	False Negative (FN) $FN_{prot} + FN_{non-prot}$ **10 (4:6)**
Actual class	**Negative -**	False Positive (FP) $FP_{prot} + FP_{non-prot}$ **9 (4:5)**	True Negative (TN) $TN_{prot} + TN_{non-prot}$ **11 (6:5)**

Fig. 1. The confusion matrix with an example

3.1 Statistical Parity

Statistical parity (denoted as SP) is a well-known group fairness measure [13], whereby the output of any classifier satisfies statistical parity if the difference (bias) in the predicted outcome ($\hat{Y}$) between any two groups under study (i.e., s and $\overline{s}$) is up to a predefined tolerance threshold ϵ:

$$P(\hat{Y}|S = s) - P(\hat{Y}|S = \overline{s}) \leq \epsilon. \tag{1}$$

We use the violation of statistical parity [27,35,40] to measure the bias of a classifier:

$$SP = P(\hat{Y} = +|S = \overline{s}) - P(\hat{Y} = +|S = s). \tag{2}$$

The value range: $SP \in [-1, 1]$, with $SP = 0$ indicating no discrimination, $SP \in (0, 1]$ designating that the protected group is discriminated, and $SP \in [-1, 0)$ standing for *reverse discrimination* (the non-protected group is discriminated). In our example (Fig. 1), this measure shows the proportion of "*pass*" students between the two demographic subgroups. $SP = \dfrac{38 + 6}{54} - \dfrac{32 + 4}{46} \approx 0.0322$.

3.2   Equal Opportunity

Equal opportunity (denoted as *EO*) is proposed by Hardt et al. [18], whereby a binary predicted outcome $\hat{Y}$ satisfies equal opportunity w.r.t. the protected attribute S and the class attribute Y if:

$$P(\hat{Y} = +|S = s, Y = +) = P(\hat{Y} = +|S = \bar{s}, Y = +). \tag{3}$$

In other words, the protected and non-protected groups should have equal true positive rates (TPR) [28,36], $TPR = \dfrac{TP}{TP + FN}$ (i.e., the classifier should give similar results for students of both genders with actual *"pass"* class). A classifier with equal false negative rates (FNR), $FNR = \dfrac{FN}{TP + FN}$, will also have equal TPR [36]. The equal opportunity can be measured by:

$$EO = |P(\hat{Y} = -|Y = +, S = \bar{s}) - P(\hat{Y} = -|Y = +, S = s)|. \tag{4}$$

The value range: $EO \in [0,1]$; with 0 standing no discrimination and 1 indicating maximum discrimination. In our example, $EO = |\dfrac{38}{38 + 6} - \dfrac{32}{32 + 4}| \approx 0.0253$.

3.3   Equalized Odds

A predictor $\hat{Y}$ is satisfied *equalized odds* (denoted as *EOd*) w.r.t. the protected attribute S and class label Y, if "$\hat{Y}$ and S are independent conditional on Y" [18]. Specifically, predicted true positive and false positive probabilities should be the same between male and female student groups.

$$P(\hat{Y} = +|S = s, Y = y) = P(\hat{Y} = +|S = \bar{s}, Y = y), \qquad y \in \{+, -\}. \tag{5}$$

Therefrom, we can measure the equalized odds as the following [21,27]:

$$EOd = \sum_{y \in \{+,-\}} |P(\hat{Y} = +|S = s, Y = y) - P(\hat{Y} = +|S = \bar{s}, Y = y)|. \tag{6}$$

The value range: $EOd \in [0,2]$; with 0 standing for no discrimination and 2 indicating the maximum discrimination. In our example, $EOd = |\dfrac{32}{32 + 4} - \dfrac{38}{38 + 6}| + |\dfrac{4}{4 + 6} - \dfrac{5}{5 + 5}| \approx 0.1253$.

3.4   Predictive Parity

Predictive parity [9] (denoted as *PP*) is satisfied if both protected and non-protected groups have an equal positive predictive value (PPV) or *Precision*,

$PPV = \dfrac{TP}{TP + FP}$, i.e., the probability of a student predicted to *"pass"* actually having *"pass"* class should be the same, for both male and female students.

$$P(Y = +|\hat{Y} = +, S = s) = P(Y = +|\hat{Y} = +, S = \bar{s}). \tag{7}$$

Therefore, we report the predictive parity measure as:

$$PP = |P(Y = +|\hat{Y} = +, S = s) - P(Y = +|\hat{Y} = +, S = \bar{s})|. \tag{8}$$

where $PP \in [0,1]$, with 0 standing for no discrimination and 1 indicating the maximum discrimination. $PP = \dfrac{32}{32 + 4} - \dfrac{38}{38 + 5} \approx 0.0052$, in our example.

3.5   Predictive Equality

Predictive equality [10] (denoted as PE), also referred as false positive error (FPR) rate balance [9] ($FPR = \dfrac{FP}{TN + FP}$), aims to the equality of decision's accuracy across the protected and non-protected groups. In detail, the probability of students with an actual *"fail"* class being incorrectly assigned to the *"pass"* class should be the same for both male and female students.

$$P(\hat{Y} = +|Y = -, S = s) = P(\hat{Y} = +|Y = -, S = \bar{s}). \tag{9}$$

In practice, researchers report predictive equality measure by the difference of $FPRs$ [21]:

$$PE = |P(\hat{Y} = +|Y = -, S = s) - P(\hat{Y} = +|Y = -, S = \bar{s})|. \tag{10}$$

The value range: $PE \in [0,1]$, 0 and 1 indicate no discrimination and maximum discrimination, respectively. $PE = |\dfrac{4}{6 + 4} - \dfrac{5}{5 + 5}| = 0.1$, in our example.

3.6   Treatment Equality

Treatment equality [8] (denoted as TE) is satisfied if the ratios of false negatives and false positives are the same for both protected and non-protected groups.

$$\dfrac{FN_{prot.}}{FP_{prot.}} = \dfrac{FN_{non-prot.}}{FP_{non-prot.}}. \tag{11}$$

In our paper, we report the treatment equality by the difference between two ratios described in Eq. 11.

The metric becomes unbounded if $FP_{prot.}$ or $FP_{non-prot.}$ is zero[2]. In our example, $TE = -0.2$, because the ratios of FN and FP are 1 and 1.2 for female and male groups, respectively.

---

[2] https://docs.aws.amazon.com/sagemaker/latest/dg/clarify-post-training-bias-metric-te.html.

3.7   Absolute Between-ROC Area

Absolute Between-ROC Area (ABROCA) [17] is based on the Receiver Operating Characteristics (ROC) curve. It measures the divergence between the protected (ROC_s) and non-protected group $(ROC_{\bar{s}})$ curves across all possible thresholds $t \in [0,1]$ of FPR and TPR. The absolute difference between the two curves is measured to capture the case that the curves may cross each other.

$$\int_0^1 \mid ROC_s(t) - ROC_{\bar{s}}(t) \mid dt. \tag{12}$$

The value range: $ABROCA \in [0,1]$. The lower value indicates a lower difference in the predictions between the two groups and, therefore, a fairer model.

4   Evaluation

In this section, we evaluate the performances of predictive models w.r.t. accuracy and fairness measures on five datasets and investigate the effect of choosing grade threshold on fairness measures.

4.1   Datasets

We evaluate the fairness measures on popular educational datasets [27,30,38], which are summarized in Table 2. All datasets are imbalanced, as shown in the imbalance ratio (IR) column.

Table 2. An overview of educational datasets

Datasets	#Instances	#Instances (cleaned)	#Attributes	Protected attribute	Class label	IR (+:-)
Law school	20,798	20,798	12	Race	Pass the bar exam	8.07:1
PISA	5,233	3,404	24	Gender	Reading score	1.35:1
Student academics	131	131	22	Gender	ESP	3.70:1
Student performance	649	649	33	Gender	Final grade	5.49:1
xAPI-Edu-Data	480	480	17	Gender	Grade level	2.78:1

Law School. The Law school dataset[3] contains the law school admission records from 163 law schools in the US in 1991. The target is to predict whether a candidate would pass the bar exam or not. The protected attribute is "race" = $\{white, non - white\}$, where *"non-white"* is the protected group.

PISA Dataset. The PISA dataset[4] contains information on the performance of American students [14] taking the exam in 2009 from the Program for International Student Assessment (PISA). The grade threshold ("readingScore" attribute) is chosen at 500 to compute the class label = $\{low, high\}$ since the mean reading score is 497.6. The experiments are performed on the cleaned version of this dataset with 3,404 instances after removing missing values.

---

[3] https://github.com/tailequy/fairness_dataset/tree/main/Law_school.
[4] https://www.kaggle.com/econdata/pisa-test-scores.

Student Academics Performance Dataset. The student academics performance dataset[5] [19] consists of socio-economic, demographic, and academic information of students from three different colleges in India with 22 attributes. The class label is ESP (end semester percentage). In this paper, we encode class label as a binary attribute with values { *"pass"*, *"good-and-higher"*}, where *"good-and-higher"* is a positive class.

Student Performance Dataset. The student performance dataset[6] [11] was collected in two Portuguese schools in 2005 - 2006. It contains 33 features describing demographics, grades, social and school-related information of students. "gender" is considered the protected attribute. The target is to predict the final outcome. The class label = $\{pass, fail\}$ is computed based on the final grade (attribute "G3") as $\{<10, \geq 10\}$ [11,27].

Students' Academic Performance Dataset (xAPI-Edu-Data). xAPI-Edu-Data[7] [4] contains 480 student records described by 17 attributes collected from *Kalboard 360* learning management system. We encode the class label as a binary attribute as $\{Low, Medium - High\}$ corresponding to $\{L, M \text{ or } H\}$ in the original dataset. The positive class is *"Medium-High"*.

4.2 Predictive Models

We select four prevalent classifiers used for student performance prediction problems based on the survey of Xiao et al. [38], and two well-known fairness-aware classifiers, namely Agarwal's [2] and AdaFair [21]. In which, Agarwal's method reduces the fair classification to a sequence of cost-sensitive classification problems with the lowest (empirical) error subject to the desired constraints, and AdaFair is based on AdaBoost that further updates the weights of the instances in each boosting round. In brief, the predictive models are: 1) Decision Tree (DT); 2) Naive Bayes (NB); 3) Multi-layer Perceptron (MLP); 4) Support Vector Machines (SVM); 5) Agarwal's; 6) AdaFair. In our experiments, we use 70% of data for training and 30% for testing (single split). Predicted models are implemented and executed with default parameters provided by Scikit-learn and Iosifidis et al. [21]. Agarwal's method is implemented in the AI Fairness 360 toolkit[8].

4.3 Experimental Results

Law School Dataset. The results are presented in Table 3. AdaFair is the best predictive model w.r.t. fairness measures, although its balanced accuracy is significantly lower than that of other models. Besides, the fairness measures

---

[5] https://archive.ics.uci.edu/ml/datasets/Student+Academics+Performance.

[6] https://archive.ics.uci.edu/ml/datasets/student+performance.

[7] https://www.kaggle.com/datasets/aljarah/xAPI-Edu-Data.

[8] https://github.com/Trusted-AI/AIF360.

show a quite large variation across the classification methods, as demonstrated in Fig. 7-a. Furthermore, the shape and position of the ROC curves, as visualized in Fig. 2, have been changed across the predictive models, which indicates the change in the performance of models w.r.t. each value in the protected attribute. Because the datasets are imbalanced, we report the performance of predictive models on both accuracy and balanced accuracy measures.

PISA Dataset. The interesting point is SVM and DT show their superiority in terms of fairness measures, although AdaFair still has very good results on fairness metrics and accuracy (Fig. 3 and Table 4). Furthermore, fairness measures have the least variability in this dataset, as shown in Fig. 7-b.

Student Academics Performance Dataset. The AdaFair outperforms other models w.r.t. fairness measures, however, the balanced accuracy is decreased considerably (Table 5). Besides, all fairness measures have significant variation across predictive models (Fig. 4 and Fig. 7-c).

Student Performance Dataset. In general, all models show good accuracy (balanced accuracy) on predicting students' performance (Table 6). MLP and AdaFair models fairly guarantee the fairness of results on most measures. Besides, the values of fairness measures also do not vary significantly across predictive models (Fig. 7-d), although the ABROCA slices are quite different in shape (Fig. 5).

Table 3. Law school: performance of predictive models

Measures	DT	NB	MLP	SVM	Agarwal's	AdaFair
Accuracy	0.8458	0.8191	**0.9042**	0.8926	0.7952	0.8921
Balanced accuracy	0.6301	**0.7784**	0.6596	0.5029	0.5848	0.5
Statistical parity	0.1999	0.5250	0.2367	0.0052	0.0326	**0.0**
Equal opportunity	0.1557	0.4665	0.1237	0.0014	0.0202	**0.0**
Equalized odds	0.3253	0.8105	0.5501	0.0169	0.0953	**0.0**
Predictive parity	0.1424	**0.0130**	0.0754	0.1857	0.1802	0.1885
Predictive equality	0.1696	0.3440	0.4265	0.0154	0.0751	**0.0**
Treatment equality	−0.0667	22.440	0.7770	0.0039	−1.9676	**0.0**
ABROCA	0.0336	**0.0316**	0.0336	0.0833	0.0365	0.0822

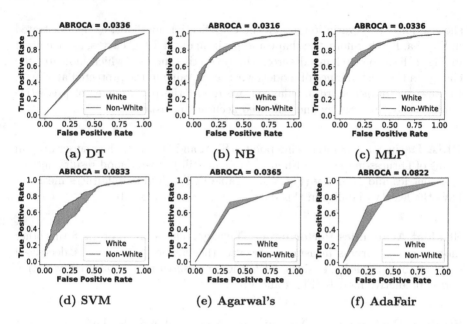

Fig. 2. Law school: ABROCA slice plots

Table 4. PISA: performance of predictive models

Measures	DT	NB	MLP	SVM	Agarwal's	AdaFair
Accuracy	0.6360	0.6624	0.6526	0.6096	0.6614	**0.6810**
Balanced accuracy	0.6224	**0.6379**	0.5732	0.5026	0.6340	0.6130
Statistical parity	−0.0200	−0.0316	−0.0771	**−0.0022**	−0.0096	−0.0573
Equal opportunity	**0.0019**	0.0262	0.0330	0.0043	0.0414	0.0164
Equalized odds	0.0165	0.0709	0.1398	**0.0068**	0.0548	0.0752
Predictive parity	0.1012	**0.0683**	0.0826	0.1108	0.0785	0.0868
Predictive equality	0.0146	0.0446	0.1067	**0.0024**	0.0134	0.0588
Treatment equality	0.5642	0.3855	−0.0251	**−0.0033**	0.4609	0.0260
ABROCA	**0.0070**	0.0330	0.0223	0.0844	0.0326	0.0216

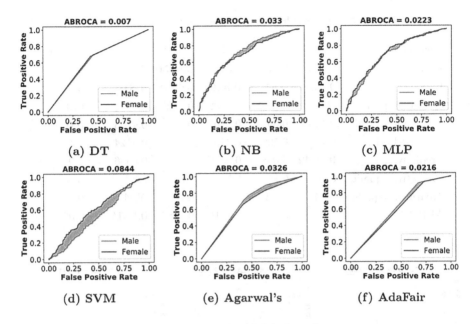

Fig. 3. PISA: ABROCA slice plots

xAPI-Edu-Data Dataset. This is a surprising dataset because the traditional classification methods show a better performance not only in terms of accuracy/balanced accuracy measures but also w.r.t. fairness measures (Table 7). In addition, variation in the values of fairness measures across the predictive models is not significant, as shown in Fig. 7-e, except for the ABROCA measure with a noticeable change in the shape (Fig. 6).

Regarding the *treatment equality* measure, this measure is entirely different from all other measures with an extensive range of values, which is visualized in Fig. 7-f[9]. On the *PISA* datasets, this TE measure shows the best values across predicted models, followed by *Law school* and *Student Academics* datasets.

Summary of Results: In general, *ABOCA* is the measure with the lowest variability across predictive methods and datasets. It also clearly presents the ML model's accuracy variation over each value of the protected attribute. *Equal opportunity* and *predictive parity* also have a slight variation across methods and datasets. *Equalized odds*, to some extent, can represent two measures *equal opportunity* and *predictive equality* as it is the sum of the other two metrics. Furthermore, *treatment equality* has a very wide range of values (sometimes the value may not be bounded), making it difficult to compare and evaluate.

---

[9] We use the abbreviations of the fairness measures and datasets in Fig. 7.

Table 5. Student academics: performance of predictive models

Measures	DT	NB	MLP	SVM	Agarwal's	AdaFair
Accuracy	0.7750	0.8750	0.8750	**0.9250**	0.8750	0.9
Balanced accuracy	0.6528	**0.8194**	**0.8194**	0.6250	**0.8194**	0.5
Statistical parity	−0.1278	−0.1328	−0.1328	0.0526	0.0677	**0.0**
Equal opportunity	0.1455	0.0991	0.2105	**0.0**	0.0123	**0.0**
Equalized odds	0.1455	0.5991	0.7105	0.5	0.5124	**0.0**
Predictive parity	**0.0042**	0.0588	0.0552	0.0397	0.0556	0.01
Predictive equality	**0.0**	0.5	0.5	0.5	0.5	**0.0**
Treatment equality	−3.0	*N/A*	*N/A*	**0.0**	*N/A*	**0.0**
ABROCA	0.0728	0.2059	0.1316	0.1285	**0.0317**	0.0372

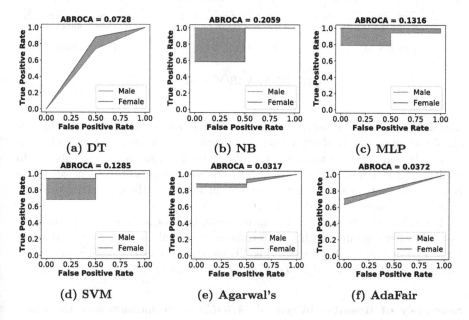

Fig. 4. Student academics: ABROCA slice plots

Table 6. Student performance: performance of predictive models

Measures	DT	NB	MLP	SVM	Agarwal's	AdaFair
Accuracy	0.9333	0.8974	0.9077	0.9231	0.8923	**0.9487**
Balanced accuracy	**0.8639**	0.8595	0.7840	0.7441	0.8565	0.8240
Statistical parity	−0.0382	−0.0509	−0.0630	**0.0151**	−0.0209	−0.0255
Equal opportunity	0.0125	0.0174	0.03	0.0183	0.0176	**0.0092**
Equalized odds	0.1316	0.2198	**0.1252**	0.3279	0.2200	0.1877
Predictive parity	**0.0456**	0.0591	0.0601	0.0944	0.0577	0.0639
Predictive equality	0.1190	0.2024	**0.0952**	0.3095	0.2024	0.1786
Treatment equality	2.0	7.5	**0.3333**	0.5	9.75	**0.3333**
ABROCA	0.0575	0.0686	0.0683	**0.0231**	0.0762	0.0887

Table 7. xAPI-Edu-Data: performance of predictive models

Measures	DT	NB	MLP	SVM	Agarwal's	AdaFair
Accuracy	0.8333	0.8750	0.8750	0.8611	**0.8681**	0.8056
Balanced accuracy	0.8	**0.8970**	0.8545	0.8505	0.8859	0.8162
Statistical parity	**−0.1274**	−0.2608	−0.2112	−0.2209	−0.2505	−0.2292
Equal opportunity	0.0282	0.0974	0.0654	**0.0308**	0.0974	0.0538
Equalized odds	0.1329	0.1954	**0.1262**	0.2706	0.1684	0.3207
Predictive parity	0.0752	0.0074	0.0654	0.0088	0.0122	**0.0057**
Predictive equality	0.1047	0.0980	**0.0608**	0.2399	0.0709	0.2669
Treatment equality	1.0667	−8.0	**0.0**	−0.2667	−2.0	−1.1667
ABROCA	0.0665	**0.0216**	0.0263	0.0796	0.0293	0.1065

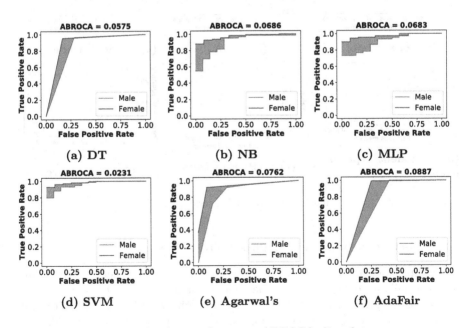

Fig. 5. Student performance: ABROCA slice plots

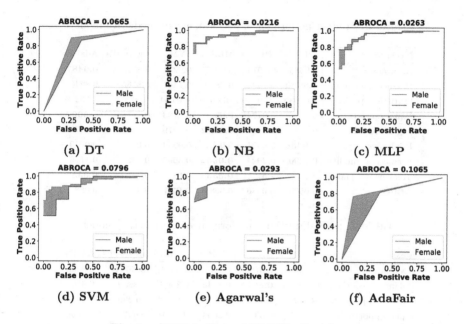

Fig. 6. xAPI-Edu-Data: ABROCA slice plots.

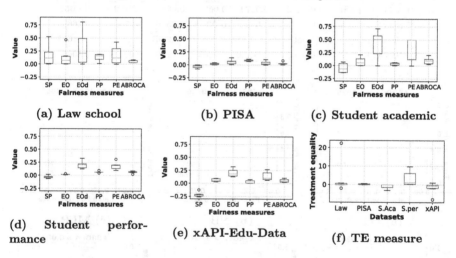

Fig. 7. Variation of fairness measures

4.4   Effect of Varying Grade Threshold on Fairness

Grade thresholds are often chosen as a basis for determining whether a candidate passes or fails an exam. In the student performance dataset, 10 (out of 20) is selected as the grade threshold [11,27]. However, the selection of a threshold can affect the fairness of the predictive models, as shown in the IPUMS Adult dataset [12]. Hence, we investigate the effect of grade threshold on fairness by varying the threshold in a range of [4, 16], corresponding to 25% to 75% of the maximum grade (20). The results in Fig. 8 show that all fairness measures are affected by the grade threshold. When the grade threshold is gradually increased, the predictive models tend to be fairer (shown on the measures: equalized odds, predictive equality, and ABROCA). The opposite trend is observed in the remaining measures (except the treatment equality measure). Regarding the balanced accuracy, two models (DT and AdaFair) tend to predict more accurately. The NB model has a decreasing accuracy after the threshold is increased.

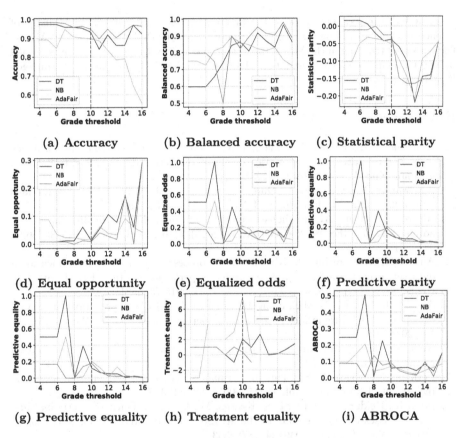

Fig. 8. Accuracy and fairness interventions with varying grade threshold on Student performance dataset (Decision Tree method).

5   Conclusion and Outlooks

In this work, we evaluate seven popular group fairness measures for student performance prediction problems. We conduct experiments using four traditional ML models and two fairness-aware ML methods on five educational datasets.

Our experiments reflect variations and correlations of fairness measures across datasets and predictive models. The results provide an overview picture for the selection of fairness measure in a specific case. Besides, we investigate the effect of varying grade thresholds on the accuracy and fairness of ML models. The preliminary results suggest that choosing the threshold is an important factor contributing to ensuring fairness in the output of the ML models. In the future, we plan to extend our evaluation of fairness w.r.t. more than one protected attribute, such as gender and race, and further explore the correlation between groups of fairness notions.

Acknowledgments. The work of the first author is supported by the Ministry of Science and Culture of Lower Saxony, Germany, within the Ph.D. program "LernMINT: Data-assisted teaching in the MINT subjects". The work of the second author is funded by the German Research Foundation (DFG Grant NI-1760/1-1), project "Managed Forgetting".

References

1. Abu Saa, A., Al-Emran, M., Shaalan, K.: Factors affecting students' performance in higher education: a systematic review of predictive data mining techniques. Technol. Knowl. Learn. **24**(4), 567–598 (2019)
2. Agarwal, A., Beygelzimer, A., Dudík, M., Langford, J., Wallach, H.: A reductions approach to fair classification. In: ICML, pp. 60–69. PMLR (2018)
3. Alvero, A., et al.: AI and holistic review: informing human reading in college admissions. In: AIES, pp. 200–206. ACM (2020). https://doi.org/10.1145/3375627.3375871
4. Amrieh, E.A., Hamtini, T., Aljarah, I.: Preprocessing and analyzing educational data set using x-api for improving student's performance. In: AEECT, pp. 1–5. IEEE (2015). https://doi.org/10.1109/AEECT.2015.7360581
5. Anders, J., Dilnot, C., Macmillan, L., Wyness, G.: Grade expectations: how well can we predict future grades based on past performance? CEPEO Working Paper No. 20–14 (2020)
6. Anderson, H., Boodhwani, A., Baker, R.S.: Assessing the fairness of graduation predictions. In: EDM (2019)
7. Berhanu, F., Abera, A.: Students' performance prediction based on their academic record. Int. J. Comput. Appl. **131**(5), 0975–8887 (2015)
8. Berk, R., Heidari, H., Jabbari, S., Kearns, M., Roth, A.: Fairness in criminal justice risk assessments: the state of the art. Soc. Methods Res. **50**(1), 3–44 (2021). https://doi.org/10.1177/0049124118782533
9. Chouldechova, A.: Fair prediction with disparate impact: a study of bias in recidivism prediction instruments. Big data **5**(2), 153–163 (2017)
10. Corbett-Davies, S., Pierson, E., Feller, A., Goel, S., Huq, A.: Algorithmic decision making and the cost of fairness. In: KDD, pp. 797–806 (2017)
11. Cortez, P., Silva, A.M.G.: Using data mining to predict secondary school student performance (2008). https://hdl.handle.net/1822/8024
12. Ding, F., Hardt, M., Miller, J., Schmidt, L.: Retiring adult: new datasets for fair machine learning. NeurIPS **34**, 6478–6490 (2021)
13. Dwork, C., Hardt, M., Pitassi, T., Reingold, O., Zemel, R.: Fairness through awareness. In: ITCS, pp. 214–226 (2012). https://doi.org/10.1145/2090236.2090255

14. Fleischman, H.L., Hopstock, P.J., Pelczar, M.P., Shelley, B.E.: Highlights from pisa 2009: Performance of us 15-year-old students in reading, mathematics, and science literacy in an international context, nces 2011–004. National Center for Education Statistics (2010)

15. Foster, I., Ghani, R., Jarmin, R.S., Kreuter, F., Lane, J.: Big data and social science: a practical guide to methods and tools. CRC Press (2016)

16. Francis, B.K., Babu, S.S.: Predicting academic performance of students using a hybrid data mining approach. J. Med. Syst. **43**(6), 1–15 (2019). https://doi.org/10.1007/s10916-019-1295-4

17. Gardner, J., Brooks, C., Baker, R.: Evaluating the fairness of predictive student models through slicing analysis. In: LAK19, pp. 225–234 (2019). https://doi.org/10.1145/3303772.3303791

18. Hardt, M., Price, E., Srebro, N.: Equality of opportunity in supervised learning. In: Advances in neural information processing systems 29 (2016)

19. Hussain, S., Dahan, N.A., Ba-Alwib, F.M., Ribata, N.: Educational data mining and analysis of students' academic performance using weka. Indonesian J. Electr. Eng. Comput. Sci. **9**(2), 447–459 (2018)

20. Hutchinson, B., Mitchell, M.: 50 years of test (un) fairness: lessons for machine learning. In: FAT, pp. 49–58 (2019). https://doi.org/10.1145/3287560.3287600

21. Iosifidis, V., Ntoutsi, E.: AdaFair: Cumulative fairness adaptive boosting. In: CIKM, pp. 781–790 (2019). https://doi.org/10.1145/3357384.3357974

22. Jiang, W., Pardos, Z.A.: Towards equity and algorithmic fairness in student grade prediction. In: AIES, pp. 608–617. ACM (2021). https://doi.org/10.1145/3461702.3462623

23. Jiang, W., Pardos, Z.A.: Towards equity and algorithmic fairness in student grade prediction. In: AIES, pp. 608–617 (2021). https://doi.org/10.1145/3461702.3462623

24. Khan, A., Ghosh, S.K.: Student performance analysis and prediction in classroom learning: a review of educational data mining studies. Educ. Inf. Technol. **26**(1), 205–240 (2021). https://doi.org/10.1007/s10639-020-10230-3

25. Khan, N.A.U., Khan, I.U., Alamri, L.H., Almuslim, R.S.: An improved early student's academic performance prediction using deep learning. Int. J. Emerg. Technol. Learn. (iJET) **16**(12), 108–122 (2021)

26. Kuzilek, J., Hlosta, M., Zdrahal, Z.: Open university learning analytics dataset. Scient. data **4**(1), 1–8 (2017). https://doi.org/10.1038/sdata.2017.171

27. Le Quy, T., Roy, A., Vasileios, I., Wenbin, Z., Ntoutsi, E.: A survey on datasets for fairness-aware machine learning. WIREs Data Mining Knowl. Disc. 12(3), e1452 (2022). https://doi.org/10.1002/widm.1452

28. Mehrabi, N., Morstatter, F., Saxena, N., Lerman, K., Galstyan, A.: A survey on bias and fairness in machine learning. ACM Comput. Surv. (CSUR) **54**(6), 1–35 (2021). https://doi.org/10.1145/3457607

29. Meyer, K.: Education, justice and the human good: fairness and equality in the education system. Routledge (2014)

30. Mihaescu, M.C., Popescu, P.S.: Review on publicly available datasets for educational data mining. Wiley Interdisc. Rev. Data Mining Knowl. Discovery **11**(3), e1403 (2021). https://doi.org/10.1002/widm.1403

31. Namoun, A., Alshanqiti, A.: Predicting student performance using data mining and learning analytics techniques: a systematic literature review. Appl. Sci. **11**(1), 237 (2020). https://doi.org/10.3390/app11010237

32. Ntoutsi, E., Fafalios, P., Gadiraju, U., Iosifidis, V., Nejdl, W., Vidal, M.E., Ruggieri, S., Turini, F., Papadopoulos, S., Krasanakis, E., et al.: Bias in data-driven artificial intelligence systems-an introductory survey. Wiley Interdisc. Rev. Data Mining Knowl. Discovery **10**(3), e1356 (2020). https://doi.org/10.1002/widm.1356
33. Saleem, F., Ullah, Z., Fakieh, B., Kateb, F.: Intelligent decision support system for predicting student's e-learning performance using ensemble machine learning. Mathematics **9**(17), 2078 (2021). https://doi.org/10.3390/math9172078
34. Shahiri, A.M., Husain, W., et al.: A review on predicting student's performance using data mining techniques. Procedia Computer Science **72**, 414–422 (2015)
35. Simoiu, C., Corbett-Davies, S., Goel, S.: The problem of infra-marginality in outcome tests for discrimination. Annals Appl. Statist. **11**(3), 1193–1216 (2017). https://doi.org/10.1214/17-AOAS1058
36. Verma, S., Rubin, J.: Fairness definitions explained. In: 2018 IEEE/ACM International Workshop on Software Fairness (FairWare), pp. 1–7 (2018). https://doi.org/10.23919/FAIRWARE.2018.8452913
37. Wightman, L.F.: LSAC national longitudinal bar passage study. LSAC Research Report Series (1998)
38. Xiao, W., Ji, P., Hu, J.: A survey on educational data mining methods used for predicting students' performance. Eng. Reports **4**(5), e12482 (2022). https://doi.org/10.1002/eng2.12482
39. Yu, R., Li, Q., Fischer, C., Doroudi, S., Xu, D.: Towards accurate and fair prediction of college success: evaluating different sources of student data. In: EDM (2020)
40. Žliobaitė, I.: On the relation between accuracy and fairness in binary classification. In: FAT/ML 2015 workshop at ICML, vol. 15 (2015)
41. Zohair, A., Mahmoud, L.: Prediction of student's performance by modelling small dataset size. Int. J. Educ. Technol. High. Educ. **16**(1), 1–18 (2019). https://doi.org/10.1186/s41239-019-0160-3

Combining Image Enhancement Techniques and Deep Learning for Shallow Water Benthic Marine Litter Detection

Gil Emmanuel Bancud(✉), Alex John Labanon, Neil Angelo Abreo,
and Vladimer Kobayashi

AIR-ES Lab, University of the Philippines Mindanao, Davao City, Philippines
{gvbancud,aclabanon,nsabreo,vbkobayashi}@up.edu.ph

Abstract. The scarcity of information about benthic marine litter especially in developing countries hampers the implementation of targeted actions to minimize the extent of its impacts. This study developed a system using image processing and deep learning methods for detecting/tracking marine macro litter that can efficiently identify and quantify its amount in benthic environments in shallow coastal areas. Shallow underwater litter detection poses several challenges. First is the low quality of images. Second is the difficulty in recognizing litter brought by their varying visual characteristics. Third is the lack of available data for training. Underwater images of litter were collected from marine litter hotspots in coastal areas in southern Philippines. This study experimented with various object detection algorithms. The best object detection model is then paired with various image enhancement techniques to determine the optimal combination. Among the combinations that were tested, YOLOv5n combined with CLAHE gave the best performance for simple binary task (litter or not litter) with a mAP@0.5 of 0.704. Furthermore, the results showed that applying underwater image enhancement techniques provides noticeable improvement for object detection models on detecting marine litter.

Keywords: Yolov5 · Image enhancement · Marine litter · Object detection

1 Introduction

Marine litter, especially plastics, is a threat to global marine biodiversity, food security and food safety [7, 16]. Most anthropogenic marine litter come from developing countries in South and Southeast Asia, however, large knowledge gaps regarding marine litter in these regions exist that impede in solving the problem [19]. With vast coastlines and numerous islands, countries like the Philippines, Malaysia and Indonesia would need to develop, or adopt, methods to study marine litter that can overcome the logistical, funding, and other challenges associated with archipelagic countries.

Developments in image processing, machine learning and artificial intelligence could overcome some of the challenges in marine litter research [18]. In fact, The use of machine learning on drone captured images, for example, is suggested to limit human

© The Author(s), under exclusive license to Springer Nature Switzerland AG 2023
I. Koprinska et al. (Eds.): ECML PKDD 2022 Workshops, CCIS 1752, pp. 137–149, 2023.
https://doi.org/10.1007/978-3-031-23618-1_9

error in quantifying and identifying marine litter [4]. Image-based analysis of marine litter was shown to have a < 5% error in estimating marine litter volume on a beach [14].

Although, there are existing studies which have used AI and image processing to tackle the litter problem most of them are limited to land-based (including beached) and floating litter. Research on benthic marine litter on the other hand is relatively uncommon with only one published literature quantifying benthic litter in Southeast Asia [20]. This is concerning as studies show that benthic areas are potential "sinks" of marine litter [20]. One possible explanation of the scarcity of studies on benthic marine litter is the difficulty of collecting training data. Another plausible reason is the task of identifying benthic litter in images or videos is extra challenging due to visibility issues.

The objectives, therefore, of this study are two-fold: 1) to collect image data that could be used to train object detection models for benthic litter detection and 2) to test and compare different existing object detection algorithms for this task. Here the detection is limited to only detecting litter without classifying the type of litter. Although simplistic, this study serves as a good starting point in quantifying the amount of litter in a rapid, replicable, and accurate manner. We then experimented on different image enhancement techniques and paired it with the best performing object detection algorithm to build the detection system. This research on benthic litter would contribute to addressing several of the UN SDGs, namely, *good health and well-being*, *clean water and sanitation*, *responsible consumption and production*, and *life below water*.

2 Related Work

In shallow water marine environments, marine litter assessments through visual census with SCUBA diving or snorkeling are the most common approaches [26]. However, both methods are prone to observer bias and are time constrained (e.g., depending on the air holding capacity of SCUBA tanks). Other researchers use ROVs (Remotely Operated Vehicles) to capture videos of underwater environments [3]. A more cost-effective alternative to ROVs is the use of towed camera systems that have been used to collect marine data [22, 27]. Captured videos and photos are post-processed to detect or identify litter contained therein. Some approaches include manual detection and classification of litter and/or the use of advanced object detection models.

Artificial intelligence (AI) and machine learning (ML) are powerful tools for litter research [31]. When paired with remote sensing, AI and ML significantly increase marine litter study area coverage [17] and possibly increase rate and accuracy of marine litter detection [15]. F-scores from ML models ranges from 44% to 78% [5, 8, 9, 18]. Meanwhile, a comparative study showed the reliability of automated detection in providing litter density map vis-a-vis manual image screening [9].

Object detection models which have been used for underwater litter detection are Mask RCNN [23], CNN [28], YOLOv2, Tiny YOLO, Faster R-CNN and SSD [6]. It was reported that YOLOv2 strikes a good balance between accuracy and inference time. The Yolov5 framework is a family of models ported from Darknet Yolov4 into the PyTorch ecosystem. Latest iterations of the model utilize CSP-Darknet53 [1] for its backbone, and a Yolov3 head [25]. Authors in [23] used Mask R-CNN for automated underwater litter detection where they reported a mAP@0.50 of .62. They noted several difficulties in detecting seafloor litter. First, some litter objects belonging to the same class have no defined geometric shapes in several categories or some litter shapes in different classes are the same. Second is some litters have been buried or degraded. And third is the presence of background objects or structures which may mislead the algorithm.

As the lack of standardized approach to marine litter is a main obstacle for tackling the marine litter threat, developments in AI and ML models for marine litter detection also provide standardized methodology that would allow data comparison at large spatial scales for a better understanding of the global marine litter problem [8, 18].

3 Materials and Methods

3.1 Underwater Imagery Acquisition

Data were collected from shallow waters at various coastal sites: Bato, Sta. Cruz, Davao del Sur; Matina Aplaya, Davao City; Samal District, Island Garden City of Samal; Madaum, Davao del Norte; and Pujada Bay, City of Mati. Socio-economic activities and water characteristics were considered in selecting the sites as these would indicate the amount and types of litter found in them and the quality of the resulting images. Most of the time the water is clear but there are also instances where the water is highly turbid. All images were taken in the natural environment.

Data were captured using waterproof point-and-shoot action cameras (Sjcam SJ40000) and a digital camera (FinePix XP120). Both camera models can take up to 16mp resolution photos. The images were taken by pointing the cameras perpendicular to the scene from varying distance depending on the depth (1–3 m). Seven data collection dives were performed and a total of 2,362 images were collected. These were subsequently labelled following the Oslo Paris Conventions marine litter classification guideline [30]. Although there are 121 marine litter classes in the OSPAR guideline, a binary marine litter guideline was explored for the collected dataset due to poor variability in most classes.

3.2 Image Processing and Labeling

Images collected from different cameras have varying properties: action cameras have intrinsic distortion (fisheye effect), and image resolutions can be different between cameras. Hence, each image was adjusted to remove distortions. To preserve image fidelity, images are set to their original quality during labeling. These images are subsequently resized to a fixed 640 by 640 pixels during training. For the labelling, five individuals were employed to label the images to increase reliability. Disagreements in the labels are resolved using the majority method. To allow for remote and collaborative labelling workflow, Supervise.ly[1], a web-based platform for computer vision project management, was used. Supervise.ly is free, easy to use, and integrates well with various object detection frameworks.

---

[1] https://supervise.ly/.

The current 2,362 manually labelled images were then randomly split into training, validation, and test sets: 1181 (~50%) training images, 707 (~30%) validation images, and 474 (~20%) test images. Augmenting the training set increases its amount threefold bringing the total dataset counts to 3543 (~75%) training images, 707 (15%) validation images, and 474 (10%) testing images; details on augmentation techniques will be further discussed. During image enhancement, the splits were maintained to reduce variability in the small dataset. A stratified split of the dataset was used for more accurate evaluations. All reported performance results are computed from the test set.

3.3 Object Detection Approach

Multiple object detection models as listed on Table 1 were considered for experiments to set a baseline performance of the dataset on different architectures. For non-Yolov5 models, model and training configurations were based on the MMDetection Library [2]. Motivations for modifying training configurations include modifying batch sizes to fit a Nvidia RTX 2070 Max-Q card, modifying epochs to ensure model convergence, and modifying heads to accommodate for the binary classes used in the dataset; all other configurations are set to default. The Yolov5 [24] family is a particular point of interest since it is accessible, easy to use, and has potential extensibility for the deployment of a real-time solution for marine litter monitoring due to its highly optimized lightweight structure for embedded devices.

Data augmentation techniques that can be used during training include mosaic data loading, copy pasting, random affine transformation, mixup, random HSV, and image flipping. Training and inference strategies such as auto-learned anchor boxes, mixed precision, learning rate scheduling, and hyperparameter evolution are supported to improve speed and performance of the model.

Table 1. Different object detection models for baseline performance testing

Model	Object detection type	Backbone
Yolov5n	Single stage	CSPNet
Yolov5m	Single stage	CSPNet
YoloX	Single stage	YOLOX-s
SSDNet	Single stage	VGG16
RetinaNet	Single stage	X-101-64x4d-FPN
Faster RCNN	Two stage	X-101-64x4d-FPN
Deformable DETR	Two stage	ResNet-50

3.4 Image Enhancement

Various underwater image enhancement methods were tested to deal with the problem of poor image quality. In contrast to restoration methods, image enhancement methods do not rely on any physical model and are mainly based on pixel intensity re-distribution which make them simpler to implement and faster to run. Five methods were tested. First is the Contrast limited adaptive histogram equalization (CLAHE) which is an adaptive contrast enhancement method based on adaptive histogram equalization (AHE) [33]. Table 2 shows the parameters of CLAHE [33]. Second is **RGHS** proposed by [10]. Table 2 also shows the parameters of RGHS [10]. Third is **ICM** which was proposed by [13]. The parameters used in this method only rely on the stretching of RGB and HSI channels to a maximum and minimum values and the minimum and maximum pixel currently present in the image. Fourth is Unsupervised color correction (UCM) method which is based on color balancing, contrast correction of the RGB model and contrast correction of the HSI model [12]. The parameters are quite similar with ICM with few modifications which set the minimum value of Red instead of zero for the contrast correction to the upper side and sets upper limit to the maximum of Blue instead of 255 for the contrast correction to the lower side. Fifth is the Histogram equalization (HE) which adjusts the contrast of an image by spreading out the most frequent pixel intensity values [11]. This method is automatically implemented using the *equalizeHist* function in OpenCV.

In evaluating the quality of an image quantitatively, methods are often divided into full reference and non-reference. Full reference image metrics require a high-quality reference image. Unfortunately, dehazed and natural reference image cannot be obtained in the case of the complexity of underwater environment unless there are generated synthetic images of underwater scenes. Thus, non-reference metrics developed specifically for underwater images were chosen, the underwater image quality measure (UIQM) and underwater color image quality evaluation (UCIQE) metrics. **UIQM** was proposed by [21] which is a linear combination of three attribute measures: underwater image colorfulness measure (UICM), underwater image sharpness measure (UISM), and underwater image contrast measure (UIConM). Each attribute measure is inspired by the properties of human visual system and can be expressed as:

$$UIQM = c_1 \times UICM + c_2 \times UISM + c_3 \times UIConM \tag{1}$$

where c_1, c_2, c_3 represent the weights of colorfulness, sharpness, and contrast parameters, respectively. **UCIQE,** on the other hand, is a linear combination of contrast, chroma, and saturation in CIE-lab color space. UCIQE quantifies the non-uniform color cast, blurring, and low contrast of an image [32], expressed as:

$$UCIQE = c_1 \times \sigma_c + c_2 \times con_l + c_3 \times \mu_s \tag{2}$$

where σ_c, con_l, and μ_s represent the standard deviation of image chromaticity, contrast of image brightness and average of image saturation, respectively, while c_1, c_2, c_3 represent the weights of these parameters.

Table 2. Parameters of CLAHE and RGHS

CLAHE		RGHS	
Variable	Value	Variable	Value
Clip limit	2	R	0.83
Grid size	16	G	0.95
		B	0.97
		Estimation distance	3
		L component	[0, 100]
		a and b components	[−128, 127]
		Stretching range	0.5%
		Experimental value φ	1.3

3.5 Combining Image Enhancement and Deep Learning

The best object detection model will then be paired with each image enhancement technique to determine the best combination. The mean average precision at IoU = 0.5 was used to assess performance. Figure 1 depicts the entire workflow of the study.

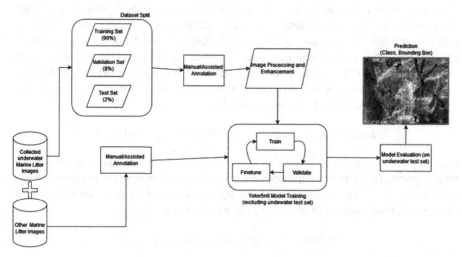

Fig. 1. Overview of the workflow implemented on underwater litter imagery.

4   Results and Discussion

4.1   Underwater Image Enhancement

Our collected dataset was used to evaluate the performance of each image enhancement method which includes 2,362 labelled underwater images in shallow water environments.

The dataset includes four types of underwater images commonly observed in shallow areas, which are also used in the literature [29]. One is relatively clear scene and three challenging underwater images under the greenish, yellowish, and turbid or low-visibility scene [29] (Fig. 2(a)). We show parts of the experimental results with representatives for each underwater type.

The best parameters for each method were determined before feeding the algorithm to the images as shown in Tables 3 and 4. The settings for CLAHE that produced better image quality was region size 32 with clip level 2. For RGHS, experimental value φ of 1.5 produced better results. No parameters were modified for ICM, UCM, and HE (Tables 5, 6 and 7).

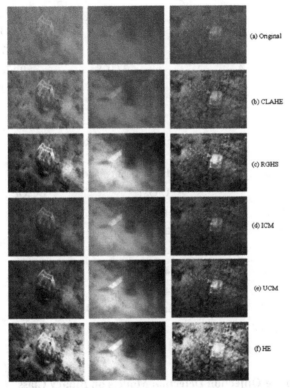

Fig. 2. Comparison of underwater image enhancement methods on collected dataset. (Color figure online)

Figure 2 shows the results of five classic underwater image enhancement methods applied to the collected dataset. Performances were assessed using qualitative and quantitative analysis on the enhanced underwater images. Images enhanced by UCM method present an immense amount of red tone and increased the noises of the original image as shown in Fig. 2(e). HE method (Fig. 2(f)) also produced over-saturated images and introduced unwanted noises. It can be observed that RGHS, CLAHE, and ICM did not present over enhanced results as shown in Fig. 2(b–d). However, CLAHE was not very effective in removing the greenish or bluish and yellowish effect of underwater images as shown in Fig. 2(b). Both RGHS and ICM were successful in removing effects of different underwater types, but RGHS method show a better dehazing effect compared to ICM (Fig. 2(c)).

Table 3. Parameter setting for CLAHE.

Region size	Clip level	Image quality assessment metrics	
		UIQM	UCIQE
8	2	2.5548	0.4382
16	2	3.0421	0.6086
32	2	**3.0644**	**0.6131**
8	4	2.7589	0.4876
16	4	3.0078	0.5720
32	4	3.0247	0.5231

Table 4. Parameter setting for RGHS.

Experimental value (φ)	Image quality assessment metrics	
	UIQM	UCIQE
1.1	4.0152	0.6522
1.3	4.1171	0.6712
1.5	**4.1395**	**0.6828**
1.7	4.0629	0.5316
1.8	4.1056	0.5877
1.10	4.0223	0.6219

4.2 Comparison of Objection Detection Models on Binary Class

To establish a baseline performance of different object detection models on the binary dataset we trained and evaluated seven models. The models were trained using their default configurations as provided in their library. After training, the models were evaluated using the testing set. The results show that YOLOX-s achieved the highest mAP@0.5 while Yolov5m had the highest mAP@0.5:0.95. The results show that the dataset is trainable and that newer models tend to achieve higher scores. Furthermore, it can be observed that one stage detectors (Yolov5m, YOLOX-s, SSDNet, and RetinaNet) performed better compared to two stage detectors (Faster R-CNN, and Deformable DETR).

Table 5. Quantitative analysis of enhanced results based on different methods.

Method	Image quality assessment metrics	
	UIQM	UCIQE
Original (no enhancement)	0.9851	0.1865
CLAHE	3.0644	0.6131
RGHS	**4.1395**	**0.6828**
ICM	3.3228	0.6567
UCM	2.1782	0.5291
HE	2.0333	0.4892

Table 6. Performance metrics of different models on the test set

Model	mAP@0.5	mAP@0.5:0.95
Yolov5n	0.667	0.322
Yolov5m	0.701	**0.359**
YOLOX-s	**0.715**	0.323
SSDNet	0.688	0.284
RetinaNet	0.706	0.311
Faster RCNN	0.673	0.286
Deformable DETR	0.658	0.335

4.3 Combining Image Enhancement and Object Detection

We further trained the YOLOv5n by combining it with image enhancement techniques to determine if performance can be improved. We selected YOLOv5n since it is lightweight (and hence fast), and the performance is also at par with other algorithms. This is also driven by the fact that we plan to integrate the model in a device that can be deployed for real-time litter monitoring. Figure 3 shows each model's true labels and predicted labels for each image enhancement technique.

There is difficulty in objectively differentiating the performance benefits of the candidate image enhancement technique. While there are improvements observed by separately applying each technique (see Sect. 4.1), these do not necessarily translate to better detection accuracy when used in conjunction with Yolov5n. The highest performance is achieved when CLAHE is applied to the dataset.

Additionally, noting the smoothed training curves of each method as seen in Fig. 4 demonstrating an increase in performance during training in select methods, most noticeably CLAHE. While there are only minor improvements in the results derived from each image enhancement technique, model training is improved; the minor improvement in the test result may simply be attributed to the extreme variability of the data due to the nature of the problem, made worse by the lack of ample data.

| Base
True La- | Base
Predic- | GC
Predic- | HE
Predic- | RGHS
Predic- | CLAHE
Predic- |

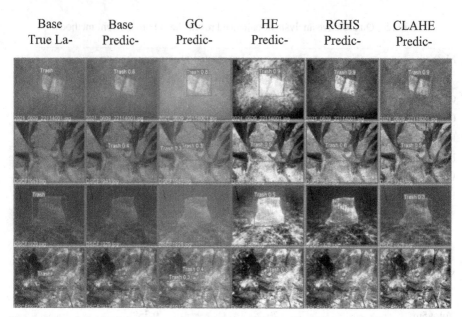

Fig. 3. Image enhanced sample images and their predictions. (From left to right) Base images with True Labels, Base Images with Predicted Labels, GC with Predicted Labels, HE with Predicted Labels, RGHS with Predicted Labels, CLAHE with Predicted Labels.

Table 7. Performance metrics of Yolov5n with different classes and image enhancement techniques on the test set.

Image enhancement method used	mAP @0.5	mAP @0.5:0.95
None	0.667	0.322
HE	0.677	0.353
CLAHE	**0.704**	**0.379**
GC	0.689	0.347
RGHS	0.658	0.361

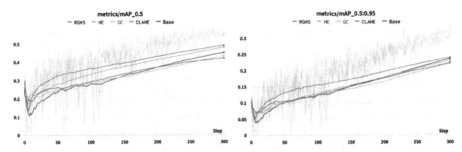

Fig. 4. Validation metrics/mAP curve of Yolo5n on different image enhanced binary datasets.

5 Conclusion and Future Work

In this study we confronted the challenge of automatically detecting benthic litter found in shallow water environments from images using deep learning techniques. Whereas many studies demonstrated the feasibility of this approach, this is still an exceptionally difficult problem as highlighted in [23].

Apart from the visual aspects, it is also hard to find underwater images of litter which can be used for training. We have addressed this by collecting underwater benthic images. This has resulted to improve performance. The visual aspect was dealt with using image enhancement techniques, although it did not significantly improved detection accuracy, it contributed to stability during training.

For the practical implications, to the best of our knowledge, this is the only study in the Philippines that used deep learning techniques for this application. The Philippines has consistently been ranked at the top of main contributors of marine litter. Hence, rapid and cheap ways to quantify, assess the distribution, and determine marine litter types would definitely help address the marine litter problem in the country. Moreover, marine litter in the country is markedly different from the marine litter found in other countries hence, naively using models developed from other countries would not be as effective.

The models developed here will be integrated to a device that can be easily deployed in towed camera systems or UAV that would allow on-board object detection which will make the quantification and assessment of marine litter faster. This plan also influenced our choice of the object detection algorithms as we want to make a trade-off between precision and speed.

Finally, we plan to further enhance the object detection performance by collecting more data and experimenting on different image processing techniques and object detection models as well as expanding the classes of litter we will detect.

References

1. Bochkovskiy, A. et al.: YOLOv4: optimal speed and accuracy of object detection. arXiv: 2004.10934 [cs, eess] (2020)
2. Chen, K. et al.: MMDetection: open MMLab detection toolbox and benchmark. arXiv:1906. 07155 (2019). https://doi.org/10.48550/arXiv.1906.07155

3. Consoli, P., et al.: Composition and abundance of benthic marine litter in a coastal area of the central Mediterranean Sea. Mar. Pollut. Bull. **136**, 243–247 (2018). https://doi.org/10.1016/j.marpolbul.2018.09.033

4. Deidun, A., et al.: Optimising beached litter monitoring protocols through aerial imagery. Mar. Pollut. Bull. **131**, 212–217 (2018). https://doi.org/10.1016/j.marpolbul.2018.04.033

5. Fallati, L., et al.: Anthropogenic Marine Debris assessment with Unmanned Aerial Vehicle imagery and deep learning: a case study along the beaches of the Republic of Maldives. Sci. Total Environ. **693**, 133581 (2019). https://doi.org/10.1016/j.scitotenv.2019.133581

6. Fulton, M. et al.: Robotic detection of marine litter using deep visual detection models. Presented at the 2019 International Conference on Robotics and Automation (ICRA), Montreal, Canada (2019)

7. Bergmann, M., Gutow, L., Klages, M. (eds.): Marine Anthropogenic Litter. Springer, Cham (2015). https://doi.org/10.1007/978-3-319-16510-3

8. Gonçalves, G., et al.: Mapping marine litter with unmanned aerial systems: a showcase comparison among manual image screening and machine learning techniques. Mar. Pollut. Bull. **155**, 111158 (2020). https://doi.org/10.1016/j.marpolbul.2020.111158

9. Gonçalves, G., et al.: Quantifying marine macro litter abundance on a sandy beach using unmanned aerial systems and object-oriented machine learning methods. Remote Sens. **12**(16), 2599 (2020). https://doi.org/10.3390/rs12162599

10. Huang, D., Wang, Y., Song, W., Sequeira, J., Mavromatis, S.: Shallow-water image enhancement using relative global histogram stretching based on adaptive parameter acquisition. In: Schoeffmann, K., et al. (eds.) MMM 2018. LNCS, vol. 10704, pp. 453–465. Springer, Cham (2018). https://doi.org/10.1007/978-3-319-73603-7_37

11. Hummel, R.: Image enhancement by histogram transformation. Comput. Graphics Image Process. **6**(2), 184–195 (1977). https://doi.org/10.1016/S0146-664X(77)80011-7

12. Iqbal, K. et al.: Enhancing the low quality images using unsupervised colour correction method. In: 2010 IEEE International Conference on Systems, Man and Cybernetics, pp. 1703–1709 (2010). https://doi.org/10.1109/ICSMC.2010.5642311

13. Iqbal, K., et al.: Underwater image enhancement using an integrated colour model. IAENG Int. J. Comput. Sci. **34**, 2 (2007)

14. Kako, S., et al.: Estimation of plastic marine debris volumes on beaches using unmanned aerial vehicles and image processing based on deep learning. Mar. Pollut. Bull. **155**, 111127 (2020). https://doi.org/10.1016/j.marpolbul.2020.111127

15. Kylili, K., Kyriakides, I., Artusi, A., Hadjistassou, C.: Identifying floating plastic marine debris using a deep learning approach. Environ. Sci. Pollut. Res. **26**(17), 17091–17099 (2019). https://doi.org/10.1007/s11356-019-05148-4

16. Lebreton, L.C.M., et al.: Numerical modelling of floating debris in the world's oceans. Mar. Pollut. Bull. **64**, 653–661 (2012). https://doi.org/10.1016/j.marpolbul.2011.10.027

17. Martin, C., et al.: Enabling a large-scale assessment of litter along Saudi Arabian red sea shores by combining drones and machine learning. Environ. Pollut. **277**, 116730 (2021). https://doi.org/10.1016/j.envpol.2021.116730

18. Martin, C., et al.: Use of unmanned aerial vehicles for efficient beach litter monitoring. Mar. Pollut. Bull. **131**, 662–673 (2018). https://doi.org/10.1016/j.marpolbul.2018.04.045

19. Omeyer, L.C.M., et al.: Priorities to inform research on marine plastic pollution in Southeast Asia. Sci. Total Environ. **841**, 156704 (2022). https://doi.org/10.1016/j.scitotenv.2022.156704

20. Onink, V., et al.: Global simulations of marine plastic transport show plastic trapping in coastal zones. Environ. Res. Lett. **16**(6), 064053 (2021). https://doi.org/10.1088/1748-9326/abecbd

21. Panetta, K., et al.: Human-visual-system-inspired underwater image quality measures. IEEE J. Oceanic Eng. **41**(3), 541–551 (2016). https://doi.org/10.1109/JOE.2015.2469915

22. Pham, C.K., et al.: Marine litter distribution and density in European Seas, from the shelves to deep basins. PLoS ONE **9**(4), e95839 (2014). https://doi.org/10.1371/journal.pone.0095839

23. Politikos, D.V., et al.: Automatic detection of seafloor marine litter using towed camera images and deep learning. Mar. Pollut. Bull. **164**, 111974 (2021). https://doi.org/10.1016/j.marpolbul.2021.111974

24. Redmon, J. et al.: You only look once: unified, real-time object detection. In: Proceedings of the IEEE Conference on Computer Vision and Pattern Recognition, pp. 779–788 (2016)

25. Redmon, J., Farhadi, A.: YOLOv3: An incremental improvement. arXiv:1804.02767 [cs] (2018)

26. Spengler, A., Costa, M.F.: Methods applied in studies of benthic marine debris. Mar. Pollut. Bull. **56**(2), 226–230 (2008). https://doi.org/10.1016/j.marpolbul.2007.09.040

27. Tekman, M.B., et al.: Marine litter on deep Arctic seafloor continues to increase and spreads to the North at the HAUSGARTEN observatory. Deep Sea Res. Part I **120**, 88–99 (2017). https://doi.org/10.1016/j.dsr.2016.12.011

28. Valdenegro-Toro, M.: Submerged marine debris detection with autonomous underwater vehicles. In: Proceedings of the 2016 International Conference on Robotics and Automation for Humanitarian Applications (RAHA), pp. 1–7 (2016). https://doi.org/10.1109/RAHA.2016.7931907

29. Wang, Y., et al.: An experimental-based review of image enhancement and image restoration methods for underwater imaging. IEEE Access **7**, 140233–140251 (2019). https://doi.org/10.1109/ACCESS.2019.2932130

30. Wenneker, B., Oosterbaan, L.: Guideline for monitoring marine litter on the beaches in the OSPAR maritime area. OSPAR Commission (2010). https://doi.org/10.25607/OBP-968

31. Wolf, M., et al.: Machine learning for aquatic plastic litter detection, classification and quantification (APLASTIC-Q). Environ. Res. Lett. **15**(11), 114042 (2020). https://doi.org/10.1088/1748-9326/abbd01

32. Yang, M., Sowmya, A.: An underwater color image quality evaluation metric. IEEE Trans. Image Process. **24**(12), 6062–6071 (2015). https://doi.org/10.1109/TIP.2015.2491020

33. Zuiderveld, K.: Contrast limited adaptive histogram equalization. In: Graphics Gems, pp. 474–485 (1994)

Ethical and Technological AI Risks Classification: A Human Vs Machine Approach

Sónia Teixeira[1,3](✉), Bruno Veloso[1,2], José Coelho Rodrigues[1,3], and João Gama[1,3]

[1] INESC TEC, Porto, Portugal
sonia.c.teixeira@inesctec.pt, jgama@fep.up.pt
[2] University Portucalense, Porto, Portugal
[3] University of Porto, Porto, Portugal

Abstract. The growing use of data-driven decision systems based on Artificial Intelligence (AI) by governments, companies and social organizations has given more attention to the challenges they pose to society. Over the last few years, news about discrimination appeared on social media, and privacy, among others, highlighted their vulnerabilities. Despite all the research around these issues, the definition of concepts inherent to the risks and/or vulnerabilities of data-driven decision systems is not consensual. Categorizing the dangers and vulnerabilities of data-driven decision systems will facilitate ethics by design, ethics in design and ethics for designers to contribute to responsible AI. The main goal of this work is to understand which types of AI risks/ vulnerabilities are Ethical and/or Technological and the differences between human vs machine classification. We analyze two types of problems: (*i*) the risks/ vulnerabilities classification task by humans; and (*ii*) the risks/vulnerabilities classification task by machines. To carry out the analysis, we applied a survey to perform human classification and the BERT algorithm in machine classification. The results show that even with different levels of detail, the classification of vulnerabilities is in agreement in most cases.

Keywords: Ethics · Technology · Human classification · Machine classification

1 Introduction

Over the last few years, news on social media about discrimination, privacy issues, and especially accidents with autonomous cars highlighted the vulnerabilities of data-driven decision systems. One step for defining strategies in data-driven decision systems based on Artificial Intelligence (AI) is identifying and characterizing the risks associated with these systems. Publications related to AI systems' risks, vulnerability and challenges appear in *Ethics, Law* or *Computer Science* journals. However, when we investigate these concerns/vulnerabilities,

I. Koprinska et al. (Eds.): ECML PKDD 2022 Workshops, CCIS 1752, pp. 150–166, 2023.
https://doi.org/10.1007/978-3-031-23618-1_10

there is not just one definition for each concept. Sometimes different areas mention different concepts as the same, for example, in *Bias* and *Fairness* concepts. On the other hand, *Privacy* issues arise in AI publications and publications on ethical issues. Which in itself makes it challenging to characterize each of these vulnerabilities.

One branch of research that has grown in recent years is the field that studies the Ethics of AI, with several works addressing the challenges of AI for a Responsible Artificial Intelligence. *Ethics in Design, Ethics by Design* and *Ethics for Design* constitute the three pillars of the care to be taken in the Design of Ethical AI systems. *Ethics in Design* focuses on AI systems' regulation, and ethical implications as their adoption in society increase [2]. Integrating ethical reasoning capabilities into the algorithms is considered in *Ethics by Design* [2]. In [2] *Ethics for Design* is characterized by integrity, and transversal to the entire ecosystem, from research integrity to how manufacturers design, construct, use and manage those AI systems. Awareness of the three design levels is necessary to ensure trust in the users and society, in general, in the technology [3].

For data-driven decision systems to have some level of trust on the part of citizens, they must involve technical and non-technical considerations [11]. In this sense, and considering the published journals which mention AI risks, vulnerabilities and challenges, we assume *Technological* risks as those that occur through the AI process and *Ethical* risks as those that arise in the outcome. The first focus on the technical issue and the second on the non-technical issue. For example, the risks that occur in the outcome are relevant for public policy decision-makers to analyse the effects on society [12]. Classifying the type of risks/vulnerabilities/challenges, essentially ethical or technological, helps clarify their nature. In addition, it facilitates their allocation and research regarding the kind of design for data-driven systems based on AI.

We can find other works related to human vs machine text classification in the literature (Sect. 2). However, as far as we know, this is the first work that uses a survey for human classification in human vs machine comparative approaches and focuses on the classification of theoretical concepts.

This paper aims to contribute to classifying risks/vulnerabilities in their nature. In addition, we intend to understand whether the classification of risks or vulnerabilities by humans and machines is similar. In order to do that, we used a survey and applied a text mining approach (BERT algorithm) to answer:

- RQ1: What are the ethical risks?
- RQ2: What are the technological risks?
- RQ3: What are the differences between risk classification by humans and machines?

We conclude that with different levels of detail, the classification of vulnerabilities is in agreement in most cases. This agreement means that humans classified a large part of the risks/vulnerabilities presented with the exact nature of concern that the machine classified the research papers (where the concepts were).

Overall this document is structured as follows: in Sect. 2 we present the related work regarding human vs machine classification; in Sect. 3 we present the proposed methodology; in Sect. 4 we present the results and discussion. Finally, in Sect. 5, we draw the conclusions and future work.

2 Human Vs Machine Classification

In this section, we present existing approaches in the literature for text classification in human vs machine comparison. One of these studies focuses on the application of the legal text. In [8], the task of classifying legal text based on machine learning is opposed to the same task performed by legal experts from different legal domains knowledge. The machine uses SVM to solve the multi-labelling task classification problem. The results showed that the precision of the machine corresponds to the accuracy of legal experts with extensive experience. However, the machine need knowledge and attention to the domain.

Another example in the literature is the work carried out by [4], the authors describe an SVM-based topic classification task applied to scientific abstracts. Results compared advantageously with those obtained by similarly tasked human volunteers, based on accuracy, recall and F1 scores.

On the other hand, [6] studied the immediate effect on the model by introducing perturbations in the text, *i.e.*, with the input of words in the text. The authors studied how humans generated adversarial examples compared to attack algorithms such as *TextFooler, Genetic, BAE*, and *SememePSO*. For this case, although the performance of humans does not outperform the machine, the authors concluded that they achieve similar performance more efficiently.

Nonetheless, this comparative approach between human vs machine is also used for word deletion evaluation measures and prediction confidence of classifiers. For example, [7] contributes to this aspect by comparing these approaches in local explanations for text classification. First, logistic regression and neural networks were the models used to classify the text. Then, based on the explanations, humans were asked to predict the output of the classifiers.

In [10] the authors studied the attention mechanisms for human vs machine text classification. The authors use deep learning in machine classification and human attention maps. They obtained relationships at the level of overlap in word selection, lexical categories and context-dependency of sentiment polarity.

3 Case Study

For this work, we have two key objectives: (*i*) classify risks extracted from literature as *Ethical, Technological* or *Both*; and (*ii*) to understand whether the classification of risks by humans and machines is similar.

In this work we use *Literature Review, Survey* and *Text Mining* in order to analyse classification of risks in different perspectives, humans vs machine (Fig. 1). The following subsections present the methods involved and how we proceed.

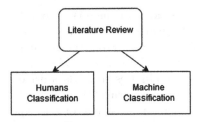

Fig. 1. Flowchart of research

3.1 Risks Extraction from Literature Review

The research was carried out on the *Web of Science*, a multidisciplinary data source, covering the period between January 1st, 1999 and May 19th, 2020. The papers belongs to five research areas, of *Web of Science* classification until 2019 [14]. In the sense of researching on *Ethical risks* and *Technological risks* of algorithmic systems based on Artificial Intelligence, namely in Data-Driven Decision Models, we used the following words for the search: *(("ethics" OR "ethical" OR "technologic" OR "technological") AND ("risk" OR "risks") AND ("artificial intelligence" OR "AI" OR "machine learning" OR "data-driven")).* The search gave rise to 412 published papers.

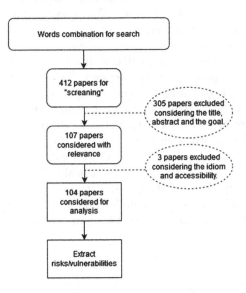

Fig. 2. Flowchart of literature review

Three experts reviewed all 412 papers. The three experts are from different fields and backgrounds, although from fields related to the topic. The experts classify the 412 papers as "Must be considered", "Can be considered", and "Do not consider". The three experts agree on excluding 305 papers according to the title, the abstract, the field, and the goal. From this selection, from which 305 papers have been excluded once they are not relevant for our research, 107 papers remained under analysis. From the 107 papers, three were excluded due to idiom and accessibility. After this process, 104 papers remained to be used to extract risks/ vulnerabilities from data-driven systems based on AI. The described process led to considering 104 papers as presented in Fig. 2. This means that in the 104 papers, at least one of the experts classified the paper as "Must be considered". Only 21 of the 104 papers were classified as "Must be considered" by the three experts and are available. From these papers, we extract the 24 risks/vulnerabilities present in Annex I, Table 2.

3.2   Humans Approach

This subsection presents the approach adopted for the human classification of risks (Fig. 3). In order to do that, we present our survey construction, data collection, and the methods of analysis involved.

Survey Construction. The survey consists of two groups of questions. The first group characterizes the respondent positioning in the Artificial Intelligence (AI) area and includes five questions. The second group of questions seeks to assess opinion regarding the current state of concerns about data-driven systems based on AI and includes eight questions. The questionnaire contains 13 questions, 1 of which is an open answer, 1 of multiple-choice, 5 of single-choice, 1 of Yes/No, four with five Likert scales, and one open optional question. We comprehensively explain the concern/risk/vulnerability for both questions (Annex II, Table 3), including the participant's perception. We mean in the classification of concerns question and their severity. The survey's last question is optional and allows the respondents to comment thoughts about the topic under analysis. In one of the survey questions, the participants addressed the classification of risks/ vulnerabilities identified in the literature. The question is a single-choice question, and the answer option is *Ethical, Technological, Both,* or *None.* The survey also mentioned what we assumed as ethical risks and technological risks. The survey was written in English. In order to ensure the feasibility of the survey and that it would have a proper understanding, it was pre-tested with two researchers with experience in AI, both Portuguese native speakers.

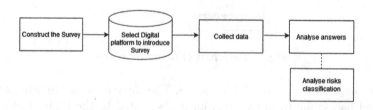

Fig. 3. Flowchart of survey research

Data Collection. The data was collected from the 23rd of March to the 29th of June. We used *LimeSurvey* to develop the survey, collect answers and later download the results in *Microsoft Office Excel* format. The sample was of 20 answers.

3.3   Machine Approach

This subsection presents the approach adopted for the machine classification of risks. We present the data set and the machine's method in the classification task.

Data Set. The data set consists of papers considered relevant by the three experts. We extracted risks/vulnerabilities of data-driven systems based on AI from those papers. Twenty-one papers compose the list of documents selected for the machine classification. Among the 21 papers, two are from 2017, five from 2018, eleven from 2019 and three from 2020. The publication locations for these papers are varied and are primarily related to Engineering, Medicine, Philosophy, Social Sciences, Ethics, Information Technologies, Law, and Policy.

Experimental Setup. With the growing explosion of online information, the difficulty of processing text manually became evident. Therefore, text classification is one of the most relevant tasks. Thus, several methods have emerged in recent decades that facilitate text classification. According [5], there are generic models used in text classification such as *KNN*, *SVM* and *Random Forest*; more recent algorithms with good performance, such as *XGBoost* and *LightGBM*, and deep learning as *TextCNN*. Finally, the *BERT* algorithm is also used for text classification, and it is considered a state-of-the-art and strong baseline, although it is not specifically for this purpose [5].

Given the good results of BERT in text classification problems, we decided to use this algorithm to classify research papers (which contain the concepts extracted for the survey). We use PyTorch to perform machine classification. In this case, the SoftMax function to predict a Multinomial probability distribution which acts as the activation function [9], is used. Furthermore, Luce's axiom of choice allows discovering the probability distribution of the output classes [9]. The loss function used to optimize the BERT model is the cross entropy loss. The pipeline used to classify the documents comprises two steps: i) pre-processing, i.e., extracting the text from the PDFs, removing the punctuation, removing stopwords and applying lemmatization; and ii) tuning a BERT-based case classifier with 32 documents split into equal parts for ethical and technological, the training phase consists in 50 epochs with a learning rate of $1e^{-6}$. The evaluation phase uses 20 documents to be classified.

3.4   Methods Used in Human and Machine Analysis

In Data Analysis, we used: i) Multiple Factor Analysis, ii) Descriptive Analysis and iii) Clustering. We use *Descriptive Data Analysis* in the variables to characterize the participants and characterize the class classification of risks/ vulnerabilities by humans and machines. We use *Multiple Factor Analysis*, an appropriate method when we intend to analyze different groups. Multiple Factor Analysis (MFA) is a multivariate method that allows the simultaneous analysis of data from several sources. The purpose of the MFA is to assess the individuals described by the groups, their contributions and variability [1]. In our case, we intend to evaluate the risks/vulnerabilities through human and machine classification. After using MFA, we also used Clustering to understand the proximity of risks/ vulnerabilities in each classification group. We use the R software for these analyses, namely the package *Factoshiny* [13]. In our case, Clustering is performed in the sequence of results from MFA. Factoshiny [13] allows us to select between Euclidean or Manhattan distance. Moreover, we have low dimensionality data, and all data is between 0 and 1, so the results will be identical for comparing risks/vulnerabilities with these distances. We choose Euclidean distance.

4   Results and Discussion

In this section, we discuss the obtained results for the classification problem, *i.e.*, comparing the human and machine classification perspectives.

4.1   Classification Task by Humans

Among the survey participants, 12 are men, and 8 are women. None of the participants works in the government. The academy is the predominant category, with 16 participants and 4 from the industry. In the educational level variable, the Master predominates, with 8 participants, followed by the PhD with 7 participants and the Bachelor with 5 participants. The predominant background area is Informatics Engineering with 6 participants, as well as the category "Others" with an equal number of participants, four from Computer Science, three from Electronic Engineering and one from Mathematics.

Question 10 of our survey asks participants to assign a class to the risks/ vulnerabilities according to the type of concern they associate. The survey presents twenty-four risks/vulnerabilities of the systems identified in the literature (Annex 2). The possible classes are *Ethical, Technological, Both*, or *None*. However, the question is a single-choice question, i.e., the participants can select one of the possible classes for each risk/vulnerability. No participant classified the risks/vulnerabilities presented as *None*. So this means that participants consider all risks for classification in the survey as *Ethical* and/or *Technological*.

Figure 4 presents the probability of survey answers; this is human classification, considering the risks/vulnerabilities concepts under analysis. As we can see from Fig. 4, the concepts with a higher probability of responses for the classification only in *Ethical* were: Moral, Power, Diluting Rights, and Extinction. Next came the Transparency, Systemic, Liability and Responsibility risks. Finally, regarding the classification as just *Technological* risks, those with the highest

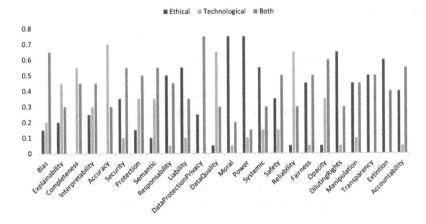

Fig. 4. Risk concepts classification by Humans.

probability were: Accuracy, Data Quality, Reliability, Completeness and Explainability. However, participants consider that there are *Ethical and Technological* risks. DataProtection/Privacy, Bias, Opacity and Accountability are the cases with the highest probability.

4.2 Classification Task by Machine

The concepts of risks/vulnerabilities presented to the participants in the survey were extracted from papers (explained in the Sect. 3). The machine now classifies these same papers as *Ethical* or *Technological*. Some papers under review address more than one AI risk/vulnerability. We used the BERT algorithm (Sect. 3.3) for this. The evaluation phase uses 20 documents to be classified. However, two papers were not considered in the table, as they included the risk/vulnerabilities present in other papers. Table 1 presents the probability that each document belongs to a specific class.

The Table 1 also includes the risks/vulnerabilities extracted from those papers. As seen from Table 1, there are papers with a high probability of being classified in a specific class. An example is papers 72, 75, 87 and 28, which have a probability greater than 0.8 of being classified as Ethical class. The same happens with some papers for the Technological class, for example, papers 53, 54, 70 and 81. In some cases, the probability of being classified between Ethical and Technological is very close, for example, in paper 12.

4.3 Human Vs Machine

We used the *Factoshiny*, a package from R, to perform Multiple Factor Analysis and Clustering (Sect. 3.4).

Table 1. Probability of BERT classification for papers as Ethical or Technological.

PaperID	Ethical	Technological	Risk/Vulnerability
12	0.4998	0.5002	Protection
14	0.3886	0.6114	Accuracy
26	0.6182	0.3818	Data protection
28	0.9154	0.0846	Moral power
40	0.4891	0.5109	Systemic
43	0.6106	0.3894	Privacy
53	0.0631	0.9369	Safety extintion
54	0.1500	0.8500	Bias
55	0.2972	0.7028	Completeness interpretability
64	0.5457	0.4543	Data quality
70	0.0737	0.9263	Manipulation security
72	0.8452	0.1548	Fairness
75	0.8584	0.1416	Diluting rights
76	0.2348	0.7652	Explainability capacity
81	0.0596	0.9404	Transparency
87	0.9430	0.0570	Reliability
97	0.6803	0.3197	Accountability
98	0.6272	0.3728	Responsability liability

As seen from Fig. 5, the distribution of machine and human classification seems to be more different in classifying technological concepts and technological papers. However, in the case of classifying ethical concepts and papers as ethical, the median of both cases is very close.

Let us assume the highest probability as the classification in a specific class, with all the conditions already mentioned throughout the work. In that case, the classifications of humans and machines do not agree on ten types of risks/vulnerabilities (Annex IV). This occurs for the risks: Security (humans (H) = Ethical; machine (M) = Technological), Liability (H = Ethical; M = Technological), Data Quality (H = Technological; M = Ethical), Systemic (H = Ethical; M = Technological); Safety (H = Ethical; M =Technological), Reliability (H = Technological; M = Ethical), Fairness (H = Ethical; M = Technological), Manipulation (H = Ethical; M = Technological), Transparency (H = Ethical; M = Technological) and Extinction (H = Ethical; M = Technological). In the case of humans, the classification of vulnerability concepts is carried out at a more abstract level (they only have the definition of the vulnerability to perform the classification). In contrast, in the case of the machine, it is carried out at a more contextual level (they have the entire document, including the definition of the concept, to carry out the classification). Despite this, even with different levels of detail, the perception of vulnerabilities is in agreement in most cases.

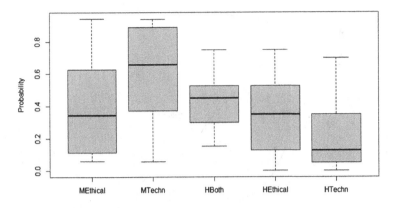

Fig. 5. Distribution of the Machine(M) and Humans(H) classifications.

Therefore, when humans classify with high values for the class Both, in general, is when there is no consensus (Table 6).

The group constituted by the human classification has the most significant contribution on axis 3, while the machine classification has the most significant contribution on axis 1 (Fig. 6 and Annex III, Table 5). In this case, it is necessary to retain three axes so that the explained inertia reaches 80 % (Pearson's criteria). In Annex III, Table 4, the risk contribution and humans/machine contributions (relative and absolute) can be observed. The risks that contribute most to the first axis are 1 (Bias), 3 (Completeness), 5 (Accuracy) and 19 (Opacity), as opposed to risks 9 (Responsibility), 11 (Data Protection/ Privacy) and 20 (Diluting Rights). In the second axis, the most significant contributions are from risks 18 (Fairness), 21 (Manipulation), 22 (Transparency) and 23 (Extinction), as opposed to risks 3 (Completeness), 5 (Accuracy), 12 (Data Quality) and 17 (Reliability). However, risks 8 (Semantic) and 10 (Liability) are not well represented on any axis. On axis 3, only risks 2 (Explainability), 11 (Data Protection/ Privacy), and 24 (Accountability) are well represented, with Explainability as opposed to the other two risks. However, the best represented on the first axis are *Moral, Diluting Rights* and *Power*. On the second axis, *Reliability, Extinction, Transparency* and *Fairness* are better represented. Finally, on the third axis, the best represented are *DataProtection/ Privacy*.

After using MFA, we also used Clustering to understand the proximity of risks/ vulnerabilities in each classification group. The inertia explained by the partition suggests three clusters. The same was also suggested by the dendrogram. Thus, we choose three clusters.

In Fig. 7 we can see the three clusters of risks/ vulnerabilities created:

- Cluster 1: *Bias, Interpretability, Protection, Explainability, Semantic, Opacity, Completeness, Accuracy, Data Quality* and *Reliability*;
- Cluster 2: *Extinction, Transparency, Fairness, Manipulation, Safety* and *Security*;

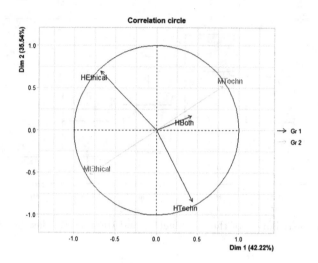

Fig. 6. Correlation circle

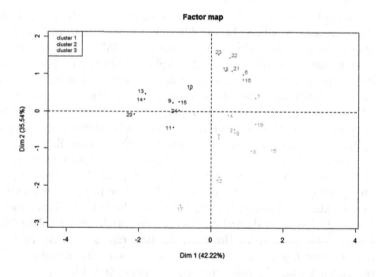

Fig. 7. Cluster groups in Factor Map

– Cluster 3: *Moral, Power, Diluting Rights, Responsibility, Systemic, Liability, Accountability* and *Data Protection.*

Cluster one comprises six of the ten risks/ vulnerabilities in which human and machines did not have a consensus. Humans classified the six vulnerabilities as ethical and the machine as technological. Cluster two consists of eight risk concepts in which humans and machines agree in their classification, a classification of a technological nature. The exceptions in this cluster are the *DataQuality* and *Reliability* vulnerabilities, which humans consider technological and ethical the machine. Although *DataQuality* and *Reliability* do not have consensus in the classifications, there is proximity to the technological group. In turn, cluster three includes risk concepts essentially classified as ethical. This is the case for six risks, which humans and machines rated as ethical. However, in *Systemic* and *Liability*, humans classify as ethical and the machine as technological. *Systemic* and *Liability* are considered the ethical group.

5 Conclusion

In this work, we aim to contribute to classifying risks/vulnerabilities in their nature. In addition, we intend to understand how different the classification of risks/vulnerabilities by humans and machines is. For that, we use a Survey to collect the classification of humans in terms of risk/vulnerabilities concepts. These risks and/or vulnerabilities were extracted through a literature review. For machine classification, we use the BERT algorithm to classify the papers from which the risks/vulnerabilities were extracted.

For the analysis of the human vs machine results, we used i) Multiple Factor Analysis, ii) Descriptive Analysis and iii) Clustering. In the first case, the analysis groups include the classifications performed in both cases as variables, and the individuals correspond to the risks/vulnerabilities. In humans' case, the group includes *Ethical, Technological* and *Both*. In the machine case, the group is constituted by *Ethical* and *Technological.* Finally, we apply Clustering to understand which types of risks are closest to each other, according to the classifications of humans and machines.

It is possible to conclude that some risk concepts have a higher contribution to the map and are better represented than others in their classification. *Responsibility, Moral, Diluting Rights* and *Power* are best represented on the first axis. On the second axis, *Reliability, Extinction, Transparency* and *Fairness* are better represented. Finally, on the third axis, the best represented are *DataProtection/ Privacy.* It is also possible to conclude that even with different levels of detail for the classification, the classification of vulnerabilities is in agreement in most cases. Therefore, when humans are classified with high values for the class *Both*, in general, is when there is no consensus. Risk concepts considered technological by humans and machines through the papers correspond to risks: *Bias, Interpretability, Protection, Explainability, Semantic, Opacity, Completeness* and *Accuracy.* Although *DataQuality* and *Reliability* do not have consensus in the classifications, there is proximity to the technological group. Similarly, regarding the classification as ethical, we have *Moral, Power, Diluting Rights, Responsibility, Accountability* and *Data Protection. Systemic* and *Liability* are close to the ethical group.

In future work, we intend to use an algorithm for text classification to classify a paper as not belonging to the classes identified in training. This way, a possible new class by the machine could bring value to the comparison with human classification. So, it would be possible to compare both approaches in an equal number of classes (Ethical, Technological and Both). In addition, we intend to extend the search to other databases and perform a machine model sensitivity to each concept's description. From this analysis, it would be possible to perceive the relevance of the difference in size and syntax between the descriptions accessed by humans and machines for classification.

Acknowledgments. The research reported in this work was partially supported by the European Commission funded project "Humane AI: Toward AI Systems That Augment and Empower Humans by Understanding Us, our Society and the World Around Us" (grant #820437). The support is gratefully acknowledged.

Annex

Annex I

Table 2. Main concerns/risks identified.

Accountability	Data Protection/Privacy	Extintion	Manipulation	Protection	Security
Accuracy	Data Quality	Fairness	Moral	Reliability	Semantic
Bias	Diluting Rights	Interpretability	Opacity	Responsability	Systemic
Completeness	Explainability	Liability	Power	Safety	Transparency

Annex II
See Tables 3, 4, 5 and 6

Table 3. Description of risk/vulnerability concepts

Concept	Description
Bias	A systematic error, a tendency to learn consistently wrongly
Explainability	Any action or procedure performed by a model to clarify or detail its internal functions
Completeness	Describe the operation of a system accurately
Interpretability	Describe the internals of a system in a way that is understandable to humans
Accuracy	The assessment of how often a system performs the correct prediction
Security	Implications of the weaponization of AI for defence (the embeddedness of AI-based capabilities across the land, air, naval and space domains may affect combined arms operations)
Protection	"Gaps" that arise across the development process where normal conditions for a complete specification of intended functionality and moral responsibility are not present

(continued)

Table 3. (*continued*)

Concept	Description
Semantic	Difference between the implicit intentions on the system's functionality and the explicit, concrete specification used to build the system
Responsability	The difference between a human actor being involved in the causation of an outcome and having the sort of robust control that establishes moral accountability for the outcome
Liability	When it causes harm to others, the losses caused by the harm will be sustained by the injured victims themselves and not by the manufacturers, operators or users of the system, as appropriate
Data Protection/Privacy	Vulnerable channel by which personal information may be accessed. The user may want their data to be kept private
Data Quality	Data quality measures how well-suited a data set is to serve its specific purpose
Moral	Less moral responsibility humans will feel regarding their life-or-death decisions with the increase of machines' autonomy
Power	The political influence and competitive advantage obtained by having technology
Systemic	Ethical aspects of people's attitudes to AI and other problems associated with AI
Safety	Set of actions and resources used to protect something or someone
Reliability	Reliability is the probability that the system performs satisfactorily for a given period under stated conditions
Fairness	Impartial and just treatment without favouritism or discrimination
Opacity	Stems from the mismatch between mathematical optimization in a high-dimensionality characteristic of machine learning and the demands of human-scale reasoning and styles of semantic interpretation
Diluting rights	A possible consequence of self-interest in AI generation of ethical guidelines
Manipulation	The predictability of behaviour protocol in AI, particularly in some applications, can act as an incentive to manipulate these systems
Transparency	The quality or state of being transparent
Extinction	Risk to the existence of humanity
Accountability	The ability to determine whether a decision was made by procedural and substantive standards and to hold someone responsible if those standards are not mine.

Annex III

Table 4. Risks/Vulnerabilities contributions using MFA

Individuals	Dim.1	ctr	cos2	Dim.2	ctr	cos2	Dim.3	ctr	cos2
1	1.244	5.776	0.650	0.352	0.551	0.052	0.842	5.025	0.298
2	0.651	1.581	0.282	−0.499	1.106	0.166	−0.906	5.825	0.547
3	1.120	4.681	0.521	−1.067	5.048	0.473	−0.120	0.102	0.006
4	0.485	0.878	0.944	−0.110	0.054	0.049	−0.041	0.012	0.007
5	1.686	10.614	0.521	−1.038	4.780	0.198	−1.237	10.857	0.281
6	0.890	2.961	0.435	0.980	4.262	0.527	0.261	0.484	0.037
7	0.215	0.172	0.058	−0.738	2.414	0.684	0.453	1.456	0.258
8	0.670	1.677	0.405	−0.576	1.471	0.299	0.574	2.334	0.297
9	−1.046	4.087	0.816	0.217	0.210	0.035	0.447	1.415	0.149
10	−0.578	1.247	0.409	0.581	1.495	0.412	−0.382	1.036	0.179
11	−1.036	4.010	0.156	−0.440	0.860	0.028	2.372	39.887	0.816
12	0.239	0.213	0.016	−1.773	13.937	0.877	−0.618	2.711	0.107
13	−1.813	12.268	0.779	0.467	0.969	0.052	−0.846	5.077	0.170
14	−1.839	12.627	0.713	0.326	0.472	0.022	−1.121	8.902	0.265
15	−0.877	2.872	0.691	0.248	0.273	0.055	−0.532	2.005	0.254
16	0.893	2.977	0.519	0.859	3.274	0.481	−0.026	0.005	0.000
17	−0.840	2.635	0.099	−2.529	28.377	0.899	−0.125	0.111	0.002
18	0.403	0.606	0.122	1.076	5.137	0.869	0.113	0.091	0.010
19	1.241	5.751	0.747	−0.333	0.492	0.054	0.641	2.917	0.199
20	−2.134	17.004	0.998	−0.073	0.024	0.001	−0.042	0.013	0.000
21	0.584	1.273	0.217	1.080	5.176	0.742	−0.256	0.464	0.042
22	0.522	1.016	0.116	1.440	9.193	0.884	0.017	0.002	0.000
23	0.205	0.158	0.016	1.533	10.424	0.891	−0.496	1.747	0.093
24	−0.884	2.917	0.424	0.016	0.001	0.000	1.030	7.521	0.576

Table 5. Risks/Vulnerabilities contributions using MFA

	Dim.1	ctr	cos2	Dim.2	ctr	cos2	Dim.3	ctr	cos2
HEthical	−0.680	22.731	0.463	0.695	28.192	0.483	−0.231	4.955	0.053
HTechn	0.441	9.526	0.194	−0.841	41.197	0.706	−0.315	9.244	0.099
HBoth	0.427	8.945	0.182	0.170	1.691	0.029	0.888	73.519	0.789
MEthical	−0.810	29.399	0.656	−0.521	14.460	0.272	0.269	6.141	0.072
MTechn	0.810	29.399	0.656	0.521	14.460	0.272	−0.269	6.141	0.072

Annex IV

Table 6. Human vs Machine classifications

Concept	MEthical	MTechn	HBoth	HEthical	HTechn
Bias	0.15	0.85	0.65	0.15	0.2
Explainability	0.2348	0.7652	0.3	0.2	0.45
Completeness	0.2972	0.7028	0.45	0	0.55
Interpretability	0.2972	0.7028	0.45	0.25	0.3
Accuracy	0.0596	0.9404	0.3	0	0.7
Security	0.0737	0.9263	0.55	0.35	0.1
Protection	0.4998	0.5002	0.5	0.15	0.35
Semantic	0.3886	0.6114	0.55	0.1	0.35
Responsability	0.6272	0.3728	0.45	0.5	0.05
Liability	0.3886	0.6114	0.35	0.55	0.1
DataProtectionPrivacy	0.9154	0.0846	0.75	0.25	0
DataQuality	0.5457	0.4543	0.3	0.05	0.65
Moral	0.6272	0.3728	0.2	0.75	0.05
Power	0.6272	0.3728	0.15	0.75	0.1
Systemic	0.4891	0.5109	0.3	0.55	0.15
Safety	0.0631	0.9369	0.5	0.35	0.15
Reliability	0.943	0.057	0.3	0.05	0.65
Fairness	0.15	0.85	0.5	0.45	0.05
Opacity	0.2348	0.7652	0.6	0.05	0.35
DilutingRights	0.8584	0.1416	0.3	0.65	0.05
Manipulation	0.0737	0.9263	0.45	0.45	0.1
Transparency	0.0596	0.9404	0.5	0.5	0
Extintion	0.0631	0.9369	0.4	0.6	0
Accountability	0.6803	0.3197	0.55	0.4	0.05

References

1. Abdi, H., Valentin, D.: Multiple factor analysis (MFA). In: Encyclopedia of Measurement and Statistics, January 2007
2. Dignum, V.: Ethics in artificial intelligence: introduction to the special issue. Ethics Inf. Technol. **20**(1), 1–3 (2018)
3. Dignum, V., et al.: Ethics by design: necessity or curse? In: Proceedings of the 2018 AAAI/ACM Conference on AI, Ethics, and Society, pp. 60–66. AIES 2018, Association for Computing Machinery, New York, NY, USA (2018)
4. Goh, Y.C., Cai, X.Q., Theseira, W., Ko, G., Khor, K.A.: Evaluating human versus machine learning performance in classifying research abstracts. Scientometrics. **125**(2), 1197–1212 (2020)

5. Li, Q., et al.: A survey on text classification: from traditional to deep learning. ACM Trans. Intell. Syst. Technol. **13**(2), 1–41 (2022)
6. Mozes, M., Bartolo, M., Stenetorp, P., Kleinberg, B., Griffin, L.D.: Contrasting human- and machine-generated word-level adversarial examples for text classification. CoRR abs/2109.04385 (2021)
7. Nguyen, D.: Comparing automatic and human evaluation of local explanations for text classification. In: Proceedings of the 2018 Conference of the North American Chapter of the Association for Computational Linguistics: Human Language Technologies, Volume 1 (Long Papers), pp. 1069–1078. Association for Computational Linguistics, New Orleans, Louisiana, June 2018
8. Orosz, T., Vági, R., Csányi, G.M., Nagy, D., Üveges, I., Vadász, J.P., Megyeri, A.: Evaluating human versus machine learning performance in a legaltech problem. Appl. Sci. **12**(1), 297 (2022)
9. PyTorch: Pytorch softmax. https://www.educba.com/pytorch-softmax/. Accessed 31 July 2022
10. Sen, C., Hartvigsen, T., Yin, B., Kong, X., Rundensteiner, E.: Human attention maps for text classification: Do humans and neural networks focus on the same words? In: Proceedings of the 58th Annual Meeting of the Association for Computational Linguistics. pp. 4596–4608. Association for Computational Linguistics, Online, July 2020
11. Teixeira, S., Gama, J., Amorim, P., Figueira, G.: Trustability in algorithmic systems based on artificial intelligence in the public and private sectors. ERCIM News 122 (2020). https://ercim-news.ercim.eu/en122/r-s/trustability-in-algorithmic-systems-based-on-artificial-intelligence-in-the-public-and-private-sectors
12. Teixeira, S., Rodrigues, J.C., Veloso, B., Gama, J.: Challenges of data-driven decision models: implications for developers and for public policy decision-makers. In: Banerji, P., Jana, A. (eds.) Advances in Urban Design and Engineering. DSI, pp. 199–215. Springer, Singapore (2022). https://doi.org/10.1007/978-981-19-0412-7_7
13. Vaissie, P., Monge, A., Husson, F.: Factoshiny: Perform Factorial Analysis from 'FactoMineR' with a Shiny Application (2021). https://CRAN.R-project.org/package=Factoshiny. (r package version 2.4)
14. WebofKnowledge: Web of science core collection help, March 2022). https://images.webofknowledge.com/images/help/WOS/hp_research_areas_easca.html

A Reinforcement Learning Algorithm for Fair Electoral Redistricting in Parliamentary Systems

Callum Evans$^{(\boxtimes)}$ ⓘ and Hugo Barbosa ⓘ

The University of Exeter, Exeter, UK
callumdoneevans@gmail.com

Abstract. The primary goal of a strong democracy should be to most accurately represent its electorate, and the way they are divided into electoral districts can drastically affect this. As a result, many methods have been proposed to algorithmically generate fairer boundaries, the majority of which focus on eliminating bias through qualitative measures, however, these often fail to produce truly fair results. This paper, therefore, aims to demonstrate how fairness can and should become a higher priority within our electoral systems through the development, implementation and application of a new reinforcement learning-based method for algorithmic redistricting that directly optimises for fairness. Specifically, the model has been applied to the parliamentary system of the UK, filling a significant gap within the literature, meaning the paper also outlines a new metric for measuring fairness in parliamentary systems that directly rewards proportionality, the seats-votes difference. The algorithm has then been evaluated on the current parliamentary constituency boundaries in the UK and was ultimately found to fulfil all initial goals as the algorithm was able to improve the map's fairness in all experiments performed. The paper subsequently concludes with some of the limitations of the model and the seats-votes difference and ways the redistricting algorithm could be further expanded in the future.

Keywords: Algorithmic redistricting · Reinforcement learning · Electoral fairness

1 Introduction

The way that a country decides to separate itself into electoral districts or constituencies can create meaningful impacts on the way its people are represented in government [1]. As a result, the process of drawing or updating these boundaries, called electoral redistricting, is often a long, laborious and sometimes controversial one involving many iterative stages of planning and public consultations [2]. Mostly, this is due to the many factors that have to be considered, as not only do boundaries have to follow the rules and constraints defined by law, but they also must be an accurate reflection of the country's electorate and cannot be

I. Koprinska et al. (Eds.): ECML PKDD 2022 Workshops, CCIS 1752, pp. 167–180, 2023.
https://doi.org/10.1007/978-3-031-23618-1_11

manipulated to show bias towards any political party or demographic. Despite this, there are still many examples of "gerrymandered," or biased, boundaries in recent years, especially in the US where many governing parties draw electoral boundaries [3]. Even in the UK, where independent commissions decide boundaries, one review of Westminster parliamentary constituencies was abandoned after attempts in 2013 and 2018 [4] due to criticisms including a bias towards the Conservative party and reduction of Scotland and Wales' influence [5].

Therefore, many methods have been proposed to detect or quantify the effect of biased boundaries, with one of the most well-known being the efficiency gap [6]. Meanwhile, additional research aims to create algorithmic redistricting methods to remove a bias said to be inherent to human-drawn maps through solely quantitative factors, such as population distribution or district geometries [7–9]. On the other hand, some reject this idea and propose the only fair boundaries are those created considering their impact on elections [10,11].

Following this concept and by defining a fair and unbiased electoral map as one that can most accurately represent its electorate in elections, we should be able to generate fair boundaries by rewarding a proportional representation between party vote share and seat shares. This should essentially aim towards the ability of proportional vote systems to fairly represent the electorate whilst maintaining the advantages of local representation found in first-past-the-post systems [12]. This paper, therefore, proposes a new reinforcement learning algorithm for electoral redistricting that directly optimises boundaries for fairness and this ability to represent the electorate and applies the algorithm to the UK. As a result, this paper also outlines a new metric for fairness evaluation as, to the authors' knowledge, no research has been done on applying similar redistricting or fairness evaluation methods to parliamentary systems.

This paper is organised as follows; Sect. 2 first describes the necessary datasets and the creation of a small-scale election results dataset used for fairness evaluations. Section 3 then outlines the proposed algorithm's methodology and Sect. 4 describes the fitness calculations, including the newly developed "seats-votes difference." Lastly, Sect. 5 evaluates the algorithm's performance and demonstrates some of its proposals before Sect. 6 concludes the paper.

2   Boundary & Election Datasets

There are two datasets fundamental to the proposed algorithm; firstly, the model needs a dataset of base geographic units and their geometries to construct constituencies, and secondly, it needs the distribution of each party's voters amongst these areas to be used to evaluate fairness. Here, the 9,498 2011 electoral wards in the UK are used as the base geographic unit because the four commissions that decide the constituency boundaries for each country in the UK also use this approach. This is despite the fact they can diverge due to geographical factors or where they would otherwise not be able to produce boundaries that follow legal constraints. Ultimately, this is done as these wards are generally well-defined, well-understood and broadly indicative of areas with a community of shared interest [13], and they have the advantage that ward data is readily available.

On the other hand, the election results dataset for fairness evaluations had to be created for use in the model, which was done by first collecting constituency-level election results from the 2017 general election and ward-level socio-economic data. Demographic data is often used to predict election results data at different scales [14, 15], with the data here consisting of 32 statistics from the 2011 UK census surrounding age, education, economic activity, household and ethnicity. Therefore, to create the election dataset, the ward demographic data was combined into their constituencies and was used as the input to an ordinary least squares linear regression model trained to fit demographic data to the constituency election results. This model was then used to predict the party support in each ward, with the outputs used as weights to calculate how each party's vote was distributed throughout their constituency. The final election dataset[1] was validated by combining the ward-level results back into their constituencies and comparing the output with the real election results. This approach was not able to estimate the constituency-level results with complete accuracy, although vote shares remain sufficiently close to demonstrate the proposed redistricting algorithm whilst somewhat accurately reflecting the real world. Subsequently, developing a full prediction model for ward-level election data is deemed outside the scope of this paper, and differences between the generated dataset and the real 2017 results can be seen in appendix 1.

3   Redistricter Methodology

The redistricting algorithm proposed by this paper is based on a reinforcement learning-based local search algorithm for generalised grouping problems originally applied to graph colouring, proposed by Zhou et al. in 2016 [17]. Their algorithm works iteratively with three main components; a group selection method, a descent-based local search (DBLS), and probability updating and smoothing stages, with the structure of the redistricting algorithm remaining fairly similar to this. A diagram of the main schema is displayed in Fig. 1, and each component is detailed below.

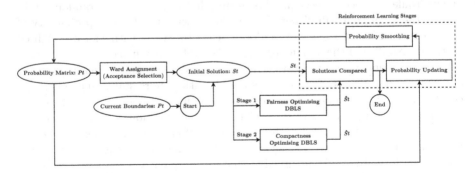

Fig. 1. A schematic diagram of the proposed redistricter algorithm.

---

[1] All data used for this paper is made available online [16].

We can define the problem of redistricting as, given a set W of n wards, find an optimal set C of k partitions, representing constituencies. As is done in the original algorithm, we define a probability matrix P of size $(n \times k)$, where each element in the matrix p_{ij} ($0 < i \leq n$ and $0 < j \leq k$), represents the probability that ward w_i should belong to the constituency c_j. To generate an initial solution that always consists of the real current boundaries, we can initialise all values in P to 0, except for when p_{ij} represents the probability a ward will be assigned to its real-world constituency, where we can set the value to 1.0.

It is also important to generate a set of ward assignments that conforms to the legal constraints of the 'Parliamentary Constituencies Act (1986)' [18] that the real boundary commissions must follow. This means constituencies cannot have an area above 13,000km^2 and their electorate must be within 5% of the electoral quota, calculated as the average electorate of mainland UK constituencies. There are Exceptions for protected or island constituencies whose boundaries cannot be changed, such as 'Ynys Môn', and those with areas above 12,000km^2 are allowed smaller electorates, however, the algorithm's proposals should follow these rules to generate relevant results. Proposed constituencies also cannot span multiple countries and are made to be geographically contiguous, with allowances for geographical factors, to remain logical and avoid enclaves or exclaves.

3.1   Selection Method

The first step of each iteration t of the algorithm is to generate our initial solution of proposed boundaries S_t by assigning wards to constituencies using probabilities from the probability matrix P. The original paper uses a hybrid greedy/random selection method as the algorithm could better avoid local minima, where the method randomly chooses to either make the assignment with the highest probability or assign items to groups randomly. However, the redistricting algorithm uses an adapted "acceptance selection" method developed to more easily follow contiguity constraints whilst fully exploiting the knowledge stored in the probability matrix.

This approach first assigns a starting ward to each constituency using a greedy/roulette wheel selection. This means that according to a random probability, the algorithm will either choose a ward with the highest probability of belonging to the constituency or randomly select the ward, with choices weighted by the probability of the assignment from the probability matrix P. Assigning a starting ward ensures each constituency is guaranteed to have at least one ward and the use of a roulette wheel makes the algorithm more stable and contiguity constraints easier to follow as wards are more likely to be assigned to closer constituencies they may have even been a part of previously. The acceptance selection method then looks at the neighbours of each ward, checking whether they are assigned to a constituency. If a neighbour has been assigned, the probability that the ward will be assigned to that same constituency is stored in a list, and once all neighbours are checked, the resulting list is sorted from the highest to lowest probability assignment. Lastly, we iterate through this list, choosing whether to "*accept*" the assignment based on its probability. This is iteratively repeated for all wards until the majority of wards are assigned, leaving only those that cannot be due to contiguity constraints, mostly including those on islands without a constituency's starting ward. Therefore, when there are no new assignments made during an iteration, we assign any remaining wards to the constituency of the closest assigned ward.

3.2   Descent-based Local Search

The next stage during each iteration is the DBLS algorithm where each solution S_t is improved by randomly swapping wards between constituencies. Each swap can then be evaluated by analysing how the fitness of the solution changes before it is chosen to be accepted or rejected, where fitness calculations are outlined in Sect. 4. This is also where the legal constraints are implemented.

First, a ward is chosen randomly, excluding those in protected constituencies, and its neighbours are examined. If the ward borders any constituencies different to its own, one of these is chosen as a potential new constituency and the swap is checked to ensure it only produces valid constituencies. This means the new areas and populations are calculated to ensure they stay within the necessary thresholds and a ward adjacency matrix is generated from all the wards in the original constituency. This is used to ensure the constituency would remain contiguous without the swapped ward, ignoring any island wards without any neighbours. Once the ward has been swapped, it is only accepted if there is an improvement in the fitness of the solution, which is the same as the hill climbing method used in the original algorithm. This was chosen over simulated annealing, where worse solutions are sometimes accepted according to a probability given by the Boltzmann distribution [19,20], to help the algorithm converge, particularly when making fewer swaps in the DBLS. The algorithm also ensures each swap improves the fitness of the country where the swap took place, which aims to ensure better national representation for the countries within the UK.

One significant change to the local search component of the original algorithm is the use of multi-stage optimisation. Specifically, the redistricter algorithm uses fairness prioritised and compactness prioritised optimisation stages. This means that the redistricter will optimise solutions solely for fairness for the majority of the algorithm's runtime, but will then change to optimise solely for compactness for a small number of iterations. The fitness calculations are detailed in Sect. 4, however, this is simply done by changing the parameters λ and μ in the fitness function. A point to note is that although the main goal of the algorithm is to optimise for fairness, implementing a compactness stage allows for the algorithm to produce more reasonable and logical results that are still fair. This ultimately follows the idea that despite many US state constitutions stating legislative boundaries should be "compact," there is usually no formal definition and they instead rely on the idea people recognise gerrymandering when they see it [21]. Multi-stage optimisation is therefore a good compromise that creates fairer constituency boundaries that are still reasonable and logical.

3.3   Probability Updating & Smoothing

Once the solution has been improved, the new DBLS improved solution is compared to the initial solution, making note of any changes and rewarding or penalising constituencies accordingly. This section of the algorithm remains identical to the probability updating and smoothing stages seen in the original method by Zhou et al. Therefore, at each iteration t, the constituency assignment for a given ward in V, w_i, is compared in the original solution S_t and the DBLS improved solution $\hat{S}_t$. If it has stayed in its original constituency, c_u, we reward c_u and update the probability vector p_i according to the reward factor α $(0 \leq \alpha \leq 1)$, using Eq. (1).

$$p_{ij}(t+1) = \begin{cases} \alpha + (1-\alpha)p_{ij}(t) & \text{if } j = u \\ (1-\alpha)p_{ij}(t) & \text{otherwise.} \end{cases} \tag{1}$$

If no swaps were made during the DBLS, it is assumed we have found the most optimal solution and the algorithm is terminated. Otherwise, when ward w_i has moved from its original constituency c_u to a new constituency c_v, where $v \neq u$, we penalise the original constituency c_u and compensate the new constituency c_v according to the penalisation and compensation factors β $(0 \leq \beta \leq 1)$ and γ $(0 \leq \gamma \leq 1)$ respectively. This is done according to Eq. (2).

$$p_{ij}(t+1) = \begin{cases} (1-\gamma)(1-\beta)p_{ij}(t) & \text{if } j = u \\ \gamma + (1-\gamma)\frac{\beta}{k-1} + (1-\gamma)(1-\beta)p_{ij}(t) & \text{if } j = v \\ (1-\gamma)\frac{\beta}{k-1} + (1-\gamma)(1-\beta)p_{ij}(t) & \text{otherwise.} \end{cases} \tag{2}$$

Lastly, values in the probability matrix are reduced by multiplying them by a coefficient ρ if they are above a defined threshold p_0. This is done so that older and potentially misleading decisions can be forgotten.

4   Fitness Metric

The proposed redistricter algorithm is designed to optimise constituency boundaries for fairness and their ability to best represent the electorate, and this is done primarily through the fitness metrics used during the algorithm's DBLS stage. Specifically, these calculations look at two aspects; compactness and fairness. Although measuring the compactness of a constituency is fairly trivial and is only used to ensure the algorithm produces reasonable and logical results, the fairness evaluations remain the primary factor in the fitness calculation. Therefore, a qualitative measure for fairness had to be developed that can be applied to parliamentary systems, as no other methods have been proposed to the authors' knowledge. As a result, the seats-votes (SV) difference was formulated for use in this algorithm and is outlined in Sect. 4.2.

Overall, this results in the fitness metric $f(S)$ for a solution S as seen in Eq. (3), where the average party SV difference is denoted by v and the average constituency compactness is denoted by c. The algorithm's priority regarding each of these factors can also be tuned using the parameters λ and μ respectively. An alternative approach to this could have been to use multi-objective optimisation techniques, however, the multi-stage optimisation used in the DBLS makes this unnecessary as each factor is optimised in isolation.

$$f(S) = \frac{\lambda(1 - v) + \mu \cdot c}{\lambda + \mu} \tag{3}$$

4.1 Compactness Evaluation

The choice in which compactness measure to use is generally fairly subjective and should not have a large impact on the results of redistricting algorithms [22], however, here, we use a modified version of the Reock score [23]. This measures compactness as the ratio of the constituency's area to the area of the smallest circle that completely encloses it, but had to be slightly changed due to the complexity and computational cost of repeatedly finding the bounding circle of a polygon, known as the "smallest-circle problem" [24]. Therefore, the compactness is calculated as the ratio of the constituency's area to that of a circle with a diameter as the length or width of the constituency, whichever is larger. If this is above 1, which cannot be the case with the original Reock score, the compactness is taken as the reciprocal of this value. The average compactness for constituencies in the dataset used here is 0.49996, with the most compact constituency being "Bristol South" (0.8969) and the least compact being "Orkney and Shetland" (0.0588).

4.2 Fairness Evaluation

As mentioned previously, a majority of the literature surrounding redistricting and gerrymandering uses the US as a case study even though many other countries, including the UK, use first-past-the-post electoral systems where the candidate with the most vote wins even if they receive less than 50% of the vote. As a result, many proposed methods for measuring electoral fairness cannot be applied to parliamentary systems which can have many more than the two parties considered in the US. For example, the efficiency gap is simply the ratio between two parties' wasted votes, defined as votes cast either towards the losing candidate or those towards the winning candidate above the threshold needed to win, and this cannot scale to any number of parties. It has also been criticised for the way it can penalise proportionality as an election with a 60:40 split in the proportional vote and seat share would be described as 8% biased towards the losing party [25]. In parliamentary systems, it can also be common to have a mix of larger and smaller parties and the UK adds another layer of complexity with national parties for Scotland, Wales and Northern Ireland, such as the SNP or Plaid Cymru, who all must be fairly represented.

Therefore, as we have held the aim that a fair map is one that most accurately represents the electorate, the "seats-votes difference" was developed for use in this algorithm to optimise for proportionality between party seat shares and vote shares. This simply calculates the average absolute difference between a party's overall vote share and their seat share in government, as a percent of their vote share. This has the advantage that it scales well for any number of parties, is easy to calculate, directly rewards proportionality and equally penalises under and over-representation. A formalised definition of the measure can be seen in Eq. 4, where n is the number of parties, p is the set of proportional votes and s is the set of seat shares for each party, both of length n.

$$v = \frac{1}{n}\left(\sum_{i=0}^{n} \frac{|(p_i - s_i)|}{p_i} \right) \tag{4}$$

The UK has an average SV difference of 65.0% for the 13 parties used in the generated 2017 election results dataset; the Conservatives, Labour, the Liberal Democrats, the Green Party, UKIP, Plaid Cymru, SNP, DUP, Sinn Fein, SDLP, UUP, Alliance and independents (including the Speaker). Northern Ireland is the least fair country in the UK, with an average SV difference of 82.7%, whilst England, Scotland and Wales have 62.2%, 63.2% and 69.7% respectively.

5   Evaluation & Results

Overall, the algorithm's results were evaluated over 106 runs, covering 24 experiments, and the results showed that the redistricter was able to improve the current constituency boundaries' fairness in all runs. Also, whilst all runs showed an improvement in fairness, only some increased average constituency compactness except for where it was explicitly prioritised by only using compactness prioritised stages. For example, as seen in Table 1, the 5 control experiment runs saw an average improvement of 1.5% after 45 fairness and 5 compactness stages using reward and compensation factors α and γ of 0.8 and a penalisation factor β of 0.6. These values were used as the base parameters during all other experiments because they were used throughout the algorithm's development where they showed decent results and helped the algorithm to converge.

The fairest set of boundaries produced by the algorithm can be seen to the far right of Fig. 2 which shows their predicted election results in comparison with the current boundaries. This run produced a fairness score of 0.4201, an improvement of 7%, and was achieved using reinforcement learning parameters of $\alpha = 0.9$, $\beta = 0.1$ and $\gamma = 0.9$. Notable seat differences predicted with the proposed map include; the Ulster Unionist Party (UUP) gaining a seat in Northern

Table 1. Final solution fairness and compactness for the control experiments, with 45 stage 1 iterations and 5 stage 2 iterations. Here, $\alpha = 0.8$, $\beta = 0.6$, $\gamma = 0.8$ and 100 steps were taken during the DBLS.

Metric	Run 1	Run 2	Run 3	Run 4	Run 5	Average	Initial solution
SV Difference	0.36373	0.36810	0.36021	0.36979	0.36426	0.36522	0.3501 (+0.015)
Compactness	0.49814	0.49351	0.49475	0.49595	0.49583	0.49563	0.49996 (−0.004)

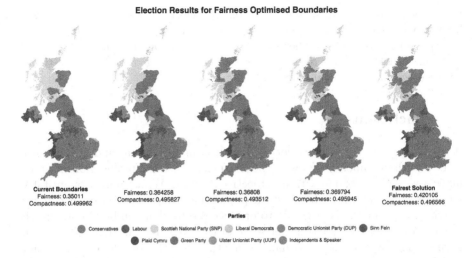

Fig. 2. A comparison of predicted election results using current constituency boundaries and 3 maps generated during the control experiments. The furthest left was the fairest generated in all experiments, with $\alpha = 0.9$, $\beta = 0.1$, $\gamma = 0.9$.

Ireland, Plaid Cymru gaining a set and Labour gaining 2, whilst the Democratic Unionist Party (DUP) and the Scottish National Party (SNP) each lost 1 and 2 respectively. More specifically, Labour's SV difference decreased from 0.6% to 0.3% with 264 seats, whilst the SNP's SV difference decreased from 77.2% to 68.7% with 31 seats. There is also a high concentration of UUP supporters in the southwest of Northern Ireland, yet they do not have any seats in Parliament and so giving them a seat reduced their SV difference from 100% to 46%. This meant the algorithm was able to do this fairly often, signifying some level of partisan bias in the current boundaries, which is further supported by the SV difference metric denoting Northern Ireland as the least fair country in the UK.

Significant parameter tuning was also performed on the reinforcement learning parameters and although some of the larger fairness improvements were produced with higher reward and compensation factors and lower penalisation factors, the trend was still fairly marginal. Similarly, increasing the number of iterations or steps made during the DBLS also did not produce a clear pattern in the fairness of maps generated by the model. These are likely due to two main reasons; a limitation of the SV difference in its application to redistricting and the impacts of the current boundaries as the algorithm's initial solution. Firstly, unlike metrics such as the efficiency gap, the SV difference is not able to recognise a favourable swap unless there is a change in seats which of course is not guaranteed to happen. Therefore, although the SV difference would still work in analysing or comparing elections, the DBLS may struggle to optimise solutions as there is not always a strong pressure to converge on a solution. Secondly, the initial solution used by the algorithm will affect the possible improvements as it is still only using a local search improvement algorithm and so there is likely a limit to what can be done by swapping individual wards.

Appendix 2 outlines further evaluation of the algorithm that aims to evaluate the initial proposals from the currently undergoing review of constituency boundaries, due to be completed in 2023.

6   Conclusions

It should be clear from the variety of redistricting algorithms and fairness measures and the number of factors to be considered that the problem of redistricting is a very complex one with no objective solution. Whilst purely quantitative methods can accurately distribute a population amongst a series of compact districts, these methods often fail to produce results that can best represent the electorate as they do not consider some of the other factors that influence the fairness of a map. On the other hand, those that directly consider election results and fairness, such as the algorithm proposed here, should be able to ensure that accurate representation remains a primary goal of a strong democracy.

Ultimately, ensuring this was possible was one of the main intentions behind the development of the redistricting algorithm, and we are very confident that these results show these ambitions have been filled. This is because, despite somewhat marginal improvements seen during evaluation, it is worth reiterating that the algorithm was still able to improve the fairness of the current constituency map in every experiment performed. Even a few seats changing hands to parties that would otherwise be significantly under-represented in government should demonstrate a positive shift in how the electorate is being represented. It could also be said that smaller changes in the constituency map are desirable as current boundaries likely reflect long-standing cultural or historical ties which could evidently be upset by drastically changing the boundary of every constituency.

We also believe that the SV difference performs well in its ability to reward proportionality between seat share and vote share, especially due to its scalability and ease of use in parliamentary systems. Of course, further evaluation of the metric should be undertaken to analyse its performance with other applications or elections as well as its potential limitations in evaluating small changes in electoral maps. There are also potential expansions for the redistricting algorithm itself, such as the implementation of population-based optimisation to enhance the improvement algorithm or multi-objective optimisation techniques to be able to consider more factors in redistricting. The algorithm could also evidently be run using newer data, such as results from more recent general elections or census data from the 2021 UK census which has not yet been released.

Overall, whilst the political landscape in the UK is constantly changing, we believe that aiming for proportionality and ensuring the electorate is fairly and accurately represented by their government could only be beneficial. Therefore, through the implementation and application of this model, as well as the fairness metric, this project should hopefully demonstrate that fairness can and should be considered a higher priority within our electoral systems.

Appendix 1

See Table 2.

Table 2. The number of parliamentary seats won by each party and their vote share in the 2017 general election, according to the real results and the linear regression model results.

Party	2017 seats	Model seats	2017 vote (%)	Model vote (%)
Conservatives	317	321 (+4)	42.4	41.91 (−0.49)
Labour	262	260 (−2)	40.0	40.45 (+0.45)
SNP	35	33 (−2)	3.0	3.03 (+0.03)
Liberal Democrats	12	13 (+1)	7.4	7.32 (−0.08)
DUP	10	10 (−)	0.9	0.92 (+0.02)
Sinn Fein	7	7 (−)	0.7	0.79 (+0.09)
Plaid Cymru	4	3 (−1)	0.5	0.50 (−)
Green	1	1 (−)	1.6	1.60 (−)
UKIP	0	0 (−)	1.8	1.77 (−0.03)
SDLP	0	0 (−)	0.3	0.31 (+0.01)
UUP	0	0 (−)	0.3	0.28 (−0.02)
Alliance	0	0 (−)	0.2	0.23 (+0.03)
Other Parties	2	2 (−)	0.9	0.89 (−0.01)

Appendix 2

Alongside the experiments using the current boundaries, the model was also tested using those from the initial proposals for the 2023 boundary review, released in June 2021. The proposed map was found to be 6% less fair than the current boundaries, with a fairness score of only 0.2986 as opposed to 0.3501, and compactness also decreased, but only from 0.49996 to 0.4916. The model predicted the Conservatives would gain 6 seats from the changes whilst Labour, the Liberal Democrats, DUP and Plaid Cymru, notably with Plaid Cymru losing 2 of their 3 seats. It is also worth noting the Conservatives would win 327 seats in total, meaning they would have above the 325 needed to hold a majority, something they were not able to achieve in the real 2017 election. This is ultimately supported by many criticisms of the proposals, including how the map would benefit the Conservatives and neglect Scotland and Wales, although the predictions here were not as pessimistic as others. For example, Electoral Calculus' model predicted the Conservatives would gain 13 seats and Labour would lose 8 [26], however, this would be using more recent election data to make predictions. A detailed outline of the model's predicted seat changes is in Table 3.

The boundaries themselves can be seen in Fig. 3, alongside the optimised maps generated by the redistricting algorithm, which were able to give a slight improvement to 0.3274. This is still below the fairness of the current boundaries but does have the Conservatives with one less seat and Labour 4 more seats. However, this potentially again highlights how the initial boundaries affect the model's proposals as the model was not able to have Plaid Cymru regain its seats.

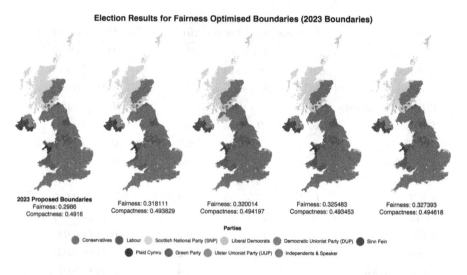

Election Results for Fairness Optimised Boundaries (2023 Boundaries)

Fig. 3. A comparison of predicted election results using the proposed 2023 boundaries and four fairness optimised versions, along with their respective fairness and compactness scores. These were generated using the control experiment parameters.

Table 3. A comparison of seats gained using the current boundaries and the 2023 proposals with the generated 2017 dataset.

Party	2017 seat share	2023 seat share	Difference
Conservatives	321	327	+6
Labour	260	258	−2
SNP	33	33	0
Liberal Democrats	13	11	−2
DUP	10	9	−1
Sinn Fein	7	8	+1
Plaid Cymru	3	1	−2
Green	1	1	0
UKIP	0	0	0
SDLP	0	0	0
UUP	0	0	0
Alliance	0	0	0
Other Parties	2	2	0

References

1. Johnston, R.: Manipulating maps and winning elections: measuring the impact of malapportionment and gerrymandering. Polit. Geogr. **21**(1), 1–31 (2002). https://doi.org/10.1016/S0962-6298(01)00070-1
2. F.H.: How Britain draws its electoral boundaries. The Economist, September 2018. https://www.economist.com/the-economist-explains/2018/09/20/how-britain-draws-its-electoral-boundaries
3. Witherspoon, A., Levine, S.: These maps show how Republicans are blatantly rigging elections. The Guardian, November 2021. https://www.theguardian.com/us-news/ng-interactive/2021/nov/12/gerrymander-redistricting-map-republicans-democrats-visual
4. Johnston, N., Uberoi, E.: Constituency boundary reviews and the number of MPs. Research Briefing 5929, House of Commons Library, London, November 2021
5. Walker, P.: Labour accuses Tories of constituency boundary 'power grab'. The Guardian, September 2018. https://www.theguardian.com/politics/2018/sep/10/uk-parliamentary-boundary-changes-final-plans-unveiled
6. Stephanopoulos, N., McGhee, E.: Partisan gerrymandering and the efficiency gap. Univ. Chicago Law Rev. **82**(2), 831–900 (2015)
7. Fifield, B., Higgins, M., Kosuke, I., Tarr, A.: Automated redistricting simulation using Markov Chain Monte Carlo. J. Comput. Graph. Stat. **29**(4), 715–728 (2020). https://doi.org/10.1080/10618600.2020.1739532
8. Olson, B.: BDistricting, November 2021. https://bolson.org/dist/
9. Smith, W.D.: Splitline districtings of all 50 states+DC+PR, July 2011. https://rangevoting.org/SplitLR.html
10. Baas, K.: Auto-Redistricter, September 2018. gitHub repository. https://github.com/happyjack27/autoredistrict/releases/tag/1.32
11. Gurnee, W., Shmoys, D.B.: Fairmandering: A column generation heuristic for fairness-optimized political districting. arXiv:2103.11469. June 2021
12. Reynolds, A., Reilly, B., Ellis, A.: Electoral System Design: The New International IDEA Handbook. Handbook Series, International Institute for Democracy and Electoral Assistance, Stockholm, Sweden (2005)
13. Boundary Commission for England: Guide to the 2023 Review of Parliamentary constituencies, May 2021. https://boundarycommissionforengland.independent.gov.uk/2023-review/guide-to-the-2023-review-of-parliamentary-constituencies/page/3/
14. Sanders, E., de Gier, M., van den Bosch, A.: Using demographics in predicting election results with twitter. In: Spiro, E., Ahn, Y.-Y. (eds.) SocInfo 2016. LNCS, vol. 10047, pp. 259–268. Springer, Cham (2016). https://doi.org/10.1007/978-3-319-47874-6_18
15. Electoral Calculus: Predicting the election with modern statistics, November 2019. https://www.electoralcalculus.co.uk/blogs/ec_pred_regress_20191130.html
16. Evans, C.: UK Ward Demographic Data and 2017 Election Results Dataset, July 2022. https://doi.org/10.34740/kaggle/dsv/3706511
17. Zhou, Y., Hao, J.K., Duval, B.: Reinforcement learning based local search for grouping problems: a case study on graph coloring. Expert Syst. Appl. **64**, 412–422 (2016). https://doi.org/10.1016/j.eswa.2016.07.047
18. Parliamentary Constituencies Act 1986, c. 56, Parliament of the United Kingdom. Queen's Printer of Acts of Parliament, November 1986

19. Kirkpatrick, S., Gelatt, C.D., Vecchi, M.P.: Optimization by simulated annealing. Science **220**(4598), 671–680 (1983). https://doi.org/10.1126/science.220.4598.671
20. Černý, V.: Thermodynamical approach to the traveling salesman problem: an efficient simulation algorithm. J. Optim. Theory Appl. **45**(1), 41–51 (1985). https://doi.org/10.1007/BF00940812
21. Kaufman, A.R., King, G., Komisarchik, M.: How to measure legislative district compactness if you only know it when you see it. Am. J. Polit. Sci. **65**(3), 533–550 (2021). https://doi.org/10.1111/ajps.12603
22. Barnes, R., Solomon, J.: Gerrymandering and compactness: implementation flexibility and abuse. Polit. Anal. **29**(4), 448–466 (2021). https://doi.org/10.1017/pan.2020.36
23. Reock, E.C.: A note: measuring compactness as a requirement of legislative apportionment. Midwest J. Polit. Sci. **5**(1), 70 (1961). https://doi.org/10.2307/2109043
24. Sylvester, J.J.: A question in the geometry of situation. Q. J. Pure Appl. Math. **1**(1), 79–80 (1857)
25. Bernstein, M., Duchin, M.: A formula goes to court: Partisan gerrymandering and the efficiency gap. Am. Math. Soc. **64**(9), 1020–1024 (2017). https://doi.org/10.1090/noti1573
26. Electoral Calculus: New Constituency Boundaries for 2023, April 2020. https://www.electoralcalculus.co.uk/boundaries2023.html

Study on Correlation Between Vehicle Emissions and Air Quality in Porto

Nirbhaya Shaji[1,2(✉)] , Thiago Andrade[1,2] , Rita P. Ribeiro[1,2] ,
and João Gama[1,3]

[1] INESC TEC, 4200-465 Porto, Portugal
nirbhaya.shaji@inesctec.pt
[2] Faculty of Sciences, University of Porto, 4169-007 Porto, Portugal
[3] Faculty of Economics, University of Porto, 4200-464 Porto, Portugal

Abstract. Road transportation emissions have increased in the last few decades and have been the primary source of pollutants in urban areas with ever-growing populations. In this context, it is important to have effective measures to monitor road emissions in regions. Creating an emission inventory over a region that can map the road emission based on the vehicle trips can be helpful for this. In this work, we show that it is possible to use raw GPS data to measure levels of pollution in a region. By transforming the data using feature engineering and calculating the vehicle-specific power (VSP), we show the areas with higher emissions levels made by a fleet of taxis in Porto, Portugal. The Uber H3 grid system is used to decompose the city into hexagonal grids to sample nearby data points into a region. We validate our experiments on real-world sensor datasets deployed in several city regions, showing the correlation with VSP and true values for several pollutants attesting to the method's usefulness.

Keywords: Road emission · Vehicle specific power · City decomposition · Particle matter · Air pollution · Uber H3

1 Introduction

A quarter of the EU's greenhouse emissions can be traced back to transport, with road transportation representing the greatest share, measuring up to 72% in 2019 [5]. Unlike many sectors that have shown significant reductions in greenhouse gas emissions by implementing climate and energy policies over the last decades, transport greenhouse gas emissions have increased by more than 33% between 1990 and 2019 and **road transport emissions** by almost 28%. On average, traffic is the biggest source of air pollution, responsible for one-quarter of particulate matter in the air [18]. According to all existing policy measures, transport carbon dioxide (CO_2)emissions are projected to be 3.5% higher in 2030 than in 1990 and to fall by only 22% by 2050 compared to 1990 levels [4]. The case for other emission pollutants is also similar to projected growth, considering

I. Koprinska et al. (Eds.): ECML PKDD 2022 Workshops, CCIS 1752, pp. 181–196, 2023.
https://doi.org/10.1007/978-3-031-23618-1_12

the increase in road emission, which is one of the major sources of air pollution in urban areas.

Urban areas are large population clusters that contribute to continuous growth in private transport, with negative consequences for air quality and human health [1,2,8]. Results obtained for the continental region of Portugal [2] revealed all the districts will be negatively affected with higher effects on human health in major urban areas. Recently, Portugal has reported having exceedingly higher values, continually and persistently, in its annual nitrogen dioxide (NO_2) limits in their three air quality zones ('Lisboa Norte', 'Porto Litoral', and 'Entre Douro e Minho'). The air pollutant NO_2 results mostly from human activities, such as road traffic, in particular diesel vehicles, and industry. This type of pollution is the cause of serious illnesses such as asthma and reduced lung function. Hence, detecting high emission spatial and temporal patterns in the urban areas and developing ways to keep the exceedance period as short as possible is of extreme importance for Portugal [12].

Even though point sources like industries, factories, and electric power plants can also cause emissions, traffic congestion, and additional traffic can significantly increase exposures and risks. Also, risks and exposures are not simply proportional to traffic volumes alone. Incremental risks depend on site-specific factors including *road type* [29], *geographical topography*, [17] or *wind speed* [19]. Along with spatial characteristics, traffic emissions have high temporal characteristics, stemming from the *behavioral patterns* of the road users [26].

To take effective steps to mitigate and control vehicle emissions in a city, understanding the temporal and spatial distribution of vehicle emissions at the landscape scale is essential. This can support management decisions at the regional level for keeping the air quality acceptable for decision-makers and non-governmental organizations [12], especially in countries like Portugal with a growing urban population.

An emissions inventory (EI) of a region indicates the number of air pollutants in the atmosphere during a year or other period in that given region. EIs are an essential input to mathematical models that estimate air pollution [22]. An emission framework that maps the vehicle emission over the road transport of a region can be used to study the influence of site-specific factors on the emission. Policymakers can use these EIs to help determine significant air pollutants sources and target regulatory actions.

This work explores the importance of an EI framework for a city like Porto, Portugal, as a tool to monitor the relationship between vehicle emissions and air pollutants in the city. Mapping the vehicle emission on the city topology can also contribute to finding the spotting sectors that require further action like the addition of sensors [23]. A geospatial framework that can map a city's vehicle trajectory and users' driving behaviour can also help find locations that need to be monitored for driving behaviours that can contribute to higher emissions.

The paper is organized as follows. After introducing the case of road emission and the need for an emission inventory for an urban city like Porto, Sect. 2 briefly reviews the related works in this area and the city decomposition method we used to map the emission over the region. Section 3 explains the data set and the methods used in detail. Section 4, describes the experimental setup and discusses the factors that may have constrained the study. In Sect. 5, we conclude the paper with pointers for future work.

2 Related Work

2.1 Emission Inventory Over Regions to Study Road Emission

A previous study of the effects of air pollution from traffic emission in Porto, Portugal, was done by [26], emphasising the damaging effects of traffic pollutants on the historical heritages. The levels of pollutants were measured for 40 days during autumn-winter 2008, and the black cluster samples, which indicate the damage to the buildings, were collected in December 2008. Values of potential health risks associated with exposure were also assessed, considering that people spend about 20% of their time outdoors. It was shown that traffic emissions were the main source of polycyclic aromatic hydrocarbons (PAHs) in the air of the metropolitan area studied. The health risk analysis of PAHs in air showed that the estimated values of lifetime lung cancer risks considerably exceeded the health-based guideline level. The study confirmed that historical monuments in urban areas act as passive repositories for air pollutants in the surrounding atmosphere, making these spots interesting stationary points for further study of urban air pollution effects.

Gonzalez et al.'s [17] work on the emission inventory of Manizales - a medium-sized Andean city - used the Vehicle Specific Power (VSP) model [15] to get realistic emission estimates to create a baseline in atmospheric modelling and urban air quality indexes. More specifically, the VSP method was shown to be effective in detecting the high emissions in the city of Manizales, Colombia. This happens due to the unique characteristics dominated by a complex topography with hills that put more stress on the vehicle engines, which results in higher fuel emissions.

Another notable work by [19] explored the visually observable patterns and basic relationships among multiple variables related to emissions to effectively represent the spatio-temporal information contained in air pollution data for Beijing using two sets of data ranging over 2009 to 2014. The work's conclusions helped guide residents' daily lives and support government decisions. These included detecting a strong correlation between pollutants and wind speed, finding temporal characteristics indicating long-term moderate pollution, and spatial distribution indicating the longer span of vegetation diffusing and absorbing atmospheric pollutants. The work standouts exemplify what a detailed visual analysis alone can contribute to understanding an area's pollution/emission inventory.

2.2 Geo-Spatial Frameworks for Region Decomposition

When processing large-scale GPS trace data for research, user privacy and the cost of frequently accessing the data can be a challenge. Ge and Fukuda [16] used meshes or cells to aggregate peoples' location data over several areas of $500 \times 500\,m^2$, which enabled to access the relevant information from the data as needed at a lower cost with better privacy.

Variations of these grid-based (cell-based) techniques are frequently used to decompose a geographical area into k disjoint sub-regions to perform data analysis of interest [11]. These **city decompositions** enable any finite amount of locations to be mapped to a region. These can be evaluated using a threshold-based (0–1) function over user-defined continuous criteria such as density or aggregate measure of a secondary variable associated with the initial location. This **Region of Interest** (ROI) identification is a problem of high relevance, especially in the EI space. It needs to be able to stress the regions that need to be monitored for the high emission/pollution contribution, i.e. emission hot-spots. However, a naive city decomposition based on politically predefined boundaries or equally spaced boundaries will always stay independent from the actual spatial distribution of the data resulting in regions containing an excess/deficit of data samples. And this is important in finding regions of emission/pollution in a city that could be affected by other sources like industrial or commercial locations. Moreira-Matias et al. [21] successfully address this problem by using Half-Space trees to divide the city area into dense sub-regions of equal mass. This mass-based city decomposition outperforms the naive grid-based one, discovers equal-mass ROIs, and maintains equally-sized cells on the data space.

In grid-based geospatial frameworks, when a point data sample is used to characterize the larger unit as a whole, a smaller perimeter to diameter ratio is essential so that each unit closely resembles a circle and has less bias from edge effects. Due to this, hexagonal grids are more efficient than square grids [7]. Square units have eight neighbours; the four neighbours sharing a side are at one distance, whereas the other four diagonal neighbours sharing a vertex are at a greater distance. In contrast, with hexagon structure, the centroids (centre points) of all six neighbouring hexagons are equidistant, making it a better choice for connectivity and path analysis.

Hexagonal grids are currently widely used for geospatial frameworks [27], with various methods for sampling the points to set the centroids for the grids [25]. Hexagons are also generated to fill the area based on the desired number of data samples, chosen hexagon area, or a consistent distance between hexagon centroid. A Discrete Global Grid System (DGGS) has been put forth as an alternative for an arbitrary starting point for the hexagonal grids. A DGGS is a hierarchical data structure covering the surface of the earth with a consistent grid of regular shaped, equal-area units. In this case, the earth is treated as an icosahedron divided into hexagons. Units spatially reference locations, bypassing transformation issues related to planar representations of coordinates [9]. EI works in urban areas can benefit from a DGGS geospatial framework with grid systems to convert, aggregate, scale and interpolate the vehicle emissions to see their effect on overall air pollution in the area.

In this work, we use the H3, a grid system developed by Uber, to efficiently divide the region to analyze large spatial data sets by bucketing the data points into hexagonal areas.

3   Data and Methods

3.1   Porto Taxi Data

The dataset comprises 442 taxis running in the city of Porto, in Portugal, for an entire year (from 2013-07-01 to 2014-06-30) [3]. These taxis operate through a taxi dispatch central, using mobile data terminals installed in the vehicles. It contains a total of 9 (nine) features in total and following are the ones used in this work:

- TRIP ID: (String) It contains an unique identifier for each trip;
- TAXI ID: (integer): It contains a unique identifier for the taxi driver that performed each trip;
- TIMESTAMP: (integer) Unix Timestamp (in seconds). It identifies the trip's start;
- MISSING DATA: (Boolean) It is FALSE when the GPS data stream is complete and TRUE whenever one (or more) locations are missing
- POLYLINE: (String): It contains a list of GPS coordinates (i.e. WGS84 format) mapped as a string. The string's beginning and end are identified with brackets (i.e. [and], respectively). The same brackets also identify each pair of coordinates as [LONGITUDE, LATITUDE]. This list contains one pair of coordinates for every 15 s of the trip. The last list item corresponds to the trip's destination while the first one represents its start;

The dataset has $1,710,670$ instances in total and $1,704,759$ rows without missing values.

3.2   Sensor Data

The sensor data was collected from July/2014 to August/2017 for the UrbanSense project [20], a city-wide platform for continuous environmental monitoring. The project deployed data collection units (DCUs) containing sensors for weather, environmental, and noise parameters capable of monitoring multiple interest points of a city, allowing for the creation of local and global representations of the current status and history of relevant environmental parameters. The sensors were deployed over several zones with different characteristics: industrial, park, traffic, touristic, and waterside.

Each dataset contains data from 23 stations. The true location of the sensors are nearby the center of the hexagonal grids shown in the Figs. 2, 3, 4, 5 and 6. Most of the data is concentrated in the summertime, with August being the month with more records. The data is logged in one reading per minute. For this study we are using data from CO, NO_2, O_3, PM_{10} and $PM_{2.5}$ particles sensors. Particle matter (PM) sensors have their values in counts while the rest of the sensors have the values in volts (V) [20].

In this work, we used the part of the datasets corresponding to the days when there was more taxi activity. The range of the taxi dataset spans from July/2013 to June/2014. The period chosen was August/2013 as it represents the holiday season that repeats itself every year. During this time the city is full and busy with tourists and locals enjoying the peak of summertime which contributes to in increase in traffic. For validation, we use the sensor data from August 2015.

3.3   Feature Extraction

For the taxi data, we used the latitude, longitude, and timestamp to generate new features that are further used to calculate the VSP.

Calculating Speed. The average speed of an object in an interval of time is the distance travelled by the object divided by the duration of the interval [14]; If d is the length of the path (also known as the distance) travelled until time t, the speed equals the distance d divided by the time t :

$$s = \frac{d}{t}. \tag{1}$$

Calculating Acceleration. Acceleration is the rate of change of velocity with time. At any point on a trajectory, the magnitude of the acceleration is given by the rate of change of velocity in both magnitude and direction at that point [14].

$$\bar{a} = \frac{\Delta v}{\Delta t}. \tag{2}$$

Calculating the Road Inclination. Road inclination or road grade or slope at each point is the sin of the central angle θ between that point and the previous point along the Earth's great circle. This indicates how much the highway is inclined from the horizontal. For example, if a section of road is flat and level, then its grade along that section is zero.

To get $\sin(\theta)$ between two points on the Earth, we need d, the shortest distance between the points over the Earth's surface, an 'as-the-crow-flies' distance, and e, the altitude or elevation at those points. So the slope or $\sin(\theta)$ will be the ratio between the elevation difference and distance between the points along the Earth's surface.

$$\sin(\theta) = \frac{e_i - e_{i+1}}{d_{(i,i+1)}}. \tag{3}$$

The distance d was calculated using the Haversine formula [6] (cf. Eq. 3), which calculates the shortest distance between two points on a sphere (Earth) using the latitudes and longitudes measured along the surface. The elevation e for the data point was obtained using Open-Elevation API[1].

---

[1] https://open-elevation.com/.

3.4   Vehicle Specific Power (VSP)

Vehicle Specific Power (VSP) is conventionally defined as instantaneous vehicle engine power. It has been widely utilized to reveal the impact of vehicle operating conditions on emission and energy consumption estimates dependent upon speed, roadway grade and acceleration or deceleration based on the second-by-second vehicle operation, as shown in the formula below [15].

$$VSP = v[1.1a + 9.81\sin(\arctan(grade)) + 0.132] + 0.000302v^3 \qquad (4)$$

where VSP is vehicle specific power $[KW/ton]$; v is vehicle speed $[m/s]$ each second; a is acceleration $(+)$ or deceleration $(-)$ $[m/s^2]$ each second; and $grade$ is terrain gradient $[\pm\%]$.

The calculation of VSP, on a second-to-second basis, allows obtaining the vehicle's power distribution throughout a trip. To ease the visualization and the analysis, it is then possible to group VSP points into 14 classes of required power, as shown in Table 1. This power range division allows vehicle fuel consumption and emissions mapping according to the VSP category.

Table 1. VSP modes from VSP values.

VSP Mode	VSP $[KW/ton]$
1	VSP < -2
2	$-2 \leq$ VSP < 0
3	$0 \leq$ VSP < 1
4	$1 \leq$ VSP < 4
5	$4 \leq$ VSP < 7
6	$7 \leq$ VSP < 10
7	$10 \leq$ VSP < 13
8	$13 \leq$ VSP < 16
9	$16 \leq$ VSP < 19
10	$19 \leq$ VSP < 23
11	$23 \leq$ VSP < 28
12	$28 \leq$ VSP < 33
13	$33 \leq$ VSP < 39
14	$39 \leq$ VSP

3.5   VSP as an Indication of Vehicle Emission

According to Rodríguez et al. [24], VSP can be used as an appropriate metric to obtain correlations between driving patterns and air pollutant emissions. The work showed real-time results for the test conducted on vehicles, demonstrating the advantage of using VSP as a proxy for emissions instead of methodologies exclusively based on speed or acceleration. The (positive) correlation between emissions (CO_2, CO, HC and NO_x) and VSP was significantly higher than that for just speed and acceleration [24]. This shows that VSP is a valuable concept for estimating mobile source emissions. Since VSP is a function of slope (road grade), speed and acceleration, VSP is also effective in studying instantaneous emission and their relationship with driving patterns over different road, environmental and temporal conditions that affect the user's driving behaviour. Road conditions can range from roads with regular traffic congestion to roads with fixed speed limits, while the environmental condition can be temperature or atmospheric pressure.

This work uses VSP modes as an indicator of vehicle emission, with a higher VSP mode corresponding to higher emission potential. We are not considering the vehicles' fuel type, engine type, or displacement for the current work.

3.6   H3: Uber's Hexagonal Hierarchical Spatial Index

Grid systems are critical to analyzing large spatial data sets and partitioning areas of the Earth into identifiable grid cells. Some techniques involve using squares or Voronoi diagrams to partition a plane into regions close to each of a given set of objects. With this in mind, Uber developed H3[2], a grid system for efficiently optimizing ride pricing and dispatch for visualizing and exploring spatial data. The method uses a grid system to bucket the data points into hexagonal areas, in other words, cells. The H3 grid is constructed by laying out 122 base cells over the Earth, with ten cells per face. Some cells are contained by more than one face. Since it is impossible to tile the icosahedron with only hexagons, the system uses twelve pentagons, one at each of the icosahedron vertices. H3 supports 16 resolutions [10]. Each fine-grained resolution has cells with a one-seventh area of the coarser resolution. Hexagons cannot be perfectly subdivided into seven hexagons, so the finer cells are only approximately contained within a parent cell. The identifiers for these child cells can be easily truncated to find their ancestor cell at a coarser resolution, enabling efficient indexing. Because the children's cells are only approximately contained, the truncation process produces a fixed amount of shape distortion. This distortion is only present when performing truncation of a cell identifier; when indexing locations at a specific resolution, the cell boundaries are exact.

For this work, we will use the eight and nine resolutions as they better fit the sensors' reach radius, roughly $2\,km$. In this sense, we can get the sensor location with a finer resolution and extrapolate to its neighbours by getting the hexagon's parent or simply growing one value in the resolution.

3.7   Index Levels Based on the Emission and Pollution

To have a standardized value, after data pre-processing, we performed a transformation over both the sensor values and the VSP modes separately to divide

---

[2] https://eng.uber.com/h3/.

the pollution for VSP emission and sensor pollutant readings. We used a classification similar to that used by openweathermap.org[3].

For the sensor values, from the true location of the sensor, we identified the H3 equivalent index for the resolution 8, which is ≈ 730 meters. Then we summed all the values inside that hexagon for the desired hour and standardized the values. We then convert these values into levels from 1 to 5 to have a common reference for all the types of sensor readings. Similarly to what was done to the sensors data, to have a standardized value, we perform a data transformation step over the VSP mode values for each data point in the taxi trajectories. From the GPS point coordinates, we identified the H3 equivalent index for the resolution 8, which is ≈ 730 meters. Then we summed all the VSP values inside that hexagon for the desired hour and standardized the values. We then convert these values into levels from 1 to 5 to have a common reference that will match the sensor's readings enabling us to find the correlations for the emissions. Figure 1 shows the vehicle emission over the city of Porto over a period of a day (2013-08-01) with the scale color indicating the emission levels from *Good* (1) to *Very Poor* (5) as listed in the Table 2.

Table 2. Air Quality Index levels

Name	Index	VSP	PM_{10}	$PM_{2.5}$	NO_2	CO	O_3
Good	1	1–36	1–863	1–16094	1–122	1–67	1–72
Fair	2	37–116	864–1148	16095–19415	123–125	68–72.06	73–101
Moderate	3	117–350	1149–1392	19416–25690	126–128	72.07–72.21	102–105
Poor	4	351–1531	1393–2750	25691–36941	129–135	72.22–73	106–110
Very Poor	5	1532–56178	2751–233767	36942–762797	136–239	74–258	111–210

4   Obtained Results

4.1   Experiment Setup

We processed one hour of data from one day in 2015-08-01 from 12:00:01 to 12:59:59. This corresponds to 956 observations on average for each of the sensors.

In Fig. 2 with PM_{10} values, one can notice a clear pattern cross-sectioned through all the sensors over the riverside in a region called 'Ribeira' in the lower part of the city center. Note the four lower hexagons and the pair of yellow ones with high levels of emissions. This region has various landmarks, sightseeing places, restaurants, and cafes. Mainly during summer, the area also receives street artists and other performances. There is also a pier from where the famous touristic Portuguese boats depart all day. It is then possible to assume that the region is a strong hub for emissions as many public and private transport vehicles have this area as the origin or destination for their trips. For the $PM_{2.5}$ sensors, the pattern is similar and can be verified in Fig. 3.

---

[3] https://openweathermap.org/api/air-pollution.

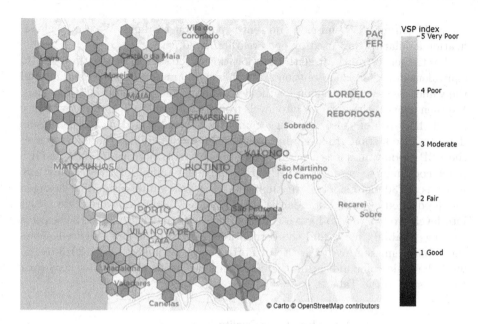

Fig. 1. VSP emissions for grids over Porto city for the whole day of 2013-08-03

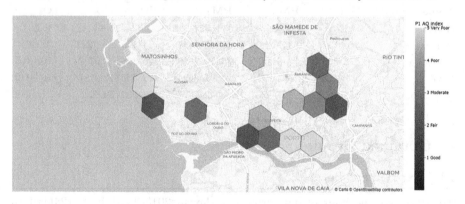

Fig. 2. PM_{10} emissions around sensors over Porto city on 2015-08-01

The values for CO, NO_2, and O_3 are shown in Figs. 4, 5, and 6 with the difference that the yellow pair of hexagons (representing the highest emission values) shifted from the right to the middle of the lower four items.

Fig. 3. PM$_{2.5}$ emissions around sensors over Porto city on 2015-08-01

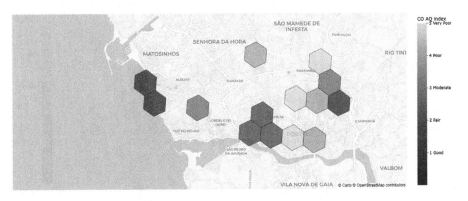

Fig. 4. CO emissions around sensors over Porto city on 2015-08-01 (Color figure online)

Regarding the VSP emissions, the sample of data used in the experiment has 196, 487 instances. The inner city has a clear pattern with higher emission values encompassing all but one hexagon in the middle of Fig. 1. It is also possible to notice that the peripheral parts have the lowest values with the exception for the two hexagons that fall over the highway that connects Porto city with Porto airport (5 consecutive yellow hexagons lined towards north-west direction).

By looking on a broader area for the day 2013-08-03 over the great Porto (Porto, Maia, Matosinhos, Gaia) - cf. Fig. 1, one can see the VSP emissions with high levels for Porto and the city ring that connects to the other regions. There is also a clear line of yellow hexagons representing high emissions over the highway that connects Porto to Matosinhos and Maia as shown in Fig. 7.

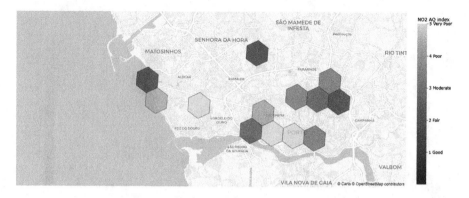

Fig. 5. NO$_2$ emissions around sensors over Porto city on 2015-08-01(Color figure online)

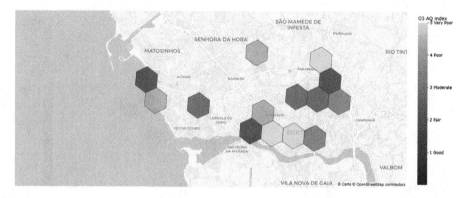

Fig. 6. O$_3$ emissions around sensors over Porto city on 2015-08-01 (Color figure online)

4.2   Discussion

This work focused on developing a framework that can be used as the first step toward a road-emission inventory of the city of Porto in Portugal. Using the VSP mode methods to determine the severity of the vehicle's emission through it's trip trajectory helps give an idea of the vehicle emissions around locations in the city with different traffic levels. A grid-based system is used to bucket the data points into hexagonal cells, which help map aggregate values to the city locations. This work also validates the VSP emission in city locations by using several air pollutant sensors around the city.

We used only light-duty vehicle (taxi) trips from Porto. A much more diverse data set that considers trips from other types of vehicles (e.g., public bus transport) also is needed to get a better picture of the road-emission contribution in the city. However, the method discussed to transform the VSP modes in each grid into air pollution indicators allows the use of Table 2 over any vehicle type or mode of transportation. In future, we intend to use different data sets that have trajectories of different types of vehicles with more information about fuel

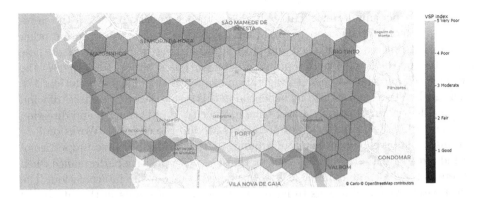

Fig. 7. VSP emissions for sensors over Porto city on 2013-08-03

and engine type. This study is also constrained because the taxi and sensor data are from other years. So we had to subset the data to periods that would indicate seasonal variations, in this case, the first Saturday of the corresponding years' August, around the usual vacation time. Until we have trip and sensor data from the same time, we will have to restrict our sampling to periods with similar behaviours over the year, e.g., public holidays, festival periods, etc. Another limitation of this study is not having sensors located at points in the city that would relate to road traffic. This affected the quality of the comparison we could make on the pollution indicators. Locations in the town like highways, side roads, tourist spots, landscapes etc., would give us better data related to road emissions. If we can have sufficient data, we will validate the proposed idea in the future. Another limitation of this study is not considering meteorological factors like wind and rain, which have been shown to affect the dispersion of pollution around a geographical region [17], [28], [13]. However, the grid-based method we used allows us to explore this in our future works, as discussed in the next session.

5   Conclusion and Future Work

In this work, we show that raw GPS data can be used to measure pollution levels in a region. By transforming the data using feature engineering and calculating the instantaneous vehicle-specific power (VSP), we show the areas with higher emissions levels made by a fleet of taxis in Porto, Portugal. We validate our experiments on real-world sensor datasets deployed in several regions of the city, showing the correlation with VSP and true values for several pollutants, demonstrating the method's usefulness.

For future work, we intend to perform more extensive experiments on different real-world datasets on various vehicles and provide detailed analysis on the effects of different vehicle characteristics such as fuel type, engine displacement, revolutions per minute etc. This will give a deeper understanding of the influence of vehicle specifications on-road emissions. We also intend on using other sensor data such as wind speed and precipitation to verify the influence of these variables on the level of pollution in a greater area as several studies suggest the wind speed and the closeness to vegetation can affect the index of pollution [17]. The grid system we used will be beneficial in this case to study the effects of wind on the dispersion of pollution over time in the city. Wind strength and direction are crucial in the propagation of pollutants around the city [28]. Works on how to interpolate vehicle emission all around a city considering these properties of wind already exits [13] and have shown that there is a positive performance when there is a significant number of known points to use in the interpolation. The grid-based system allows us to have a varying range of points in the city based on the traffic, which could help us better interpolate.

Acknowledgement. This work was developed under the project "City Analyser" (POCI-01-0247-FEDER-039924), financed by European Regional Development Fund (ERDF), through the Research and Technological Development Incentive System, within the Portugal2020 Competitiveness and Internationalization Operational Program.

This work is also financed by National Funds through the Portuguese funding agency, FCT - Fundação para a Ciência e a Tecnologia within project : UI/BD/152697/2022.

References

1. Tchepel, O., Dias, D.: Quantification of health benefits related with reduction of atmospheric pm levels: implementation of population mobility approach. Sci. World J. **21**(3), 189–200 (2011). https://doi.org/10.1080/09603123.2010.520117
2. Dias, D., Tchepel, O., Carvalho, A., Miranda, A.I., Borrego, C.: Particulate matter and health risk under a changing climate: assessment for Portugal. Int. J. Environ. Health Res. **2012**, 409546 (2012). https://doi.org/10.1100/2012/409546
3. Ecml/pkdd 15 competition: Taxi trajectory prediction (i) (2015). https://www.kaggle.com/competitions/pkdd-15-predict-taxi-service-trajectory-i/overview/evaluation
4. Agency, E.E.: Decarbonising road transport - the role of vehicles, fuels and transport demand. Transport and Environment Report 2021 (2021)
5. Agency, E.E.: Greenhouse gas emissions from transport in Europe (2021). https://www.eea.europa.eu/ims/greenhouse-gas-emissions-from-transport
6. Azdy, R.A., Darnis, F.: Use of haversine formula in finding distance between temporary shelter and waste end processing sites. J. Phys. Conf. Ser. **1500**(1), 012104 (2020). https://doi.org/10.1088/1742-6596/1500/1/012104
7. Birch, C.P., Oom, S.P., Beecham, J.A.: Rectangular and hexagonal grids used for observation, experiment and simulation in ecology. Ecol. Model. **206**(3), 347–359 (2007). https://doi.org/10.1016/j.ecolmodel.2007.03.041, https://www.sciencedirect.com/science/article/pii/S0304380007001949
8. Borrego, C., Tchepel, O., Costa, A., Amorim, J., Miranda, A.: Emission and dispersion modelling of Lisbon air quality at local scale. Atmos. Environ. **37**(37), 5197–5205 (2003). https://doi.org/10.1016/j.atmosenv.2003.09.004, https://www.sciencedirect.com/science/article/pii/S1352231003007404

9. Bousquin, J.: Discrete global grid systems as scalable geospatial frameworks for characterizing coastal environments. Environ. Model. Softw. **146**, 105210 (2021). https://doi.org/10.1016/j.envsoft.2021.105210, https://www.sciencedirect. com/science/article/pii/S1364815221002528

10. Brodsky, I.: H3: Uber's hexagonal hierarchical spatial index (2018). https://eng. uber.com/h3/[22 June 2019]

11. Castro, P.S., Zhang, D., Chen, C., Li, S., Pan, G.: From taxi GPS traces to social and community dynamics: a survey. ACM Comput. Surv. **46**(2), 1–34 (2013). https://doi.org/10.1145/2543581.2543584

12. Commission, E.: Air quality: Commission refers Portugal to the court of justice of the European union for high levels of nitrogen dioxide (2021). https://ec.europa. eu/commission/presscorner/detail/en/ip_21_5353

13. Contreras, L., Ferri, C.: Wind-sensitive interpolation of urban air pollution forecasts. Procedia Comput. Sci. **80**, 313–323 (2016). https://doi. org/10.1016/j.procs.2016.05.343, https://www.sciencedirect.com/science/article/ pii/S187705091630758X

14. Elert, G.: The physics hypertextbook. In: The Physics Hypertextbook. hypertextbook (2021)

15. Frey, H., Unal, A., Chen, J., Li, S., Xuan, C.: Methodology for developing modal emission rates for EPA's multi-scale motor vehicle & equipment emission system. US Environmental Protection Agency, Ann Arbor, Michigan (2002)

16. Ge, Q., Fukuda, D.: Updating origin-destination matrices with aggregated data of GPS traces. Transp. Res. Part C: Emerg. Technol. **69**, 291–312 (2016). https:// doi.org/10.1016/j.trc.2016.06.002, https://www.sciencedirect.com/science/article/ pii/S0968090X16300705

17. González, C., Gómez, C., Rojas, N., Acevedo, H., Aristizábal, B.: Relative impact of on-road vehicular and point-source industrial emissions of air pollutants in a medium-sized Andean city. Atmos. Environ. **152**, 279–289 (2017). https:// doi.org/10.1016/j.atmosenv.2016.12.048, https://www.sciencedirect.com/science/ article/pii/S135223101631024X

18. Karagulian, F., et al.: Contributions to cities' ambient particulate matter (PM): a systematic review of local source contributions at global level. Atmos. Environ. **120**, 475–483 (2015). https://doi.org/10.1016/j.atmosenv.2015.08.087, https:// www.sciencedirect.com/science/article/pii/S1352231015303320

19. Li, H., Fan, H., Mao, F.: A visualization approach to air pollution data exploration- a case study of air quality index (pm2.5) in Beijing, china. Atmosphere. **7**, 35 (2016). https://doi.org/10.3390/atmos7030035

20. Luis, Y., Santos, P.M., Lourenco, T., Pérez-Penichet, C., Calcada, T., Aguiar, A.: UrbanSense: an urban-scale sensing platform for the internet of things. In: 2016 IEEE International Smart Cities Conference (ISC2), pp. 1–6. IEEE (2016)

21. Moreira-Matias, L., Gama, J., Ferreira, M., Mendes-Moreira, J., Damas, L.: Time-evolving o-d matrix estimation using high-speed GPS data streams. Expert Syst. App. **44**, 275–288 (2016). https://doi.org/10.1016/j.eswa.2015.08.048, https:// www.sciencedirect.com/science/article/pii/S0957417415006053

22. Ntziachristos, L., Gkatzoflias, D., Kouridis, C., Samaras, Z.: COPERT: a European road transport emission inventory model. In: Athanasiadis, I.N., Rizzoli, A.E., Mitkas, P.A., Gómez, J.M. (eds.) Inf. Technol. Environ. Eng., pp. 491–504. Springer, Berlin Heidelberg, Berlin, Heidelberg (2009)

23. Oreggioni, G., et al.: The impacts of technological changes and regulatory frame-works on global air pollutant emissions from the energy industry and road trans-port. Energy Policy. **168**, 113021 (2022). https://doi.org/10.1016/j.enpol.2022. 113021, https://www.sciencedirect.com/science/article/pii/S0301421522002464

24. Rodríguez, R.A., Virguez, E.A., Rodríguez, P.A., Behrentz, E.: Influence of driving patterns on vehicle emissions: a case study for Latin American cities. Transp. Res. Part D: Transp. Environ. **43**, 192–206 (2016). https://doi.org/10.1016/j.trd.2015. 12.008, https://www.sciencedirect.com/science/article/pii/S1361920915002187

25. Russell, M., Harvey, J., Ranade, P., Murphy, K.: EPA h2o user manual. US EPA Office of Research and Development, Washington, DC (EPA/600/R-15/090) (2015)

26. Slezáková, K., et al.: Air pollution from traffic emissions in Oporto, Portugal: health and environmental implications. Microchem. J. **99**, 51–59 (2011). https:// doi.org/10.1016/j.microc.2011.03.010

27. Smith, L., Nestlerode, J., Harwell, L., Bourgeois, P.: The areal extent of brown shrimp habitat suitability in mobile bay, Alabama, USA: targeting vegetated habi-tat restoration. Environ. Monitor. Assess. **171**, 611–20 (2010). https://doi.org/10. 1007/s10661-009-1303-0

28. Tian, Y., Yao, X.A., Mu, L., Fan, Q., Liu, Y.: Integrating meteorological factors for better understanding of the urban form-air quality relationship. Landsc. Ecol. **35**(10), 2357–2373 (2020). https://doi.org/10.1007/s10980-020-01094-6

29. Zhang, K., Batterman, S.: Air pollution and health risks due to vehicle traffic. Sci. Total Environ. **450**, 307–316 (2013). https://doi.org/10.1016/j.scitotenv.2013.01. 074, https://www.sciencedirect.com/science/article/pii/S0048969713001290

Intelligently Detecting Information Online-Weaponisation Trends (IDIOT)

Fawzia Zehra Kara-Isitt[(⊠)] [iD], Stephen Swift[iD], and Allan Tucker[iD]

Intelligent Data Analysis Group, Department of Computer Science, Brunel University, Kingston
Lane, Uxbridge UB8 3PH, UK
{Fuzzy.Kara-Isitt,Stephen.Swift,Allan.Tucker}@brunel.ac.uk

Abstract. This paper discusses a detailed study on existing natural language processing open source and commonly used sentiment analysis toolboxes and looks at how various combinations of those toolboxes' results can be used to accurately classify a sinister intent in a statement. For example, can the toolboxes' results for different features, such as Attacks, Toxicity and Aggression be combined together predict an Attacks class with more accuracy than just the Attacks classification alone? Can that combination be used to predict any other intimidating intent within text, and can it also help identify a trajectory of an online threatening trend quicker? The main findings so far conclude that the open sourced and massively used sentiment analysis toolboxes for the English language provided by Python and Java work better for Attacking and Aggressive language, compared to general Toxic language. Also, within this experiment, Support Vector machines, although have the largest overheads and take the longest time, give a more reliable accuracy prediction. Finally, Multi-class aggregates of the toolboxes provide on average a much-improved performance result than just using a single class from a single toolbox.

Keywords: Text mining · Data wrangling · Sentiment analysis · Natural language processing · Machine learning

1 Introduction

Online harm and related sentiment analysis findings have so far brought to light the fact that the main challenges to effectively and accurately monitor online abuse at present are; that the data, tools, processes and systems needed are not fully available. The field is beset with terminological, methodological, legal and theoretical challenges in both horizontal and vertical frameworks around which it occurs [40]. Online harm, abuse, or 'hate-speech' (including both interpersonal attacks, such as harassment and bullying, and verbal attacks against individuals or groups) is finally receiving more attention in the UK and EU policy making departments [3, 43]. Toxifying public discourse motivate other forms of extremist and hateful behaviour through a cycle of 'cumulative extremism' [10]. A report from the Commission for Countering Extremism found that 56% of the public believe 'a lot more' should be done to counter extremism online [7].

I. Koprinska et al. (Eds.): ECML PKDD 2022 Workshops, CCIS 1752, pp. 197–214, 2023.
https://doi.org/10.1007/978-3-031-23618-1_13

The Analysis of Oxford Internet Survey [7, 15] showed that experiences of online abuse vary considerably across demographics. Xenophobia (including anti-migrant hatred) was the most commonly reported grounds of hate speech (17%) followed by sexual orientation, transphobic (16%) and Islamophobic hatred (13%).

This problem of finding online harm is difficult to deal with since it has many "faces" and exhibits complex interactions among social media users. Such multifaceted, abusive behaviour involves instances of hate speech, such as offensive, sexist and racist language, aggression, cyberbullying, harassment, and trolling [43].

Social media platforms generally provide a sense of community, connection and commonality at one level, but have also proven to be 'fatal' at another level as discussed above, as it triggered not only everyday irritating, offensive harm; but it has, unfortunately even instigated the finality of death for some people in the form of aggressive attacks, suicide and genocide. The findings on the rate of removal of hate speech came in an update on the EU Code of Conduct, "Code of conduct on countering illegal hate speech online", depict that IT companies removed 62.5% of the content notified to them, while 37.5% remained online [34].

This paper presents a review on the classification and analysis of negative sentiments of aggression, attack and toxicity in text using the easily accessible and quite popularly used open-source toolboxes within everyday application packages. The use of a combination of their rapid analysis can facilitate more reliable conclusions. Those sentiment combinations can then be used to expedite catching the trajectory of incitement, hopefully, in the next paper to be written, utilizing the results from this paper's experiment, in the near future as the subsequent step. This research also focuses on text in the English language as a base to ascertain online harm.

In its present state, the experiments answer the following:

RQ1: Does any single trait signify or indicate another class trait more than its original?

RQ2: Does any combination trait signify or indicate another class trait?

RQ3: Does the Multiclass (Even 1 of 10 AND Average) or Multi-Class classify better for any one trait or any combination of traits?

RQ4: Which classifier worked most accurately for which trait?

RQ5: Which is the least accurate classifier model?

Shah [38] showed that the prevalence of Internet users was positively correlated with general population suicide in men ($P = 0.001$) and approached statistical significance for women ($P = 0.074$).

Thus, thankfully, such observations have also led to the use of social media platforms and the data gathered for social good for suicide prevention and surveillance and that has been a focus of many mental health focus groups and NLP forums lately. The Online Harms White Paper [27] stated that the suicide-related internet use (i.e. searching the internet for information on suicide methods) were reported for about 23% of 595 children and young people attempting suicide in the UK between 2014 and 2016.

The application of algorithms in L.Tong et al.'s 'Cost-sensitive Boosting Pruning Trees for depression detection on Twitter", in other platforms may help reduce this dreadful harm [39].

Another ongoing issue was demonstrated using a Bartik-type empirical strategy by Schwarz and Müller (2017) [25] which showed that right-wing anti-refugee sentiment on Facebook predicted violent crimes against refugees and that it is more likely to occur in areas with higher exposure to anti-refugee hate speech online.

What is offensive, really? The lack of clarity in Government laws, the lack of precise definitions of hate in the privately-owned channels, the lack of proper basic classification of, or even a generic outline of what entails offence and hate within the numerous global cultures and sub-cultures; really makes online offence hard to capture. Neither has it been clearly defined by the public, as perhaps, what this researcher finds offensive may not be offensive for the various other readers of this paper, there is no real single static model defined and developed for what is known as 'online weaponisation'.

This experiment so far concludes that on combining similar toxic text features' scores, it is generally possible to obtain better results for classifying the presence of other similar forms of rudeness. Overall this document is structured as follows: in Sect. 2 we present the related work regarding capture of online weaponisation; in Sect. 3 we present the proposed methodology; at Sect. 4 we present the whole experiment, and Sect. 5 the Experimental Results, Evaluation and Discussion. Finally, in Sects. 6, 7 and 8 we draw the conclusions, discuss the challenges and future work, and end at plan for the next stage of the research.

2 Related Work (Online-Weaponisation)

Allahyari, M. et al. (2017) [2] explained that text data is a good example of unstructured information, which is one of the simplest and basic forms of data that can be generated in most scenarios. Unstructured text is easily processed and perceived by humans but is significantly harder for machines to understand.

Knowledge Discovery from Data/Text (KDD/T) – as introduced by Feldman et al. [12]; refers to the process of extracting high quality of information from text, some semi-structured and unstructured resources such as word documents, videos, and images. These approaches can be Information Extraction from text (IE), Text Summarization, Unsupervised Learning Methods, Supervised Learning Methods, Probabilistic Methods for Text Mining, Text Streams and Social Media Mining, Opinion Mining and Sentiment Analysis, Biomedical Text Mining.

Natural Language Processing (NLP) techniques are a subfield of computer science, artificial intelligence and linguistics aiming to understanding of the extracted natural language text using computers. Many text mining algorithms make use of NLP techniques broadly, as part of speech tagging (POG), syntactic parsing and other types of linguistic analysis, such as sentiment analysis. Opinion Mining and Sentiment Analysis expertise flourished with the advent of e-commerce, e-services, online shopping and social media, as a huge amount of text is created and continues to grow about different product reviews or user's opinions and comments and statements. This research aims to predict what factors could lead to an inciteful transgression by a potential harmer through their weapon of toxic language.

Various feature selection approaches are used to eliminate irrelevant and superfluous characteristic [1, 42] from the feature list and thus increases the sentiment classification accuracy. That idea was put into practice in this research, and will be developed to be made even more reliable and faster to predict negativity in the next paper after this one by using the outcomes from this present paper.

Transfer learning methodology techniques have grown because they can produce great accuracy and results while requiring significantly less training time than training a new model from scratch [5]. By using the combined features multi-classes which were concluded to be more reliable in this experiment (See Sect. 6), as a weight to fine tune a pre-existing hate detecting model like HateBERT [4], may perhaps, lead to more reliable results.

This research uses three similar, but defined and annotated separately, datasets on Aggression, Attacks and Toxicity [33], from 15 years' worth of the Wikipedia Talk Corpus. The negatively scored sentiments of this corpus (using open-sourced toolboxes) are stored as features in a file. The results are then augmented as a combination feature to increase the negative classification accuracy results applying a KDD approach of the model. The annotated conclusions are used for classification. This improves the reliability of finding that negative sentiment. The motivation behind using a number of widely used toolboxes is to assess if the aggregate results deal with the uncertainty, bias and ambiguity that may be present in just one single toolbox.

3   Methodology

This research has a non-standard approach, and is not strongly related to most literature reviews which focus on a combination of machine learning and NLP tools yet, instead it is focusing on the combination of results from data that has already been analysed by open-sourced tools, commonly used in other well distributed applications of business, entertainment, industry and academia. Thus, in order to make it more systematic, this approach aligns to a (Knowledge Discovery from Data) KDD process, which depends heavily on data pre-processing [47], as in this research. To obtain useful knowledge from data, the following steps are performed iteratively. Refer to Key and the Fig. 1 below.

4   Data Collection and Annotation Description

As discussed in Sect. 2, the Wikipedia Talk Corpus [44] has been the chosen dataset for this research paper for its large size and easy and free accessibility, and its previous reliable results and uses in other research experiments by academics and companies like Meta (https://meta.wikimedia.org/wiki) and Jigsaw© (https://jigsaw.google.com/); and thus easy to compare the results with. 'Detox' [44], originally used by Ellery Wulczyn et al.'s [45] paper 'Ex-Machina' on online personal attacks at scale. In order to get reliable estimates of whether a comment is a personal attack, each comment was labelled by at least 10 different Crowdflower annotators and their aggregate judgments from the 10 separate people was used when constructing a single label for each comment, making it extremely reliable. All data collected or generated for this project is available under free licenses on Figshare (https://figshare.com/), per their open access policy. This human

Key Abbreviation (Meaning)
A (Aggression)
AAC (Aggression Attacks Class)
AACA (Aggression Attacks Class Average)
Ac (Accuracy)
AC (Aggression Class)
ACA (Aggression Class Average)
At (Attacks)
ATC (Aggression Toxicity Class)
AtCA (Attacks Class Average)
AtTC (Attacks Toxicity Class)
AtTCA (Attacks Toxicity Class Average)

C (Class)
D (Data)
F1 (F1)
M (Model)
MC (Multi-Class)
MCA (Multi-Class Average)
P (Precision)
R (Recall)
ROC (Receiver Operating Characteristic)
T (Toxicity)
TC (Toxicity Class)
TCA (Toxicity Class Average)

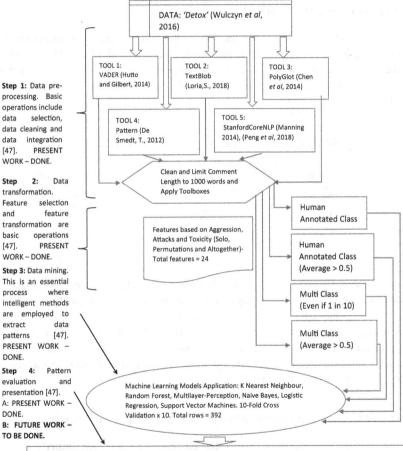

Fig. 1. Research methodology

annotated dataset of 1M crowd-sourced annotations cover 100K user and article talk pages made between 2001–2015 [33]. This corpus also stores the data using a timestamp in UTC, or Universal Time Coordinated, and is the most precise and commonly referred to time standard. The time-based aspect for posts will help with the subsequent study using Markov Chain models. This experiment has certain limitations and thus restricted to pre-determined and commonly used machine learning techniques and the thoroughly annotated pre-selected toxicity, attacking and aggression datasets. It is designed to test the hypothesis within the data dimensionality of these domain-specific datasets and their criteria.

4.1 Dataset Choice (KDD Step 1)

Wulczyn et al. (2017) [45] had used the very same data and had its performances listed in Table 1. by Karan et al.'s (2018) [19] and Fortuna, P. et al. (2021) [13] where 'Id': identifier we use as reference; 'Category': annotation categories; 'Size': number of instances, 'Performance': best score on the dataset and reference (F1 for all datasets) by [13, 19].

Table 1. F1 readings for Karan et al.'s (2018) [19] experiment

Id	Category	Size Instances	Performance
Wul1	Aggressive	69,526	0.70
Wul2	Attack	69,526	0.71
Wul3	Toxic	95,692	0.75

Fortuna, P. et al. (2021) [13] concluded that cross-dataset model generalization in the context of abusive online language should be considered when creating models that generalize when the nature of the categories within the datasets are relevant. Thus, this research model experiments only inter and cross combination of the datasets (Step 2) generalization evaluation of Attacking, Aggression and Toxicity only and compare the Accuracy, Precision, Recall, F1, ROC values to predict one of those respected features of Attack, Aggression or Toxicity.

4.2 Data Cleaning and Feature Allocation. (KDD Step 1 and Step 2)

The comments had to go through several data cleaning steps and then limited to fixed size of 1000 words before being sent through the open sourced sentiment analysis toolboxes. Nulls (NaN), blanks and unrecognized characters were removed. The comment id was maintained for random record verification to follow the trail of annotation. (Step 2) On applying the chosen open-source java and python language model sentiment analysis (See Sect. 4.3), and using only the common comment review ids, the leftover total rows were: 70,336, Aggression + Toxic: 70,343 and Attacks + Toxic: 70,336. This resulted in 24 features separately, 8 class outputs per each trait set. The model considered all the inputs of an individual trait (eg: Aggression) and a combination feature (eg: Aggression plus Toxicity) as well as the all-inclusive feature set. Hence, 7 separately run machine learning models, 4 class combinations, each of the 3 traits and the binary string based Multiclass, giving us a total of 8 different ways to form the class sets.

4.3   Sentiment Analysis Open Sourced Toolboxes (KDD Step 2)

'A basic task in sentiment analysis is classifying the polarity of a given text at the document, sentence, or feature/aspect level—whether the expressed opinion in a document, a sentence or an entity feature/aspect is positive, negative, or neutral. Advanced, "beyond polarity" sentiment classification looks, for instance, at emotional states such as enjoyment, anger, disgust, sadness, fear, and surprise.' [16]. The performance of the aggregate outputs on using the toolboxes would be used for comparison against the annotated class scores, after all the complete runs through the models. Chosen toolboxes are TextBlob [23], VADER [18], PolyGlot [6], Pattern [8], Stanford CoreNLP [24, 32] processing all the three data sources in Java and Python [31] (Table 2).

Table 2.   Toolboxes and their sentiment range.

Toolbox	TextBlob	VADER	PolyGlot	Pattern	Stanford CoreNLP
Sentiment range	− 1, 0, 1	− 1 to 1	− 1 to 1	− 1 to 1	0 to 4

Algorithm 1. Experimental Setup.

```
1.INPUT 'Comments.txt'
2.RUN 'Sentiment_Analysis_Tool' ON 'Comments.txt'
3.  OUTPUT 'Sentiment_Scores.txt'
4.START time
5 FOR Every Row in Sentiment_Score.txt DO
6.   FOR Every Annotated Class DO
7.      FOR Every Chosen Machine Learning Model DO
8.         FOR 1 to 10 DO
9.            STRATIFY CROSS-VALIDATION FOLDS Train and Test 10 times
10.         END FOR
11.      END FOR
12.   END FOR
13.END FOR
14.END time
15.STORE accuracy, roc, precision, recall, f1
16.time_taken = end time - start time
17.OUTPUT data, class, model, mean accuracy, mean roc, mean precision,
mean recall, mean f1, total time_taken INTO 'Final_Values.txt'
```

4.4 Experimental Design (Step 2)

The dataset for each of the experiments was created by concatenating the corresponding 24 fields columns of each set of sentiment analysis toolbox output. The observed classification or compound class is added as the final feature. Machine learning classifiers were stratified over 10-fold 10 times to preserve the class ratios (1/10) in each training and validation fold for the 70K + samples from the unbalanced dataset. A mean of the metrics is then concatenated at the end for a comparison result. Finally, the Time taken (in minutes) to run the entire Model × Data Feature × Class 10-fold cycle from start to finish per record is recorded. This process is detailed in the Algorithm 1. The code is available at: https://github.com/FuzzyLogic9/ECMLPKDD_IDIOT.git.

4.5 Machine Learning Model Selection (KDD Step 3 and Step 4)

Scores were observed on models commonly recommended for semantic and linguistic sentiment analysis use cases namely; Logistic Regression (LR), Naive Bayes (NB), and linear Support Vector Machines (SVM) by Kumar et al.'s Systemic Literature Review [21]. Default parameters for the large data were applied on various machine learning models so that all experiments were at an equal advantage. This was to reduce and potential bias from applying parameter optimization. Scikit-learn machine learning Python libraries were used for the experiments [30].

5 Experimental Results, Evaluation and Discussion (Step 4)

The metrics used for comparison were: Accuracy, Precision, Recall, F1, ROC score, and Time (Table 3). There was a final total of 392 different sets of results. On completion of the entire set of results, at first instance it was obvious that multi-classes were producing the better overall results, suggesting that creating a more intuitive class variable is a better negative sentiment holistic detector (See Tables 4 and 5). Classes based on an average of annotated scores per comment performed better than the class based on a single "vote" (at least 1 of 10 annotators voting for a negative score). However, if there are any incorrect annotations, these may have a significant bias on the class variables, thus the motivation behind the creation of a compound (multi-class) variable.

Figures in shaded ' blue' cells within Tables 4, 5, 6, 7, 8, 9, 10, 11, 12 and 13 reflect the best results per table.

Table 3. Header example of 392 records derived from the 10-fold cross validated runs of each of the 8 classes for the 7 selected features and for each of the 7 machine learning models.

No	Dataset	Class	Model	Accuracy	ROC	Precision	Recall	F1	Time taken
1	A	AC	KN5	0.65	0.67	0.71	0.72	0.71	121.95
2	A	AC	NB	0.64	0.72	.	.	.	.

The various metric readings are as follows and Tables 4 and 5 show how Multi-Class Accuracies have fared better than all the others followed by average and combination classes then single classes, apart from Multi-class averages.

Table 4. Aggregates of Multi-class accuracies vs the total of all the others indicates a better average overall.

Multiclass Averages	No	Yes
Accuracy	0.73	0.76
ROC	0.74	0.76
Precision	0.67	0.65
Recall	0.57	0.47
F1	0.60	0.51

Table 5. All metric averages for all classes.

Class	Accuracy	ROC	Precision	Recall	F1
MC	0.84	0.79	0.71	0.35	0.47
ACA	0.79	0.77	0.63	0.46	0.51
TCA	0.79	0.77	0.61	0.49	0.52
AtCA	0.76	0.76	0.60	0.48	0.51
AC	0.69	0.73	0.73	0.68	0.70
TC	0.68	0.72	0.72	0.64	0.67
AtC	0.68	0.71	0.73	0.65	0.68
MCA	0.67	0.72	0.58	0.59	0.56

RQ1: Table 6 shows Toxicity, Aggression and Attacks single class trait average best respectively, a close follow up is Attacks predicting Aggression average. Best F1 metrics was Aggression in Table 5.

RQ2: All four major combinations predict accuracy Aggression class average equally and the best in Table 7 and it is a massive improvement of 10% combination of traits:

Aggression and Attacks, Attacks and Toxicity and ALL considered;

and a humble improvement of 2% on the single trait of Attacks.

RQ3: The performance of Multi-class is 5% to 8% better than the Average classes and 16% better than that of a single class. Multi-class average performs worst at 17% on a total average but much more stable overall and performs at maximum on some individual cases (See Tables 5, 8 and 9).

RQ4: Support Vector Machine classifiers worked (in terms of performance metrics) most accurately as an average for all the traits in Table 8. Support Vector Machines as seen in Table 9.

RQ5: Naive Bayes and K-Nearest Neighbour were less accurate over an average over all the traits. SVCLINEAR performed best over per class as well. (Multiclass / MultiClassAvg) and Gaussian NB was the poorest performer overall in Table 10.

Table 6. Single classed metric averages indicating each unique class best predicting its own class, the best being at 0.83 (Toxicity predicting Toxicity Class Average).

D	C	Ac	ROC	P	R	F1
A	AC	0.68	0.72	0.73	0.72	0.72
At	AC	0.69	0.73	0.73	0.70	0.71
T	AC	0.69	0.73	0.73	0.70	0.71
A	ACA	0.82	0.77	0.69	0.46	0.54
At	ACA	0.70	0.75	0.54	0.49	0.49
T	ACA	0.68	0.73	0.54	0.48	0.48
A	AtC	0.68	0.72	0.74	0.68	0.70
At	AtC	0.65	0.71	0.72	0.68	0.69
T	AtC	0.68	0.71	0.73	0.70	0.71
A	AtCA	0.66	0.73	0.53	0.57	0.53
At	AtCA	0.70	0.75	0.53	0.52	0.50
T	AtCA	0.66	0.72	0.54	0.48	0.49
A	TC	0.68	0.73	0.72	0.68	0.70
At	TC	0.68	0.73	0.72	0.68	0.70
T	TC	0.68	0.73	0.72	0.68	0.70
A	TCA	0.67	0.74	0.53	0.58	0.54
At	TCA	0.69	0.74	0.51	0.52	0.49
T	TCA	0.83	0.78	0.62	0.48	0.53

The most obvious conclusions from the readings we have is that the open sourced and massively used sentiment analysis toolboxes provided by Python and Java do not work as well for Toxicity, as they do for Attacks and Aggression. Support Vector Machine's accuracy predictions are considerably good as seen in Table 11 albeit having the largest overheads and taking the longest time. Finally, the accuracy readings over the different 7 class sets in Table 12 show generally improved accuracies on combining classes proving that Multi-class aggregates do on an average perform better than single classes. Lastly, the F1 readings over the different class sets show a slight improvement of over that of those in Table 1 F1 performances from Karan et al.'s (2018) [19] experiment.

Table 7. Combined classed metric averages indicating each unique class best predicting its own class, the best being at 0.84 (AggAtt, AggTox, AttTox and ALL predicting Aggression Class Average).

D	C	Ac	ROC	P	R	F1
AAt	ACA	0.84	0.78	0.64	0.45	0.51
AT	ACA	0.84	0.79	0.66	0.44	0.51
AtT	ACA	0.84	0.79	0.66	0.44	0.51
AtT	AtCA	0.84	0.78	0.67	0.44	0.52
ALL	ACA	0.84	0.79	0.65	0.45	0.51
AT	TCA	0.84	0.79	0.67	0.45	0.53
ALL	TCA	0.83	0.79	0.66	0.46	0.52
AtT	TCA	0.83	0.79	0.66	0.46	0.52
AAt	AtCA	0.83	0.78	0.63	0.49	0.53
AT	AtCA	0.83	0.78	0.67	0.43	0.51
AAt	TCA	0.83	0.78	0.62	0.49	0.53
ALL	AtCA	0.82	0.78	0.66	0.44	0.51
AT	AC	0.69	0.72	0.73	0.64	0.67
AtT	AC	0.69	0.72	0.73	0.64	0.67
ALL	AC	0.69	0.72	0.73	0.64	0.67
AAt	AC	0.69	0.73	0.73	0.70	0.71
AtT	TC	0.69	0.72	0.72	0.61	0.65
AAt	TC	0.69	0.71	0.72	0.61	0.65
AT	TC	0.69	0.71	0.72	0.61	0.65
ALL	TC	0.69	0.71	0.72	0.61	0.65
AAt	AtC	0.68	0.71	0.73	0.63	0.66
AtT	AtC	0.68	0.71	0.73	0.63	0.66
AT	AtC	0.68	0.71	0.73	0.63	0.66
ALL	AtC	0.68	0.71	0.73	0.63	0.66

Table 8. Best model performances over classes.

M	C	MaxAcc
SVCL	MC/MCA	0.86
SVCG	TC	0.86
LRl	MC/AtCA	0.86
RF	MC/MCA/ACA	0.86
RF6	MC/AtCA	0.86
ML3	MC/AtCA/ACA	0.86
KN5	MC/ACA	0.86
BNB	MC	0.86
GNB	ACA	0.84

Table 9. Worst model performances over classes.

M	C	MinAcc
SVCL	MCA	0.86
SVCG	AtCA	0.79
LRl	AtC/TC	0.66 / 0.68
RFC	AC/TC/AtC	0.67 / 0.69
RF6	AC/TC/AtC	0.69
ML3	AC/TC/AtC	0.69
KN5	A/AtC	0.65
BNB	MCA	0.81
GNB	A/At	0.64 / 0.66

Table 10. Total Average model performances over all classes.

M	Ac	ROC	P	R	F1
BNB	0.73	0.75	0.62	0.47	0.50
GNB	0.68	0.74	0.63	0.53	0.56
KN5	0.70	0.72	0.62	0.54	0.56
LRl	0.75	0.76	0.70	0.53	0.58
ML3	0.76	0.76	0.67	0.54	0.58
RF	0.71	0.75	0.64	0.52	0.56
RF6	0.75	0.76	0.67	0.54	0.58
SVCG	0.80	0.75	0.72	0.66	0.66
SVCL	0.80	0.72	0.74	0.44	0.52

Table 11. Total average metrics over all class performances, SVC being the most accurate overall.

M	A	AAt	AT	ALL	At	AtT	T
BNB	0.65	0.67	0.82	0.78	0.68	0.83	0.68
GNB	0.63	0.73	0.73	0.72	0.58	0.73	0.61
KN5	0.65	0.76	0.76	0.76	0.60	0.76	0.63
LRl	0.66	0.78	0.77	0.78	0.74	0.78	0.74
ML3	0.72	0.77	0.78	0.78	0.74	0.78	0.73
RF	0.71	0.73	0.74	0.74	0.66	0.73	0.68
RF6	0.74	0.73	0.78	0.78	0.73	0.78	0.73
SVCG	0.78	0.82	0.81	0.81	0.77	0.82	0.79
SVCL	0.85	0.85	0.85	0.68	0.85	0.69	0.85

Table 12. Average model accuracy performances of all the different classes.

M	A	AAt	AT	ALL	At	AtT	T
BNB	0.65	0.67	0.82	0.78	0.68	0.83	0.68
GNB	0.63	0.73	0.73	0.72	0.58	0.73	0.61
KN5	0.65	0.76	0.76	0.76	0.60	0.76	0.63
LRl	0.66	0.78	0.77	0.78	0.74	0.78	0.74
ML3	0.72	0.77	0.78	0.78	0.74	0.78	0.73
RF	0.71	0.73	0.74	0.74	0.66	0.73	0.68
RF6	0.74	0.73	0.78	0.78	0.73	0.78	0.73
SVCG	0.78	0.82	0.81	0.81	0.77	0.82	0.79
SVCL	0.85	0.85	0.85	0.68	0.85	0.69	0.85

Table 13. Average model F1 performance of all classes.

M	A	AAt	AT	ALL	At	AtT	T
BNB	0.44	0.45	0.60	0.58	0.43	0.59	0.43
GNB	0.54	0.58	0.58	0.58	0.53	0.58	0.55
KN5	0.54	0.59	0.58	0.58	0.53	0.59	0.53
LRl	0.65	0.59	0.58	0.58	0.54	0.59	0.55
ML3	0.54	0.60	0.60	0.60	0.57	0.60	0.57
RF	0.55	0.56	0.56	0.56	0.55	0.56	0.55
RF6	0.57	0.57	0.59	0.59	0.56	0.60	0.57
SVCG	0.74	0.64	0.59	0.59	0.73	0.59	0.74
SVCL	0.44	0.44	0.44	0.74	0.44	0.73	0.42

6 Conclusions

It is worth noting that the Karan et al.'s (2018) [19] experiment's F1 measures of 0.70, 0.71, 0.75 reported from the literature within Table 1 are comparable to the corresponding F1 measures of 0.74, 0.73, 0.74 from this paper as shown in Table 13. The slightly improved differences (apart from Toxicity) can be accounted for by considering the slight variation in the number of records and model implementation limitations and differences (packages used, parameters, etc.). The main findings showed that the open sourced and massively used sentiment analysis toolboxes for the English language provided by Python and Java work better for Attacking and Aggressive language, compared to general Toxic language. Using a single class from a single toolbox does not perform as reliably as Multi-class aggregates of the toolboxes which provide on average much-improved performance results. Finally, Support Vector Machines take the longest time and consume the largest overheads but give a much more reliable accuracy prediction.

7 Challenges

Identifiable challenges as discussed by Kumar, A. and Jaiswal, [21] in ' Systemic literature review of sentiment analysis on Twitter using soft computing techniques', are mostly to do with context behind the language such as; multiple racial or homophobic slurs, racism, sarcasm and irony detection, slang, different mixed up languages within a word or a sentence, the same word having two difference meanings depending on the text origin or user's native slang perchance, multi-modal inferences, misclassification of words and their meanings. Other challenges include mining, analyzing and classifying sentiments directly from web data is challenging as effective feature selection is computationally hard. The tools and software are useable and affordable only by organizations (both private and government) but currently unavailable to generic users for assisting intelligent and personalized data analysis. Most of the work in the field of SA majorly ponders on polarity detection and classification. Analyzing negated expressions and man-made words and expressions for such informal and mashed-up web content has become altogether a very challenging task in the area of sentiment analysis.

As such, hate detection models can be used to flag comments for human moderation, following the human-in-the-loop paradigm [17] as even the best model struggles in "boundary cases" where also a human would struggle to determine if a comment is hateful or not (e.g., when more contextual information is needed to judge) as the performance of hate detection models deteriorates over time. Automatic hate speech detection systems need to keep up the changing of attitudes towards topics over time and historical context as well. A situation similar to the statues standing for hundreds of years now deemed offensive since the #BlackLivesMatter movement and thus recently taken down. Another remaining challenge is that automatic hate speech detection needs a closed-loop system; individuals are aware that it is happening, and actively try to evade detection and find loopholes, thus a regular feedback in the system is mandatory.

The haters will, of course, keep trying till the end of time itself. Given all the challenges that remain, there is a need for more research on this problem within both technical and practical matters constantly and ubiquitously.

8 Future Work

Research still needs more unique solutions to counteract the actual spread of online harm and understand its taxonomy in depth [41]. Today there are many projects, hunting down and mitigating hate (Hatebase since 2013) [14], or provide a positive mental well-being (Kooth, 2021) [20], via empathic technology; which is a beautiful use of machines aiding humans and towards which the aim of this particular research is: to contribute towards detecting and insightfully arbitrating hate speech. This is still an extremely challenging task as the literature reviews and journal publishing show. Hate-speech really should be flagged like spam, and can be used not only by social media platforms, but also law enforcement agencies, consulates, or the Home Office and businesses and academic administration offices.

Aspect [37] and context-based sentiment analysis research [22] avenues lead to a clearer and better understanding of the intent in any comment, for marketing (opinion mining) and crime-solving [11] and as suggested in the introduction, more focus to prevent unnecessary social media instigated death in the form of suicide and genocide.

Sequential Pattern Mining techniques for predicting hate-speech path trends within forum based social media discussions will also be used to harness a possibility of a viral hateful trajectory incitement prediction by following the pattern along the timeline like Olteanu, A. et al. [26] and Paul, D. et al's election study [29]. The next step with this research intended here is to use Markov Chains models to assess the when combined features aggregate scores begin to peak, implying a conversation to be getting more inciteful. The direction of this research will be to focus on using Sequential Pattern Mining techniques for predicting hate-speech path trends within forum based social media discussions will also be used to harness a possibility of a viral harmful trajectory prediction by following patterns of time scale using temporal abstraction. A similar approach was also used to study the communication flow to understand how evaluated politeness, sentiment and emotions of comments posted by the developer interacted in the presence of impolite and negative comments (and vice versa) [26, 28]. The time data (UTC) within the present chosen datasets will be used to harness a possibility of a viral harmful trajectory prediction by following patterns of time scale.

Röttger, P et al. (2021) [35] have also introduced HateCheck, https://hatecheck.ai/; a suite providing extremely reliable functional tests for hate speech detection models providing 29 model functionalities, covering 11 languages; motivated by a complete review of previous hate speech research considering both practical and academic applications of hate speech detection models and a series of interviews with civil society stakeholders [35, 41]. Using the above model samples and research direction, the aim will be to improve the scoring received on the Wikipedia Assertive, Aggression and Toxicity datasets using open sources toolboxes, the results of which have been demonstrated above.

Using a hybrid accurate classifier, with a more holistic approach of a quick surface pre-sifted multi-class selection, (initial trial review pilot test run using the sentiment toolboxes presented here) we may be able interpret Toxicity more accurately. Thus, the next step in this experiment of combining the findings of the results in Table 12 of using multi-classes and combination feature traits, in conjunction with a transformer model, such as BERT-based (Bidirectional Encoder Representations from Transformers developed at Google in 2018) [9, 46], to finetune a pre-trained transformer similar to HateBERT and DistilBERT models [4, 36] on a dynamically generated hate dataset and evaluating on comparison against the best scoring HateCheck benchmark.

The final hybrid research hypothesis is then to test the speed of trajectory detection and mitigation of a particular aggressive, attacking and toxic stance. The underlying weaponised nuance of that online harmful speech would be finally tested on a live comment text data block online, and moderated using congruent communication over apt counter-speech. Thus, web scraping technology and live data testing to detect and police a sinister trajectory is also part of the future plans.

Acknowledgements. Sincerely grateful to the EPSRC Funded DTP PhD in Computer Science, Machine Learning studentship program (Full time) since October 1st 2019 with the The Intelligent Data Analysis Research Group (https://ida-research.net/) at Brunel University. Especially indebted to my Primary and Secondary supervisors, Dr Stephen Swift and Dr Allan Tucker respectively and my Research Development Advisor, Professor Steve Counsell. Last but not the least, I truly appreciate the ongoing heartfelt support and encouragement my brilliant family, cohort peers and dear friends endlessly offer.

References

1. Ahmad, I.S., Bakar, A.A., Yaakub, M.R.: A review of feature selection in sentiment analysis using information gain and domain specific ontology. Int. J. Adv. Comput. Res. **9**, 283–292 (2019)
2. Allahyari, M., et al.: A brief survey of text mining: classification, clustering and extraction techniques (2017)
3. Brown, A.: What is hate speech? Part 1: the myth of hate. Law Philos. **36**(4), 419–468 (2017)
4. Caselli, T., Basile, V., Mitrovic, J., Granitzer, M.: HateBERT: retraining BERT for abusive language detection in English. arXiv:2010.12472 (2021)
5. Celik, Y., Talo, M., Yildirim, O., Karabatak, M., Acharya, U.: Automated invasive ductal carcinoma detection based using deep transfer learning with whole-slide images. Pattern Recogn. Lett. **133**, 232–239 (2020)
6. Chen, Y., Skiena, S.: Building sentiment lexicons for all major languages. In: Proceedings of the 52nd Annual Meeting of the Association for Computational Linguistics, ACL 2014, pp. 383–389. Association for Computational Linguistics (ACL) (2014)
7. Commission for Countering Extremism: Statistical summary of responses from our call for evidence (2019)
8. De Smedt, T., Daelemans, W.: Pattern for Python. J. Mach. Learn. Res. **13**(1), 2063–2067 (2012)
9. Devlin, J., Chang, M.-W., Lee, K., Google, K. T.: Language, A.I.: BERT: pre-training of deep bidirectional transformers for language understanding (2019). https://github.com/tensorflow/tensor2tensor
10. Eatwell, R.: Community cohesion and cumulative extremism in contemporary Britain. Polit. Q. **77**, 204–216 (2006)
11. El-Halees, A., Elyezj, N.: Investigating crimes using text mining and network analysis. Int. J. Comput. Appl. **126**, 19–25 (2015)
12. Feldman, R., Dagan, I.: Knowledge Discovery in Textual databases (KDT) (1995)
13. Fortuna, P., Soler-Company, J., Wanner, L.: How well do hate speech, toxicity, abusive and offensive language classification models generalize across datasets? Inf. Process. Manage. **58**(3), 102524 (2021)
14. Hatebase | The sentinel project (2013). https://thesentinelproject.org/project/Hatebase/
15. HateLab research featured on ITV news special report – HateLab (2020). https://hatelab.net/2020/03/03/Hatelab-Research-Featured-On-ITV-News-Special-Report/
16. Ho, V.A., et al.: Emotion recognition for vietnamese social media text. In: Nguyen, L.-M., Phan, X.-H., Hasida, K., Tojo, S. (eds.) PACLING 2019. CCIS, vol. 1215, pp. 319–333. Springer, Singapore (2020). https://doi.org/10.1007/978-981-15-6168-9_27
17. Holzinger, A.: Interactive machine learning or health informatics: when do we need the human-in-the-loop? Brain Inf. **3**(2), 119–131 (2016)
18. Hutto, C.J., Gilbert, E.: "Vader: a parsimonious rule-based model for sentiment analysis of social media text. In: Proceedings of the 8th International Conference on Weblogs and Social Media, ICWSM 2014, pp. 216–225 (2014)
19. Karan, M., Snajder, J.: Cross-domain detection of abusive language online. In: Proceedings of the 2nd Workshop on Abusive Language Online (ALW2), pp. 132–137. Association For Computational Linguistics, Brussels (2018)
20. Kooth. https://www.kooth.com/. Accessed 01 Aug 2022
21. Kumar, A., Jaiswal, A.: Systematic literature review of sentiment analysis on Twitter using soft computing techniques. Concurrency Comput. Pract. Experience **32**(1), e5107 (2020)
22. Kumar, A., Garg, G.: Systematic literature review on context-based sentiment analysis in social multimedia. Multimed. Tools Appl. **79**, 15349–15380 (2020)

23. Loria, S.: TextBlob documentation. Release 0.15, 2 (2018)
24. Manning, C.D., Surdeanu, M., Bauer, J., Finkel, J., Bethard, S.J., Mcclosky, D.: The stanford CoreNLP natural language processing toolkit (2014)
25. Müller, K., Schwarz, C.: Fanning the flames of hate: social media and hate crime. Elsevier (2017)
26. Olteanu, A., Castillo, C., Boy, J., Varshney, K.R.: The effect of extremist violence on hateful speech online (2018)
27. Online Harms Paper. https://Www.Gov.Uk/Government/Consultations/Online-Harms-White-Paper/Online-Harms-White-Paper. Accessed 01 Aug 2022
28. Ortu, M., Conversano, C., Marchesi, M., Tonelli, R., Counsell, S., Destefanis, G.: Describing software developers affectiveness through Markov chain models. Electron. J. Appl. Stat. Anal. **13**, 1–35 (2020)
29. Paul, D., Li, F., Teja, M.K., Yu, X., Frost, R.: Compass: spatio temporal sentiment analysis of US election what twitter says! In: Proceedings of the ACM SIGKDD International Conference on Knowledge Discovery and Data Mining, pp. 1585–1594. Association for Computing Machinery (2017)
30. Pedregosa, F., et al.: Scikit-learn: machine learning in python. J. Mach. Learn. Res. **12**, 2825–2830 (2011)
31. Priegue, L.B.: Intro to Stanford's CoreNLP for Pythoners, CoreNLP_Tutorial. Github Repository (2020). https://Github.Com/Laurabravopriegue/Corenlp_Tutorial, https://Towardsdatascience.Com/Intro-To-Stanfords-Corenlp-And-Java-For-Python-Programmers-C2586215aab6
32. Qi, P., Dozat, T., Zhang, Y., Manning, C.D.: Universal dependency parsing from scratch. In: Proceedings of the CoNLL 2018 Shared Task: Multilingual Parsing from Raw Text to Universal Dependencies, pp. 160–170 (2018)
33. Research: Detox/Data Release - Meta.wikimedia.org. https://Meta.Wikimedia.Org/Wiki/Research:Detox/Data_Release
34. Reynders, D.: 6th Evaluation of the Code of Conduct (2021)
35. Röttger, P., Vidgen, B., Nguyen, D., Waseem, Z., Margetts, H., Pierrehumbert, J.B.: Hatecheck: functional tests for hate speech detection models. arXiv preprint arXiv:2012.15606 (2020)
36. Sanh, V., Debut, L., Chaumond, J., Wolf, T.: DistilBERT, a distilled version of BERT: smaller, faster, cheaper and lighter (2020). https://github.com/huggingface/transformers
37. Sarno, R., Fatihah, C., Faisal, E.: Aspect based sentiment analysis: a systematic literature review. J. Appl. Intell. Syst. **5**, 8–22 (2020)
38. Shah, A.: The relationship between general population suicide rates and the internet: a cross-national study. Suicide Life-Threat. Behav. **40**(2), 146–150 (2010)
39. Tong, L., et al.: Cost-sensitive boosting pruning trees for depression detection on Twitter. IEEE Trans. Affective Comput. (2022)
40. Vidgen, B., Harris, A., Nguyen, D., Tromble, R., Hale, S., Margetts, H.: Challenges and frontiers in abusive content detection, pp. 80–93 (2019)
41. Vidgen, B., et al.: Introducing CAD: the contextual abuse dataset. In: Proceedings of the 2021 Conference of the North American Chapter of the Association for Computational Linguistics: Human Language Technologies, pp. 2289–2303. Association for Computational Linguistics (2021)
42. Wankhade, M., Rao, A.C.S., Kulkarni, C.: A survey on sentiment analysis methods, applications, and challenges. Artif. Intell. Rev. **55**, 5731–5780 (2022). https://doi.org/10.1007/s10462-022-10144-1
43. Waseem, Z., Davidson, T., Warmsley, D., Weber, I.: Understanding abuse: a typology of abusive language detection subtasks (2017)

44. Wulczyn, E., Thain, N., Dixon, L.: Wikipedia Detox. Figshare (2017). https://doi.org/10.6084/M9.Figshare.4054689
45. Wulczyn, E., Thain, N., Dixon, L.: Ex machina: personal attacks seen at scale. In: Proceedings of the 26th International Conference on World Wide Web, WWW 2017, pp. 1391–1399 (2016)
46. Xiao, H. (2018). https://github.com/hanxiao/bert-as-service
47. Xu, L., Jiang, C., Wang, J., Yuan, J., Ren, Y.: Information security in big data: privacy and data mining. IEEE Access **2**, 1–28 (2014). https://doi.org/10.1109/Access.2014.2362522

Workshop on New Frontiers in Mining Complex Patterns (NFMCP 2022)

New Frontiers in Mining Complex Patterns (NFMCP 2022)

The analysis of complex data represents the new frontier in data mining and knowledge discovery. There are several emerging technologies and applications where complex patterns can be extracted: examples are blogs, event or log data, medical data, spatio-temporal data, social networks, mobility data, sensor data, and streams. The abundance, variety, and velocity of data pose new challenges which can't be easily resolved with traditional data mining techniques. This asks for new contributions which allow for efficiently identifying patterns and enable effective decision making.

The Tenth International Workshop on New Frontiers in Mining Complex Patterns (NFMCP 2022) was held in Grenoble in conjunction with the European Conference on Machine Learning and Principles and Practice of Knowledge Discovery in Databases (ECML-PKDD 2022) on September 19, 2022. It was aimed at bringing together researchers and practitioners of data mining and knowledge discovery interested in the advances and latest developments in mining complex data. The workshop is establishing itself as a premier event with this goal.

The workshop received 15 submitted papers, of which seven papers were accepted for presentation at the workshop. These papers went through a rigorous review process in which each paper was reviewed by at least three reviewers in a single-blind manner. The individual contributions illustrate advanced data mining techniques which preserve the informative richness of complex data and allow for efficient and effective identification of complex information units present in such data.

We would like to thank all the authors who submitted papers for publication and all the workshop participants and speakers. We are also grateful to the members of the Program Committee for their excellent work in reviewing submitted and revised contributions with expertise and patience. A special thanks is due to both the ECML-PKDD workshop chairs and the ECML-PKDD organizers who made the event possible. We would like to acknowledge the support of the Apulia Region through the REFIN project "Metodi per l'ottimizzazione delle reti di distribuzione di energia e per la pianificazione di interventi manutentivi ed evolutivi" (CUP H94I20000410008, Grant no. 7EDD092A).

October 2022

Elio Masciari
Paolo Mignone
Zbigniew Ras
Ettore Ritacco

Organization

Program Chairs

Elio Masciari   ICAR-CNR, Italy
Paolo Mignone   University of Bari Aldo Moro, Italy
Zbigniew Ras   University of North Carolina at Charlotte, USA
Ettore Ritacco   ICAR-CNR, Italy

Program Committee

Giuseppina Andresini   University of Bari Aldo Moro, Italy
Annalisa Appice   University of Bari Aldo Moro, Italy
Michelangelo Ceci   University of Bari Aldo Moro, Italy
Roberto Corizzo   American University, USA
Claudia Diamantini   Marche Polytechnic University, Italy
Hadi Fanaee-T   Halmstad University, Sweden
Bettina Fazzinga   ICAR-CNR, Italy
Stefano Ferilli   University of Bari Aldo Moro, Italy
Dragi Kocev   Jožef Stefan Institute, Slovenia
Angelica Liguori   University of Calabria, Italy
Vincenzo Pasquadibisceglie   University of Bari Aldo Moro, Italy
Ruggero G. Pensa   University of Turin, Italy
Gianvito Pio   University of Bari Aldo Moro, Italy
Francesco S. Pisani   ICAR-CNR, Italy
Gennaro Vessio   University of Bari Aldo Moro, Italy

Multi-modal Terminology Management

Corpora, Data Models, and Implementations in TermStar

Enrico Giai[(✉)], Nicola Poeta, and David Turnbull

STAR7, S.p.A., Alessandria, Italy
enrico.giai@star-7.com

Abstract. Terminology is a key part of the translation process. Nonetheless, the benefits of implementing a terminology management workflow using specialist tools and processes is sometimes disregarded, as the benefits in terms of ROI are not always easy to evaluate. As a result, the use of spreadsheets and other inappropriate tools leads to fragmented and inefficient terminology management processes.

In this paper we set out to describe an efficient terminology management workflow which has been developed for real terminology projects. We will also assess the benefits of implementing a proper terminology management workflow where all stakeholders (terminologists, linguists, authors, and end users) are involved. We will highlight the benefits of using a Terminology Management System (TMS) such as TermStar, which can make use of parallel corpora and collaboration functions to streamline the entire process, from terminological extraction to glossary approval and maintenance.

Keywords: Terminology management · TMS

1 Introduction

Computer-Assisted Translation (CAT) has been at the core of the localisation industry for over three decades. Using CAT tools, linguists can translate more efficiently thanks to Translation Memory (TM) suggestions: CAT tools can leverage TMs to pre-translate content that has been translated in the past or offer 'fuzzy match' suggestions for similar source texts. Consequently, texts translated using a CAT tool are usually more consistent and can be delivered in less time.

While the importance of TMs in terms of quality assurance and economic profit is self-explanatory and can easily be calculated, the added value of setting up a TermBase (TB) is not always evident.

A TB can be defined a "a database comprising information about special language concepts and terms designated to represent these concepts, along with associated conceptual, term-related, and administrative information." [3]. This definition is based on the strict definition of 'term' as being "an expression that designates a particular concept within a given subject field" [9]. As such, it comes as no surprise that assessing the benefits of investing in terminological work is a hard task: not all organisations make

© The Author(s), under exclusive license to Springer Nature Switzerland AG 2023
I. Koprinska et al. (Eds.): ECML PKDD 2022 Workshops, CCIS 1752, pp. 219–226, 2023.
https://doi.org/10.1007/978-3-031-23618-1_14

use of highly specialised terminology in their texts, especially in the case of marketing and e-commerce, where the need for technical terminology is scarce.

In this context, the concept of 'termhood' (i.e., the degree to which a term is justified being included in a TB [10]) can be broadened to include a range of words that are vital to corporate communication, despite not being part of a specialised language. These may include product names, organisation and entity names, slogans, frequently used words, or words that appear in sensitive contexts, to name just a few.

Another pain point is the format in which the TB is presented. Commonly, terminological entries are not stored in specialised Terminology Management Systems (TMSs); rather, they are collected in text document lists or in spreadsheets, at best. This is a great obstacle when it comes to organising and sharing terminological assets.

At STAR7 we are aware of the value of a well-structured, centralised TB. Ideally, this can be accessed by all stakeholders in different modes. STAR Group's TermStar has been acknowledged as a TMS that can meet the needs of everyone in the information lifecycle: terminologists, who can take advantage of the highly customisable data model; linguists, who can use TermStar in STAR's CAT tool Transit to have morphology-based term suggestions and use the right terms for each context; authors, who can use TermStar in their authoring tool; and clients, who can access the terminology online via WebTerm – STAR7's solution for online terminology management.

In this paper, we will present STAR7's terminology management workflows and tools aimed at extracting terminology from bilingual corpora, adapting our data models to best fit each term entry, and facilitating the validation and distribution processes for all stakeholders.

2 Related Work

The importance of Terminology Management has been clear since the early days of modern terminology studies as pioneered by Wüster [14]. The onomasiological approach is still a founding pillar of terminology work, and data models in terminography have been shaped to accommodate this concept [10, 11].

While these assumptions are still valid, in recent years the focus has shifted towards a more pragmatic approach. The role of the Corporate Terminologist [11] has surged, and a question has been raised with it: what is a term in a corporate context?

Warburton [10] broadens Pavel's definition [6] of term to "any lexical unit that might help a potential consumer of the termbase". The Terminology for Large Organizations Consortium (TerminOrgs) builds on that by stating:

"To support the communicative aims of large organisations, the notion of a 'term' extends beyond the conventional view to include any expression that, if it is managed according to the methods outlined in this document, brings some benefit to the organization such as improved communication and reduced translation costs. This includes, sometimes, words from general language, marketing slogans, short sentence fragments, and so forth." [9].

Lexicology and its lexicographic applications have developed significantly over recent decades [4], thanks to corpus research [8] and increasingly powerful technology. However, terminology management in CAT tools often plays second fiddle to translation memory management. Terminology can be confined to easy to use but poorly organised TBs. Specialised terminology is often considered monosemic, but even the most specific term needs contextual details. Technology can offer suitable solutions, such as structured entries, examples, definitions and images.

Despite the high number of TMSs available, not all of them are flexible enough to allow the end user to harness the benefits of the system, especially when used with a CAT tool [5]. TermStar has been praised for its highly customisable data model, which can be adapted to the glossary's needs and even used for lexicography work [7].

3 Methodology

While previous literature on the topic has been the basis for our enquiry, the findings shown in this paper are the result of processes developed empirically over the years while working on actual terminology projects. These involved several different domains, including automotive and agriculture, luxury and fashion, finance and banking, sport and fitness, and pharma. Overall, STAR7 manages over 400 termbases in TermStar and 150 termbases in other TMSs, counting more than 200,000 data records ranging from bilingual to 36-language entries.

Text types also vary accordingly: owner's manuals, service manuals, marketing leaflets, product catalogues, websites, financial reports, and many other text types were used as source texts in the terminology extraction process.

Despite the different nature of these contents, the workflows described in this paper can still be considered valid. The process has been validated internally and well received by all stakeholders. Improvements have been made based on clients' and linguists' feedback.

We have identified five steps which contribute to successfully completing a terminology project. These are described in further detail in the next chapter.

4 Results

4.1 Preliminary Analysis

The first step consists of analysing the scope of the project. This can be done by considering the elements listed below with their reasoning:

- Domain: Each domain has its own lexicon and specialised terminology. Determining the domain helps in limiting the scope of the project.
- Text type: Identifying the text type helps in setting the termhood level for the project. The termhood bar for technical documentation might be higher than that for marketing material.
- Languages: Helps in identifying the number of language resources to be involved in the project.
- Budget & Timeframe: Budget is key in determining the resources that can be spent on glossary creation in terms of number of records and data granularity.

- Reference material: Parallel corpora facilitate the terminology extraction process, enabling linguists to extract terms that are actually in use. When not available, open-source corpora can be used. Existing glossaries can also be used as a basis for the terminology work.
- Final audience: Considering the end users is key to understanding how the glossary is to be published. If the glossary is for linguists, it can be implemented in a CAT tool; if the end user is the client, it can be published online.

4.2   Data Model Setup

Once the project scope is clear, the next step is to understand which data model to adopt. TermStar offers a high level of customisation – the result of lexicography and terminography studies.

A TermStar terminological card follows the traditional onomasiological approach, in that each card represents a single concept. However, TermStar's data record structure allows for a deeper level of content organisation: each term can have sub-entries defined as abbreviations, synonyms, irregular forms, alternatives and disallowed terms (Fig. 1).

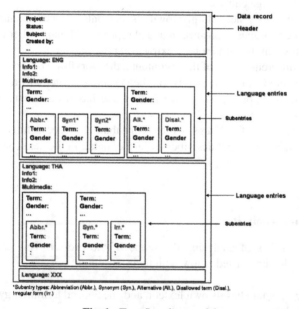

Fig. 1. TermStar data model

This approach is deeply embedded into Transit, whose morphological search capabilities makes it possible for terms to be recognised in texts even if they appear declined or conjugated, while being classified in their base form in the glossary.

In addition, each language entry can be classified using a number of different attributes, including status, data source, definition, definition source, gender, remark, subject, part of speech, and many others. This level of detail is particularly useful to clarify the use of homographs or to distinguish term use based on context (e.g., one term should be used in technical documents and another in marketing texts). Pictures can also be inserted to better clarify complex terms (Fig. 2).

Fig. 2. TermStar data record sample

4.3 Terminology Extraction

The terminology extraction step is the most time-consuming part of the process. It can be divided into three steps: (1) source term and (2) target term extraction; and (3) term tagging and consolidation.

Based on budget and time constraints, the terminologist can agree with the customer the number of terms to be extracted and the level of additional information that can be collected.

Despite the number of (semi-)automatic terminology extraction tools on the market, their effectiveness is still far from satisfactory. Most tools are based on frequency and stop-words rules, and even if contexts are offered for each candidate term, the risk of not grasping the correct context or not considering a term in its entirety is high.

For these reasons, source term extraction is usually performed manually, by reading the source texts in their entirety and extracting terms in the process. For us, this is the most effective approach, since terms are not extracted in isolation, but directly from the texts. This also makes it easier to collect context and usage notes.

The whole process takes place in the CAT tool: the terminologist can import source files and create an empty termbase, which will be used for the entire workflow. Terms will be added to the TB, which can be configured to ease the work of the terminologist (e.g., by setting input verification rules to maintain consistency in the attributes used for each label).

While reading the texts and extracting source terms, the terminologist is able to fine-tune the termhood level and get the most out of the source material. The following table lists possible terms that can be included in a selection of domains (Table 1).

Table 1. Possible terms in a glossary based on selected domains

Domain/text type	Candidate terms
Luxury & Fashion	Product names, colour names, taglines
Law/Finance & Banking	Law names, entity and body names
Corporate communication	Division names, corporate role names
IT & Software	Button names, menu items
Technical documentation	Acronyms, abbreviated forms, technology names

Once the source terms have been extracted, the CAT tool can be used to leverage existing parallel corpora (TMs) to facilitate the work of translators. Linguists will be able to run 'concordance searches' to look up source terms in the TM and get a list of already translated sentences. From there, translators can extract any matching term in the target language and insert it in the data record in just a few clicks.

4.4   Terminology Validation

Once the glossary is completed, the validation step can take place. This is an essential part of the workflow: without subject-matter expert validation, the glossary cannot be considered as complete.

Usually, validation is performed by clients, or by different client branches around the world. Performing such a task in a spreadsheet would not be efficient. For this reason, STAR7 offers clients a terminology validation process in WebTerm – TermStar's web interface. With it, clients are able to see the glossary without the need for a TMS and can easily add comments and suggestions that can be read by the terminologist and implemented in real time.

WebTerm can also be offered in 'read and write mode', meaning that clients can make changes directly in each data record and changes are immediately available for all stakeholders (Fig. 3).

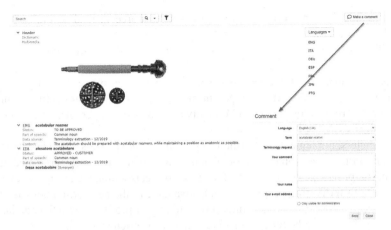

Fig. 3. WebTerm7 comment function

At the end of the validation step, any 'status' metadata associated with approved terms should be updated consequently.

4.5 Termbase Deployment and Update

Finally, the termbase can be deployed to all stakeholders. When using STAR7's technologies, the TermStar TB can be accessed during the entire information lifecycle:

- Technical authors using selected authoring tools can connect to the TermStar database, or look up terms in WebTerm;
- Linguists using Transit as their CAT tool have direct access to TermStar;
- Clients and reviewers using WebTerm can look up terms, insert comments, make terminology requests, or even edit data records.

Terminology is never static, but it constantly evolves. Technological changes in technical texts, new products launched in marketing material, and changes in term use and preferences should be all recorded as updates in the termbase. For this reason, it is vital to plan a TB update schedule that, based on the available budget and expected workloads, can either be triggered for each new project, for any project which may be particularly important or belonging to a new domain, or on a monthly/half-yearly basis.

5 Conclusion

In this paper we have described in detail a standardised process for implementing a terminology workflow for all use cases. A glossary shared among all stakeholders (clients, authors, linguists, reviewers, etc.) is beneficial in terms of:

- consistency, as a centralised termbase helps to reduce the use of variants;
- prescription, as non-allowed words can be noted;

- time, as linguists can look up terms in a single source instead of multiple, often unreliable sources;
- overall quality, as the corporate terminology will be used instead of general words.

That said, quantifying the benefits in terms of time and money is difficult, as not all texts may contain the terms mapped in the glossary. General productivity can also depend on external factors such as TM quality and linguists' experience and know-how in the subject.

Nonetheless, implementing a terminology management process is still widely recognised as important. We would point out that the fundamental research performed during the TermStar project has laid the basis for further projects within the group. An example of this is the **StarPrinting** project that took advantage of the new terminology management techniques for performing further research on user profiling, with the crucial goal of providing a new and better printing and delivery experience to users.

References

1. Cruse, D.A.: Lexical Semantics. Cambridge University Press, Cambridge (1986)
2. ISO 12616–1:2021: Terminology work in support of multilingual communication—Part 1: Fundamentals of translation-oriented terminography
3. ISO 30042:2019: Management of terminology resources—TermBase eXchange (TBX)
4. Landau, S.: Dictionaries: The Art and Craft of Lexicography, 2nd edn. Cambridge University Press, Cambridge (2001)
5. Magris, M., Musacchio, M.T., Rega, L., Scarpa, F.: Manuale Di Terminologia: Aspetti Teorici, Metodologici E Applicative. Ulrico Hoepli Editore, Milano (2017)
6. Pavel, S., Nolet, D.: Handbook of Terminology. Minister of Public Works and Government Services Canada, Ottawa (2001)
7. Poeta, N.: Terminologia, corpora e contesto negli strumenti di traduzione assistita. In: Collesi, P., Serpente, A., Zanola, M. T.: Terminologie e ontologie. Definizioni e comunicazione fra norma e uso, pp. 87–94. EDUCatt, Milano (2013)
8. Sinclair, J. (ed.): Corpus, Concordance, Collocation. Oxford University Press, Oxford (1991)
9. TerminOrgs.: Terminology Starter Guide. http://www.terminorgs.net/. Accessed 26 Jul 2022
10. Warburton, K.: A practical approach to terminology: developing lexical resources for companies. http://www.ccaps.net/blog/lets-talk-terminology/. Accessed 27 Jul 2022
11. Warburton, K.: The Corporate Terminologist. John Benjamins Publishing Company, Philadelphia (2021)
12. Wright, S.E.: Data categories for terminology management. In: Wright, S.E., Budin, G.: Handbook of Terminology Management, vol. 2, pp. 552–571. John Benjamins Publishing Company, Philadelphia (2001)
13. Wright, S.E.: Terminology management entry structures. In: Wright, S.E., Budin, G.: Handbook of Terminology Management, vol. 2, pp. 572–599. John Benjamins Publishing Company, Philadelphia (2001)
14. Wüster, E.: The Machine Tool – An Interlingual Dictionary of Basic Concepts, Comprising an Alphabetical Dictionary and a Classified Vocabulary with Definitions and Illustrations. Technical Press, London (1968)

Cluster Algorithm for Social Choice

Emanuele d'Ajello, Davide Formica, Elio Masciari, Gaia Mattia,
Arianna Anniciello[(✉)], Cristina Moscariello, Stefano Quintarelli,
and Davide Zaccarella

The 10th Edition of the Workshop New Frontiers in Mining Complex Patterns
(NFMCP) in Conjunction with the European Conference on Machine Learning
and Principles and Practice of Knowledge Discovery in Databases (ECML-PKDD
2022), Grenoble, France
ariannaanniciello@gmail.com

Abstract. In order to overcome the classical methods of judgement, in
the literature there is a lot of material about different methodology and
their intrinsic limitations. One of the most relevant modern model to
deal with votation system dynamics is the Majority Judgement.

It was created with the aim of reducing polarization of the electorate
in modern democracies and not to alienate minorities, thanks to its use
of a highest median rule, producing more informative results than the
existing alternatives. Nonetheless, as shown in the literature, in the case
of multiwinner elections it can lead to scenarios in which minorities,
albeit numerous, are not adequately represented.

For this reason our aim is to implement a clustered version of this
algorithm, in order to mitigate these disadvantages: it creates clusters
taking into account the similarity between the expressed judgements and
then for, each of these created groups, Majority Judgement rule is applied
to return a ranking over the set of candidates. These traits make the
algorithm available for applications in different areas of interest in which
a decisional process is involved.

Keywords: Decision making · Social choice · Cluster · Majority
judgement · K-Medoids

1 Introduction

Voting rules are different and behave differently according to their limitations
or sometimes paradoxal traits. Asking for a more inclusive democracy also represents a modern citizens' quest, but what does exactly it mean? First of all,
we want to underline why a majority voting system embodies the best option
between the classical judgement methods.

Consider three agents who express their binary judgement ("Yes" or "No")
for two statements A, B, $A \wedge B$ and $A \longleftrightarrow B$. Premised-based rule take majority
decisions on A and B and then infers conclusions on the other two propositions.

As shown in the Table 1, results are quite different based on the used rule.

I. Koprinska et al. (Eds.): ECML PKDD 2022 Workshops, CCIS 1752, pp. 227–237, 2023.
https://doi.org/10.1007/978-3-031-23618-1_15

We now focus on Agent 2 case: he's represented in just one of the single proposition (A), and his judgement doesn't agree with the outcome, in the other cases. So, a huge liability of this model could appear: Agent 2 could think about manipulating the outcome, pretending a disagreement for A. The premised model reacts by providing as final outcome on 3 agents' votation a "No" for both $A \land B$ and $A \longleftrightarrow B$, as originally expressed by Agent 2.

Table 1. Three agent case of voting

	A	B	$A \land B$	$A \longleftrightarrow B$
Agent 1	Yes	Yes	Yes	Yes
Agent 2	Yes	No	No	No
Agent 3	No	Yes	No	No
Premised rule	Yes	Yes	Yes	Yes
Majority	Yes	Yes	No	No

In such a way, a strategical approach on voting could lead to a deviation effect, providing as result the best tricker's choice.

Looking at the table, we can also highlight another paradoxal aspect: considering majority-based outcome, the latest two propositions are inconsistent with "Yes" value assigned to both A and B.

This is known as *discursive dilemma* and deals with inconsistency problem in judgement aggregation based on majority rule [10].

Both premised and majority rule present drawbacks, but the latter has one important feature: it doesn't suffer from deficiency shown by the first, so that, if an Agent care about the number of propositions agreeing with his own judgement, then it is always in his best interest to report his true preference. For this reason we focus our attention on majority rule as a transparent asset in decisional process, while trying to deal with its intrinsic problems related to judgement aggregation [11].

Our attempt is not aimed to solve above-mentioned dilemma, rather joining a more refined majority rule (*Majority Judgement*) with cluster approach's advantages in aggregating similar patterns.

2   Majority Judgement

2.1   Formal Aspects

To introduce social choice theory formally, consider a simple decision problem: a collective choice between two alternatives. The first involves imposing some 'procedural' requirements on the relationship between individual votes and social decisions and showing that majority rule is the only aggregation rule satisfying them. May (1952) [9,32] introduced four such requirements for majority voting rule must satisfies:

– **Universal domain**: the domain of admissible inputs of the aggregation rule consists of all logically possible profiles of votes $< v_1, v_2, ..., v_n >$, where each $v_i \in [-1,1]$ (to cope with any level of 'pluralism' in its inputs);
– **Anonimity**: applying any kind of permutation on individual preferences does not affect the outcome (to treat all voters equally), i.e.,

$$f(v_1, v_2, ..., v_n) = f(w_1, w_2, ..., w_n) \qquad (1)$$

– **Neutrality**: each alternative has the same weight and for any admissible profile $< v1, v2, ..., vn >$, if the votes for the two alternatives are reversed, the social decision is reversed too (to treat all alternatives equally), i.e.

$$f(-v_1, -v_2, ..., -v_n) = -f(v_1, v_2, ..., v_n) \qquad (2)$$

– **Positive responsiveness**: For any admissible profile $<v_1, v_2, ..., v_n>$, if some voters change their votes in favour of one alternative (say the first) and all other votes remain the same, the social decision does not change in the opposite direction; if the social decision was a tie prior to the change, the tie is broken in the direction of the change, i.e., if $[w_i > v_i$ for some i and $w_j = v_j$ for all other $j]$ and $f(v_1, v_2, ..., v_n) = 0$ or 1, then $f(w_1, w_2, ..., w_n) = 1$.

The May theorem (Theorem: *"An aggregation rule satisfies universal domain, anonymity, neutrality, and positive responsiveness if and only if it is majority rule"*) provides an argument for the majority rule based on four plausible procedural desires and the theorem helps us characterize other aggregation rules in terms of which desiderata they violate.

But that's with regards to binary choice. Now, we consider a set $N = [1, 2, ..., n]$ of individuals ($n \geq 2$). Let $X = [x, y, z, ...]$ be a set of social alternatives, for example possible policy platforms, election candidates, or other [8]. Each individual $i \in N$ has a preference ordering R_i over these alternatives that rapresents a complete and transitive binary relation on X. For any $x, y \in X$, xR_iy means that individual i weakly prefers x to y. We write xP_iy if xR_iy and not yR_ix ('individual i strictly prefers x to y'), and xI_iy if xR_iy and yR_ix ('individual i is indifferent between x and y'). But we must specify that at the heart of social choice theory is the analysis of preference aggregation [33], understood as the aggregation of several individuals' preference rankings of two or more social alternatives into a single, collective preference ranking (or choice) over these alternatives [7]. In case of many successful alternatives, we need a more sophisticated model to deal with preferences' aggregation [6]. A multi-winner election (V,C,F,k) is defined by a set of voters V expressing preferences over a number of candidates C, and then a voting rule F returns a subset of size k winning candidates. A voting rule can perform its role on different types of ordered preferences, even though the most common refers to a pre-fixed linear order on the alternatives. In most of cases, these are chosen *a priori*.

Formally we denote set of judgements performed by the i-th voter as profile preferences P_i. Each profile contains information about the grade of candidates by voters. The voting rule F associates with every profile P a non-empty subset of winning candidates.

In multi-winner elections more precise traits are required, compared to the ones stated in May's theory [12]. Indeed:

- **Representation**: for each partition of voters

$$V_i \in V \left(\text{with } |V_i| \geq \left\lfloor \frac{n}{k} \right\rfloor \right) \qquad (3)$$

at least one successful candidate is elected from that partition;
- **Proportionality**: for each partition of voters

$$V_i \in V \left(\text{with } |V_i| \geq \left\lfloor \frac{n}{k} \right\rfloor \right) \qquad (4)$$

number of elected candidate is proportional to the partition's size.

An implicit assumption so far has been that preferences are ordinal and not interpersonally comparable: preference orderings contain no information about each individual's strength or about how to compare different individuals' preferences with one another. Statements such as 'Individual 1 prefers alternative x more than Individual 2 prefers alternative y' or 'Individual l prefers a switch from x to y more than Individual 2 prefers a switch from x* to y*' are considered meaningless. In voting contexts, this assumption may be plausible, but in welfare-evaluation contexts-when a social planner seeks to rank different social alternatives in an order of social welfare-the use of richer information may be justified.

2.2   Single-Winner Majority Judgement

In order to describe the majority judgement, we need to use a table that refers to ranking for all the candidates C, by using tuples [5]. Suppose having six possible choices we may use the words: *excellent, very good, good, discrete, bad, very bad*.

So each candidate is described by a bounded set of vote.

In general, letting $\alpha = (\alpha_1, \alpha_2, ..., \alpha_n)$ be a candidate A's set of n grades (written from highest to lowest, $\alpha_i \geq \alpha_{i+1}$ for all i), there is a majority of (at least) $n - k + 1$ for n A's grade to beat most α_k and at least α_{n-k+1}, for all $1 \leq k \leq \frac{(n+1)}{2}$. We call this the (n-k+1) - majority for $[\alpha_k , \alpha_{n-k+1}]$.

As already mentioned any possible ranking tuple that we choose to describe must follow ordering relations.

So the ranking should respect domination: namely, evaluate one candidate above another when that candidate's grades dominate the other's.

The described majority judgement is a single winner system, found comparing recursively median grade between candidates: first, grades are ordered in columns from the highest to the lowest according to the order relation, then the middle column (lower middle if number of grades are even) with the highest grade between candidates'row is selected. If there's a tie, algorithm keeps on discarding grades equal in value to the shared median, until one of the tied candidate is found to have the highest median (Fig. 1). Before describing how it's possible to generalize this single winner system to a multi winner strategy, thanks to the use of clusters, we focus our attention on how these works, analyzing in particular *K-medoids*.

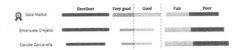

Fig. 1. Example with 5 grades, between the dashed lines it's reported the median grade. Highest occurrences in "Good" determines the winner.

3 Clustering Approach

3.1 How Clusters Work

There's no precise definition of clustering, mostly due to the huge variety in different clustering algorithms. We can state that they share the ability to divide data into groups with some common features. According to some general traits, we can distinguish types of clustering:

1. **Connectivity models**: data points in a sample space exhibits similarity according to the distance between them. Two approaches are equally valid: *bottom-up* where each observation constitutes a group and then pairs of clusters are merged; *top-down*, where observation are included in one cluster and then it's segregated; but in both approaches is not included the possibility of modifying a cluster once created;

2. **Distribution models**: once created a cluster, model check probabilities on observations following a particular distribution. Good performances are not always guaranteed since these models are prone to overfit data if no constraint on complexity is made;

3. **Density models**: areas of higher density are identified and local cluster are there created, while remaining data can be grouped into arbitrary shaped region, with no assumption about da ta distribution; for their flexibility, these models are fit to handle noise better than organizing data on fixed required body.

Since we would like to model clusters that satisfy requirements expressed before, based on pretty fixed structure with no assumption about distribution followed by data, it seems more accurate considering a different class of clustering algorithm known as *centroid models*.

3.2 K-Medoids

Clustering is the process of grouping a set of objects in order to have each similar object to each other in one cluster, that are dissimilar to objects in other clusters.

For our goal, namely selecting winners from a group of candidates, *K-medoids* clustering are used, because medoids are the representative objects that are considered, in order to have a result that belongs to the group of candidates: it is based on the most centrally located object in a cluster, so it is less sensitive to outliers in comparison with the K-means clustering, which is not the best model in our case since it could result in something that is not present in the candidate list due to the fact that is an average-based method rather than median. In fact, the medoid is a data point (unlike the centroid) which has the least total distance to the other members of its cluster.

Another advantage for this choice is that the mean of the data points is a measure that gets highly affected by the extreme points; so, in K-Means algorithm, the centroid may get shifted to a wrong position and hence result in incorrect clustering if the data has outliers because then other points will move away from. On the contrary, the K-Medoids algorithm is the most central element of the cluster, such that its distance from other points is minimum. Thus, K-Medoids algorithm is more robust to outliers and noise than K-Means algorithm.

The K-medoid we use is part of the python sklearn library [13], which is oriented to machine learning. This library supports *partitioning around medoids* (PAM) [2] proposed by Kaufman and Rousseeuw (1990), that is known to be most powerful. The workflow of PAM is described below [1].

The PAM procedure consists of two phases: *BUILD* and *SWAP*:

- In the BUILD phase, primary clustering is performed, during which k objects are successively selected as medoids.
- The SWAP phase is an iterative process in which the algorithm makes attempts to improve some of the medoids. At each iteration of the algorithm, a pair is selected (medoid and non-medoid) such that replacing the medoid with a non-medoid object gives the best value of the objective function (the sum of the distances from each object to the nearest medoid). The procedure for changing the set of medoids is repeated as long as there is a possibility of improving the value of the objective function.

Suppose that n objects having p variables each should be grouped into k ($k < n$) clusters, where k is known. Let us define j-th variable of object i as X_{ij} ($i = 1, ..., n; j = 1, ..., p$). As a dissimilarity measure is used the Euclidean distance, that is defined, between object i and object j, by:

$$d_{ij} = \sqrt{\sum_{a=1}^{p}(X_{ia} - X_{ja})^2} \tag{5}$$

where i and j range from 1 to n. The medoids is selected in this way:

- calculate the Euclidean distance between every pair of all objects;
- calculate $v_j = \sum_{i=1}^{n} \frac{d_{ij}}{\sum_{l=1}^{n} d_{il}}$;
- sort all v_j for $j = 1, ..., n$ in ascending order and select the first k object that have smallest initial medoids value;
- from each object to the nearest medoid we can obtain the initial cluster result;

- calculate the sum of distances from all objects to their medoids;
- update the current medoid in each cluster by replacing with the new medoid, selected minimizing the total distance from a certain object to other objects in its cluster;
- assign each object to the nearest medoid and obtain the cluster result;
- calculate the sum of distance from all objects to their medoids, so if the sum is equal to the previous one, then stop the algorithm; otherwise, go back to the update step.

In our case, prior knowledge about the number of winners is required, and identified clusters are restricted in minimum size that is number of voters on the number of candidates ($\frac{n}{k}$).

3.3 Clustered Majority Judgement

Multi winner majority judgement exploits clustering approach to apply to each group majority judgement [4]. Given k the number of candidates to be elected, algorithm seeks the optimal number of cluster to create.

This ranges from 1 to k and has to satisfy an important additional requirement: once selected a number of clusters, if a tie occurs and so k' vacant seats are left, algorithm is repeated k' times until tie's broken. In case there's no broken tie, fixed number of cluster is changed.

3.4 Algorithm

In order to explain how the algorithm deals with polarization problem, most relevant steps are described in pseudocode and in annotated strides:

1. set the number of winners as maximum number of clusters;
2. cluster are created decreasing the previous maximum number of clusters until the optimal number is not achieved. This number is bound by the size of cluster, that satisfies the following proportion: *number of voters : number of winners = number of voters in one cluster : one winner* (line 8 in pseudocode);
3. the function *winners* calculates the median for every created cluster (line 15 of pseudocode);
4. check that winners from cluster are different between each other (line 29 in pseudocode); in case it's not true (condition="ko" on pseudocode) algorithm goes back to step 2 with a maximum number of cluster equal to number of vacant seats and the proceedings are held until all seats have been filled.

Algorithm 1

Require: $k \geq 0$
Ensure: $n\_winners = (n_1, ..., n_k), k > 1$
   $k \leftarrow number\_winners$
   $max\_cluster \leftarrow k$
   $condition \leftarrow \text{``}ko\text{''}$
   while $condition = \text{``}ko\text{''}$ **do**
      $cluster\_list \leftarrow cluster(vote\_list)$
      for all list_cluster **do**
         $winners\_per\_cluster \leftarrow compute\_winners(cluster)$
         $all\_winners \leftarrow list\_of\_all\_winners(winners\_per\_cluster)$
      end for
      $list\_winner\_distinct = list\_of\_all\_distinct\_winners(all\_winners)$
      $option\_remaining \leftarrow number\_winners - len(list\_winner\_distinct)$
      if $option\_remaining = 0$ **then**
         $condition =' ok'$
      else
         $k \leftarrow option\_remaining$
         $condition \leftarrow' ko'$
      end if
   end while

3.5   Case Studies

In this section, we describe two interesting comparisons of majority judgement (MJ) and clustered majority judgement (CMJ).

Case Study 1: President of the Republic Election In order to test our algorithm, we asked an heterogeneous group of voters to express judgements on a pre-defined list of possible candidates as President of the Republic before the elections took place. This list has been created according to the rumours circulated on that period, creating a bias effect on our results, as it was excluded a possible rielection of Sergio Mattarella.

In spite of it, we focus on how the algorithm has worked in order to balance polarization, returning a subset of winners with size chosen *a priori*, that we may interpret as best solutions for majority of people who took part into the venture.

Input parameters of Clustered Majority Judgement test are *Excellent, Very Good, Good, Acceptable, Poor, To Reject, No Opinion* and the number of winners is set a priori equal to 3. 125 voters took part into this election and the algorithm form three clusters, exactly like the number of winners.

Testing our algorithm on the described election has shown how difference preference has a leverage on judgement aggregation: for example, voters in Cluster 1 are more bound to express "Good" judgement for candidates considered neutral in terms of political ideas, than the cluster 3 in which voters have a tendency in judging neutral ones as "Fair" or "Poor". Cluster 2 has intermediate

Table 2. CMJ results

Cluster	Cluster size	Winner
Cluster 1	65	Mario Draghi
Cluster 2	35	Paolo Gentiloni
Cluster 3	25	Anna Finocchiaro

Table 3. Top 3 of single-winner Majority Judgement applied to voters

Ranking MJ	Candidate
1	Mario Draghi
2	Paolo Gentiloni
3	Emma Bonino

traits and no particular tendency is emphasized. We can compare CMJ results with single-winner MJ ranking, comparing the Tables 2 and 3. The comparison shows different results for the third candidate, highlighting how clustering influences outcome, giving more weight to minorities' judgement.

3.6 Case Study 2: Working Hours per Week

The last case study is a good paradigm for deciding how to manage working hours in the office, given a fixed number of working hours to be done (18 h). In this case, we asked 160 students of University Federico II of Naples to choose the best combination of working hours, in presence (P) or with online lectures (O). We used again the grades *Excellent, Very Good, Good, Acceptable, Poor, To Reject, No Opinion* and the five options are:

1. 6 h (P) - 6 h (O) - 6 h (P or O)
2. 10 h (P) - 4 h (O) - 4 h (P or O)
3. 8 h (P) - 6 h (O) - 4 h (P or O)
4. 7 h (P) - 9 h (O) - 2 h (P or O)
5. 5 h (P) - 5 h (O) - 8 h (P or O)

The results of MJ method, with the traditional compute of medians takes back as winner the option 4 (7 h (P) - 9 h (O) - 2 h (P or O)) that has the highest number of "Good" votes.

Instead the compute of winner with CMJ method takes back a different situation: we fixed 2 as number of winners (and number of clusters) and the first one is the option 3 (8 h (P) - 6 h (O) - 4 h (P or O)) and the second one is the option 4, the same winner of MJ method.

As we can see, probably because the number of voters is quite high, the results are not the same like in case study 2. With CMJ, we take into account the wide spectrum of preferences, with special regards for the most polarising ones, which are the most influent in creating different clusters.

Especially for this reason, we may prefer CMJ to MJ for this case-study's lookalike situations, where a shared solution should be taken, considering the different impact it can have on the heterogenous groups (*clusters*) the judgement is made by.

Conclusions

In Sect. 1, we dealt with logical issues involved in voting rules and judgement aggregation, highlighting majority rule's resistance to strategical vote.

In Sect. 2, a more fined model of majority rule, Majority Judgement, has been presented as an option to better estimate the most shared candidate.

In Sect. 3, the related works have been shown and in Sect. 4, all possible categories of clustering approach has been reported in order to choose the fittest one for our generalization of Majority Judgement as a multi-winner strategy. After that, three different case studies are reported, with a particular attention to the comparison between MJ and CMJ results.

In spite of non-deterministic nature of K-Medoids, Clustered Majority Judgement is thought to be used in high populated disputes. For these reasons, we feel confident about clustering's role of taking into account all different perspectives could be shown in such situation.

Moreover, our implementation is not strictly linked to political field, as is clearly shown in the case studies, mostly because it requires only some fixed parameters: number of winners, number of grades and grades themselves.

An important future challenge could be speeding up the algorithm or making a more flexible structure, even though all the constraints already explained in previous sections need to be satisfied.

References

1. Park, H.-S., Jun, C.-H.: A simple and fast algorithm for K-medoids clustering. POSTECH
2. Kaufman, L., Rousseeuw, P.J.: Partitioning around medoids. In: Finding Groups in Data: An Introduction to Cluster Analysis. Wiley (2015)
3. Balinski, M., Laraki, R.: Majority judgement vs. majority rule. Social Choice and Welfare. HAL Open Science (2016)
4. Loreggia, A., Mattei, N., Quintarelli, S.: Artificial intelligence research for fighting. In: Political Polarisation: A Research Agenda, pp. 1–2. Publisher (2020)
5. Balinski, M.: Fair Majority Voting (or How to Eliminate Gerrymandering) (2006)
6. Nehring, K., Pivato, M.: Incoherent Majorities: The McGarvey Problem in Judgement Aggregation. Elsevier (2011)
7. Garcia-Bermejo, J.C.: A plea for the majority method in aggregating judgements. Oxford J. (2011)

8. Christian, L.: Social Choice Theory, The Stanford Encyclopedia of Philosophy (2022)
9. May, K.O.: A set of indipendent necessary and sufficient conditions for simple majority decision (1952)
10. Bellec, G., Scherr, F., Subramoney, A.: A solution to the learning dilemma for recurrent networks of spiking neurons (2020)
11. Kleinberg, J.: An impossibility theorem for clustering (2002)
12. Fabre, A.: Tie-Breaking the Highest Median: Alternatives to the Majority Judgment (2018)
13. Pedregosa, F., et al.: Scikit-Learn Machine Learning in Python (2011)
14. Streibel, B.J.: The manager's guide to effective meetings (2003)
15. Tannenbaum, R.S., Schmidt, W.H.: How to Choose a Leadership Pattern (2009)
16. Blake, R.R., Mouton, J.S., Barnes, L.B., Greiner, L.E.: Breakthrough in organization development(1964)
17. Vroom, V.H., Yetton, P.W.: Leadership and decision-making (1973)
18. Verzuh, E., American Psychological Association and Others: A Guide to the Project Management Body of Knowledge: PMBOK Guide (2021)
19. Balinski, M., Laraki, R.: Election by majority judgment: Experimental evidence (2011)
20. Balinski, M., Laraki, R.: A theory of measuring, electing, and ranking (2007)
21. Brandt, F., Conitzer, V., Endriss, U., Lang, J., Procaccia, A.D.: Handbook of computational social choice (2016)
22. Serafini, P.: La Matematica in Soccorso Della Democrazia: Cosa Significa Votare e Come Si Può Migliorare il Voto (2019)
23. Arrow, K.J.: Social choice and individual values (2012)
24. Costa, B.E., Carlos, A., Vansnick, J.-C.: The MACBETH approach: Basic ideas, software, and an application (1999)
25. Angilella, S., Mazzù, S.: The financing of innovative SMEs: A multicriteria credit rating model (2015)
26. Wang, K., Shao, Y., Shu, L., Zhu, C., Zhang, Y.: Mobile big data fault-tolerant processing for ehealth networks (2016)
27. Chi, G., Zhang, Z.: Multi Criteria Credit Rating Model for Small Enterprise Using a Nonparametric Method (2017)
28. Balinski, M., Laraki, R.: Judge: Don't Vote! (2014)
29. Fazzinga, B., Flesca, S., Furfaro, F., Masciari, E.: RFID data compression for supporting aggregate queries
30. Ceci, M., et al.: Big data techniques for supporting accurate predictions of energy production from renewable sources (2015)
31. Caroprese, L., Zumpano, E.: Aggregates and priorities in P2P data management systems (2011)
32. Caroprese, L., Zumpano, E.: Declarative Semantics for P2P Data Management System (2020)
33. Caroprese, L., Zumpano, E.: A Logic Framework for P2P Deductive Databases (2020)

Sentimental Analysis of COVID-19 Vaccine Tweets Using BERT+NBSVM

Areeba Umair[1]([⊠])(iD), Elio Masciari[1]([⊠]), Giusi Madeo[2],
and Muhammad Habib Ullah[1]

[1] University of Naples, Federico II, 80125 Naples, Italy
areeba.umair@unina.it
[2] IC Rende Commenda, Rende, CS, Italy

Abstract. The development of the vaccine for the control of COVID-19
is the need of hour. The immunity against coronavirus highly depends
upon the vaccine distribution. Unfortunately, vaccine hesitancy seems to
be another big challenge worldwide. Therefore, it is necessary to analysis
and figure out the public opinion about COVID-19 vaccines. In this era
of social media, people use such platforms and post about their opinion,
reviews etc. In this research, we proposed BERT+NBSVM model for the
sentimental analysis of COVID-19 vaccines tweets. The polarity of the
tweets was found using TextBlob(). The proposed BERT+NBSVM outperformed other models and achieved 73% accuracy, 71% precision, 88%
recall and 73% F-measure for classification of positive sentiments while
73% accuracy, 71% precision, 74% recall and 73% F-measure for classification of negative sentiments respectively. Thus, these sentimental and
spatial analysis helps in world-wide pandemics by identify the people's
attitudes towards the vaccines.

Keywords: Sentimental analysis · Vaccine · COVID-19 · Vaccine
hesitancy

1 Introduction

The COVID-19, caused by coronavirus, started spreading an infectious disease
in December, 2019 in Wuhan, China [4,14]. The preventive measures of social
distancing and wearing masks were observed in different countries. However,
the long-term solution of this disease was the development of vaccines [6,30].
Moreover, after the vaccines were developed, the acceptance of vaccines among
the general public was next milestone [16]. Most of the population from all over
the world was not willing to get themselves vaccinated because of the its side-
effects and other misinformation [2,12,17]. To overcome this situation, it is a
good strategy if the agencies put their efforts in understanding what people are
thinking about vaccines and design their strategies accordingly [1,28].

The increasing number of social media platforms users made it easy for
researchers to find and extract the user-generated freely data [31]. Such kind
of data can easily be used for public sentiments analysis [10]. This data can be

I. Koprinska et al. (Eds.): ECML PKDD 2022 Workshops, CCIS 1752, pp. 238–247, 2023.
https://doi.org/10.1007/978-3-031-23618-1_16

very helpful in investigating the people's behaviour during this disease, during lockdown and for the vaccine campaign [15,34]. Twitter is considered as the most popular social media app which has been used worldwide for sharing the feeling, opinion and ideas [7,25]. Tweets can be useful for analysing the people's feedback on any trending topic [18]. Sentimental analysis is the most famous method by which people's feelings are extracted [9]. It uses machine learning and deep learning for this purpose [13,15]. For performing the sentimental analysis, the polarity of the tweet is found [22].

In this study, we used tweets related to COVID-19 vaccine and used them for extracting the sentiments of people towards vaccination of COVID-19. This research can bring fruitful results for government and policy makers for designing the vaccination campaign according to the sentiments of people. We used freely available twitter data from Kaggle website and found out the polarity of the tweets. At the end of the method, we used BERT+NBSVM model for classification of positive and negative sentiments.

The objectives of this research paper are:

- Using freely available twitter data about COVID vaccines and categorize the text into different sentiment classes.
- To categorize the tweets based on their polarity values using python script.
- To propose BERT+NBSVM model for positive and negative tweet classification.

2   Methods

Machine learning and natural language processing are used for sentimental analysis.

2.1   Sentimental Classification Framework

Our proposed sentimental classification framework consists of three stages as we can see in Fig. 1.

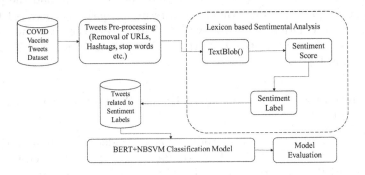

Fig. 1. Our proposed sentimental classification framework

First, the dataset is collected and pre-processing is performed.

Secondly, the sentiment polarity is extracted using TextBlob() function.

Third, polarity values are used to classify the positive and negative tweets with the help of BERT+NBSVM model.

2.2 Collection and Pre-processing of Data

In this study, we used freely available twitter data. The dataset contains tweets about COVID-19 vaccines. The dataset is then further processed by removing URLs, hashtags, and stop-words using python script. In Table 1, column 1 shows the dummy tweets, column 2 shows tweets after hashtag removal, column 3 shows tweets after URLs removal.

Table 1. Comparison of tweets before and after pre-processing

Dummy samples	After removing Hashtags	After removing URLs
Fever after first dose #PfizerBioNTech https://t.co/xffiee77	Fever after first dose PfizerBioNTech https://t.co/xffiee77	Fever after first dose PfizerBioNTech
Vaccine scheduling available online https://t.co/jgeeityc	Vaccine scheduling available online https://t.co/jgeeityc	Vaccine scheduling available online
Any update on booster dose?? https://t.co/hdrryuugy	Any update on booster dose https://t.co/hdrryuugy	Any update on booster dose

2.3 Finding Values of Sentiments Polarity

The sentiment analysis depends upon the polarity of the sentence. The polarity shows that either the given text is neutral, negative or positive. We categorized the tweets into seven classes of sentiments [27] based on the polarity values. The classes includes neutral, weakly positive, mild positive, strongly positive, weakly negative, mild negative and strongly negative. We used principles of [27] as given in Table 2 to fix the polarity range of each class. We find the polarity using TextBlob() library of Python, which returns polarity between -1 to $+1$.

We find the polarity values (between $[-1$ to $+1]$) of the given tweets using the TextBlob() library function of Python. The working principle of TextBlob() can be seen in Fig. 2.

2.4 Combining BERT and Naive Bayes-SVM for Sentimental Classification

In this research, we combined the Bidirectional encoder representation of transformers (BERT) with hybrid of Naive Bayes and Support Vector Machine (NBSVM). BERT is the transformer based model which used attention mechanism. In transformer, encoder and decoder both are used, while in BERT model,

Table 2. Rules for sentimental classes

Polarity	Sentiment class
0	Neutral
> 0 and ≤ 0.3	Weakly Positive
> 0.3 and ≤ 0.6	Mild Positive
> 0.6 and ≤ 1	Strongly Positive
> −0.3 and ≤ 0	Weakly Negative
> −0.6 and ≤ −0.3	Mild Negative
> 1 and ≤ −0.6	Strongly Negative

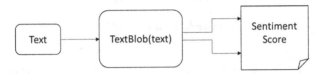

Fig. 2. How TextBlob() works?

only encoder layers of transformers are used [20,32]. The two famous architectures of BERT are base and large models. Both of the models have four
differences between them [20].

Naive Bayes and Support vector machines are the machine learning algorithms, the former works good on short sentimental tasks while the later on
longer documents. The hybrid of NB and SVM uses the variances of SVM and
ratio of log NB for better accuracy [19].

BERT+NBSVM System Architecture. The combination of deep learning
and classical machine learning results in the BERT+NB-SVM model, which is
estimated on DTM (document term frequency) features. The DTM is used to
compute the NB log-count ratios. These ratios helps to calculate the word probability of positive and negative classes in a document. The system architecture of
BERT+NB-SVM is shown in Fig. 3. It can be seen from the figure that, the left
side shows the process of training while the right side shows the classification.

The following steps are adopted for training and classification:

- The training dataset was used in fine tuning of BERT model
- The NB log-count ratios are used for SVM model training
- While prediction, final score is calculated as the weighted sum of the fitted
  NB-SVM model and best fine-tuned BERT model.
- The best fine tuned model indicates the model with best performances with
  different epochs and batch sizes.

BERT+NBSVM Model Training. To train the model, we used pre-training
and fine tuning. As a loss function, Adam optimizer is used to train the model

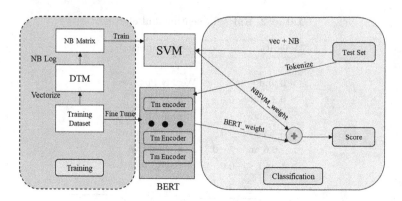

Fig. 3. System architecture of BERT+ NBSVM

and grid search was used for parameter tuning. These best weight for BERT model is 0.87 and NB-SVM is 0.08. Two classification models, (positive and negative). The precision, recall and F_1 score are used, as shown in Eqs. (1), (2) and (3) respectively.

$$Precision = \frac{TP}{TP + FP} \tag{1}$$

$$Recall = \frac{TP}{TP + FN} \tag{2}$$

$$FMeasure = \frac{2 \times Precision \times Recall}{Precision + Recall} \tag{3}$$

where:
TP occurs when both item and the result are positive.
TN occurs when both item and the result are negative
FP occurs when item is negative while model is giving positive result.
FN occurs when item is positive while model is giving negative result.

State-of-the-Art. We performed the experiments with state-of-the-art in order to evaluate our proposed model. We used K-nearest neighbour (KNN) algorithm, Support Vector Machine (SVM) algorithm, Random Forest (RF) algorithm, Naive Bayes (NB) algorithm and DT (Decision Tree) algorithm because of their being mostly used in literature [4,15,24].

Decision tree and random forest have ability to learn from uses [33]. Random forest works good on non-linear datasets. It chooses randoms samples and features from the dataset [23]. While, decision tree works on decision rules from the entire dataset. It works well on small dataset [5]. Naive Bayes uses the principles of probability for its working. It considers all the features statistically independent [3,5]. Naive Bayes uses Bayesian theorem and calculates the probability of the items as we can seen in Eq. 4:

$$P(H|X) = P(X|H)P(H)/P(X) \tag{4}$$

The simplest machine learning algorithm, KNN, looks for the most similar item among its neighbours. It requires alot of time, as it needs to search from the entire dataset. Therefore, it is good for the small datasets. Moreover, it is the algorithm, that does not follow test-train mechanism. User provides the number of neighbours during search [3]. The Eq. 5) is used for find the most similar item.

$$di = \sqrt{[(xi - x)^2 + (yi - y)^2]} \tag{5}$$

SVM is the effective algorithm when the dataset contains high dimensional feature space. It works by generating the hyperplane. The hyperplane thus helps in classification. It combines features from different sources and make one feature to train the model. The higher the separation of hyperplane, the more accurate the classification. Linear function, polynomial function and radial basis function are the kernels functions used in SVM [8].

BERT works on the principles of masked languages (MLM) by using word representation model. It has [SEP] and [CLS] as two special tokens. BERT takes input as [CLS] and then transfers it to the upper layer. At that step, the self attention is applied. The output from this step is transferred to the feed-forward network. The vector C, output of the model, is used for classification and translation. The probability of sentimental classes can be calculated by following Eq. 6 [29].

$$P = softmax(CW^T) \tag{6}$$

3   Results and Discussion

3.1   Sentiment Polarity

The polarity value helps to find the sentiment of the text. Table 3, shows the polarity values for each text with the sentiments category, described in Sect. 2.3

Table 3. Categorization of sentiments on sample data

Data Sample	Polarity	Category
Fever after first dose PfizerBioNTech	−0.5	Mild Negative
Vaccine scheduling available online	0.7	Strongly Positive
Any update on Booster	0	Neutral

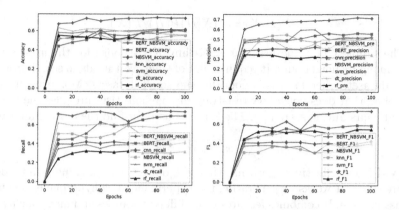

Fig. 4. Graph showing the results of experiments for positive sentiments

3.2 Sentimental Classification

The results of the experiments are shown in the Figure below:

Figure 4 shows the sub-graphs depicting the classification accuracy, precision, recall and F1 score of our proposed BERT+NBSVM model in comparison with BERT, NBSVM, Decision tree, KNN, random forest and SVM for the classification of positive sentiments. The classification results of positive tweets classification show that our proposed approach outperformed all other state of the art models. The proposed BERT+NBSVM showed the best accuracy.

Figure 5 shows the sub-plots of accuracy, precision, recall and F1 score for our proposed BERT+NBSVM model in comparison with BERT, NBSVM, Decision tree, KNN, random forest and SVM for the classification of negative sentiments. The BERT+NBSVM showed best performance among all other state of the art neural network and machine learning models that have been used in literature. Deep learning has attracted the attention due to its prediction performance in the social media domain. Out of all baseline neural network models, BERT+NBSVM outperformed all others.

Among machine learning models, the performance of SVM was high among other baseline algorithms because SVM does not show any effect of hyper-parameters related to data [26]. KNN and decision trees were found with similar accuracy and they show a significant effect in the classification [11]. Random forest shows the intermediate performance in both of the scenarios of our study, because random forest draws observation strategies randomly and requires a hyper-parameter tuning for good performance [21].

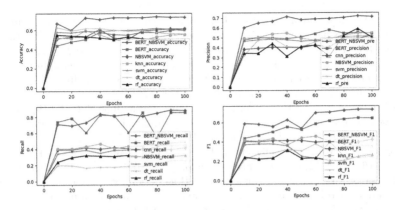

Fig. 5. Graph showing the results of experiments for negative sentiments

4 Conclusion

Twitter based sentimental analysis for extraction people's response towards any general issue or topic is a very fruitful and efficient way for policy makers. Vaccine hesitancy is a hurdle in the control of COVID-19 disease and is emerged as a bigger challenge worldwide. In this research, people's reaction during COVID-19 vaccination campaigns are analyzed using twitter data. We categorized the data into seven categories of sentiments using their polarity. We proposed the BERT+NBSVM classification models (positive and negative) for sentiment classification. Hence, such kind of research can help the policy makers and government to understand what people are thinking about their campaigns and initiatives. So, they can educate people timely about any misinformation regarding any campaigns and thus can save the lives of citizens from any disease or epidemic.

References

1. Examining Australian public perceptions and behaviors towards a future COVID-19 vaccine. medRxiv, pp. 1–9 (2020). https://doi.org/10.1101/2020.09.29.20204396
2. Hogan, C., et al.: Knowledge and attitudes of us adults regarding COVID-19. Int. J. Emerg. Med. **13**(1), 1–6 (2020). https://doi.org/10.1186/s12245-020-00309-6
3. Abdulrahman, N., Abedalkhader, W.: KNN classifier and Naive Bayse classifier for crime prediction in San Francisco context. Int. J. Datab. Manag. Syst. **9**(4), 1–9 (2017). https://doi.org/10.5121/ijdms.2017.9401
4. Adamu, H., Lutfi, S.L., Malim, N.H.A.H., Hassan, R., Di Vaio, A., Mohamed, A.S.A.: Framing twitter public sentiment on Nigerian government COVID-19 palliatives distribution using machine learning. Sustainability **13**(6), 1–13 (2021). https://doi.org/10.3390/su13063497
5. Almanie, T., Mirza, R., Lor, E.: Crime prediction based on crime types and using spatial and temporal criminal hotspots. Int. J. Data Min. Knowl. Manag. Process **5**(4), 1–19 (2015). https://doi.org/10.5121/ijdkp.2015.5401

6. Chou, W.Y.S., Budenz, A.: Considering emotion in COVID-19 vaccine communication: Addressing vaccine hesitancy and fostering vaccine confidence. Health Commun. **35**(14), 1718–1722 (2020). https://doi.org/10.1080/10410236.2020.1838096

7. Das, S., Dutta, A.: Characterizing public emotions and sentiments in COVID-19 environment: A case study of India. J. Hum. Behav. Soc. Environ. **31**(1–4), 1–14 (2020). https://doi.org/10.1080/10911359.2020.1781015

8. Dqj, L.X., et al.: IEEE Int. Conf. Syst. Man Cybern. 4056–4062 (2019)

9. Flesca, S., Furfaro, F., Masciari, E.: On the minimization of xpath queries. J. ACM **55**(1), 2:1–2:46 (2008). https://doi.org/10.1145/1326554.1326556

10. Flesca, S., Masciari, E.: Efficient and effective web change detection. Data Knowl. Eng. **46**(2), 203–224 (2003). https://doi.org/10.1016/S0169-023X(02)00210-0

11. George, J., Skariah, S.M., Xavier, T.A.: Role of contextual features in fake news detection: a review. In: 2020 International Conference on Innovative Trends in Information Technology (ICITIIT), pp. 1–6. IEEE (2020)

12. Green, M.S., Abdullah, R., Vered, S., Nitzan, D.: A study of ethnic, gender and educational differences in attitudes toward COVID-19 vaccines in Israel - implications for vaccination implementation policies. Isr. J. Health Policy Res. **10**(1), 1–12 (2021). https://doi.org/10.1186/s13584-021-00458-w

13. Manguri, H.K.N., Ramadhan, R.R., Mohammed Amin, P.: Twitter Sentiment Analysis on Worldwide COVID-19 Outbreaks. Kurdistan J. Appl. Res. pp. 54–65 (2020). https://doi.org/10.24017/covid.8

14. Huang, H., Peng, Z., Wu, H., Xie, Q.: A big data analysis on the five dimensions of emergency management information in the early stage of COVID-19 in China. J. Chinese Gov. **5**(2), 213–233 (2020). https://doi.org/10.1080/23812346.2020.1744923

15. Jelodar, H., Wang, Y., Orji, R., Huang, H.: Deep sentiment classification and topic discovery on novel coronavirus or COVID-19 online discussions: NLP using LSTM recurrent neural network approach. arXi **24**(10), 2733–2742 (2020)

16. Kourlaba, G., et al.: Willingness of Greek general population to get a COVID-19 vaccine. Glob. Heal. Res. Policy **6**(1), 1–10 (2021). https://doi.org/10.1186/s41256-021-00188-1

17. Lazarus, J.V., et al.: A global survey of potential acceptance of a COVID-19 vaccine. Nat. Med. **27**(2), 225–228 (2021). https://doi.org/10.1038/s41591-020-1124-9

18. Luo, Y., Xu, X.: Comparative study of deep learning models for analyzing online restaurant reviews in the era of the COVID-19 pandemic. Int. J. Hosp. Manag. **94**, 102849 (2021). https://doi.org/10.1016/j.ijhm.2020.102849

19. Muhammad, A.N., Bukhori, S., Pandunata, P.: Sentiment analysis of positive and negative of Youtube comments using Naïve Bayes-support vector machine (NBSVM) classifier. In: 2019 International Conference on Computer Science, Information Technology, and Electrical Engineering (ICOMITEE), pp. 199–205. IEEE (2019)

20. Pota, M., Ventura, M., Catelli, R., Esposito, M.: An effective bert-based pipeline for twitter sentiment analysis: A case study in Italian. Sensors (Switzerland) **21**(1), 1–21 (2021). https://doi.org/10.3390/s21010133

21. Probst, P., Wright, M.N., Boulesteix, A.L.: Hyperparameters and tuning strategies for random forest. Wiley Interdiscip. Rev. Data Mining Knowl. Discov **9**(3), e1301 (2019)

22. Raheja, S., Asthana, A.: Sentimental analysis of twitter comments on COVID-19. In: 2021 11th International Conference on Cloud Computing, Data Science & Engineering, pp. 704–708 (2021). https://doi.org/10.1109/Confluence51648.2021.9377048

23. Rangnekar, R.H., Suratwala, K.P., Krishna, S., Dhage, S.: Career prediction model using data mining and linear classification. In: 2018 Fourth International Conference on Computing Communication Control and Automation (ICCUBEA), pp. 1–6 (2018). http://ieeexplore.ieee.org/abstract/document/8697689/

24. Rustam, F., Khalid, M., Aslam, W., Rupapara, V., Mehmood, A., Choi, G.S.: A performance comparison of supervised machine learning models for Covid-19 tweets sentiment analysis. PLoS One **16**(2), 1–23 (2021). https://doi.org/10.1371/journal.pone.0245909

25. Samuel, J., et al.: Feeling positive about reopening? New normal scenarios from COVID-19 US reopen sentiment analytics. IEEE Access **8**, 142173–142190 (2020). https://doi.org/10.1109/ACCESS.2020.3013933

26. Schratz, P., Muenchow, J., Iturritxa, E., Richter, J., Brenning, A.: Hyperparameter tuning and performance assessment of statistical and machine-learning algorithms using spatial data. Ecol. Model. **406**, 109–120 (2019)

27. Singh, M., Jakhar, A.K., Pandey, S.: Sentiment analysis on the impact of coronavirus in social life using the BERT model. Soc. Netw. Anal. Min. **11**(1), 1–11 (2021). https://doi.org/10.1007/s13278-021-00737-z

28. Sv, P., Ittamalla, R., Deepak, G.: Analyzing the attitude of Indian citizens towards COVID-19 vaccine text analytics study (2020)

29. Umair, A., Masciari, E.: Using high performance approaches to COVID-19 vaccines sentiment analysis. In: 2022 30th Euromicro International Conference on Parallel, Distributed and Network-Based Processing (PDP), pp. 197–204. IEEE (2022)

30. Umair, A., Masciari, E., Habib Ullah, M.H.: Sentimental analysis applications and approaches during COVID-19: a survey. In: 25th International Database Engineering & Applications Symposium. IDEAS 2021, pp. 304–308. Association for Computing Machinery, New York (2021). https://doi.org/10.1145/3472163.3472274

31. Umair, A., Sarfraz, M.S., Ahmad, M., Habib, U., Ullah, M.H., Mazzara, M.: Applied Sciences Spatiotemporal Analysis of Web News Archives for Crime Prediction (2020). https://doi.org/10.3390/app10228220

32. Yadav, N., Singh, A.K.: Bi-directional encoder representation of transformer model for sequential music recommender system. ACM International Conference Proceeding Series, pp. 49–53 (2020). https://doi.org/10.1145/3441501.3441503

33. Yi, F., Yu, Z., Xu, H., Guo, B.: Talents recommendation with multi-aspect preference learning. Green Pervasive Cloud Comput. **11204**, 409–423 (2018). https://doi.org/10.1007/978-3-030-15093-8-29

34. Zhou, B., Cheng, C., Ma, G., Zhang, Y.: Remaining useful life prediction of lithium-ion battery based on attention mechanism with positional encoding. IOP Conf. Ser. Mater. Sci. Eng. **895**(1), 9 (2020). https://doi.org/10.1088/1757-899X/895/1/012006

Rules, Subgroups and Redescriptions as Features in Classification Tasks

Matej Mihelčić[1]([⊠]) and Tomislav Šmuc[2]

[1] Department of Mathematics, Faculty of Science, University of Zagreb,
Bijenička cesta 30, 10000 Zagreb, Croatia
`matmih@math.hr`
[2] Ruđer Bošković Institute, Bijenička cesta 54, 10000 Zagreb, Croatia
`tomislav.smuc@irb.hr`

Abstract. We evaluate the suitability of using supervised and unsupervised rules, subgroups and redescriptions as new features and meaningful, interpretable representations for classification tasks. Although using supervised rules as features is known to allow increase in performance of classification algorithms, advantages of using unsupervised rules, subgroups, redescriptions and in particular their synergy with rules are still largely unexplored for classification tasks. To research this topic, we developed a fully automated framework for feature construction, selection and testing called DAFNE – Descriptive Automated Feature Construction and Evaluation. As with other available tools for rule-based feature construction, DAFNE provides fully interpretable features with in-depth knowledge about the studied domain problem. The performed results show that DAFNE is capable of producing provably useful features that increase overall predictive performance of different classification algorithms on a set of different classification datasets.

Keywords: Feature construction · Classification · Redescription mining · Rule mining · Subgroup discovery · CLUS-RM · JRip · M5Rules · CN2-SD

1 Introduction

With the rise of popularity and awareness of different predictive machine learning algorithms able to provide huge number of often highly accurate predictions for various tasks, there is also an increasing need to provide tools and techniques to aid in the construction, extraction and selection of predictive attributes.

The main aim of feature construction is to find new features which capture non-trivial, possibly non-linear interactions between existing, original features [21,29]. Its utility is assessed via increase in the predictive performance, high importance of newly constructed features for the predictive task and through better understanding of the underlying problem. Various types of feature construction have been studied: creating rules [31] or using decision tree based algorithms (Random Forest [40], Deep Forest [45]). The main advantage of rules is that they can simultaneously offer interpretative and performance improvement for various classifiers [28,31,32,44]. Rules can also be used as local predictors [5,11,27] to form global classification models.

In this work, we extend the study of rule-based feature construction to include subgroups, descriptive (unsupervised) rules and redescriptions. The main goal is to assess if and when the latter can be more informative than supervised rules or be used in synergy with supervised rules to improve performance. Subgroups [17,42] have the same form of a logical formula as regular rules, but describe subsets of instances such that their distribution of target labels significantly deviates from the target label distribution on the entire dataset. Redescriptions [9,33] are tuples of logical formulae that can contain a conjunction, disjunction or negation operator, with the constraint that each formula in a tuple (also called a query) should describe very similar, or the same subsets of entities. Redescription mining is an unsupervised, descriptive task, with redescriptions representing a second order constructs (tuples of rules that are in a near equivalence relation), forming complex but fully interpretable features.

As previously mentioned, rule-based features necessarily increase the dimensionality of data. The detrimental effect of such increase can be alleviated using different feature selection techniques [14,21]. These techniques aim to eliminate features that provide no or very little information about the target concept. Alternatively, feature extraction techniques [21,39] map existing features, to a new, very often smaller set of features that capture important information about the relation of original features and the target concept. Such features can be used independently of the original feature set, but can also be added and used in synergy with original features.

2   Notation and Related Work

In this section, we define the most important terms necessary to understand the approach and provide an overview of related work.

2.1   Notation and Definition

In this work, we use one-view datasets $\mathcal{D}$ (one data table), containing $|\mathcal{A}|$ attributes and $|E|$ entities. Since we deal with a classification task, each entity is assigned a target label $y \in \{c_1, \ldots, c_k\}$, where a special case of Binary classification has $y \in \{0, 1\}$. We use $\mathcal{M}$ to denote an arbitrary machine learning classification model that is trained on some data $\mathcal{D}_{train}$, and it outputs a prediction $\hat{y}$ for each entity $e \in E_{test}$, where $E_{train} \cap E_{test} = \emptyset$.

The input data is used to create rules, subgroups and redescriptions. Rules and subgroups are logical formulae containing conditions and conjunction logical operator, whereas redescriptions contain tuples of logical formulae containing conditions and conjunction, disjunction and negation logical operators. Each query in a redescription can contain only attributes that are disjoint from attribute of other queries in the redescription. In this work, we use redescriptions formed by pairs of queries.

2.2 Related Work

Feature selection [14,21] and feature construction [21,29] are often used jointly in predictive tasks. As feature construction increases the number of variables, feature selection aims to choose the attributes containing the important information about the target variable, allowing faster training/predicting with machine learning models and increasing their accuracy in practice (e.g. [16,23]).

Feature selection approaches [14,21] include correlation-based, forward selection using Gram-Schmidt orthogonalization, mutual information or model-based feature ranking, hybrid approaches, various feature subset selection methods, wrapper and filter methods [22]. Some ensemble algorithms (e.g. random forest) provide feature ranking which can be used for feature selection (see [15]). Feature selection methods using models can be divided in performance-based approaches and test-based approaches [15].

Performance-based approaches (e.g. [6,35]) combine feature selection with a classifier-based feedback on the quality of the selected set of features. Test-based approaches (e.g. [1,41]) combine permutation testing of attribute values with feature ranking obtained by random forest algorithm to assess the real significance of importance of original features.

Feature construction includes constructive induction [22], construction using fragmentary knowledge [22], greedy feature construction [29] and hybrid approaches (e.g. [36]). Self-supervised learning frameworks [2,37] learn useful new representations for tabular data.

Constructive induction approaches such as [28,31,32,44] construct new attributes from subsets of existing attributes. Attributes in the subset can be combined using conjunction, disjunction and negation logical operator [31,32], or more complex operators such as M-of-N [28] (at least one conjunction of m out of N attributes is true), X-of-N [44] (for a given instance, it denotes the number of attribute-value pairs that are true) or using arithmetic combination of attributes [19]. Gomez and Morales [12] created a learning algorithm RCA, which tries to build a single rule for each class with a predetermined number of terms. FRINGE by Pagallo et al. [30] is a decision-tree based feature construction algorithm (it adaptively enlarges the initial attribute set using NOT and AND logical operators for learning DNF concepts). CITRE [25] and DC Fringe [43] combine existing attributes using conjunction and disjunction operators to construct new features. FICUS [24] generalizes previous approaches to allow combining existing features by some user-predefined function. Garcia et al. [10] create a fuzzy rule-based feature construction approach. A part of research uses rules as local patterns to form global prediction models [5,11] or to rectify predictions of existing classification algorithms [27].

Subgroups have been used as local patterns to build a global regression model [13], as dummy variables to improve regression fit [7] and as local patterns to understand the behaviour of spammers in a classification use-case [3].

Redescription mining [33] aims to find subsets of entities that can be described in multiple ways (re-described), discovering in that manner strong, equivalence-like relations between different subsets of attributes.

3   The DAFNE Framework

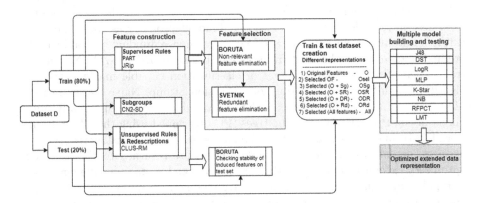

Fig. 1. DAFNE, framework for automated feature construction and evaluation.

The DAFNE framework (Fig. 1) takes a standard, tabular dataset representing some kind of classification problem, creates a stratified split to train (80%) and test (20%) dataset. Train set is used to create supervised rules using state-of-the-art algorithms JRip and PART implemented in Weka [8], subgroups are created using the well known CN2-SD algorithm [20]. Descriptive (unsupervised) rules and redescriptions are created using the state-of-the-art redescription mining algorithm CLUS-RM [26] on the entire dataset. The CLUS-RM algorithm does not require knowledge about target labels and can thus utilize all entities to create rules and redescriptions. Descriptive rules are obtained as a by-product of redescription mining, these are actually query candidates for redescriptions. The fact that in many applications rule-pairs match accurately for groups with homogeneous target label (since these share many common properties) and the fact that CLUS-RM aims to find pairs of rules that describe common subsets of entities, led us to believe that this process might create useful unsupervised rules and redescriptions for classification tasks. After descriptive objects (rules, subgroups and redescriptions) have been obtained, the tool creates Binary features representing each obtained object and enriches the attribute set of both train and test data. The Boruta framework [18], which utilizes a random forest of decision trees, is used to detect a subset of provably useful attributes to predict the given target label on the train set (these features will be used in further evaluation). In this evaluation setting, we also apply Boruta to obtain provably important set of features on the test set (users can observe changes in percentages of important attributes for different types of objects compared to train set). The selected set of provably useful features on a train set is further reduced using the feature selection approach proposed by Svetnik et al. [35] which returns the non-redundant set of features useful to predict the target label. To analyse the usefulness of different types of objects, DAFNE creates a train/test dataset containing: a) all original features (O), b) all non-redundant provably useful original features (O_{sel}), c) all non-redundant provably useful features (All_{sel}), d) non-redundant provably useful original and features obtained from supervised rules (OSR_{del}), e) non-redundant provably useful original and features obtained from descriptive rules (ODR_{sel}), f) non-redundant provably useful original and features obtained from subgroups (OSg_{sel}), g) non-redundant provably useful original and features obtained from redescriptions (ORd_{sel}). DAFNE further trains each of the 8 different types of classification capable machine learning algorithms: multilayer perceptron, $J48$, Decision Stump, Naive Bayes, Logistic Model Trees, Logistic Regression and KStar available in Weka [8] and a Random Forest of 600 Predictive Clustering trees (PCTs) trained using the CLUS framework [4]. Trained models are evaluated on a test set and all constructed, selected features, model evaluation results and analyses are returned to the user. The optimized, extended feature set (Optimized extended data representation in Fig. 1) can be used to produce predictive models with improved performance and/or use these new features for better interpretation and understanding of the data and the problem domain.

The feature evaluation procedure performed by DAFNE is rigorous. From provably important Boruta computed features to non-redundant set of features and finally evaluation of selected features using different types of classifiers. It is well known that adding useless features reduces classification accuracy of many types of classification algorithms, thus newly constructed features on a train set must be predictive in order to increase classifier score on a separate test set. To further ensure that increase in classifier score is achieved only due to newly constructed features or their synergy with original features, default parameters are used to train all 8 classification algorithms. Using default parameters also greatly reduces the execution time of feature evaluation. Parameters of each classification algorithm would need to be tuned for every of 6 newly created datasets, which is unfeasible for large scale experimentation.

If classification performance of one or more classification algorithms is increased on a test set compared to using only original features, DAFNE has achieved the goal of detecting predictive features. Since using supervised rules as features is known to improve classification accuracy and there exists use-cases where using subgroups is beneficial as well in this setting, we aim to broaden the evaluation of subgroups to more different datasets, investigate the use of descriptive rules and redescriptions and to evaluate the effects of synergy of these objects on classification accuracy.

3.1   Parameters Used in DAFNE Components

We fixed the parameters of DAFNE components as follows:

- JRip - default options, with minimal weight of entities per rule set to 1.0, 500 batch optimization runs and batch size of 200. Changes compared to defaults were made to obtain larger number of rules.
- PART - default options with a constraint of minimal 10 entities per rule.

- CN2-SD - default options (8 iterations, beam size of 5 and $\gamma = 0.7$).
- CLUS-RM - default options (redescription accuracy of 0.6) with 20 random runs, 10 iterations per run, tree depth of 8, using conjunctive refinement procedure [26], conjunction, disjunction and negation operator, support size in $[10, 0.8|E|]$, maximal redescription p-value of 0.01 and output non-redundant redescription set of maximal size 1000 [26]. The main aim is to increase the number of produced redescriptions. Maximal support enables pruning uninteresting redescriptions and tautologies, and is often set to $0.8 \cdot |E|$.

Rules and subgroups are filtered to eliminate redundant objects; subgroups must have p-value ≤ 0.01. Fine-grained selection was performed by the Boruta [18] and the feature selection approach by Svetnik et al. [35]. We use default options for Boruta as suggested in [18] and increase the number of trees in a forest to 2000 as suggested in [6]. For non-redundant feature selection [35], we use default parameters, as these are well justified in the varSelRF R package.

Classification algorithms were trained with default Weka options with maximal number of iterations of Logistic regression classifier set to 10000 to disallow lengthy executions. The random forest of PCTs contains 600 trees with standard $\sqrt{|\mathcal{A}|} + 1$ number of random subspaces. A maximal tree depth of 8 is used.

3.2 Use Case Scenario

DAFNE is constructed to tackle realistic problems in which one data table ($\mathcal{D}_{train}$) with target labels is available. Also, obtaining additional data table ($\mathcal{D}_{test}$) without target labels is possible (through data collection, domain-level experimentation or similar). The task is to predict the target label y for instances in $\mathcal{D}_{test}$. When both data tables are available, the DAFNE uses $\mathcal{D}_{train}$ to create supervised rules and subgroups and $\mathcal{D} = \mathcal{D}_{train} \cup \mathcal{D}_{test}$ to create unsupervised rules and redescriptions. Notice that it is possible to iteratively extend the feature set with newly constructed unsupervised rules and redescriptions for any consecutive test set. DAFNE simulates this process by dividing the annotated data into artificial train and test set, performing the aforementioned feature construction procedure and evaluating newly constructed features using several machine learning algorithms and the target labels for $\mathcal{D}_{test}$, which were not used during any step of rule or model creation. The fact that DAFNE can utilize knowledge available in the test set is considered to be a significant advantage compared to the majority of other state-of-the-art feature construction approaches.

4 Data Description

We used 5 datasets: Abalone, Arrhythmia, Breast cancer, Wine and Sports Articles, downloaded from the UCI Machine learning repository [38], to evaluate the proposed methodology. We removed rows containing missing values in all datasets since these are not supported by Boruta and tested DAFNE on the Arrhythmia dataset in the original multi-class and the derived binary classification setting. The binary setting simply predicts existence of arrhythmia (yes/no).

5   Experiments and Results

DAFNE was run 40 times on each dataset to obtain statistics about the usefulness of supervised/descriptive rules, subgroups and redescriptions to predict a
target concept on each of the aforementioned 5 datasets. Supervised rules and
subgroups are created using the same seed every time, effectively returning the
same set of rules and subgroups, redescriptions and descriptive rules change at
each run. Thus, we assess what is the overall change of the system depending on
the introduced descriptive rules and redescriptions.

Median percentage of selected rules, subgroups and redescriptions on a train
and test set by Boruta is reported in Table 1. This table also contains the number of times (out of 40) at least one member of the object type was found in the
non-redundant set of features. In Table 2, we report the median and maximal
$AUPRC$ measure [34] for each classifier on each dataset. We underline the original or selected original features if they lead to the best performance of a given
model, or boldface every combination of features that allow this model to outperform an identical model using the original or selected original set of features.
We also boldface the maximal $AUPRC$ score if the model achieves the same
maximal score as using original features, but there exist runs where using newly
constructed features allowed outperforming a model trained only on original features or using newly constructed features in synergy with original features allows
obtaining the same (maximal) result. If maximal result is achieved utilizing only
original features, the result is not displayed in boldface.

Results presented in Table 1 suggest that Boruta found that high percentage
of created subgroups are significant, followed by supervised rules, redescriptions
and descriptive rules. This is the expected trend since subgroups and supervised rules utilize target label information during creation. It is important to
notice that both redescriptions and descriptive rules are deemed important on
the majority of datasets, and that there are representatives of these objects in
the non-redundant sets of features used to train and evaluate classification mod-

Table 1. Median percentages of supervised rules (SR), descriptive rules (DR), subgroups (Sg) and redescriptions (Rd) deemed provably important for predicting the
target class by the Boruta approach on the train (Tr) and test (Ts) set obtained
from each dataset. *Num. nn.* reports numbers of runs in which at least one subgroup,
supervised rule, descriptive rule and redescription occurred in the non-redundant set
of features used for training/testing of different classifiers.

$\mathcal{D}$	Sg_{Tr}	SR_{Tr}	DR_{Tr}	Rd_{Tr}	$Num.nn$	Sg_{Ts}	SR_{Ts}	DR_{Ts}	Rd_{Ts}
Abalone	85	42	11	34	32/12/23/9	49	7	3	3
Arrhythmia	100	71	2	<1	40/40/22/3	33	0	0	0
Arrhythmia$_b$	100	69	1	0	40/37/0/0	50	0	0	0
Breast cancer	100	83	5	13	40/37/2/1	100	33	3	11
Wine	100	100	19	27	40/38/30/20	100	100	10	27
Sports articles	100	61	1	1	40/40/2/1	33	11	1	1

els. Boruta also determined that large number of objects, found important on the train set, remains important for the prediction of target label on the test set.

Results presented in Table 2 show that newly created features improve performance (or allow obtaining the same maximal performance) of every of the 8 chosen classification models on at least 3 different datasets. Results confirm that subgroups seem to be the most important features, however other types of objects have a very important role as well. It is evident that using descriptive rules and redescriptions can significantly increase classifier performance. For example, the Decision Stump model has achieved the best performance using redescriptions as features on the Breast Cancer dataset or using descriptive rules on the Arrhythmia dataset. If there existed supervised rules or subgroups more useful to predict the target label, these would surely be chosen instead by the feature selection procedure. Also, if there existed supervised, descriptive rules or subgroups with similar predictive power as redescriptions on the Breast Cancer dataset, these would be used in at least some of the runs (where the predictive redescriptions were not present) to obtain similar predictive performance. Redescriptions and descriptive rules can also improve performance of complex classifiers such as Multilayer perceptron, Logistic model trees, Decision trees and Random Forest of PCTs. Thus, synergy or complementarity of different types of objects has played an important role, as noticeable from the results (there are instances where using a selected subset from the set of all features yields the highest score, e.g. Arrhythmia with binary class label).

Table 2. Evaluation results of 8 selected classifiers.

$\mathcal{M}$	$\mathcal{D}$	O	O_{sel}	All_{sel}	OSg_{sel}	OSR_{sel}	ODR_{sel}	ORd_{sel}
MLP	AB	0.203	0.179	0.194	0.195	0.179	0.194	0.183
		0.203	0.202	**0.223**	**0.233**	**0.217**	**0.219**	**0.227**
	AR	0.668	0.608	0.653	**0.691**	0.569	0.594	0.611
		0.668	0.722	**0.733**	**0.729**	**0.738**	0.722	0.722
	AR_B	0.798	0.508	**0.825**	**0.822**	0.659	0.508	0.508
		0.798	0.526	**0.849**	**0.849**	0.694	0.526	0.526
	BC	0.984	0.966	0.911	0.939	0.956	0.966	0.966
		0.984	0.983	0.965	0.968	0.977	0.982	0.983
	W	1.0	0.905	0.988	0.927	0.923	0.968	0.905
		1.0	1.0	**1.0**	0.989	0.994	1.0	**1.0**
	SA	0.868	0.855	0.788	0.806	0.842	0.855	0.855
		0.868	0.892	0.848	0.855	0.877	0.892	0.892
LMT	AB	0.217	0.217	0.206	0.207	0.217	0.212	0.217
		0.217	0.217	**0.229**	**0.230**	**0.225**	**0.229**	**0.223**
	AR	0.788	0.717	0.718	0.715	0.682	0.714	0.717
		0.788	0.796	0.780	0.793	0.789	0.792	0.796

(*continued*)

Table 2. (*continued*)

$\mathcal{M}$	$\mathcal{D}$	O	O_{sel}	All_{sel}	OSg_{sel}	OSR_{sel}	ODR_{sel}	ORd_{sel}
	AR_B	0.841	0.662	**0.859**	0.835	0.666	0.662	0.662
		0.841	0.662	**0.870**	**0.846**	0.726	0.662	0.662
	BC	<u>0.992</u>	0.967	0.948	0.939	0.969	0.967	0.967
		<u>0.992</u>	0.982	0.958	0.939	0.976	0.983	0.982
	W	<u>1.0</u>	0.928	0.948	0.890	0.887	0.985	0.952
		1.0	<u>1.0</u>	0.948	0.995	0.981	**1.0**	**1.0**
	SA	0.884	0.855	**0.888**	0.866	0.868	0.855	0.855
		0.884	0.881	**0.902**	**0.895**	**0.896**	0.881	0.881
NB	AB	0.160	0.160	0.160	**0.160**	0.160	0.160	0.160
		0.160	<u>0.168</u>	0.167	0.167	0.168	0.167	0.168
	AR	0.472	0.645	**0.713**	**0.714**	**0.656**	**0.647**	0.643
		0.472	0.715	**0.753**	**0.758**	**0.729**	0.708	0.715
	AR_B	0.719	0.617	**0.863**	**0.846**	0.719	0.617	0.617
		0.719	0.618	**0.872**	**0.858**	**0.720**	0.618	0.618
	BC	<u>0.983</u>	0.966	0.970	0.971	0.970	0.966	0.966
		<u>0.983</u>	0.979	0.974	0.976	0.978	0.979	0.979
	W	<u>0.991</u>	0.901	0.976	0.945	0.945	0.975	0.920
		0.991	<u>1.0</u>	**1.0**	0.998	0.998	**1.0**	1.0
	SA	<u>0.845</u>	0.819	0.838	0.828	0.830	0.819	0.819
		0.845	0.827	**0.855**	0.837	0.841	0.827	0.827
DSt	AB	<u>0.08</u>	<u>0.08</u>	0.08	0.08	0.08	0.08	0.08
		<u>0.08</u>	0.08	0.08	0.08	0.08	0.08	0.08
	AR	<u>0.163</u>	<u>0.163</u>	0.162	0.162	0.138	0.163	0.163
		0.163	0.163	0.162	0.162	0.138	**0.20**	0.163
	AR_B	0.518	0.551	**0.682**	**0.682**	**0.620**	0.551	0.551
		0.518	0.551	**0.682**	**0.682**	**0.620**	0.551	0.551
	BC	0.816	0.816	**0.839**	**0.839**	0.790	0.816	0.816
		0.816	0.864	0.839	0.839	0.790	**0.867**	**0.881**
	W	0.570	0.570	**0.604**	**0.604**	**0.630**	**0.605**	0.570
		0.570	0.610	**0.630**	**0.630**	**0.630**	**0.667**	**0.667**
	SA	<u>0.724</u>	<u>0.724</u>	0.722	0.722	0.724	0.724	0.724
		<u>0.724</u>	<u>0.724</u>	0.722	0.722	**0.724**	**0.724**	**0.724**
$LogR$	AB	<u>0.199</u>	<u>0.199</u>	0.197	0.199	0.199	0.199	0.199
		0.199	<u>0.210</u>	0.210	0.210	0.210	0.210	0.210
	AR	0.40	<u>0.707</u>	0.647	0.640	0.660	0.707	0.707
		0.40	<u>0.776</u>	0.729	0.719	0.734	0.776	0.776
	AR_B	0.678	0.508	**0.857**	**0.835**	0.666	0.508	0.508
		0.678	0.520	**0.868**	**0.859**	**0.701**	0.520	0.520
	BC	<u>0.985</u>	<u>0.965</u>	0.894	0.962	0.890	0.965	0.965
		0.985	0.986	0.952	0.974	0.962	**0.986**	0.986

(*continued*)

Table 2. (*continued*)

$\mathcal{M}$	$\mathcal{D}$	O	O_{sel}	All_{sel}	OSg_{sel}	OSR_{sel}	ODR_{sel}	ORd_{sel}
	W	<u>0.995</u>	0.910	0.966	0.942	0.926	0.938	0.914
		0.995	<u>1.0</u>	**1.0**	**1.0**	**1.0**	**1.0**	**1.0**
	SA	0.883	0.867	**0.890**	**0.886**	0.865	0.865	0.867
		0.883	0.882	**0.90**	**0.891**	**0.903**	0.882	0.882
KS	AB	<u>0.187</u>	<u>0.187</u>	0.173	0.173	1.0	0.187	0.187
		0.187	<u>0.194</u>	0.191	0.192	0.194	0.193	0.194
	AR	0.468	0.50	**0.571**	**0.568**	**0.513**	**0.510**	0.50
		0.468	0.590	**0.644**	**0.640**	**0.607**	0.590	0.590
	AR_B	0.577	0.634	**0.814**	**0.792**	**0.737**	0.634	0.634
		0.577	0.634	**0.849**	**0.821**	**0.745**	0.634	0.634
	BC	<u>0.975</u>	0.966	0.969	0.970	0.968	0.966	0.966
		<u>0.975</u>	<u>0.981</u>	0.973	0.970	0.968	0.966	0.966
	W	0.980	0.878	**0.981**	0.946	0.955	**0.988**	0.926
		0.980	<u>1.0</u>	**1.0**	**1.0**	**1.0**	**1.0**	**1.0**
	SA	0.792	0.796	0.784	0.770	**0.814**	0.796	0.96
		0.792	0.837	0.831	0.813	**0.862**	0.837	0.837
J_{48}	AB	0.10	0.10	**0.107**	**0.102**	0.10	**0.101**	0.10
		0.10	<u>0.129</u>	0.129	0.129	0.129	0.129	0.129
	AR	<u>0.543</u>	0.331	0.396	0.40	0.351	0.344	0.331
		0.543	0.542	0.527	0.530	0.433	**0.573**	0.542
	AR_B	0.697	0.575	**0.727**	**0.737**	0.658	0.575	0.575
		0.697	0.575	**0.730**	**0.754**	0.677	0.575	0.575
	BC	<u>0.875</u>	0.816	0.844	0.853	0.837	0.816	0.816
		0.875	0.922	0.853	0.853	**0.934**	0.922	**0.960**
	W	<u>0.95</u>	0.738	0.880	0.886	0.880	0.852	0.781
		0.95	0.954	0.886	0.886	0.880	**1.0**	**0.963**
	SA	0.664	0.739	**0.793**	**0.777**	**0.785**	0.739	0.739
		0.664	0.773	**0.849**	**0.792**	**0.807**	0.773	0.773
RF_{PCT}^{600}	AB	<u>0.180</u>	<u>0.176</u>	0.174	0.173	0.176	0.176	0.176
		0.180	0.176	**0.194**	**0.185**	**0.199**	**0.196**	**0.189**
	AR	<u>0.767</u>	0.612	0.672	0.681	0.577	0.606	0.612
		<u>0.767</u>	0.728	0.747	0.744	0.707	0.734	0.728
	AR_B	<u>0.826</u>	0.633	0.812	0.791	0.752	0.633	0.633
		0.826	0.633	**0.830**	0.825	0.765	0.633	0.633
	BC	<u>0.988</u>	0.956	0.964	0.960	0.968	0.956	0.956
		<u>0.988</u>	<u>0.977</u>	0.973	0.966	0.976	0.976	0.977
	W	<u>1.0</u>	0.850	0.991	0.928	0.923	0.986	0.895
		<u>1.0</u>	<u>1.0</u>	**1.0**	0.998	0.998	**1.0**	**1.0**
	SA	<u>0.938</u>	0.827	0.868	0.827	0.860	0.827	0.827
		<u>0.938</u>	0.867	0.875	0.852	0.880	0.867	0.867

6   Conclusion and Future Work

In this work, we created a framework for improving the representation of tabular data. A new feature construction and evaluation framework DAFNE, includes a set of feature generating algorithms, producing supervised and unsupervised rules, subgroups and redescriptions, and advanced feature selection methodology to construct relevant and non-redundant feature sets. These are used to extend original problem representation with new interpretable and informative features for downstream supervised learning tasks. Evaluation results across 5 different datasets confirmed benefits of using supervised rules as features in classification tasks and showed that subgroups represent highly relevant features across tested datasets. Our study also shows that rules and redescriptions, constructed in a specific unsupervised manner, can form informative features that help increase performance of various classification algorithms. This is especially interesting in cases when unlabelled data is abundant in comparison to labelled data. Finally, the synergy of different types of features often allowed increasing classification performance compared to the original representation. Future work includes evaluating DAFNE on more challenging datasets or tasks and comparison against the state-of-the-art self-supervised learning frameworks for learning useful new representations for tabular data.

Acknowledgement. The authors acknowledge support by the Research Cooperability Program of the Croatian Science Foundation, funded by the European Union from the European Social Fund under the Operational Programme Efficient Human Resources 2014–2020, through the Grant 8525: Augmented Intelligence Workflows for Prediction, Discovery, and Understanding in Genomics and Pharmacogenomics.

References

1. Altmann, A., Toloşi, L., Sander, O., Lengauer, T.: Permutation importance: a corrected feature importance measure. Bioinformatics **26**(10), 1340–1347 (2010)
2. Arik, S.O., Pfister, T.: TabNet: attentive interpretable tabular learning. In: AAAI vol. 35, no. 8, pp. 6679–6687 (2021)
3. Atzmueller, M., Lemmerich, F., Krause, B., Hotho, A.: Towards understanding spammers-discovering local patterns for concept description. In: LeGo ECML/PKDD Workshop (2009)
4. Blockeel, H., Raedt, L.D., Ramon, J.: Top-down induction of clustering trees. In: ICML, pp. 55–63. Morgan Kaufmann (1998)
5. Dembczyński, K., Kotłowski, W., Słowiński, R.: A general framework for learning an ensemble of decision rules. In: LeGo ECML/PKDD Workshop (2008)
6. Díaz-Uriarte, R., Alvarez de Andrés, S.: Gene selection and classification of microarray data using random forest. BMC Bioinform. **7**(1), 3 (2006)
7. Duivesteijn, W., Feelders, A.J., Knobbe, A.: Exceptional model mining. Data Min. Knowl. Disc. **30**(1), 47–98 (2016)
8. Eibe, F., Hall, M.A., Witten, I.H.: The WEKA workbench. Online appendix for data mining: practical machine learning tools and techniques. In: Morgan Kaufmann. Morgan Kaufmann Publishers (2016)

9. Galbrun, E., Miettinen, P.: Redescription Mining. SCS, Springer, Cham (2017). https://doi.org/10.1007/978-3-319-72889-6

10. García, D., Stavrakoudis, D., González, A., Pérez, R., Theocharis, J.B.: A fuzzy rule-based feature construction approach applied to remotely sensed imagery. In: IFSA-EUSFLAT. Atlantis Press (2015)

11. Giacometti, A., Miyaneh, E.K., Marcel, P., Soulet, A.: A generic framework for rule-based classification. In: LeGo ECML/PKDD Workshop, pp. 37–54 (2008)

12. Gomez, G., Morales, E.F.: Automatic feature construction and a simple rule induction algorithm for skin detection. In: ICML Workshop on Machine Learning in Computer Vision, pp. 31–38 (2002)

13. Grosskreutz, H.: Cascaded subgroups discovery with an application to regression. In: ECML/PKDD, vol. 5211, p. 33 (2008)

14. Guyon, I., Elisseeff, A.: An introduction to variable and feature selection. J. Mach. Learn. Res. **3**, 1157–1182 (2003)

15. Hapfelmeier, A., Ulm, K.: A new variable selection approach using random forests. Comput. Stat. Data Anal. **60**, 50–69 (2013)

16. Haury, A.C., Gestraud, P., Vert, J.P.: The influence of feature selection methods on accuracy, stability and interpretability of molecular signatures. PLoS ONE **6**(12), 1–12 (2011)

17. Herrera, F., Carmona, C.J., González, P., del Jesus, M.J.: An overview on subgroup discovery: foundations and applications. Knowl. Inf. Syst. **29**(3), 495–525 (2011)

18. Kursa, M.B., Jankowski, A., Rudnicki, W.R.: Boruta-a system for feature selection. Fund. Inform. **101**(4), 271–285 (2010)

19. Langley, P., Bradshaw, G.L., Simon, H.A.: Rediscovering chemistry with the bacon system. In: Michalski, R.S., Carbonell, J.G., Mitchell, T.M. (eds.) Machine Learning. Symbolic Computation, pp. 307–329. Springer, Heidelberg (1983). https://doi.org/10.1007/978-3-662-12405-5_10

20. Lavrac, N., Kavsek, B., Flach, P., Todorovski, L.: Subgroup discovery with CN2-SD. J. Mach. Learn. Res. **5**(2), 153–188 (2004)

21. Liu, H., Motoda, H., Yu, L., Ye, N.: Feature Extraction, Selection, and Construction. The Handbook of Data Mining, pp. 409–424 (2003)

22. Liu, H., Motoda, H.: Feature Extraction, Construction and Selection: A Data Mining Perspective, vol. 453. Springer, New York (1998). https://doi.org/10.1007/978-1-4615-5725-8

23. Mansbridge, N.: Feature selection and comparison of machine learning algorithms in classification of grazing and rumination behaviour in sheep. Sensors **18**(10), 3532 (2018)

24. Markovitch, S., Rosenstein, D.: Feature generation using general constructor functions. Mach. Learn. **49**(1), 59–98 (2002)

25. Matheus, C.J., Rendell, L.A.: Constructive induction on decision trees. In: IJCAI - Volume 1, pp. 645–650. Morgan Kaufmann Publishers Inc., San Francisco (1989)

26. Mihelčić, M., Džeroski, S., Lavrač, N., Šmuc, T.: A framework for redescription set construction. Expert Syst. Appl. **68**, 196–215 (2017)

27. Mozina, M., Bratko, I.: Rectifying predictions of classifiers by local rules. In: LeGo ECML/PKDD Workshop (2008)

28. Murphy, P.M., Pazzani, M.J.: ID2-of-3: constructive induction of M-of-N concepts for discriminators in decision trees. In: Machine Learning Proceedings 1991, pp. 183–187. Elsevier (1991)

29. Oglic, D., Gärtner, T.: Greedy feature construction. In: NIPS, pp. 3945–3953. Curran Associates, Inc. (2016)

30. Pagallo, G.: Learning dnf by decision trees. In: IJCAI - Volume 1. pp. 639–644. Morgan Kaufmann Publishers Inc., San Francisco, CA, USA (1989)
31. Pagallo, G.M.: Adaptative decision tree algorithms for learning from examples (PH.D. thesis). Technical report, Santa Cruz, CA, USA (1990)
32. Ragavan, H., Rendell, L.A.: Lookahead feature construction for learning hard concepts. In: ICML, pp. 252–259. Morgan Kaufmann Publishers Inc. (1993)
33. Ramakrishnan, N., Kumar, D., Mishra, B., Potts, M., Helm, R.F.: Turning cartwheels: an alternating algorithm for mining redescriptions. In: KDD, pp. 266–275. ACM, New York (2004)
34. Saito, T., Rehmsmeier, M.: The precision-recall plot is more informative than the roc plot when evaluating binary classifiers on imbalanced datasets. PLoS ONE 10(3), 1–21 (2015)
35. Svetnik, V., Liaw, A., Tong, C., Wang, T.: Application of Breiman's random forest to modeling structure-activity relationships of pharmaceutical molecules. In: Roli, F., Kittler, J., Windeatt, T. (eds.) MCS 2004. LNCS, vol. 3077, pp. 334–343. Springer, Heidelberg (2004). https://doi.org/10.1007/978-3-540-25966-4_33
36. Tran, B., Xue, B., Zhang, M.: Using feature clustering for GP-based feature construction on high-dimensional data. In: McDermott, J., Castelli, M., Sekanina, L., Haasdijk, E., García-Sánchez, P. (eds.) EuroGP 2017. LNCS, vol. 10196, pp. 210–226. Springer, Cham (2017). https://doi.org/10.1007/978-3-319-55696-3_14
37. Ucar, T., Hajiramezanali, E., Edwards, L.: SubTab: subsetting features of tabular data for self-supervised representation learning. In: NeurIPS, pp. 18853–18865 (2021)
38. UCI: UCI machine learning repository. https://archive.ics.uci.edu/ml/index.php. Accessed 05 July 2022
39. Van Der Maaten, L., Postma, E., Van den Herik, J.: Dimensionality reduction: a comparative review. J. Mach. Learn. Res. 10, 66–71 (2009)
40. Vens, C., Costa, F.: Random forest based feature induction. In: Cook, D.J., Pei, J., Wang, W., Zaïane, O.R., Wu, X. (eds.) ICDM, pp. 744–753. IEEE Computer Society (2011)
41. Wang, M., Chen, X., Zhang, H.: Maximal conditional chi-square importance in random forests. Bioinformatics 26(6), 831–7 (2010)
42. Wrobel, S.: An algorithm for multi-relational discovery of subgroups. In: Komorowski, J., Zytkow, J. (eds.) PKDD 1997. LNCS, vol. 1263, pp. 78–87. Springer, Heidelberg (1997). https://doi.org/10.1007/3-540-63223-9_108
43. Yang, D.S., Rendell, L., Blix, G.: A scheme for feature construction and a comparison of empirical methods. In: IJCAI - Volume 2, pp. 699–704. Morgan Kaufmann Publishers Inc., San Francisco (1991)
44. Zheng, Z.: Constructing nominal X-of-N attributes. In: IJCAI - Volume 2, pp. 1064–1070. Morgan Kaufmann Publishers Inc., San Francisco (1995)
45. Zhou, Z., Feng, J.: Deep forest: towards an alternative to deep neural networks. In: Sierra, C. (ed.) IJCAI, pp. 3553–3559. ijcai.org (2017)

Bitpaths: Compressing Datasets Without Decreasing Predictive Performance

Loren Nuyts[(✉)][iD], Laurens Devos[iD], Wannes Meert[iD], and Jesse Davis[iD]

Department of Computer Science, KU Leuven, Celestijnenlaan 200A,
Leuven, Belgium
{loren.nuyts,laurens.devos,wannes.meert,jesse.davis}@kuleuven.be

Abstract. The ever growing amount of data that becomes available necessitates more memory to store it. Machine learned models are becoming increasingly sophisticated and efficient in order to navigate this growing amount of data. However, not all data is relevant for a certain machine learning task and storing that irrelevant data is a waste of memory and power. To address this, we propose bitpaths: a novel pattern-based method to compress datasets using a random forest. During inference, a KNN classifier then uses the encoded training examples to make a prediction for the encoded test example. We empirically compare bitpaths' predictive performance with the uncompressed setting. Our method can achieve compression ratios up to 80 for datasets with a large number of features without affecting the predictive performance.

Keywords: Feature-encoding · Tree-embedding · Dataset-compression

1 Introduction

The ever increasing sizes of data poses challenges. On the one hand, more storage is needed. On the other hand, machine learning (ML) approaches runtime scales with size and dimensionality of the data. From a ML perspective, ideally the data could be compressed in a way that still enables good predictive performance [17]. A variety of techniques have been proposed for this task such as product quantization-based approach [11], using a neural network [15], or the pattern-mining based KRIMP [12,18]. A drawback to product quantization is that it is only applicable to real-valued data whereas KRIMP is based on itemsets and hence is only applicable to discrete data.

This paper proposes a pattern-mining-based compression scheme using random forests. Random forests are a popular and powerful method that construct an ensemble of decision trees learned on random subsets of the data. The value predicted for an input example is determined by its *output configuration* [4] – the ordered set of leaves that are activated by the example in each tree – and is obtained by combining the predictions of the individual leaves using e.g. a voting scheme. A decision tree effectively compresses the data by (1) identifying

I. Koprinska et al. (Eds.): ECML PKDD 2022 Workshops, CCIS 1752, pp. 261–268, 2023.
https://doi.org/10.1007/978-3-031-23618-1_18

relevant patterns by automatically selecting predictive features, and (2) grouping together examples that are similar, ignoring differences that are irrelevant to the task at hand. As the number of trees in an ensemble is relatively small, and because each leaf can be represented by a small code (at most d bits, with d the tree's depth), the concatenation of the leaf codes in an example's output configuration is an effective compressed representation of the example. A tree-based scheme has the added benefit that it can naturally cope with data that contains both discrete and real-valued features.

Based on these insights, we developed *bitpaths*, a method that trains a random forest on the original feature space $\mathscr{F}$. The random forest maps each example from the original feature space $\mathscr{F}$ to the encoded output configuration space $\mathscr{B}$. During inference, the encoded output configuration of the test example is computed and a KNN classifier is used on the encoded output configurations of the training examples to make a prediction for the encoded test example.

The method we developed for compressing the dataset is similar to the method Pliakos et al., 2016 [16] used for unsupervised learning tasks: Extremely Random Clustering tree Paths (ERCP). However, they use a different encoding for the output configurations that is not suitable for compression (Sect. 2). Indeed, depending on the dimensions of the random forest, ERCP usually expands the size of the dataset. Bitpaths uses a more memory-efficient encoding while maintaining the same predictive accuracy for supervised learning tasks.

This paper investigates the following 2 key questions to determine whether our proposed method is suitable for compression.

1. How well in terms of accuracy does bitpaths perform when compared to KNN on the original feature space $\mathscr{F}$, RF on the original feature space $\mathscr{F}$ and the related method ERCP [16] (Q1)?
2. How much compression of the training set can be achieved by transforming the original feature space $\mathscr{F}$ to the binary code space $\mathscr{B}$ using *bitpaths* without decreasing predictive performance (Q2)?

2   Preliminaries

Random Forest. A random forest, first proposed by Breiman, 2001 [1], is a randomized decision tree ensemble that is widely used for both classification [2,8] and regression tasks [9,13]. A decision tree ensemble consists of several, independently constructed decision trees. By combining the predictions of all individual trees, the ensemble can overcome the large variance that individual decisions trees usually have [16]. A random forest is such a decision tree ensemble, but it consists of randomized decision trees, which means that each decision tree can only split on a randomly chosen subset of the features.

Output Configuration. Given a random forest with m trees, the output configuration (OC) [4] of an example x is the ordered set of leaf nodes $(l_1, .., l_m)$ where each leaf node l_i of the output configuration contains x. The output configuration corresponds to a combination of root-to-leaf paths and the corresponding leaf nodes, where there is one such path and leaf node for each tree in the ensemble. The output configuration of an example x completely determines the prediction of the random forest for x.

Extremely Random Clustering Tree Paths (ERCP). Pliakos et al., 2016 [16] developed a similar method: Extremely Random Clustering tree Paths (ERCP). They use an ensemble of extremely randomized trees instead of a random forest with randomized trees. The most important difference however is the encoding of the output configurations. Instead of encoding the root-to-leaf path, they encode the presence of an example in each node of the tree. Given a tree T with nodes $n_1, .., n_k$, an example $x \in \mathcal{F}$ is encoded as a binary string $b_1..b_k$, where $b_i = 1$ if $x \in n_i$ and 0 otherwise. This results in a very sparse encoding of the example.

3   Bitpaths

The goal of bitpaths is to transform the original feature space $\mathcal{F}$ to the encoded output configuration space $\mathcal{B}$ without losing the essential predictive information. The essential predictive information is extracted by training a random forest on the training set using the original feature space $\mathcal{F}$. By encoding the root-to-leaf paths of each example, the information that the random forest uses to make predictions is kept, while the other information is discarded (Sect. 3.1).

Inference in the encoded output configuration space $\mathcal{B}$ is done with a KNN classifier, which has excellent performance as long as the number of irrelevant features is small. Since our compression scheme removes irrelevant information, KNN is an excellent match.

3.1   Feature Construction

First, a random forest of m trees with maximal depth d is trained on the training set using the original feature space $\mathcal{F}$. Second, the path of each training example in each tree is encoded in a binary string. At each node of a tree, the example can take the left branch, in which case a 0 bit is added to the binary code, or the right branch, in which case a 1 bit is added. This results in a binary code of d bits. Figure 1 shows a toy example of a random forest with 3 trees and maximal depth 2. Each leaf node additionally contains the binary code that represents the path from the root to the leaf node. Finally, the encoded OC for the training example is obtained by concatenating the binary codes of each tree in the random forest. In the toy example of Fig. 1, the training example with $f_1 = f_2 = f_3 = f_4 = 1$ is represented by the encoded OC 01 10 01 and the training example with $f_1 = f_2 = f_3 = f_4 = 5$ is represented by 10 01 00.

3.2   Inference

At inference time, a k-nearest neighbours model predicts the target variable of an encoded test example, based on the encoded OC's of the training examples. The k-nearest neighbours are determined by the Hamming distance between the

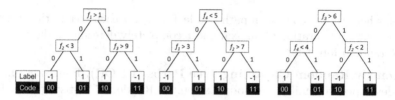

Fig. 1. Example random forest with 3 trees and maximal depth 2. The leaf nodes contain the label and the binary code that represents the root-to-leaf path.

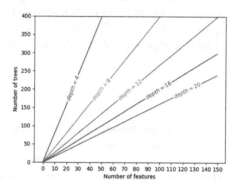

Fig. 2. Lines of equal memory usage in function of the number of trees in the ensemble, the maximal depth of each tree and the number of features in the original feature space.

encoded training examples and the encoded test example. The prediction of the test example is then the average of the predictions of the k-nearest neighbours.

3.3   Compression

For a random forest of m trees and maximal depth d, bitpaths represents each example by an encoded OC of $m * d$ bits. If we assume that each feature in the original feature space $\mathscr{F}$ is represented by a 4 byte float and that there are k features, an example in $\mathscr{F}$ consists of $8 * 4 * k = 32 * k$ bits. Figure 2 shows the lines of equal memory usage in terms of the number of features in $\mathscr{F}$, the number of trees in the random forest and the maximal depth of each tree. If the number of trees and maximal depth is chosen such that you fall below the corresponding depth line, compression is achieved.

The encoding of the related method ERCP on the other hand is not suitable for compression. ERCP represents each example by a binary string of $(2^{d+1} - 1) * m$ bits. This quickly explodes with increasing depth and number of trees and compression would only be possible for datasets with an enormous number of features.

4   Experimental Evaluation

In this section, the following research questions will be answered.

Table 1. Characteristics of the datasets used for evaluation

	Nb of instances	Nb of features
BreastCancer	699	9
Covertype	581 012	54
Higgs	3 468	33
Gina agnostic	601	970
monks-problem-2	250 000	6
ijcnn1	141 691	22
Webspam	350 000	254
tic-tac-toe	958	9
Scene	2 407	299
Fashion MNIST	14 000	784

1. How does bitpaths compare to KNN on the original feature space $\mathscr{F}$, RF on the original feature space $\mathscr{F}$, and the related method ERCP [16] in terms of predictive performance (Q1)?
2. How much compression of the training set can be achieved by transforming the original feature space $\mathscr{F}$ to the binary code space $\mathscr{B}$ using *bitpaths* without decreasing the predictive performance (Q2)?

We used 10 datasets[1] that vary in the number of instances and features (Table 1) for our experiments. Min-max normalization is first applied to all datasets. We used the implementation of the *RandomForestClassifier* class of scikit-learn version 1.0 with Gini impurity for all random forests used in the experiments. The exact number of trees and the maximal depth depend on the specific experiment. For the other parameters, the default setting of the *RandomForestClassifier* class is used. The evaluation is done with 10-fold cross-validation.

4.1   Experimental Evaluation Bitpaths (Q1)

For the first research question, we used a random forest with 50 trees with a maximal depth of 8 and selected the 10 nearest neighbours during inference. Table 2 compares bitpaths with KNN evaluated on the original feature space $\mathscr{F}$, the same random forest as was used for feature construction and ERCP [16] (see Sect. 2). It also contains the average and the standard deviation of the rank per method. Although bitpaths has the best average rank and the lowest standard deviation, both the Friedman test [6,7] and the test developed by Iman and Davenport [10] imply that all compared methods do not significantly differ from each other ($\alpha = 0.05$). Furthermore, following the approach proposed by Demsar, 2006 [3] to compare multiple classifiers in a statistically correct way, the

---

[1] For the Fashion MNIST dataset, only the examples belonging to class 2 and 4 are used to make the classifier binary. This will be denoted as Fashion MNIST (2, 4).

Table 2. Accuracy results for regular k-nearest neighbours (KNN, $k = 10$), the random forest used for feature construction in the bitpaths method (RF), the method proposed by Pliakos et al., 2016 (ERCP) [16] and our proposed method (bitpaths). For each dataset, the rank of each method is given between brackets. The achieved compression (not in percent) by ERCP and bitpaths on each dataset is also included, where a higher compression ratio means that there is more compression and is thus better. The last column gives the average duration (in seconds) of the compression for bitpaths.

	KNN	RF	ERCP	Bithpaths	Compression ERCP	Compression bitpaths	Compression time bitpaths (s)
BreastCancer	0.964 (4)	0.969 (1)	0.968 (2)	0.966 (3)	1.13e−2	7.20e−1	1.15e−1
Covertype	0.971 (1)	0.770 (4)	0.905 (3)	0.908 (2)	6.76e−2	4.32	159
Higgs	0.807 (4)	0.826 (1)	0.820 (3)	0.825 (2)	4.13e−2	2.64	11.7
Gina agnostic	0.826 (4)	0.922 (3)	0.937 (1)	0.935 (2)	1.21	77.6	3.55e−1
monks-problem-2	0.809 (4)	0.960 (1)	0.942 (2.5)	0.942 (2.5)	7.51e−3	4.80e−1	1.44e−1
ijcnn1	0.975 (3)	0.964 (4)	0.979 (2)	0.983 (1)	2.76e−2	1.76	8.10
Webspam	0.982 (3)	0.959 (4)	0.984 (1)	0.983 (2)	3.18e−1	20.3	73.4
tic-tac-toe	0.824 (4)	0.926 (2)	0.918 (3)	0.948 (1)	1.13e−2	7.20e−1	1.34e−1
Scene	0.950 (1)	0.908 (4)	0.926 (3)	0.931 (2)	3.74e−1	23.9	2.59e−1
Fashion MNIST (2, 4)	0.870 (3)	0.868 (4)	0.875 (2)	0.881 (1)	9.82e−1	62.7	1.40
Average rank	3.05	2.80	2.25	1.90	–	–	–
Standard deviation rank	1.150	1.327	0.750	0.663	–	–	–

Nemenyi test [14], that performs a pair-wise comparison, and the Bonferroni-Dunn test [5], that additionally corrects for the family-wise error in multiple hypothesis testing, conclude that our proposed method doesn't significantly differ from any of the other methods in terms of accuracy. However, 7 of the 10 datasets are compressed with a compression ratio ranging between 1.76 and 77.6 (not in percent), depending on the dataset. This implies that bitpaths can compress datasets without affecting the predictive performance. This stands in contrast with ERCP that uses more memory for 9 of the 10 evaluated datasets. Furthermore, bitpaths compresses datasets quickly: depending on the size of the dataset it takes less than a second or up to a few minutes.

4.2   Compression Versus Accuracy (Q2)

For the second research question, we varied the compression ratio of the bitpaths algorithm to investigate its effect on the accuracy. The number of trees in each ensemble are chosen such that a compression ratio of 1, 2, 4, 6, 8, 10, 20, 30, 40, 50, 60, 70 and 80 is achieved. The maximal depth of each tree always remained 8. Figure 3 shows that the datasets can be divided in two categories:

1. For the datasets with a low number of features, the best accuracy is found when no compression takes place (compression ratio = 1) and the accuracy gradually decreases with a higher compression ratio. The decrease in accuracy is because the ensembles get smaller and smaller, until eventually they are unable to accurately capture the relationship between the features and target variable. For the breastcancer, monks-problem-2 and tic-tac-toe datasets, a

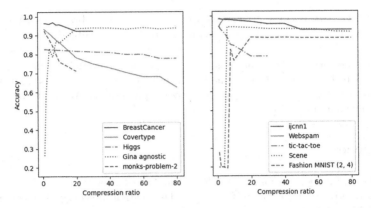

Fig. 3. Evolution of the accuracy of bitpaths in terms of the compression ratio (not in percent) for each example in the training set. We evaluated the following ratios: 1, 2, 4, 6, 8, 10, 20, 30, 40, 50, 60, 70, 80. The number of trees in each ensemble are chosen to achieve such a compression ratio. The maximal depth always remained 8.

compression ratio beyond 40, 30 and 30 respectively couldn't be achieved because these datasets are a very low dimensionality (<10) and because we look at depth 8 trees, our codes are always one byte.

2. For the datasets with a high number of features, the initial accuracy is low (except for Webspam) and gradually increases with increasing compression until it reaches its peak. From that point, the accuracy has a steady course and doesn't drop like the datasets with a low number of features. This behaviour can be explained by the extremely large number of trees that are needed when no compression takes place (1000–3000 trees) while this is substantially fewer for the other datasets (maximum 216 trees with no compression). The datasets of this category are too small to properly train such a huge forest, which results in low accuracy results for small compression rates. Webspam on the other hand is large enough to train its large forest, which explains its good initial accuracy. The steady course can also be explained by the number of trees in the ensemble, which for higher compression ratios is still large enough to make good predictions. It is expected that for even higher compression ratio's, the accuracy will also drop.

5 Conclusion

This paper explored how to compress datasets without losing predictive performance. Our approach can handle both real-valued and discrete data by using a random forest to compress the data. The experiments showed that bitpaths can achieve high compression ratios for datasets with many features without affecting the predictive accuracy. One limitation of our approach is that the encoded output configuration is suboptimal in terms of compression when working with non-balanced trees where most examples take the long branches. A different encoding of the output configurations might be more suitable in that case.

Acknowledgements. This work was supported by the Research Foundation-Flanders (1SB1320N to LD), iBOF/21/075, the KU Leuven Research Fund (C14/17/070), and the Flemish Government under the "Onderzoeksprogramma Artificiële Intelligentie (AI) Vlaanderen" program.

References

1. Breiman, L.: Random forests. Mach. Learn. **45**, 5–32 (2001)
2. Cutler, D.R., et al.: Random forests for classification in ecology. Ecology **88**(11), 2783–2792 (2007)
3. Demsar, J.: Statistical comparisons of classifiers over multiple data sets. J. Mach. Learn. Res. **7**, 1–30 (2006)
4. Devos, L., Meert, W., Davis, J.: Adversarial example detection in deployed tree ensembles (2022)
5. Dunn, O.J.: Multiple comparisons among means. J. Am. Stat. Assoc. **56**(293), 52–64 (1961)
6. Friedman, M.: The use of ranks to avoid the assumption of normality implicit in the analysis of variance. J. Am. Stat. Assoc. **32**(200), 675–701 (1937)
7. Friedman, M.: A comparison of alternative tests of significance for the problem of m rankings. Ann. Math. Stat. **11**(1), 86–92 (1940)
8. Gislason, P.O., Benediktsson, J.A., Sveinsson, J.R.: Random forests for land cover classification. Pattern Recogn. Lett. **27**(4), 294–300 (2006). Pattern Recognition in Remote Sensing (PRRS 2004)
9. Gong, H., Sun, Y., Shu, X., Huang, B.: Use of random forests regression for predicting IRI of asphalt pavements. Constr. Build. Mater. **189**, 890–897 (2018)
10. Iman, R.L., Davenport, J.M.: Approximations of the critical region of the Friedman statistic. Commun. Stat., 571–595 (1980)
11. Jégou, H., Douze, M., Schmid, C.: Product quantization for nearest neighbor search. IEEE Trans. Pattern Anal. Mach. Intell. **33**(1), 117–128 (2011)
12. Makhalova, T., Kuznetsov, S.O., Napoli, A.: Numerical pattern mining through compression, pp. 112–121 (2019)
13. Montillo, A., Ling, H.: Age regression from faces using random forests. In: 16th IEEE International Conference on Image Processing, pp. 2465–2468 (2009)
14. Nemenyi, P.B.: Distribution-free multiple comparisons. Ph.D. thesis, Princeton University (1963)
15. Park, J., Park, H., Choi, Y.J.: Data compression and prediction using machine learning for industrial IoT. In: 2018 International Conference on Information Networking (ICOIN), pp. 818–820 (2018)
16. Pliakos, K., Vens, C.: Feature induction based on extremely randomized tree paths. In: Online Proceedings, pp. 3–18 (2016)
17. Sculley, D., Brodley, C.: Compression and machine learning: a new perspective on feature space vectors. In: Data Compression Conference, pp. 332–341 (2006)
18. Vreeken, J., Van Leeuwen, M., Siebes, A.: KRIMP: mining itemsets that compress. Data Mining Knowl. Discov. **23**(1), 169–214 (2011)

3D Detection of ALMA Sources Through Deep Learning

Michele Delli Veneri[1,2](✉) ⬤, Lukasz Tychoniec[3] ⬤, Fabrizia Guglielmetti[3] ⬤,
Eric Villard[3] ⬤, and Giuseppe Longo[4] ⬤

[1] INFN Section of Naples, via Cintia, 1, 80126 Naples, Italy
[2] Department of Electrical Engineering and Information Technology,
University of Naples "Federico II", Via Claudio, 21, 80125 Naples, NA, Italy
michele.delliveneri@unina.it
[3] ESO, Karl-Schwarzschild-Straße 2, 85748 Garching bei München, Germany
[4] Department of Physics "Ettore Pancini", University of Naples "Federico II",
Via Cintia, 1, 80126 Naples, Italy

Abstract. We present a Deep Learning pipeline for the detection of
astronomical sources within radiointerferometric simulated data cubes.
Our pipeline is constituted by two Deep Learning models: a Convolutional Autoencoder for the detection of sources within the spatial domain
of the cube, and a RNN for the denoising and detection of emission peaks
in the frequency domain. The combination of spatial and frequency information allows for higher completeness and helps to remove false positives.
The pipeline has been tested on simulated ALMA observations achieving better performances and faster execution times with respect to traditional methods. The pipeline can detect 92% of sources up to a flux
of 1.31 Jy/beam with no false positives thus providing a reliable source
detection solution for future astronomical radio surveys.

Keywords: Deep learning · Object detection · Radio interferometry

1 Introduction

In the last two decades, astronomical measurements underwent a rapid growth in
size and complexity thus driving Astronomy in the big data regime [3,14,18,26]
requiring a redesign of data reduction techniques capable to provide robust
results and substantial speed-up in the solution being sought. Machine learning demonstrated to be capable to solve a wide spectrum of problems spanning all aspects of the astronomical data cycle, from instrument monitoring to data acquisition and ingestion, to data analysis and interpretation
[1,9,10,13,16,22,25]. Particularly challenging are the problems posed by exis-
tent and future infrastructures for radio astronomy, such as the Atacama Large
Millimeter/sub-millimeter Array (ALMA), the Low Frequency Array (LOFAR)
and the Square Kilometer Array (SKA) which are pushing astronomy in the
exabyte and exascale computing. After the initial correlation and calibration of

I. Koprinska et al. (Eds.): ECML PKDD 2022 Workshops, CCIS 1752, pp. 269–280, 2023.
https://doi.org/10.1007/978-3-031-23618-1_19

the raw signals in Fourier space, these observatories are capable to provide data in the form of cubes. We consider 3-dimensional cubes provided by an image space (coordinates on the celestial sphere) combined with a spectrum in frequency. The extraction of the celestial signal from the data cubes requires the solution of an ill-posed inverse problem:

$$I^D(x,y) = R \times I(x,y) + n \tag{1}$$

where $I^D(x,y)$ are the observed measurements, $I(x,y)$ is the unknown signal, R is a degradation operator due to the response capabilities of the observatories and n is the additional noise propagated from the observation process to the calibrated signal. R, also known as *forward operator*, takes up the very complex underlying physical processes involved in the observational process. The deconvolution process ideally provides the noiseless observation $I(x,y)$ from the observed measurements and it is traditionally performed making assumptions about the signal and the forward operator. Many attempts have been made at solving this problem using Machine Learning (ML) based approaches [4,7,19,21,27]. In this paper, we present a deep-learning-based pipeline for the detection of sources within "uncleaned" data cubes $I^D(x,y)$, i.e. data which have not undergone any prior deconvolution (hereafter "dirty" datacubes). In a first order approximation, a dirty cube represents the inverse Fourier transform of the observed visibilities convolved with the instrumental point spread function (dirty beam). Visibilities are recorded complex values of the interference pattern provided by each antenna pair. The number of sampled visibilities is limited and a direct inversion of Eq. 1 is not feasible for reconstructing the sky brightness. The most popular deconvolution technique for image reconstruction in the radio wave region of the electromagnetic spectrum is CLEAN [12]. Given the information of the point-spread function, bright point sources are identified and subtracted from the dirty image using an iterative process. The identified point sources are recorded in the model image. When all point sources are removed from the dirty image, the remaining dirty image should consist only of noise. A multiscale CLEAN approach extends the work of [12] allowing point sources to be Gaussian distributed instead of a delta function [8]. In this work we introduce a new design to the image reconstruction problem capable to overcome some of the limitations introduced by the traditional CLEAN algorithm. These limitations are

1. the iterative cleaning procedure optimize the best possible image reconstruction employing a minor cycle operating in the image domain and a major cycle to handle residuals from the observed data and the estimated model image (through a transformation from data and image domains). Hence, each cube undergoes a time-consuming cleaning procedure which is demanding for current and future radio interferometers [5].
2. by working on each slice independently, CLEAN completely ignores possible correlations between pixels along the frequency axis of the cube, and this leads to the introduction of biases and artifacts in the cleaned cube. For example, a noise peak would be deconvolved several time with the PSF of the instrument and then the recovered delta function would be convolved with

the *clean beam* thus producing a structure morphologically similar to actual sources that underwent the same iterative deconvolution process.

The main novelty of our proposed pipeline with respect to other architectures [7,19,21] is to include frequency information (which is usually discarded) to help detect the sources and remove false detections. As we shall demonstrate, frequency information can help both in deblending spatially blended (overlapping) sources and in the detection of faint sources.

Our paper is structured as it follows: In Sect. 2 we describe the architectures of the deep learning models used in our pipeline, the complete data flow within the pipeline in order to explain its inner workings, and the training strategies for all the models. In Sect. 3 we present the simulation algorithm used to generate the realistic ALMA observations needed to train and test our pipeline, and we analyse the pipeline performances in detecting sources within the test set. A comparison is also made with the performances of *blobcat* and *Sofia-2*: two classical source detection algorithms widely used within the community [11,24]. Finally, in Sect. 4 we draw our concluding remarks, and lay the prospect for future work. We wish to emphasize that while this paper focuses mainly on the analysis of ALMA data cubes, the methodology is general and can easily be exported to the processing of similar data (e.g. LOFAR and SKA) as well as to other fields (such as radiology) requiring an accurate analysis of data cubes.

2   Methodologies

The pipeline can be described as a decision graph interconnecting two deep learning models, each one taking a specialised role in the detection process. The architectures were chosen on the basis of their strengths: a convolutional architecture (we shall call it "Blobs Finder") to process spatial information and a Recurrent Neural Network (Deep GRU) to process frequency information. Before describing the details of the Deep Learning models in the pipeline, we hereby describe the full flow of data within the pipeline.

2.1   The Pipeline

The pipeline can be divided into tree logical blocks: 2D source detection, frequency denoising and emission detection, and source focusing (these blocks are marked in Fig. 1). To ease the logical flow of the pipeline, we assume that all DL models have been trained to act as simple, functional map between their inputs and outputs.

1. **2D Sources Detection (1–4).** The image cube is normalized to the [0,1] range and then it is integrated along frequency (1) to create a 2D image. We refer to this image as the "dirty image". The dirty image is then cropped to a size of [256, 256] pixels (which is large enough to contain the whole source and removes the edge of the images which are characterized by low SNR), normalized to the [0, 1] range (2) and then fed to the first DL model **Blobs Finder**.

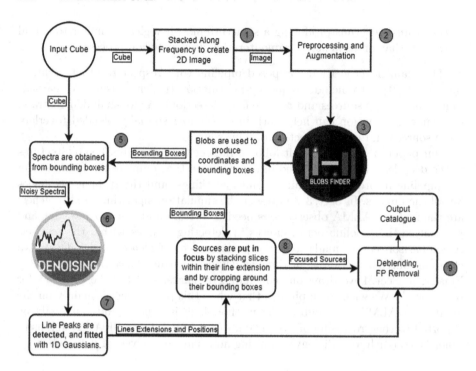

Fig. 1. The full pipeline schema, the numbers show the logic flow of the data within the pipeline (see the text for explanations).

The autoencoder processes the image and predicts a 2D probabilistic map (normalized to the $[0, 1]$ range) of source detection (3). A hard thresholding value of 0.1 is used to binarize the probabilistic map and then the *scikit-learn* [17] *label* and *regionprops* algorithms are used to extract bounding boxes around all blobs of pixels (4). The thresholding value is chosen to be 0.1 in order to peak all the signal detected by Blobs Finder, while excluding small fluctuation in the background. We refer to these blobs as source candidates. Figure 2 shows, respectively, an example of an input dirty image containing 6 simulated sources (outlined by green bounding boxes and of which two are spatially blended), the target sky model image (with in green the target bounding boxes and in red the predicted bounding boxes extracted through thresholding of the predicted 2D probabilistic map), and the 2D prediction map with in red the predicted bounding boxes.

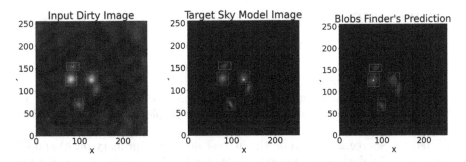

Fig. 2. Left: Input dirty image; center: target sky model image; right: blobs finder prediction image (green = true bounding boxes, red = predicted). (Color figure online)

2. **Frequency Denoising (5–7):** bounding boxes around source candidates (blobs) are used to extract dirty spectra from the input cube. The spectrum of each source candidate is extracted by adding the pixels inside its bounding box for each of the 128 frequency slices of the cube. The spectra are standardized, i.e. rescaled to have null mean and standard deviation with unity value, and then fed to **Deep GRU**. The Deep Gated Recurrent Unit denoises the standardized spectra and outputs 1D probabilistic maps of source emission lines (hereafter, cleaned spectra (6)). In order to detect emission peaks, the cleaned spectra are analysed with the *scipy* [23] *find_peaks* algorithm (threshold value of 0.1). Each peak is fitted with a Gaussian [2]. All detected peaks are recorded alongside their FWHMs (7). At this stage, to account for possible false positives produced by Blobs Finder, all potential candidates that show no meaningful peak in their spectra are removed. If more than one peak is found inside a given spectrum, the candidate likely is the superimposition of two or more blended sources and thus is flagged for deblending.

3. **Source Spectral Focusing (8–9):** this phase has two main objectives; deblend sources and remove false positives. The first is tackled via *spectral focusing* aimed at increasing the Signal to Noise Ratio (SNR) of the source (by cropping a $[64, 64]$ pixel box around its bounding box and integrating only within the peak FWHM. In order to measure sources SNRs, we introduce two diverse SNR metrics defined as follows:

   – **Global SNR:**

$$SNR = \frac{median(x_s(r))}{var(x_n(R-r))} \tag{2}$$

   where $x_s(r)$ are the values of the source pixels contained within the circumference of radius r that inscribes the source bounding box, and $x_n(R-r)$ are the pixel values within an annulus of internal radius r and external radius R which has the same area of the inscribed circumference;

– **Pixel SNR:**

$$snr = \frac{x_i}{var(X)} \tag{3}$$

where x_i is the value of the given pixel, and $var(X)$ is the variance computed on the full image.

These two SNR estimators are used respectively to disentangle false positives from true sources and to deblend possible multiple sources within a given blob.

First, the source is focused on the highest flux peak (primary peak) and the global SNR calculation is made to understand if the potential source must be discarded. Also, the pixel SNR measurement is used to find the highest SNR pixel in the image, which will act as a reference for the next phase of the deblending process. The candidate source is focused around the secondary peaks. If the secondary peaks are outside the emission range of the brightest source, then the latter should disappear from the focused image (because the image is produced by integrating the cube outside the source emission range), and the pixel SNR measurement is used to find the highest SNR pixel in the image. If this pixel is different from the previously found reference pixel, then the neighboring pixels around this pixel are linked with a friend of friends algorithm in an iterative manner. At each iteration, the Global SNR is measured. Pixels are added in this fashion until a plateau in the global SNR is reached. If the highest SNR pixel and the reference pixel are within 1 pixel and the global SNR measured in the integrated cube image is higher than the measured SNR in the spectrally focussed image, then the source is discarded as a False Positive. A bounding box is finally created in order to encompass all the selected pixels, and a $[64, 64]$ pixel image is cropped around the bounding box.

2.2 Blobs Finder

Blobs Finder is a 2D Deep Convolutional Autoencoder trained to solve the image deconvolution problem:

$$D[x, y] = P[x, y] \times M[x, y] + N[x, y] \tag{4}$$

where $D[x, y]$ is the dirty (stacked) image produced integrating along the frequency the dirty cube, $P[x, y]$ is the dirty PSF, $N[x, y]$ is the combination of all noise patterns in the data and $M[x, y]$ is the true sky model, i.e. the unaltered radio signal emitted from the simulated astronomical sources. Blobs Finder is trained with the dirty images as inputs, and the sky model images as targets. Both input and target images are normalized to the $[0, 1]$ range. The Blobs Finder architecture is constituted by an Encoder Network and a Decoder Network. The Encoder consists of four convolutional blocks and a final fully connected layer.

Each block contains a 2D Convolution layer with stride 2 and a kernel size of 3, a Leaky ReLU (Rectified Linear Unit) activation function and a 2D Batch Normalization layer. Each block halves the spatial extent of its input and doubles the number of channels. The Decoder is constituted by a fully connected layer, followed by four deconvolutional blocks and a final layer. Each deconvolutional block contains a bilinear interpolation function with a stride of 2 which up-samples spatially the input, a 2D Transposed Convolution with a kernel size of 3 and a stride of 1 which reduces the number of channels while preserving the spatial dimensions, a leaky ReLU activation function and a 2D Batch Normalization layer. The final layer (used to normalize the input to the $[0, 1]$ range) is a 2D Convolution with a kernel size of 1 and a stride of 1 followed by a Sigmoid activation function. To train Blobs Finder, we use as a loss function the weighted combination of two well-known losses in the DL image reconstruction and denoising framework: the l_1 loss and the Structural dissimilarity loss $DSSIM$.

2.3   The Deep GRU

The Deep Gated Recurrent Unit (GRU) is a Recurrent Neural Network (RNN) [20] constructed by combining together two layers of GRUs [6] and a fully connected layer. In our implementation, each layer of GRUs outputs 32 hidden states (or channels to keep the nomenclature homogeneous) which are then concatenated to form a latent vector of size $[b, 64 \times 128]$ before being fed to a fully connected layer. The layer transforms its input in a vector with the same size as the input signal and then a Sigmoid activation function is applied to normalize it to the $[0, 1]$ range. As loss function, we use the l_1 loss.

3   Experiments

To train and test the proposed pipeline, we need a statistically significant sample of ALMA model and dirty cube pairs. To this effect we generated our own simulations of ALMA data cubes by combining python and bash scripting with the Common Astronomy Software Application (CASA) v. 6.5.0.15 [15] python libraries. CASA provides a set of simulator methods allowing one to create realistic ALMA observations at any given configuration and observing time. Corrupting effects as thermal noise and atmospheric pollution are possible. ALMA simulations are reliable and can also be used to tune parameters of the (real) data reduction. Each model cube was created by first generating a central source and then by adding between 2 and 5 additional sources such that each source emission flux is lower or equal to that of the central source. In order to simulate 3D sources, we combined 2D Gaussian Components in the spatial plane with 1D Gaussian components (emission lines) in frequency space. The source morphological parameters are sampled from the intervals reported in Table 1.

Table 1. Sampling intervals of the model source parameters. Sources are generated by randomly sampling from the outlined uniform distributions. The first column shows the parameter name, the second the range from which the parameter values are sampled, and the third the unit.

Parameter name	Range	Unit
Number of components	[2–5]	–
Amplitude of 2D Gaussian compoment	[1–5]	Arbitrary
FWHM of the 2D Gaussian component	[2–8]	Pixel
Spectral index	[-2–2]	–
Position in the xy plane	[100–250]	Pixel
Position angle	[0–90]	Deg
Line amplitude	[1–5]	Arbitrary
Line center	[10–110]	Chan
Line FWHM	[3–10]	Chan

We then feed the sky models to the CASA *simobserve* taks which simulates interferometric measurements sets through a series of observing parameters. The dirty data cubes are then obtained by performing the fast Fourier transform of the visibility data and gridding. We generate $5,000$ simulated cube pairs containing a total of $22,532$ simulated sources and divide them into train, validation, and test sets ($60\%, 20\%, 20\%$). The three sets contain respectively $13,512$, $4,465$, and $4,556$ simulated sources. While the two models are trained indipendently in parallel on the same training data, the predictions are made sequentially given that the input of each model is the output of the previous one.

3.1   Source Detection

Hereafter, we present the performances of Blobs Finder and Deep GRU in detecting sources within the $1,000$ cubes in the Test set. To check if a source has been detected by Blobs Finder, we measure the 2D Intersection over Union (2D IoU) between the true 2D bounding box and the predicted one, while for Deep GRU we measure the 1D IoU between the true emission ranges and the detected ones. In both cases, we use a threshold of 0.8. To ensure that the central part of the source emission of a True Positive (TP) is always detected, we require the distance between the centres of the true and predicted bounding boxes is smaller then 3 pixels. Blobs Finder predicts 4056 (89%) sources (TP). Matching them with the true $4,556$ sources in the Test set, $4,205$ (92.3%) pass the 2D IoU criterion, meaning that an additional 149 sources are detected by Blobs

Finder but are spatially blended with another source. Blobs Finder misses 354 sources (FN) and detects no False Positives (FP). The 4056 bounding boxes are used to extract a corresponding number of dirty spectra from the dirty cubes. The Deep GRU detects 4,202 emission peaks out of the 4,205 present in the extracted spectra but also produces 62 false positives. Sources are then "spectrally focused" within the predicted frequency emission ranges and SNR checks are made to detect false positives and, in the case, deblend multiple sources. At the end of this phase all 62 false positives are correctly identified and eliminated. In order to compare with BLOBCAT ([11]) and SOFIA-2 ([24]), we run them on the 1000 dirty images (cubes in the case of SOFIA-2) in the test set. BLOBCAT requires two parameters: a detection (T_d) and cut (T_f) SNR threshold to decide which peaks in the image are candidates for blobs and where to cut the blobs boundaries around them (in other words: pixels with a SNR higher than T_f are selected to form islands and island boundaries are defined by T_d). We measured BLOBCAT performances with different choices of T_d and T_f through a grid-search strategy ($T_d \in [2, 15]$, $T_f \in [1, 10]$) and, in this paper, we report the best results ($T_d = 8\sigma$, $T_f = 4\sigma$). SOFIA-2 was run with its default set of parameters with the exception of the filter sizes that were set to $[3, 5, 7, 11]$ in both spatial and frequency directions and the *autokernel* parameter that was set to *True* to automatically determine the reliability kernel size. We run the SOFIA-2 smooth and clip algorithm with a spatial and frequency kernel sizes of $[3, 5, 7, 9, 11]$, a source finding threshold of 0.5, a spatial linking radius of 1, a frequency linking radius of 3 and a SNR threshold of 2. We let the algorithm automatically select the other thresholds. We limit the detection area of SOFIA-2 by setting the masking to a 256 pixel size square centered in the image. BLOBCAT successfully detects 2,779 (61%) sources, produces 2,429 false detections and misses 1777 sources. The majority of sources missed by BLOBCAT are spatially blended with brighter sources, or present a $SNR \leq 5.0$, or are located at the edges of the images. *Sofia-2* detects 1010 (22%) sources, produces 4011 false detections and misses 3546 sources. Regarding SOFIA-2 predictions, most false positives are located at the spatial edges of the image, while it misses most blended sources by merging their emissions with other sources which leads to all involved sources failing the 2D IoU or distance based thresholds. Table 2 summarises the source detection performances. Regarding the execution time to process an ALMA cube, the DL pipeline, BLOBCAT and SOFIA-2 take on average 3.2 ms, 32 s and 67 s, respectively. This is a crucial factor for ALMA (which is transitioning to a TB data regime [5]) and for other future radio interferometers such as SKA.

Table 2. Comparison between the sequential proposed source finding pipeline composed by Blobs Finder, DeepGRU and Spectral Focusing, and BLOBSCAT. Columns show true positives (TP), false positives (FP), false negatives (FN), precision, recall and mean intersection over union (Mean IoU) between true bounding boxes and predicted ones. TP and FN are also expressed as fractions over the total number of sources.

Algorithm	TP/	FP	FN	Precision	Recall	Mean IoU
Pipeline	4202 (92.3%)	0	354 (7.7%)	1.0	0.923	0.84
Blobcat	2779 (61%)	2429	1777 (39%)	0.53	0.609	0.81
Sofia-2	1010 (22%)	4011	3546 (78%)	0.20	0.22	0.83

4   Conclusions

In this paper, we present a novel pipeline for source detection in radio-interferometric data cubes. The pipeline is constituted by two DL models: Blobs Finder (Deep Convolutional Autoencoder) and Deep GRU (RNN). Blobs Finder detects sources within the integrated data cubes (2D images produced by integrating the cubes along the frequency axis) and the found candidate sources are used to extract spectra which are then fed to the Deep GRU algorithm. Deep GRU is capable of denoising the spectra in order to detect emission lines. Spatial and Spectral information is combined to remove false positives and spatially deblend sources. To test the pipeline capabilities, we produce our own realistic simulations of ALMA observations, $5,000$ data cubes containing $22,532$ simulated sources with fluxes ranging from 1 to 380 $Jy/beam$. We also compare the pipeline performances with BLOBCAT and SOFIA-2, two standard source finding algorithms extensively used within the community, showing that our proposed pipeline achieves better performances and faster execution times. The DL pipeline is 33% and 76% more efficient than BLOBCAT and SOFIA-2, respectively, when compared at the purity level. The DL pipeline is also capable to improve by a factor of 10 the imaging procedure's speed. The application to ALMA dirty cubes shows that the DL pipeline is capable to support CASA redesigning the imaging procedure in view of the big data era.

References

1. Akhazhanov, A., et al.: Finding quadruply imaged quasars with machine learning - I. Methods. Mon. Not. R. Astron. Soc. **513**(2), pp. 2407–2421 (2022). https://doi.org/10.1093/mnras/stac925
2. Collaboration, A., et al.: "The astropy project: building an openscience project and status of the v2.0 core package. Astron. J. **156**(3), 123 (2018). https://doi.org/10.3847/1538-3881/aabc4f. arXiv: 1801.02634 [astro-ph.IM]
3. Baron, D.: Machine learning in astronomy: a practical overview (2019). https://doi.org/10.48550/ARXIV.1904.07248

4. Bowles, M., et al.: Attention-gating for improved radio galaxy classification. Mon. Not. R. Astron. Soc. **501**(3), 4579–4595 (2020). https://doi.org/10.1093/mnras/staa3946

5. Carpenter, J., et al.: The ALMA development program: roadmap to 2030 (2020). https://doi.org/10.48550/ARXIV.2001.11076. https://arxiv.org/abs/2001.11076

6. Chung, J., et al.: Empirical evaluation of gated recurrent neural networks on sequence modeling. CoRR abs/1412.3555 (2014). arXiv:1412.3555

7. Connor, L., et al.: Deep radio-interferometric imaging with POLISH: DSA-2000 and weak lensing. Mon. Not. R. Astron. Soc. **514**(2), pp. 2614–2626 (2022). https://doi.org/10.1093/mnras/stac1329

8. Cornwell, T.J.: Multiscale CLEAN deconvolution of radio synthesis images. IEEE J. Sel. Top. Sig. Process. **2**(5), 793–801 (2008). https://doi.org/10.1109/JSTSP.2008.2006388

9. Duarte, R., Nemmen, R., Navarro, J.P.: Black hole weather forecasting with deep learning: a pilot study. Mon. Not. R. Astron. Soc. **512**(4), 5848–5861 (2022). https://doi.org/10.1093/mnras/stac665

10. Goode, S., et al.: Machine learning for fast transients for the deeper, wider, faster programme with the removal Of BOgus transients (ROBOT) pipeline. Mon. Not. R. Astron. Soc. **513**(2), 1742–1754 (2022). https://doi.org/10.1093/mnras/stac983

11. Hales, C.A., et al.: BLOBCAT: software to catalogue flood-filled blobs in radio images of total intensity and linear polarization. Mon. Not. R. Astron. Soc. **425**(2), 979–996 (2012). https://doi.org/10.1111/j.1365-2966.2012.21373.x

12. Hogbom, J.A.: Aperture synthesis with a non-regular distribution of interferometer baselines. Astron. Astrophys. **15**, 417 (1974)

13. Lin, S.-C., et al.: Estimating cluster masses from SDSS multiband images with transfer learning. Mon. Not. R. Astron. Soc. **512**(3), 3885–3894 (2022). https://doi.org/10.1093/mnras/stac725

14. Longo, G., Merényi, E., Tiňo, P.: Foreword to the focus issue on machine intelligence in astronomy and astrophysics. Publ. Astron. Soc. Pac. **131**(1004), 1–6 (2019). ISSN: 00046280, 15383873. https://www.jstor.org/stable/26874447. Visited 24 June 2022

15. McMullin, J.P., et al.: CASA architecture and applications. In: Shaw, R.A., Hill, F., Bell, D.J. (eds.) Astronomical Data Analysis Software and Systems XVI ASP Conference Series, vol. 376, Proceedings of the Conference Held 15–18 October 2006 in Tucson, Arizona, USA, p. 127 376, October 2007

16. Nousi, P., et al.: Autoencoder-driven spiral representation learning for gravitational wave surrogate modelling. Neurocomputing **491**, 67–77 (2022). https://doi.org/10.1016/j.neucom.2022.03.052

17. Pedregosa, F., et al.: Scikit-learn: machine learning in Python. J. Mach. Learn. Res. **12**, 2825–2830 (2011)

18. Pesenson, M.Z., Pesenson, I.Z., McCollum, B.: The data big bang and the expanding digital universe: high-dimensional, complex and massive data sets in an inationary epoch. Adv. Astron. 2010 (2010), pp. 1–16. https://doi.org/10.1155/2010/350891

19. Rezaei, S., et al.: DECORAS: detection and characterization of radio-astronomical sources using deep learning. Mon. Not. R. Astron. Soc. **510**(4), 5891–5907 (2021). https://doi.org/10.1093/mnras/stab3519

20. Rumelhart, D.E., Hinton, G.E., Williams, R.J.: Learning internal representations by error propagation. In: Rumelhart, D.E., Mcclelland, J.L. (eds.) Parallel Distributed Processing: Explorations in the Microstructure of Cognition, Volume 1: Foundations, pp. 318–362. MIT Press, Cambridge (1986)

21. Schmidt, K., et al.: Deep learning-based imaging in radio interferometry. Astron. Astrophys. (2022). https://doi.org/10.1051/0004-6361/202142113

22. Sweere, S.F., et al.: Deep learning-based super-resolution and de-noising for XMM-Newton images (2022). https://doi.org/10.48550/ARXIV.2205.01152

23. Virtanen, P., et al.: SciPy 1.0: fundamental algorithms for scientific computing in Python. Nat. Methods **17**, 261–272 (2020). https://doi.org/10.1038/s41592-019-0686-2

24. Westmeier, T., et al.: sofia2 an automated, parallel H source finding pipeline for the WALLABY survey. Mon. Not. R. Astron. Soc. **506**(3), 3962–3976 (2021). https://doi.org/10.1093/mnras/stab1881

25. Yi, Z., et al.: Automatic detection of low surface brightness galaxies from Sloan Digital Sky Survey images. Mon. Not. R. Astron. Soc. **513**(3), 3972–3981 (2022). https://doi.org/10.1093/mnras/stac775

26. Zelinka, I., Brescia, M., Baron, D. (eds.): Intelligent Astrophysics. ECC, vol. 39. Springer, Cham (2021). https://doi.org/10.1007/978-3-030-65867-0

27. Zeng, Q., Li, X., Lin, H.: Concat convolutional neural network for pulsar candidate selection. Mon. Not. R. Astron. Soc. **494**(3), 3110–3119 (2020). https://doi.org/10.1007/978-3-030-65867-0

Anomaly Detection for Physical Threat Intelligence

Paolo Mignone[1,2]([⊠]) [iD], Donato Malerba[1,2] [iD], and Michelangelo Ceci[1,2] [iD]

[1] Department of Computer Science, University of Bari Aldo Moro,
Via Orabona, 4, 70125 Bari, Italy
`paolo.mignone@uniba.it`
[2] Big Data Lab, National Interuniversity Consortium for Informatics (CINI),
Via Ariosto, 25, 00185 Rome, Italy

Abstract. Anomaly detection is a machine learning task that has been investigated within diverse research areas and application domains. In this paper, we performed anomaly detection for Physical Threat Intelligence. Specifically, we performed anomaly detection for air pollution and public transport traffic analysis for the city of Oslo, Norway. To this aim, the state-of-the-art method SparkGHSOM was considered to learn predictive models for normal (i.e. regular) scenarios of air quality and traffic jams in a distributed fashion. Furthermore, we extended the main algorithm to make the detected anomalies explainable through an instance-based feature ranking approach. The results showed that SparkGHSOM is able to detect anomalies for both the real applications considered in this study, despite the fact it was designed for different tasks.

Keywords: Anomaly detection · Air pollution · Public transport traffic

1 Introduction

Anomaly detection is a machine learning task that refers to the problem of identifying data that do not conform to patterns observed in historical data. These patterns represent the expected behaviour in normal conditions. Therefore, anomaly detection is usually performed through a data-driven algorithm to construct a model which will be able to detect a specific measurement/object/instance/observation as anomalous with respect to the historical data already seen. Anomaly detection is a very general task that finds applications in many real-domain scenarios such as fraud detection for credit cards, insurance, or health care, intrusion detection for cyber-security, fault detection in safety-critical systems, and military surveillance for enemy activities [6].

In this paper, we consider the Anomaly Detection task for the purposes of Physical Threat Intelligence. Specifically, we propose an algorithm for anomaly detection which works on data continuously collected by geo-located sensors located in urban areas. The data refer to physical information (e.g. temperature, number of vehicles crossing a gate, number of pedestrians in a given area, PM10 level at certain points in the town, etc.). The goal is to identify an anomalous, not expected, behaviour for one or many values simultaneously, considering the specific time, date and spatial coordinates of the considered observation. This would give the opportunity to Security Operators to understand potentially dangerous situations and take the appropriate actions in time.

The task we consider hereby is particularly challenging since data generated by sensors are big in size and have spatial and temporal coordinates that make the data not independent. Indeed, the spatial proximity of sensors introduces spatial autocorrelation in functional annotations and violates the usual assumption that observations are independently and identically distributed (i.i.d.) [1]. Although the explicit consideration of these spatial dependencies brings additional complexity to the learning process, it generally leads to increased accuracy of learned models [9]. In addition, data generated by sensors are also affected by temporal autocorrelation, since they *i)* tend to have similar values at the same time on close days; *ii)* have a cyclic and seasonal (over days and years) behavior; *iii)* tend to show the same trend over time.

While stream mining algorithms deal with both i) and ii), they may fail to consider iii), since they tend to better represent the most recently observed concepts, forgetting previously learned ones [2]. On the contrary, time series-based approaches are able to deal with iii), but may fail to consider i) and ii). In fact, they typically require the size of the temporal horizon as an input: Considering a short-term horizon (e.g., daily) excludes a long-term horizon (e.g., seasonal) and vice versa. On the contrary, in the approach presented in this paper, we propose a time-series approach that exploits both spatial and temporal features, in order to take into account all the aspects mentioned before. In particular, the method addresses the problem of identifying complex spatio-temporal patterns in sensor data by means of Self-Organizing Maps (SOMs).

A SOM [5] is a neural-network-based clustering algorithm that operates by mapping high-dimensional input data into a 2-dimensional space implemented by a grid of neurons called *feature map*. In this paper, we consider GHSOMs, (Growing Hierarchical SOMs) that are particularly suitable for time series data and better capture spatio-temporal information thanks to the hierarchical organization of the SOMs that better adapt to complex data distribution. Specifically, we consider the distributed extension Spark-GHSOM [6], that exploits the Spark architecture to process massive data, like those coming from sensors. Since GHSOMs are designed for clustering and not for anomaly detection tasks, we extend the learning algorithm Spark-GHSOM in order to learn GHSOMs for anomaly detection, in an unsupervised fashion.

2   Spark-GHSOM

Spark-GHSOM [6] was introduced to overcome two limitations of the classical GHSOMs. Indeed, a GHSOM *i)* requires multiple iterations over the input dataset making it intractable on large datasets; *ii)* it is designed to handle datasets with numeric attributes only, representing an important limitation as most modern real-world datasets are characterized by mixed attributes (numerical and categorical). Therefore, Spark-GHSOM exploits the Spark platform to process massive datasets in a distributed fashion. Furthermore, it exploits the distance hierarchy [3] to modify the optimization function of GHSOM so that it can (also) coherently handle mixed-attribute datasets. Spark-GHSOM showed high accuracy, scalability, and descriptive power on different datasets.

The first step in the GHSOM algorithm is to compute the inherent dissimilarity in the input data with different types of attributes. Classical GHSOMs exploit the *mean quantization error*. However, this error is suitable for numerical attributes only. While there is no standard definition of mean for categorical attributes, SparkGHSOM replaces the mean quantization error by considering instead the variance in order to assess the quality of map and neurons. For categorical attributes, *unlikability* is a good measure to estimate how often the values differ from one another [4]. Formally, let $\mathbb{D}$ the dataset under analysis, the unlikability for a categorical attribute A of $\mathbb{D}$ is defined as:

$$\mathbb{U}(A) = \sum_{i \in domain(A)} p_i(1 - p_i) \tag{1}$$

where $p_i = \frac{frequency(A_i, \mathbb{D})}{|\mathbb{D}|}$, A_i is the i-th value of the attribute A and $frequency(A_i, \mathbb{D})$ is the absolute frequency of the value A_i for the attribute A in $\mathbb{D}$. Therefore, SparkGHSOM computes the overall variance of the dataset as follows:

$$\sigma = \sum_{A \in featureset} \mathbb{1}^{num(A)} \sigma(A) + \mathbb{1}^{cat(A)} \frac{\mathbb{U}(A)}{2} \tag{2}$$

where $\mathbb{1}^{num(A)}$ (resp. $\mathbb{1}^{cat(A)}$) is 1 when the attribute A is numerical (resp. categorical), 0 otherwise. $\sigma(A)$ represents the classical variance for the attribute A when it is numerical.

The distance hierarchy [3] is considered to compute the similarities among the categorical values. To compute the distance among categorical values, a distance hierarchy for each categorical attribute must be provided in advance. Similar values according to the concept hierarchy are placed under a common parent which represents an abstract concept. The GHSOM training process takes into account mixed attributes and consists in finding the *winner* (closest) neuron of the SOM w.r.t. the single input instance according to the distance hierarchy.

In the first step, the winner neuron is identified for the input instance according to the distance hierarchy. Therefore, the neuron's weight vector is modified by a certain amount to match the instance vector. In the hierarchy tree of the concepts, where the leaves represent the actual values of the instances and the non-leaf nodes represent the neurons, this process pulls the neuron point towards its leaf in order to "specialize" what the neuron describes.

In the second step, the closest winner neuron and its surrounding neighbor neurons of the SOM are adapted moving them towards the input instance. This training process requires a defined number training epochs over the input dataset. The training is governed by the Mean Quantization Error (MQE) of a neuron, that is the total deviation of the neuron from its mapped input instances. The MQE for a SOM layer is computed as the average MQE of all the neurons representing instances. A higher value of the MQE means that the layer does not represent the input data well and requires more neurons to better represent the input domain. Moreover, when a single neuron is still not representing the surrounding instances, then the neuron is expanded as a SOM hierarchically (see Fig. 1).

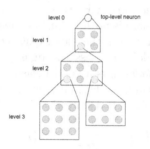

Fig. 1. A growing hierarchical self organizing map.

3   Spark-GHSOM for Anomaly Detection

The training process of the Spark-GHSOM follows the classical process of the GHSOM training, except for the use of a different function for the calculation of the distance between the input vector and the neurons of the feature map, since the Euclidean distance is not computable on categorical attributes. For this reason, the hierarchical distance was chosen [3, 6].

The hierarchy obtained can thus be used to solve an anomaly detection task. In particular, when a new input vector is supplied to the hierarchy, the algorithm looks for the SOM that succeeds in better approximating the input data (that is, the SOM with the shortest distance with respect to the input vector). Once found, it is used to carry out the prediction for the new input data, based on the distance between the input vector and the closest neuron (the *winner neuron*) in the map.

More formally, let x_i be the new example to be considered, and let $e(x_i) = \arg\min_e dist(x_i, e)$ the closest neuron to x_i according to the distance measure described before, the example is considered an anomaly if the following inequality holds:

$$dist(x_i, e(x_i)) > (d_{avg} + tf * \sigma) \tag{3}$$

In the formula, d_{avg} is the average distance among the training instances and the neurons of the model after the training, σ the standard deviation of such distances, and tf the user-defined threshold.

As data distributions tend to change over time, it may be necessary to update the knowledge of the anomaly detector using more recent data. For this reason, Spark-GHSOM for anomaly detection provides the possibility to update the weights vectors of the neurons while keeping the generated hierarchy unchanged. This process can be particularly useful if end users do not have enough time or data availability to train a new anomaly detector from scratch. Consequently, having a pre-trained model already available, it is possible to provide the model with a micro-batch of data, in order to update the knowledge extracted by the model and adapt it to the user's needs. This aspect is particularly useful in our case, where data generated by the sensors can be relatively few.

The anomaly detector could produce different types of output depending on the level of detail. The simplest approach provides feedback for the current data in the form of a Boolean response. This kind of output could support raising an alert if the response is equal to "anomaly".

This approach presents the advantage that is simple to handle and transmits the prediction as a binary variable (e.g., anomaly/normal, 0/1, true/false). Its drawback is that it makes it difficult for the end-user to interpret the raised alert/anomaly. Therefore, a more informative approach could be considered by combining the previous one with a ranking of the variables (feature ranking) according to their importance, indicating the contribution to catching the variable's anomaly.

Feature ranking is a ranking of the entire set of features composing the data collection, ordered with respect to the feature importance. Feature importance is a numerical value between 0 and 1, which expresses how anomalous the value expressed by the feature is with respect to the data collection, such that the sum of all the features importance in the feature ranking is equal to 1. The importance score is determined starting from a distance function between the current data under analysis and the winner neuron. Specifically, the ranking is proportional to the contribution provided by the single feature in the Euclidean distance between x_i and $e(x_i)$. More formally, the ranking function for the instance x_i, $r_f(x_i)$, is computed as follows:

$$r_f(x_i) = \frac{(x_i[l] - e(x_i)[l])^2}{\sum_{l'}(x_i[l'] - e(x_i)[l'])^2} \tag{4}$$

where l represents the feature index.

This approach helps to identify the feature(s) that most contributed to the anomaly and, therefore, the "reason" for the anomaly.

4   Experiments

The experiments were conducted for the city of Oslo (Norway) by considering two real domains for the following analyses: air pollution and public transport traffic.

Air Pollution Analysis

The proposed method was tested using data coming from air quality monitoring sensors to identify pollutant concentrations deemed abnormal.

At each location, different pollutants are monitored by the sensors:

– Hjortnes: NO, NO2, NOx, PM10 and PM2.5
– Loallmenningen: NO, NO2, NOx, PM1, PM10 and PM2.5
– Spikersuppa: PM10 and PM2.5

The information on the concentration of pollutants comes with both a timestamp and the geo-coordinates (latitude and longitude), so that the time series can be reconstructed. Data, which is publicly available, can be downloaded through a REST API[1].

The period considered for training was from January 2021 to September 2021, with an hourly sampling rate, totalling 18.286 data points from the chosen locations. The period considered for testing is October 2021, totalling 720 acquisitions from the chosen locations. The best value for the parameter tf has been selected according to an internal cross-validation on the training instances in the interval $[0, 15]$.

Figure 2 shows the concentrations per hour of NO, NOx, and NO2 pollutants during the identified test period, i.e., October 2021, from the station of Hjortnes. The choice fell on these pollutants because they are present within the top-3 of the feature ranking, for those time instants considered anomalous by the algorithm, indicated with black arrows in the graph.

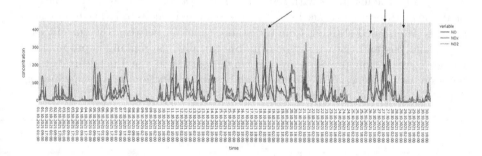

Fig. 2. Concentrations per hour of NO, NOx and NO2 pollutants during October 2021, from Hjortnes station.

It is worth to note that we did not find an abnormal situation during October 21 at 10 a.m., indicated with a green arrow in Fig. 3, when very high concentrations of PM1 were recorded, even though at this time point the pollutant PM1 is correctly present in the first position of the feature ranking.

---

[1] https://api.nilu.no/.

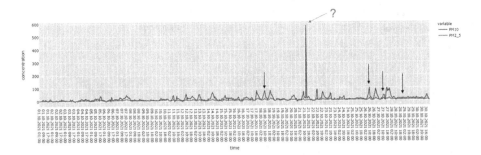

Fig. 3. Concentrations per hour of PM10 and PM2.5 pollutants during October 2021, from Hjortnes station.

The motivation is because several pollutants are being observed together and the sudden increase of concentrations of one of them is sometimes not sufficient to classify the time instant as a potential abnormal situation.

Figure 4 shows the concentration per hour of PM1 pollutant during the test period, from Loallmenningen. For this place, PM1 is the most decisive pollutant for the detection of abnormal situations that occurred during October 2021.

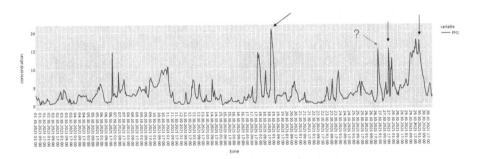

Fig. 4. Concentrations per hour of PM1 pollutant during October 2021, from Loall-menningen station.

As in the previous graphs, the black arrows indicate the time instants in which we detected abnormal concentrations of the pollutants considered. As expected, the algorithm was able to correctly detect high concentrations of the PM1 pollutant.

However, on October 26 at 9 p.m., indicated by the green arrow, the concentrations of PM1 were very similar to those of October 27 at 4 p.m., but only in the latter case, an anomalous situation was found by the algorithm. A more detailed graph is shown in Fig. 5.

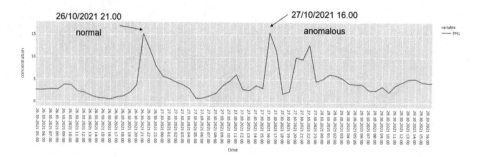

Fig. 5. A zoom in with respect to the time interval for PM1 pollutant during October 2021, from Loallmenningen station.

The reason is due to a sudden increase in concentrations of the remaining pollutants, which occurred on October 27 at 4 p.m. This situation, as shown in Fig. 6, allowed the algorithm to identify an anomalous situation at this timestamp.

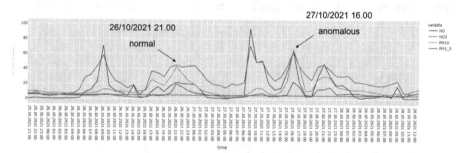

Fig. 6. Concentrations per hour of NO, NO2, PM10 and PM2.5 pollutants during October 2021, from Loallmenningen station.

Figure 7 shows the concentrations per hour of PM10 and PM2.5 pollutants during the test period, from the area of Spikersuppa. The pollutants shown in the graph are the only ones the station can monitor. As expected, the algorithm did not identify any situations deemed abnormal for this place, as the concentrations of October are quite regular.

Public Transport Traffic

This data consists of one week of data regarding Oslo's public transport. The instances represent GPS-tracked busses with latitude and longitude. Each instance is timestamped according to the standard ISO 8601 with a resolution in seconds. The Service Interface for Real time Information - Vehicle Monitoring

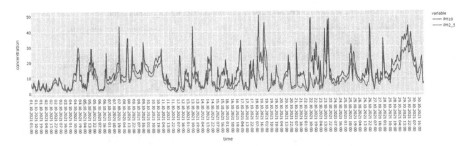

Fig. 7. Concentrations per hour of PM10 and PM2.5 pollutants during October 2021, from Spikersuppa station.

(SIRI-VM) is used to model vehicle-movements and their progress compared to a planned timetable[2].

Fig. 8. The data processing pipeline

For this dataset, the processing pipeline illustrated in Fig. 8 was executed. Therefore, starting from the week of data from Oslo traffic transport, we performed data cleaning in order to fix some encoding issues. We also aggregated data by 5-minutes interval periods and by spatial areas according to some preliminary clustering. This step was crucial since the data provided refer to movable points in the map making the aggregation operations unfeasible. Clustering on the spatial location was performed by exploiting K-Means algorithm. The variables of the considered data were extended by considering the cluster identifier (cluster ID) and the cluster's centroid latitude and longitude to the data. Since K-Means algorithm needs the number of clusters to identify, we performed the well-known silhouette cluster analysis [8] with the aim to identify the number of areas for monitoring the traffic. According to silhouette analysis, we considered 100 different regions for traffic monitoring (see Fig. 9).

The instances are therefore grouped by two levels: first the time, then the cluster id previously identified. Various new features are computed as part of the aggregation (e.g., the average "delay" of the buses in seconds) for each identified clustered monitoring area. Multiple train and test sets were created as illustrated in Fig. 10. The n-th evaluation step uses n hours for training, and the $(n + 1)$-th hour for testing. The 10% of the available test windows are perturbed

---

[2] https://api.entur.io/realtime/v1/rest/vm?datasetId=RUT.

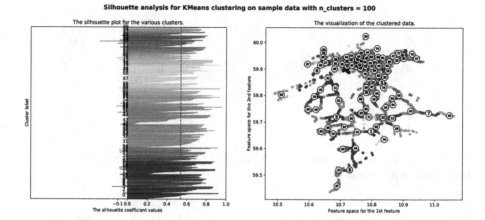

Fig. 9. The Oslo street map and the best locations for monitoring traffic according to the clustering step.

randomly selecting 3 columns for each instance and randomly assigning a new value for each selected feature. These test windows are considered as anomalous. The remaining 90% of the available test windows are used without perturbation and considered non-anomalous for the evaluation. The aim of this setting is to perform an evaluation based on landmark windows. The best value for the parameter tf has been selected according to an internal cross-validation on the training instances in the interval $[0, 15]$.

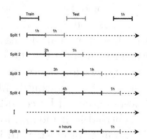

Fig. 10. Training and testing sets.

In Fig. 11 hour-by-hour histograms are reported for the first day. Stacked green bars indicate the correct predictions, while the red ones the wrong predictions. The red text in the date indicates that the window is perturbed (anomaly). The top label contains the total number of instances in the test set. During normal windows, the anomaly detector results are effective since false positives are generally avoided. Most of the normal scenarios that occurred during different time slots (in the morning, afternoon, evening, and night) were recognized as normal situations: 99.7% accuracy (we have only 5 false positives at the beginning, when the model is still unstable). From the figure, we can also see that the system identifies many false negatives at the beginning [01:40–03:40]. This is expected since the model is still unstable to detect anomalies. Moreover, the lack of data, due to the lack of public transport late in the night (or early in the morning, only 48 instances), further complicated the problem. During the day, after 22 h of training, the anomaly detector appears to be much more stable and capable to predict most of the anomalies occurred during the two-hours anomalous time slot [16:40–18:40] in the afternoon. After 26 h of training, the anomaly detector becomes further stable and capable to predict most of the anomalies occurred during the anomalous time slot [20:40–21:40] in the evening. After 28 h of training, the anomaly detector becomes further more stable and capable to predict most of the anomalies occurred during the anomalous time slot [05:40–06:40] in the evening/early morning. In Table 1, where we report the overall quantitative results which confirm the fact that the algorithm, after sufficient data for training, shows very high prediction scores, with very high precision.

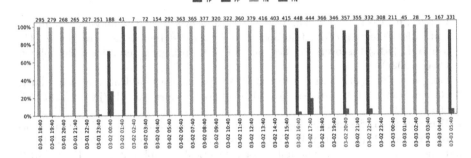

Fig. 11. Hour-by-hour histograms indicating True positives, True negatives, False positives and False negatives for the first day of data.

Table 1. Oslo public transport traffic: quantitative results in terms of accuracy, precision, recall, and f1-score.

Accuracy	Precision	Recall	f1-score
91.33%	99.77%	85.74%	92.22%

5   Conclusions

In this paper, we tackle the task of anomaly detection. For this purpose we extended the algorithm SparkGHSOM, originally designed for the clustering task, in order to consider the task at hand. Furthermore, the main algorithm has been made more explainable by providing the reasons for each detected anomaly in the form of an instance-based feature ranking. The results show the effectiveness of the proposed approach both qualitatively and quantitatively in real application scenarios. For future work, we aim to perform further and more robust experiments with the aim to better evaluate the predictive quality, the explainability, and the scalability of this new extended version of SparkGH-SOM. From an architectural viewpoint, we aim to provide anomaly detection as an additional service according to the a model-based approach for Big Data Analytics-as-a-service [7].

Acknowledgment. We acknowledge the project IMPETUS (Intelligent Management of Processes, Ethics and Technology for Urban Safety) that receives funding from the European Union's Horizon 2020 research and innovation programme under grant agreement No. 883286. https://cordis.europa.eu/project/id/883286. Dr. Paolo Mignone acknowledges the support of Apulia Region through the REFIN project "Metodi per l'ottimizzazione delle reti di distribuzione di energia e per la pianificazione di interventi manutentivi ed evolutivi" (CUP H94I20000410008, Grant n. 7EDD092A).

References

1. Corizzo, R., Ceci, M., Pio, G., Mignone, P., Japkowicz, N.: Spatially-aware autoencoders for detecting contextual anomalies in geo-distributed data. In: Soares, C., Torgo, L. (eds.) Discovery Science, pp. 461–471. Springer International Publishing, Cham (2021)
2. Gonçalves, P.M., Jr., Barros, R.S.: RCD: a recurring concept drift framework. Patt. Recogn. Lett. **34**(9), 1018–1025 (2013). https://doi.org/10.1016/j.patrec.2013.02.005
3. Hsu, C.C.: Generalizing self-organizing map for categorical data. IEEE Trans. Neural Networks **17**(2), 294–304 (2006). https://doi.org/10.1109/TNN.2005.863415
4. Kader, G.D., Perry, M.: Variability for categorical variables. J. Stat. Educ. **15**(2) (2007). https://doi.org/10.1080/10691898.2007.11889465
5. Kohonen, T.: The self-organizing map. Proc. IEEE **78**(9), 1464–1480 (1990). https://doi.org/10.1109/5.58325
6. Malondkar, A., Corizzo, R., Kiringa, I., Ceci, M., Japkowicz, N.: Spark-GHSOM: growing hierarchical self-organizing map for large scale mixed attribute datasets. Inf. Sci. (2018). https://doi.org/10.1016/j.ins.2018.12.007
7. Redavid, D., Corizzo, R., Malerba, D.: An owl ontology for supporting semantic services in big data platforms. In: 2018 IEEE International Congress on Big Data (BigData Congress), pp. 228–231 (2018). https://doi.org/10.1109/BigDataCongress.2018.00039
8. Rousseeuw, P.J.: Silhouettes: a graphical aid to the interpretation and validation of cluster analysis. J. Comput. Appl. Math. **20**, 53–65 (1987). https://doi.org/10.1016/0377-0427(87)90125-7
9. Stojanova, D., Ceci, M., Appice, A., Džeroski, S.: Network regression with predictive clustering trees. Data Mining Knowl. Disc. **25**(2), 378–413 (2012). https://doi.org/10.1007/s10618-012-0278-6

Workshop on eXplainable Knowledge Discovery in Data Mining (XKDD 2022)

International Workshop on eXplainable Knowledge Discovery in Data Mining (XKDD 2022)

The 4th International Workshop on eXplainable Knowledge Discovery in Data Mining (XKDD 2022) was held in conjunction with the European Conference on Machine Learning and Principles and Practice of Knowledge Discovery in Databases (ECML PKDD 2022) on Monday, September 19, 2022. Previous editions of the workshop were also held jointly with ECML-PKDD in 2019, 2020, and 2021. In line with the organization of ECML-PKDD 2022, the XKDD 2022 workshop was run in a hybrid mode, with speakers and participants able to connect remotely but also able to present their research on-site. The majority of papers were presented on-site. Discussed results were made available on the workshop website[1].

In the past decade, machine learning-based decision systems have been widely used in a wide range of application domains, like for example credit score, insurance risk, and health monitoring, in which accuracy is of the utmost importance. Although the support of these systems has a big potential to improve the decision in different fields, their use may present ethical and legal risks, such as codifying biases, jeopardizing transparency and privacy, and reducing accountability. Unfortunately, these risks arise in different applications and they are made even more serious and subtle by the opacity of recent decision support systems, which often are complex and have internal logic that is usually inaccessible to humans.

Nowadays most of the artificial intelligence (AI) systems are based on machine learning algorithms. The relevance and need of ethics in AI is supported and highlighted by various initiatives arising from research to provide recommendations and guidelines in the direction of making AI-based decision systems explainable and compliant with legal and ethical issues. These include the EU's General Data Protection Regulation (GDPR), which introduces, to some extent, a right for all individuals to obtain "meaningful explanations of the logic involved" when automated decision making takes place, the "ACM Statement on Algorithmic Transparency and Accountability", Informatics Europe's "European Recommendations on Machine-Learned Automated Decision Making", and "The ethics guidelines for trustworthy AI" provided by the EU High-Level Expert Group on AI.

The challenge to design and develop trustworthy AI-based decision systems is still open and requires a joint effort across technical, legal, sociological, and ethical domains.

The purpose of XKDD, the Workshop on eXplainable Knowledge Discovery in Data Mining, is to encourage principled research that will lead to the advancement of explainable, transparent, ethical, and fair data mining and machine learning. This year the workshop also called for submissions addressing uncovered important issues in specific fields related to eXplainable AI (XAI), such as privacy and fairness,

---

[1] https://kdd.isti.cnr.it/xkdd2022/.

application in real case studies, benchmarking, and explanation of decision systems based on time series and graphs, which are becoming more and more important in current applications. The workshop sought top-quality submissions presenting research results in any of the topics of interest, as well as tools and promising preliminary ideas. XKDD 2022 asked for contributions from researchers in academia and industry, working on topics addressing these challenges primarily from a technical point of view but also from a legal, ethical, or sociological, perspective.

Topics of interest included, but were not limited to, the following:

- Explainable Artificial Intelligence (XAI)
- Interpretable Machine Learning
- Transparent Data Mining
- XAI for Fairness Checking Approaches
- XAI for Privacy-Preserving Systems
- XAI for Federated Learning
- XAI for Time Series-based Approaches
- XAI for Graph-based Approaches
- XAI for Visualization
- XAI in Human-Machine Interaction
- XAI Benchmarking
- Counterfactual Explanations
- Ethics Discovery for Explainable AI
- Privacy-Preserving Explanations
- Transparent Classification Approaches
- Explanation, Accountability, and Liability from an Ethical and Legal Perspective
- Iterative Dialogue Explanations
- Explanatory Model Analysis
- Human-Model Interfaces
- Human-Centered Artificial Intelligence
- Human-in-the-Loop Interactions
- XAI Case Studies and Applications

The XKDD workshop papers were selected through a single-blind peer-review process in which each submitted paper was assigned to at least three members of the Program Committee. The main selection criteria were the novelty of the proposal and its impact in explanation/privacy/fairness processes. XKDD 2022 received a total of 29 submissions (over 30% more than in the previous year). In total, 16 papers were accepted for presentation (an acceptance rate of 55%). We registered an audience of at least 80 partcipants on site and 20 participants who joined remotely (across the whole workshop).

The workshop was divided into two parts. The first was mainly focused on XAI themes. It started with the excellent keynote "From Attribution Maps to Concept-Level Explainable AI" by Wojciech Samek, Professor at TU Berlin, Head of the AI Department at Fraunhofer HHI, and Fellow at BIFOLD, Germany. The second part was more focused on privacy-related themes. It was opened by the second keynote titled "The Relationship between Explainability & Privacy in AI" by Anna Monreale, Computer Science Department to the University of Pisa. The workshop concluded with a panel discussion on emerging trends in human-centered AI. The panelists included Andrea Passarella, Anna Monreale, Francesca Naretto, Andreas Theissler, Przemyslaw Biecek, Wojciech Samek, and Dino Pedreschi.

More information about the workshop, including the papers, can be found on the workshop website: https://kdd.isti.cnr.it/xkdd2022/. We would like to thank all the participants for making XKDD 2022 a success, the authors for their interesting works and presentations, and all workshop attendees for their engagement and the questions. A special thanks goes to the wonderful Program Committee for their effective and timely reviews.

The organization of XKDD 2022 was supported by the European Community H2020 program under the funding schemes INFRAIA-1-2014-2015 Res. Infr. G.A. 871042 *SoBigData++* (sobigdat), G.A. 952026 *HumanE AI Net* (humane-ai), G.A. 825619 *AI4EU* (ai4eu), G.A. 834756 *XAI* (xai), and NCN Sonata Bis-9 grant 2019/34/E/ST6/00052 (HOMER).

September 2022   Riccardo Guidotti
                                                            Francesca Naretto
                                                            Andreas Theissler
                                                            Przemysław Biecek

Organization

XKDD 2022 Program Chairs

Riccardo Guidotti — University of Pisa, Italy
Francesca Naretto — Scuola Normale Superiore, Italy
Andreas Theissler — Aalen University of Applied Sciences, Germany
Przemysław Biecek — Warsaw University of Technology, Poland

XKDD 2022 Program Committee

Leila Amgoud — CNRS, France
Francesco Bodria — Scuola Normale Superiore, Italy
Umang Bhatt — University of Cambridge, UK
Miguel Couceiro — Loria, France
Menna El-Assady — ETH Zurich, Switzerland
Josep Domingo-Ferrer — Universitat Rovira i Virgili, Spain
Françoise Fessant — Orange Labs, France
Andreas Holzinger — Medical University of Graz, Austria
Thibault Laugel — AXA, France
Paulo Lisboa — Liverpool John Moores University, UK
Marcin Luckner — Warsaw University of Technology, Poland
John Mollas — Aristotle University of Thessaloniki, Greece
Amedeo Napoli — CNRS, France
Antonio Rago — Imperial College London, UK
Jan Ramon — Inria, France
Xavier Renard — AXA, France
Mahtab Sarvmaili — Dalhousie University, Canada
Christin Seifert — University of Duisburg-Essen, Germany
Udo Schlegel — Konstanz University, Germany
Mattia Setzu — University of Pisa, Italy
Dominik Slezak — University of Warsaw, Poland
Fabrizio Silvestri — Università di Roma, Italy
Francesco Spinnato — Scuola Noramle Superiore, Italy
Vicenc Torra — Umea University, Sweden
Cagatay Turkay — University of Warwick, UK
Marco Virgolin — CWI, Netherlands
Martin Jullum — Norwegian Computing Center, Norway
Albrecht Zimmermann — Université de Caen Normandie, France
Guangyi Zhang — KTH Royal Institute of Technology, Sweden

XKDD 2022 Keynotes:
Extended   Abstracts

From Attribution Maps to Concept-Level Explainable AI

Wojciech Samek[1,2]

[1] EECS Department, Technical University of Berlin
[2] AI Department, Fraunhofer Heinrich Hertz Institute

The field of Explainable AI (XAI) has recently developed various techniques to explain and interpret the predictions of state-of-the-art AI models. Two popular types of methods are local and global XAI techniques. While the former methods explain individual predictions by highlighting the relevant input dimensions (e.g., in form of an attribution map), global XAI techniques shed light on the features and concepts generally encoded by intermediate neurons of the model (e.g., are not prediction specific). However, by design both techniques only provide partial insights into the prediction behavior of the model. For instance, an attribution map explaining the prediction of an age classifier only shows us "where" the relevant information is in the image (i.e., which pixels are relevant), but leaves the burden of interpretation of "what" this information is to the human. More precisely, even if the attribution map tells us that the mouth is relevant for the prediction "young woman", we still do not know whether it is the fact that the person is laughing or the fact that the person has particularly white teeth which triggers the model output. By connecting the best of the two worlds (local and glocal XAI), this talk will introduce a next-generation XAI technique, termed Concept Relevance Propagation (CPR), which explains individual predictions in terms of localized and human-understandable concepts. CRP is based on the popular Layer-wise Relevance Propagation (LRP) framework, which not only explains predictions by computing an attribution map, but also assigns relevance scores to hidden-layer neurons (encoding concepts which are relevant to this prediction). By relating explanation to the encoded concepts, CRP overcomes the ambiguities described before and provides more detailed, human-interpretable explanations. This talk will discuss several experiments demonstrating the improved explanation capabilities of CRP. In particular, we will show how CRP can be used for an in-depth understanding of the model's internal representations and decision making strategies and how it can be used for model debugging and the identification of Clever Hans filters focusing on spurious correlations in the data. By lifting local XAI to the concept level, CRP opens up a new way to understand and interact with ML models, which can be of particular interest when designing explainable AI systems.

Bio: Wojciech Samek is a professor at the Technical University of Berlin and is jointly heading the AI Department at Fraunhofer Heinrich Hertz Institute. He studied computer science in Berlin and Edinburgh, was a visiting researcher at the NASA Ames Research Center, Mountain View, USA, and received the Ph.D. degree with distinction from TU Berlin in 2014. He then founded the Machine Learning Group at Fraunhofer HHI, which he headed until 2020. Dr. Samek is Fellow at BIFOLD - Berlin Institute for the Foundation of Learning and Data and associated faculty at the ELLIS Unit Berlin and the DFG Graduate School BIOQIC. Furthermore, he is a senior editor of IEEE TNNLS, an editorial board member of Pattern Recognition, and an elected member of the IEEE MLSP Technical Committee. He is recipient of multiple best paper awards, including the 2020 Pattern Recognition Best Paper Award, and part of the expert group developing the ISO/IEC MPEG-17 NNR standard. He is the leading editor of the Springer book "Explainable AI: Interpreting, Explaining and Visualizing Deep Learning" (2019), co-editor of the open access Springer book "xxAI – Beyond explainable AI" (2022), and organizer of various special sessions, workshops and tutorials on topics such as explainable AI, neural network compression, and federated learning. Dr. Samek has co-authored more than 150 peer-reviewed journal and conference papers; some of them listed as ESI Hot (top 0.1%) or Highly Cited Papers (top 1%).

The Relationship Between Explainability and Privacy in AI

Anna Monreale

Computer Science Department of the University of Pisa

In recent years we are witnessing the diffusion of AI systems based on powerful machine learning models which find application in many critical contexts such as medicine, financial market, credit scoring, etc. In such contexts it is particularly important to design Trustworthy AI systems while guaranteeing interpretability of their decisional reasoning, privacy protection and awareness. In this talk we will explore the possible relationships between these two relevant ethical values to take into consideration in the design of Trustworthy AI system. We will answer research questions such as: *how explainability may help privacy awareness? Can explanations jeopardize individual privacy protection?*

Concerning the first research question, we will present EXPERT, an EXplainable Privacy ExposuRe predicTion framework that exploits (i) machine learning models for predicting a user's individual privacy risk and (ii) *local* explainers for producing explanations of the predicted risk. First, EXPERT extracts from human data individual profiles describing the behavior of any user. Second, for each user it computes the associated privacy risk. Third, it uses the profiles of the users with their associated privacy risks to train a machine learning model. For the prediction task, EXPERT exploits tree-based ensemble models to effectively handle the class-imbalance problem. Finally, for a new user, along with the prediction of risk, EXPERT also generates an explanation of the predicted risk exploiting local explainers, such as SHAP, LORE and LIME.

Concerning the second research question, we will present a methodology for assessing the privacy risk of local and global explainers based on the learning of surrogate models. We applied our methodology for attacking the global explainer TREPAN and the local explainers LORE and LIME. The privacy risk evaluation is based on the simulation of the well-known membership inference attack.

Bio: Anna Monreale is an associate professor at the Computer Science Department of the University of Pisa and a member of the Knowledge Discovery and Data Mining Laboratory (KDD-Lab), a joint research group with the Information Science and Technology Institute of the National Research Council in Pisa. She has been a visiting student at Department of Computer Science of the Stevens Institute of Technology (Hoboken, NewJersey, USA) (2010). Her research interests include big data analytics, social networks and the privacy issues raising in mining these kinds of social and human sensitive data. In particular, she is interested in the evaluation of privacy risks during analytical processes and in the design of privacy-by-design technologies in the era of big data. She earned her Ph.D. in computer science from the University of Pisa in June 2011 and her dissertation was about privacy-by-design in data mining.

Is Attention Interpretation?
A Quantitative Assessment on Sets

Jonathan Haab, Nicolas Deutschmann[(✉)], and María Rodríguez Martínez

IBM Research Europe, Saümerstrasse 3, 8803 Zürich, Switzerland
jonathan.haab@ibm.com, {deu,mrm}@zurich.ibm.com

Abstract. The debate around the interpretability of attention mechanisms is centered on whether attention scores can be used as a proxy for the relative amounts of signal carried by sub-components of data. We propose to study the interpretability of attention in the context of set machine learning, where each data point is composed of an unordered collection of instances with a global label. For classical multiple-instance-learning problems and simple extensions, there is a well-defined "importance" ground truth that can be leveraged to cast interpretation as a binary classification problem, which we can quantitatively evaluate. By building synthetic datasets over several data modalities, we perform a systematic assessment of attention-based interpretations. We find that attention distributions are indeed often reflective of the relative importance of individual instances, but that silent failures happen where a model will have high classification performance but attention patterns that do not align with expectations. Based on these observations, we propose to use ensembling to minimize the risk of misleading attention-based explanations.

Keywords: Attention mechanism · Multiple-instance learning · Interpretable machine learning

1 Introduction

Attention mechanisms have become a popular tool in multiple areas of machine learning, in particular in natural language processing (NLP) where their introduction significantly increased performance [2]. Attention-based models have also been successful in the context of computer vision [4] and have in particular been attractive in digital histopathology applications (cancer diagnosis based on stained microscopy images) [6,10,15,19], where a patch-based approach is particularly well-adapted to analyse the large whole-slide images (WSIs) with corrupting artefacts typically exploited in this field.

Besides the performance gain provided by attention mechanisms in many applications, one of their alluring aspects is the promise of interpretability: attention relies on a dynamically weighted average of representations of data subcomponents, and it feels natural that these weights should be informative

© The Author(s), under exclusive license to Springer Nature Switzerland AG 2023
I. Koprinska et al. (Eds.): ECML PKDD 2022 Workshops, CCIS 1752, pp. 303–321, 2023.
https://doi.org/10.1007/978-3-031-23618-1_21

of the relative importance of these subcomponents for the final prediction. This potential interpretability is particularly attractive for biomedical applications, both in a clinical setting and for research. Indeed, insights into automatic diagnostic tools is both a regulatory requirement [16] and a necessary safeguard to understand and diagnose failure modes for critical decisions [1]. In a biomedical research context, attention-based interpretability could lead to new breakthroughs in understanding the mechanisms that underlie diseases and help find new targets for diagnosis and therapy.

While intuitively promising, there is still no clear understanding of the extent to which attention distributions provide meaningful information about the amount of signal carried by data subcomponents. This has been the object of a debate within the context of NLP [7,22], which started at a conceptual level but was then moved forward by experimental assessments [17,20]. These studies found imperfect and task-dependent agreement between attention and other importance attribution metrics, but are limited by the constraints inherent to NLP: the difficulty of building robust ground truths and evaluation metrics for token importance [11].

Given the recent interest in using attention in the context of biomedical applications, we propose to study the quality of attention-based explanations of instance importance in a simpler context, where we can conceive synthetic tasks with a well-defined ground truth, therefore allowing more control on the evaluation. Indeed, histopathological (and biomolecular) applications of attention can be characterised as multiple-instance learning (MIL) problems or simple extensions thereof. The goal of this work is to establish synthetic analogies for the MIL-like problems encountered in biomedical applications, with well-defined instance-level importance labels, and to quantitatively assess the quality of attention-based explanations, how frequently they are misleading, and potential solutions.

Our manuscript is organised as follows: we first introduce MIL as an abstract set classification problem, as well as some multi-population extensions. We show how these problems permit a quantitative assessment of instance importance attributions and why they map satisfyingly to some biomedical problems. We then describe the synthetic datasets we constructed as analogies and the attention-based models used to classify them, and conduct experiments to show to which extent attention-based explanations can be trusted. Finally, we argue for an ensemble-based solution to respond to the potential weaknesses of single-model explanations.

2   Importance Attribution as a Binary Classification Task

2.1   Multiple-Instance Learning and Its Extensions

2.1.1   Problem Formulation. Multiple-instance learning (MIL) is a classical weakly-supervised learning binary classification problem [3,12,14] in which data points X_i are made of unordered collections of vectors $X_i = \{x_{i1}, \ldots, x_{iM_i}\}$. The individual vectors x_{im} are referred to as "instances", while the data points X_i

are called bags of instances. Each instance x_{im} has a binary label $y_{im} \in \{1,0\}$ (also referred to as positive and negative), which is not available at training time, but defines the label Y_i of the bag X_i as:

$$Y_i = \min \left(1, \sum_{m=1}^{M_i} y_{im} \right), \tag{1}$$

which simply means that Y_i is 1 if at least one of the y_{im} is 1, and is 0 otherwise.

This is a formalization of classification problems used in multiple biomedical applications, such as patient diagnosis from histopathology images. Images are typically processed as collections of patches, of which only a few might contain clinically relevant regions. Another interesting medical application of MIL is the classification of tumors using single-cell molecular profiles. In this case, samples are a mixture of healthy and cancerous cell profiles, but only patient-level labels are available.

2.1.2   Multi-population MIL. Inspired by the biological applications of MIL, especially in the context of cancer, we propose to extend MIL to a multi-population setting with non-trivial interactions, which we can formalise as logical problems.

Multi-population AND

- There are three instance populations with three instance labels: $y_{im} \in \{0, 1, 2\}$.
- Bags have a binary label Y_i given as "the set of $\{y_{im}\}$ contains 1 AND contains 2". Namely, Y_i is one only if it contains population 1 and 2, but 0 if only one of the two is present. Population 0 is irrelevant.

This problem can model tumours where multiple cell communities can develop and support each other's growth by collaboration: the presence of both cellular communities accelerates disease progression and leads to worse prognosis [18]. In this case, population 0 would correspond to uninformative cells such as healthy cells in the tumour microenvironment while populations 1 and 2 would represent two cancerous populations that can collaborate.

Multi-population XOR

- There are three instance populations with three instance labels: $y_{im} \in \{0, 1, 2\}$.
- Bags have a binary label Y_i given as "the set of $\{y_{im}\}$ contains 1 XOR contains 2", *i.e.* Y_i is one only if it contains population 1 but not 2 or 2 but not 1. Population 0 is irrelevant.

This problem can model tumours where two cell communities can co-evolve but reduce their joint fitness such as by increasing drug response when both are present [13].

2.2   Quantifying Key Instance Attribution

The simple setting of MIL lends itself to quantifying the interpretability of importance distributions over bags of instances such as those provided by attention. For
standard MIL this is often called key-instance attribution [9], which amounts to
identifying positive instances inside positive bags. When ground truth instance-
level labels are known, this can be formulated as a supervised binary classification problem. In this work, we train models with weak, bag-level labels but want
to evaluate the attention scores as a prediction score to identify positive label
instances.

Of course, we cannot expect attention scores to be well calibrated and to allow
their immediate interpretation as a probability score for being "important". We
therefore need to be careful with some of the standard classification metrics based
on discretising prediction scores, such as accuracy or F_1. What we require of our
attention scores is that they discriminate well between positive and negative
instances for some threshold, which can be verified by inspecting the area under
the receiver operating characteristic curve (AUROC or AUC). For the sake of
clarity, we will refer to the AUC of importance attribution as IAUC, so as not to
confuse metrics for the bag-level classification and those for evaluating attention-
based explanations.

The multi-population extensions of MIL, *i.e.* AND and XOR don't have
canonically defined importances. We propose to extend the "key instance" label
by assigning it to populations 1 and 2 for both problems defined in Sect. 2.1.2,
while classifying population 0 as unimportant, since its presence or absence does
not impact the bag labels.

3   Methods

3.1   Attention-Based Deep MIL

Permutation-invariant models are best-suited to handle MIL tasks as they introduce an inductive bias tailored to sets of instances where order does not matter.
To this end, the Deep Sets architecture [23] was designed to produce an independent latent representation of each instance, which are then aggregated with
a permutation invariant function such as the mean. The aggregated latent representation is further processed to produce a bag label, as shown in Fig. 1.

Attention-based aggregation is another permutation-invariant operation that
dynamically performs weighted averages using the attention scores. This was
shown to improve performance and provide insights into the data through
the assigned weights [6]. With attention-based aggregation, a data point $X =
\{x_1, \ldots, x_M\}$ is mapped to a prediction y as follows:

$$z_i = \phi(x_i), \quad Z = \sum_{m=1}^{M} a_m z_m,$$
$$y = \rho(Z), \tag{2}$$

where ϕ and ρ are approximated by neural networks and a_m is the attention scores of instance x_m, defined as:

$$a_m = \frac{\exp\{\mathbf{w}^\top \tanh[\mathbf{V}\phi(x_m)^\top]\}}{\sum\limits_{j=1}^{M} \exp\{\mathbf{w}^\top \tanh[\mathbf{V}\phi(x_j)^\top]\}}, \qquad (3)$$

and, $\mathbf{V} \in \mathbb{R}^{L \times K}$ and $\mathbf{w} \in \mathbb{R}^{L \times 1}$ are trainable parameters. Notice that as $\sum\limits_{j=1}^{M} a_m = 1$, Eq. 3 defines normalized discrete weights over the instances.

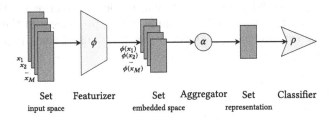

Fig. 1. Deep-Sets-like permutation invariant networks map bags of instances x_i to bags of latent representations $\phi(x_i)$ which are then aggregated as a set representation. This set representation is processed by a classifier to obtain a prediction ρ. In all experiments in this paper, the aggregator α is the attention mechanism described in Eq. 2.

3.2   Synthetic Datasets

We generate synthetic datasets with well-defined ground truth instance labels using three data modalities. These instance labels were kept hidden from the model at all times and only used to evaluate the performance of the attention attribution.

The first type of datasets, referred to as *Gaussian MIL*, *Gaussian AND* or *Gaussian XOR*, was built by sampling instances from normal distributions, $\mathcal{N}(\mu, \sigma = 1)$ with $\mu \in \mathbb{R}^4$. Populations 0,1 and 2 correspond to three choices of μ: $\mu_0 = (0,0,0,0)^\top$, $\mu_1 = (1,1,1,1)^\top$ and $\mu_2 = (-1,1,1,1)^\top$.

The second type of datasets trades 4-dimensional vectors for 28×28 pixels images of MNIST handwritten digits and are referred to as *MNIST MIL*, *MNIST AND* or *MNIST XOR*. The bags defined by first specifying the list of digits allowed in each population and then randomly sampling images of the specified digits from the original MNIST dataset [8]. Images of the digit "3" are given the instance label 1 in every problem while images of the digit "9" have instance label 2 in the XOR and AND cases. Any other digits are considered unimportant (label 0).

The last data modality mimics data produced by single-cell proteomics experiments. We used experimental single-cell mass-cytometry (CyTOF) measurements from breast cancer tumours [21] to produce pseudo-samples by randomly selecting epithelial cells. Each cell is characterised by 27 protein abundance measurements from a panel of markers chosen for cell phenotyping. The work that collected and published these data [21] grouped cells into 9 super-clusters of functionally and phenotypically distinct cells, including 7 clusters of luminal cells and two clusters of basal cells (B1 and B2). Basal cells are indicative of more dangerous tumours, in particular, super-cluster B2 was found to be strongly associated with triple-negative tumours [5]. We therefore define the *CyTOF MIL*, *CyTOF AND* or *CyTOF XOR* with populations 0, 1, and 2 respectively corresponding to luminal cells, B2 cells and B1 cells.

In all settings, we generate bags of 250 instances, which are drawn from bi- or trinomial distributions of populations 0, 1 and 2. In the MIL setting, we use a binomial distribution with equi-probable outcomes while in the multi-population settings we use a trinomial distribution where population 0 has probability 0.4 and populations 1 and 2 have probability 0.3. While not described in this paper, we have confirmed that our results are quite robust to changes in these parameters except for extreme cases (extremely low fractions of some population or very small bags).

4   Results

The basis of our analysis is a hyperparameter search for each task and data modality. We perform a grid search through possible configurations for our models and train each configuration with five random initialisations. Models are then ranked and selected on the basis of their performance on a validation set, and evaluated on a separate test set. More details on the hyperparameter search are provided in Appendix A.

4.1   Models with High Accuracy Can Have Poorly Behaved Attention

To reproduce the process of selecting models in a setting where instance-level importances are unknown, we select five candidate model configurations from our hyperparameter search based on their validation accuracy and evaluate the interpretability of their attention distributions. We train 100 repetitions of each of those top five configurations with different random seeds and evaluate how well the attention scores separate negative from positive instances in bags with a positive label. As we show in Fig. 2, some configurations have narrow distributions of IAUC centred around a reasonable value (0.75), meaning that all model realisations provide meaningful interpretations through their attention distributions while others have a non-negligible fraction of outliers with a very poor identification of important instances (IAUC around 0.5).

This pattern repeats over all problems and data modalities we evaluated. We summarise the results of our analysis in Table 1, where we report the mean test IAUC across all configurations and the number of "bad" configurations, defined as those having 10% or higher fraction of realisations with an IAUC less than 0.65. Detailed results with all IAUC distributions are available in Appendix B.

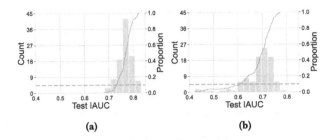

(a)   (b)

Fig. 2. (a) Configuration with stable IAUC. **(b)** Configuration with significant fraction of low IAUC. Both configurations were trained on the Gaussian MIL setting. The left Y-axis refers to the histogram (in green), while the right Y-axis refers to the cumulative frequency plot (orange line). The magenta line is a guide for the eye showing the 10% threshold used to define bad configurations in Table 1. (Color figure online)

Table 1. Evaluation of attention explanations performances. Multi-population problems tend to have more bad configurations than MIL, which can still have poor explanations. In general, AND problems also have an overal lower IAUC.

Data	Problem	Mean IAUC	# bad config.
Gaussian	MIL	0.75	1/5
	AND	0.59	5/5
	XOR	0.72	5/5
MNIST	MIL	0.80	0/5
	AND	0.69	2/5
	XOR	0.84	2/5
CyTOF	MIL	0.76	1/5
	AND	0.75	3/5
	XOR	0.77	3/5

To further illustrate the difference in behavior between "good" and "bad" models, we show low-dimensional representations of both of our numerical datasets (Gaussian and CyTOF) in Fig. 3, where the attention distributions are visible. "Good" models have an essentially constant attention over unimportant instances and show a sharp gradient on positive instances moving away from the class boundary, while "bad" models essentially have uniform attention over much of the dataset, with the exception of a small minority of the data, which is not necessarily a subset of the positive instances.

4.2   Repetitions of the Same Model Have Little Correlation Between Performance and Interpretability

The stochasticity of training multiple neural networks with the same hyperparameters leads to the variability in the quality of the explanations provided by

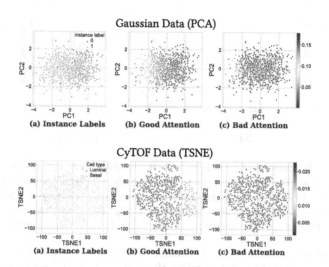

Fig. 3. Low-dimensional projections of MIL data with showing attention scores for an example of a "good" and a "bad" model, as well as the instance labels shown for reference.

their attention maps. Of course, this stochasticity also leads to variability in the validation and test performance of these models. It is therefore natural to investigate whether, for a fixed configuration, there is a correlation between the classification performance at the bag level and the quality of the attention-based explanations. This analysis might provide a way to weed out problematic models at the validation stage.

For each problem and data modality, we use the top 5 configurations defined in Sect. 4.1 to evaluate how well validation-time classification performance discriminates between models with low and high-quality explanations. As we show in Fig. 4, high performance is not a good indicator of good explanations, and the correlation between accuracy and IAUC exists but is rather mild. A more detailed picture separated by problem and data modality is available in Appendix C. In the case of MIL problems on Gaussian data (Fig. 14a), all models with the top configurations reach a validation accuracy of 100% while having varying IAUC values. On more complex problems, not all realisations reach perfect accuracies, and a limited amount of correlation can be observed. Indeed, as shown in Fig. 14e, it is often the case that only the models with top validation accuracies reach the top values for the IAUC. Nevertheless, there is still significant variability among the models with top validation accuracies so that filtering out models with a poorer validation performance is not enough to avoid models with poor explanations.

We measure the Spearman correlation ρ between the validation-time accuracy of the 100 repetitions of each top configurations for all our classification tasks and the IAUC score and report them in Table 2. For each problem, we further report the configurations with the highest and lowest spreads of IUAC values

(ΔIAUC) between individual top-performing realisations. Namely, to compute ΔIAUC, we select the models in the highest decile of validation accuracy for each configuration and measure the spread between their maximum and minimum IAUC values. This provides a way of observing how specific configurations have a large variability of IAUC even when filtering for models with high classification performance.

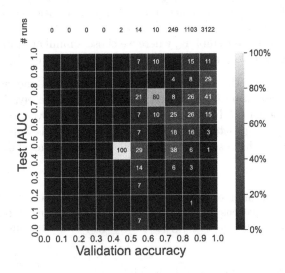

Fig. 4. Relationship between validation accuracy and test IAUC for top configurations. Models are binned by validation accuracy and IAUC and each bin displays the fraction of total models *per column* (*i.e.* per accuracy bin). The total number of models in each column is reported at the top.

Table 2. Predictivity of classification performance for informative explanations. We report the Spearman correlation between the validation accuracy and the IAUC as well as the highest and lowest ΔIAUC found among the models. When all trained models have accuracy 1, we report the Spearman correlation as 0 since accuracy cannot provide any information about IAUC.

Data	Problem	Spearman ρ	High ΔIAUC	Low ΔIAUC
	MIL	0	0.74	0.13
Gaussian	AND	0.50 ± 0.18	0.69	0.12
	XOR	0.65 ± 0.16	0.28	0.11
	MIL	-0.03 ± 0.06	0.41	0.13
MNIST	AND	-0.01 ± 0.12	0.42	0.10
	XOR	0.12 ± 0.24	0.83	0.06
	MIL	0	0.62	0.23
CyTOF	AND	0.07 ± 0.12	0.81	0.26
	XOR	0.04 ± 0.06	0.63	0.27

4.3 Ensembling Improves Explanation Robustness

While the risk of poor explanations is real, most trained models with good performance achieve satisfying interpretation-based explanation quality. We therefore propose to use ensembling to reduce the risk of encountering poorly-performing single models. Two strategies are possible:

- Single-configuration ensembling, where a fixed hyperparameter set is chosen based on validation performance and multiple realisations are trained with different random seeds.
- Multi-configuration ensembling, where we chose a number of high-performing models and ensemble realisations of each hyperparameter choice.

For both approaches, the ensembling is performed with the goal of obtaining *more robust attention-based explanations.* More concretely, for each bag of instances, each model produces an attention distribution over the instances and we compute the average attention scores across models. This yields a valid attention distribution for the ensemble in the sense that the averaged distribution also sums to 1.

Table 3. Impact of ensembling on the fraction of models with bad explanations. We compare three situations: no ensembling ($N=1$), and ensembling 20 models with either single configuration ensembling ($N=20$, single) or multi-configuration ensembling ($N=20$, mult.).

Data	Problem	% bad configs.		
		$N=1$	$N=20$ (single)	$N=20$ (mult.)
Gaussian	MIL	5.3	5.3	0.0
	AND	69.3	32.0	15.3
	XOR	42.3	0.0	0.0
MNIST	MIL	1.3	0.0	0.0
	AND	12.3	5.3	6.0
	XOR	11.3	0.0	0.0
CyTOF	MIL	6.0	0.0	0.0
	AND	10.0	0.0	0.0
	XOR	10.7	0.0	0.0

As we show in Table 3, ensembling does improve the fraction of models with bad explanations (as defined in Sect. 4.1), and multi-configuration ensembling provides the best option for most cases. The results we report for single-configuration ensembling are the average of the results obtained for the top five configurations found for each problem through hyperparameter search. As we show in more details in Appendix D, this average hides the fact that single-configuration ensembling fails badly for some configurations, while multi-configuration ensembling does not present this failure mode.

5   Discussion

Our experiments confirm that, most of the time, attention mechanisms provide meaningful information about the relative importance of instances in set classification problems like MIL. Nevertheless, silent failure modes exist where individual models can have good performance at the main weakly supervised task but produce attention maps that are not aligned with the amount of signal carried by data sub-components. This finding is somewhat worrying: with a bit of bad luck, a researcher could train a good model with poor interpretability and generate new hypotheses based on nonsensical explanations, which could lead to resource waste if they are the basis for experimental studies. However, attention-based explanations should not altogether be discarded, but be considered with care. As our ensembling experiments show, sporadically appearing bad-behaving models can be mitigated, but not altogether avoided in a multi-model setup as silent failures seem to fall in the minority. In some settings, however, ensembling by averaging attention scores does not improve the failure rate. We suspect that this is due to poor agreement between the attention assignment of different models, leading to poor ensemble performance, which could be improved by switching to majority voting. If this is the case, we could avoid false positive labelling of important instances by requiring a clear consensus between different models, which we hope to explore in future work. In any case, some responsible downstream analysis and validation of patterns highlighted by attention mechanisms is warranted when trying to discover new features in data, keeping in mind that there is a small but non-zero probability that the patterns might be misleading.

6   Conclusion

We showed across a variety of set-classification tasks and data modalities that silent failure modes exist for attention-based key instance attributions, where attention does not correlate with instance importance. While ensembling multiple random initialisations of the same model and multiple model architecture mitigates the issue, there often remains a probability that explanations based on attention could be misleading, which can range from problematic for scientific discovery to dangerous when using explanations to verify predictions in application settings. This should not be a reason to abandon attention as a tool for identifying important sub-components of data for a given model, but shows that downstream verification of potential patterns is necessary. We have hinted at the fact that a more fine-grained approach to ensembling could help filter false positives and this is definitely an interesting avenue for further research. Other important directions which we plan to pursue is the identification of the features of tasks where silent failure is less common, as well as understanding which aspects of model architecture impact the quality of importance attribution.

Acknowledgments. We thank the Systems Biology group at IBM Research Europe for useful discussions, as well as Mattia Rigotti and Janis Born. This project was support by SNF grant No. 192128 and the H2020 grant "iPC" (No. 826121).

A   Hyperparameter Searches

A.1   Gaussian Data

Table 4. Parameter grid for Gaussian data.

Parameter	Values
Batch size	100
Epoch	100, 200, 500
Learning rate	0.001, 0.005, 0.01, 0.02
Weight decay	0.0001
Loss function	Cross entropy
Optim. algorithm	Adam
Hidden layer size	2, 4, 8
Attention size	1, 2, 4, 8
Featurizer depth	0, 1, 2
Classifier depth	1, 2, 3

A.2   Image Data

Table 5. Parameter grid for image data.

Parameter	Values
Batch size	100
Epoch	500
Learning rate	0.001, 0.005, 0.01, 0.02
Weight decay	0.0001
Loss function	Cross entropy
Optim. algorithm	Adam
Hidden layer size	8, 16, 32, 64
Attention size	1, 2, 4, 8, 10
Featurizer depth	1, 2
Classifier depth	1, 2

A.3   CyTOF Data

Table 6. Parameter grid for CyTOF data.

Parameter	Values
Batch size	100
Epoch	500
Learning rate	0.001, 0.005, 0.01, 0.02
Weight decay	0.0001
Loss function	Cross entropy
Optim. algorithm	Adam
Hidden layer size	4, 8, 16
Attention size	1, 2, 4, 8
Featurizer depth	1, 2, 3
Classifier depth	1, 2, 3

B   IAUC Distributions for Top Models

Models marked with an asterisk have a significant proportion of bad runs, i.e. 10% or more of them achieved an IAUC below 0.65 (Figs. 5, 6, 7, 8, 9, 10, 11, 12 and 13).

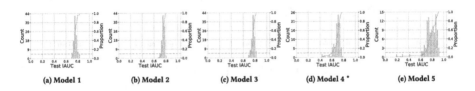

(a) Model 1   (b) Model 2   (c) Model 3   (d) Model 4 *   (e) Model 5

Fig. 5. Gaussian MIL

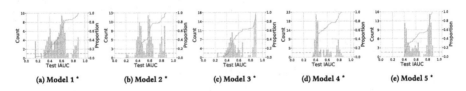

(a) Model 1 *   (b) Model 2 *   (c) Model 3 *   (d) Model 4 *   (e) Model 5 *

Fig. 6. Gaussian AND

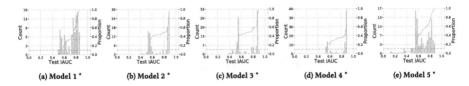

(a) Model 1 *   (b) Model 2 *   (c) Model 3 *   (d) Model 4 *   (e) Model 5 *

Fig. 7. Gaussian XOR

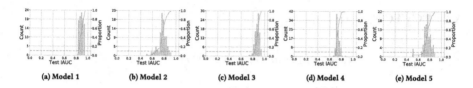

Fig. 8. MNIST MIL

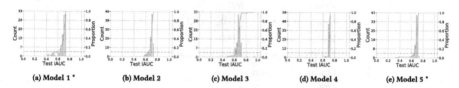

Fig. 9. MNIST AND

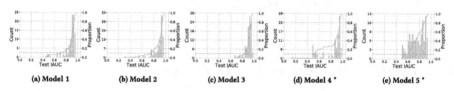

Fig. 10. MNIST XOR

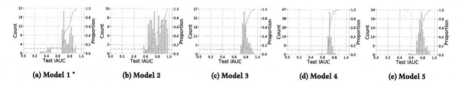

Fig. 11. CyTOF MIL

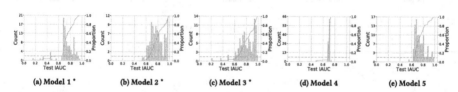

Fig. 12. CyTOF AND

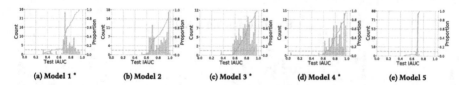

Fig. 13. CyTOF XOR

C Correlations Between IAUC and Accuracy

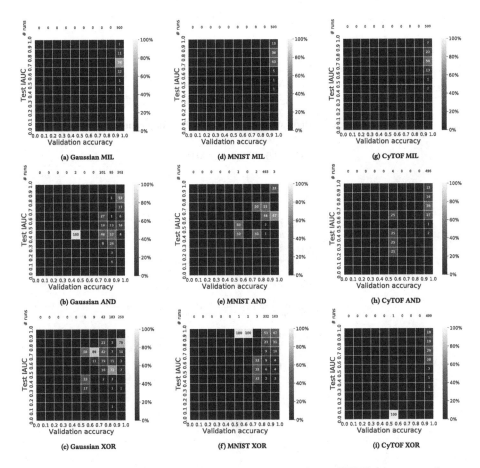

Fig. 14. Relationship between validation accuracy and test IAUC for top configurations, separated by problem and data modality. Models are binned by validation accuracy and IAUC and each bin displays the fraction of total models *per column* (*i.e.* per accuracy bin). The total number of models in each column is reported at the top.

D Ensembling

Proportion of bad ensembles for single- and multi-configuration ensembles. Bad ensembles are characterised by an IAUC of 0.65 or below. For each ensemble size, 30 different ensembles were produced. In the single-configuration plots, the light grey lines show the results for the individual configurations while the black line shows their average. In the multi-configuration case, the process was repeated five times. The 95% confidence interval is indicated by the grey area (Figs. 15, 16, 17, 18, 19 and 20).

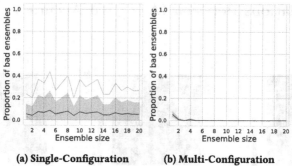

(a) Single-Configuration   (b) Multi-Configuration

Fig. 15. Gaussian MIL

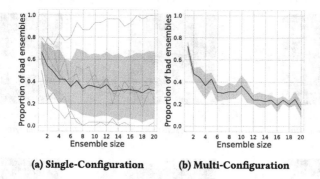

(a) Single-Configuration   (b) Multi-Configuration

Fig. 16. Gaussian AND

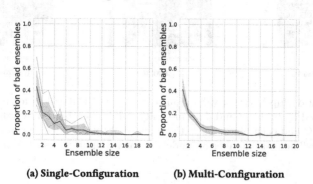

(a) Single-Configuration   (b) Multi-Configuration

Fig. 17. Gaussian XOR

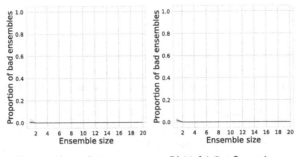

(a) Single-Configuration   **(b) Multi-Configuration**

Fig. 18. MNIST MIL

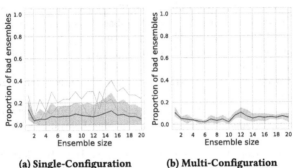

(a) Single-Configuration   **(b) Multi-Configuration**

Fig. 19. MNIST AND

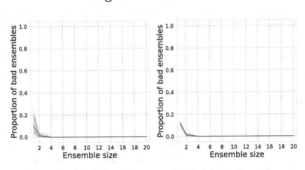

(a) Single-Configuration   **(b) Multi-Configuration**

Fig. 20. MNIST XOR

References

1. Cluzeau, J.M., et al.: Concepts of design assurance for neural networks (CoDANN) - AI roadmap. Technical report, EASA (2020)
2. Devlin, J., Chang, M.-W., Lee, K., Toutanova, K.: BERT: pre-training of deep bidirectional transformers for language understanding (2018). https://doi.org/10.48550/ARXIV.1810.04805
3. Dietterich, T.G., Lathrop, R.H., Lozano-Pérez, T.: Solving the multiple instance problem with axis-parallel rectangles. Artif. Intell. **89**(1), 31–71 (1997). https://doi.org/10.1016/S0004-3702(96)00034-3
4. Dosovitskiy, A., et al.: An image is worth 16 × 16 words: transformers for image recognition at scale. In: International Conference on Learning Representations (2020)
5. Elias, A.D.: Triple-negative breast cancer: a short review. Am. J. Clin. Oncol. **33**(6), 637–645 (2010). https://doi.org/10.1097/COC.0b013e3181b8afcf
6. Ilse, M., Tomczak, J., Welling, M.: Attention-based deep multiple instance learning. In: International Conference on Machine Learning, pp. 2127–2136. PMLR (2018)
7. Jain, S., Wallace, B.C.: Attention is not explanation (2019). https://doi.org/10.48550/ARXIV.1902.10186
8. LeCun Y., Cortes, C.: The MNIST database of handwritten digits. Undefined (2005)
9. Liu, G., Wu, J., Zhou, Z.-H.: Key instance detection in multi-instance learning. In: Proceedings of the Asian Conference on Machine Learning. PMLR, pp. 253–268 (2012)
10. Lu, M.Y., Williamson, D.F.K., Chen, T.Y., Chen, R.J., Barbieri, M., Mahmood, F.: Data-efficient and weakly supervised computational pathology on whole-slide images. Nat. Biomed. Eng. **5**(6), 555–570 (2021). https://doi.org/10.1038/s41551-020-00682-w
11. Madsen, A., Reddy, S., Chandar, S.: Post-hoc interpretability for neural NLP: a survey (2022). https://doi.org/10.48550/arXiv.2108.04840arxiv:2108.0484 [cs]
12. Maron, O., Lozano-Pérez, T.: A framework for multiple-instance learning. In: Advances in Neural Information Processing Systems, vol. 10. MIT Press (1997)
13. Miller, B.E., Machemer, T., Lehotan, M., Heppner, G.H.: Tumor subpopulation interactions affecting melphalan sensitivity in Palpable Mouse Mammary tumors. Cancer Res. **51**(16), 4378–4387 (1991)
14. Oquab, M., Bottou, L., Laptev, I., Sivic, J.: Is object localization for free? - Weakly-supervised learning with convolutional neural networks. In: Proceedings of the IEEE Conference on Computer Vision and Pattern Recognition (2015)
15. Redekop, E., et al.: Attention-guided prostate lesion localization and grade group classification with multiple instance learning. In: Medical Imaging with Deep Learning (2021)
16. Selbst, A.D., Powles, J.: Meaningful information and the right to explanation. Int. Data Privacy Law **7**(4), 233–242 (2017). https://doi.org/10.1093/idpl/ipx022
17. Serrano, S., Smith, N.A.: Is attention interpretable? In: Proceedings of the 57th Annual Meeting of the Association for Computational Linguistics. Association for Computational Linguistics, Florence, Italy, pp. 2931–2951 (2019). https://doi.org/10.18653/v1/P19-1282
18. Tabassum, D.P., Polyak, K.: Tumorigenesis: it takes a village. Nat. Rev. Cancer **15**(8), 473–483 (2015). https://doi.org/10.1038/nrc3971

19. Tourniaire, P., Ilie, M., Hofman, P., Ayache, N., Delingette, H.: Attention-based multiple instance learning with mixed supervision on the Camelyon16 dataset. In: Proceedings of the MICCAI Workshop on Computational Pathology, pp. 216–226. PMLR (2021)

20. Vashishth, S., Upadhyay, S., Tomar, G.S., Faruqui, M.: Attention interpretability across NLP tasks. arXiv:1909.11218 [cs], September 2019

21. Wagner, J., et al.: A single-cell atlas of the tumor and immune ecosystem of human breast cancer. Cell **177**(5), 1330–1345.e18 (2019). https://doi.org/10.1016/j.cell. 2019.03.005

22. Wiegreffe, S., Pinter, Y.: Attention is not explanation (2019). https://doi.org/10. 48550/ARXIV.1908.04626

23. Zaheer, M., Kottur, S., Ravanbakhsh, S., Poczos, B., Salakhutdinov, R., Smola, A.: Deep sets. arXiv:1703.06114 [cs, stat], April 2018

From Disentangled Representation to Concept Ranking: Interpreting Deep Representations in Image Classification Tasks

Eric Ferreira dos Santos[(✉)] and Alessandra Mileo

Collins Ave Ext - Whitehall, Dublin City University, Dublin, Ireland
eric.ferreiradossantos2@mail.dcu.ie, alessandra.mileo@dcu.ie
https://www.dcu.ie/courses/undergraduate/school-computing/
computer-science

Abstract. Deep Learning models such as Convolutional Neural Networks (CNNs) are particularly successful in computer vision tasks. They have proven to be tremendously effective and popular in the last decade, reaching great accuracy in tasks such as image classification and object recognition. Despite their success, it is well known that conveying what the model learnt to humans remains challenging. This is due to the fact that a CNN is still mostly a black-box model, and images are very rich input data. In this work, we build upon the idea of disentangled representation produced from a trained CNN, and explore how such disentangled representation can be used to describe what the model has learned in terms of semantic concepts. Specifically, we aim at providing a ranked list of the concepts that are related to both a specific instance or image (local explainability) and a class (global explainability). In this preliminary work we use a simple linear classifier for concept ranking. Results are promising since we reached 95% precision at both local and global level. This indicates potential in developing our idea further by leveraging external knowledge bases to associate and validate specific properties and relations among the ranked concepts at both local and global level as discussed in the final section of this paper.

Keywords: Explainable AI · Disentangled representation · Convolutional Neural Network

1 Introduction and Overview

Computer Vision is a branch of Artificial Intelligence that looks into how computer programs can interpret, represent, and act on visual inputs (such as pictures and videos). Deep Learning models such as Convolutional Neural Networks (CNNs) are specifically tailored to computer vision tasks, and in the last decade

Supported by Science Foundation Ireland - Grant No. 18/CRT/6223.

they have become remarkably successful and popular, achieving incredible accuracy in tasks such as image classification and object detection.

Despite their success, CNNs are still mostly a black-box model, in that how and what the model learns is intelligible to the users and cannot be easily presented in human terms. The difficulty in generating a human-understandable explanation of the model outcome is hindering the use of CNNs in critical environments such as diagnostic imaging, disaster management and security surveillance to mention a few. In these scenarios it is crucial to understand how the model came to a given outcome and what the model has learned from the training data, not only to identify and correct mistakes, but also to detect potential bias in the data or the model.

The majority of approaches for interpreting directly the output of a trained CNN in a classification task have been focusing on the use of visual cues and more in general attention-based methods. For example, work in [8] and [5] have highlighted image pixels or areas contributing to a specific classification. [8] describes a technique for visualising how the model behaves in each layer for a particular image. Both approaches aid in localising which parts of the image were relevant to a specific class. However, because the image concepts are not declared in the image or the dataset, this visualisation does not represent them, and there is no guarantee that the model will highlight the same parts for other images in the same class.

In order to tackle the limitation of visual approaches, other explainability methods have been proposed in recent years, and the field of Explainable AI has began to be characterised in different survey papers.

Among others, [4] examines many strategies that employ textual justification when textual data is learnt and coupled with visual data, increasing the model's explainability. This method was utilised in the medical domain to clarify categorisation by combining image and textual diagnostics. Other techniques include simplification, which involves creating a white-box model from a complex model to achieve performance while simplifying the explanation. Feature relevance is another method which consists of considering each feature's value and using it to describe the learning process.

Another perspective in [2] is to explore using human expertise to explain how the model is learnt in a way that a layperson may comprehend, explained is rooted in real-world principles. This survey also provides links to the code for each approach discussed.

Based on the classification in these surveys, our approach would relate to the feature-relevant method, which in computer vision we would convert to real-world concepts. Ranking them, we intend to present the concepts more relevant from a singular image and to an entire class. In further work, we would combine this approach with the common-sense knowledge database, creating explanations that an AI system and a regular person can understand.

In this study, we will look at how a basic linear classifier can be used to rank concepts that characterise not only an instance, but more generally a class from local disentangled representations, which was not provided in previous works. We aim to provide a semantic explanation of what the model has learned in terms of the most relevant concepts. This is only the first step towards providing an alternative human-understandable and self-explainable representation of a trained CNN model. In fact, we plan on building on the ability to not only identify semantic concepts as in disentangled representations, but also rank them based on their semantic relevance to an instance or a class (which is our key contribution in this work). Leveraging such ranking, we believe we can then go one step further in extracting semantic relations and subsequently learning logic rules from deep representations, as discussed in the final section of this paper.

The rest of the paper is structured as follows: in Sect. 2 we discuss related paper that specifically introduce and use the disentangled technique for improving model interpretability in image classification tasks; Sect. 3 describes our approach, specifically how we retrieved the local and global disentangled concepts from the trained model; our preliminary experimental evaluation and discussion of results is provided in Sect. 4, where we also outline how the evaluation should be extended and strengthened; we conclude in Sect. 5 presenting our ongoing research which builds upon the work in this paper towards a deeper understanding of the deep CNN model in a self-explainable and human-understandable way.

2   Related Work

Disentangled representation is a method that divides each characteristic (of an image) into carefully specified variables and encodes them as distinct dimensions. The idea is to emulate humans' fast intuitive process.[1] This method can characterise semantic concepts gained by a model throughout its training phase. This section will list the principal works that employed this strategy to characterise concepts learned in deep representations: Network Dissection, Decision Trees-based approach to learn disentangled filters and Concept Activation Vectors.

Network Dissection. Networks Dissection is a method for extracting meaning from each layer or filter, using the distillation approach to explain a CNN. Authors in [11] claim that a DNN may spontaneously learn disentangled representations. In order to demonstrate that, they developed a framework for connecting human notions to each filter in a CNN model (Fig. 1). The objective is to provide meaningful labels to individual filters. The initial stage was to generate the Broden dataset, which contains pixel-annotated low-level notions like colours and high-level concepts like objects. They then used a trained model and passed through it the Broden dataset, to assess each filter and comparing the binary map from each picture and each filter activation map. If the convolutional filter is strongly activated in parts of the picture containing a human-labelled notion, authors claim that the filter is "searching for" that idea or concept.

---

[1] https://deepai.org/machine-learning-glossary-and-terms/disentangled-representation-learning.

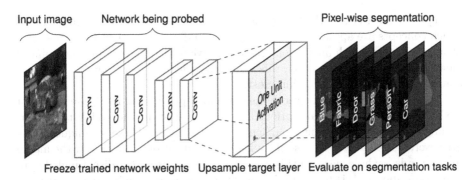

Fig. 1. Network dissection framework [11]

Examining different CNN designs, authors discovered certain important notions, such as the number of unique concepts for each layer in each architecture and the number of objects increasing into deeper convolutional layers.

Decision Trees Approach. In [10], the authors suggested learning a decision tree from a trained CNN, detailing the exact reasons for categorisation at a semantic level. The proposed technique describes which image components activate, which filters for categorisation and how much each part contributes. In this approach the authors use simplification method, to extract from a complex model a simple explanation.

The first part of the approach is training a CNN with disentangled filters on the high convolution layers to each filter learn a specific concept and associate each one to semantic meaning since they do not have any annotations of the concepts. This approach is presented in [9], where a loss function is applied for each filter in the top convolutional layer.

The trained disentangled filters extract information from each image and input it into a decision tree that understands its composition. There is no link between a filter and a human notion at this time, thus the authors use other datasets to assign a concept to a specific filter. They concentrated on a single topic (bird) and only used concepts relating to that issue. This method differs from [11] because it does not employ an extensive concept dataset to assign the concept to each filter. It can, however, be used to search for ideas that are not available in the Broaden dataset.

Concept Activation Vectors. Another relevant work in [3] proposes determining how human notions influence categorisation results. Authors defined and developed the CAV (Concept Activation Vectors) to transform a neural network's internal state into human-friendly notions. The method is useful because a human concept, such as "stripes," may be shown to impact the "zebra" class.

The core idea is retrieved from a trained model, a vector that characterises a particular concept, and then a directional derivative is used to assess concept sensitivity for a specific class. This method gives a local explanation for a specific concept within a class, which may be required if the user already understands which concepts are applicable to a given class and wants to identify among a set of such concepts which ones are more descriptive for that class from the point of view of the deep representation, this validating which concepts among the given ones are affecting a classification most.

The papers and approaches discussed above provide some explanations for CNNs, incorporating human notions that might assist a non-specialist in determining how the model learnt a particular categorisation. These techniques, however, were not employed to describe a global classification, such as how the model understands a whole class. In this paper, we suggest using the disentangled approach described in [11] to determine how the classes may be interpreted using a global ranking of semantic concepts. We use a different dataset [7] to examine the ideas used to categorise a specific image. The model processed the dataset, and the total of each activation map of a unit in the final layer was used as input for an SVM classifier. We then use the top-ranked unit weighted by the SVM model for a particular image to order the identified concepts. Section 3 describes our naive technique in more detail.

3   Extracting Concepts for Action Classification

This section will outline the approach for concept extraction and ranking we propose in this paper.

The first step in this process is to extract semantic concepts about a class or a single instance from a trained CNN model using transfer-learning on an action classification task on a dataset containing forty actions. We decided to build upon previous research [11] that has already obtained promising results on semantic concept identification for a trained CNN model. One of the outcomes of such work is the ability to quantify how interpretable a CNN is by discovering how individual hidden units align to semantic concepts at each hidden layer. Concepts were identified as being part of six categories: object, part, material, colour, texture and scene. The architecture that identified more unique concepts among those tested was ResNet-152, as indicated in Fig. 2; therefore this is the architecture we adopt.

We extend this technique for concept detection by identifying and connecting such concepts to output classes as well as individual input images (or instances). We chose to focus on the last CNN layer to maximise the number of unique high-level semantic concepts discovered; once more different concepts are harnessed, more concepts may be connected with local or individual examples.

We start from the semantic concepts identified by *Network Dissection* [11] from the trained CNN model and build upon the relationship between the convolutional filter and the semantic concept from the *Broden* [1] dataset. A transfer-learning approach makes it possible to adapt the *Network Dissection* method to be used on different data sets (and classification tasks) and determine which filters are activated by each new input. With this approach, the concepts learned

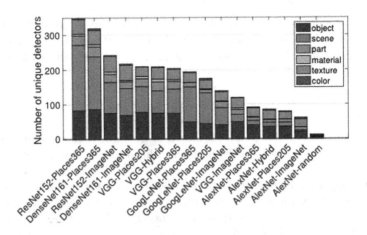

Fig. 2. Unique detectors for each CNN architecture [11]

from *Network Dissection* are extended to new input images: the top K highest-scoring filters for each input image are chosen as the identified concepts, considering the mean of each activation map.

Note that an activation map is a matrix that represents which image part was activated after the convolution function. It can be represented by a matrix $A_{M \times N}$ of the elements a_{ij}, where $M = 1..i$ and $N = 1..j$. We define the mean of the activation map matrix $M_{Activation\_map}$ as follows:

$$M_{Activation\_map} = \frac{\sum_{i=1}^{M} \sum_{j=1}^{N} a_{ij}}{\#E} \tag{1}$$

where $\#E$ is the number of elements of A.

We then rank the K filters from highest to lowest based on the mean activation map for each picture, assuming that the highest value identifies the most representative concept contained in an image. Once the model has identified other concepts for each image, the order of the pictures of the same class may be readjusted.

As a result, the approach produces as output a list of K different semantic concepts that are considered meaningful for each image. For the global concepts, a linear classifier with model-extracted features is applied to the same dataset for each class; subsequently, based on feature significance we determine which semantic concepts are relevant for the global separation. As mentioned previously, the dataset used for the investigation is the *Action40* dataset [7], which contains action photos labelled for 40 different action classes.

As a first metric for evaluation, we assess a simple precision from the ranked semantic concepts from local instances to the ranked semantic concepts for their class using the list of top K high-scored concepts from local and global examples. To do so, we compare the notions for each local example (image) belonging to a specific category to the top concepts that best linearly separate the class. We consider the globally rated concepts to make sense with the local ones if at least one concept is offered between them. The formula for this can be expressed as:

$$P_c = \frac{\sum C_{l_c, g_c}}{\#L_c} \tag{2}$$

where P_c is the precision of the specific class c, $\sum C_{l_c, g_c}$ is the sum of the instances where the global and local shared at least one ranked semantic concept in the class c, and the $\#L_c$ is the number of local instances that belongs to the class c.

In this paper we assess the relationship between the top-ranked concepts from local and global examples using this metric. This gives us an indication of how well the global characteristics, separated linearly, reflect the semantic concepts acquired by the model for each class. We are aware this is a simplistic metric and we will discuss in the next section other possible variations that we will test and compare in future work.

The experimental evaluation of the extracted concepts following this approach will be presented in the next section.

4   Experimental Evaluation

As mentioned in Sect. 3, we build upon the *Network Dissection* technique to extract local and global concepts. The task we consider in our investigation is action classification (*Action40* dataset)[2]. The concepts associated to each filter in the CNN model are provided by *Network Dissection*, which was trained on the *Imagenet* dataset[3], considering only a limited set of categories, namely *object*, *part*, *material* and *colour*. We only collected the concepts identified in the CNN's last layer, which created 162 distinct concepts. Then, using a transfer-learning approach, we used the *Action40* dataset to capture the concepts learnt for this data, based on the *Network Dissection* results.

The local semantic features from the new data were recovered using the mean of the activation map from each filter in the final layer as per Formula 1. The same formula was used for global concepts, i.e. concepts for each class, but this time it is used as feature extraction for the classification input. Following the intuition in [3] that meaningful higher-level concepts may be simpler to grasp, we used the SVM linear classifier to detect such concepts per class. We ran the algorithm using a 5-fold cross-validation, using the learning rate (C) equal to 0.001[4] and took the model with the best F1 score. The classification algorithm produced the confusion matrix in Fig. 3, which displays the precision obtained for each class. The linear model achieved the precision of 80% in the class separation (classification task).

---

[2] http://vision.stanford.edu/Datasets/40actions.html.

[3] https://www.image-net.org/download.php.

[4] Best results from a grid-search technique using: https://scikit-learn.org/stable/modules/generated/sklearn.model_selection.GridSearchCV.html,.

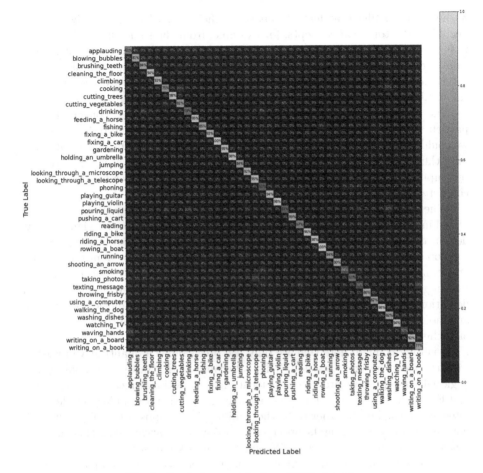

Fig. 3. Confusion matrix from SVM classifier

Based on the top-ranked concepts extracted, we calculate the precision (Formula 2) between the images and their class in four different ways:

- Top 5 L - Top 1 G: The top 5 local concepts for each instance and the top 1 global concept for each class.
- Top 5 L - Top 5 G: The top 5 local concepts for each instance and the top 5 global concepts for each class.
- Top 5 L - Top 10 G: The top 5 local concepts for each instance and the top 10 global concepts for each class.
- Top 10 L - Top 10 G: The top 10 local concepts for each instance and the top 10 global concepts for each class.

The rationale behind varying the number of top concepts is to determine how many top global ranking concepts may best represent images from the same class. We discovered that a linear classifier will provide the feature relevance depending on how successfully that feature separated the class, which is not always connected to the top local concepts, for example, from the same class. This means that in the model, the most common concepts provided in a group of images from the same class are not necessarily chosen as the best representative characteristics for that class. Therefore, we used this variation to precision between the local and global concepts belonging to the same class.

The first assessment evaluated whether the top one global concept from a particular class was present in the top five local concepts. Figure 4 shows that we could not identify a relevant precision for the majority of the classes utilising only the top 1 global concept. This behaviour supports the previous intuition by emphasising that the feature relevance in a linear classifier is aimed at the characteristics that best distinguish (or separate) the classes.

When we examine the precision between the top ten concepts in local and global instances (Fig. 5), we can observe that the precision improves significantly, demonstrating that the global top ten concepts are represented in the local top ten concepts. Given that the model identified 162 different semantic concepts, and our technique could identify a mean precision of 95% between only ten ranking concepts, this is a significant result. The precision mean and standard deviation for all classes for each different number of global and local concepts are shown in Fig. 6. Note that all the code is is available in an open repository on github[5] for reproducibility of results.

It is important to note that we only use precision as a quantitative measure for our concept ranking method. This is because in this instance we only check if global concepts are presented in local ones. Additional measures like recall and F1 would not change this result but we agree that they could provide other interesting insights. In order to further validate the proposed technique, we will not only explore the insights provided by using alternative evaluation metrics, but also compare results across different benchmark datasets.

In order to illustrate our outcome qualitatively with an example, we chose one of the greatest and lowest precision classes, "cutting_trees" and "phoning", respectively. The class "cutting_trees" had a significant separation result from the linear classifier (98%) and obtained 100% precision between the global and local concepts. Based on the feature significance from the linear model, the global concepts for this class are: "snow", "tree", "bird", "motorbike", "house", "bicycle", "plant" and "hand". When we look at all of the photographs in the same class, the top ten local concepts are: "house", "tree", "plant", "bird", "person", "bicycle", "hand", "motorbike", "snow" and "food".

This result demonstrates that there is an interesting overlap between global and local concepts for the class "cutting_trees," which we can use to describe what the model learned as the pattern of this class. Simultaneously, we may manually check that the presented notions appear plausible when we consider the activity of cutting the tree and its images on the dataset. This is just an intuition, as we said, and a more systematic evaluation (either manually by humans or automatically via labels) should be conducted.

---

[5] https://github.com/EricFerreiraS/disentangled_representation-concept_ranking.

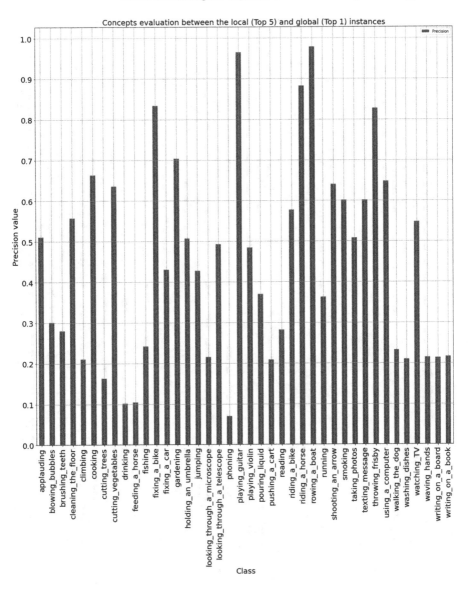

Fig. 4. Top 5 local concepts X Top 1 Global concept

When we look at the "phoning" class, the linear classifier did not produce an flattering result (precision of 51%), and when compared to the global and local concepts, the result was the poorest in the method (about 67%). This result might indicate two possibilities: the linear model did not segregate the concepts properly (an issue with the linear model) or there is a lack of concepts that could better describe this class (issue with concept generation). These concerns will be investigated upon in future work.

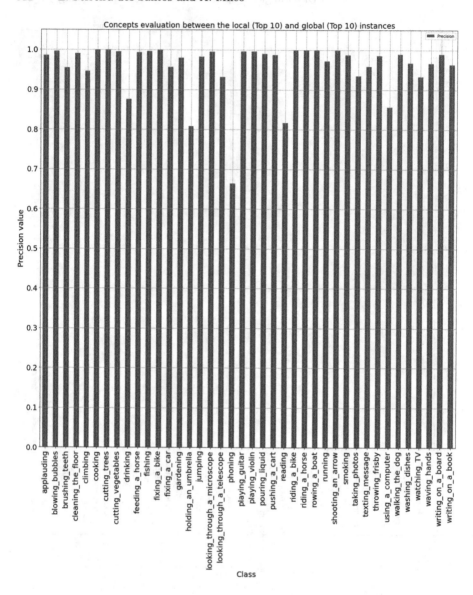

Fig. 5. Top 10 local concepts X Top 10 global concept

To summarise, our quantitative experimental analysis so far showed that our approach was able to successfully retrieve the top 10 concepts from disentangled representation that best characterise the local instances (as per *Network Dissection*) as well as the global instances. We assessed the method by comparing the existence of concepts in local and global occurrences. In the next section we will present the ongoing research we are conducting in this area and our next steps.

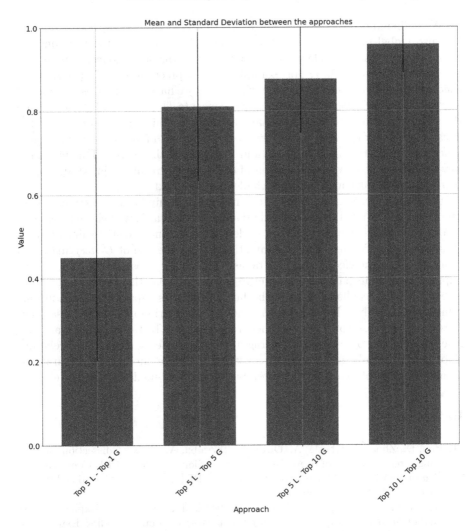

Fig. 6. Mean and standard deviation between the precision

5   Ongoing Work

CNN has shown impressive accuracy in computer vision applications, but the absence of an explanation for what the model learnt remains an open challenge for its adoption in high-risk scenarios. This study investigated the potential of building upon disentangled representations to provide a semantically meaningful interpretation of classification results produced by a CNN in terms of relevant semantic concepts. We demonstrate how even using a linear classifier such as SVM, we are able to meaningfully rank top ten concepts that characterise not only an instance, but more generally a class from local disentangled representations.

We define and test a method for extracting not only the top local concepts but also global ones. We demonstrated that we can identify the top concepts for an image of a given class, and that these are the same concepts necessary to best separate this class. For example, with a precision of 95% between the concepts presented in the images and their class, we have that images categorised as "riding a bike" contain the top local concepts "bicycle" and "wheel", and the same top concepts were necessary to separate this class according to the linear classification. As a result, we argue that the model has learned those concepts related to a specific class (and instances of that class). This paves the way for a concept-driven explanation of classification results using disentangled representations, although different challenges lie ahead.

For example, we notice that no semantic relationship between extracted concepts can be extracted with our method alone. To this aim, we believe leveraging an external knowledge base can aid in detecting semantic relationships between those concepts. We are currently investigating on the use of *Conceptnet* [6], a common-sense knowledge graph database, to acquire those relationships, thus improving the transparency and interpretability of what the model has learned.

Another key challenge is that the human expert's capacity to explain outcomes semantically is limited due to a lack of information regarding causal linkages between those concepts and their relationships. To tackle this we are also investigating the possibility of leveraging the extracted concepts and relationships to learn symbolic rules about causality, therefore offering a structural and human-like way of explaining the results of a decision made by the model.

References

1. Bau, D., Zhou, B., Khosla, A., Oliva, A., Torralba, A.: Network dissection: quantifying interpretability of deep visual representations. In: 2017 IEEE Conference on Computer Vision and Pattern Recognition (CVPR), pp. 3319–3327 (2017). https://doi.org/10.1109/CVPR.2017.354
2. Holzinger, A., Saranti, A., Molnar, C., Biecek, P., Samek, W.: Explainable AI methods-a brief overview. In: International Workshop on Extending Explainable AI Beyond Deep Models and Classifiers, pp. 13–38. Springer (2022). https://doi.org/10.1007/978-3-031-04083-2_2
3. Kim, B., Wattenberg, M., Gilmer, J., Cai, C., Wexler, J., Viegas, F., et al.: Interpretability beyond feature attribution: quantitative testing with concept activation vectors (TCAV). In: International Conference on Machine Learning, pp. 2668–2677. PMLR (2018)
4. Minh, D., Wang, H.X., Li, Y.F., et al.: Explainable artificial intelligence: a comprehensive review. Artif. Intell. Rev. **55**, 3503–3568 (2022). https://doi.org/10.1007/s10462-021-10088-y
5. Selvaraju, R.R., Cogswell, M., Das, A., Vedantam, R., Parikh, D., Batra, D.: Gradcam: visual explanations from deep networks via gradient-based localization. In: Proceedings of the IEEE International Conference on Computer Vision, pp. 618–626 (2017)
6. Speer, R., Chin, J., Havasi, C.: ConceptNet 5.5: an open multilingual graph of general knowledge. In: Thirty-First AAAI Conference on Artificial Intelligence (2017)

7. Yao, B., Jiang, X., Khosla, A., Lin, A.L., Guibas, L., Fei-Fei, L.: Human action recognition by learning bases of action attributes and parts. In: 2011 International Conference on Computer Vision, pp. 1331–1338. IEEE (2011)
8. Zeiler, M.D., Fergus, R.: Visualizing and understanding convolutional networks. In: European Conference on Computer Vision, pp. 818–833. Springer (2014). https://doi.org/10.1007/978-3-319-10590-1_53
9. Zhang, Q., Wu, Y.N., Zhu, S.C.: Interpretable convolutional neural networks. In: Proceedings of the IEEE Conference on Computer Vision and Pattern Recognition, pp. 8827–8836 (2018)
10. Zhang, Q., Yang, Y., Ma, H., Wu, Y.N.: Interpreting CNNs via decision trees. In: Proceedings of the IEEE/CVF Conference on Computer Vision and Pattern Recognition, pp. 6261–6270 (2019)
11. Zhou, B., Bau, D., Oliva, A., Torralba, A.: Interpreting deep visual representations via network dissection. IEEE Trans. Pattern Anal. Mach. Intell. **41**(9), 2131–2145 (2018)

RangeGrad: Explaining Neural Networks by Measuring Uncertainty Through Bound Propagation

Sam Pinxteren[(⊠)], Marco Favier, and Toon Calders

University of Antwerp, Antwerp, Belgium
sam.pinxteren@uantwerpen.be

Abstract. When generating local neural network explanations, many methods remove or obfuscate information at the input and observe the effect on the neural network output. If the lack of certain information causes meaningful changes to the output, we assume it was important and forms part of the explanation for the prediction result. It is not trivial, however, to decide on a clear definition for the absence of information. Previous methods have blurred, darkened or added normally distributed noise to certain portions of the input. In this paper, we propose using interval bounds as a proxy for uncertainty about, or absence of, information. Using this insight, we developed RangeGrad, a novel method for generating saliency maps for neural networks. This method exploits the relationship between uncertainty on the input with prediction uncertainty. We show that the uncertainty framework produces valid explanations in line with existing methods.

Keywords: Explainable artificial intelligence · Saliency maps · Interval bound propagation

1 Introduction

Machine learning is an ever-developing field. These developments, however, often lead to large and complex models. This is especially the case in the field of neural networks. At the same time, due to regulatory [4], fairness, and bias concerns, understanding our models is more important than ever. For this reason, explainability is gaining attention and importance in recent years.

For neural networks, explainability takes many forms. One of the main qualifiers in the taxonomy of neural network explanation methods is global versus local explanations. Global explanations provide insight into how the network generally performs its function, independent of a certain given data point. For example, Pedapati et al. [10] developed a method to convert a black box model to

S. Pinxteren—Supported by FWO (Flanders) and M. Favier—Supported by the AXA joint research initiative (CS15893).

a decision tree model without losing much of the original model's performance, while this derived model can be interpreted more easily than the original model.

In contrast to global explanations, the goal of local explanations is to give insight into a single prediction of the neural network. For example, if the network classifies a certain image as containing a cat, we would like to know which parts of the image were important for this prediction. This insight could come in the form of rules [3,11], dataset examples [8], or saliency maps. The latter is the subject of this work. With saliency maps, the goal is to identify those input dimensions which are most critical for a certain prediction of a neural network. In the example of images, we wish to know which pixels mattered most for the observed prediction outcome.

There are various ways of defining what makes an input dimension *important* for a certain prediction. Here, we use a model based on uncertainty. Intuitively, if we can be very uncertain about a certain input dimension without a model gaining much uncertainty about the output, that dimension is less important for the prediction. If, however, any small uncertainty about an input dimension introduces large uncertainty about the output, that dimension must be more important. For example, in image classification, if a pixel value could be any possible value without having a large effect on the final classification, it was not important. We then equate uncertainty with intervals on the data. For example, when evaluating an image, calling a pixel value uncertain means it *could* be several steps darker, lighter, or a slightly different color. Guided by this intuition and definition, we propose RangeGrad. This novel explanation method finds a correlation between uncertainty at the input and uncertainty at the output of a neural network through interval-bound propagation. The key insight of this paper is the assumption of the equality of all following concepts:

- importance of an input
- uncertainty or *"lack of information"* at the input/output
- interval-bound of an input/output

We will, therefore, use these concepts interchangeably. We then find dimensions of an input where uncertainty has a large effect on the output uncertainty. We call these dimensions more important for the prediction.

For the sake of readability and clearer examples, we will mostly be discussing explanations in the context of image classification models. However, most methods and theories can be applied to other machine learning settings straightforwardly. For example, inputs are not limited to images and the output can represent any predicted value besides class scores without any changes to the method.

The organization of the paper is as follows. In Sect. 2 we will review earlier research most similar to ours. Section 3 outlines the formal framework this paper uses to generate explanations. Next, Sect. 4 describes RangeGrad, our implementation of the framework, applicable to neural network image classification models. In Sect. 5, we apply RangeGrad to different DNN architectures and compare results to existing and state-of-the-art methods. Next, we perform various experiments to show the strengths and weaknesses of RangeGrad. The final Sect. 6 reflects on the results and outlines future possible research topics that this paper has created.

2 Related Work

2.1 Saliency Maps

The earliest method for generating saliency map explanations for a single prediction was based on a point gradient [2]. Here, backpropagation is used to compute the gradient of the output in function of the input. The idea is that we get a correlation between change at the input and the output. So we can observe which input dimensions have little effect on the output and are therefore considered less important. These gradients are crucial for training a neural network. Therefore, obtaining a sensitivity map in this way is trivial in most Deep Neural Network (DNN) frameworks. However, as again shown in our experiments, noise is an issue using this method.

One early method addressing the noise issue is SmoothGrad [16], developed by Smilkov et al. Instead of only observing the gradients at a single point, observations are made at multiple samples around the point. These samples are created by adding normally distributed noise to the input vector and measuring the gradient at that point. These different measurements can then be combined to yield a more robust view of the behavior of the network around a given input.

In [18], Sundararajan et al. developed Integrated Gradients (IG). There is a similarity with SmoothGrad, in that the method aims to take more samples to eliminate noise in the local gradients. The main difference, however, is the part of the input space where samples are taken from. SmoothGrad samples from a normal distribution around the input image, IG samples on the line between the input image, and a "null" point. The latter point represents the complete lack of information. In image-based experiments, this is often a black image. This line, therefore, represents all samples ranging from the input under evaluation to no input to the network.

Another method for finding important dimensions in the input is Guided Back-propagation [17,21] (GP). Like other saliency map methods, the goal here is to find the inputs which contribute most to the output of a neural network. In this case, this is done by finding those inputs that positively contribute to an output value. This is done by removing or setting to zero the negative gradients during the backpropagation.

Selvaraju et al. have proposed Grad-Cam [14], a generalization of Class Activation Mapping [22]. Convolutional layers retain spacial information, meaning, a value in every channel directly relates to a defined region in the input image. This method, therefore, analyses the last convolutional layer in particular. Through backpropagation, Grad-Cam finds the values in this layer which, for all channels combined, have a positive gradient with regards to the predicted class score. That is, those values that increased the score during the forward propagation. These gradients can then be further back propagated to get a saliency map for the input. The full procedure is generally referred to as Guided Grad-Cam.

The main difference between existing methods and RangeGrad is the gradient that is calculated. Existing methods compute a gradient on the input for one or more samples. This finds the input dimensions which have the strongest impact on the output. RangeGrad, however, computes the gradient of an interval on the input and output. That is, we view an interval as uncertainty or *"lack of information"* at the input. Intuitively, when a value has a larger range, there are more possible values and the uncertainty is greater. We then look for the input uncertainty that has the largest effect on output uncertainty.

2.2 Interval-Bound Propagation

Our method uses interval-bound propagation to estimate the effect of *"lack of information"* at the inputs on the uncertainty of the output of a neural network. Here, an interval, or range of possible values, is defined in the input space and propagated through all layers of the network. The interval at the network output always contains any possible point the network can produce given any input in the input interval. This idea is commonly used by formal verification methods. In this field, the ultimate goal is to give formal guarantees on the output of a neural network given a certain input range. For example, Wang et al. [20] use such bounds to prove the safety of a neural network under certain conditions. In this way, it becomes possible to prove that certain behaviors of a neural network are impossible. The bounds have also been used to improve robustness at the training stage [5,19]. Here, the aim is to ensure that not only the training samples are classified correctly, but also the samples which lie close in the input space. As shown in the cited works, networks trained in this way are usually more resilient to adversarial attacks.

Modern formal verification and interval-bound propagation methods, such as [9,13], provide strict bounds for a neural network. RangeGrad does not require that bounds are strictly lower and upper bounds. There are two important differences in the requirements for the bounds used by RangeGrad and those used in formal verification or robustness training:

1. Our bounds *do not need to be strict*. That is, even though our method propagates bounds, we do not need a formal guarantee that any input which lies in the input range is covered by the output range. This stands in contrast with the formal verification setting, where this property is critical. For our purposes, we are mainly interested in the relative sizes of the intervals in each dimension. It is, in our case, preferable to sacrifice bound strictness for relative accuracy.
2. The functions that transform the input bounds to the output bounds need to be *derivable* in our case. This is an important factor in deciding which bounding method to use. We don't just want a bound on the output, we want to know which dimensions at the input have a larger impact on this bound.

3 Problem Statement

We want to find the correlation between the inputs and outputs of a deep neural network. We propose that those inputs where the uncertainty has a larger impact on the uncertainty of the outputs are more important to the prediction. The inputs with more correlation to the output are then more important and form an explanation.

Take a neural classification network $f : \mathbb{R}^d \rightarrow \mathbb{R}^C$ with d input dimensions and C output classes. We are interested in a local explanation of the network around some data point $\mathbf{x} \in \mathbb{R}^d$. We consider a d-dimensional interval $I_r \subseteq \mathbb{R}^d$ centered around $\mathbf{x}$ depending on a range vector $\mathbf{r} \in \mathbb{R}^d_+$, that is

$$I_{\mathbf{r}} := [x_1 - r_1, x_1 + r_1] \times \cdots \times [x_d - r_d, x_d + r_d]$$

We aim to find an uncertainty function $U : \mathbb{R}^d_+ \rightarrow \mathbb{R}^C_+$ such that

$$U_c(\mathbf{r}) = \max_{\mathbf{p} \in I_{\mathbf{r}}} f_c(\mathbf{p}) - \min_{\mathbf{p} \in I_{\mathbf{r}}} f_c(\mathbf{p})$$

for any class $c \in \{1, \ldots, C\}$; in that case, we call the gradient of the function $U_c(\mathbf{r})$ our explanation for the class c at the point $\mathbf{x}$:

$$E(\mathbf{x}, c) = \nabla U_c(\mathbf{r})$$

If $c = \arg \max_{i \in \{1, \ldots, C\}} f_i(\mathbf{x})$ then $E(\mathbf{x}, c)$ corresponds to the explanation for the prediction of f at the point $\mathbf{x}$ since dimensions where this gradient is larger have a larger impact on the output range of f. In other words, there is a correlation between the uncertainty of $\mathbf{x}$ and the uncertainty of $f_i(\mathbf{x})$ or the predicted class. Note that this explanation is of the same dimensionality as input point $\mathbf{x}$. Therefore, for every dimension in $\mathbf{x}$, there is a measure of importance. This forms a saliency map in the image classification setting.

In practice, it is infeasible to create this exact uncertainty function for a neural network, as evidenced by the work done in the formal verification field (see Sect. 2.2). However, what is most important to us are relative gradients. As long as U *correlates* to the true bound, the explanations generated are valid. This implies that we could use an approximation $\tilde{U}$ instead of U itself and change the explanation accordingly

$$\tilde{U}_c(\mathbf{r}) \approx \max_{\mathbf{p} \in I_{\mathbf{r}}} f_c(\mathbf{p}) - \min_{\mathbf{p} \in I_{\mathbf{r}}} f_c(\mathbf{p})$$

$$\tilde{E}(\mathbf{x}, c) = \nabla \tilde{U}_c(\mathbf{r})$$

The way to approximate U by some $\tilde{U}$ is considered an implementation choice. This section is focused on the theory behind the uncertainty framework. Therefore, the method for computing $\tilde{U}$ in our setting is discussed in Sect. 4.1.

4   RangeGrad

In this section, we explain the RangeGrad algorithm. The algorithm consists of the following steps described in detail in the remainder of this section:

- Define an interval around the input sample, indicating the uncertainty added to each of the input dimensions.
- Forward propagate the bounds, where for each linear part of the neural network we estimate the bounds after the linear transformation. Since these bounds are generally too loose, compensate for the loss in bound tightness before applying any activation functions.
- Take the bounds on the output, and backpropagate the gradient such that the bound on the value for the predicted class increases. That is, the gradient related to increasing the uncertainty about the predicted class. As with existing methods, the bound on the output is taken before any softmax or similar layers.
- Measure the gradients on the interval added to the input initially. Here larger values indicate the dimension was more important for creating uncertainty at the output. We then take these larger values to mean the dimension is more important for the prediction.

4.1   Interval Bound Propagation

To implement an uncertainty function we first define a way to generate true lower and upper bounds. For this, we need an upper and lower bound for each neuron in the network. This can be done by correctly rewiring the connections in the network. An example is shown in Fig. 1. When a neuron is weighted by a positive weight, the upper bound of that neuron affects the upper bound of a neuron in the next layer. For negative weights, the lower bound is used to compute the upper bound for a neuron in the next layer. It is clear that this process is not computationally expensive. Propagating bounds (together with the center value) in this manner has the same cost as propagating a single sample 3 times.

Using the neuron model, lower and upper bound layers can be developed for many common layer types such as linear and convolutional layers. Also, a sum of two signals as is needed for residual neural networks [6] can be implemented using this procedure. Monotonic layers such as max-pool, avg-pool, dropout, and normalization layers can simply be applied to the lower bound and upper bound separately. Many functions such as softmax can also be converted into a bounded equivalent. However, as with existing methods, during the RangeGrad backpropagation, the output gradient is applied to the final output before the softmax layer.

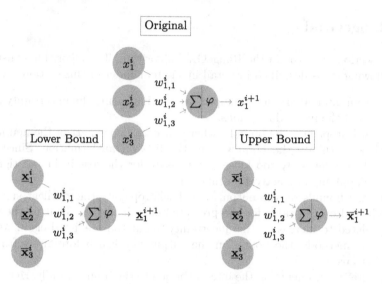

Fig. 1. This figure shows an example of part of a network layer (Original) rewired for lower and upper bounds respectively. In this example $w^i_{1,1}, w^i_{i,2} > 0$ and $w^i_{1,3} < 0$. Note the impact of the sign of the weight on which bound (lower or upper) of the earlier neuron is used. Using these rewired networks, forward and backward propagation can be done as if they were regular neural networks.

Using the notation common for a neural network layer, bounds are propagated through a layer as follows:

$$\mathbf{y}^i = W^i * \mathbf{x}^i + \mathbf{b}^i$$
$$\underline{\mathbf{y}}^i = W^i_+ * \underline{\mathbf{x}}^i + W^i_- * \overline{\mathbf{x}}^i + \mathbf{b}^i$$
$$\overline{\mathbf{y}}^i = W^i_+ * \overline{\mathbf{x}}^i + W^i_- * \underline{\mathbf{x}}^i + \mathbf{b}^i$$
$$\mathbf{x}^{i+1} = \varphi\left(\mathbf{y}^i\right)$$
$$\underline{\mathbf{x}}^{i+1} = \varphi\left(\underline{\mathbf{y}}^i\right)$$
$$\overline{\mathbf{x}}^{i+1} = \varphi\left(\overline{\mathbf{y}}^i\right)$$

where

- W^i_+ and W^i_- are the positive and negative weights of layer i respectively.
- $\mathbf{b}^i$ is the bias term of the layer.
- φ is any monotonic activation function. A non-monotonic activation function can be used but is outside of the scope of this work. In short, it introduces extra computation but no fundamental changes to RangeGrad are needed.
- $\underline{\mathbf{x}}^i$ and $\overline{\mathbf{x}}^i$ are respectively the lower and upper bound for the output of f at the i-th layer. In particular $\underline{\mathbf{x}}^0 := \mathbf{x} - \mathbf{r}$ and $\overline{\mathbf{x}}^0 := \mathbf{x} + \mathbf{r}$.
- $\underline{\mathbf{y}}^i$ and $\overline{\mathbf{y}}^i$ are the bounds for the neurons *before* the application of the activation function φ.

Using this expression, we can replace each linear transformation in the neural network.

4.2 Rescaling

This way of propagating bounds provides true lower and upper bounds. However, the bounds are not tight. There is a single and clear cause for this; neuron value dependencies. That is, when we combine values of previous neurons, for example in a sum, we compute the minimum output by summing the minima of both. For example, Fig. 2 shows a small network where we know the output range should be $[0, 0]$, but the described procedure will bound the output as $[-1, 1]$. This is because the bounding method completely omits any dependence between the neurons. Whenever two dependent neurons are combined, our bound will loosen.

As a practical example, when the input interval is an image where every pixel can be $1/256$ brighter or darker, the output interval is problematically loose. Even using such a small input interval, the output bounds often enclose every output the network generates on any sample in the dataset. We have stated before that the bounds can be approximate, however, the ranges need to cover a functional part of the network. That is, in every layer i, the lower ($\mathbf{\underline{x}}^i$) and upper ($\mathbf{\overline{x}}^i$) bounds need to be close enough to the true sample ($\mathbf{x}^i$) to be meaningful.

As mentioned in Sect. 2, computing a tighter true bound introduces several issues, such as non-derivability and expensive computation. Therefore, we propose a scaling factor to compensate for the loss of meaning due to bound approximation error:

$$\mathbf{\underline{y}}_\lambda^i = \lambda * \mathbf{\underline{y}}^i + (1 - \lambda) * \mathbf{y}^i$$
$$\mathbf{\overline{y}}_\lambda^i = \lambda * \mathbf{\overline{y}}^i + (1 - \lambda) * \mathbf{y}^i$$
$$\mathbf{\underline{x}}^{i+1} = \varphi\left(\mathbf{\underline{y}}_\lambda^i\right)$$
$$\mathbf{\overline{x}}^{i+1} = \varphi\left(\mathbf{\overline{y}}_\lambda^i\right)$$

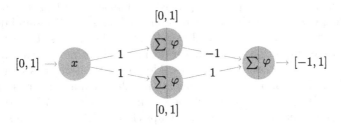

Fig. 2. This figure shows an example of how dependent neurons in earlier layers can cause the bounds to loosen in subsequent layers. Assume no other neurons are connected to the ones shown and $\varphi := Relu$, it is clear the output range should be $[0, 0]$ instead of $[-1, 1]$.

Note that the lower and upper bounds are always scaled relative to $\mathbf{y}^i$. This ensures our bounds undergo similar non-linearities of the network as $\mathbf{x}$ during the forward propagation.

There are numerous ways to set this λ. It can be set as a constant, that is, in every layer, the bounds are scaled by the same relative amount. The main purpose of scaling, however, is to mitigate the effects of dependent values. Therefore, a constant λ can be used when each layer contains the same relative dependency between neurons. However, we cannot make this assumption for an arbitrary neural network.

In our experiments, we used a dynamic scaling method, producing a different λ for every layer. The metric used for scaling is:

$$\lambda = \sup\{\mu \colon \dim \mathbf{y}^i - (\text{sign } \underline{\mathbf{y}}^i_\mu)^\mathsf{T}(\text{sign } \overline{\mathbf{y}}^i_\mu) \le 2k \dim \mathbf{y}^i\}$$

with $\dim \mathbf{y}^i$ the number of neurons in layer i. This method does this in such a way that there are only $k \dim \mathbf{y}^i$ neurons for which the lower bound lies below 0 and the upper bound lies above 0. Most activation functions change the most around an input of 0 and display the least linear behavior in that region. Therefore this scaling method ensures that some but not too many of the dimension bounds enclose regions with this behavior in the activation functions.

This scaling method introduces a parameter k. In our experiments we set $k = \frac{1}{C}$. However, in the experiments, we show that the explanations are not sensitive to this value. That is, explanations change little under different values for k.

Besides scaling the data in the propagation steps, we can use this same k value to set the range vector r on the input data point. That is, we set r to be the largest value for which the data does not need to be scaled in the first layer.

5   Experiments

In this section, we do 4 types of experiments. First, we compare RangeGrad to existing saliency map methods. Here, we show that even though RangeGrad uses fundamentally different assumptions, explanations fall in line with those from existing methods, with notable differences. The similarities and differences are best illustrated with these real-world data experiments. For this reason, with the space limitation in mind, we do not include numerical experiments and experiments with other data types. Moreover, the former is non-trivial as illustrated by the lack of such experiments in saliency map papers such as [16]. Secondly, we study the sensitivity of the scaling parameter k. We show that this parameter is not sensitive, and saliency maps change little under different values of k. In the third experiment, we observe that RangeGrad explanations lose quality when applied to deeper neural networks. Finally, we apply some sanity checks to RangeGrad to ensure the resulting explanations are not meaningless. Note that most saliency map figures are better visible in full color.

All code needed to run these experiments or develop further bounding layers can be found at https://github.com/SamPinxteren/RangeGrad.

Original	Gradient	SmoothGrad	Grad-Cam	pxpxRangeGrad

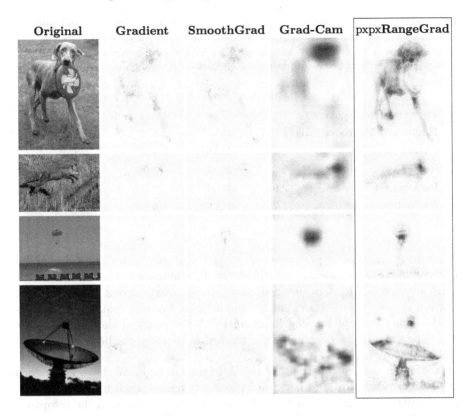

Fig. 3. A set of images from ImageNet classified correctly using VGG19. We show a comparison of explanations by simple gradients, SmoothGrad, Grad-Cam and Range-Grad. No filtering or post-processing was applied to any of the explanations. (Color figure online)

5.1 Method Comparison

First, we compare RangeGrad explanations or saliency maps to those of existing methods. Here, we use the VGG19 [15] neural network. The model was trained on the ImageNet [12] dataset. Figure 3 shows a comparison of RangeGrad to the simple gradient (baseline), SmoothGrad, and Grad-Cam. No post-processing was applied to the saliency maps, what is shown is the output of each method, linearly scaled such that the lowest value is white and the highest is red. In the related work, we have also discussed guided backpropagation and integrated gradients. Given the limited space, we do not include these methods here. Grad-Cam already uses guided backpropagation and SmoothGrad is similar in principle to integrated gradients.

It is common for filters to be applied to the output of explanation methods. This is because, in many cases, the explanations generated are often focused mainly on a few pixels. When applying smoothing or blurring to these saliency maps, larger sensible regions of an image are marked. During this process, however, a lot of the detail in the explanation is lost. With RangeGrad, there is

Table 1. This table shows run times (in seconds) for different methods and samples. These results were obtained using the VGG19 network on a CPU-only system. The times are mostly explained by how many samples (or sample-equivalent operations) each method needs to propagate forward and backward through the neural network.

	Gradient	SmoothGrad	Grad-Cam	RangeGrad
Forward Propagations	1	35	≈ 1	3
Backward Propagations	1	35	≈ 1	2
Weimaraner (Dog)	2.16	40.70	1.48	4.48
Red Fox	1.35	28.31	1.06	3.07
Parachute	2.96	45.44	2.30	9.02
Radio Telescope	5.73	242.98	5.45	18.63

no need for this type of post-processing. As is the case with Grad-Cam, larger areas of importance are marked. However, in comparison to Grad-Cam, the areas are also much more detailed. RangeGrad clearly shows the boundaries between regions of larger and smaller importance. For example, on the Range-Grad saliency map of the dog image in Fig. 3 the edges of the dog can more clearly be seen. In the example of the red fox, far more of the body can be seen in the saliency map.

Table 1 shows the run times of the different methods. We have also added the number of forward and backward propagation steps each method requires. These values explain most of the differences in run times. Note the 3 forward propagation steps RangeGrad needs. This consists of two passes for the bounds, and one for the center. During backpropagation, only the bounds are propagated. This means taking two backpropagation steps. RangeGrad is, therefore, in terms of run times, in line with other non-sampling-based methods. We conclude that RangeGrad run times are not prohibitive. For example, it takes more time to train a DNN than to generate a saliency map for every sample in the used dataset.

5.2   Scaling Factor Impact

In this section, we investigate the impact of the scaling factor on the explanation results. Figure 4 shows the resulting explanation under various scale factors.

The main finding is that the method is not too overly sensitive to this parameter. That is, it is not difficult to set a scaling factor that generates sensible results. Moreover, explanations do not change much for all scaling factors in the interval $k \in [0.01\%, 5\%]$. Note that in all other experiments we are using $k = \frac{1}{C} = 0.001$. This insensitivity is important since it avoids selecting a k that works for a few observed samples but generates unusable or non-sensible explanations for others. It is clear, however, that at high factors the explanation does not relate in any way to the input image or the predicted class. This is to be expected since, at these levels, we are exploring regions of the network which

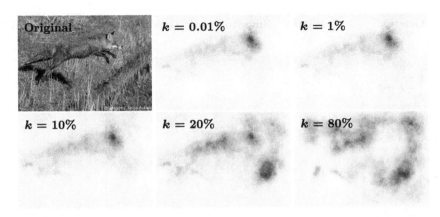

Fig. 4. This figure shows the impact of the scaling factor on the saliency map. The percentages indicate the maximum allowed number of non-linear activations for any layer. In other words, how many dimensions are allowed to have a minimum below 0 and a maximum above 0 before the activation function. It is clear that the explanations change little for any $k \in [0.01\%, 5\%]$. Note, for all other experiments $k = 0.1\%$ is used.

are not in any way related to the class. That as an example a network using ReLU activation functions. In that case, within the bounds, some neurons are activated or deactivated which normally would never do so under any sample of the given class.

5.3 Performance on Deeper Networks

As was described earlier in Sect. 4.1, our uncertainty function is an approximation. While propagating bounds through any layer, the size of the bounds is influenced by two factors:

1. The underlying true minimum and maximum. This is the factor we are interested in. This factor leads to usable explanations under our model and assumptions.
2. The omitted dependency between neurons. This factor will increase the bounds for the value of a neuron more when the value of the neurons it depends on are more correlated. That means, using our method, we are partially measuring which nodes are more dependent. We do not expect this to increase the quality of the explanations.

With more layers, the signal of the first factor can get lost in the noise of the second. We, therefore, expect the method to perform worse when used with very deep networks.

We show several examples in Fig. 5. These explanations are generated for Densenet121, a 121-layer image classification network. These results show that RangeGrad explanations are far less focused on the subject of the image. One

Original	Gradient	SmoothGrad	Grad-Cam	pxpxRangeGrad

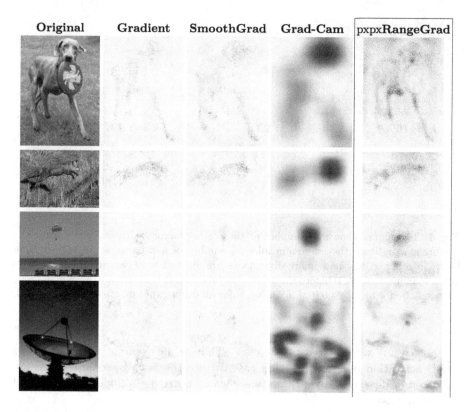

Fig. 5. A set of images from ImageNet classified correctly using DenseNet121 [7]. We show a comparison of explanations by simple gradients, SmoothGrad, Grad-Cam and RangeGrad. No filtering or post-processing was applied to any of the results. It is clear that performance is degraded when compared to results on the VGG19 network.

could argue that this is because these deeper networks are inherently more complex. The context around the subject may be taken into account more than for more shallow neural networks. However, we can see a clear deviation between the explanations of RangeGrad and SmoothGrad. Since the latter uses a sampling method, the neuron-neuron dependencies are inherently accounted for. If the background was truly more important for these deeper networks, we would expect this signal to show up in the saliency maps of the other networks.

The relevant parts of the image are still marked in the saliency map of a 121-layer network. However, this is the deepest network this version of the method should be applied to. The signal-to-noise ratio gradually degrades when adding more layers.

5.4   Sanity Checks

It is hard to numerically assess the quality of an explanation. Moreover, humans are not always accurate in their visual assessment of these methods. To address this issue, Adebayo et al. [1] propose certain sanity checks to perform on explainability methods. These checks do not prove that an explanation is valid, but failing these checks implies that an explanation is guided more by network architecture or other factors. Since the assumption is that an explanation should be guided by network training and sensible training data, eliminating these two factors should yield no sensible explanation. Moreover, we expect the generated saliency maps to change significantly when these factors are removed.

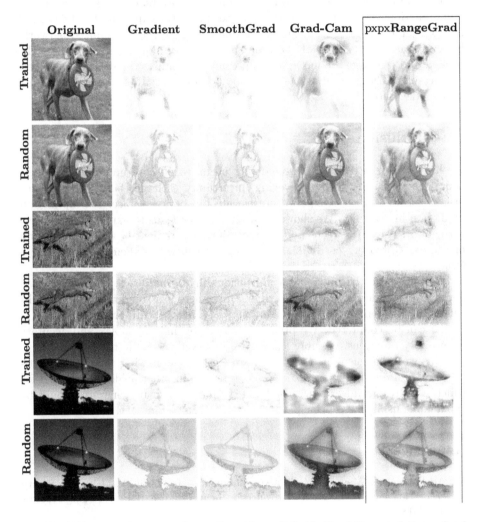

Fig. 6. This figure shows simple gradient, SmoothGrad, Grad-Cam and RangeGrad explanations for a trained and untrained VGG19 network. To clearly show which parts are marked as important, the saliency maps are used to decide transparency in the images. When a pixel is more important for the prediction, it has the original color. Less important pixels are turned white. It is clear that RangeGrad, like other methods, clearly marks important regions for a trained network. However, no clear preference for these regions is shown when explaining an untrained network.

Figure 6 shows the explanations for a trained and untrained VGG19 network. Both the trained and random networks follow the VGG19 architecture, so the only difference is the set of network weights. In these images, we have used the saliency maps as transparency layers. That is, a pixel is closer to the true color when it was important and more white if it was less important. These results show that RangeGrad falls in line with other methods. Some details are still marked as more important than others, but this is largely due to network architecture and is true for all methods. Convolutional layers, even when untrained, often function as edge detectors. It can be seen that the explanations of a trained network largely focus on the subject. Explanations of the randomized network, however, mark every part of the input as equally important. In all cases, the background is marked as far more important as compared to the trained network results. These results show us we should not reject RangeGrad for being a simple edge detector.

6   Conclusion

We have shown that interval bounds are useful to obscure information from a neural network, effectively conveying uncertainty as larger bounds. With this insight, we were able to explore the relationship between uncertain inputs and prediction uncertainty. We showed that this model leads to explanations in line with, or in certain aspects better than, current gradient-based methods and principles. Moreover, sensible saliency maps are generated when applying Range-Grad.

We have seen that correlated dimensions in the hidden layers degrade the performance of deeper neural networks. Since there is a trend towards networks with many hidden layers, the method would be more future-proof if this degradation can be countered. We propose to focus on more complex and accurate uncertainty functions, possibly leading to improved results in the future.

This work has also opened the way to explore the newly proposed theoretical *"explanation through uncertainty"* framework in other fields. Any model for which a derivable uncertainty (or bound) function can be generated could be explainable using these principles.

References

1. Adebayo, J., Gilmer, J., Muelly, M., Goodfellow, I., Hardt, M., Kim, B.: Sanity checks for saliency maps. In: Advances in neural information processing systems 31 (2018)
2. Baehrens, D., Schroeter, T., Harmeling, S., Kawanabe, M., Hansen, K., Müller, K.R.: How to explain individual classification decisions. J. Mach. Learn. Res. 11, 1803–1831 (2010)

3. Dhurandhar, A., Chen, P.Y., Luss, R., Tu, C.C., Ting, P., Shanmugam, K., Das, P.: Explanations based on the missing: towards contrastive explanations with pertinent negatives. In: Advances in neural information processing systems 31 (2018)
4. Goodman, B., Flaxman, S.: European union regulations on algorithmic decision-making and a "right to explanation". AI magazine **38**(3), 50–57 (2017)
5. Gowal, S., et al.: On the effectiveness of interval bound propagation for training verifiably robust models. arXiv preprint arXiv:1810.12715 (2018)
6. He, K., Zhang, X., Ren, S., Sun, J.: Deep residual learning for image recognition. In: Proceedings of the IEEE Conference on Computer Vision and Pattern Recognition, pp. 770–778 (2016)
7. Huang, G., Liu, Z., Van Der Maaten, L., Weinberger, K.Q.: Densely connected convolutional networks. In: Proceedings of the IEEE Conference on Computer Vision and Pattern Recognition, pp. 4700–4708 (2017)
8. Koh, P.W., Liang, P.: Understanding black-box predictions via influence functions. In: International conference on machine learning, pp. 1885–1894. PMLR (2017)
9. Mirman, M., Gehr, T., Vechev, M.: Differentiable abstract interpretation for provably robust neural networks. In: International Conference on Machine Learning, pp. 3578–3586. PMLR (2018)
10. Pedapati, T., Balakrishnan, A., Shanmugam, K., Dhurandhar, A.: Learning global transparent models consistent with local contrastive explanations. Adv. Neural. Inf. Process. Syst. **33**, 3592–3602 (2020)
11. Ribeiro, M.T., Singh, S., Guestrin, C.: Anchors: high-precision model-agnostic explanations. In: Proceedings of the AAAI Conference on Artificial Intelligence, vol. 32 (2018)
12. Russakovsky, O., et al.: ImageNet large scale visual recognition challenge. Int. J. Comput. Vision **115**(3), 211–252 (2015). https://doi.org/10.1007/s11263-015-0816-y
13. Salman, H., Yang, G., Zhang, H., Hsieh, C.J., Zhang, P.: A convex relaxation barrier to tight robustness verification of neural networks. In: Advances in Neural Information Processing Systems 32 (2019)
14. Selvaraju, R.R., Cogswell, M., Das, A., Vedantam, R., Parikh, D., Batra, D.: Grad-cam: visual explanations from deep networks via gradient-based localization. In: Proceedings of the IEEE International Conference on Computer Vision, pp. 618–626 (2017)
15. Simonyan, K., Zisserman, A.: Very deep convolutional networks for large-scale image recognition. In: Bengio, Y., LeCun, Y. (eds.) 3rd International Conference on Learning Representations, ICLR 2015, San Diego, CA, USA, 7–9 May 2015, Conference Track Proceedings (2015). http://arxiv.org/abs/1409.1556
16. Smilkov, D., Thorat, N., Kim, B., Viégas, F., Wattenberg, M.: Smoothgrad: removing noise by adding noise. arXiv preprint arXiv:1706.03825 (2017)
17. Springenberg, J., Dosovitskiy, A., Brox, T., Riedmiller, M.: Striving for simplicity: the all convolutional net. In: ICLR (workshop track) (2015)
18. Sundararajan, M., Taly, A., Yan, Q.: Axiomatic attribution for deep networks. In: International Conference on Machine Learning, pp. 3319–3328. PMLR (2017)
19. Wang, S., Chen, Y., Abdou, A., Jana, S.: Mixtrain: scalable training of verifiably robust neural networks. arXiv preprint arXiv:1811.02625 (2018)
20. Wang, S., Pei, K., Whitehouse, J., Yang, J., Jana, S.: Formal security analysis of neural networks using symbolic intervals. In: 27th {USENIX} Security Symposium ({USENIX} Security 18), pp. 1599–1614 (2018)

21. Zeiler, M.D., Fergus, R.: Visualizing and understanding convolutional networks. In: Fleet, D., Pajdla, T., Schiele, B., Tuytelaars, T. (eds.) ECCV 2014. LNCS, vol. 8689, pp. 818–833. Springer, Cham (2014). https://doi.org/10.1007/978-3-319-10590-1_53
22. Zhou, B., Khosla, A., Lapedriza, A., Oliva, A., Torralba, A.: Learning deep features for discriminative localization. In: Proceedings of the IEEE Conference on Computer Vision and Pattern Recognition, pp. 2921–2929 (2016)

An Empirical Evaluation of Predicted Outcomes as Explanations in Human-AI Decision-Making

Johannes Jakubik[(✉)], Jakob Schöffer, Vincent Hoge, Michael Vössing, and Niklas Kühl

Karlsruhe Institute of Technology (KIT), Karlsruhe, Germany
{johannes.jakubik,jakob.schoeffer,michael.voessing,niklas.kuehl}@kit.edu,
vincent.hoge@alumni.kit.edu

Abstract. In this work, we empirically examine human-AI decision-making in the presence of explanations based on predicted outcomes. This type of explanation provides a human decision-maker with expected consequences for each decision alternative at inference time—where the predicted outcomes are typically measured in a problem-specific unit (e.g., profit in U.S. dollars). We conducted a pilot study in the context of peer-to-peer lending to assess the effects of providing predicted outcomes as explanations to lay study participants. Our preliminary findings suggest that people's reliance on AI recommendations increases compared to cases where no explanation or feature-based explanations are provided, especially when the AI recommendations are *incorrect*. This results in a hampered ability to distinguish correct from incorrect AI recommendations, which can ultimately affect decision quality in a negative way.

Keywords: Explainable AI · Prescriptive AI · Predicted outcomes · Human-AI decision-making

1 Introduction

In real-world decision-making, human decision-makers are confronted with a range of available decision options with diverging future outcomes. For this reason, several approaches in the field of prescriptive AI emerged to support human decision-makers by not only recommending a decision option but also quantifying the predicted outcomes of *all* available decision options (e.g., expected profit in U.S. dollars). For decades, these approaches have been leveraged in a range of real-world high-stakes decision-making scenarios, such as in medical and healthcare [6,7,44], financial [19], manufacturing [3,27], or strategic management [33] domains. In line with this, large tech companies such as GE [45], IBM [46], or Microsoft [47] have been investing in prescriptive AI. However, there is a lack of empirical analyses on the effects of these predicted outcomes on human-AI decision-making in general. We hypothesize that presenting predicted outcomes

I. Koprinska et al. (Eds.): ECML PKDD 2022 Workshops, CCIS 1752, pp. 353–368, 2023.
https://doi.org/10.1007/978-3-031-23618-1_24

of decision options to human decision-makers can influence their reliance on AI recommendations (e. g., a human decision-maker might refrain from choosing decision options with a negative predicted outcome and, therefore, follow the AI even when the AI is incorrect). Hence, this work sets out to empirically assess the influence of predicted outcomes on the performance of human-AI decision-making in general and on humans' reliance on AI recommendations specifically.

Predicted outcomes inform human decision-makers why a certain decision option is recommended instead of an alternative one (e.g., "do *not* lend money to this person because the predicted financial return of lending the money is negative"). This is in line with the definition of *why not* explanations [25]. *Why not* explanations provide information on why an inferred recommendation and not an alternative one was produced. Hence, these explanations are *contrastive* in the sense that they allow for a pairwise comparison between the inferred and an alternative recommendation (see, e.g., [28]). Typically, *why not* explanations take into account current input values to inform human decision-makers why a specific decision option is recommended instead of alternative options. In contrast to this, predicted outcomes explain why a decision option is recommended based on expected future returns of all decision options, which are inferred by the model together with a decision recommendation. Thus, instead of descriptive information about the model input, predicted outcomes explain decision recommendations based on expected future consequences. This characteristic makes studying predicted outcomes of decision alternatives especially relevant for the XAI community.

The results of our in-progress work indicate that study participants tend to follow AI recommendations more often when these recommendations are supplemented with predicted outcomes, as compared to other conditions where they are given no explanation or feature-based explanations. This effect is particularly pronounced when AI recommendations are incorrect—a phenomenon commonly referred to as *over-reliance*. Importantly, when the AI recommendation is supplemented with predicted outcomes, we observe a tendency towards a reduced ability of study participants to distinguish between correct and incorrect AI recommendations. Thus, our preliminary findings suggest that using predicted outcomes as explanations can be detrimental to human-AI decision-making.

2   Related Work

In the following subsections, we present related literature on XAI and reliance in human-AI decision-making.

2.1   Explainable AI

AI algorithms can provide powerful decision support and have already become ubiquitous in many domains [21,40]. Problematically, many AI algorithms are opaque, which means it is difficult for users to gain insight into the internal processes and to understand why the AI suggests a specific decision [1]. XAI is concerned with making AI-based systems more transparent by providing explanations for black-box models [16] or by using interpretable machine learning models [35]. Transparency is widely assumed to improve human-AI decision-making by enabling users to detect and correct errors of the AI and by ensuring that AI decisions are fair [8,13,14,42]. Additionally, there is a demand for explanations to comply with legislation, for example, the EU General Data Protection Regulation (GDPR).

Despite these claims, recent research shows that XAI does not necessarily improve human-AI decision-making over cases where no explanations are provided [2,15,37]. Even worse, [34] find that providing people with an interpretable model can result in less accurate predictions. Yet, some studies show better human-AI decision performance when AI predictions are supplemented with explanations, compared to the performance when only predictions are provided (e.g., [9,22]).

Common XAI methods are feature-based and rule-based explanation approaches [2]. Feature-based models provide the most important features responsible for the output of the machine learning algorithm and its associated weights. Rule-based explanations output *if-then-else* rules which state the decision boundary between the given and contrasting predictions [2,43]. Since feature-based explanations are among the most commonly employed XAI approaches, we include them in our study as a baseline.

2.2   Reliance in Human-AI Decision-Making

Reliance is defined as a behavior [24] that, in the context of human-AI decision-making, is referred to as following an AI recommendation [36,41]. However, it is not always beneficial to rely on AI recommendations, given that AI may be imperfect and may provide incorrect recommendations. People following incorrect AI recommendations—also referred to as *over-reliance*—is a major issue that can inhibit human-AI complementarity [10]. To establish human-AI complementarity, humans need to *appropriately* rely on AI recommendations, meaning people must be able to distinguish correct and incorrect AI recommendations and act upon that differentiation [36,39].

Prior findings regarding the effects of XAI on reliance are inconclusive but show a tendency towards increased over-reliance. For example, [43] discovered an increased reliance for example- and rule-based explanations—also on incorrect AI recommendations. In the study of [22], study participants followed AI recommendations significantly more often when provided with example- and feature-based explanations, even if they contained random content. [34] observed that study participants supplemented with an interpretable model were less able to detect mistakes of the model compared to study participants provided with a black-box model—likely due to information overload. Besides information overload, over-reliance in human-AI decision-making may be caused by, for example, heuristic decision-making [10]. The authors of the study hypothesize that people develop heuristics about the overall competence of the AI [10]. In this context, explanations are interpreted as a general sign of competence of the AI, which then leads people to follow AI recommendations without thoroughly vetting them.

In prior XAI research, many approaches for explaining AI systems have been developed and evaluated with respect to their effects on human-AI complementarity. However, the effects of predicted outcomes as explanations have not been studied yet. As predicted outcomes play an important role in scenario analyses and high-stakes decision-making (e.g., medical [6], financial [19], or strategic management [33] domains), we aim to better understand the effects of such explanations on human-AI decision-making.

3   On the Relationship of Reliance and Human-AI Decision-Making Accuracy

In the following, we discuss the general influence of reliance r on human-AI decision-making accuracy $\mathcal{A}$ for a given AI performance. For this, we define reliance as the proportion to which people follow AI recommendations in human-AI decision-making. Over-reliance then refers to a situation in which people follow the AI not only in cases when the AI recommendation is correct but even when the given recommendation is incorrect. We define the opposite phenomenon as *under-reliance*. We then model the human-AI decision-making accuracy as a function of reliance $\mathcal{A}(r)$. We observe that for $r \longrightarrow 1$, the human-AI decision-making performance will converge to the accuracy of the AI. For $r \in (0,1)$, the human-AI decision-making accuracy ranges in an interval $\mathcal{A}(r) = [min, max]$ that indicates the minimum and maximum of the possible human-AI accuracy. Imagine, for example, an AI accuracy of 66.7% and a reliance of $r = 66.7\%$. People may correct the AI in all cases where the AI recommendation is incorrect, which would result in a human-AI decision-making accuracy of 100%. However, when people incorrectly override the AI in all cases where the AI recommendation is correct, the resulting human-AI decision-making accuracy would be 33.3%, i.e., $\mathcal{A}(r = 66.7\%) = [33.3\%, 100\%]$.

4   Study Design

In this section, we first formulate our research hypotheses. Then, we outline the use case and dataset chosen for this study, and we address technical preliminaries. Finally, we introduce our experimental design and the process of recruiting study participants.

4.1   Hypotheses

Prior research already discovered that XAI can have effects on reliance. While many studies report XAI leading to over-reliance [38], the effect demands further investigation [37]. The results of multiple studies remain inconclusive, some pointing towards over-reliance [10,39], some to under-reliance [31,36]. When it comes to the effects of *predicted outcomes*, multiple researchers raise the question on their influence on reliance and accuracy [4, 29]—with some suspecting a trend towards over-reliance [18, 30]. Thus, we conducted an exploratory pilot study to examine the effects of predicted outcomes as explanations on human-AI decision accuracy and human reliance on AI recommendations.

H1 People provided with predicted outcomes as explanation follow an AI recommendation more often than people provided with an AI recommendation without explanation.

We further hypothesize that on average and for a certain level of reliance, the empirical human-AI decision-making performance will be close to the mean value $\overline{\mathcal{A}(\mathbf{r})} = (max - min)/2$ of the interval, as introduced previously. Thus, even when people follow the AI in too many cases (i. e., over-reliance), we hypothesize that the human-AI decision-making accuracy is still given by $\overline{\mathcal{A}(\mathbf{r})}$.

H2 The empirical human-AI decision-making accuracy is close to the mean value $\overline{\mathcal{A}(\mathbf{r})}$ of the theoretical function $\mathcal{A}(\mathbf{r})$.

For many use cases, human-AI decision-making represents a special form of decision-making under risk, as defined by [17]. When predicted outcomes as explanations come into play (e.g., in terms of potential future consequences of the available decision options), we follow prospect theory in assuming that *losses loom larger than gains*. We thus expect that people tend to follow AI recommendations supplemented by negative predicted outcomes more often in order to avoid potential losses in the future.

H3 People follow AI recommendations supplemented by predicted outcomes more often when the predicted outcomes are negative.

4.2   Preliminaries

Use case. For our study, we train the prescriptive AI on a real-world dataset. We use a publicly available dataset on peer-to-peer loans from the financial company Lending Club[1]. Lending scenarios have been frequently studied in prior XAI user studies (e. g., [12, 15]) and constitute a relevant use case for prescriptive AI. The Lending Club dataset comprises real-world observations from a peer-to-peer lending platform that enabled individuals to lend money to others. As borrowers potentially fail to completely pay back the owed money, it is essential for lenders to accurately assess the risk of defaulting. In this scenario, prescriptive AI could provide valuable decision support.

---

[1] https://www.kaggle.com/datasets/wordsforthewise/lending-club (last accessed July 27, 2022).

Dataset. Our dataset contains 2,260,701 loans issued from 2007 until the end of 2018. We only consider loans that were either fully paid off or defaulted, resulting in a dataset of 1,331,863 loans. About 80% of these loans were fully repaid. The dataset contains 150 features and the label whether the borrower defaulted on the loan or not. To achieve a reasonable task complexity for human-AI decision-making, we limit the data to 6 features: *borrower's monthly income, FICO credit score, interest rate, loan amount, number of months to pay off the loan,* and the *amount of each monthly installment.* This selection of features from the Lending Club dataset is consistent with related literature (e. g., [15]).

Technical Preliminaries. Prescriptive AI methods recommend (i. e., prescribe) the best option among a set of available decision alternatives—typically by maximizing the predicted outcome of the set of available decision options. In our case, we utilize prescriptive trees as an exemplary prescriptive AI to calculate predicted outcomes and the resulting AI recommendation [6]. Several other approaches of prescriptive AI utilize predicted outcomes as well (e. g., [5,11]). Note, that prescriptive trees provide a range of additional measures designed for human experts to increase the interpretability of the prescriptive AI, which are not part of our study. A major challenge for decision-making in general (and, therefore, also for prescriptive AI), is that the true outcome can only be observed for the selected decision option in real-world use cases. Hence, outcomes of alternative decision options and the overall correct decision are unknown [23]. These unknown outcomes are often called *counterfactuals.* The prescriptive AI is, therefore, trained for an accurate estimation of the counterfactual outcomes.

In the following, we outline the technical approach behind several prescriptive AI. The prescriptive AI is trained on observational data $\{(x_i, y_i, z_i)\}_{i=1}^{n}$, including feature values $x_i \in \mathbb{R}^d$ of each observation i with d-dimensional feature vectors, the assigned decision $z_i \in \{1, ..., m\}$ and the corresponding outcome $y_i \in \mathbb{R}$ under the decision for $n \in \mathbb{N}$ realizations. For the accurate estimation of the counterfactual outcomes, the model aims at minimizing the squared prediction error for the observed data: $\sum_{i=1}^{n} (y_i - \hat{y}_i(z_i))^2$. Here, $\hat{y}_i(t)$ refers to the unknown outcome that would have been observed if decision t had been chosen for sample i. The overall goal of the prescriptive AI is to simultaneously estimate counterfactual outcomes for *all* decision options and to prescribe the option that optimizes the predicted outcome. Thus, in contrast to predictive AI, the prescriptive AI implicitly infers both predicted outcomes and a recommended decision option within a single model.

We evaluate the performance of the prescriptive AI by comparing the prescribed decision with the optimal decision based on synthetic ground truth, following, for example, [6]. The model achieves an accuracy of 85% accompanied by an area under receiver operating characteristic (AUROC) score of 86%. The model prescribes to lend money to the borrower for approximately 62% of the instances.

4.3   Experimental Design

The purpose of our study is to examine how supporting humans with predicted outcomes affects human-AI decision accuracy and the reliance of humans on AI recommendations. Therefore, we conduct a scenario-based online experiment. In our experiment, we present loan applications to the study participants and ask them to decide whether to lend money to the applicant or not. The study participants are assisted by AI recommendations and different types of explanations. We use a between-subjects design with three experimental conditions as outlined in Table 1. We utilize feature-based explanations as a baseline to better understand the effect sizes of explanations based on predicted outcomes. As the utilized prescriptive AI is tree-based, we follow [6] and calculate the global feature importance. The importance of each feature is denoted by the total decrease in the loss function as a result of each split in the trees that include this feature. The resulting scores are normalized so that the feature importance sums to 100%.

Table 1. Experimental conditions of our study design.

Condition	Explanation
AI without explanation	Study participants are provided only with an AI recommendation, not with predicted outcomes associated with the decision options
AI with predicted outcomes	Study participants are provided with an AI recommendation and, additionally, with the predicted outcomes for both decision options
AI with feature-based explanation	The AI recommendation is shown to the study participants and, additionally, the feature importance scores calculated by the model. This condition represents a common XAI approach and therefore serves as a baseline

The study participants are randomly assigned to one of the conditions. In each condition, study participants are working on the same set of loan applications. Each loan application is characterized by the 6 observational features. A description of the features and the range of values (in the entire dataset) are displayed throughout the decision-making task (see Fig. 1). By varying only the type of explanation, we can measure the effect of each treatment on the decision-making behavior. Human-AI decision-making accuracy is measured by the percentage of instances where study participants select the correct decision option (i.e., the option the reward estimation suggests). We quantify reliance by measuring the share of instances for which humans follow the AI recommendation. Over-reliance is given by the share of instances for which human decision-makers follow an *incorrect* recommendation.

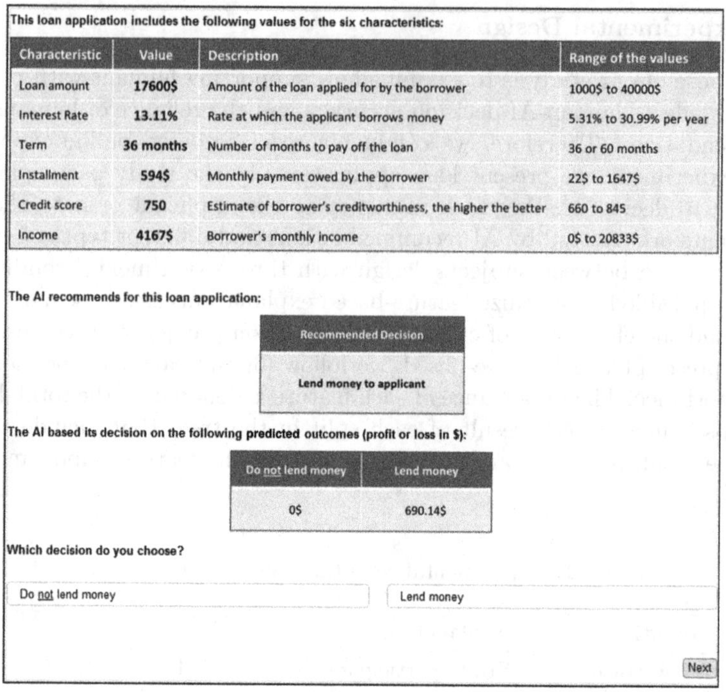

Fig. 1. Exemplary trial from our study presenting the task and relevant information in the *AI with predicted outcomes* condition.

Our study includes a consent form followed by an introduction to the task, a training and testing phase, as well as questions about demographic information and proficiency in the fields of AI and lending. In the training phase, study participants are familiarized with the procedure of the experiment, the domain, and the AI recommendations. The training phase consists of three randomly ordered trials. In each trial, study participants are shown the instructions for the task specific to the assigned condition, a loan application, the AI recommendation, and the corresponding explanation depending on the assigned condition (see Fig. 1 for an exemplary trial with predicted outcomes as explanations, and Fig. 2 with feature-based explanations). The study participants must then choose whether they would lend money to the applicant. In the training phase, after submitting a decision, the study participants are informed about what would have been the correct decision. For the training phase, we randomly sample two loan applications where the model recommends the correct decision option and one application where the model is incorrect. Thus, the study participants learn that the AI recommendation could be incorrect. We do not report results from this training phase.

In the testing phase, study participants decide on 12 loan applications. Similar to the training phase, the AI recommendation is correct for 8 loan applications and incorrect for the remaining 4 trials. Thus, in our sampling, the AI recommendation is correct in 66.7% of the cases. The cases where the AI recommendation is incorrect are composed of two trials where the AI *incorrectly* recommends to give a loan, and two trials where the AI *incorrectly* recommends to reject a loan application. The incorrect AI recommendations later allow us to determine whether study participants over-rely on the AI by following wrong AI recommendations. The trials are then presented to the study participants in random order. The procedure in the testing phase resembles the one in the training phase, except that we do not provide information on which decision would have been correct after study participants submit their decision. We collect the decisions of the study participants throughout the testing phase and later report our results based on the study participants' decisions.

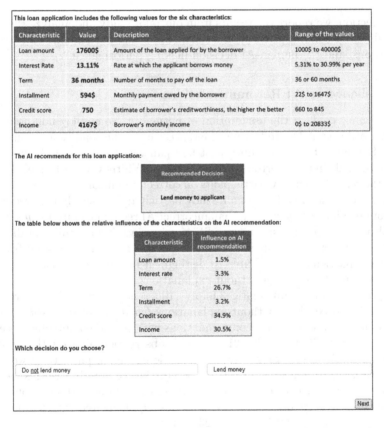

Fig. 2. Exemplary trial from our study presenting the task and relevant information in the *AI with feature-based explanation* condition.

4.4   Study Participants

We recruited 121 study participants via Prolific—a crowdworking platform for online research[2] [32]. Study participants were not required to have explicit expertise in lending or loan applications to participate in our study. The study participants were randomly assigned to one of the three conditions. Each study participant received a base payment of $1.50 for completing the study. As an incentive for study participants to do their best during the test phase, they were rewarded with an additional bonus payment of $0.04 for each correct decision, resulting in a maximum total bonus of $0.48. The median time to complete the study was approximately 10 min.

5   Results

In this section, we report the results from our pilot study and analyze the effects of the different conditions on (a) the reliance of study participants on AI recommendations, and (b) human-AI decision-making performance.

5.1   Reliance on AI Recommendations

As we cannot confirm the assumption of normality, we employ non-parametric Kruskal-Wallis tests [20] to test for differences across the conditions in our experiment. Subsequently, we conduct post-hoc pairwise comparisons between conditions by utilizing Bonferroni-corrected Mann-Whitney U tests [26]. Figure 3 shows the reliance of study participants on correct and incorrect AI recommendations for each condition. First of all, study participants generally followed correct AI recommendations more often than incorrect AI recommendations ($p < 0.001$). This also applies to each specific condition, where we find a significant difference in reliance on correct versus incorrect AI recommendations. We infer from this that study participants were able to distinguish between correct and incorrect AI recommendations—even without explanations.

Importantly, our results in Fig. 3 imply a difference between the over-reliance[3] on AI recommendations without explanations ($mean = 62.0\%$, $std = 26.2\%$) and the over-reliance on AI recommendations with predicted outcomes as explanations ($mean = 70.9\%$, $std = 21.7\%$). This observation aligns with hypothesis **H1**. However, due to the relatively small sample size in our pilot study, we cannot report statistical significance ($p = 0.14$). We further do not observe this tendency when comparing the over-reliance on AI recommendations without explanations with the over-reliance on AI recommendations supplemented with feature-based explanations ($mean = 62.5\%$, $std = 23.8\%$).

We additionally analyze the influence of positive and negative predicted outcomes on the reliance on AI recommendations in Fig. 4. The results indicate that study participants tend to follow AI recommendations more often when

---

[2] https://www.prolific.co/ (last accessed July 27, 2022).
[3] Recall that we define *over-reliance* as following *incorrect* AI recommendations.

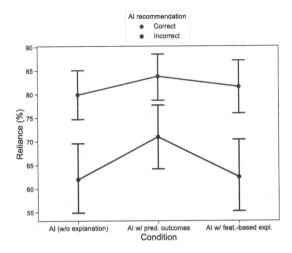

Fig. 3. Reliance of study participants on correct and incorrect AI recommendations per condition. Error bars represent 95% confidence intervals.

negative predicted outcomes are displayed compared to the conditions where no predicted outcomes are displayed (*negative* predicted outcomes: *mean* = 80.6%, *std* = 21.3%; no explanation: *mean* = 70.7%, *std* = 28.4%; feature-based explanation: *mean* = 68.4%, *std* = 24.8%). This behavior is not observed when predicted outcomes are positive. Here, reliance is relatively similar across conditions. Thus, the observed over-reliance for predicted outcomes in general can be largely attributed to an increasing reliance on recommendations to not lend money due to a *negative* predicted outcome. This is in line with our hypothesis **H3**. In our pilot study, we find a p-value of $p = 0.08$ for the observed difference in reliance across the conditions when AI recommendations are supplemented with negative predicted outcomes.

5.2   Human-AI Decision-Making Accuracy

In addition to the (over-)reliance behavior of study participants, we analyze the effect of each condition on human-AI decision-making accuracy in general. These results are summarized in Table 2. Our preliminary results indicate that accuracy is not affected by an increasing over-reliance based on predicted outcomes, which is in line with our expectation based on the relationship of reliance and human-AI decision-making accuracy (see hypothesis **H2**). Importantly, the observed human-AI decision-making accuracy in each condition (65.9% / 65.5% / 66.9%) closely resembles $\overline{\mathcal{A}(\mathbf{r})} = 66.7\%$, i.e., the mean value from the interval defined by our theoretical function $\mathcal{A}(\mathbf{r})$. In fact, we observe two compensating effects of reliance on human-AI decision-making accuracy: first, study participants seem to override fewer incorrect AI recommendations that are supplemented with predicted outcomes (29.1% of incorrect AI recommendations). Second, study participants tend to follow correct AI recommendations including predicted outcomes

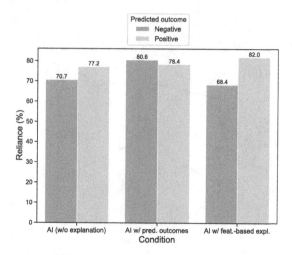

Fig. 4. Reliance of study participants on AI recommendations with negative and positive predicted outcomes per condition.

more often (83.8%). The overall human-AI decision-making accuracy over the three conditions is 66.1% ($std = 11.0\%$), thus surpassing the accuracy of random guessing (50.0%). On average over all three conditions, study participants over-rode 35.1% of incorrect AI recommendations, thus recognizing errors of the AI to a certain degree. However, study participants did not always adopt correct AI recommendations (81.6%), which reduces the overall human-AI decision-making accuracy. Similar to the previous analysis of reliance, we conduct Kruskal-Wallis tests to evaluate differences in the human-AI decision-making accuracy between conditions. Here, we find no significant difference in accuracy across the conditions ($p = 0.70$).

Table 2. Observed decision-making accuracy (in %) by condition.

Condition	Overall	AI correct	AI incorrect
	Mean ($\pm$ Std)	Mean ($\pm$ Std)	Mean ($\pm$ Std)
AI without explanation	65.94 ($\pm$ 9.91)	79.89 ($\pm$ 17.97)	38.04 ($\pm$ 26.21)
AI with pred. outcomes	65.54 ($\pm$ 9.65)	83.78 ($\pm$ 14.98)	29.05 ($\pm$ 21.66)
AI with feat.-based expl.	66.89 ($\pm$ 13.49)	81.58 ($\pm$ 17.85)	37.50 ($\pm$ 23.79)
Average	66.11 ($\pm$ 11.01)	81.61 ($\pm$ 17.00)	35.12 ($\pm$ 24.28)

6   Discussion and Outlook

In our pilot study in the context of peer-to-peer lending, study participants followed correct AI recommendations significantly more often than incorrect ones, regardless of the condition they were assigned to. Our results thus suggest that study participants were able to recognize when the AI recommendations were incorrect—even when provided with no additional explanation.

> **Preliminary finding 1:** Across all conditions, study participants were able to distinguish correct from incorrect AI recommendations.

Our results further indicate that study participants tend to be *less* able to distinguish correct from incorrect AI recommendations when AI recommendations are supplemented with predicted outcomes. This implies that providing predicted outcomes can be detrimental to human-AI decision-making.

> **Preliminary finding 2:** In contrast to other explanations, predicted outcomes may lead to over-reliance on AI recommendations.

However, we find that over-reliance does not necessarily translate to worse human-AI decision-making performance. In fact, our empirical results indicate that the human-AI decision-making is similar across conditions while reliance levels differ.

> **Preliminary finding 3:** The empirical human-AI decision-making performance closely resembles the mean of the interval $\overline{\mathcal{A}(\mathbf{r})}$ of the theoretical function $\mathcal{A}(\mathbf{r})$.

We further aim at better understanding potential causes of the observed over-reliance when AI recommendations are supplemented by predicted outcomes. Following prospect theory, we hypothesized that over-reliance is particularly pronounced when predicted outcomes are negative.

> **Preliminary finding 4:** The empirical over-reliance observed for predicted outcomes can be largely attributed to a higher reliance on recommendations to not lend money given a negative predicted outcome.

All our preliminary findings will have to be tested more thoroughly in follow-up work. As we conducted a pilot study with relatively few study participants, most observed effects are not statistically significant. However, we observe several interesting patterns in our results regarding the effects of predicted outcomes on human-AI decision-making that we will investigate in more depth in our main study. Additionally, we will examine potential reasons for the increase in over-reliance when AI recommendations are supplemented with predicted outcomes.

References

1. Adadi, A., Berrada, M.: Peeking inside the black-box: a survey on explainable artificial intelligence (XAI). IEEE Access **6**, 52138–52160 (2018)
2. Alufaisan, Y., Marusich, L.R., Bakdash, J.Z., Zhou, Y., Kantarcioglu, M.: Does explainable artificial intelligence improve human decision-making? In: Proceedings of the AAAI Conference on Artificial Intelligence, vol. 35, pp. 6618–6626 (2021)
3. Ansari, F., Glawar, R., Nemeth, T.: PriMa: a prescriptive maintenance model for cyber-physical production systems. Int. J. Comput. Integr. Manuf. **32**(4–5), 482–503 (2019)
4. Antoniadi, A.M., et al.: Current challenges and future opportunities for XAI in machine learning-based clinical decision support systems: a systematic review. Appl. Sci. **11**(11), 5088 (2021)
5. Bastani, H., Bayati, M.: Online decision making with high-dimensional covariates. Oper. Res. **68**(1), 276–294 (2020)
6. Bertsimas, D., Dunn, J., Mundru, N.: Optimal prescriptive trees. J. Optim. **1**(2), 164–183 (2019)
7. Bertsimas, D., Li, M.L., Paschalidis, I.C., Wang, T.: Prescriptive analytics for reducing 30-day hospital readmissions after general surgery. PLoS ONE **15**(9), e0238118 (2020)
8. Binns, R., Van Kleek, M., Veale, M., Lyngs, U., Zhao, J., Shadbolt, N.: 'It's reducing a human being to a percentage': perceptions of justice in algorithmic decisions. In: Proceedings of the 2018 CHI Conference on Human Factors in Computing Systems, pp. 1–14 (2018)
9. Buçinca, Z., Lin, P., Gajos, K.Z., Glassman, E.L.: Proxy tasks and subjective measures can be misleading in evaluating explainable AI systems. In: Proceedings of the 25th International Conference on Intelligent User Interfaces, pp. 454–464 (2020)
10. Buçinca, Z., Malaya, M.B., Gajos, K.Z.: To trust or to think: cognitive forcing functions can reduce overreliance on AI in AI-assisted decision-making. Proc. ACM Human-Comput. Interac. **5**, 1–21 (2021)
11. Chen, X., Owen, Z., Pixton, C., Simchi-Levi, D.: A statistical learning approach to personalization in revenue management. Manage. Sci. **68**(3), 1923–1937 (2022)
12. Confalonieri, R., Weyde, T., Besold, T.R., del Prado Martín, F.M.: Using ontologies to enhance human understandability of global post-hoc explanations of black-box models. Artif. Intell. **296**, 103471 (2021)
13. Das, A., Rad, P.: Opportunities and challenges in explainable artificial intelligence (XAI): a survey. arXiv preprint arXiv:2006.11371 (2020)
14. Dodge, J., Liao, Q.V., Zhang, Y., Bellamy, R.K.E., Dugan, C.: Explaining models: an empirical study of how explanations impact fairness judgment. In: Proceedings of the 24th International Conference on Intelligent User Interfaces, pp. 275–285 (2019)
15. Green, B., Chen, Y.: The principles and limits of algorithm-in-the-loop decision making. In: Proceedings of the ACM on Human-Computer Interaction **3**(CSCW), 1–24 (2019)
16. Guidotti, R., Monreale, A., Ruggieri, S., Turini, F., Giannotti, F., Pedreschi, D.: A survey of methods for explaining black box models. ACM Compu. Surv. (CSUR) **51**(5), 1–42 (2018)
17. Kahneman, D., Tversky, A.: Prospect theory: an analysis of decision under risk. Econometrica **47**(2), 263–292 (1979)

18. Keane, M.T., Kenny, E.M., Delaney, E., Smyth, B.: If only we had better counterfactual explanations: five key deficits to rectify in the evaluation of counterfactual XAI techniques. In: IJCAI (2021)
19. Khatri, V., Samuel, B.M.: Analytics for managerial work. Commun. ACM **62**(4), 100 (2019)
20. Kruskal, W.H., Wallis, W.A.: Use of ranks in one-criterion variance analysis. J. Am. Stat. Assoc. **47**(260), 583–621 (1952)
21. Kuncel, N.R., Klieger, D.M., Ones, D.S.: In hiring, algorithms beat instinct. Harvard Business Review (2014)
22. Lai, V., Tan, C.: On human predictions with explanations and predictions of machine learning models: a case study on deception detection. In: Proceedings of the Conference on Fairness, Accountability, and Transparency, pp. 29–38 (2019)
23. Lakkaraju, H., Kleinberg, J., Leskovec, J., Ludwig, J., Mullainathan, S.: The selective labels problem: evaluating algorithmic predictions in the presence of unobservables. In: Proceedings of the 23rd ACM SIGKDD International Conference on Knowledge Discovery and Data Mining, pp. 275–284 (2017)
24. Lee, J.D., See, K.A.: Trust in automation: designing for appropriate reliance. Hum. Factors **46**(1), 50–80 (2004)
25. Lim, B.Y., Yang, Q., Abdul, A.M., Wang, D.: Why these explanations? IUI workshops, selecting intelligibility types for explanation goals (2019)
26. Mann, H.B., Whitney, D.R.: On a test of whether one of two random variables is stochastically larger than the other. Ann. Math. Statist. **18**(1), 50–60 (1947)
27. Matyas, K., Nemeth, T., Kovacs, K., Glawar, R.: A procedural approach for realizing prescriptive maintenance planning in manufacturing industries. CIRP Ann. **66**(1), 461–464 (2017)
28. Miller, T.: Explanation in artificial intelligence: insights from the social sciences. Artif. Intell. **267**, 1–38 (2019)
29. Mueller, S.T., Hoffman, R.R., Clancey, W., Emrey, A., Klein, G.: Explanation in human-AI systems: a literature meta-review, synopsis of key ideas and publications, and bibliography for explainable AI. arXiv preprint arXiv:1902.01876 (2019)
30. Naiseh, M., Al-Thani, D., Jiang, N., Ali, R.: How different explanations impact trust calibration: the case of clinical decision support systems. Available at SSRN 4098528 (2022)
31. Nourani, M., et al.: Anchoring bias affects mental model formation and user reliance in explainable AI systems. In: 26th International Conference on Intelligent User Interfaces, pp. 340–350 (2021)
32. Palan, S., Schitter, C.: Prolific.ac - a subject pool for online experiments. J. Behav. Exper. Finan. **17**, 22–27 (2018)
33. Postma, T.J., Liebl, F.: How to improve scenario analysis as a strategic management tool? Technol. Forecast. Soc. Chang. **72**(2), 161–173 (2005)
34. Poursabzi-Sangdeh, F., Goldstein, D.G., Hofman, J.M., Wortman Vaughan, J.W., Wallach, H.: Manipulating and measuring model interpretability. In: Proceedings of the 2021 CHI Conference on Human Factors in Computing Systems, pp. 1–52 (2021)
35. Rudin, C.: Stop explaining black box machine learning models for high stakes decisions and use interpretable models instead. Nat. Mach. Intell. **1**(5), 206–215 (2019)
36. Schemmer, M., Hemmer, P., Kühl, N., Benz, C., Satzger, G.: Should I follow AI-based advice? Measuring appropriate reliance in human-AI decision-making. In: ACM CHI 2022 Workshop on Trust and Reliance in AI-Human Teams (trAIt) (2022)

37. Schemmer, M., Hemmer, P., Nitsche, M., Kühl, N., Vössing, M.: A meta-analysis on the utility of explainable artificial intelligence in human-AI decision-making. arXiv preprint arXiv:2205.05126 (2022)
38. Schemmer, M., Kühl, N., Benz, C., Satzger, G.: On the influence of explainable AI on automation bias. In: European Conference on Information Systems (2022)
39. Schoeffer, J., De-Arteaga, M., Kuehl, N.: On the relationship between explanations, fairness perceptions, and decisions. In: ACM CHI 2022 Workshop on Human-Centered Explainable AI (HCXAI) (2022)
40. Townson, S.: AI can make bank loans more fair. Harvard Business Review (2020)
41. Vereschak, O., Bailly, G., Caramiaux, B.: How to evaluate trust in AI-assisted decision making? A survey of empirical methodologies. Proc. ACM Human-Comput. Interac. 5(CSCW2), 1–39 (2021)
42. Vössing, M., Kühl, N., Lind, M., Satzger, G.: Designing transparency for effective human-AI collaboration. Inf. Syst. Front. (2022). https://doi.org/10.1007/s10796-022-10284-3
43. van der Waa, J., Nieuwburg, E., Cremers, A., Neerincx, M.: Evaluating XAI: a comparison of rule-based and example-based explanations. Artif. Intell. **291**, 103404 (2021)
44. Wang, T., Paschalidis, I.C.: Prescriptive cluster-dependent support vector machines with an application to reducing hospital readmissions. In: 2019 18th European Control Conference (ECC), pp. 1182–1187. IEEE (2019)
45. https://www.cio.com/article/244505/ge-pitney-bowes-team-up-on-predictive-andprescriptive-analytics.html. Accessed 27 July 2022
46. https://www.ibm.com/analytics/prescriptive-analytics. Accessed 27 July 2022
47. https://appsource.microsoft.com/en-us/product/web-apps/river-logic.riverlogic_analytics?tab=overview. Accessed 27 July 2022

Local Multi-label Explanations
for Random Forest

Nikolaos Mylonas[ID], Ioannis Mollas$^{(\boxtimes)}$[ID], Nick Bassiliades[ID],
and Grigorios Tsoumakas[ID]

Aristotle University of Thessaloniki, Thessalonik, Greece
{myloniko,iamollas,nbassili,greg}@csd.auth.gr

Abstract. Multi-label classification is a challenging task, particularly
in domains where the number of labels to be predicted is large. Deep
neural networks are often effective at multi-label classification of images
and textual data. When dealing with tabular data, however, conventional
machine learning algorithms, such as tree ensembles, appear to outperform competition. Random forest, being a popular ensemble algorithm,
has found use in a wide range of real-world problems. Such problems
include fraud detection in the financial domain, crime hotspot detection
in the legal sector, and in the biomedical field, disease probability prediction when patient records are accessible. Since they have an impact
on people's lives, these domains usually require decision-making systems
to be explainable. Random Forest falls short on this property, especially
when a large number of tree predictors are used. This issue was addressed
in a recent research named LionForests, regarding single-label classification and regression. In this work, we adapt this technique to multi-label
classification problems, by employing three different strategies regarding the labels that the explanation covers. Finally, we provide a set of
qualitative and quantitative experiments to assess the efficacy of this
approach.

Keywords: Explainable artificial intelligence · Interpretable machine
learning · Random forest · Multi-label learning

1 Introduction

Multi-label classification is a popular machine learning task, concerned with
assigning multiple different labels to a single sample [28]. There are plenty of
applications employing multi-label classification, such as semantic indexing [21]
and object detection [10]. Multi-label classification has also proven useful in
the predictive maintenance [16] and financial sectors [3], where tabular data
are mainly used. When this sort of data is available, ensemble methods are
typically outperforming other families of methods [25,29]. Ensembles, however,
are intrinsically not explainable. This is an important weakness, as explainability
is useful for the vast majority of ML applications, and a necessity when they
impact human lives or incur economic costs [1,12].

© The Author(s), under exclusive license to Springer Nature Switzerland AG 2023
I. Koprinska et al. (Eds.): ECML PKDD 2022 Workshops, CCIS 1752, pp. 369–384, 2023.
https://doi.org/10.1007/978-3-031-23618-1_25

This paper focuses on the explainability of random forest (RF) [4] models in the context of multi-label classification. There is a lot of work on the explainability of RF for regression and single-label classification tasks [6,13,14,17]. However, adapting these methods to multi-label tasks, where RF models find frequent use [15,26,30], is not straightforward. There are also techniques that have been specifically designed for multi-label tasks [20,27]. These are, however, independent of the explained model's architecture, and therefore cannot exploit the specific properties of RF models to their benefit.

To address the lack of RF-specific explainability techniques for multi-label classification in the literature, we propose an extension of LionForests [17] towards explaining multi-label classification decisions. We introduce three different strategies concerning the scope of the provided explanation (single-label, predicted labelset, label subsets). We compare these strategies against similar state-of-the-art techniques, through a set of quantitative and qualitative experiments. The results highlight the conciseness of the explanations of the proposed approach.

The rest of this paper is organized as follows. Section 2 discusses relevant research, while Sect. 3 introduces important concepts of the LionForests method. Section 4 presents the three novel strategies for explaining multi-label RFs. The experimental procedure, along with the data sets used, and the results, are mentioned in Sect. 5. Finally, we conclude and propose future steps for this research in Sect. 6.

2   Related Work

Explainability techniques can be classified into two categories, depending on their applicability to different types of models. *Model-agnostic* techniques ignore model structure and are therefore applicable to any ML model, whereas *model-specific* techniques are designed to interpret a certain family of models. The latter can either alter the model's structure to achieve explainability, or simply leverage information from the architecture without affecting it. Another distinction is between *global* and *local* explainability techniques, with the former explaining the entire model and the latter focusing on particular predictions of instances.

We first discuss model-agnostic explainability methods, which could be applied to multi-label classification, with some modifications. The use of simpler surrogate models that mimic the behavior of more complex ones, while also being more interpretable, is a topic studied in the literature and can be applied in a multi-label setting as well. Surrogates are built based on the input and the produced output of the model, and can be used to provide both global and local interpretations.

LIME [22], one of the most well-known explainability techniques, provides local interpretations for all types of models by estimating feature importance using perturbation methods. Similarly, Anchors [23] extracts rule-based interpretations using a slightly different perturbation approach. Another interesting technique, LORE [11], uses a genetic algorithm to generate neighbors, which are then used to train a decision tree that produces rule-based explanations. By constructing a decision tree to approximate the performance of complicated models, single tree approximations are used to simplify the prediction pattern of complex black-box models. TREPAN [5] approaches this task as an inductive learning problem, aiming to represent a complex model, such as a neural network, with symbolic knowledge. This is a rule learning task, according to RuleFit [9], in which each rule covers a small portion of the input space. RuleFit extracts rules from each decision tree to build a sparse linear model that incorporates both the original features and the retrieved rules, using decision trees as base learners for the various input variables. The final interpretation is based on feature importance.

We continue with explainability methods designed specifically for RF. A model-specific approximation technique for RF called DefragTrees [13] formulates the simplification of tree ensembles as a model selection problem. The aim of this work is to derive the simplest model possible that has similar performance to the whole ensemble. To do so, they employ a Bayesian model selection method to optimize the simplified model. InTrees [6], on the other hand, approaches the same problem by providing a framework for selecting and pruning specific rules from the entire ensemble, effectively summarizing the relevant rules into a new simpler and more interpretable learner that can be used for future predictions.

The RF explainability techniques discussed so far concern global explanations covering the whole model. We now move to local explanation methods. [18] introduces a local explainability method, which provides rule-based explanations exploiting feature importance. CHIRPS [14] extracts the relevant paths for an instance from each decision tree and filters them to reduce the complexity of the explanation. LionForests (LF) [17] provides explanations for the decisions of a random forest in the form of rules. A key advantage of LF is that it distills the interpretation from the knowledge already present in RF, while also providing complete explanations. This in turn means that these explanations are provided without any demerits in the model's performance or complexity. LF can be used in binary or multi-class classification and regression problems.

Finally, we discuss RF explainability methods with a focus on visualization. iForest [31] supports the visualization of relevant paths by multi-dimensional projection. It further allows the summarization of those paths into a final one that can be used as an explanation. Another visualization tool that can provide a global overview of a random forest model in conjunction with local explanations is ExMatrix [19]. Both the global and local explanations provided by this method come in the form of a table.

We close the related work section with a method that has been designed specifically for multi-label classification, which is applicable to RF as well. MARLENA [20] is a model-agnostic approach that can provide local interpretations for black-box models by creating a neighborhood of similar instances to the one to be explained and training a decision tree. This approach is applicable to any black-box model and was evaluated mainly on health applications.

3   LionForests

This section introduces the fundamental concepts of LF. LF does not affect the performance of the RF model, because it is applied post-hoc and only explains decisions. The main step behind the interpretation extraction process of the technique is the estimation of the minimum number of paths across the different estimators of the RF model that cover the examined instance. From each tree estimator, we extract one path responsible for the instance's prediction. Then, the set of paths that positively vote for that instance is identified. Through feature and path reduction, as well as feature-range formulation upon those paths, LF builds the interpretation. The estimation of the minimum number of paths is not a straightforward task, especially since it needs to comply with LF's main property, namely *conclusiveness*. This property requires the rules produced by an explainability technique to be free of misleading or erroneous elements.

Since a multi-label classification task can be decomposed into multiple binary classification tasks, one for each label, we will further discuss how LF computes the minimum number of paths for binary classification tasks. To better understand the following statements, we first need to mention Proposition 1 introduced in the original paper, which is pivotal in LF's procedure.

Proposition 1. *An RF model with a set of trees (T), casting $|T|$ votes, always predicts class M if and only if class M has at least a quorum of votes or more, where $quorum = \lfloor \frac{|T|}{2} + 1 \rfloor$ out of $|T|$ votes.*

Proposition 1 states that the minimum number of paths needed for the RF model to maintain its original prediction is $\lfloor \frac{|T|}{2} + 1 \rfloor$. The validity of this statement is proved in the original paper. With that in mind, the minimum number of paths which cover the examined instance that LF tries to compute is actually the quorum based on Proposition 1.

Given the minimum number of paths, LF reduces the paths extracted from each RF decision tree using a sequence of procedures, obtaining the reduced set of paths extracted from the reduced trees (T'). In this order, they are a) reduction through association rules, b) reduction through clustering, and c) reduction by random selection. Each procedure serves a different purpose. Reduction by association rules and by clustering aim to reduce features by selecting paths with similar feature sets, whereas reduction by random selection reduces the number of paths to the quorum.

Finally, after obtaining the reduced paths, LF identifies the common features and their ranges, merging them to obtain a single range for each feature, which we call *feature-range*. The lower (upper) bound of the combined range is the maximum (minimum) of the lower (upper) bounds found across all ranges. This step is called feature aggregation. When categorical features are present, LF performs OneHot encoding on them, effectively obtaining OneHot features equal to the number of possible values the initial one had.

These new OneHot features are handled based on the following principle: if a OneHot encoded feature is present in at least one path, with a value of 1, then the categorical feature it originates from is added to the final rule with the encoded feature as its value. For example, in a categorical feature regarding *Country*, if the examined instance has the value *Greece*, then the OneHot feature would be *Country_ Greece*= 1. In this case, we would include in the final rule this statement *Country=Greece*. The reduced paths cannot contain any other OneHot encoded feature of *Country* with a value of 1, as that would mean that the path would not cover the instance. In contrast, if it is absent from all paths, this value of the categorical feature does not affect the outcome. In that case, LF searches for the other OneHot features originating from the same categorical one that have value of 0 and adds them to the rule as values of the original feature, which can affect the outcome. Following our example, if *Country_ Japan* = 0, *Country_ United-States* = 0 (or any other), appears in the reduced paths, and given that *Country_ Greece*= 1 does not exist in any, these features are included in the final rule in the following form *Country* ≠ [*Japan, United States, ...*]. This procedure is called categorical feature handling.

4 LionForest Multi-label Explainability

In multi-label classification, predictions come in vectors of size $|L|$, with L denoting the set of all labels. In this case, an explanation could concern: i) the set of positively predicted labels, $L_p \subseteq L$, ii) subsets of it, $L'_p \subseteq L_p$, or iii) each one of its individual labels, $l \in L_p$. We propose three corresponding strategies that allow LF to output multi-label explanations, each calculating the quorum in a different way, based on the subset of L_p that we want our explanation to cover. As in the original, the three strategies do not meddle with the performance of the RF model.

We also introduce an example, which will be used for all strategies. Consider an RF model with $|T| = 9$ estimators, that outputs its prediction concerning $|L| = 5$ labels for a given input. Based on the theory presented before, the quorum equals $\lfloor \frac{9}{2} + 1 \rfloor = \lfloor 5.5 \rfloor = 6$. For a given instance, RF predicts the following labelset $[0, 1, 0, 1, 1]$. From each $t \in T$ tree estimator, we extract the path and the prediction for this instance. Then, based on the strategy, we proceed to the appropriate reduction and eventually the formulation of the final rule interpretation. In Fig. 1, the predicted labelsets from each t tree are visible.

4.1 Explaining Each Predicted Label Separately

The first step of this strategy (LF-l) is the extraction of all paths regarding a decision from the tree predictors comprising the RF model. Then, for each predicted label $l \in L_p$, a multi-stage process takes place, which first identifies the paths that vote for its prediction. The next step is the reduction of T, as explained in Sect. 3, to the number denoted by the quorum, obtaining the minimum number of paths from T' trees. The rule building steps remain the same as those in the original technique, namely feature aggregation and handling of

RF: Prediction: [0, 1, 0, 1, 1]	Per Label: [0, 1, 0, 1, 1]	[0, 1, 0, 1, 1]	[0, 1, 0, 1, 1]	All: [0, 1, 0, 1, 1]	Frequent Set: [0, 1, 0, 1, 1]
[0, 1, 0, 1, 1]	[0, 1, 0, 1, 1]	[0, 1, 0, 1, 1]	[0, 1, 0, 1, 1]	[0, 1, 0, 1, 1]	[0, 1, 0, 1, 1]
[1, 1, 1, 1, 1]	[1, 1, 1, 1, 1]	[1, 1, 1, 1, 1]	[1, 1, 1, 1, 1]	[1, 1, 1, 1, 1]	[1, 1, 1, 1, 1]
[0, 0, 0, 0, 0]	[0, 0, 0, 0, 0]	[0, 0, 0, 0, 0]	[0, 0, 0, 0, 0]	[0, 0, 0, 0, 0]	[0, 0, 0, 0, 0]
[0, 1, 0, 0, 1]	[0, 1, 0, 0, 1]	[0, 1, 0, 0, 1]	[0, 1, 0, 0, 1]	[0, 1, 0, 0, 1]	[0, 1, 0, 0, 1]
[0, 1, 0, 1, 1]	[0, 1, 0, 1, 1]	[0, 1, 0, 1, 1]	[0, 1, 0, 1, 1]	[0, 1, 0, 1, 1]	[0, 1, 0, 1, 0]
[0, 1, 0, 0, 0]	[0, 1, 0, 0, 0]	[0, 1, 0, 0, 0]	[0, 1, 0, 0, 0]	[0, 1, 0, 0, 0]	[0, 1, 0, 0, 0]
[0, 1, 0, 1, 1]	[0, 1, 0, 1, 1]	[0, 1, 0, 1, 1]	[0, 1, 0, 1, 1]	[0, 1, 0, 1, 1]	[0, 1, 0, 1, 1]
[1, 1, 0, 1, 1]	[1, 1, 0, 1, 1]	[1, 1, 0, 1, 1]	[1, 1, 0, 1, 1]	[1, 1, 0, 1, 1]	[1, 1, 0, 1, 1]
[0, 1, 0, 1, 1]	[0, 1, 0, 1, 1]	[0, 1, 0, 1, 1]	[0, 1, 0, 1, 1]	[0, 1, 0, 1, 1]	[0, 1, 0, 1, 1]
	8→5	6→5	7→5	6→5	6→5

Fig. 1. Running example. Greyed out predictions do not cover the examined label/labelset, whereas black and red (underlined) do. The predictions whose paths were decreased are shown in red (Color figure online)

categorical features. After formulating a rule for each predicted label l, we use these rules as an explanation for the examined instance.

In columns 2 to 4 (*Per Label*) in Fig. 1, we can see how LF selects and reduces the paths to the quorum. It identifies the paths that voted for each of the three predicted labels (black and red font). If the number of paths exceeds the quorum, the LF reduction strategies are used to decrease them to the bare minimum (black font). Treating each label separately can result in smaller feature sets in the final interpretation. This is because LF has a greater number of possible paths to reduce to the minimum.

4.2   Explaining All the Predicted Labelset

This strategy is largely similar to the previous one, with the main difference being that instead of an iterative process for each label (*LF-a*), this time a single process is executed for the whole predicted labelset. This in turn means that LF must now identify the paths from the T trees that include the whole predicted labelset in its prediction, greatly limiting the number of available paths to be reduced in the following step, if possible. Furthermore, during the path reduction step, each produced path set must cover the whole prediction, restricting the number of paths LF can safely remove to obtain $|T'|$.

It is worth noting that, due to the above conditions, the final rule obtained after applying the rule-building steps is very specific to the examined instance. There is a possibility that the number of recognized paths covering all predicted labels will be less than the quorum. This prevents us from further decreasing them, but also prohibits us from using them alone to form the final rule. In this scenario, regardless of their vote, we use all the paths.

Connecting this strategy with the running example of Fig. 1, we focus on the third column, *All*. Only 6 paths include all the predicted labels at the same time. LF will use the reduction strategies to decrease those pathways to 5 (quorum). However, because there is so little room for reduction, the strategy's effectiveness is limited, and therefore, we might not observe the desired feature reduction. This strategy is more effective in confident classifiers, where the number of individual estimators voting the whole predicted labelset is larger.

4.3 Explaining Frequent Label Subsets

This strategy provides explanations for subsets (*LF-p*) of the predicted labelset that frequently appear inside the examined data set. These subsets are identified with the use of association rules and specifically the *fpgrowth* algorithm. Then, a process comparable to the one present in the first strategy is performed. For each subset, the paths that vote for all the labels present inside it are identified and then reduced to $|T'|$, before the rule building steps that formulate the final rule for this subset are implemented. The final explanation for the frequent subsets is an aggregation of the rules built by the aforementioned process.

In case of larger labelsets, as well as a large set of predicted labels, the number of activated subsets can be very high. Therefore, the end-user is given an option to limit the number of subsets. Hence, if the activated subsets are X and the user asks for $N < X$, the first N subsets and their explanation will be provided, ordered based on the support of the subset across the labelsets of the training data set.

In the example (Fig. 1), the last column presents the explanation of one identified subset $[0, 1, 0, 1, 0] \subset [0, 1, 0, 1, 1]$, the paths which cover this set, and the removed path.

5   Experiments

This section summarizes the experiments that we carried out to compare the performance of our strategies to state-of-the-art techniques frequently used in the literature. To further the reliability of our results we performed a 10-fold cross validation and present the standard deviation of our showcased results in each table. We performed three distinct sets of experiments. The first compares our various strategies to each other, in order to gain insight into their effectiveness with multi-label data. The second focuses on techniques that explain the entire predicted labelset, pitting our second strategy against MARLENA, due to its relevance to our task, and two baselines: local (LS) and global (GS) tree surrogates. The third and final set compares our first strategy to Anchors and CHIRPS. Anchors was selected for its prominence in the literature, and CHIRPS for its similarity to our approach, concerning the per label experiments. Both techniques have been adjusted to provide explanations for each of the predicted labels. The code for these experiments is available in GitHub[1] and DockerHub[2].

5.1   Data Sets

Here, we present the data sets used and the pre-processing steps we followed for each one of them. We selected four multi-label tabular data sets, whose main statistics and performance[3] can be found in Table 1. The values inside the parentheses concern the numbers after the pre-processing steps for each data set.

Table 1. Data set information

ID	Dataset	Performance	Instances	Features	Labels	Cardinality
D1	Food Truck	51.73%	407	21 (29)	12	2.29
D2	Water Quality	51.79%	1060	16	14	5.07
D3	Flags	76.82%	194	19	7	3.39
D4	AI4I	88.77%	10K (339)	7 (6)	6 (4)	1.04

D1: Food Truck. This data set was compiled from the replies of 407 survey participants, concerning their food preferences, personal information, time of meal (input variables) and types of food trucks they eat from (target variables) [24]. We replaced missing values with the mean value across their column. Furthermore, four categorical features were present. As such, two of them were handled as ordinal (gender and time of the day) and the rest were one-hot encoded (motivation and marital status). Finally, the data were min-max scaled.

D2: Water Quality. This scientific data set was used for modeling the quality of water in Slovenian rivers. It contains features like the water's temperature, pH, and concentration of different chemicals. The target variables correspond to different water quality indicators [2]. The pre-processing was minimal only including min-max scaling.

D3: Flags. The third data set used in our experiments contains information about certain countries and their culture. The target variables concern the colors that are present on the flag of each country [7]. No pre-processing took place for this data set other than min-max scaling.

---

[1] https://tinyurl.com/c5y8uxm4.
[2] https://tinyurl.com/2nh4zyj3.
[3] Performance was estimated following a grid search, and is estimated based on micro averaged F_1 score.

D4: AI4I. The last data set employed in our experiments is a synthetic predictive maintenance data set concerning the prediction of certain types of machine failures [16]. Aiming to emulate real predictive maintenance problems encountered in the industry, the data set contains features like temperature, torque, rotational speed of different machines to predict possible failures. There is a single categorical feature (type) inside the data set which we handle as ordinal, and a feature without information (product ID). We then min-max scale all features. Regarding the labels, there is a strong dependency between the first denoting whether there is a failure or not and the rest of the labelset, which are the types of failures. As such, we only keep the examples exhibiting some kind of failure, while removing the first. Finally, we also remove the final label which denotes a random failure, of which very few instances exist in the data set.

5.2   Quantitative Experiments

In order to perform our quantitative experiments, we made use of four different metrics, each one covering a different aspect of a produced rule. Rule length (L) denotes the number of feature-ranges present inside the rule. Smaller lengths are easier for the end-user to comprehend but can also indicate that the explanation is problematic. Furthermore, expert users tend to prefer larger rules, due to their richer information [8]. It is worth noting that for techniques providing rules for each label or label subset separately, the final rule length is the sum of the lengths of those individual rules. Coverage (C) describes the average number of instances each rule satisfies. Precision (P) refers to the fraction of correctly covered instances among the ones covered by each rule. Higher values on both metrics correspond to better performance. Time response (T) describes the run time of the technique in seconds.

Table 2. Comparison between the different strategies of LF

Datasets	Algorithm	L	T
D1	LF-a	$20.33_{\pm 0.70}$	$6.25_{\pm 0.96}$
	LF-l	$30.06_{\pm 3.47}$	$10.30_{\pm 0.86}$
	LF-p	$44.71_{\pm 9.04}$	$11.33_{\pm 1.16}$
D2	LF-a	$16.37_{\pm 0.40}$	$0.94_{\pm 0.04}$
	LF-l	$57.64_{\pm 5.71}$	$1.37_{\pm 0.11}$
	LF-p	$153.34_{\pm 16.76}$	$2.87_{\pm 0.29}$
D3	LF-a	$18.24_{\pm 0.49}$	$1.05_{\pm 0.10}$
	LF-l	$62.58_{\pm 5.24}$	$5.66_{\pm 0.40}$
	LF-p	$111.72_{\pm 7.32}$	$7.38_{\pm 0.48}$
D4	LF-a	$4.92_{\pm 0.46}$	$1.38_{\pm 0.30}$
	LF-l	$5.04_{\pm 0.48}$	$1.41_{\pm 0.31}$
	LF-p	$5.04_{\pm 0.48}$	$1.41_{\pm 0.30}$

We first discuss the results of the comparison among our proposed strategies that can be seen in Table 2. The goal of this setup was to compare the length of the rules produced by each strategy, along with the time needed to produce them. As expected, the strategy providing one rule for the whole predicted labelset results in shorter rules and smaller run times. This can be seen in all four data sets, albeit the differences are minimal in the last one. The frequent pair strategy seems to be the one with the longest run times and lengthiest rules. Such an outcome was anticipated, given that in most cases the number of frequent subsets present in a labelset is higher than the number of distinct labels comprising it.

The comparison regarding the techniques providing explanations for the whole predicted labelset can be seen in Table 3. Exploring each metric separately reveals that all four techniques evaluated have rather poor Coverage, with MARLENA having the best performance and LF-a having the worst. In terms of Precision, LF-a always achieves perfect precision due to its conclusiveness property, while both surrogate models surpass MARLENA. In all datasets, LF-a produces the lengthiest rules, while MARLENA produces the shortest. Finally, save for LF-a's poor performance on the first dataset, there is no clear winner among the other local techniques in terms of time response, except for GS which is a global technique trained only once and has zero inference time.

Table 3. Comparison between techniques explaining the whole predicted labelset

Dataset	Algorithms	C	L	P	T
D1	LF-a	$0.02_{\pm0.00}$	$20.32_{\pm0.65}$	$1.00_{\pm0.00}$	$6.25_{\pm0.98}$
	GS	$0.06_{\pm0.03}$	$7.81_{\pm1.39}$	$0.77_{\pm0.08}$	$0.00_{\pm0.00}$
	LS	$0.07_{\pm0.02}$	$6.96_{\pm0.59}$	$0.75_{\pm0.07}$	$1.52_{\pm0.02}$
	MARLENA	$0.15_{\pm0.04}$	$4.42_{\pm0.27}$	$0.73_{\pm0.05}$	$2.40_{\pm0.02}$
D2	LF-a	$0.01_{\pm0.00}$	$16.36_{\pm0.40}$	$1.00_{\pm0.00}$	$0.94_{\pm0.04}$
	GS	$0.02_{\pm0.00}$	$8.78_{\pm0.36}$	$0.66_{\pm0.05}$	$0.00_{\pm0.00}$
	LS	$0.03_{\pm0.00}$	$6.67_{\pm0.20}$	$0.65_{\pm0.03}$	$1.41_{\pm0.03}$
	MARLENA	$0.05_{\pm0.01}$	$5.97_{\pm0.33}$	$0.62_{\pm0.05}$	$2.04_{\pm0.01}$
D3	LF-a	$0.05_{\pm0.00}$	$18.24_{\pm0.48}$	$1.00_{\pm0.00}$	$1.05_{\pm0.10}$
	GS	$0.08_{\pm0.01}$	$5.22_{\pm0.65}$	$0.90_{\pm0.05}$	$0.00_{\pm0.00}$
	LS	$0.08_{\pm0.02}$	$5.31_{\pm0.62}$	$0.91_{\pm0.03}$	$3.41_{\pm0.06}$
	MARLENA	$0.13_{\pm0.03}$	$4.41_{\pm0.20}$	$0.85_{\pm0.05}$	$0.86_{\pm0.00}$
D4	LF-a	$0.03_{\pm0.00}$	$4.92_{\pm0.46}$	$1.00_{\pm0.00}$	$1.38_{\pm0.30}$
	GS	$0.24_{\pm0.15}$	$3.62_{\pm0.57}$	$0.92_{\pm0.07}$	$0.00_{\pm0.00}$
	LS	$0.24_{\pm0.14}$	$3.41_{\pm0.38}$	$0.94_{\pm0.04}$	$1.43_{\pm0.04}$
	MARLENA	$0.33_{\pm0.13}$	$2.52_{\pm0.26}$	$0.75_{\pm0.06}$	$0.80_{\pm0.01}$

The last set of experiments concerns explanations for each predicted label and can be seen in Table 4. This setup allows us to use single-label interpretation

Table 4. Comparison between techniques explaining each predicted label separately

Dataset	Algorithms	C	L	P	T
D1	LF-1	$0.03_{\pm 0.00}$	$41.85_{\pm 4.8}$	$1.00_{\pm 0.00}$	$10.26_{\pm 0.90}$
	Anchors	$0.06_{\pm 0.02}$	$8.95_{\pm 2.3}$	$0.99_{\pm 0.02}$	$341.62_{\pm 105.93}$
	CHIRPS	$0.73_{\pm 0.09}$	$3.66_{\pm 1.1}$	$0.89_{\pm 0.03}$	$8.47_{\pm 0.35}$
D2	LF-1	$0.01_{\pm 0.00}$	$57.64_{\pm 5.71}$	$1.00_{\pm 0.00}$	$1.37_{\pm 0.11}$
	Anchors	$0.04_{\pm 0.01}$	$31.05_{\pm 3.47}$	$0.96_{\pm 0.02}$	$302.07_{\pm 44.43}$
	CHIRPS	$0.38_{\pm 0.05}$	$10.36_{\pm 1.37}$	$0.76_{\pm 0.05}$	$8.24_{\pm 0.50}$
D3	LF-1	$0.05_{\pm 0.00}$	$62.58_{\pm 5.24}$	$1.00_{\pm 0.00}$	$5.77_{\pm 0.42}$
	Anchors	$0.31_{\pm 0.05}$	$7.36_{\pm 1.24}$	$0.97_{\pm 0.02}$	$63.00_{\pm 17.91}$
	CHIRPS	$0.71_{\pm 0.05}$	$2.09_{\pm 0.45}$	$0.94_{\pm 0.03}$	$2.35_{\pm 0.19}$
D4	LF-1	$0.03_{\pm 0.00}$	$5.04_{\pm 0.48}$	$1.00_{\pm 0.00}$	$1.41_{\pm 0.31}$
	Anchors	$0.14_{\pm 0.05}$	$3.98_{\pm 0.52}$	$0.92_{\pm 0.07}$	$29.53_{\pm 3.42}$
	CHIRPS	$0.33_{\pm 0.14}$	$2.44_{\pm 0.66}$	$0.93_{\pm 0.06}$	$1.25_{\pm 0.09}$

techniques like Anchors and CHIRPS. In all datasets, CHIRPS outperforms its competitors in terms of Coverage. The longest rules are provided by LF-1, while the shortest are provided by CHIRPS. In terms of precision, LF-1 works flawlessly, with Anchors ranking second with a small advantage over CHIRPS. Regarding the time response, LF-1 and CHIRPS produce similar results with small deviations. Anchors, on the other hand, requires a significant amount of computational resources, leading to longer time responses.

5.3 Qualitative Experiments

Our qualitative experiments focus on the AI4I (D4) data set, as its small feature set makes it easier to present and analyze an example. The features available in this data set along with their ranges and the values of a sample instance can be found in Table 5.

Table 5. Dataset features, their ranges, and the values of a sample instance

Feature	Range	Instance values
Type	$[1, 3]$	3
Air temperature [K]	$[295.6, 304.4]$	300.7
Process temperature [K]	$[306.1, 313.7]$	310.2
Rotational speed [rpm]	$[1212, 2874]$	1364
Torque [Nm]	$[4.2, 76.2]$	65.3
Tool wear [min]	$[0, 251]$	208

Table 6. Example Rules by the proposed strategies

Techniques	Interpretation
LF-a	**If** $2.5 \leq Type \leq 3$ and $300.6 \leq Air\ temperature \leq 301.7$ and $310 \leq Process\ temperature \leq 313.7$ and $1351 \leq Rotational\ speed \leq 1380$ and $65.2 \leq Torque \leq 65.5$ and $207.5 \leq Tool\ wear \leq 209$ **then** TWF PWF OSF
LF-l	**If** $2.5 \leq Type \leq 3$ and $295.6 \leq Air\ temperature \leq 301.7$ and $1322.5 \leq Rotational\ speed \leq 1419.5$ and $65.2 \leq Torque \leq 76.2$ and $206.5 \leq Tool\ wear \leq 251.0$ **then** TWF **If** $2.5 \leq Type \leq 3$ and $295.6 \leq Air\ temperature \leq 301.7$ and $1351 \leq Rotational\ speed \leq 1380$ and $65.2 \leq Torque \leq 76.2$ and $188 \leq Tool\ wear \leq 251$ **then** PWF **If** $2.5 \leq Type \leq 3$ and $300.6 \leq Air\ temperature \leq 300.8$ and $65.2 \leq Torque \leq 65.5$ and $207.5 \leq Tool\ wear \leq 251$ **then** OSF
LF-p	**If** $2.5 \leq Type \leq 3$ and $295.6 \leq Air\ temperature \leq 301.7$ and $1351 \leq Rotational\ speed \leq 1380$ and $65.2 \leq Torque \leq 76.2$ and $185 \leq Tool\ wear \leq 251$ **then** PWF OSF

The first qualitative comparison found in Table 6 includes the rules produced by the different strategies of LF for the examined instance. As the quantitative experiments in Table 2 suggested, we can see that LF-a, the strategy explaining all predicted labels, provides the lengthier and more specific individual rule. When LF-l is employed, we can see that for the predicted label 'OSF', the rule is 2 feature-ranges smaller, while the rule regarding the predictions 'PWF' and 'TWF' are 1 feature-range smaller and have wider ranges. The third strategy, LF-p, produces rules explaining frequent label subsets. In this example, it produces a rule explaining the labels 'PWF' and 'OSF', a frequent labelset present in the prediction, and the rule is 1 feature-range smaller. Therefore, the user can choose between the available strategies based on their needs. We should mention that all these rules are conclusive, therefore, any change on the features between the given ranges, or any change on the features not appearing in the rules will not impact the prediction.

Table 7. Example rules for the whole labelset

Technique	Interpretation
GS	**If** $Air\ temperature \leq 301.7$ and $Tool\ wear > 176.5$ and $Torque > 65.2$ **then** TWF PWF OSF
LS	**If** $Air\ temperature \leq 301.7$ and $Tool\ wear > 188$ and $Torque > 48.4$ and $Type > 2.5$ **then** TWF PWF OSF
MARLENA	**If** $Air\ temperature \leq 303$ and $Rotational\ speed \leq 1382.4$ and $Type > 2.97$ **then** TWF PWF OSF

Continuing our comparisons, Table 7 presents the explanations given by GS, LS, and MA for the whole predicted labelset. These techniques provide rules that are substantially shorter and have broader feature-ranges than LF-a. However, the trade-off for these properties is the loss of conclusiveness. To support our claim, we perform three separate modifications on the values of the examined instance (one feature at a time), to demonstrate that the rules provided by the competitors do not account for these changes, in contrast to LF-a. GS does not contain a feature-range for *Type*, suggesting that it does not impact the prediction. Nonetheless, changing the value of this feature to either 1 or 2 alters the prediction to 'OSF'. The feature-range given by LS for *Torque* is deceptively wide. Lowering the value of this feature from 65.3 to 50 changes the prediction like before. Additionally, the range displayed by MA regarding *Air temperature* is inaccurate, as increasing its value from 300.7 to 302 causes the prediction to change from 'TWF', 'PWF', and 'OSF' to 'OSF'. Finally, both LS and MA incorrectly ignore a feature, *Air temperature* and *Torque*, respectively, since both affect the prediction as seen before.

Table 8. Example rules per label

Technique	Interpretation
Anchors	**If** *Air temperature* $\leq$ 301.6 and *Type* > 2 and *Tool wear* > 207.5 and *Torque* > 61.2 and *Rotational speed* $\leq$ 1365 **then** TWF **If** *Torque* > 61.2 and *Air temperature* $\leq$ 301.6 and *Type* > 2 and 1326.5 < *Rotational speed* $\leq$ 1365 and 309.5 < *Process temperature* $\leq$ 311.2 **then** PWF **If** *Tool wear* > 207.5 and *Torque* > 61.2 **then** OSF
CHIRPS	**If** {} **then** TWF **If** *Air temperature* $\leq$ 302.5 and *Torque* > 65 **then** PWF **If** *Tool wear* > 176.5 and *Torque* > 65 **then** OSF

Concluding our qualitative study, we present the rules provided by Anchors and CHIRPS in Table 8. We can see that Anchors provides rules of similar length to LF-l, compared to the significantly shorter ones of CHIRPS. Nevertheless, similarly to before, the shorter rules are inconclusive. Rules provided by CHIRPS have a lot of inaccuracies, with the most obvious being the empty rule for the 'TWF' prediction. We also spot few inaccuracies in the lengthier rules of Anchors. For example, the explanations for labels 'TWF' and 'PWF' suggest that values above 61.2 for *Torque* lead to predictions containing these 2 labels. However, increasing the value to 65 results in both not being predicted by the model. Contrarily, the rules provided by LF-l contain the correct feature ranges for *Torque*.

6 Conclusion

This paper proposed three different strategies that extend LF, so it can also be used to provide explanations for multi-label classification problems. Each of these strategies, explain the predicted labelset from a different point of view, resulting in rules of different length for each one of them, as well as different time responses. All three, however, retain the conclusiveness property of the original technique, providing concise explanations.

This was validated by our experimental procedure, where all strategies achieve a Precision of 1 throughout all the different setups and data sets, something that no other competitor manages to reach. Having said that, our strategies tend to produce lengthier rules that cover a smaller portion of instances than the competitors, meaning they are more specific. This attribute is not necessarily a shortcoming, considering that expert users prefer longer, more informative explanations. In addition, the low rule length of the other techniques can be misleading, as they tend to provide even empty explanations as showcased in our qualitative experiments. However, the user is also given the option to reduce the quorum, resulting in smaller rules losing the conclusiveness property.

Some of the future steps of this research include the extension of the technique, so it can also be applied to multi target regression problems, in conjunction to an extensive experimental procedure including new competitors, more data sets and additional metrics. Furthermore, a user study to assess the quality of the rules the three different strategies produce, can be performed. Doing so, will allow us to obtain insight from different types of users about the strategies and their applicability in various domains. Finally, applying a similar strategy to produce explanations for other ensemble models can also be explored in another work.

Acknowledgments. The research work was supported by the Hellenic Foundation for Research and Innovation (H.F.R.I.) under the "First Call for H.F.R.I. Research Projects to support Faculty members and Researchers and the procurement of high-cost research equipment grant" (Project Number: 514).

References

1. Adadi, A., Berrada, M.: Peeking inside the black-box: a survey on explainable artificial intelligence (XAI). IEEE Access **6**, 52138–52160 (2018)
2. Blockeel, H., Džeroski, S., Grbović, J.: Simultaneous prediction of multiple chemical parameters of river water quality with TILDE. In: Żytkow, J.M., Rauch, J. (eds.) PKDD 1999. LNCS (LNAI), vol. 1704, pp. 32–40. Springer, Heidelberg (1999). https://doi.org/10.1007/978-3-540-48247-5_4
3. Bogaert, M., Lootens, J., Van den Poel, D., Ballings, M.: Evaluating multi-label classifiers and recommender systems in the financial service sector. Eur. J. Oper. Res. **279**(2), 620–634 (2019)
4. Breiman, L.: Random forests. Mach. Learn. **45**(1), 5–32 (2001)

5. Craven, M., Shavlik, J.: Extracting tree-structured representations of trained networks. In: Touretzky, D., Mozer, M.C., Hasselmo, M. (eds.), Advances in Neural Information Processing Systems, vol. 8. MIT Press, Cambridge (1995)

6. Deng, H.: Interpreting tree ensembles with inTrees. Int. J. Data Sci. Anal. **7**(4), 277–287 (2018). https://doi.org/10.1007/s41060-018-0144-8

7. Dua, D., Graff, C.: UCI machine learning repository (2017)

8. Freitas, A.A.: Comprehensible classification models: a position paper. SIGKDD Explor. Newsl. **15**(1), 1–10 (2014)

9. Friedman, J.H., Popescu, B.E.: Predictive learning via rule ensembles. Ann. Appl. Stat. **2**(3), 916–954 (2008)

10. Gong, T., Liu, B., Chu, Q., Nenghai, Yu.: Using multi-label classification to improve object detection. Neurocomputing **370**, 174–185 (2019)

11. Guidotti, R., Monreale, A., Giannotti, F., Pedreschi, D., Ruggieri, S., Turini, F.: Factual and counterfactual explanations for black box decision making. IEEE Intell. Syst. **34**(6), 14–23 (2019)

12. Guidotti, R., Monreale, A., Ruggieri, S., Turini, F., Giannotti, F., Pedreschi, D.: A survey of methods for explaining black box models. ACM Comput. Surv. **51**(5), 1–42 (2018)

13. Hara, S., Hayashi, K.: Making tree ensembles interpretable: a bayesian model selection approach. In: Storkey, A., Perez-Cruz, F. (eds.), Proceedings of the Twenty-First International Conference on Artificial Intelligence and Statistics, volume 84 of Proceedings of Machine Learning Research, pp. 77–85. PMLR, 09–11 April 2018

14. Hatwell, J., Gaber, M.M., Muhammad Atif Azad, R.: CHIRPS: explaining random forest classification. Artif. Intell. Rev. **53**(8), 5747–5788 (2020)

15. Samaneh Kouchaki, Yang Yang, Alexander Lachapelle, Timothy M. Walker, A. Sarah Walker, CRyPTIC Consortium, Timothy E. A. Peto, Derrick W. Crook, and David A. Clifton. Multi-label random forest model for tuberculosis drug resistance classification and mutation ranking. Frontiers in Microbiology, 11, 2020

16. Matzka, S.: Explainable artificial intelligence for predictive maintenance applications. In: 2020 Third International Conference on Artificial Intelligence for Industries (AI4I), pp. 69–74. IEEE (2020)

17. Mollas, I., Bassiliades, N., Tsoumakas, G.: Conclusive local interpretation rules for random forests. Data Min. Knowl. Disc **36**, 1521–1574 (2022). https://doi.org/10.1007/s10618-022-00839-y

18. Moore, A., Murdock, V., Cai, Y., Jones, K.: Transparent tree ensembles. In: The 41st International ACM SIGIR Conference on Research & Development in Information Retrieval, SIGIR 2018, pp. 1241–1244, New York, NY, USA, Association for Computing Machinery (2018)

19. Neto, M.P., Paulovich, F.V.: Explainable matrix - visualization for global and local interpretability of random forest classification ensembles. IEEE Trans. Vis. Comput. Graph. **27**(2), 1427–1437 (2021)

20. Panigutti, C., Guidotti, R., Monreale, A., Pedreschi, D.: Explaining multi-label black-box classifiers for health applications. In: Shaban-Nejad, A., Michalowski, M. (eds.) W3PHAI 2019. SCI, vol. 843, pp. 97–110. Springer, Cham (2020). https://doi.org/10.1007/978-3-030-24409-5_9

21. Papanikolaou, Y., Tsoumakas, G., Laliotis, M., Markantonatos, N., Vlahavas, I.: Large-scale online semantic indexing of biomedical articles via an ensemble of multi-label classification models. J. Biomed. Semant. **8**(1), 43:1–43:13 (2017). https://doi.org/10.1186/s13326-017-0150-0

22. Ribeiro, M.T., Singh, S., Guestrin, C.: Why should i trust you?: Explaining the predictions of any classifier. In: Proceedings of the 22nd ACM SIGKDD International Conference on Knowledge Discovery and Data Mining, pp. 1135–1144. ACM (2016)

23. Ribeiro, M.T., Singh, S., Guestrin, C.: Anchors: high-precision model-agnostic explanations. In: Thirty-Second AAAI Conference on Artificial Intelligence (2018)

24. Rivolli, A., Parker, L.C., de Carvalho, A.C.P.L.F.: Food truck recommendation using multi-label classification. In: Oliveira, E., Gama, J., Vale, Z., Lopes Cardoso, H. (eds.) EPIA 2017. LNCS (LNAI), vol. 10423, pp. 585–596. Springer, Cham (2017). https://doi.org/10.1007/978-3-319-65340-2_48

25. Rokach, L., Schclar, A., Itach, E.: Ensemble methods for multi-label classification. Expert Syst. Appl. **41**(16), 7507–7523 (2014)

26. Sharma, S., Mehrotra, D.: Comparative analysis of multi-label classification algorithms. In: 2018 First International Conference on Secure Cyber Computing and Communication (ICSCCC), pp. 35–38 (2018)

27. Tabia, K.: Towards explainable multi-label classification. In: 2019 IEEE 31st International Conference on Tools with Artificial Intelligence (ICTAI), pp. 1088–1095 (2019)

28. Tsoumakas, G., Katakis, I.: Multi-label classification: an overview. Int. J. Data Warehous. Min. **3**(3), 1–13 (2007)

29. Qingyao, W., Tan, M., Song, H., Chen, J., Michael, K.N.: Ml-forest: a multi-label tree ensemble method for multi-label classification. IEEE Trans. Knowl. Data Eng. **28**(10), 2665–2680 (2016)

30. Wu, X., Gao, Y., Jiao, D.: Multi-label classification based on random forest algorithm for non-intrusive load monitoring system. Processes **7**(6), 337 (2019)

31. Zhao, X., Wu, Y., Lee, D.L., Cui, W.: iforest: interpreting random forests via visual analytics. IEEE Trans. Vis. Comput. Graph. **25**(1), 407–416 (2019)

Interpretable and Reliable Rule Classification Based on Conformal Prediction

Husam Abdelqader[1,2(✉)], Evgueni Smirnov[1], Marc Pont[2],
and Marciano Geijselaers[2]

[1] Maastricht University, Maastricht, The Netherlands
h.husamfuadsalehabdelqader@student.maastrichtuniversity.nl,
smirnov@maastrichtuniversity.nl
[2] Integrin, Geleen, The Netherlands
{marc.pont,marciano.geijselaers}@intergrin.nl

Abstract. This paper deals with the challenging problem of simultaneously integrating interpretablility and reliability into prediction models in machine learning. It proposes to combine the interpretable models of decision rules with the reliable models based on conformal prediction. The result is a new technique of conformal decision rules. Given a test instance, the technique is capable of providing a point prediction, an explanation, and a confidence value for that prediction plus a prediction set. The experiments show when and how conformal decision rules can be used for interpretable and reliable machine learning.

Keywords: Interpretable machine learning · Reliable machine learning · Decision rules · Conformal prediction

1 Introduction

Machine learning in critical domain applications needs to provide predictions that are both interpretable and reliable [7]. Following [8] we informally define, interpretablility of a prediction as the degree that the cause for the prediction can be understood by a user. Analogously, we define reliability of a prediction as the degree that a user can trust the prediction [13]. Thus, the acceptance process of a prediction can be facilitated using additional information on the interpretablility and reliability of the prediction.

Integrating interpretable and reliable machine learning is usually implemented using the Mondrian scheme summarized in [1]. The scheme consists of two steps:

(1) train an interpretable prediction model (e.g. a decision tree) on the available data T and view that model as a taxonomy that partitions the data into categories r (i.e. through leaf nodes).
(2) train a reliable prediction model on the data T_r of each category r.

© The Author(s), under exclusive license to Springer Nature Switzerland AG 2023
I. Koprinska et al. (Eds.): ECML PKDD 2022 Workshops, CCIS 1752, pp. 385–401, 2023.
https://doi.org/10.1007/978-3-031-23618-1_26

In this context, when a test instance is processed, it is first handled by the interpretable prediction model that provides a point prediction plus a cause for that prediction. In addition, the model identifies the category that fits the instance and calls the reliable prediction model that corresponds to that category. The latter outputs a confidence value in the point prediction and/or a region prediction, i.e. a set of labels that with a high probability contains the true label of the test instance.

To provide a data-distribution free guarantee integrating interpretable and reliable machine learning is realized using the conformal prediction framework [13,14]. This framework provides a set of techniques for establishing precise level of confidence in new predictions in the presence of finite training data and without any assumption on data distribution. It allows computing valid region predictions, i.e. regions that contain the true labels of test instances within a user-acceptable error probability.

In general, the conformal prediction framework operates as follows [14]. Given a test instance x, it first provisionally labels x with label y; i.e. it considers hypothetically labeled instance (x, y). Then the (confidence) p-value p_y for label y is calculated as the proportion of the instances in $T \cup \{(x, y)\}$ whose nonconformity scores α are greater than or equal to that of the instance (x, y). If $p_y > \epsilon$ for a chosen significance level ϵ, label y is added to the region prediction set Γ for test instance x.

To apply conformal prediction we need to compute for each instance nonconformity score α that indicates how untypical the instance is w.r.t. the rest of the data. This computation is realized by a nonconformity function A that is trained on the data. There are different scenarios for this based on different validation procedures which result in different conformal predictors.

Conformal prediction was integrated with interpretable prediction models for regression and classification using variations of the Mondrian integration scheme presented above [1,5,6,11]. The interpretable prediction models used were regression/decision trees while the reliable prediction models were conformal predictors. The proposed integrations employed a *global* approach to train conformal predictors. The regression/decision tree trained is viewed as a taxonomy that imposes a partition P_h on training data T. Each element $T_r \subset T$ of this partition corresponds to a concrete leaf node r. Conformal predictors are trained, one for each node r, however, in a *global* manner. This means that first each T_r is split into a proper training set T_r^t and a calibration set T_r^c. Then the global proper training set $\sum_r T_r^t$ is used to train the global nonconformity function A shared by all the conformal predictors. The conformal predictor for each leaf node r employs the global function A to compute the nonconformity scores of the calibration training instances in T_r^c associated with that leaf node. Thus, each test instance receives label p-values and region prediction from the conformal predictor of the leaf node in which it arrives.

The *global* approach to train conformal predictors is based on the assumption that larger data result in more accurate nonconformity functions that in turn decrease the sizes of the region prediction sets. However, in this paper we argue that the *global* approach has a fundamental problem that concerns integrating interpretable and reliable machine learning following the Mondrian scheme. This problem is a *label-imbalanced problem*: the probability distributions that generate the global proper training set $\sum_r T_r^t$ and leaf-node calibration subsets T_r^c can be very different since the trees are learned by minimizing the class entropy or output-variable variance in leaf nodes. This implies that the global nonconformity function can be inaccurate on test data that arrive in a particular leaf node. This is due to the fact that this function is trained on the global proper training set $\sum_r T_r^t$ while the test data is generated from the distribution similar to that of subset T_r associated with that node.

In this paper we propose a *local* approach to train conformal predictors to address the label-imbalanced problem. The key idea is to train the nonconformity functions of the conformal predictors locally, i.e. on the proper training subsets T_r. We show that this approach has a potential to improve integrating interpretable and reliable machine learning for large data.

The second contribution of our paper is that we propose to combine decision rules [4] and conformal prediction according to the Mondrian integration scheme, i.e., we continue the research line of conformal interpretable models in classification as outlined in [5,11]. Following the criteria for model interpretablility in [9] we motivate our choice for decision rules as follows. First, decision rules are more interpretable than decision trees [4]. On a model level decision rules are usually shorter, i.e. more general, than the rules encoded by decision trees[1]. This implies that for the same classification problem we need less decision rules; i.e. we need less modules for global interpretability (in terms of [9]). On a prediction level decision rules provide individual prediction explanations. For the reason given before these explanations are usually shorter than those of decision trees. Thus, (again in terms of [9]) the local interpretability for a single prediction is better. Finally, we note that while still disputable decision rules are algorithmically more transparent than decision rules. We believe that it is easier to explain the separate-and-conquer strategy of decision rules than the divide-and-conquer strategy of decision trees [4] (check the pseudo-code in Algorithm 1).

The rest of the paper is organized as follows. In the next section we formalize the classification task in the context of point estimation and prediction-set estimation. In Sect. 3, we present decision rules. The conformal prediction and its basic set predictors are presented in Sect. 4. In Sect. 5, we propose our approach and explain the underlying algorithms. The experiments and results are provided in Sect. 6. Section 7 concludes the paper.

2   Classification

Let X be an instance space, Y be a finite discrete class variable, and P be a probability distribution over $X \times Y$. Training data set T is a multi set of M instances $(x_m, y_m) \in X \times Y$ drawn from the distribution P under the randomness

---

[1] The decision tree rules partition the data which assumes these rules are longer; i.e. more specific.

assumption. In this context, we can define two possible tasks: point classification task and region classification task.

The point classification task is to find an estimate $y \in Y$ of the true class for a test instance $x \in X$ according to P. To solve the task we first learn a point predictor h in a hypothesis space H using training data T. The predictor h is a function of type $h : X \rightarrow Y$. It first computes for test instance x a distribution of posterior scores $\{s_y\}_{y \in Y}$ over all the classes in Y. Then, h outputs class y with the highest score s_y as the estimated class for test instance x.

The region classification task is to estimate a prediction set $\Gamma(x) \subseteq Y$ that contains possible classes for a test instance $x \in X$ according to P. To solve the task we need a class set predictor. The two most desired properties of such predictor are validity and informational efficiency. A class set predictor is said to be valid iff the probability that the prediction set $\Gamma^\epsilon(x) \subseteq Y$ does not contain the class for the test instance x is at most the chosen significance level $\epsilon \in [0, 1]$. A class set predictor is said to be informationally efficient if the prediction set $\Gamma^\epsilon(x) \subseteq Y$ is non-empty and small. In Sect. 4 we briefly introduce the conformal framework that is used for designing valid set predictors [14].

3   Decision Rules

Decision rules form an approach to point classification [4]. They are "if-then" rules that can be learned from training data T. The antecedent of any rule r is a condition that can be tested for any instance $x \in X$. The consequent part of r consists of a single class value $y \in Y$ that is assigned to any test instance $x \in X$ as a class point estimate. The final point predictor h is a set of decision rules r.

Decision rules can be used for descriptive and classification tasks. For descriptive tasks they provide interpretations/summarization of the training data w.r.t. class information. For classification tasks decision rules provide class predictions plus their explanations based on the conditions in the rule antecedents. This makes decision rules an important tool in interpretable machine learning.

The separate-and-conquer learning algorithm of decision rules is given in Algorithm 1. In an iterative manner it executes the following steps. First, the algorithm learns one rule r from T. If rule r is acceptable (e.g. a high TPr rate for the class assigned by r), it is added to point predictor h and subset T_r of training instances covered by r is removed from T. In this way the algorithm focuses only on those training instances in each new iteration that have not been covered so far. The iteration process ends when a stopping criterion is met. The criterion can be a threshold on the percentage of covered data, the validation performance of the final point predictor h etc. Once the criterion holds, the algorithm adds the default rule r that holds when all other rules logically fail.

To use point predictor h of decision rules r, a classification procedure has to be defined. We assume that the rules are ordered in decreasing order of their performance on a separate validation data. A test instance x receives a class value of that rule $r \in h$ that matches x first in the order.

There are several techniques for implicit regularization of decision rules due their sensitivity to over-fitting. One of the most accurate of those is Incremental

---

Algorithm 1: Decision Rule Learning

Input: Training set T;
Output: Point predictor h of decision rules;

1 Set h equal to empty set $\emptyset$;
2 **repeat**
3   Learn rule r from T;
4   **if** *rule r is acceptable* **then**
5   Add rule r to point predictor h;
6   Remove set T_r of instances covered by r from T;

7 **until** *stopping criterion is met*;
8 Add default rule r to point predictor h;
9 **return** point predictor h.

Algorithm 2: Incremental Reduced Error Pruning (IREP)

Input: Training set T;
Output: Point predictor h of decision rules;

1 Set h equal to empty set $\emptyset$;
2 **repeat**
3   Split T into growing set T^g and prune set T^p;
4   Learn rule r from T^g;
5   Prune r on T^p;
6   **if** *rule r is acceptable* **then**
7   Add rule r to point predictor h;
8   Remove instances covered by r from T;

9 **until** *stopping criterion is met*;
10 Add default rule r to point predictor h;
11 **return** point predictor h.

Reduced Error Pruning (IREP) given in [4]. The pseudo-code of IREP is provided in Fig. 2 and it is very similar to that of decision rule learning. The only difference is the manner of learning new rules (steps 3 to 5). IREP first splits the current training data T into growing set T^g and prune set T^p. Then it trains a new rule r on T^g and subsequently prunes that rule on T^p. Since the data covered by rule r are removed from T, the next rule will have a small overlap with r on instance space X if at all. If we extrapolate this finding over the whole sequence of rules r in the final point predictor h, we may conclude that IREP minimizes the overlap between the (subsequent) rules. This in turn reduces the number of decision rules r in h compared with any other technique for decision rule pruning. Thus, IREP is an excellent candidate for prediction interpretability.

The order of decision rules r in final point predictor h, that we have assumed for classification purposes, imposes a partition P_h on training set T. Each element $T_r \subset T$ of this partition corresponds to a concrete decision rule r and, thus, it is biased toward class $y \in Y$ that r assigns. This implies that the probability distributions that generate sets T and T_r can be very different.

In addition, we note that partition P_h can be viewed as a rule-induced taxonomy. The categories of this taxonomy are intensionally represented by rules r while extensionally by training sets T_r. This property is used for combining decision rules and conformal prediction following the Mondrian integration scheme.

4 Conformal Prediction

This section provides a short intro to conformal prediction. First, it considers transductive and inductive conformal prediction. Then, it proceeds with Mondrian conformal prediction.

4.1 Transductive and Inductive Conformal Prediction

The conformal prediction framework [12,13] allows us to train class set predictors that are automatically valid. They operate as follows. Given a test instance $x_{M+1} \in X$, to decide whether to include a class $y \in Y$ in prediction set $\Gamma^\epsilon(x_{M+1}) \subseteq Y$, the labeled instance (x_{M+1}, y) is provisionally considered. Then the nonconformity scores α_m of all the instances (x_m, y_m) in $T \cup \{(x_{M+1}, y)\}$ are computed. The p-value p_y of class y for test instance x_{M+1} is computed as follows:

$$p_y = \frac{\#\{(x_m, y_m) \in T | \alpha_m > \alpha_{M+1}\} + \tau \#\{(x_m, y_m) \in T | \alpha_m = \alpha_{M+1}\}}{M + 1} \quad (1)$$

where α_{M+1} is the nonconformity score of (x_{M+1}, y) and τ is an uniformly distributed random variable in $[0, 1]$.

Once we have fixed significance level ϵ, class y is included in prediction set $\Gamma^\epsilon(x_{M+1})$ of test instance x_{m+1} if $p_y > \epsilon$. Thus, in a long run we get validity: the error e when prediction sets do not include the true classes is bounded from below by ϵ.

The art to apply conformal prediction is to decide how to compute nonconformity scores. A nonconformity score α_m for any instance (x_m, y_m) is a score that indicates how untypical is (x_m, y_m) w.r.t. the instances in data $(T \cup \{(x_{M+1}, y)\}) \setminus \{(x_m, y_m)\}$. To compute such a score we need a nonconformity function A. Formally, this function is of type $A : (X \times Y)^{(*)} \times (X \times Y) \to \mathbb{R}^+ \cup \{+\infty\}^2$. Given a data set $T \subseteq X \times Y$ and an instance $(x_m, y_m) \in (X \times Y)$, it returns a nonconformity score $\alpha_m \in \mathbb{R}^+ \cup \{+\infty\}$ indicating how untypical the instance (x_m, y_m) is for the instances in $(T \cup \{(x_{M+1}, y)\}) \setminus \{(x_m, y_m)\}$. An example of function A is the general nonconformity function applicable for any point predictor $h(x)$ [14]. Given an instance (x_m, y_m), the function outputs $\sum_{y \neq y_m} s_y$, i.e. the sum of the scores s_y of all the classes $y \in Y$ computed by h without that of y_m. This makes the conformal prediction predictor-agnostic.

We note that in general the nonconformity score α_m for any instance (x_m, y_m) is w.r.t. all the remaining instances in data $(T \cup \{(x_{M+1}, y)\}) \setminus \{(x_m, y_m)\}$.

---

[2] $(X \times Y)^{(*)}$ denotes the set of all multi sets defined over $X \times Y$.

Thus, computing the nonconformity scores α_m for all the instances (x_m, y_m) in $T \cup \{(x_{M+1}, y)\}$ is realized by a leave-one-out process implemented in so-called transductive conformal predictors (TCPs). To reduce the computational complexity of TCPs [10] proposed inductive conformal predictors (ICPs). ICPs use a hold-out process and thus they split the training data set T of size M into the proper training set $T^t \subseteq T$ of size $L < M$ and the calibration set $T^c \subseteq T$ of size $M - L$. Set T^t is used to train the nonconformity function A. The function is then applied over all the instances in data $T^c \cup \{(x_{M+1}, y)\}$ to compute their nonconformity scores. The p-value p_y of class y for test instance x_{M+1} is computed in a similar manner, however, over nonconformity scores of instances in $T^c \cup \{(x_{M+1}, y)\}$ only; i.e.,

$$p_y = \frac{\#\{(x_m, y_m) \in T^c | \alpha_m > \alpha_{M+1}\} + \tau \#\{(x_m, y_m) \in T^c | \alpha_m = \alpha_{M+1}\}}{M - L + 1} \quad (2)$$

where α_{M+1} is the nonconformity score of (x_{M+1}, y) and τ is an uniformly distributed random variable in $[0, 1]$.

We note that ICPs are computationally more efficient than TCPs. However, their informational efficiency (prediction set size) is usually lower than that of TCPs. Still, in the rest of the paper will be using ICPs.

4.2   Mondrian Conformal Prediction

Assume that we have a taxonomy P of disjointed categories. P partitions T into disjointed subsets T_r intensionally represented by categories r from P. Due to the disjointedness the probability distributions behind sets T and T_r can be very different. In this case any conformal predictor trained on T is valid for any data set generated by the probability distribution that generates T. However, it may be invalid for data sets generated by the probability distributions that generate subsets T_r for some categories r in P. To guarantee predictor validity within the categories, Mondrian conformal prediction was introduced in [14].

The key idea is to train a separate conformal predictor for each subset T_r. In case of ICP this is realized as follows. First, each subset T_r is split into proper training set T_r^t and calibration set T_r^c. Then, a global proper training set T^t is formed equal to $\bigcup_{r \in P} T_r^t$ to train the global nonconformity function A. The function is used to compute the nonconformity scores of the instances in calibration set T_r^c of each ICP_r. Once this process is complete, we receive individual ICP_r for each category r in taxonomy P.

The process of region classification is simple. Given a test instance x_{M+1}, we first determine category r from taxonomy P that matches x_{M+1}. Then we apply the corresponding ICP_r on x_{M+1} to compute a prediction set $\Gamma^\epsilon(x_{M+1})$. We note that each ICP_r is a valid conformal predictor on data sets generated by the probability distributions that generate the corresponding subset T_r. Thus, we receive a local validity within the categories and, thus, a global validity of the conformal predictors.

5   Conformal Decision Rules

In this section we propose to integrate decision rules and conformal prediction. The key idea is simple: decision rules imposes a taxonomy on training data, and, thus, we integrate by training a Mondrian conformal predictor on the taxonomized data. This implies that a conformal decision rule is a decision rule r with its own ICP_r and the final predictor is a set of conformal decision rules.

The learning algorithm of conformal decision rules is given in Algorithm 3. The algorithm input consists of the training set T, calibration set ratio c, and Boolean variable *global*. First, the algorithm trains point predictor h of decision rules r on training set T using Algorithm 1 (step 1). Since rules r are ordered, they represent intensionally a taxonomy that can be employed for Mondrian conformal prediction. Therefore, the algorithm uses the rules to partition training data T into disjointed subsets $T_r \subseteq T$ s.t. each rule r covers exactly one T_r (steps 3–4). Then, to prepare the data for training ICPs, all the subsets T_r are divided in a *class-stratified manner* into proper training sets T_r^t and calibration sets T_r^c according to calibration set ratio c in a class-stratified manner (step 5).

In steps 7–16 a Mondrian conformal predictor is trained on the partitioned data; i.e. an ICP_r is trained for each rule r. Two strategies are employed to train ICPs: global (steps 7–11) and local (steps 12–15). The global strategy is similar to that from [1]: a global nonconformity function A is trained on the union of proper training sets T_r^t over all the rules r, and each ICP_r employs A on its own calibration set T_r^c. The local strategy is a new strategy that we propose: each ICP_r gets its own local nonconformity function A_r trained on its own proper training set T_r^t and this function is applied on its own calibration set T_r^c.

Once all the ICPs have been trained, the algorithm outputs point predictor h of all decision rules and the set of all ICPs. Thus, each conformal decision rule is given a rule r and its corresponding ICP_r.

The classification procedure is straightforward. Given a test instance x_{M+1}, the decision rules $r \in h$ are visited in the order imposed on h (see the explanation of Algorithm 1). If x_{M+1} matches the antecedent of the current rule r, its receives a point (class) prediction $y \in Y$ associated with r, an explanation (of how x_{M+1} matches the antecedent) plus a prediction set $\Gamma^\epsilon(x_{M+1}) \subseteq Y$ provided by ICP_r on a given significance level ϵ.

We note that conformal decision rules are valid class set predictors; i.e. the probability that the prediction set $\Gamma^\epsilon(x) \subseteq Y$ does not contain the class for the test instance x is at most ϵ. This is due to the fact that they are essentially Mondrian conformal predictors (see above).

The global and local strategies for setting up ICPs of decision rules are rather different. The global strategy trains global nonconformity functions A that are accurate on data generated by the original data distribution P. However, the calibration sets T_r^c of decision rules r might come from different distributions since the rules usually cover subsets that are class biased. Thus, *the label imbalanced problem* might be present. As a result, global nonconformity functions A can be less accurate on these sets which can result in less accurate nonconformity functions (which in turn will decrease the informational efficiency).

Algorithm 3: Conformal Decision Rule Learning

Input: Training set T, calibration set ratio $c \in (0, 1.0)$, and Boolean variable *global*;

Output: Point predictor h of decision rules r and set $\{ICP_r\}_{r \in h}$;

1 Train point predictor h of decision rules r on training set T;
2 **for** *each rule* $r \in h$ **do**
3 $\quad$ Determine training subset $T_r \subseteq T$ covered by rule r;
4 $\quad$ $T := T \setminus T_r$;
5 $\quad$ Split T_r into proper training set T_r^t and calibration set T_r^c according to c;

6 **if** *global* **then**
7 $\quad$ $T^t := \bigcup_{r \in h} T_r^t$;
8 $\quad$ **for** *each rule* $r \in h$ **do**
9 $\quad\quad$ Set up inductive conformal predictor ICP_r using T^t and T_r^c;

10 **else**
11 $\quad$ **for** *each rule* $r \in h$ **do**
12 $\quad\quad$ Set up inductive conformal predictor ICP_r using T_r^t and T_r^c;

13 **Output** Point predictor h of decision rules r and set $\{ICP_r\}_{r \in h}$.

The local strategy does not suffer from the label-imbalanced problem above: the local nonconformity functions A_r are trained on the proper training sets T_r^t and process calibration sets T_r^c that if stratified can be viewed coming from the same data distribution. Thus, the functions A_r can be accurate on T_r^c which can result in accurate nonconformity functions (which in turn will boost the informational efficiency). However, this happens only if the proper training sets T_r^t and calibration sets T_r^c are not small. Due to the nature of decision rule learning, the size of the covered set T_r of each new rule usually decreases. This implies that the local strategy has to be used for relatively large data.

6 Experiments and Results

This section presents our experiments. The data sets used for this research are described in Subsect. 6.1. The experimental setup is provided in Subsect. 6.2. The results are given in Subsect. 6.4.

6.1 Data Sets

In the experiments, we consider 10 binary classification data sets from the UCI machine learning repository [3]. The sets are summarized in Table 1. We note they are pre-processed where necessary: missing values are replaced by mean for numeric features and by mode for discrete features.

Table 1. Public data sets characteristics

Data set	Short hand	Instances	Majority class
Heart cleaveland	HC	303	54%
Heart VA	HV	200	74%
Haberman	HM	306	74%
Spam base	SB	4601	61%
Australian credit card	AC	1372	56%
Cancer	C	569	63%
Ionosphere	I	351	64%
Hepatitis	H	155	79%
German credit	GC	1000	70%
Indian liver	IL	583	71%

6.2 Experimental Settings

We experiment with two types of conformal set predictors: pure ICP and conformal decision rules based on IREP and ICP denoted by IREP-ICP. IREP-ICP employs the local strategy and global strategy denoted by IREP-ICP(L) and IREP-ICP(G), respectively. The minimal number of training instances per rule is set to 30 for IREP. The pure ICP predictors and ICP predictors in IREP-ICP use the nearest-neighbor nonconformity function from [14]. This function outputs for any instance (x, y) a nonconformity score α equal to $\frac{D_K^y}{D_K^{-y}}$, where D_K^y (D_K^{-y}) is the sum of distances between x and K nearest neighbors of x that do (not) belong to class y. For all ICPs $\frac{2}{3}$ of the training data is used for the proper training set and $\frac{1}{3}$ for the calibration set.

The set predictors are tested using a stratified 5-fold cross validation procedure. We employ several metrics to estimate the performance of the models. To test experimentally the validity of a conformal set predictor we use the error rate e. The error rate e for a significance level ϵ is defined as proportion of test instances whose predicted prediction-sets Γ^ϵ do not contain the correct class. To show experimentally that a conformal set predictor is valid, we need to show that for any significance level $\epsilon \in [0, 1]$ we have $e \leq \epsilon$.

To test experimentally the informational efficiency of a set predictor on significance level ϵ we employ three main metrics: rate r^e of empty prediction sets, rate r^s of single prediction sets, and rate r^m of multiple prediction sets. The empty prediction sets, single prediction sets, and multiple prediction sets have their own errors. Rate r^e of empty prediction sets is an error, since the correct classes are not in the prediction sets. Error rate e^s (e^m) on single (multiple) prediction sets is defined as the proportion of the single (multiple) prediction sets that do not contain the correct classes.

6.3 Algorithm Output

For any test instance the output of conformal decision rules consists of a point prediction, an explanation, confidence values for all possible predictions plus a prediction set for a chosen significance level ϵ. We provide the output of IREP-ICP(L) on the Indian Liver data. This data consists of 583 liver patients records divided into two classes, patients with a *liver problem* and patients with *no liver problem*. The input variables are presented in Table 2. IREP-ICP(L) was trained on the data and tested on two instances given in Table 3. The output for these instances for significance level $\epsilon = 0.05$ is as follows:

Table 2. Indian liver data set input variables

Name	Description	Name	Description
Age	Age of the patient	Sgpt	Alamine Aminotransferase
Gender	Gender of the patient	Sgot	Aspartate Aminotransferase
TB	Total Bilirubin	TP	Total Protiens
DB	Direct Bilirubin	ALB	Albumin
Alkphos	Alkaline Phosphotase	A/G	Albumin and Globulin Ratio

Table 3. Indian liver data Set examples

Instance	Age	Gender	TB	DB	Alkphos	Sgpt	Sgot	fTP	ALB	A/G	Class
58	48	Female	0.9	0.2	175	24	54	5.5	2.7	0.9	*no liver problem*
206	45	Male	2.5	1.2	163	28	22	7.6	4	1.1	*liver problem*

– **Instance 58:**
  - **Point Prediction:** *liver problem*
  - **Explanation:** *liver problem* since *Alkphos* is between 21.0 and 25.0
  - **p-value** of *no liver problem* is 0.49; **p-value** of *liver problem* is 0.51
  - **Prediction Set for** $\epsilon = 0.05$: { *no liver problem, liver problem* }
– **Instance 206:**
  - **Point Prediction:** *liver problem*
  - **Explanation:** *liver problem* since *TB* is between 0.88 and 1.6
  - **p-value** of *no liver problem* is 0.04; **p-value** of *liver problem* is 0.84
  - **Prediction Set for** $\epsilon = 0.05$: { *liver problem* }

6.4 Results

Illustrative Comparison. In this sub-subsection we study pure ICP versus IREP-ICP as well as the local strategy versus the global strategy of IREP-ICP. The performance of the rules created by IREP has been studied in [2]. The results are presented in Figs. 1(a) and 2(a) for the Haberman data and Spam base data. Figures 1(a) and 2(a) show that ICP, IREP-ICP(L) and IREP-ICP(G)

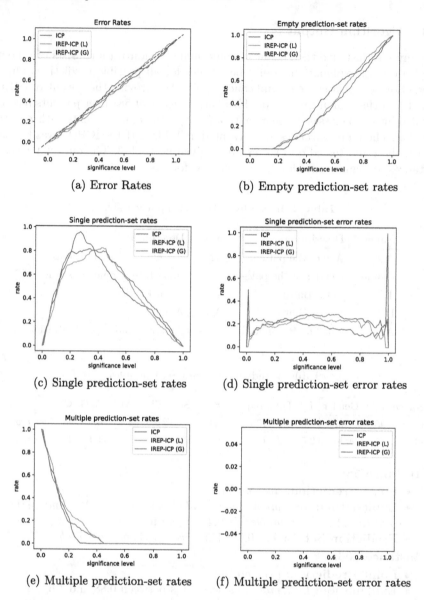

(a) Error Rates

(b) Empty prediction-set rates

(c) Single prediction-set rates

(d) Single prediction-set error rates

(e) Multiple prediction-set rates

(f) Multiple prediction-set error rates

Fig. 1. Error and prediction-set size plots for the haberman dataset

are valid set predictors. Their informational efficiency, however, are different. For the Haberman dataset ICP is more informationally efficient than both IREP-ICP predictors. Figure 1(e) shows that rate r^m of ICP decreases faster with significance level ϵ while Fig. 1(c) shows that the max rate r^s of ICP is 0.96 against 0.71 and 0.79 of IREP-ICP(L) and (G), respectively. In addition, we note that in Fig. 1(d) error rate e^s of ICP is always lower than those of IREP-ICP predictors.

For the Spam base dataset IREP-ICP(L) is more informationally efficient than ICP and IREP-ICP(G) for significance level $\epsilon < 0.2$. Figure 2(e) shows that rate r^m of IREP-ICP(L) decreases faster with significance level ϵ while Fig. 2(c) shows that the rate r^s of IREP-ICP(L) is 0.93 against 0.78 of ICP and

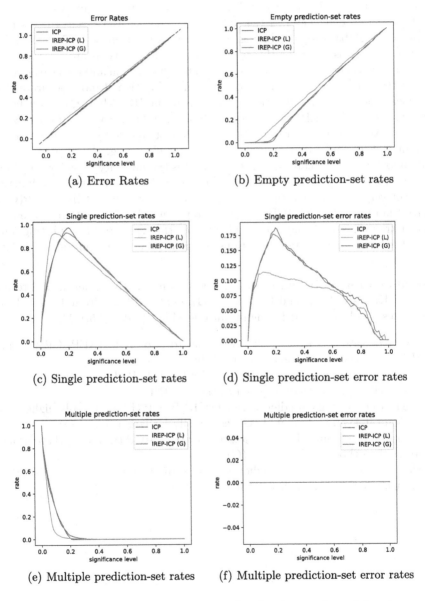

(a) Error Rates

(b) Empty prediction-set rates

(c) Single prediction-set rates

(d) Single prediction-set error rates

(e) Multiple prediction-set rates

(f) Multiple prediction-set error rates

Fig. 2. Error and prediction-set size plots for the spambase data set

IREP-ICP(G), respectively. In addition, we note that in Fig. 2(d) error rate e^s of IREP-ICP(L) is always lower than those of ICP.

The results from Figs. 1 and 2 can be explained as follows. The informational efficiency of ICP is usually better than that of the IREP-ICP(L) and (G) since ICP employs all the available data for training nonconformity functions A and calibration. However, there are cases similar to one we observed for the Spam base data when IREP-ICPs are better. This happens when decision rules impose taxonomies that make easier learning local nonconformity functions A_r.

Information efficiency of IREP-ICP(G) depends on the extent the distributions of the global proper training set T^t and calibration sets T_r^c of the ICP_r predictors are close. For the Haberman data the distributions are close (e.g. the majority class is positive over all the sets). This observation and a relatively small size of the data make the global nonconformity function A more accurate than the local nonconformity functions A_r. As a result IREP-ICP(G) has a better performance than IREP-ICP(L) on the Haberman data. However, for the Spam base data the situation is rather different: the distributions of the global proper training set T^t and calibration sets T_r^c are not close (e.g. the positive class is the majority class for calibration sets T_r^c and is the minority class for the global proper training sets T^t). This implies that the global nonconformity function A is not very accurate which explains why the performance of IREP-ICP(G) is worse than that of IREP-ICP(L). The latter keeps the distribution of the local proper training set T_r^t and calibration sets T_r^c through stratified splitting, and, thus, the local nonconformity functions A_r are more accurate on the Spam data.

Results on ten UCI Data Sets. Table 4[3] contains the experimental results for ICP, IREP-ICP (L), and IREP-ICP (G) on all data sets from Table 1. From the tables we observe that for significance level $\epsilon \in \{0.01, 0.05, 0.1\}$

- the error rate e is smaller than or equal to ϵ for ICP, IREP-ICP (L), and IREP-ICP (G) up to some statistical fluctuations;
- the rates r^e of empty prediction sets for IREP-ICP (L) and IREP-ICP (G) are usually greater than or equal to those of ICP;
- the rates r^s of single prediction sets for IREP-ICP (L) are usually higher than those of ICP and IREP-ICP (G), especiallly for larger data sets;
- the rates r^m of multiple prediction sets for IREP-ICP (L) and ICP are usually lower than those of IREP-ICP (G);
- the error rates e^s of single prediction sets for IREP-ICP (L) and IREP-ICP(G) are usually lower than those of ICP.

---

[3] Multiple prediction set error rate e^m is excluded from the table as it equals 0.0.

Table 4. Public data sets results

Set	ϵ	ICP					IREP-ICP (L)					IREP-ICP (G)				
		e	r^e	r^s	r^m	e^s	e	r^e	r^s	r^m	e^s	e	r^e	r^s	r^m	e^s
HC	0.01	0.01	0.0	0.069	0.931	0.143	0.003	0.0	0.05	0.95	0.067	0.003	0.0	0.026	0.974	0.125
	0.05	0.026	0.0	0.195	0.805	0.136	0.036	0.0	0.267	0.733	0.136	0.046	0.0	0.172	0.828	0.269
	0.1	0.086	0.0	0.386	0.614	0.222	0.099	0.0	0.538	0.462	0.184	0.096	0.0	0.386	0.614	0.248
HV	0.01	0.005	0.0	0.005	0.995	1.0	0.005	0.0	0.04	0.96	0.125	0.005	0.0	0.055	0.945	0.091
	0.05	0.04	0.0	0.13	0.87	0.308	0.035	0.0	0.255	0.745	0.137	0.06	0.0	0.285	0.715	0.211
	0.1	0.075	0.0	0.305	0.695	0.246	0.095	0.0	0.53	0.47	0.179	0.09	0.0	0.5	0.5	0.18
HM	0.01	0.003	0.0	0.007	0.993	0.5	0.0	0.0	0.039	0.961	0.0	0.013	0.0	0.059	0.941	0.222
	0.05	0.026	0.0	0.242	0.758	0.108	0.029	0.0	0.212	0.788	0.138	0.056	0.0	0.245	0.755	0.227
	0.1	0.075	0.0	0.458	0.542	0.164	0.069	0.0	0.425	0.575	0.162	0.108	0.0	0.471	0.529	0.229
SB	0.01	0.007	0.0	0.191	0.809	0.037	0.01	0.0	0.233	0.767	0.044	0.008	0.0	0.196	0.804	0.042
	0.05	0.047	0.0	0.489	0.511	0.097	0.063	0.002	0.692	0.307	0.089	0.053	0.0	0.537	0.463	0.099
	0.1	0.102	0.0	0.744	0.256	0.137	0.128	0.024	0.924	0.051	0.113	0.1	0.0	0.744	0.255	0.134
AC	0.01	0.01	0.0	0.049	0.951	0.206	0.01	0.0	0.177	0.823	0.057	0.01	0.0	0.071	0.929	0.143
	0.05	0.048	0.0	0.206	0.794	0.232	0.051	0.0	0.557	0.443	0.091	0.042	0.0	0.223	0.777	0.188
	0.1	0.104	0.0	0.443	0.557	0.235	0.107	0.016	0.87	0.114	0.105	0.109	0.0	0.438	0.562	0.248
C	0.01	0.007	0.0	0.568	0.432	0.012	0.007	0.0	0.23	0.77	0.031	0.004	0.0	0.16	0.84	0.022
	0.05	0.053	0.005	0.928	0.067	0.051	0.032	0.0	0.547	0.453	0.058	0.032	0.002	0.489	0.51	0.061
	0.1	0.093	0.033	0.967	0.0	0.062	0.074	0.04	0.938	0.021	0.036	0.1	0.044	0.926	0.03	0.061
I	0.01	0.006	0.0	0.473	0.527	0.012	0.003	0.0	0.425	0.575	0.007	0.003	0.0	0.41	0.59	0.007
	0.05	0.043	0.0	0.689	0.311	0.062	0.037	0.0	0.664	0.336	0.056	0.026	0.0	0.661	0.339	0.039
	0.1	0.074	0.0	0.769	0.231	0.096	0.1	0.014	0.849	0.137	0.101	0.094	0.011	0.849	0.14	0.097
H	0.01	0.0	0.0	0.032	0.968	0.0	0.0	0.0	0.045	0.955	0.0	0.0	0.0	0.071	0.929	0.0
	0.05	0.045	0.0	0.271	0.729	0.167	0.052	0.0	0.477	0.523	0.108	0.026	0.0	0.361	0.639	0.071
	0.1	0.058	0.0	0.452	0.548	0.129	0.097	0.0	0.665	0.335	0.146	0.052	0.0	0.503	0.497	0.103
GC	0.01	0.01	0.0	0.077	0.923	0.13	0.011	0.0	0.077	0.923	0.143	0.01	0.0	0.064	0.936	0.156
	0.05	0.038	0.0	0.214	0.786	0.178	0.048	0.0	0.273	0.727	0.176	0.045	0.0	0.27	0.73	0.167
	0.1	0.079	0.0	0.422	0.578	0.187	0.093	0.0	0.488	0.512	0.191	0.087	0.0	0.453	0.547	0.192
IL	0.01	0.003	0.0	0.017	0.983	0.2	0.007	0.003	0.021	0.976	0.167	0.009	0.003	0.036	0.961	0.143
	0.05	0.039	0.007	0.276	0.717	0.118	0.034	0.005	0.144	0.851	0.202	0.036	0.005	0.178	0.816	0.173
	0.1	0.089	0.007	0.484	0.509	0.17	0.079	0.015	0.381	0.604	0.167	0.11	0.029	0.419	0.552	0.193

From the above we may conclude that for significance level $\epsilon \in \{0.01, 0.05, 0.1, 0.2\}$ on the experimental data:

- ICP, IREP-ICP(L), and IREP-ICP(G) are valid class set predictors; i.e. they comply with the theory of conformal prediction.
- ICP is more informationally efficient than IREP-ICP(G).
- IREP-ICP(L) is more informationally efficient than IREP-ICP(G). Its superiority grows with the size of the data.
- IREP-ICP(L) is comparable with ICP in terms of informational efficiency (i.e. there is no clear winner although IREP-ICP has more wins).

From the above we provide the following recommendations:

- ICP and IREP-ICP(L) can be used interchangeably for reliable prediction. However, if interpretability is need, IREP-ICP(L) has to be employed.

– IREP-ICP(G) can be used for relatively small data sets when the number of final rules is small. If this is not the case IREP-ICP(L) has to be preferred.

7 Conclusion

This paper used the Mondrian scheme to integrate decision rules and conformal prediction. The result is a new technique of conformal decision rules capable of providing a point prediction, an explanation, and confidence values for all possible predictions plus a prediction set for any test instance.

An analysis of the Mondrian integration scheme showed that the global approach for computing the nonconformity scores can cause the label imbalance problem. To address this problem we proposed a local approach. We experimentally compared both approaches using conformal decision rules and showed when they can be used.

References

1. Boström, H., Johansson, U.: Mondrian conformal regressors. In: Proceedings of the 9th Symposium on Conformal and Probabilistic Prediction with Applications, COPA 2020. Proceedings of Machine Learning Research, vol. 128, pp. 114–133. PMLR (2020)
2. Cohen, W.W.: Fast Effective Rule Induction. In: Proceedings of the Twelfth International Conference on Machine Learning, pp. 115–123. Morgan Kaufmann (1995)
3. Dua, D., Graff, C.: UCI machine learning repository (2017) http://archive.ics.uci.edu/ml
4. Furnkranz, J., Gamberger, D., Lavrac, N.: Foundations of Rule Learning. Springer, Berlin (2012). https://doi.org/10.1007/978-3-540-75197-7
5. Johansson, U., Linusson, H., Löfström, T., Boström, H.: Conformal prediction using decision trees. In: Proceedings of the 13th IEEE International Conference on Data Mining, pp. 330–339. IEEE Computer Society (2013)
6. Johansson, U., Linusson, H., Löfström, T., Boström, H.: Interpretable regression trees using conformal prediction. Expert Syst. Appl. **97**, 394–404 (2018)
7. Johansson, U., Sönströd, C., Löfström, T., Boström, H.: Rule extraction with guarantees from regression models. Pattern Recogn. **126**, 1–9 (2022)
8. Miller, T.: Explanation in artificial intelligence: Insights from the social sciences. J. Artif. Intell. **267**, 1–38 (2019)
9. Molnar, C.: Interpretable Machine learning: a guide for making black Box Models Explainable (2022)
10. Papadopoulos, H., Proedrou, K., Vovk, V., Gammerman, A.: Inductive confidence machines for regression. In: Elomaa, T., Mannila, H., Toivonen, H. (eds.) ECML 2002. LNCS (LNAI), vol. 2430, pp. 345–356. Springer, Heidelberg (2002). https://doi.org/10.1007/3-540-36755-1_29
11. van Prehn, J., Smirnov, E.N.: Region classification with decision trees. In: Proceedings of the 8th IEEE International Conference on Data Mining Workshops, pp. 53–59 (2008)

12. Shafer, G., Vovk, V.: A tutorial on conformal prediction. arXiv:0706.3188 [cs, stat], June 2007
13. Toccaceli, P.: Introduction to conformal predictors. Pattern Recogn. **124**, 108507 (2022)
14. Vovk, V., Gammerman, A., Shafer, G.: Algorithmic Learning in a Random World. Springer, New York (2005). https://doi.org/10.1007/b106715

Measuring the Burden of (Un)fairness Using Counterfactuals

Alejandro Kuratomi[1](✉), Evaggelia Pitoura[2](✉), Panagiotis Papapetrou[1](✉),
Tony Lindgren[1](✉), and Panayiotis Tsaparas[2](✉)

[1] Department of Computer and Systems Sciences, Stockholm University,
Borgarfjordsgatan 12, 16455 Kista, Sweden
{alejandro.kuratomi,panagiotis,tony}@dsv.su.se
[2] Department of Computer Science and Engineering, University of Ioannina,
45110 Ípeiros, Ioannina, Greece
{pitoura,tsap}@uoi.gr

Abstract. In this paper, we use counterfactual explanations to offer a
new perspective on fairness, that, besides accuracy, accounts also for the
difficulty or burden to achieve fairness. We first gather a set of fairness-
related datasets and implement a classifier to extract the set of false negative test instances to generate different counterfactual explanations on
them. We subsequently calculate two measures: the false negative ratio
of the set of test instances, and the distance (also called *burden*) from
these instances to their corresponding counterfactuals, aggregated by
sensitive feature groups. The first measure is an accuracy-based estimation of the classifier biases against sensitive groups, whilst the second is a
counterfactual-based assessment of the difficulty each of these groups has
of reaching their corresponding desired ground truth label. We promote
the idea that a counterfactual and an accuracy-based fairness measure
may assess fairness in a more holistic manner, whilst also providing interpretability. We then propose and evaluate, on these datasets, a measure
called Normalized Accuracy Weighted Burden, which is more consistent
than only its accuracy or its counterfactual components alone, considering both false negative ratios and counterfactual distance per sensitive
feature. We believe this measure would be more adequate to assess classifier fairness and promote the design of better performing algorithms.

Keywords: Algorithmic fairness · Counterfactual explanations · Bias

1 Introduction

Machine Learning (ML) models assist decision-making in different applications,
such as recommender systems [16,18], vehicle localization [7], student grading [6],
credit assessment [1], disease diagnoses [9] and recidivism prediction [3]. These
decisions should be taken impartially across sensitive features, such as religion,
gender, ethnicity and age [20,27]. In order to achieve fair outcomes, the ML
models must avoid making decisions based on these qualities. There are several

I. Koprinska et al. (Eds.): ECML PKDD 2022 Workshops, CCIS 1752, pp. 402–417, 2023.
https://doi.org/10.1007/978-3-031-23618-1_27

challenges in attaining these unbiased model decisions, and we hereby describe and focus on three of them, namely **fairness evaluation, interpretability** and **fairness accuracy trade-off**:

1. **Fairness evaluation:** The first challenge refers to the fact that the difficulty of defining a measure for model fairness assessment lies on its selection. While there exist at least 20 such measures [8,20], none of them is perfectly suitable for all situations. More importantly, Kusner et al. [8] argue that some measures might exacerbate the perceived discrimination, and may not eliminate the biases entirely even after optimizing for them [2].

2. **Interpretability:** The second challenge is knowing the models' features weighting. The increase in model complexity and capacity to represent highly nonlinear functions to achieve superior prediction performance has raised a new challenge, that of providing trustable model explanations to understand how different features are prioritized [5,14,21,22,26]. Given that highly complex and opaque models may focus on sensitive features to elaborate a decision (even when the sensitive features are omitted from the data due to correlations with other nonsensitive, proxy features [8,18,20]), it is important to obtain model explanations to understand whether this is occurring or not. A subfield of ML, called ML Interpretability, aims to provide these model explanations. Specifically, an interpretability technique known as Counterfactual Explanations (CE) answers the following question: *how should an instance change its feature values so as to switch a model's predicted label from an undesired to a desired label?* An analogous nontrivial problem to the fairness evaluation challenge exists for CE generation: there are several different CE algorithms, each minimizing a distinct cost function and producing fairly contrasting CEs [27].

3. **Fairness-accuracy trade-off:** The third challenge refers to the fact that altering the model to deter biases naturally found in the datasets, due to highly correlated sensitive features and labels, may reduce the models performance, leading to a fairness-accuracy trade-off [13,18,20].

In this paper, we address these challenges by combining two fairness measures: one accuracy-based and one counterfactual-based.

In particular, we assume that for each sensitive feature, there are at least two sensitive groups, e.g. the sensitive feature *Sex* has two sensitive groups *Male* and *Female*, and that we have a binary classification task. To measure accuracy, we use *predictive equality* [27], which states that the False Negative Ratio (*FNR*), i.e., the fraction of false negative predictions, should be the same across sensitive groups. Other accuracy-based fairness definitions, such as predictive parity, are left for future work.

The CE x' of an item x is a similar item to x for which the classifier produces an outcome different than the outcome of x. Let x be an item in a sensitive group that was falsely predicted to belong to the negative class. Intuitively, the distance between x and its counterfactual x' measures the amount of change that is needed to counteract unfairness in accuracy, that is, to correctly classify x in the positive class. We call *Burden* the average such distance for all items in the sensitive group that were falsely assigned to the negative class. In a sense, Burden captures the cost of achieving fairness.

The main advantages of counterfactual-based fairness are three-fold: first, it aligns with a fair treatment intuition, since the difficulty of achieving a desired output among sensitive groups should be similar [8]. This similar difficulty may be seen as a similar burden value among different groups; second, burden is calculated using a generated CE (x'), which inherently indicates the models features relevances, providing important information to tackle the models opacity; and third, it may provide both individual and group fairness assessment [23], while other metrics, like statistical parity and equalized odds, focus on group fairness.

Hence, the first contribution of this paper is a study between the FNR and the measure of burden, where the set of CEs are generated by minimizing different cost functions. The study uses 11 fairness-related, binary classification datasets from four different fields. We analyze the differences in burden among different CE methods and their relation to FNR. Moreover, the second contribution of the paper is a new measure, *Normalized Accuracy Weighted Burden* (NAWB), that assesses fairness holistically and may be used to optimize classifiers training and address the accuracy-fairness trade-off challenge.

2   Related Work

In this work, two areas converge: machine learning fairness and counterfactual explainability. From the perspective of machine learning fairness, different approaches have been taken to both measure and correct biases in different applications [18–20, 25, 29].

2.1   Fairness and Bias Measurement

To avoid model discrimination biases, the biases must be first detected [8]. Quy et al. compiled 15 datasets from different fields that are frequently used for fairness-related research in ML and use statistical parity, equalized odds and Absolute Between-ROC Area (ABROCA) to detect biases among a set of sensitive features in each dataset [20]. Machine learning models may amplify the users input biases according to common user preferences [25]. Zafar et al. relate the recommendation bias increase to stereotypical-based biases, and highlight the strong relation of false positive rates with sensitive groups in recidivism prediction biases against African Americans, and in less-paid jobs for women [29].

2.2   Counterfactual Explainability

Verma et al. propose a rubric to compare different CE generation algorithms, reviewing 39 papers where methods and metrics are discussed [27]. They highlight the existence of linear and mixed-integer programming CE methods, such as the Actionable Recourse algorithm by Ustun et al. [26], that provides action-ability (actionable decisions) with low computational demand, at the cost of using low-accuracy, linear classifiers.

Among the metrics discussed by Verma et al. are likelihood (the closeness of the CE to the data distribution) and sparsity (the number of changed features) [27]. Related to actionability is the property of feasibility, which considers the feature direction of change and the plausibility of the obtained feature values. Linked to sparsity is proximity, which is the inverse of the distance between the Instance of Interest (IOI) and its CE [12,26]. Finally, faithfulness may also be prioritized, as it indicates how likely (through likelihood) or justified [11] a CE is according to the data. Different algorithms prioritize different metrics.

The Nearest Neighbor Tweaking (NN) method selects the *closest* positive ground truth label instance in the training set to the IOI. The Minimum Observable (MO) method selects the closest counterfactual instance from the whole dataset (including the test instances with their predicted labels). These two methods minimize the euclidean distance function and preserve the plausibility of the feature values [12,28]. The Random Forest Tweaking (RT) method selects the *most frequent* counterfactual training instance inside the same leaves that the IOI falls in, in a Random Forest (RF) classifier, providing plausibility and faithfulness. The Counterfactual Conditional Heterogeneous Autoencoder (CCHVAE) CE method prioritizes likelihood, outputting counterfactual instances that are likely according to the data. The method uses a variational autoencoder and creates random perturbations in its latent space. These perturbations are brought to the original space and become the generated counterfactuals [17].

Other notable more complex methods exist. Model-Agnostic CE (MACE) [4] delivers best-in-class proximity performance but with the longest computational times; Growing Spheres (GS) [10] attempts to obtain close counterfactuals by growing spheres from the IOI; Diverse CE (DiCE) [15] allows users to obtain a set of CEs instead of a single one, where the set is chosen to provide diverse feature changes. Local Rule-based Explainability (LORE) is able to provide feature relevances and CEs through the training of a local rule generation model.

2.3   Counterfactual Fairness

At the intersection of these two areas lies counterfactual fairness: a characteristic of decision processes treating individuals equally in the as-is situation, and in a world where their sensitive features are different [8]. Currently, CEs provide insights on why a decision was taken and potential actionability, but cannot indicate whether these decisions are fair [13]. On the other hand, fairness measures lack the actionability and feature relevance that CEs ellicit.

Ustun et al. propose an interesting measure between the classifier model and the instances attributes, and use this to design a fair model. This measure uses the covariance between the sensitive features values and the distance between the subjects and the decision boundary. If this covariance is high, that means the distance between the instances and the decision boundary are highly related, indicating that the model may be biased according to those features [26]. This measure is however intended for linear classifiers and assumes a linear relation between classifiers and features. The authors also present an interesting evaluation of the relation between the cost of achieving a given counterfactual (cost of recourse) and split it by false and true negative prediction groups.

Coston et al. argue that traditional measures of fairness, like parity, may not necessarily lead to fairness in counterfactual scenarios. Therefore, they indicate that counterfactual reasoning must be implemented to measure fairness, and apply a set of methods to achieve fairness in a policy design framework [2]. Finally, Sharma et al. define the counterfactual-based fairness metric called burden, and indicate its usage for both individual and group fairness assessment. The authors use this metric as part of the fitness function in a genetic algorithm that generates counterfactuals [23].

3   Methodology

Given a dataset X, with labels $Y \in \{-, +\}$, $+$ being the desired, positive label, a classification function f, such that $f : X \to Y$ and a set of sensitive features S_i, $i \in \{1, 2, ..., M\}$, where M is the number of sensitive features, the accuracy-based metric of False Negative Ratio (FNR) per sensitive group is defined as follows:

$$\text{FNR}_s = P(f(x) = -|S = s, Y = +), \tag{1}$$

where FNR_s is the false negative ratio of the sensitive group s.

For the counterfactual-based measure, we first formally define the counterfactual search as [12,24]:

$$x^* = \underset{x'}{\arg\min}\, c(x, x')|f(x) = y \wedge f(x') = y' , \tag{2}$$

where $c(x, x')$ is a distance-based cost function, and y' is the opposite label to y. The counterfactual reasoning is mainly applied by analyzing whether it is equally *difficult* to change the model outcome, from an undesired label $f(x) = y = -$, to a desired predicted label $f(x') = y' = +$, among sensitive groups or individuals [23,26]. Hence, the counterfactual-based measure may be obtained by calculating the average cost function $c(x, x')$ with $x \in X^s$, where X^s is the set of instances belonging to the sensitive feature group s, and the counterfactuals found x' for each x. This measure is defined as *Burden* and is formulated as follows:

$$Burden_s = \frac{1}{|X^s|} \sum_{x_i \in X^s} c(x_i, x_i'), \tag{3}$$

where $Burden_s$ is the average value of the cost function $c(.)$, which may be defined as the euclidean distance, based on the concept defined by [23].

We propose and examine a combined measure based on $Burden_s$ and FNR_s that could potentially be used to design a fair and accurate classifier. The proposed measure is called the *Accuracy Weighted Burden* or AWB. To derive it, we define the set of false negative instances per sensitive group s as:

$X_{FN}^s = \{x \in X | f(x) = -, S = s, Y = +\}$ and multiply Burden$_s$ and FNR$_s$ as shown:

$$\text{AWB}_s = P(f(x) = - | S = s, Y = +) \frac{1}{|X_{FN}^s|} \sum_{x_i \in X_{FN}^s} d(x_i, x_i') \qquad (4)$$

$$\text{AWB}_s = \frac{|X_{FN}^s|}{|\{x \in X | S = s, Y = +\}|} \frac{1}{|X_{FN}^s|} \sum_{x_i \in X_{FN}^s} d(x_i, x_i') \qquad (5)$$

$$\text{AWB}_s = \frac{\sum\limits_{x_i \in X_{FN}^s} d(x_i, x_i')}{|\{x \in X | S = s, Y = +\}|} \qquad (6)$$

where x_i' represents the CE of the x_i instance, and function $d(.)$ is the euclidean distance or burden. If we plot Burden$_s$ versus FNR$_s$, and locate each sensitive group as a point in this plane, a point located in the upper-right corner would present a higher general bias than one located in the lower-left corner. The FNR$_s$ is the ratio of instances falsely classified as belonging to the negative class, whilst the Burden$_s$ measures how far the IOI is from an existing, desired counterfactual instance, per group. In this sense, a high FNR$_s$ and a high Burden$_s$ indicates a high number of difficult-to-correctly classify points for a given group and classifier f. This may be translated to the *area* of the box formed between the location of the dots and the origin. This area is calculated by multiplying these variables, leading to Eq. 6.

By normalizing each of the L features in the dataset inside the $[0,1]$ range, the range of values for $d(.)$ is $[0,L]$, so we divide Eq. 6 by L to obtain the *Normalized Accuracy Weighted Burden* or NAWB:

$$\text{NAWB}_s = \frac{\sum\limits_{i \in X_{FN}^s} d(x_i, x_i')}{L | \{x \in X | S = s, Y = +\}|} \qquad (7)$$

After defining the basic metrics, let us outline the steps of our methodology. In order to study classifier fairness, for each dataset and classification task, we test several classifiers and search for the model parameters that provide the best performance in each case (see Sect. 4). A single classifier (the one with the best F1 score) is used per dataset. We then execute a four-step process: (1) Calculate the FNR per sensitive group, (2) obtain CEs for the false negative instances using different CE methods (different ways and cost functions in solving Eq. 2, (3) estimate the aggregated Burden per sensitive group, per CE method, and (4) study the relation of Burden$_s$ and FNR$_s$ to provide a holistic view on the classifier fairness and evaluate AWB, our new combined measure.

The first step of the process is carried out using Eq. 1, where s is the sensitive group of a feature (Male, Female or White, Non-white, etc.). Ultimately, a fair classifier would have a similar FNR$_s$ among the different s values belonging to each S sensitive feature.

The second step is using NN, MO, RT and CCHVAE to generate the CEs. We concentrate on the four mentioned algorithms, as they represent a set of relevant objectives currently prioritized in CE algorithms, namely proximity, feasibility and faithfulness (through likelihood), whilst maintaining relatively low complexity and computational times. These methods are applied to the false negative instances (X_{FN}), i.e., obtaining a set of four CEs for each of them.

The third step is calculating the aggregated burden by sensitive feature $Burden_s$ using Eq. 3. A higher burden for a given group of subjects, in comparison to another, would mean that the individuals belonging to that group have a higher difficulty, in terms of the distance, to achieve the positive class, according to the model f.

In the fourth and final step, we discuss these metrics, presenting their evaluation on the fairness-related datasets. We analyze the FNR_s per dataset and evaluate the $Burden_s$ per dataset and CE method. We then relate both measures and study their correlation and finally examine the combined measure AWB_s and its normalized version $NAWB_s$.

4   Empirical Evaluation

We describe here the datasets based on [20] and discuss the obtained results. The datasets, their main sources, and codes are available at the GitHub[1].

4.1   Datasets

The datasets and relevant characteristics are shown in Table 1. Preprocessing is carried out according to [4, 20], reducing the number of features and instances by removing duplicates, missing values and low-importance features. Further details may be observed in the repository. The test group and true positive distributions are obtained after preprocessing.

4.2   Results and Discussion

In this section we show the classification performance, analyze the FNR_s per dataset, discuss the $Burden_s$ measure per dataset and CE method, and finally present and analyze an accuracy-counterfactual combined fairness measure.

Model Selection. We implemented four different types of classifiers and used grid search with 5-fold validation to identify the optimal parameters according to the F1 score. The implemented classifiers are Support Vector Machines (SVM), Decision Trees (DT), Multilayer Perceptrons (MLP) and Random Forests (RF). The RF classifier achieved the best performance for 5 out of the 11 datasets (shown in Table 2 along with the model parameters), while the MLP classifier

---

[1] https://github.com/alku7660/counterfactual-fairness.

Table 1. Datasets instances, features, labels and sensitive groups distributions

Dataset	Items (feat.)	Classes	Sensitive groups	Test group distribution	True positive distribution
Adult	48842 (15)	+:>50kUSD -:≤50kUSD	Male/Female White/Nonwhite <25/25–60/>60	9112/4455 11666/1901 2214/10500/853	2848/499 3032/315 31/3102/214
KDD census	299285 (41)	+:>50kUSD -:≤50kUSD	Male/Female White/Nonwhite	43193/46593 75268/14518	4374/1180 5052/502
German	1000 (21)	+:low risk -:high risk	Male/Female	208/92	55/28
Dutch	60420 (12)	+:low risk -:high risk	Male/Female	9090/9036	6024/3401
Bank	45211 (17)	+:deposits -:no deposit	Sing./Marr./Divor. <25/25–60/>60	3785/8171/1608 244/12939/381	574/849/196 68/1384/167
Credit	30000 (24)	+:no default -:defaults	Male/Female Marr./NotMarr. Oth./HS/Uni./Gra.	3547/5350 4131/4756 143/1435/4122/3187	854/1118 980/992 10/355/1006/601
Compas	7214 (52)	+:improved -:recidivist	Male/Female Caucasian/African	1276/308 619/965	624/209 379/454
Diabetes	101766 (50)	+:recovered -:readmitted	Male/Female	6326/7527	4743/5767
Student	395 (33)	+:high grade -:low grade	Male/Female <18/≥18	55/64 93/26	40/45 66/19
Oulad	32593 (12)	+:pass exam -:fail exam	Male/Female	5142/4303	2393/2061
Law	20798 (12)	+:pass bar -:fail bar	Male/Female White/Nonwhite	3426/2703 5148/981	3274/2557 4990/841

achieved the best performance for the other 6 datasets (shown in Table 3 along with the model parameters). We used the best classifier for each dataset.

FNR_s Evaluation. The dataset is split into 70% train and 30% test. The models are used to predict the label of positive ground truth test instances.

The FNR_s are shown in Fig. 1. In the Adult dataset, the highest FNR_s corresponds to the *< 25* age group. This indicates that younger adults are expected to earn less than those with longer careers and higher education, both correlated to age. Additionally, *Females* present a considerable unfavorable bias, relative to *Males*. *Non-whites* are unfavored, though not as *Females* and young people. A similar behavior is observed in the KDD Census dataset FNR_s with respect to the unfavored *Female* and *Non-white* groups.

An inverted bias behavior is observed in the German and Dutch datasets, where *Males* are more likely to be incorrectly classified with bad credit or low-level occupation, respectively, than *Females*. The FNR_s is double for *Males* in the German dataset (similar in the Oulad dataset), while it is close to 5 times in the Dutch dataset, compared to *Females*.

In the Bank and Credit datasets, all FNR_s are considerable. In the Bank dataset the *>60* age group has the lowest FNR_s (<1%), while in the Credit dataset the *Other* education group has the highest FNR_s (>80%).

Table 2. Datasets with RF as best classifier and F1 score

Dataset	Adult	KDD Census	Dutch	Bank	Student
F1	0.83	0.87	0.84	0.86	0.70
Max. depth	10	10	10	10	2
Min. samples/leaf	1	5	3	1	5
Min. samples/split	5	5	5	2	2
Num. trees	100	100	50	200	200

Table 3. Datasets with MLP as best classifier and F1 score

Dataset	Credit	German	Diabetes	Oulad	Law	Compas
F1	0.72	0.70	0.61	0.67	0.82	0.66
Activation	Tanh	ReLU	Logistic	Logistic	Tanh	Tanh
Hidden layers	(50, 1)	(100, 10)	(100, 2)	(100, 10)	(50, 1)	(100, 10)
Solver	Adam	SGD	SGD	SGD	Adam	Adam

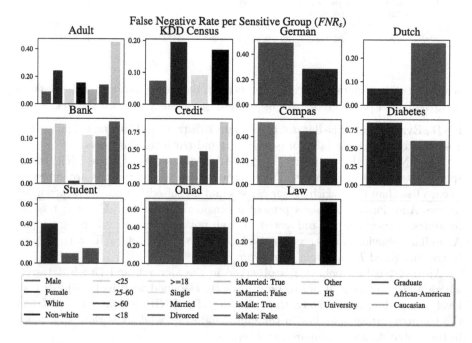

Fig. 1. FNR_s for each sensitive group

In the Compas dataset, the *African-Americans* and *Females* are more than twice as likely to be incorrectly classified as recidivist as *Caucasians* and *Males*, respectively. The Diabetes dataset shows the highest *Females* FNR_s caused by the low classifier performance. In the Student dataset, the highest FNR_s is observed in the *>=18* age group (>60%), in comparison with the lower FNR_s for the *Female*, *Male* and *< 18* groups with 40% or lower. Finally, in the Law dataset, all FNR_s are close to 20%, except for the *Non-white* group with 50%.

Burden$_s$Evaluation. Figure 2 present datasets in rows and CE methods in columns. In general, all datasets show a similar relative burden among sensitive groups for NN and MO methods, since they prioritize distance and pick the counterfactual from the pool of observations (MO's Burden$_s$ measure is lower because it also considers test instances). RT and CCHVAE present a relative different Burden$_s$ behavior in both magnitude and relative position among sensitive groups, since these two prioritize frequency and likelihood, respectively, over proximity. The CEs obtained through CCHVAE are particularly further from their respective IOIs because they are closer to the data distribution centers to maximize likelihood. Specifically, for the Adult dataset, in the age feature, we may see that *>60* has a high Burden$_s$, compared to *< 25* and *25–60*, specially in the NN, MO and RT methods. This could indicate a bias against older people who may have a higher difficulty of achieving a high income.

In the KDD Census dataset, the relative Burden$_s$ magnitude is the same for all methods: higher for *Females* than *Males* and higher for *Non-whites* than *Whites*. The KDD Census dataset presents a similar behavior in terms of relative burden with the Law dataset.

In the German dataset, the correlation of burden with FNR_s is inverted in CCHVAE, while NN, MO and RT preserve the same higher bias for *Males* than *Females*. In the Dutch dataset, Burden$_s$ is higher for *Females*, while the FNR_s ratio was higher for the *Males* (Fig. 1).

In the Bank dataset, there is a higher burden for the *< 25* and *Divorced* groups relative to their counterparts in the NN, MO and RT methods, however, it is the *>60* group that has a higher burden according to CCHVAE. These behaviors are contrasting with the FNR_s in the age groups, because the *>60* has a significantly lower FNR_s.

In the Credit dataset, the behavior among groups is similar to the FNR_s relative behavior in the NN, MO and RT methods. However, it drastically changes in the CCHVAE, where the burden is high and similar across groups.

In the Compas dataset note that the RT FNR_s shows a different relative magnitude: the *Males* and *African-Americans* FNR_s is higher, whilst the burden is higher for *Females* and *Caucasians*.

In the Diabetes dataset the FNR_s of *Females* is higher than that of *Males* (even though the data is balanced among genders) but Burden$_s$ shows a relative similar behavior for both *Females* and *Males*.

In the Student dataset, all methods showed a similar relative Burden$_s$ behavior, which is a strong contrast with the highly unfavored age group of *>18*

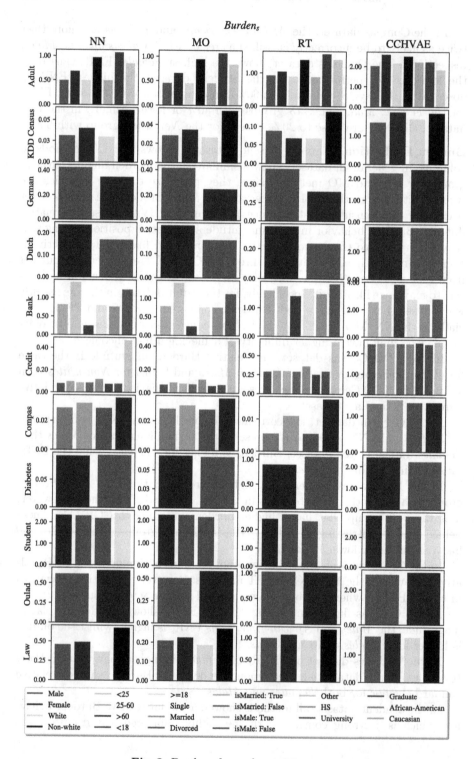

Fig. 2. Burden$_s$ for each sensitive group

according to FNR$_s$. Finally, in the Oulad dataset, *Females* present a slightly higher Burden$_s$ than *Males* in all methods except RT.

FNR$_s$ and Burden$_s$. The relation between FNR$_s$ and each CE method's Burden$_s$ is observed in Fig. 3 for some of the datasets. Each scatter plot shows the FNR$_s$ in the x-axis and Burden$_s$ in the y-axis. The dots represent the sensitive groups location in the $Burden - FNR$ plane. Each color indicates a sensitive feature and each dot has its group name. Positively correlated Burden$_s$ and FNR$_s$ measures show dots of the same color (belonging to the same feature) scattered across the positive diagonal, whilst a negative correlation shows these dots closer to the negative diagonal. For example, in the Diabetes dataset, *Male* and *Female* dots are located in the negative diagonal in NN, and RT, whilst in the positive one in MO and CCHVAE.

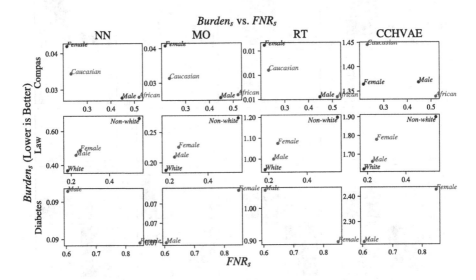

Fig. 3. False negative ratio (FNR$_s$) versus Burden (Burden$_s$)

A dot located in the upper-right corner of Fig. 3 has the highest area and therefore the highest general bias. This area measure is the *Accuracy Weighted Burden* or AWB, shown in Eq. 6. We then calculate its normalized version, NAWB$_s$, for all the datasets and models and show it in Fig. 4.

Normalized Accuracy Weighted Burden (NAWB). The NAWB$_s$ measure is not as sensitive to the CE method used, due to the FNR factor, however, the magnitude may still change significantly. This is observed throughout all the datasets. In the Adult dataset, *Females*, *Non-whites* and < 25 are the most unfavored in terms of bias, and the ordering of the age groups is the same across methods. This was not true for the Adult Burden$_s$ measure alone, in which (see

Normalized Accuracy Weighted Burden ($NAWB_s$) (%)

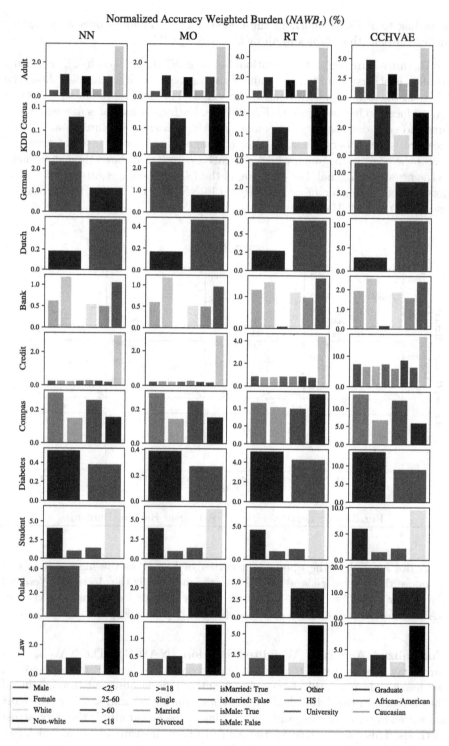

Fig. 4. Normalized Accuracy Weighted Burden (AWB) for each dataset and sensitive group

Fig. 2) the Burden$_s$ was higher for the >60 group. In the German dataset the NAWB$_s$ measure shows a higher bias against *Males* than *Females* than FNR$_s$ or Burden$_s$ alone indicating that the difficulty of each IOI to change its label brings an added level of bias against *Males* to the already higher ratio of false negatives in that group, compared to *Females*. This indicates that it is important to consider both metrics and in that way improve the overall perspective on the relative biases among groups. Additionally, the consistency between these relative measures is greatly improved. For example, the German and Dutch datasets Burden$_s$ measure showed a different behavior among groups, compared to the more holistic NAWB$_s$ measure. However, in terms of magnitude, the NAWB$_s$ measure indicates a higher value for the RT and CCHVAE methods, which is still justified by the objectives they prioritize, as mentioned before. This may indicate that, although relative NAWB$_s$ among the groups is more consistent across diverse CE methods, the magnitude is still dependent on the CE method. Further improvements may be done on normalization of the measures with respect to each sensitive feature, or across the features, for example, considering the NAWB$_s$ fraction over the sum of all NAWB$_s$ to make this metric less dependent on which CE method is applied.

5 Conclusions and Future Work

In this study, we performed an evaluation of four different CE methods to assess the burden on different sensitive groups due to a classifier model. The distance between the CEs and the instances are seen as a measure of fairness through counterfactual reasoning. We compared this measure with an accuracy-based fairness measure, the False Negative Ratio per sensitive group, and propose a combined product of these measures that attempts to more consistently measure the (un)fairness of classifiers. Hence, we proposed NAWB$_s$ as a normalized, accuracy and counterfactual-based measure to determine the existence of classifier bias, proving that it may enhance the evaluation of biases among sensitive groups. We assessed the difference among the groups burden identified by different CE methods, and that future work may deal with a further normalization process to make this measure independent of the CE method used.

Additionally future work should also consider other methods, such as MACE, GS, DiCE and LORE. Finally, an extension to multi-class tasks and the application of the combined measure in the design of a classifier may be done, in order to make a generalized system that optimizes for both fairness and accuracy.

References

1. Boer, N., Deutch, D., Frost, N., Milo, T.: Just in time: personal temporal insights for altering model decisions. In: 2019 IEEE 35th International Conference on Data Engineering (ICDE), pp. 1988–1991. IEEE (2019)

2. Coston, A., Mishler, A., Kennedy, E.H., Chouldechova, A.: Counterfactual risk assessments, evaluation, and fairness. In: Proceedings of the 2020 Conference on Fairness, Accountability, and Transparency, pp. 582–593. ACM, Barcelona Spain, January 2020. https://doi.org/10.1145/3351095.3372851

3. Dodge, J., Liao, Q.V., Zhang, Y., Bellamy, R.K., Dugan, C.: Explaining models: an empirical study of how explanations impact fairness judgment. In: Proceedings of the 24th International Conference on Intelligent User Interfaces, pp. 275–285 (2019)

4. Karimi, A.H., Barthe, G., Balle, B., Valera, I.: Model-agnostic counterfactual explanations for consequential decisions. In: International Conference on Artificial Intelligence and Statistics, pp. 895–905. PMLR (2020)

5. Karlsson, I., Rebane, J., Papapetrou, P., Gionis, A.: Locally and globally explainable time series tweaking. Knowl. Inf. Syst. **62**(5), 1671–1700 (2020)

6. Kearns, M., Neel, S., Roth, A., Wu, Z.S.: An empirical study of rich subgroup fairness for machine learning. In: Proceedings of the Conference on Fairness, Accountability, and Transparency, pp. 100–109 (2019)

7. Kuratomi, A., Lindgren, T., Papapetrou, P.: Prediction of global navigation satellite system positioning errors with guarantees. In: Dong, Y., Mladenić, D., Saunders, C. (eds.) ECML PKDD 2020. LNCS (LNAI), vol. 12460, pp. 562–578. Springer, Cham (2021). https://doi.org/10.1007/978-3-030-67667-4_34

8. Kusner, M.J., Loftus, J.R., Russell, C., Silva, R.: Counterfactual fairness. arXiv:1703.06856 [cs, stat], March 2018. http://arxiv.org/1703.06856

9. Kyrimi, E., Neves, M.R., McLachlan, S., Neil, M., Marsh, W., Fenton, N.: Medical idioms for clinical Bayesian network development. J. Biomed. Inform. **108**, 103495 (2020)

10. Laugel, T., Lesot, M.J., Marsala, C., Renard, X., Detyniecki, M.: Inverse classification for comparison-based interpretability in machine learning. arXiv preprint arXiv:1712.08443 (2017)

11. Laugel, T., Lesot, M.-J., Marsala, C., Renard, X., Detyniecki, M.: Unjustified classification regions and counterfactual explanations in machine learning. In: Brefeld, U., Fromont, E., Hotho, A., Knobbe, A., Maathuis, M., Robardet, C. (eds.) ECML PKDD 2019. LNCS (LNAI), vol. 11907, pp. 37–54. Springer, Cham (2020). https://doi.org/10.1007/978-3-030-46147-8_3

12. Lindgren, T., Papapetrou, P., Samsten, I., Asker, L.: Example-based feature tweaking using random forests. In: 2019 IEEE 20th International Conference on Information Reuse and Integration for Data Science (IRI), pp. 53–60. IEEE (2019)

13. Loi, M., Ferrario, A., Viganò, E.: Transparency as design publicity: explaining and justifying inscrutable algorithms. Ethics Inf. Technol. **23**(3), 253–263 (2021). https://doi.org/10.1007/s10676-020-09564-w

14. Molnar, C.: Interpretable machine learning: a guide for making black-box models explainable (2021). https://christophm.github.io/interpretable-ml-book/limo.html

15. Mothilal, R.K., Sharma, A., Tan, C.: Explaining machine learning classifiers through diverse counterfactual explanations. In: Proceedings of the 2020 Conference on Fairness, Accountability, and Transparency, pp. 607–617 (2020)

16. Nobrega, C., Marinho, L.: Towards explaining recommendations through local surrogate models. In: Proceedings of the 34th ACM/SIGAPP Symposium on Applied Computing. SAC 2019, pp. 1671–1678. Association for Computing Machinery, New York (2019). https://doi.org/10.1145/3297280.3297443

17. Pawelczyk, M., Broelemann, K., Kasneci, G.: Learning model-agnostic counterfactual explanations for tabular data. In: Proceedings of The Web Conference 2020, pp. 3126–3132 (2020)

18. Pitoura, E., Stefanidis, K., Koutrika, G.: Fairness in rankings and recommendations: an overview. VLDB J. (Oct2021)

19. Pitoura, E., et al.: On Measuring bias in online information. ACM SIGMOD Rec. **46**(4), 16–21 (2018)

20. Quy, T.L., Roy, A., Iosifidis, V., Zhang, W., Ntoutsi, E.: A survey on datasets for fairness-aware machine learning. arXiv:2110.00530 [cs] (Jan 2022). https://arxiv.org/abs/2110.00530

21. Ribeiro, M.T., Singh, S., Guestrin, C.: "Why should i trust you?" Explaining the predictions of any classifier. In: Proceedings of the 22nd ACM SIGKDD International Conference on Knowledge Discovery and Data Mining, pp. 1135–1144 (2016)

22. Rudin, C.: Stop explaining black box machine learning models for high stakes decisions and use interpretable models instead. Nat. Mach. Intell. **1**(5), 206–215 (2019)

23. Sharma, S., Henderson, J., Ghosh, J.: CERTIFAI: counterfactual explanations for robustness, transparency, interpretability, and fairness of artificial intelligence models. In: Proceedings of the AAAI/ACM Conference on AI, Ethics, and Society, pp. 166–172, Februay 2020. https://doi.org/10.1145/3375627.3375812, arXiv:1905.07857

24. Tolomei, G., Silvestri, F., Haines, A., Lalmas, M.: Interpretable predictions of tree-based ensembles via actionable feature tweaking. In: Proceedings of the 23rd ACM SIGKDD International Conference on Knowledge Discovery and Data Mining, pp. 465–474 (2017)

25. Tsintzou, V., Pitoura, E., Tsaparas, P.: Bias disparity in recommendation systems. arXiv:1811.01461 [cs], November 2018, https://arxiv.org/abs/1811.01461

26. Ustun, B., Spangher, A., Liu, Y.: Actionable recourse in linear classification. In: Proceedings of the Conference on Fairness, Accountability, and Transparency, pp. 10–19 (2019)

27. Verma, S., Dickerson, J., Hines, K.: Counterfactual explanations for machine learning: a review. arXiv:2010.10596 [cs, stat], October 2020. https://arxiv.org/abs/2010.10596

28. Wexler, J., Pushkarna, M., Bolukbasi, T., Wattenberg, M., Viégas, F., Wilson, J.: The what-if tool: interactive probing of machine learning models. IEEE Trans. Vis. Comput. Graph. **26**(1), 56–65 (2019)

29. Zafar, M.B., Valera, I., Rodriguez, M.G., Gummadi, K.P.: Fairness constraints: mechanisms for fair classification. arXiv:1507.05259 [cs, stat], March 2017. https://arxiv.org/abs/1507.05259

Are SHAP Values Biased Towards High-Entropy Features?

Raphael Baudeu[1] (ID), Marvin N. Wright[2,3,4] (ID), and Markus Loecher[5(✉)] (ID)

[1] University of Glasgow, Glasgow, UK
[2] Leibniz Institute for Prevention Research and Epidemiology - BIPS, Bremen, Germany
[3] Faculty of Mathematics and Computer Science, University of Bremen, Bremen, Germany
[4] Department of Public Health, University of Copenhagen, Copenhagen, Denmark
[5] Berlin School of Economics and Law, Berlin, Germany
markus.loecher@hwr-berlin.de

Abstract. In this paper, we examine the bias towards high-entropy features exhibited by SHAP values on tree-based structures such as classification and regression trees, random forests or gradient boosted trees. Previous work has shown that many feature importance measures for tree-based models assign higher values to high-entropy features, i.e. with high cardinality or balanced categories, and that this bias also applies to SHAP values. However, it is unclear if this bias is a major problem in practice or merely a statistical artifact with little impact on real data analyses. In this paper, we show that the severity of the bias strongly depends on the signal to noise ratio (SNR) in the dataset and on adequate hyperparameter tuning. In high-SNR settings, the bias is still present but is unlikely to affect feature rankings and thus can be safely ignored in many real data applications. On the other hand, in low-SNR settings, a feature without ground-truth effect but with high entropy could be ranked higher than a feature with ground-truth effect but low entropy. Here, we show that careful hyperparameter tuning can remove the bias.

1 Introduction

With the rising popularity of machine learning also came a growing need to understand prediction models through interpretability methods. These methods can have differing aims ranging from visualising the workings of the black-box model to feature importance measures to understand which features are the most important to the model or to some underlying relationship. One such interpretability method is SHAP (SHapley Additive exPlanations) [1]. SHAP values are based on Shapley values [2], a method from game theory that was first introduced to machine learning applications by Štrumbelj & Kononenko [3]. Lundberg & Lee [1] later introduced SHAP as the only additive feature attribution method satisfying the properties of local accuracy, missingness and consistency. Lundberg et al. [4] introduced a new method for efficiently calculating SHAP values for tree based structures (TreeSHAP).

© The Author(s), under exclusive license to Springer Nature Switzerland AG 2023
I. Koprinska et al. (Eds.): ECML PKDD 2022 Workshops, CCIS 1752, pp. 418–433, 2023.
https://doi.org/10.1007/978-3-031-23618-1_28

Several feature importance methods for tree-based methods have been shown to have a bias towards high-entropy features, i.e., numerical features with many unique values, categorical features with high cardinality or balanced category frequencies. This phenomenon was already shown by Breiman et al. [5] for classification and regression trees and later made popular for model-specific random forest feature importance [6–9]. Loecher [10,11] and Adler & Painsky [12] have shown that the same kind of bias is rooted deeper in the underlying tree structure and is thus not exclusive to random forests and its model-specific feature importance measures but rather extends to SHAP values for random forests and also to other tree-based prediction methods such as gradient boosted trees.

In this paper, we show that the bias observed for SHAP values is only a problem when the signal to noise ratio (SNR) in the dataset is very low. The bias becomes less important the higher the SNR and, while it is still present, hardly matters in practice in settings with high SNR. We do this by performing simulation studies on datasets with different levels of SNR. We also use two real-world datasets with different levels of SNR to show the impact of SNR on the bias. We further show that proper hyperparameter tuning can remove the bias in SHAP values.

2   Simulation Study

To investigate whether SHAP values exhibit a bias towards high-entropy features for tree-based models we conducted a simulation study. We used a data generating process (DGP), which consists in first generating four categorical explanatory variables (features) X_1, X_2, X_3, X_4 with 2,4,10 and 20 categories [6] and one continuous explanatory variable $X_5 \sim \mathcal{N}(0, 1)$, respectively. Let X be the $n \times 5$ matrix of explanatory variables. We used a sample size of n = 100 throughout Sect. 2. All categorical variables were multinomially distributed with equal probabilities for each category. The categories were $1, .., n_c$ where n_c corresponds to the number of categories of the variable in question. The explanatory variables were simulated independently of each other. We used an outcome variable $O = f(X) + \epsilon = X \cdot \beta + \epsilon$, where β is a 1×5 vector and $\epsilon \sim \mathcal{N}(0, \sigma^2)$ with variance σ^2 selected such that we attain a pre-specified signal to noise ratio (SNR) which we define as SNR $= Var(f(X))/\sigma^2$.

Since we have an output O that is linear in $X_1, ..., X_5$ we can calculate ground-truth SHAP values. First, for SNR = 0, we set $\beta = 0$, which is analogous to the no-effect case in [6]. Second, we set β to $(1, 0, 0, 0, 0)^T$ so that only the first variable has an effect on the outcome O. With $Var(x_1) = 0.25$: SNR $= Var(\beta_1 \cdot x_1)/\sigma^2 = \beta_1^2 \cdot 0.25/\sigma^2$

For each of the generated datasets, we fitted a random forest (R package *ranger*) and gradient boosted trees (R package *xgboost*). We then calculated SHAP values with TreeSHAP (R package *treeshap*) and KernelSHAP (R package *shapr*). We ran the same data-generating process 100 times, computing SHAP values for every observation at each repetition. Further, we calculated the SHAP variable importance by calculating the mean absolute SHAP values over the instances in the dataset [13].

Figure 1 shows the results for the no-effect case (SNR=0). As we can see, SHAP importance values exhibit a very similar behavior to uncorrected impurity importance in Strobl et al. [6], where the importance of the first continuous variable X_1 is the highest and the categorical variables are more important the more categories they have. We see the same behavior with random forests and xgboost and both with KernelSHAP and TreeSHAP.

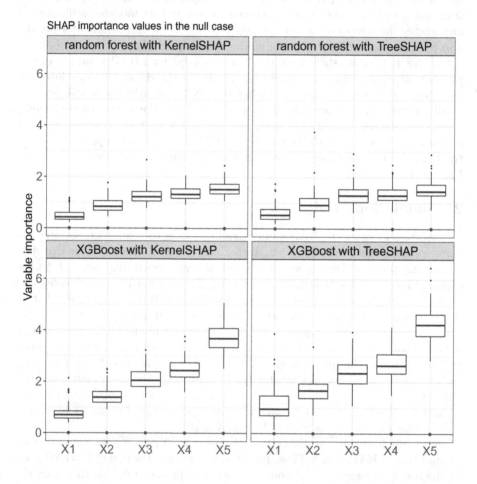

Fig. 1. Boxplots of SHAP variable importance for the no-effect case with SNR=0 with random forest and xgboost, KernelSHAP and TreeSHAP. The red dots correspond to the ground-truth SHAP values from the data-generating linear model, the red line is at 0. (Color figure online)

Figure 2 shows the result for the effect case with $\beta = (1, 0, 0, 0, 0)^T$ and increasing SNR. We see that for very low SNR (SNR = 0.01), X_1 receives the lowest variable importance on average, even though it is the only feature with a true effect. For a higher SNR (SNR = 0.1), the bias is still visible but X_1 can be clearly distinguished from $X_2, ..., X_5$. For a high SNR (SNR = 1), the bias is almost negligible. In the replicates of the experiment with SNR = 1 the SHAP importance value for X_1 was always the highest SHAP value out of the five variables.

Figure 10 (Appendix) shows boxplots of SHAP importance values for a neural network trained on the same data. The results confirm the fact that the bias is inherent to tree-based structures and is not necessarily exhibited by other methods.

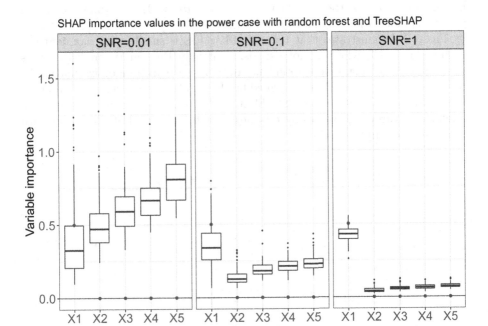

Fig. 2. Boxplots of SHAP variable importance for the effect case with $\beta = (1, 0, 0, 0, 0)^T$ and SNR set to 0.01, 0.1 and 1, with random forest and TreeSHAP. The red dots correspond to the ground-truth SHAP values from the data-generating linear model, the red line is at 0. Similar plots for xgboost and KernelSHAP can be found in the Appendix. (Color figure online)

3   Effect of Model Tuning

We are interested in the effect of optimally tuning Random Forests on the observed bias in SHAP importance values. In this section, we present results from a grid search aimed at finding those values for `max_depth` and `mtry`, which minimize the log loss or MSE on a hold-out set. Both for synthetic and real data sets (see Sect. 4) we find that the observed bias is inevitably due to a sub-optimally tuned model.

We follow the same procedure as in Sect. 2, but omit the often studied *null case* ($\beta_1 = 0$) since clearly the optimal model would just be a mean prediction. Instead we focus on the so-called *power case* ($\beta_1 > 0$) and tune the model parameters for various signal to noise ratios.

Figure 3 demonstrates that the out-of-bag loss is smallest for `max_depth` = 1 and `mtry` = 5, which is not surprising: if only the binary predictor x_1 is informative, the best model would be a stump with no randomization in the columns (`mtry` = 5) which is confirmed by the graphs. In this light, the observed bias in the simulated data by Strobl et al. [6] could be viewed simply as an artefact of "throwing" an overly complex, non-tuned model at a data set with an extremely simple structure.

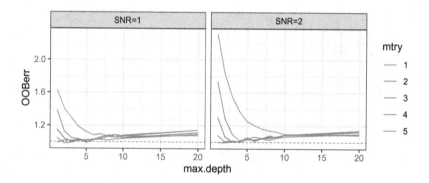

Fig. 3. Simulated data ($n = 1000$): Out-of-bag (OOB) error as a function of `max_depth` and `mtry` for SNR = 1,2 respectively. The optimal RF parameters are seen to be $max\_depth = 1$ and $mtry = 5$, consistent with the obvious fact that a tree stump would be the ideal model. The Bayes error (= 1) is added as a brown dashed horizontal line.

A similar story emerges from the effect of model tuning on SHAP values as illustrated in Fig. 4: the (global) SHAP values for the non-informative features show the familiar biased pattern - the dependence on feature cardinality $x_5 > x_4 > x_3 > x_2 > x_1$ as well as the overall increase with `max_depth`. But strikingly, for `max_depth` = 1 and `mtry` = 5, the bias completely disappears and the only non-zero SHAP scores arises for x_1. The expected/true SHAP value shown in Fig. 4 can be computed as follows: The overall expected value of y is

$$E(y) = \beta_1 E(x_1) = 1.5 \cdot \beta_1 = 1.5 \cdot \sqrt{\text{SNR}}/0.5 = 3 \cdot \sqrt{\text{SNR}}.$$

Hence

$$\phi_1 = \pm\sqrt{\text{SNR}} \Rightarrow |\phi_1| = \sqrt{\text{SNR}},$$

since $\beta_1 x_1$ takes on the values $2\sqrt{\text{SNR}}$ and $4\sqrt{\text{SNR}}$, respectively.

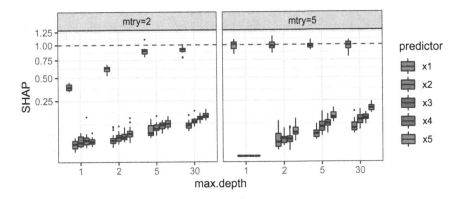

Fig. 4. Simulated data ($n = 200$): Global SHAP distributions (100 repeated simulations) as a function of max_depth for mtry $= 2,5$ respectively (SNR $= 1$). At max_depth $= 1$ and mtry $= 5$ (rightmost panel), the SHAP scores seem entirely unbiased: zero for non-informative features and centered around the expected/true SHAP value for x_1 which is added as a red dashed horizontal line. Note the square-root y-scale which greatly amplifies the small SHAP values for the non informative predictors.

We repeated these simulations for a sequence of decreasing SNRs and noticed marked deviation from this unbiasedness only for very low values of SNR< 0.08. In comparison, even a linear model fails to reliably identify the estimated slope β_1 as significantly different from zero for values of SNR< 0.05. So again, we conclude from this subsection that the well publicised bias seems to be of concern only in low SNR situations with poorly tuned models.

4 Real Data Analysis

The cervical cancer data set contains indicators and risk factors for predicting whether a woman will get cervical cancer. The features include demographic data (such as age), lifestyle, and medical history. The data can be downloaded from the UCI Machine Learning repository and was used in [13] to illustrate the utility of SHAP values to yield feature importance rankings, as illustrated in Fig. 11 in the Appendix. As there appears to be a general consensus/expectation that random forests rarely overfit [14–16] it is frequently common practice to accept its default parameters and not spend more resources in tuning the model, which is the case for the results in Fig. 11. On closer inspection though, these feature attributions may reflect a fair degree of overfitting: Fig. 5 suggests that the optimal model is simply the baseline mean prediction and that more complex ones fare worse on validation data. We speculate that this unexpected result is due to the extreme imbalance of the outcome ($\hat{y} = 0.94$).

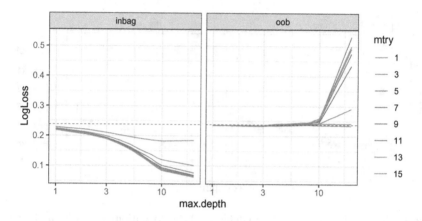

Fig. 5. Cervical cancer data: Inbag versus out-of-bag (oob) loss as a function of the two main tuning parameters of random forests. Somewhat surprisingly, the validation loss is highly insensitive to the exact choices of max-depth and mtry and is in fact minimized by the lowest complexity model, tree stumps. The baseline (mean predictions) log loss is overlaid as a dashed brown line. (Color figure online)

To study how the bias affects SHAP values on real data, we added permuted versions of the original features, fitted random forests with default parameters and calculated TreeSHAP variable importance values. We applied this procedure to the cervical cancer (see above) and Boston housing data sets. The Boston housing dataset contains various measures related to housing for the census tracts of Boston recorded in the 1970 census. The dataset was first published in Harrison et al. [17] Fig. 6 shows the results on both data sets: For the cervical cancer data, half of the top ten features are permuted ones, the two top permuted features are the ones with highest cardinality (age and hormonal contraceptives years) and for some features the permuted version even ranks higher than the original (e.g. age). Thus, the top ten feature selection appears to be mostly random, with a tendency to rank high-cardinality features high. On the other hand, on the boston housing data, all top ten features are original features. These results confirm our findings from the simulation studies: The bias towards high-cardinality features is notable in low-SNR settings (cervical cancer) but does not affect high-SNR settings (boston housing) much.

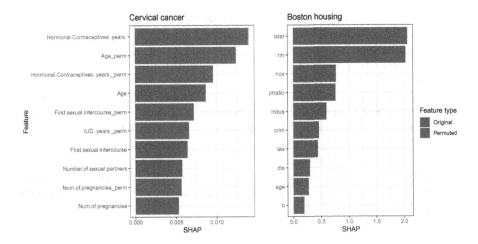

Fig. 6. SHAP variable importance (top 10) for the cervical cancer and boston housing data sets with original and permuted features. Permuted features are permuted versions of the original features in the data.

5 Related Work

Strobl et al. [6] showed that variables with more categories have a higher Gini importance. Permutation importance was also shown to be unbiased but variables with more categories have higher variance which leads to higher false positive rates for global importance measures. The authors argued that the bias is inherent to the tree structure. Many solutions have been proposed to address this bias, often by modifying the tree-building algorithm: Strobl et al. [6] suggest using conditional inference trees or forests [18] and sub-sampling without replacement to solve the problem. Wright et al. [8] make use of maximally selected rank statistics to avoid the bias, whereas Loh & Shih [19] use ANOVA F-statistics.

Loecher [20] showed that SHAP values exhibit the bias just like Gini and permutation importance in the null and power case for random forests. Adler & Painsky [12] extended the result by showing that gradient boosting machines exhibit the same bias in importance measures for Gini, permutation and SHAP importance. SHAP is originally a local measure of variable importance. To use SHAP as a global importance measure we are forced to first calculate SHAP values for each individual observation before taking the mean of the absolute value of SHAP values for each variable across observations [13]. An alternative method to calculate global SHAP values is SAGE [21], which estimates Shapley values for each variable to explain the reduction in the risk function induced by adding this variable to a coalition of variables instead of explaining each model prediction individually. Sutera et al. [22] shows that SAGE applied to tree-based models is very similar to the Gini importance. Further methods to calculate global SHAP values have been proposed [23–25]. However, as argued above the bias is due to the underlying tree-structure and thus, all of these methods inherit it, as long as the tree-building algorithm is unchanged.

Through comprehensive experiments, Yasodhara et al. [26] evaluate both the accuracy and stability of estimated global feature importance scores such as SHAP and Gini and report disappointingly low correlations with the true feature rankings even in the absence of added noise. When inputs or models are perturbed, the correlations drop even lower. The authors did not investigate the influence of uninformative variables of varying cardinality. The stability of local explainability methods has been studied by Alvarez et al. [27] who show that LIME [28] and (Kernel) SHAP [1] lack stability for complex black-box models. Perhaps the most interesting take-away from these studies is the possible coexistence of stable predictions with fragile explanations that change drastically in response to the perturbations.

6   Discussion

SHAP variable importance measures show a bias when trying to infer an inherent relationship in the data similar to the bias observed by Strobl et al. [6]. The bias towards high-entropy variables, i.e. variables with more categories and continuous variables, is present not just for random forests, but also for trees and XGBoost trees, suggesting that this bias is due to the tree structure itself, as was put forward in [6]. We showed that SHAP variable importance inherits this bias but that the signal to noise ratio (SNR) plays an important role: In low-SNR settings, the bias is evident, up to the point where a variable with many categories and no effect on the outcome can have a higher SHAP importance value than a variable with few categories but an effect on the outcome. On the other hand, in high-SNR settings, the bias is still there but its magnitude is vanishingly small, compared to true effects and thus of no major concern for the practitioner.

The real world examples show the importance of SNR to determining the importance of the bias. On the cervical cancer dataset with low SNR, some of the variables with the highest SHAP values were permuted copies with high cardinality. On the Boston housing dataset with high SNR, the permuted features were not in the top ten most important features by SHAP importance. We also showed that in the power case, careful tuning of the hyperparameters of a random forest can effectively eliminate the bias. Picking the mtry and maximum tree depth combination with the lowest validation error, we end up with mtry=5 and max_depth=1. If we let the model have a maximum depth of 1 and let it choose between all five variables at each split, the bias disappears.

It is important to note that the bias studied in this paper can only be considered a bias when we use variable importance measures to infer which variable is important for some underlying relationship in the data [29]. If we are instead interested in understanding the tree-based model itself, than this "bias" in fact corresponds to a true effect, as the tree-based structure does in fact use variables with more categories more often and closer to the top of trees than variables with fewer categories. This leads to an important distinction between biases: A variable importance measure can be biased for identifying which variable is important in determining the true outcome and it can also be biased for identifying which variable is important in determining the predicted outcome, i.e. the model output. If the model to be explained is not a perfect rendition of the underlying relationship in the data, then any variable importance measure will exhibit one of these biases. Thus, when using a variable importance measure one should always consider what the measure should explain, the model output or the real-world outcome (Fig. 7).

In conclusion, recommend practitioners to consider the bias towards high-entropy features when interpreting SHAP-based variable importance. If low prediction performance on validation data indicates a low signal to noise ratio, the bias can affect feature rankings and careful hyperparameter tuning is particularly important. A strategy to detect the impact of the bias in sensitivity analyses could be to add permuted feature copies as *fake* feature to the data. One step further, one could also apply a correction method, as e.g. proposed by Nembrini et al. [9].

Funding Information. MNW received funding for this project from the German Research Foundation (DFG), Emmy Noether Grant 437611051.

A   Appendix

Figures 7, 8, 9, 10 and 11 provide more results and additional details on the simulations as well as the cervical cancer data.

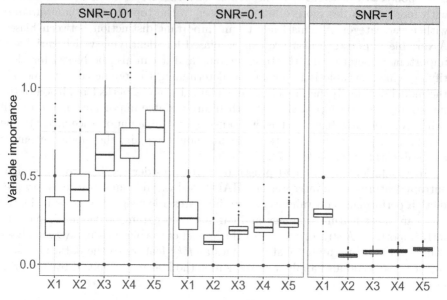

Fig. 7. Boxplots of SHAP variable importance for the effect case with $\beta = (1, 0, 0, 0, 0)^T$ and SNR set to 0.01, 0.1 and 1, with random forest and KernelSHAP. The red dots correspond to the ground-truth SHAP values from the data-generating linear model, the red line is at 0. (Color figure online)

SHAP importance values in the power case with XGBoost and TreeSHAP

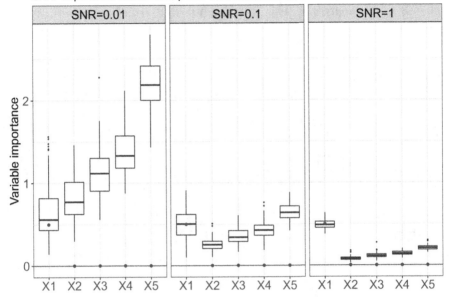

Fig. 8. Boxplots of SHAP variable importance for the effect case with $\beta = (1,0,0,0,0)^T$ and SNR set to 0.01, 0.1 and 1, with XGBoost and TreeSHAP. The red dots correspond to the ground-truth SHAP values from the data-generating linear model, the red line is at 0. (Color figure online)

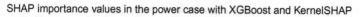

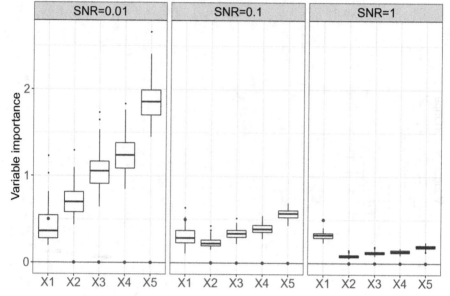

Fig. 9. Boxplots of SHAP variable importance for the effect case with $\beta = (1, 0, 0, 0, 0)^T$ and SNR set to 0.01, 0.1 and 1, with XGBoost and KernelSHAP. The red dots correspond to the ground-truth SHAP values from the data-generating linear model, the red line is at 0. (Color figure online)

SHAP importance values for each variable in a two-layer neural network

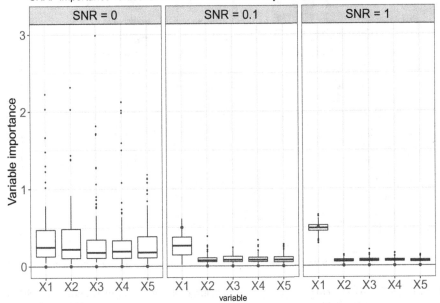

Fig. 10. Boxplots of SHAP variable importance for a neural network with two layers of 64 units with relu activation, Adam optimization and a linear output layer. The first plot is for the no effect case and the second and third plots are for the effect case with $\beta = (1,0,0,0,0)^T$ and SNR set to 0.1 and 1. The red dots correspond to the ground-truth SHAP values from the data-generating linear model, the red line is at 0 (Color figure online)

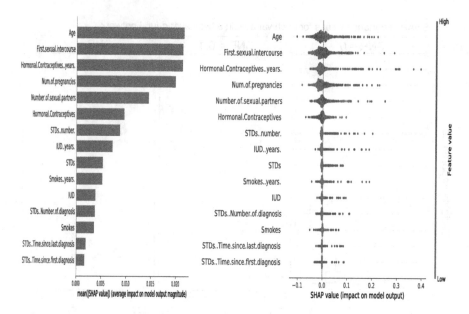

Fig. 11. left: SHAP feature importance measured as the mean of the absolute SHAP values. **right**: SHAP "beeswarm" plot showing the distributions of SHAP values per feature color coded by the sign and magnitude of the corresponding feature value. Low number of years on hormonal contraceptives reduce the predicted cancer risk, a large number of years increases the risk. (Random Forest with default parameter settings, ntree = 100) (Color figure online)

References

1. Lundberg, S.M., Lee, S-I.: A unified approach to interpreting model predictions. In: Advances in Neural Information Processing Systems (2017)
2. Shapley, L.S.: A Value for N-Person Games, pp. 307–318. Princeton University Press (2016). https://doi.org/10.1515/9781400881970-018
3. Štrumbelj, E., Kononenko, I.: Explaining prediction models and individual predictions with feature contributions. Knowl. Inf. Syst. **41**(3), 647–665 (2014)
4. Lundberg, S.M., Erion, G.G., Lee, S-I.: Consistent individualized feature attribution for tree ensembles. arXiv preprint arXiv:1802.03888 (2018)
5. Leo, B., Friedman, J.H., Olshen, R.A., Stone, C.J.: Classification and Regression Trees. CRC Press, Boca Raton (1984)
6. Strobl, C., Boulesteix, A.-L., Zeileis, A., Hothorn, T.: Bias in random forest variable importance measures: illustrations, sources and a solution. BMC Bioinf. **8**(1), 1–21 (2007)
7. Boulesteix, A.L., Bender, A., Lorenzo Bermejo, J., Strobl, C.: Random forest GINI importance favours snps with large minor allele frequency: impact, sources and recommendations. Briefings Bioinf. **13**(3), 292–304 (2012)
8. Wright, M.N., Dankowski, T., Ziegler, A.: Unbiased split variable selection for random survival forests using maximally selected rank statistics. Stat. Med. **36**(8), 1272–1284 (2017)

9. Nembrini, S., König, I.R., Wright, M.N.: The revival of the GINI importance? Bioinformatics **34**(21), 3711–3718 (2018)
10. Loecher, M.: From unbiased mdi feature importance to explainable AI for trees. arXiv preprint arXiv:2003.12043 (2020)
11. Loecher, M.: Debiasing MDI feature importance and SHAP values in tree ensembles. In: Holzinger, A., Kieseberg, P., Tjoa, A.M., Weippl, E. (eds.) Machine Learning and Knowledge Extraction. CD-MAKE 2022. Lecture Notes in Computer Science, vol. 13480, pp. 114–129. Springer, Cham (2022). https://doi.org/10.1007/978-3-031-14463-9_8
12. Adler, A.I., Painsky, A.: Feature importance in gradient boosting trees with cross-validation feature selection. Entropy **24**(5), 687 (2022)
13. Molnar, C.: Interpretable machine learning (2019)
14. Breiman, L.: Random forests. Mach. Learn. **45**(1), 5–32 (2001)
15. Probst, P., Wright, M.N., Boulesteix, A.L.: Hyperparameters and tuning strategies for random forest. Wiley Interdisc. Rev. Data Min. Knowl. Disc. **9**(3), e1301 (2019)
16. Probst, P., Boulesteix, A.-L., Bischl, B.: Tunability: importance of hyperparameters of machine learning algorithms. J. Mach. Learn. Res. **20**(1), 1934–1965 (2019)
17. Harrison, D., Rubinfeld, D.: Hedonic housing prices and the demand for clean air. J. Environ. Econ. Manage. **5**, 81–102 (1978)
18. Hothorn, T., Hornik, K., Zeileis, A.: Unbiased recursive partitioning: a conditional inference framework. J. Comput. Graph. Stat. **15**(3), 651–674 (2006)
19. Loh, W.-Y., Shih, Y.: Split selection methods for classification trees. Stat. Sinica **7**, 07 (1999)
20. Loecher, M.: Unbiased variable importance for random forests. Commun. Stat. Theor. Methods **51**(5), 1–13 (2020)
21. Covert, I., Lundberg, S.M., Lee, S-I.: In: Advances in Neural Information Processing Systems (2020)
22. Sutera, A., Louppe, G., Huynh-Thu, V.A., Wehenkel, L., Geurts, P.: From global to local mdi variable importances for random forests and when they are shapley values. Adv. Neural Inf. Process. Syst. **34**, 3533–3543 (2021)
23. Casalicchio, G., Molnar, C., Bischl, B.: Visualizing the feature importance for black box models. In: Berlingerio, M., Bonchi, F., Gärtner, T., Hurley, N., Ifrim, G. (eds.) ECML PKDD 2018. LNCS (LNAI), vol. 11051, pp. 655–670. Springer, Cham (2019). https://doi.org/10.1007/978-3-030-10925-7_40
24. Frye, C., Rowat, C., Feige, I.: Asymmetric Shapley values: incorporating causal knowledge into model-agnostic explainability. Adv. Neural Inf. Process. Syst. **33**, 1229–1239 (2020)
25. Williamson, B., Feng, J.: Efficient nonparametric statistical inference on population feature importance using Shapley values. In: International Conference on Machine Learning, pp. 10282–10291. PMLR (2020)
26. Yasodhara, A., Asgarian, A., Huang, D., Sobhani, P.: On the trustworthiness of tree ensemble explainability methods. In: Holzinger, A., Kieseberg, P., Tjoa, A.M., Weippl, E. (eds.) CD-MAKE 2021. LNCS, vol. 12844, pp. 293–308. Springer, Cham (2021). https://doi.org/10.1007/978-3-030-84060-0_19
27. Alvarez-Melis, D., Jaakkola, T.S.: On the robustness of interpretability methods. arXiv preprint arXiv:1806.08049 (2018)
28. Ribeiro, M.T., Singh, S., Guestrin, C.: Why should i trust you? explaining the predictions of any classifier. In: Proceedings of the 22nd ACM SIGKDD International Conference on Knowledge Discovery and Data Mining, pp. 1135–1144 (2016)
29. Chen, H., Janizek, J.D., Lundberg, S., Lee, S-I.: True to the model or true to the data? arXiv preprint arXiv:2006.16234 (2020)

Simple Explanations to Summarise Subgroup Discovery Outcomes: A Case Study Concerning Patient Phenotyping

Enrique Valero-Leal[1,2] , Manuel Campos[2,3] , and Jose M. Juarez[2(✉)]

[1] Technical University of Madrid, Madrid, Spain
[2] AIKE Group (INTICO), University of Murcia, Murcia, Spain
jmjuarez@um.es
[3] Murcian Bio-Health Institute (IMIB-Arrixaca), Murcia, Spain

Abstract. Phenotyping is essential in medical research, as it provides a better understanding of healthcare problems owing to the fact that clinical phenotypes identify subsets of patients with common characteristics. Subgroup discovery (SD) appears to be a promising machine learning approach because it provides a framework with which to search for interesting subgroups according to the relations between the individual characteristics and a target value. Each single pattern extracted by SD algorithms is human-readable. However, its complexity (the number of attributes involved) and the high number of subgroups obtained make the overall model difficult to understand. In this work, we propose a method with which to explain SD, designed for the clinical context. We have employed a two-step process in order to obtain SD model-agnostic explanations based on a decision tree surrogate model. The complexity involved in evaluating explainable methods led us to adopt a multiple strategy. We first show how explanations are built, and test a selection of state-of-the-art SD algorithms and gold-standard datasets. We then illustrate the suitability of the method in a clinical use case for an antimicrobial resistance problem. Finally, we study the utility of the method by surveying a small group in order to validate it from a human-centric perspective.

Keywords: Explainable artificial intelligence · Subgroup discovery · Biomedical informatics

1 Introduction

Although explainability is a term that predates this century, there is now an increasing interest in explainable artificial intelligence (XAI). Much of the work in this field revolves around classification and Deep Learning techniques, while some areas - such as unsupervised and semi-supervised learning - are barely explored.

This is the case of subgroup discovery (SD) [15, 36], a family of descriptive induction algorithms that find subgroups of interesting members of a particular

© The Author(s), under exclusive license to Springer Nature Switzerland AG 2023
I. Koprinska et al. (Eds.): ECML PKDD 2022 Workshops, CCIS 1752, pp. 434–451, 2023.
https://doi.org/10.1007/978-3-031-23618-1_29

population with regard to a certain characteristic (target attribute). SD techniques are, in practice, particularly helpful in biomedical science for the purpose of patient phenotyping, i.e. the characterisation of groups of patients given their traits and clinical evidence [9,12,25]. However, from the XAI point of view, the main limitations as regards making SD outcomes understandable are the volume of subgroups obtained and their complexity (the number of descriptors involved in order to define each pattern discovered). In this work, we tackle both aspects of the problem with the objective of providing a more compact and understandable representation of the whole SD model. The main contributions of this paper are the following:

- A new SD model-agnostic explanation method based on a global surrogate model.
- The evaluation of the explanatory SD capacity of our proposal: (1) using gold-standard datasets, (2) illustrating the utility of the proposal with a real clinical phenotype problem concerning infectious diseases, and (3) carrying out an empirical survey analysis to study subjective human satisfaction.

The paper is organised as follows. In Sect. 2, we introduce the background knowledge and the notation used. The SD explainer is described in Sect. 3, while Sect. 4 shows the preliminary experimental results obtained with synthetic data, a proof of concept in the antimicrobial infection domain and a study of the usefulness of our proposal by means of a survey. Finally, Sects. 5 and 6 respectively provide a discussion of the results obtained and our conclusions.

2   Background

2.1   XAI Methods and Healthcare

In XAI, it is possible to distinguish between model-specific and model-agnostic explanations. The objective of the former is to explain the model itself and can be understood as explainability by design, whereas model-agnostic explanations are independent of the model. Model agnostic methods are post-hoc, i.e. we first train a machine learning (ML) model and we then attempt to explain it by considering the outputs of that model.

An example of a model-agnostic technique is the global surrogate model, which consists of approximating the results obtained by a black box using a simple and intrinsically interpretable model [24]. We first train the original (black box) model, and the outputs obtained are then used to train the interpretable model, after which it is necessary only to study the interpretable model. Similar works have already been carried out using this approach in the context of explaining neural networks [6].

Given the importance of transparency in the healthcare domain, there has been a growing interest in improving the explainability of opaque yet powerful models, such as random forests [20] and different types of artificial neural networks [13,22]. The use of model-agnostic methods, such as local explanations provided by LIME [30] or SHAP [21], makes it possible to both maintain high accuracy in the system and provide approximate explanations of the reasoning.

Although the aforementioned methods have yielded relatively good results, they are designed to explain classification tasks. We are, therefore, of the opinion that the current state of the art lacks an exploratory analysis of descriptive methods, and believe that a promising approach would be to adapt the philosophy of the global explanations to these methods. The use of a global surrogate approach might, for example, make it possible to gain further insights into the relations between the data and the output, which is exactly what doctors require when SD is explained to them.

Decision trees have been adopted by the healthcare community as a graphical method with which to express most of the medical decisions described in clinical guidelines and protocols [27]. The later success of decision tree algorithms in the 1990s s contributed to these structures becoming gold standards for clinical knowledge extraction using ML [29]. Clinicians' familiarity with decision trees helps to answer questions about the importance of features, data distribution and the output (subgroups) obtained [8].

Other models that could be considered as surrogates are the state-of-the-art algorithms designed with the philosophy of being interpretable and transparent. Generalized linear rule models [35] generate a linear combination of interpretable rules for classification and regression using column generation to deal with the explosion of possible conjunctions/disjunctions of the rules. Similarly, in [7], an algorithm with which to construct rules in conjunctive and disjunctive normal forms, denominated as boolean decision rules via column generation, is presented. However, both methods generate a set of rules rather than compacting all the information into a single structure.

2.2   Subgroup Discovery

SD can be defined [15,36] as a ML task at the intersection of predictive and descriptive modelling [26] whose objective is to discover the most interesting subgroups within a given population according to a certain set of characteristics of interest and to a target variable.

In this work we provide the following conventions based on [3]:

Given a dataset $D = (I, A)$ where I defines the set of individuals and $A = \{a_1, \ldots, a_m\}$ is the set of attributes, a selector condition sc describes a constraint on the values of an attribute $a_i \in A$ of the dataset.

A selector is a function $s_{sc} : I \rightarrow Boolean$ that returns $True$ if an individual $i \in I$ of the dataset has the characteristics described by the selector condition sc.

A pattern P is a finite set of selectors $P = \{s_1, \ldots, s_l\}$, interpreted as a conjunctive or disjunctive form. For the sake of simplicity, in this work we restrict the patterns to their conjunctive form.

A subgroup is a 2-tuple $SG = (P, s_t)$, where P is a pattern and s_t is a selector. The subgroup can be interpreted as an IF-THEN rule. For example, given the selector condition $s_t = (susceptibility = Resistant)$ and the pattern $P = \{age >$

$35, culture = EnterococcusFaecium\}$ the following subgroup can be defined: $IF\ (age > 35 \wedge culture = EnterococcusFaecium)\ THEN\ susceptibility = Resistant$. Given a dataset $D = (I, A)$ and the subgroup $SG = (P, s_t)$, the instances of a subgroup are formalised as $SG(\cdot) = \{\forall i \in I | s_{sc}(i) = True, \forall sc \in P\}$. It is worth mentioning that $SG(\cdot)$ also includes false positive instances, that is $i \in I$ where $s_t(i) = False$.

The interest of a subgroup is computed by employing a quality function $qf(P, D) \in \mathbb{R}^+$ that maps every pattern P in the search space onto a real number that reflects the quality of the subgroup. For example, in Eq. (1) we formalise the weighted relative accuracy (WRAcc) [16], a widely used quality measure that provides a trade-off between the generality and distributional unusualness of the subgroup [5,17]. The first part of the product refers to the support of the subgroup, whereas the second refers to the relative accuracy, i.e., the accuracy minus the proportion of (true and false) positives instances.

$$WRAcc(SG) = \frac{|SG(\cdot)|}{|I|} \cdot \left(\frac{|\{\forall i \in SG(\cdot)| s_t(i) = True\}|}{SG(\cdot)} - \frac{|\{\forall i \in I | s_t(i) = True\}|}{|I|} \right). \quad (1)$$

2.3 SD Algorithms and Explainability

SD algorithms generally follow a top-down search approach in order to find subgroups of interest. The algorithm starts from the most basic subgroup descriptions, and explore the search space by specialising the most promising subgroup descriptions. According to [31], it is possible to distinguish between exhaustive and beam search approaches. For reduced data sets, the whole space is often traversed using adapted versions of frequent pattern mining algorithms, such as $SD\text{-}MAP$ [4], $Dp\text{-}Subgroup$ [11] or BSD [18]. If an exhaustive search is not possible (owing to, e.g., certain medical problems), beam search is frequently adopted in order to explore only a portion of the vast space of solutions by relying on heuristics such as SD [9], $CN2\text{-}SD$ [17] or $SD4TS$ [25] algorithms. Finally, other local-search strategies, such as evolutionary techniques [34], have also been considered.

To the best of our knowledge, little attention is paid to SD algorithms and explainability principles. In [19], the utility of employing SD strategies to provide model-agnostic local (or even global) explanations for recommending systems is discussed. However, rather than use SD to explain other more complex systems, we are interested in studying how explainable is SD itself.

Some proposals use ontologies to generate Subgroup explanations [32,33]. In these works, a SD algorithm is first used to obtain subgroups, after which the dataset is labelled with the subgroups that cover each example, an algorithm ranks the attributes according to their capability to discriminate between subgroups and, finally, a semantic SD algorithm is applied, taking more generic ontology terms as characteristics and the induced subgroups as the target. Other than this approach, as far as we know, there is no literature regarding SD explainability that does not rely on additional knowledge.

3 Methods

In this section, we propose an approach with which to explain SD: the Subgroup-Explainer methodology, which can be summarized as follows: (0) We apply a SD algorithm. Any algorithm can be used without restrictions, since our proposal is model agnostic; (1) the dataset is automatically labelled, according to the subgroup coverage of the examples; (2) the surrogate model is learnt from the labelled dataset taking the newly created label as the target attribute. This will build an explainable model for the dataset that has the objective of helping to interpret the SD task. The key elements of the SubgroupExplainer methodology are shown in Fig. 1.

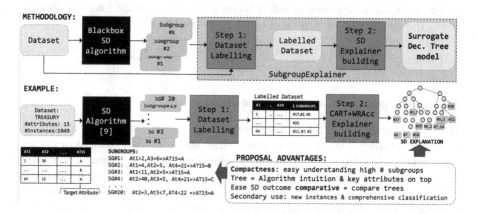

Fig. 1. Intuitions of SubgroupExplainer methodology

The **first step** in our methodology with which to explain SD is that of labelling each instance of the dataset according to the subgroups to which the instance belongs. The fact that an instance belongs to each of the k induced subgroups can be expressed as a k-dimensional boolean label, where $true$ in i signifies that the instance belongs to the i-th subgroup and $false$ is the opposite, with $i \in 1..k$.

Formally, let $S_{SG} = \{SG_1, \ldots, SG_k\}$ be the set of subgroups discovered by a SD algorithm from a given dataset $D(I, A)$. We temporally label the dataset by adding to A a new k-dimensional binary attribute $L' = (l'_1, \ldots, l'_k)$ which expresses the fact that the individual $i \in I$ belongs to the subgroup $SG_j \in S_{SG}$ (Eq. (2)). We then transform the vector of labels L' into a single label L, using a label powerset. Working with binary numbers, this equates to transform each label l'_j of the vector L' into one-hot encoding with a 1 bit in the position j if the instance belongs to subgroup j and then sum all of them, getting then a single binary string L in which, consequently, a 1 in the position j means that the instance belongs to subgroup j and a 0 means the opposite. Finally, we label the dataset, $D' = (I, A \cup L)$ (Eq. (3)).

$$l'_j(i) = \begin{cases} 1 \text{ if } i \in SG_j(\cdot) \\ 0 \text{ } otherwise \end{cases} \tag{2}$$

$$L(i) = \sum_{j=1}^{k} l'_j(i)^j \tag{3}$$

The **second step** consists of building a global surrogate model in order to explain SD outcomes. This methodology specifically employs a decision tree, which is a human-interpretable graphical model that has been widely used by clinicians to represent medical decision knowledge and can potentially be interactive and improved by using visual tools to make it more user-friendly. Moreover, the tree will make it possible to visualise the overlapping between subgroups, as the instances that belong to multiple subgroups will be represented by their own branches on the tree.

Although the SubgroupExplainer methodology states that any decision tree algorithm can be used, we illustrate the suitability of our approach by using the CART algorithm [10]. This decision was motivated by the binary nature of the selectors, which allows them to be used as *splits* for a binary tree.

We propose a new strategy with which to simplify and accelerate the construction of the tree described in Algorithm 1 using the information obtained from the subgroups. The algorithm considers only as possible splits for the nodes the selectors present in the subgroups, and we have prioritised the use of splits (selectors) that are present in generic subgroups (the one with fewer selectors). We additionally decided to split each node using the selector with the highest WRAcc rather than computing the Gini impurity or entropy of the possible splits, thus giving the splits a semantic sense closer to that of the SD framework. When Gini is employed, the branching maximises the classification accuracy of a random instance, whereas our proposal distinguishes between those examples that (according to the WRAcc) belong to the best one-selector subgroup and those that do not.

4   Experiments

Explainable AI is a multi-disciplinary field that involves computer science, human-computer interaction and social sciences [23], signifying that a more complex evaluation that is not limited to numerical experiments is required. Our evaluation method, therefore, comprised three stages: (1) the scalability and computational properties of the proposal were studied using various SD algorithms and gold-standard datasets commonly used in the SD domain, as shown in Sect. 4.1; (2) the suitability of the method was studied by employing it in a clinical use case for an antimicrobial resistance problem, as described in Sect. 4.2, and (3), since the ultimate goal of XAI is for it to be understood by actual people, the utility of the method was studied by surveying a small group in order to validate it from a human-centric perspective, as explained in Sect. 4.3. The results obtained are preliminary and will be discussed in Sect. 5.

Algorithm 1. Selection of the SD-split attribute

Input: D', qf, *Output*   ▷ Labeled dataset D', a quality function qf, the set *Output* of subgroups founded by the black-box algorithm

Output: *split*   ▷ Split attribute

1: $S_{SG} \leftarrow \emptyset$ ▷ List of all possible one-selector-pattern subgroups of D
2: $S \leftarrow \emptyset$
3: $L \leftarrow$ Set of all feasible labeled-classes   ▷ Target-value tuples
4: $i \leftarrow 1$
5: **repeat**
6:    $S \leftarrow$ selectors present in patterns of *Output* whose $length = i$
7:    **if** $S \neq \emptyset$ **then**
8:       $\forall s \in S,\ \forall l \in L$, add $SG = (s, l)$ to S_{SG} ▷ "IF s THEN l"
9:       $(s, l) \leftarrow \arg\max_{SG \in S_{SG}} qf(SG, D')$ ▷ "best pattern subgroup"
10:       $split \leftarrow s$
11:       **return** *split*
12:    **else**
13:       $i \leftarrow i + 1$
14: **until** $length(out) < i,\ \forall out \in Output$
15: **return** $\varnothing$ ▷ No possible split was found

Table 1. Dataset description

Dataset	$|D|$	Categorical	Numerical	Dataset	$|D|$	Categorical	Numerical
autoMPG8	392	0	6	abalone	4177	0	8
dee	365	0	6	puma32h	8192	0	32
ele-1	495	0	2	elevators	16599	0	18
forestFires	517	0	12	bikesharing	17379	2	10
concrete	1030	0	8	california	20640	0	8
treasury	1049	0	15	house	22784	0	16

With regard to SD algorithms, we selected a local search strategy, since these strategies perform better than exhaustive search algorithms in large databases, such as those used in biomedical and healthcare domains. We specifically selected SD, $CN2$-SD and $SD4TS$. The last two algorithms are implemented in the Pyhton3 library `Subgroups`[1], whereas the already the SD algorithm already implemented was improved in terms of execution time efficiency and the quality of the subgroups found. The other experiments were implemented outside `Subgroups`, in a separate repository[2].

4.1 Performance and Scalability

The aim of these preliminary experiments was to understand the performance and scalability of our proposal in terms of the complexity of the explanation

---

[1] Available at PyPI, https://pypi.org/project/subgroups/.
[2] Available at GitHub, https://github.com/Enrique-Val/SubgroupExplainer.

model - studying the size, branching and complexity of the tree - and its relation to: (1) the SD Algorithm selected, and (2) the characteristics of the subgroups obtained. The study was essential in order to attain a first impression of the usefulness of the tree from a computational perspective. A further evaluation will be carried out in the following sections.

The experiments were carried out using 12 gold-standard datasets for SD analysis [28], which are available in the Keel repository [1] and have a wide range of examples and features. The description of the datasets is summarised in Table 1. While most of them are not related to the healthcare domain, these datasets allowed us to study the viability of our algorithms in numerical terms (number and size of subgroups, size of the trees...). The datasets selected are intended to be used in regression tasks, and the target attribute is, therefore, numerical (discrete or real). However, we are interested in classification tasks with a discrete target for our use case and thus we grouped all the possible values of the target into five equal-sized bins that would be used as the new target attribute.

As stated previously, all of the three algorithms selected (SD, $CN2\text{-}SD$, $SD4TS$) use a beam search to traverse the space of solutions, but they require different parameters and use diverse quality measures that shape how the algorithms behave in different manners. The most noteworthy divergence concerns the quality function. SD uses the Q_g quality function, whose parameter g allows a trade-off between general and specific subgroups, while $CN2\text{-}SD$ uses a modified version of the WRAcc that considers example weighting (referred in this work as WRAcc'). In [25], the algorithm $SD4TS$ use a domain-specific quality measure, but in our experiments we selected the WRAcc. The selection of parameters is summarised in Table 2.

Since the size of the tree can sometimes grow rapidly, we decided to add an input parameter min_split to the tree. This parameter specifies the minimum number of samples of the total dataset that a node should contain in order to be split. If $min\_split = 0$, we will split each node regardless of the number of examples that it contains and, as a result, the leaf nodes of the tree will be *completely pure*, whereas if $min\_split \geq 0$ some leaf nodes might be *impure* (contain instances with a different label L), but the number of nodes might decrease. This provides an interesting trade-off between accurate trees and small trees that will be discussed in the following sections.

Table 2. Algorithms and parameters used

Algorithm	Quality measure	Beam width	Min. support	Weighting scheme
SD	Q_g ($g = 10$)	20	15%	*None*
$CN2\text{-}SD$	WRAcc'	3	*None* (0%)	Multiplicative ($\gamma = 0.3$)
$SD4TS$	WRAcc	20	15%	*None*

The results of the experiments are depicted in Tables 3 and 4. The study parameters regarding SD will be the number of induced subgroups $|S_{SG}|$, the total number of selectors $|S|$ of the set S_{SG}, the number of non-repeated selectors of S, namely $|S_u|$, and the mean cardinality of the subgroups $card = \frac{|S|}{|S_{SG}|}$. The study parameters of the tree, will be the number of nodes (T), the depth of the tree ($Depth$), the depth of the shortest branch of the tree (Min_depth) and a purity ratio ($Purity$), which is a measure that we defined as the proportion of examples of the training set that have been perfectly classified, i.e. the number of instances that attain a pure leaf node that label them correctly divided by the total number of instances. Two trees will be generated for each SD algorithm: one with the parameter min_split set to 0 and the other with a min_split value of 0.05, thus allowing for some degree of impurity in the leaf nodes.

Table 3. Results (1)

Dataset	SG alg.	SG metrics				min split	SGExplainer metrics			
		$|S_{SG}|$	$|S|$	$|S_u|$	$card$		$|T|$	$Depth$	Min_depth	$Purity$
autoMPG8	SD	20	117	9	5.85	0	9	5	2	1.0
						0.05	9	5	2	1.0
	CN2-SD	24	63	33	2.62	0	413	17	5	1.0
						0.05	73	13	4	0.16
	SD4TS	20	**67**	**13**	**3.35**	0	**5**	**3**	**2**	1.0
						0.05	5	3	2	1.0
dee	SD	20	112	10	5.6	0	9	5	2	1.0
						0.05	9	5	2	1.0
	CN2-SD	24	68	33	2.83	0	457	17	5	1.0
						0.05	79	12	4	0.09
	SD4TS	20	68	11	3.4	0	59	8	4	1.0
						0.05	43	8	3	0.81
ele-1	SD	11	20	4	1.82	0	17	5	3	1.0
						0.05	17	5	3	1.0
	CN2-SD	**29**	**59**	**15**	2.03	0	**49**	**9**	**3**	1.0
						0.05	49	9	3	1.0
	SD4TS	20	55	7	2.75	0	13	5	2	1.0
						0.05	13	5	2	1.0
forestFires	SD	20	25	16	1.25	0	455	15	5	1.0
						0.05	91	15	3	0.09
	CN2-SD	**29**	**84**	**56**	2.9	0	953	22	6	1.0
						0.05	93	12	4	0.01
	SD4TS	20	27	19	1.35	0	671	14	6	1.0
						0.05	65	8	4	0.0
concrete	SD	20	88	8	4.4	0	49	8	3	1.0
						0.05	39	7	3	0.9
	CN2-SD	38	107	40	2.82	0	945	19	5	1.0
						0.05	73	9	4	0.0
	SD4TS	20	26	17	1.3	0	711	14	6	1.0
						0.05	65	8	4	0.0
treasury	SD	**20**	117	24	**5.85**	0	21	8	2	1.0
						0.05	15	8	2	0.97
	CN2-SD	19	51	39	2.68	0	273	21	4	1.0
						0.05	97	16	3	0.34
	SD4TS	20	25	20	1.25	0	127	16	4	1.0
						0.05	**57**	16	3	**0.82**

4.2   Use Case: Patient Phenotype

The objective of this use case is to identify potential patient phenotypes of antimicrobial resistance. In this problem, we analyse the increase in its Minimum Inhibitory Concentration (MIC). The MIC is the lowest concentration of a chemical that will inhibit the growth of a microorganism, and they are considered highly important when determining the susceptibility of bacteria to an antibiotic [2].

Table 4. Results (2)

Dataset	SG alg.	SG metrics				Min split	SGExplainer metrics			
		$|S_{SG}|$	$|S|$	$|S_u|$	card		$|T|$	Depth	Min_depth	Purity
abalone	SD	20	96	14	4.8	0	9	5	2	1.0
						0.05	9	5	2	1.0
	CN2-SD	35	95	40	2.71	0	945	22	5	1.0
						0.05	135	18	3	0.32
	SD4TS	20	20	20	1	0	425	13	5	1.0
						0.05	51	13	3	0.61
puma32h	SD	20	61	5	3.05	0	21	6	3	1.0
						0.05	21	6	3	1.0
	CN2-SD	40	84	37	2.1	0	12097	26	6	1.0
						0.05	49	9	3	0.0
	SD4TS	20	21	12	1.05	0	351	10	6	1.0
						0.05	69	10	4	0.28
elevators	SD	20	111	8	5.55	0	9	5	2	1.0
						0.05	9	5	2	1.0
	CN2-SD	53	150	63	2.83	0	20757	30	6	1.0
						0.05	89	13	3	0.0
	SD4TS	20	20	20	1.0	0	135	9	5	1.0
						0.05	49	9	3	0.84
bikesharing	SD	20	72	8	3.6	0	5	3	2	1.0
						0.05	5	3	2	1.0
	CN2-SD	20	48	22	2.4	0	309	13	3	1.0
						0.05	63	10	3	0.58
	SD4TS	20	57	7	2.85	0	7	4	2	1.0
						0.05	7	4	2	1.0
california	SD	20	35	11	1.75	0	471	12	6	1.0
						0.05	77	12	3	0.4
	CN2-SD	47	115	45	2.45	0	5075	23	6	1.0
						0.05	79	10	4	0.0
	SD4TS	20	51	8	2.55	0	65	7	3	1.0
						0.05	25	7	3	0.79
house	SD	20	83	9	4.15	0	169	10	3	1.0
						0.05	39	8	3	0.63
	CN2-SD	62	164	71	2.65	0	40335	33	6	1.0
						0.05	85	13	4	0.0
	SD4TS	20	51	8	2.55	0	65	7	3	1.0
						0.05	25	7	3	0.79

For the sake of reproducibility, in this research we used a dataset obtained from the public database MIMIC-III [14], which integrates information from the health records of over 60,000 admissions. The dataset used contains 1280 samples that represent medical episodes. These contain clinical information about the episode registered, such as the sex and age of the patient, the month, year and season of the medical episode, the episode ID (the same patients that have the same episode ID) or the duration of the episode. Key attributes of the dataset are: (1) Microorganism: the bacteria observed in the study of the MIC; (2) Susceptibility: the microbiological study of the reaction of bacteria to an antibiotic; (3) MIC Increases: whether or not the Minimum Inhibitory Concentration increases. If it increases, this means that the susceptibility was lower in a previous observation, and (4) Culture service: the hospital service (ICU, cardiology, etc.) that requested the bacterial culture used in the study. The problem falls in the category of binary classification, as we are interested to study if the MIC increases or not.

Table 5 provides a summary of the dataset used for the experiments. The EiD column shows the duration of the patient episode in days.

Table 5. Dataset: Minimum inhibitory concentration (only 2 rows shown)

Sex	Age	Season	Month	Year	Episode Id	Microorganism	EiD	Susceptibility	MIC increases	Culture service
F	ELDERLY	SPRING	6	2015	10119	S. EPIDERMIDIS	1	SENSIBLE	Yes	TRA
M	ADULT	SUMMER	8	2016	12731	S. COAGULASA NEG	1	SENSIBLE	No	ORL
.	...	...	.	...	...	...	.	...	.	...

We are interested in studying the subgroups of a population in which there is a high chance of a microbiological resistance being developed. We use the $CN2\text{-}SD$ algorithm instead of the less sophisticated SD and $SD4TS$. According to our experiments (see Sect. 4.1), $CN2\text{-}SD$ tends to induce subgroups with a higher variety of non-repeated selectors. We used the same parameters as in the previous section (see Table 2). In addition, we focused the search ton only look for subgroups with the target $MIC\ Increases = yes$ rather than subgroups with any target value, since we were specifically interested in defining the population in which the resistance is prone to appear. This can be easily done in $CN2\text{-}SD$, since it launches an individual beam search procedure for every target value. As shown in Tables 3 and 4, the use of $CN2\text{-}SD$ algorithm results also in larger tree sizes, and we accordingly placed the threshold of instances on a node for it to be split by 5%. The numeric results and subgroups obtained can be seen in Table 6, while a visual representation of the tree is shown in Fig. 2.

Table 6. MIC detection results

SG metrics				Min split	SGExplainer metrics			
$|S_{SG}|$	$|S|$	$|S_u|$	card		$|T|$	Depth	Min_depth	Purity
4	12	7	4.95	0	17	7	3	1.0
				0.05	15	7	3	0.98

IF microorg not E. FAECALIS, microorg not E. FAECIUM AND microorg not MARSA THEN MIC Increases

IF age not NEWBORN, microorg not S. AUREUS, microorg not S. COAGULASE NEG. THEN MIC Increases

IF microorg not E. FAECALIS, microorg not MARSA, microorg not S. EPIDERMIDIS THEN MIC Increases

IF microorg not E. FAECIUM, microorg not S. AUREUS, microorg not S. EPIDERMIDIS THEN MIC Increases

4.3 Human Subjective Study

Interpretations are social [23] and thus have a strong cognitive and subjective factor. The usefulness of an interpretation can depend on many variables, such as the users' academic background, their cognitive abilities or their knowledge of ML and statistics. It is insufficient to study the characteristics of an explanation by simply looking at the numbers obtained. We, therefore, decided to carry out

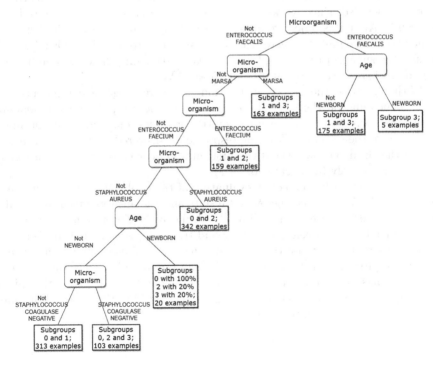

Fig. 2. SD explanation tree: global surrogate model

a survey that would allow us to study the efficacy of a decision tree with which to explain SD.

The study was carried out with a total of 18 participants, most of whom (90%) had University studies and were between 18 and 25 years old. Furthermore, 70% of the respondents had a background in Computer Science and 55% of them (a third of the total population) had knowledge of Artificial Intelligence and ML. However, SD is a highly specific task that is not usually taught at universities, and is, therefore, known only by ML practitioners.

In the survey, we first provided an intuitive explanation of what a subgroup and SD are, and the idea of SubgroupExplainer, after which we presented a set of five subgroups and posed a control question in order to validate whether the respondents had understood what the key concepts of SD are. Two thirds of the population understood the intuitive concept of subgroup, while the other third assumed that the members of a subgroup always had to have the value of the target specified by the subgroup description (which, although desirable, does not always hold true).

Three SubgroupExplainer trees were then presented, each with a different threshold with which to divide a node. The first had no threshold, in the second, a node had to have at least 15% of the examples and in the third, 30%. There were two questions for each tree regarding whether an individual belonged to the subgroups presented, showing descriptions of both the subgroup and the tree. Domain-specific and more subjective questions, such as identifying key features, were not included, since we were focusing on the actual comprehension of the subgroups. After this objective question, we then asked the users whether they found the tree helpful, complete (the tree is sufficient to be able to visualise and classify the subgroup) and simple, rating each tree along these axes on a scale of 1 to 5, where 1 was "Not at all" and 5 was "Very".

With regard to the objective question, the percentage of correct answers varied depending on the tree: (1) in the case of the first, 86% of the answers given were correct once the average for the two questions had been obtained; (2) in that of the second, 94% of the respondents answered correctly, and (3), in that of the third, 17% answered the first question correctly and 94% answered the second correctly (an average of 56%).

With regard to the subjective evaluation of the explanation, the results are shown in Table 7, in which the overall results and the answers given by AI/ML practitioners are separated. As will be noted, the average user prefers a tree with a certain trade-off between node purity and tree size (second tree). In contrast, AI students prefer a precise tree, even if it has more nodes. They actually rate the precise (first) tree as being less simple than the second, despite the fact that the second has more nodes. Both groups rate the highly-pruned tree (the third) as being the least helpful, complete and simple, showing that, overall, a more accurate tree is preferred to a small one.

Table 7. Summary about the mean user experience with the SubgroupExplainer trees.

Polled	Tree	Helpful	Complete	Simple	Mean help.-simple	Mean compl.-simple
All	No min. samples	4.94	4.56	4.06	4.5	4.32
	Min. samples = 15%	4.89	4.61	4.28	4.58	4.44
	Min. samples = 30%	4.06	3.89	4	4.03	3.94
AI/ML knowledge	No min. samples	4.83	4.33	4.33	4.58	4.33
	Min. samples = 15%	4.83	4.33	4	4.42	4.17
	Min. samples = 30%	4.33	3.83	3.83	4.08	3.83

5   Discussion

5.1   Scalability of the SD Algorithms

With regard to the results of the scalability analysis described in Tables 3 and 4, it is worth noting that the $CN2\text{-}SD$ discovers more subgroups because it is not limited to 20 subgroups, as opposed to SD and $SD4TS$. While the algorithm that generates more or less selectors is dependent on the dataset, it will be noted that the variety of selectors induced is always higher in $CN2\text{-}SD$, and that the SD algorithm discovers subgroups with a higher selector cardinality in 9 out of 12 experiments.

5.2   Decision Trees as Explainers

The trees built with the subgroups obtained with $CN2\text{-}SD$ are the largest, while those obtained with SD have a slight tendency towards being the smallest. In the cases, the trees tend to be very imbalanced - that is, there is a considerable difference between the longest and shortest branch. As expected, the purity ratio when min_split is set to 0 is maximum, since all the nodes are pure and the tree perfectly classifies the instances into subgroups. When min_split is set to 0.05 the trees that have a higher number of nodes are those that are reduced the most, possibly owing to an inefficient branching that occurs when attempting to classify very specific and unique instances. The reduction in the size of the tree comes at the cost in its $Purity$, which tends to be higher in the trees obtained with the $CN2\text{-}SD$ subgroups.

In the case of the relation between the characteristics of each set of subgroups obtained and the trees, it is possible to observe that the size and depth of the tree is independent of the number of subgroups induced and the cardinality. Although we cannot state that there is a clear dependence between the number of unique selectors and the size of the tree, the probability of the tree growing larger seems to be higher when the number of unique selectors is also large.

Our use case (Sect. 4.2) proves the potential of compacting all the subgroups are compacted into a single tree. It helps to highlight the attributes that make it possible to better discriminate between subgroups, which are the attributes that are in a higher position in the tree and that are selected more frequently as *split*. This specific use case shows us that if the microorganism is an Enterococcus Faecalis or MARSA, the individual will not belong to subgroups 0 and 2.

Visualising the tree makes it possible to see the imbalance previously identified in Sect. 4.1. The tree contains only 15 nodes, a quantity of information that is usually easy to handle, but the imbalance makes the tree look large and complex, thus potentially limiting the explanation.

5.3   Understanding of the Subgroups by Humans

Concerning the opinions gathered from the users in Sect. 4.3, we highlight that most people find it difficult to understand the fact that an individual may belong to two subgroups. The tree can be helpful as regards solving this problem, as it can explicitly show that an individual with certain characteristics can belong to multiple subgroups.

The AI/ML practitioners' preference for the larger (although more accurate) decision tree can be explained by their greater familiarity with ML models. Analogously, non ML students have favoured a smaller tree for the sake of simplicity, even if it was not as accurate because it is a completely new concept for them.

6   Conclusions

The objective of this paper is to provide clinicians with tools that will allow them to better understand SD algorithms and their outcomes for patient phenotyping. We propose SubgroupExplainer, a methodology that provides SD model-agnostic explanations. This method is based on the hypothesis that decision trees are an effective approach by which to provide global surrogate explanations for medical problems. We have evaluated the suitability of our proposal by studying the ML pipeline and by providing a clinical use case and a human-centric analysis.

Unlike the state-of-the-art approaches [32,33], SubgroupExplainer does not require additional knowledge (ontologies) in order to generate explanations. As a result, the subgroup explanations might be less compact than those obtained using higher level concepts of an ontology, but structuring the partition of the space in a tree-like form is still helpful as regards understanding the data and the subgroups.

While interviewing clinicians would have been more helpful for our study, the results obtained with our current sample are still helpful in order to validate the usefulness of the explanations of SD.

In future research it will be necessary to analyse both the explanatory potential of n-ary decision trees, as well as looking for correlations between the characteristics of the subgroups and the size of the tree. Even if subgroup discovery is not strictly designed for classification, a comparison between the accuracy of the subgroups and the surrogate tree would be another method to examine its fidelity. A baseline comparison with a tree whose split are found using the Gini impurity would also be a valuable addition. The trees could be further improved by using visual and interactive keys, such as colouring the nodes and branches and allowing user interaction. From a practical perspective, we plan to extend the study to clinicians working in MIC detection or related problems.

Acknowledgement. This work was partially funded by the CONFAINCE project (Ref: PID2021-122194OB-I00), supported by the Spanish Ministry of Science and Innovation, the Spanish Agency for Research and the IMPACT-T2D project (PMP21/00092) supported by the Spanish Health Institute Carlos III (ISCIII).

References

1. Alcalá-Fdez, J., et al.: KEEL data-mining software tool: data set repository, integration of algorithms and experimental analysis framework. J. Multiple-Valued Logic Soft Comput. **17**(2–3), 255–287 (2011)
2. Andrews, J.M.: Determination of minimum inhibitory concentrations. J. Antimicrobial Chemotherapy **48**(Suppl. 1), 5–16 (2001)
3. Atzmueller, M.: Subgroup discovery. Wiley Interdiscipl. Rev. Data Min. Knowl. Discov. **5**(1), 35–49 (2015)
4. Atzmueller, M., Puppe, F.: SD-map – a fast algorithm for exhaustive subgroup discovery. In: Fürnkranz, J., Scheffer, T., Spiliopoulou, M. (eds.) PKDD 2006. LNCS (LNAI), vol. 4213, pp. 6–17. Springer, Heidelberg (2006). https://doi.org/10.1007/11871637_6
5. Carmona, C.J., del Jesus, M.J., Herrera, F.: A unifying analysis for the supervised descriptive rule discovery via the weighted relative accuracy. Knowl.-Based Syst. **139**, 89–100 (2018)
6. Craven, M., Shavlik, J.: Extracting tree-structured representations of trained networks. Adv. Neural. Inf. Process. Syst. **8**, 24–30 (1995)
7. Dash, S., Gunluk, O., Wei, D.: Boolean decision rules via column generation. Adv. Neural. Inf. Process. Syst. **31**, 4655–4665 (2018)
8. Di Castro, F., Bertini, E.: Surrogate decision tree visualization interpreting and visualizing black-box classification models with surrogate decision tree. In: Joint Proceedings of the ACM IUI 2019 Workshops Co-located with the 24th ACM Conference on Intelligent User Interfaces of CEUR Workshop Proceedings, vol. 2327. CEUR-WS (2019)
9. Gamberger, D., Lavrac, N.: Expert-guided subgroup discovery: methodology and application. J. Artif. Intell. Res. **17**, 501–527 (2002)
10. Gordon, A.D., Breiman, L., Friedman, J.H., Olshen, R.A., Stone, C.J.: Classification and regression trees. Biometrics **40**(3), 874 (1984)
11. Grosskreutz, H., Rüping, S., Wrobel, S.: Tight optimistic estimates for fast subgroup discovery. In: Daelemans, W., Goethals, B., Morik, K. (eds.) ECML PKDD 2008. LNCS (LNAI), vol. 5211, pp. 440–456. Springer, Heidelberg (2008). https://doi.org/10.1007/978-3-540-87479-9_47
12. Helal, S.: Subgroup discovery algorithms: a survey and empirical evaluation. Knowl. Inf. Syst. **3**(29), 495–525 (2011)
13. Ibrahim, L., Mesinovic, M., Yang, K.-W., Eid, M.A.: Explainable prediction of acute myocardial infarction using machine learning and Shapley values. IEEE Access **8**, 210410–210417 (2020)
14. Johnson, A.E.W., et al.: Mimic-iii, a freely accessible critical care database. Sci. Data **3**(1), 1–9 (2016)

15. Klösgen, W.: Explora: a multipattern and multistrategy discovery assistant. In: Advances in Knowledge Discovery and Data Mining, pp. 249–271. AAAI/MIT Press (1996)
16. Lavrač, N., Flach, P., Zupan, B.: Rule evaluation measures: a unifying view. In: Džeroski, S., Flach, P. (eds.) ILP 1999. LNCS (LNAI), vol. 1634, pp. 174–185. Springer, Heidelberg (1999). https://doi.org/10.1007/3-540-48751-4_17
17. Lavrac, N., Kavsek, B., Flach, P., Todorovski, L.: Subgroup discovery with CN2-SD. J. Mach. Learn. Res. 5(2), 153–188 (2004)
18. Lemmerich, F., Rohlfs, M., Atzmueller, M.: Fast discovery of relevant subgroup patterns. In: Proceedings of the Twenty-Third International Florida Artificial Intelligence Research Society Conference (FLAIRS), pp. 428–433. AAAI Press (2010)
19. Lonjarret, C., Robardet, C., Plantevit, M., Auburtin, R., Atzmueller, M.: Why should I trust this item? Explaining the recommendations of any model. In: 2020 IEEE 7th International Conference on Data Science and Advanced Analytics (DSAA), pp. 526–535 (2020)
20. Lundberg, S.M., et al.: From local explanations to global understanding with explainable AI for trees. Nat. Mach. Intell. 2(1), 56–67 (2020)
21. Lundberg, S.M., Lee, S.-I.: A unified approach to interpreting model predictions. Adv. Neural Inf. Process. Syst. 30, 4765–4774 (2017)
22. Magesh, P.R., Myloth, R.D., Tom, R.J.: An explainable machine learning model for early detection of Parkinson's disease using LIME on DaTSCAN imagery. Comput. Biol. Med. 126, 104041 (2020)
23. Miller, T.: Explanation in artificial intelligence: insights from the social sciences. Artif. Intell. 267, 1–38 (2019)
24. Molnar, C.: Interpretable Machine Learning. Lulu.com (2019)
25. Mueller, M., Rosales, R., Steck, H., Krishnan, S., Rao, B., Kramer, S.: Subgroup discovery for test selection: a novel approach and its application to breast cancer diagnosis. In: Adams, N.M., Robardet, C., Siebes, A., Boulicaut, J.-F. (eds.) IDA 2009. LNCS, vol. 5772, pp. 119–130. Springer, Heidelberg (2009). https://doi.org/10.1007/978-3-642-03915-7_11
26. Novak, P.K., Lavrač, N., Webb, G.I., Supervised descriptive rule discovery: a unifying survey of contrast set, emerging pattern and subgroup mining. J. Mach. Learn. Res. 10(2), 377–410 (2009)
27. Podgorelec, V., Kokol, P., Stiglic, B., Rozman, I.: Decision trees: an overview and their use in medicine. J. Med. Syst. 26(5), 445–463 (2002)
28. Proença, H.M., Grünwald, P., Bäck, T., Leeuwen, M.: Discovering outstanding subgroup lists for numeric targets using MDL. In: Hutter, F., Kersting, K., Lijffijt, J., Valera, I. (eds.) ECML PKDD 2020. LNCS (LNAI), vol. 12457, pp. 19–35. Springer, Cham (2021). https://doi.org/10.1007/978-3-030-67658-2_2
29. Quinlan, J.R.: Induction of decision trees. Mach. Learn. 1(1), 81–106 (1986)
30. Ribeiro, M.T., Singh, S., Guestrin, C.: Why should I trust you?: explaining the predictions of any classifier. In: Proceedings of the 22nd ACM SIGKDD International Conference on Knowledge Discovery and Data Mining, pp. 1135–1144. ACM (2016)
31. van Leeuwen, M., Knobbe, A.: Non-redundant subgroup discovery in large and complex data. In: Gunopulos, D., Hofmann, T., Malerba, D., Vazirgiannis, M. (eds.) ECML PKDD 2011. LNCS (LNAI), vol. 6913, pp. 459–474. Springer, Heidelberg (2011). https://doi.org/10.1007/978-3-642-23808-6_30
32. Vavpetič, A., Podpečan, V., Lavrač, N.: Semantic subgroup explanations. J. Intell. Inf. Syst. 42(2), 233–254 (2013)

33. Vavpetič, A., Podpečan, V., Meganck, S., Lavrač, N.: Explaining subgroups through ontologies. In: Anthony, P., Ishizuka, M., Lukose, D. (eds.) PRICAI 2012. LNCS (LNAI), vol. 7458, pp. 625–636. Springer, Heidelberg (2012). https://doi.org/10.1007/978-3-642-32695-0_55

34. Ventura, S., Luna, J.M., et al.: Supervised Descriptive Pattern Mining. Springer, Cham (2018). https://doi.org/10.1007/978-3-319-98140-6

35. Wei, D., Dash, S., Gao, T., Gunluk, O.: Generalized linear rule models. In: International Conference on Machine Learning, pp. 6687–6696. Proceedings of Machine Learning Research (2019)

36. Wrobel, S.: An algorithm for multi-relational discovery of subgroups. In: Komorowski, J., Zytkow, J. (eds.) PKDD 1997. LNCS, vol. 1263, pp. 78–87. Springer, Heidelberg (1997). https://doi.org/10.1007/3-540-63223-9_108

Limits of XAI Application-Grounded Evaluation: An E-Sport Prediction Example

Corentin Boidot[1,2]([⊠]) [iD], Olivier Augereau[1] [iD], Pierre De Loor[1] [iD], and Riwal Lefort[2] [iD]

[1] Lab-STICC UMR CNRS 6285, École Nationale d'Ingénieur de Brest, Brest, France
{boidot,augereau,deloor}@enib.fr
[2] Crédit Mutuel Arkéa, Le Relecq-Kerhuon, France
riwal.lefort@arkea.com
https://labsticc.fr/fr/poles/interaction, https://www.cm-arkea.com/

Abstract. EXplainable AI (XAI) was created to address the issue of Machine Learning's lack of transparency. Its methods are expanding, as are the ways of evaluating them, including human performance-based evaluations of explanations. These evaluations allow us to quantify the contribution of XAI algorithms to human decision-making. This work performs accuracy and response time measurements to evaluate SHAP explanations on an e-sports prediction task. The results of this pilot experiment contradict our intuitions about the beneficial potential of these explanations and allow us to discuss the difficulties of this evaluation methodology.

1 Introduction

Machine Learning (ML) has made significant progress in the last decade, not just in research, where beating "state-of-the-art algorithms" has become a standard, but also in business. Its use is becoming commonplace, as shown by the growing need for regulation [10]. However, employing these models frequently entails putting a process under the control of a black box: an algorithm whose behavior is unknown to the user [11]. A data scientist can look back on the behavior of his model. However he will rarely be able to specify the role of each parameter in his model, let alone guarantee the calculation's logic. However, not all operations may be left in the hands of a black box for reasons of control, safety, trust, or legal liability: in industries such as medicine, banking, and the military industry, models are needed to provide not only results but also a valid interpretation of those results [3,24]. Explainable Artificial Intelligence (XAI) is a field of study that has grown in popularity in recent years to address these demands.

Depending on the specific ML framework or model, one will find various XAI methods, given that many methods try to be compatible with any model. This variety of methods matches the variety of goals of XAI, and questions about users' needs should be asked before one chooses a method. Do the explanations convey

I. Koprinska et al. (Eds.): ECML PKDD 2022 Workshops, CCIS 1752, pp. 452–466, 2023.
https://doi.org/10.1007/978-3-031-23618-1_30

accurate representations, and helpful information? Is the user overloaded by information or put off by its formulation? Algorithmic properties of the methods can be studied but the effects these explanations will have on different persons remains uncertain. That is partly because the graphical presentation of the explanations and interface ergonomics can interfere with these effects.

XAI therefore requires the implementation of explanations' evaluations in order to know whether the explanations produced the desired effects. One such evaluation technique is human task performance evaluation, also called *application-grounded evaluation*, which is one of the techniques that involve humans in the loop. In this work, we consider the user an expert without ML knowledge: explanations have to support their decision-making process. Evaluating the usefulness of XAI methods by measuring performance requires a given framework: a task, training data, a human operator, and an ML model intended as a decision aid.

The model is trained using the data, and the user makes decisions based on AI guidance and its own understanding of current data. The decision support system can thus be limited to provide the result of the model on the current data, or it can be complemented by additional information-rich interfaces in the XAI framework.

Accuracy is the main metric for binary decision, and decisions are made sequentially so that we can measure speed. Using these performance criteria, we compare the results of decisions made with and without explanations. This performance analysis should provide a quantifiable determination of the quality of human decision-making.

Hoffman et al. proposed different evaluation techniques in their review [14], and measuring performance is the closest to the human agent's actual use. That is why we find it valuable, and we want to apply it to simple data (i.e., tabular) and a simple task format: binary classification.

In this paper, we attempt to evaluate a popular XAI method, SHAP [21], on a simple task: predicting the outcome of an e-sports match. E-sport offers us possibilities because a lot of players could be treated as experts: we can hope to generalize results to other domains' expert explanations. On top of that, we can easily find open data about this game.

Our goal is to predict which of the two teams will win, using event summary data from the first few minutes of a League of Legends match. This task sets the stage for our performance evaluation. Our XAI system measures the accuracy and speed with which human users respond. The difference between human performance from data and an ML analysis explained by SHAP vs. performance without explanation should establish an evaluation of SHAP's influence on decision-making for our task with our interface.

The rest of the article is organized as follows: Sect. 2 presents the state of the art in XAI, focusing on its evaluation techniques, with the work of Jesus et al. [15] that we partially replicate. Section 3 describes our expectations of the results and the methodological framework used. Section 4 reports our results, which are then discussed more broadly in Sect. 5 before concluding in Sect. 6.

2   State of the Art

The explainability of ML models can be approached in different ways. It can be seen as the global explanation of a model's functioning, or as a process that seeks to explain the output of a model for a particular input. This study fits into the general "post-hoc" explanation framework [1], which consists in developing an explanatory method for models already designed and trained without concern for interpretability (as opposed to the development of transparent models). We can distinguish the following explanation methods: features importances [25], counterfactuals explanations [27], prototypes [2], model simplification [4], textual explanations [8] and model visualization [18]. These categories are not mutually exclusive: we can find methods at the borders of two categories [16].

One of the most famous XAI methods is SHAP [21], a post-hoc explanation method by feature importance, designed for local analysis (but it can be used for global explanation). It uses calculations from game theory to determine the positive or negative contribution of each input feature to each individual outcome. This method is particularly popular for explaining tree-based models, thanks to an optimized implementation that circumvents the computational costs of the method [20].

2.1   Evaluation of XAI

In addition to creating explanatory methods, one must also be concerned with their evaluation. One of the ongoing problems in XAI field is the lack of a fixed definition of what an explanation should be [9]. This problem is due to the subjective essence of explanations, the diversity of situations in which they are used, and the numerous and potentially conflicting objectives (simplicity, fidelity, completeness) they may pursue from one context to another. In particular, this context includes the nature of the target audience of the explanation (data scientist, layperson, application domain expert, or auditor). The methods created have therefore generally been evaluated more qualitatively than quantitatively [6,22]. However, the thoughts on how to assess XAI methods have flourished so that the main categories can be identified.

On the one hand, we can use purely computer-based evaluations: we test properties of the explanations such as the diversity of the answers or their complexity. On the other hand, we can use human evaluation, either through simple test tasks, or in real conditions. The first ones allow a quantitative evaluation but can be disconnected from the fundamental objectives of explainability, if the relevance of the tested tasks is not assessed. Moreover, these evaluations are generally adapted to the type of explanation evaluated and do not allow for comparing explanations of a different nature [19].

In the area of human evaluation, a distinction is made between two approaches. Firstly, those which are based on subjective measurements (the user is asked to rate the "comprehensibility" or various criteria related to their feeling) [7]. Then, those that will study the human-AI system from the outside, by measuring the subject response times, or the accuracy of the decisions made, and comparing the use of explanations against different baselines. Such objective measurements can also be done to evaluate more subjective properties: simulatability [12] can be measured to estimate the impact of explanations on user's mental model of the AI.

If we rely only on the former, there is a risk that the research will move towards pleasant but misleading explanations: Ehsan et al. [7] suggest that our positive biases towards AI may prevent us from adequately evaluating its outcome and result and its explanation. However, both are often performed simultaneously in the same experiment.

2.2   Application-Grounded Evaluation Methodology

We want to deploy an XAI system and evaluate it. We restricted this pilot development to a case of binary decision task with tabular data. This case has not been intensively evaluated but the work of Jesus et al. [15] seems particularly significant to us, for the conclusions they draw as for their methodology. Their study is an example of performance-based evaluation that does not rely on hypotheses about the structure of explanation or mental model [17].

Jesus et al. evaluate through practice three types of explanations (SHAP, LIME and TreeExplainer) for financial fraud detection task. Each transaction is scanned out for fraud detection, independently of the others (data is therefore tabular, not sequential). They evaluate the decisions of three expert fraud analysts, through five experimental conditions. Their tests are performed with data sampled around the decision boundary of the model: the three experts are not systematically exposed to the same data but only partially, on a sample used to establish an agreement score. The five experimental conditions are presented successively to each subject, as a long series of decisions to be made, first with the data alone (first condition), then with the data and the ML score (second condition), then with each of the three explanations in the last three conditions.

Their study raises a first half-tone analysis: if the explanations have made it possible to make decisions faster, the accuracy of the experts' judgment has not improved compared to the case where they analyze the raw data and would even degrade it.

We want to know if this conclusion generalise to other XAI systems designed to support expert decision. In the following, we adapt their methodology to an other application domain: e-sport prediction.

3   Methodology

Hypotheses. For our performance measures, our predictions are based on the work of Jesus et al. [15]. Our null hypothesis is that SHAP explanations should have the following impact:

1. The accuracy of user responses should be improved by the explanations
2. The response time should not be affected by the explanations.

These assumptions stem from the fact that we chose a "data + ML score" condition as the baseline. Otherwise, the explanation may represent a gain in time and a loss in accuracy. We measure different indicators of satisfaction, trust, and transparency (described in Appendix), where we expect to have "neutral" indicators with respect to the scales proposed to the user (answers centered on a Likert scale).

User. The subjects for these early experiments are students, with a potentially wide spectrum of expertise on the proposed task (some may spend all their free time on the game, and others may meet it for the first time through the experiment). Specifically, we could only to retain data from five research training students with little or no knowledge of machine learning. Of the five, only one knows the game well (user 5 in the results section).

Data. Data are aggregate match stats from League of Legends, taken at 10 min of play[1]. League of Legends is an competitive online game, known for its high visibility on the e-sports scene. This data thus contains a potentially engaging problem for students, given the popularity of the game; the task makes sense in that there is a market for betting on these matches.

On the presented dataset, 23 columns have been selected to be displayed to the users. Redundant columns have been removed: we preferred using direct statistics applied independently on the two teams instead of differences between both teams. The 39 games displayed were balanced regarding both blue and red teams' victories and error rates in both cases.

Model. The model chosen to perform the AI prediction is a Random Forest[2]. We would not use deep learning models but rather tree ensemble methods as they constitute state of the art for tabular data [26].

A few remarks about the data: each column corresponds to a performance of one of the two teams, and there is always a symmetrical column representing the result of the other team (except for "FirstBlood" feature). The model does not exploit this property. Moreover, this data is highly aggregated: one may wish to access individual performances for each team's different players, or even to display a video of the match to the users. These data are doubly "incomplete" since the outcome of a match is not defined after 10 min: there can be many turnovers so the problem may be considered from a probabilistic angle. Our model achieves a performance of 72% on its test data, which represents 25% of the dataset.

Experimental Procedure. We use two different experimental conditions: the first starts with explained data, the second starts with just data and row score.

---

[1] kaggle.com/bobbyscience/league-of-legends-diamond-ranked-games-10-min.
[2] sklearn implementation, scikit-learn.org.

In both conditions, the user is exposed successively to "explained" and "non-explained" views in equal proportions. Each participant is first assigned an ID that determines the condition used. The whole experiment is implemented using an interface made with streamlit[3], which presents the context of the experiment, data format, and the explanations format through two example pages before starting the prediction task. Then, the prediction task is done on each match data with the interface in Fig. 1. This graphical block is left empty for data with no explanations. Decisions are made using a cursor set on a scale of seven values, in order to express potential uncertainty on the result. We use sub-series from 4 to 10 matches, after which the interface mode changes (between explained and not explained interface[4]).

For each game, the answer and the response time are recorded. After the predictions, a form is proposed to the user to get feedback and collect information about his profile. The experiment lasted between 30 and 45 min for each candidate. In both conditions, users are exposed to the same data, in the same order, only the presence of explanations may vary.

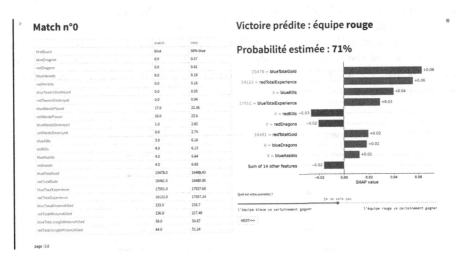

Fig. 1. Decision interface displayed to the user: on the left, the data are presented in three column: feature names, feature value for the current match and averages for reference. On the right at the top, prediction with SHAP in graphical format: the last bar of the graph represents the lesser contributions of SHAP added together. Below, a seven-step cursor that allows the user to express his prediction (translation in Appendix). (Color figure online)

---

[3] streamlit.io.

[4] The users with an odd number have first matches without SHAP explanation, the pairs start with SHAP. From match 19 on, they are exposed to the same interface mode.

4   Results

Response Accuracy. For the full analysis, we set aside the nuances in the degree of certainty of the responses to keep only three-valued data: they can only be neutral, predictions of the red team victory or the blue team victory. For the accuracy calculations, neutral responses are difficult to interpret. We decided to keep them as they represent about 10% of the responses. As correct answers were counted 1 and incorrect answers were counted 0, we decided to count the neutral as 1/2.

A first observation is that our users have mostly made decisions in accordance with the the AI's suggestions. On the 195 predictions produced, we find 23 neutral predictions (12.3%) that are not or not easily analyzable, 27 predictions going against the AI (13.3%) and 145 predictions that follow the AI (74.4%).

If we consider that AI scores near .5 express uncertainty (we will consider a score of 60% or less as uncertain), we can see that this rate of agreement increases to 86% for cases where the AI looks confident and 64% for cases where the AI looks uncertain. We can guess that the users answered intuitively in this case, while they would rather tend to follow the AI's decision.

In general, the presence of explanations seems to have little influence on users' agreement with the model. At best, we can observe a negative effect on the accuracy of the decisions, as shown in Fig. 2. This result is opposite to the results of Jesus et al. [15], which suggested that exposure to SHAP explanations should increase accuracy compared to exposure to the ML score alone.

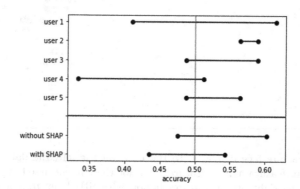

Fig. 2. Accuracy minimal and maximal estimates, considering neutral responses as misses (left points) or as good answers (right points). Our choice to count them as 1/2 equate to using the middle of these intervals as estimates. Above, we consider the global influence of the explanations' exposure on these measures, below we consider the influence of the user.

Response Time. Interestingly, it is difficult to identify any effect on response time: some decisions were made in a matter of seconds, while the longest took about 2 min. In Fig. 3, there is no observable effect of the explanations: the variance seems to be dominated by users' internal factors.

Some partial continuity appears in the sequences of response times, with explainable exceptions: peaks at the first decision and at the first change of interface (removal/addition of SHAP to indexes 10 19 25 30 35). We could also see that decision time decreases on average during the experiment, likely because of habituation, and assume that some data intrinsically require longer analysis (Fig. 4).

Table 1. Mean performances of users, with and without explanations.

User	SHAP	Accuracy	Time
1	without	0.57	31.6 ± 32.8
1	with	0.5	38.4 ± 19.7
2	without	0.65	18.7 ± 16.8
2	with	0.53	10.8 ± 10.8
3	without	0.48	52.0 ± 27.6
3	with	0.58	49.2 ± 28.7
4	without	0.55	35.6 ± 26.3
4	with	0.39	14.4 ± 17.3
5	without	0.57	24.9 ± 13.3
5	with	0.5	22.3 ± 11.0

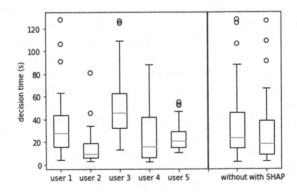

Fig. 3. On the left, box plots of the response time of the different user. On the right, the same data separated given the presence or absence of SHAP explanations.

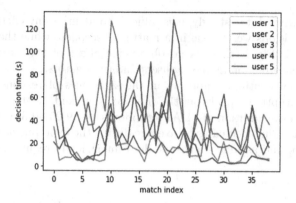

Fig. 4. Decision times graphs of the five users for each match

Although negative, these results indicate the need to solicit a large number of users and not neglect the influence of experiment construction on the measurement. The first trials of the users will necessarily be long: it is necessary to foresee a training phase and avoid changing the users' context inside the experiment too often or too abruptly.

Subjective Evaluation. This experiment used only one method of explanation, SHAP. The questions were asked in French (an English translation can be found in the appendix). Likert scales with seven levels were systematically used to collect the answers (adapting the formulation to the question). Two subjects answered the open-ended questions that were offered. Despite the explanation's lack of objective benefit, there was still some positive feedback. For example, the question "The analysis interface[5] was useful to me in making a prediction" was answered with: "somewhat agree", "agree", "agree", "strongly agree", "strongly disagree". Only the last user gave consistently negative responses, commenting in the open field: "I did not use it, it did not always give a true representation of the gap between two teams. A small gap could be represented with a large bar and therefore could be misleading. In addition, not all important values were used" (in response to "How was your experience with the model analysis interface? How did you use it?"). To the question "What would you expect from an AI trying to explain its decision to you?", he answered: "His ability to be very sure of a result but also to say when one cannot conclude anything definite". In addition to user 5, user 3 answered the same questions: "I used it to either help me with aspects I didn't understand/didn't know how to interpret, or to validate what I thought" and "Schematics but maybe also additional captions/additional explanations".

---

[5] i.e., the graphical representation of Shapley values.

5   Discussion

Our data support our second hypothesis: explanations do not seem to alter the decision time (compared to the case with ML score). However, they do not favor our first hypothesis: the accuracy was not improved but decreased. We must be cautious about drawing any conclusions about these measures. On the one hand, our users do not know much about the game: for example, the most experienced one does not play ranked games, which is however common among frequent players. Moreover, even if a subject would have a deeper experience of the game, understanding the tabular data certainly requires an effort of adaptation, which can reverse our model of what an "expert" would be. Obviously, the small number of users coupled with the small number of predictions made per user is the major limitation of our study: we will scale up the experiment a revised protocol.

One of the troublesome points of this experiment and of Jesus' et al. is the choice to work on a subsample of the data selected by the model. We can consider that the model is relatively inaccurate on these data, and therefore has little useful information to bring through the explanation. This would explain why user accuracies above 50% fall back to the mean once exposed to the explanations but not the cases where it falls below. Of course we do not already know what kind of understanding our model could have, and whether our explanation will indeed convey such an understanding to the user. Nevertheless, that is precisely why we should be cautious that our model has learnt complex patterns before using it on XAI evaluation purpose. Reciprocally, if the human capacities seem wholly exceeded by the model, the information it would provide a sort of popularization or justification (at best teaching [5]) than explanation. Considering this distinction, we see that establishing a framework of measurement to compare humans and AIs before any explanatory experiment is crucial. Only in this way can we have an a priori idea of the explanatory situation in which we are situated and of the benefit that we will draw from a method of XAI. It seems to us that the model's explanations, by analogy with its use between humans, are to be considered in a cooperative framework between entities of comparable expertise. XAI's usefulness would be demonstrated in terms of performance if it allowed a "joint decision-making" strictly more accurate than the one made by the human alone or the model alone. That was the way of proving the existence of the "wisdom of the crowds" for instance [13].

In first approach, we use the accuracy of answers as an indicator of intelligence and expertise in the task. An independent sample must be used to provide an objective comparison of the accuracies of a model and humans. Therefore, the sample should not be artificially balanced against ML's errors. However, this is open to some criticism: it potentially leaves many "simple cases" on which humans and AI would have agreed anyway and where the addition of an explanation does not seem relevant from the point of view of accuracy. It then becomes vital to estimate the intrinsic "difficulty" of each data point, but there is no general approach to this problem. We should not let a model estimate this difficulty for itself, nor humans judge it for themselves. Also, we should distinguish in this difficulty what is an actual complexity, exploitable by a calculation, and what is a simple absence of information.

Beyond this idea of local data difficulty in our experimental sample, the global nature of the task can greatly influence on the human capacity to handle the problem and the possibility for the models to reach high performances: characterizing this nature is not always easy. Two other major factors that are difficult to control for our evaluations are the user profiles, and the influence of the user interface. Beyond the selection criteria for our subjects, which of course introduce biases, humans represent noisy decision systems, which do not necessarily return the same result twice for the same problem [23]. This noise can be ignored when the number of users is high but could present an important limitation to implementing meaningful measures with small populations and should then be estimated.

Finally, there is nothing to tell us that the choice of SHAP is precisely responsible for the user's different decision-making. Maybe the simple provision of a graphical interface with importance values that are consistent with the problem but ultimately independent of the model could have an equal influence on our experience.

5.1   Future Works

In general, it seems to us that a map of datasets and corresponding tasks, accompanied by estimates of human performance (expert if possible) and model performance on these tasks, would be very useful for XAI evaluation research. It would help to direct evaluation by performance measures to promising application topics to demonstrate the usefulness of the explanations. Of course, such a census, represents a considerable amount of work for a moderate epistemic gain.

It seems reasonable to put aside possible investigations regarding interface's and local difficulty's influence. We will carry out more precise profiling of our users with respect to the task at hand. This approach must also be accompanied by the development of a training phase in the interface, which gives feedback to the user on these decisions. Otherwise, their predictions cannot fit the problem by themselves: only the response time may decrease according to the user's habituation to the interface. It will be necessary to reduce the number of inopportune changes in the interface that may have affected the experience and to keep only two series (with/without explanation), with an intermediate re-training for the user.

Ideally, our measures should be extended to other tasks and datasets but the need for some form of human expertise, in the face of an ML model, may be limiting. We could also use another explanation format: performance measures' advantage is evaluating wholly different explanations (like counterfactuals, prototypes, or model simplifications) on standard axes.

Finally, our choice for e-sport data as an application domain seems relevant to us because human decisions, although correlated a priori with those of a model, offer a significant margin of variation. For the exploitation of temporal measures, we now have to experiment a baseline without exposure to the ML score, which should allow us to observe an effect. Replicating of the experiment on a larger number of users will allow us to cope with the large variability intrinsic to this measure.

6   Conclusion

This study evaluates SHAP explanations through human performance measures on an e-sport prediction task. This methodological approach is crucial because it allows a firm grounding of XAI evaluations in the human consequences of XAI use, without any assumption about explanation type or mental model. The results of this evaluation indicate that the explanation would have caused our users to lose accuracy. The numerous methodological difficulties of the experiment have been discussed and make us hope for progress in the exploitation of the collected measures, thanks to the development of our methodologies.

Acknowledgements. This research has been supported by the group Crédit Mutuel ARKEA. We would like to thank members of the Datalabs service at the Innovation and Operation Pole at Crédit Mutuel ARKEA for their collaboration.

A   Translation of the Main Interface

On the Fig. 1, over the Shap visualisation, user could read:
"Predicted victory: *red* team
Estimated probability: 71%". Under the graph, they could read:
"What is your prediction?"
The likert scale then use the following phrasing:
"the blue team will definitely win, the blue team is likely to win, the blue team has a slight advantage over the red team, I do not know, the red team has a slight advantage over the blue team, the red team is likely to win, the red team will definitely win".

B   Translation of the Questionnaire

The following question have been asked at the end of the experiment. Questions preceded by an asterisk are open-ended, so people could write whatever they want. Most of questions were asked as affirmative sentence, and the likert scale went from "strongly disagree" to "strongly agree" (centered on "neutral"). Other likert scale went from "absolutely no" to "absolutely yes" (centered on "undecided").

- Do you know anything about the game League of Legends?
- Have you ever played or watched a full game?
- Do you play MOBAs regularly?
- Do you think you can make good predictions about winning after 10 min of play?

* (If you play ranked games) what is your rank?

- The analysis interface included all relevant information to help me make a decision.
- The analysis interface allowed me to make a decision more quickly.
- The analysis interface was helpful in making a good prediction.
- The analysis interface was easy to use.
* How was your experience with analysis interface? How did you use it?

- The analysis interface allowed me to understand how the AI worked.
- The AI used is able to make good predictions.
- The model analysis interface explained the model well, in a clear and concise way.
* What would you expect from an AI that tries to explain its decision to you?
- If you were to actually make 10-minute predictions, would you like a model to assist you?

- If you were to actually make 10-minute predictions, would you like to have the mean data?
- If you were to actually make 10-minute predictions, would you like to have the explanations of the model?
- Do you have confidence in the future development of AI?
- Would you be willing to use a similar AI system, with explained results, in another context?
* What are your expectations of using AI in a similar application setting?

- What is your level of education in computer science/engineering sciences?
- Do you have any knowledge of Artificial Intelligence?
* Do you have any other knowledge related to AI or XAI in particular?
- Do you think you are able to estimate the probability of the red team winning?
- Do you feel you made progress during use?
- Were you very focused during the experiment?
- Did the experiment make you tired?

References

1. Barredo Arrieta, A., et al.: Explainable artificial intelligence (XAI): concepts, taxonomies, opportunities and challenges toward responsible AI. Inf. Fusion **58**, 82–115 (2020)
2. Chen, C., Li, O., Tao, D., Barnett, A., Rudin, C., Su, J.K.: This looks like that: deep learning for interpretable image recognition. In: Advances in neural information processing systems 32 (2019)
3. Cirqueira, D., Nedbal, D., Helfert, M., Bezbradica, M.: Scenario-based requirements elicitation for user-centric explainable AI. In: Holzinger, A., Kieseberg, P., Tjoa, A.M., Weippl, E. (eds.) CD-MAKE 2020. LNCS, vol. 12279, pp. 321–341. Springer, Cham (2020). https://doi.org/10.1007/978-3-030-57321-8_18
4. Craven, M., Shavlik, J.: Extracting tree-structured representations of trained networks. Adv. Neural. Inf. Process. Syst. **8**, 24–30 (1995)

5. Das, D., Chernova, S.: Leveraging rationales to improve human task performance. In: Proceedings of the 25th International Conference on Intelligent User Interfaces, pp. 510–518 (2020)
6. Doshi-Velez, F., Kim, B.: Towards a rigorous science of interpretable machine learning. arXiv preprint arXiv:1702.08608 (2017)
7. Ehsan, U., et al.: The who in explainable AI: how AI background shapes perceptions of AI explanations. arXiv preprint arXiv:2107.13509. https://arxiv.org/abs/2107.13509v1 (2021)
8. Ehsan, U., Tambwekar, P., Chan, L., Harrison, B., Riedl, M.O.: Automated rationale generation: a technique for explainable AI and its effects on human perceptions. In: Proceedings of the 24th International Conference on Intelligent User Interfaces, pp. 263–274 (2019)
9. Gilpin, L.H., Bau, D., Yuan, B.Z., Bajwa, A., Specter, M., Kagal, L.: Explaining explanations: a overview of interpretability of machine learning. In: 2018 IEEE 5th International Conference on Data Science and Advanced Analytics (DSAA), pp. 80–89. IEEE (2018)
10. Goodman, B., Flaxman, S.: European Union regulations on algorithmic decision-making and a "right to explanation." AI Magazine **38**(3), 50–57 (2017)
11. Guidotti, R., Monreale, A., Ruggieri, S., Turini, F., Pedreschi, D., Giannotti, F.: A survey of methods for explaining black box models. arXiv: 1802.01933. http://arxiv.org/abs/1802.01933 (2018)
12. Hase, P., Bansal, M.: Evaluating explainable AI: which algorithmic explanations help users predict model behavior? arXiv: 2005.01831 (2020)
13. Herzog, S.M., Hertwig, R.: Harnessing the wisdom of the inner crowd. Trends Cogn. Sci. **18**(10), 504–506 (2014)
14. Hoffman, R.R., Mueller, S.T., Klein, G., Litman, J.: Metrics for explainable AI: challenges and prospects. arXiv: 1812.04608 (2019)
15. Jesus, S., et al.: How can i choose an explainer? an application-grounded evaluation of post-hoc explanations. In: Proceedings of the 2021 ACM Conference on Fairness, Accountability, and Transparency, pp. 805–815 (2021). https://doi.org/10.1145/3442188.3445941
16. Kim, B., et al.: Interpretability beyond feature attribution: quantitative testing with concept activation vectors (TCAV). In: International Conference on Machine Learning, pp. 2668–2677. PMLR (2018). http://proceedings.mlr.press/v80/kim18d.html. iSSN: 2640–3498
17. Lage, I., et al.: Human evaluation of models built for interpretability. In: Proceedings of the AAAI Conference on Human Computation and Crowdsourcing, vol. 7, issue: 1, pp. 59–67 (2019)
18. Li, J., Chen, X., Hovy, E., Jurafsky, D.: Visualizing and understanding neural models in NLP. arXiv preprint arXiv:1506.01066 (2015)
19. Lipton, Z.C.: The mythos of model interpretability. Queue **16**(3), 31–57 (2018). ACM New York, NY, USA
20. Lundberg, S.M., et al.: Explainable AI for trees: from local explanations to global understanding. arXiv preprint arXiv:1905.04610 (2019)
21. Lundberg, S.M., Lee, S.I.: A unified approach to interpreting model predictions. In: Advances in Neural Information Processing Systems, pp. 4765–4774 (2017)
22. Miller, T.: Explanation in artificial intelligence: insights from the social sciences. Artificial Intelligence **267**, 1–38 (2019)
23. Mueller, S.T., Weidemann, C.T.: Decision noise: an explanation for observed violations of signal detection theory. Psychonomic Bullet. Rev. **15**(3), 465–494 (2008). https://doi.org/10.3758/PBR.15.3.465

24. Panigutti, C., Perotti, A., Pedreschi, D.: Doctor XAI: an ontology-based approach to black-box sequential data classification explanations. In: Proceedings of the 2020 Conference on Fairness, Accountability, and Transparency. pp. 629–639. FAT* 2020, Association for Computing Machinery, New York, NY, USA (2020). https:// doi.org/10.1145/3351095.3372855
25. Ribeiro, M.T., Singh, S., Guestrin, C.: "Why should i trust you?" Explaining the predictions of any classifier. In: Proceedings of the 22nd ACM SIGKDD International Conference on Knowledge Discovery and Data Mining, pp. 1135–1144 (2016)
26. Shwartz-Ziv, R., Armon, A.: Tabular data: deep Learning is not all you need. arXiv: 2106.03253 (2021)
27. Wachter, S., Mittelstadt, B., Russell, C.: Counterfactual explanations without opening the black box: automated decisions and the GDPR. Harv. JL Tech. **31**, 841 (2017)

Improving the Quality of Rule-Based GNN Explanations

Ataollah Kamal[1], Elouan Vincent[2], Marc Plantevit[2], and Céline Robardet[1(✉)]

[1] Univ Lyon, INSA Lyon, CNRS, UCBL, LIRIS, UMR5205,
69621 Villeurbanne, France
celine.robardet@insa-lyon.fr
[2] EPITA LRE, 94276 Le Kremlin-Bicêtre, France

Abstract. Recent works have proposed to explain GNNs using activation rules. Activation rules allow to capture specific configurations in the embedding space of a given layer that is discriminant for the GNN decision. These rules also catch hidden features of input graphs. This requires to associate these rules to representative graphs. In this paper, we propose on the one hand an analysis of heuristic-based algorithms to extract the activation rules, and on the other hand the use of transport-based optimal graph distances to associate each rule with the most specific graph that triggers them.

1 Introduction

One of the purposes of artificial intelligence is to help human beings to perform cognitive tasks, especially categorization which is among the most important ones. Supporting human beings in this process can be considered in two ways: either by carrying out the process for them or by just helping them so that they keep control of the ongoing process. In this paper, we adopt the second point of view and consider the use of machine learning tools to automatically associate objects with classes in a very efficient way (generally using numerical models with many learned parameters) to then seek to interpret the classification mechanisms to understand how the classification has been made. By making the models explicit, we hope to increase their scope of application in areas with high societal challenges (medicine, justice) but also for the discovery of knowledge (scientific impact). The effectiveness of many recent learning algorithms is at the price of their interpretability, as they rely on the learning of latent variables. This is particularly the case for Graph Neural Networks (GNNs) [22] that classify graphs by learning embedding vectors to represent each of the graph nodes in a metric space so that the classification task based on these vectors is optimized. These vectors encode a lot of information that is unreadable to humans and need to be "interpreted".

Interpretation is an ill-defined concept that has been specified in [5] as covering three distinct aspects: the *comprehensibility*, i.e. the ability for the user to understand the model well enough to be able to apply it manually to new data,

I. Koprinska et al. (Eds.): ECML PKDD 2022 Workshops, CCIS 1752, pp. 467–482, 2023.
https://doi.org/10.1007/978-3-031-23618-1_31

the *justifiability*, which specifies whether the model is in line with existing knowledge, and the *plausibility*, i.e. the pragmatic value of the model for the user. In this article, we mainly address the first two aspects by identifying the main activation rules as well as the subgraph that they characterize. The first step relies on pattern mining techniques that have been shown to be valuable for interpreting machine learning black box models [19], especially by providing comprehensible interpretations of a latent space. The second step leverages techniques of Optimal Transport on graphs [17] to transform comprehensible interpretations into justifiable models that makes it possible to evaluate whether the model is in line with existing knowledge expressed in a graph language.

2   Related Work

GNNs are generating considerable interest thanks to their performance in several tasks such as node classification [14], link prediction [27] and graph classification [22,23]. Many cutting-edge techniques improve the performance of models. However, there are few studies that address the explainability of GNNs in comparison to the areas of image and text where an abundance of methods have been proposed [2,11]. As established by [26], the existing methods for the explanation of convolutional neural networks for the classification of images cannot be directly used on data which is not grid-like such as graphs. For example, the methods that computes an abstract images via back-propagation [16] provide non-exploitable results when they are applied to discrete adjacency matrices. Those that learn soft masks to find important regions of images [13] do not apply to discrete data as well. Though, some methods have been proposed to explain GNNs over the past four years. One can identify three types of explanation methods: (i) instance-level and (ii) model-level explanation methods, that both explain the output of the model, and (iii) rule-based approaches that in addition consider the latent space built by the GNN.

2.1   Instance-level Methods

Given an input graph, *instance-level* methods aim to provide input-dependent explanations by identifying important input characteristics on which the model builds its prediction. The gradient/feature-based methods [1] use the gradients or hidden feature map values to compute the importance of the input features. Perturbation-based methods [9,24] learn a graph mask by studying the prediction changes when perturbing the input graphs. GNNExplainer [24] learns a soft mask by maximizing the mutual information between the original prediction and the predictions of the perturbed graphs. PGExplainer [9] uses a generative probabilistic model to learn succinct underlying structures from the input graph data as explanations. Surrogate methods [6,20] explain an input graph by sampling its neighborhood and learning an interpretable model. GrapheLime [6] uses a Hilbert-Schmidt Independence Criterion Lasso as a surrogate model. PGM-Explainer [20] builds a probabilistic graphical model for explaining node or graph classification models. These surrogate models can be misleading because the user tends to generalize beyond its neighborhood an explanation related to a local model. GraphSVX [4] falls into these 4 categories by learning a surrogate explanation model on a perturbed dataset, the explained prediction is decomposed among input nodes and features based on their respective contribution.

2.2   Model-level Methods

The only existing model-level method is XGNN [25]. It consists in training a graph generator to maximize the predicted probability for a certain class and uses such graph patterns to explain this class. However, it is based on the strong assumption that each class can be explained by a single graph, which is unrealistic when considering complex phenomena.

2.3   Rule-based Methods

INSIDE-GNN [18] does not only consider the output of the model when building its explanations: it also considers the intern weight matrix and derive rules that associate a set of activated components to a class. This work is rooted in the FORSIED framework [3] which allows to address the problem of pattern flooding by identifying a set of non redundant and informative patterns. As our work heavily relies on it, we detail below its main characteristics.

Activation Matrix. Considering a set of graphs $\mathcal{G}$ where each graph $G = (V, E, L)$ has labels L on vertices. A Graph Neural Network classifies each graph of $\mathcal{G}$ into two categories $\{0, 1\}$: $\text{GNN} : \mathcal{G} \rightarrow \{0, 1\}$. We use a Graph Convolutional Networks (GCN) [7] that computes vectors $\mathbf{h}_v^\ell$ associated to the ego-graph centered in vertex v with radius ℓ, recursively. Such an ego-graph is the sub-graph of G induced by v and all its neighbors at distance ℓ. Each vector is of size K and ℓ varies from 0 up to L (the maximum number of layers in the GNN), two hyperparameters of the GNN. The vectors $\mathbf{h}_v^\ell$ capture the key characteristics of the graphs for the classification task, especially vector components of high value. We therefore consider the activation matrix that has to be interpreted:

$$\widehat{H^\ell}[v, k] = \begin{cases} 1 \text{ if } (\mathbf{h}_v^\ell)_k > 0, \text{ with } k = 1 \ldots K, \text{ the dimension of the embeddings} \\ 0 \text{ otherwise} \end{cases}$$

Activation Rules. Activation rules group vector components that are mostly activated together in graphs having the same GNN decision. $\mathbf{A}^\ell \rightarrow c$ is composed of a binary vector $\mathbf{A}^\ell$ of size K and $c \in \{0, 1\}$ a decision class of the GNN. A graph $g_i = (V_i, E_i, L_i) \in \mathcal{G}$ activates the rule if there is a node v in V_i such that $\widehat{H^\ell}[v, k] = (\mathbf{A}^\ell)_k, \forall k = 1 \cdots K$. The activated graphs with GNN decision c form the support of the rule. Activated rules are more interesting if their supports are largely homogeneous in term of GNN decisions, i.e. the graphs of the support are mainly classified either in class 0 or in class 1.

Measuring the Interest of an Activation Rule. As theorized in the FOR-SIED framework [3], the knowledge extracted from the activation matrix is modeled by a background model that is used to evaluate the interest of a rule. Considering the discrete random variable $H^\ell[v, k]$ associated to the activation matrix $\widehat{H}^\ell[v, k]^1$, the background knowledge is defined by the probabilities $P(H^\ell[v, k] = 1)$. Considering the assumption that all $H^\ell[v, k]$ are independent of each other, the interest of a rule is evaluated by the negative log-probability of the product of $P(H^\ell[v, k] = 1)$, for v activated by the rule and k such that $(A^\ell)_k = 1$:

$$IC(R, \mathcal{G}) = \sum_{g_i \in \mathbf{Supp}(R, \mathcal{G})} \min_{\substack{v \in V_i, \\ \mathbf{Act}(R, v)}} \sum_{(A^\ell)_k = 1} \log(P(H^\ell[v, k] = 1))$$

with $R = A^\ell \to c$, **Supp** the supporting graphs and **Act** the nodes that activate the rule. A pattern with a large IC is more informative but is more difficult to assimilate. Thus, IC value is contrasted by its description length which measures the complexity of communicating the pattern to the user:

$$SI(A^\ell \to c, \mathcal{G}) = \frac{IC(A^\ell \to c, \mathcal{G})}{\alpha.|A^\ell| + \nu}$$

with α the cost for the user to assimilate each component and ν a fixed cost for the pattern[2]. However, in order to identify rules specific to a GNN decision, we consider the difference of subjective interestingness of the measure evaluated on the two groups of graphs. We denote by $\mathcal{G}^0$ (resp. $\mathcal{G}^1$) the graphs $g_i \in \mathcal{G}$ such that $\mathrm{GNN}(g_i) = 0$ (resp. $\mathrm{GNN}(g_i) = 1$). The subjective interest of the rule $A^\ell \to c$ with respect to the classes is evaluated by

$$SI\_SG(A^\ell \to c) = \omega_c \, SI(A^\ell \to c, \mathcal{G}^c) - \omega_{1-c} \, SI(A^\ell \to c, \mathcal{G}^{1-c}).$$

The weights ω_0 and ω_1 are used to counterbalance the measure in unbalanced decision problems. The rational is to reduce the SI values of the majority class. We set $\omega_0 = \max(1, \frac{|\mathcal{G}^1|}{|\mathcal{G}^0|})$ and $\omega_1 = \max(1, \frac{|\mathcal{G}^0|}{|\mathcal{G}^1|})$.

Computing the Background Model. The background model is initialized with basic assumptions about the activation matrix:

$$\sum_v P(H^\ell[v, k] = 1) = \sum_v P(\widehat{H}^\ell[v, k] = 1), \quad \sum_k P(H^\ell[v, k] = 1) = \sum_k P(\widehat{H}^\ell[v, k] = 1).$$

However, these constraints do not completely specify the probability matrix. and we choose the probability distribution with the maximum entropy.

Once a rule $A^\ell \to c$ has been extracted, it brings some information about the activation matrix that can be integrated into P: $P(H^\ell[v, k] = 1)$ is set to 1, $\forall k$ such that $(A^\ell)_k = 1$ and v such that $\widehat{H}^\ell[v, k] = (\mathbf{A}^\ell)_k, \forall k = 1 \cdots K$.

---

[1] We use hats to signify the empirical values.

[2] We set $\nu = 1$ and $\alpha = 0.6$, as the constant parameter ν does not influence the relative ranking of the patterns, and with a value of 1, it ensures that the DL value is greater than 1. With $\alpha = 0.6$, we express a slight preference toward shorter patterns.

2.4 Limitations and Desiderata

Most of the introduced methods attempt to explain a GNN model from its final decision. INSIDE_GNN [18], is the only one to analyze the internal structure of the network and to build an explication on the different layers of GNN. However, due to the exhaustive search employed to construct the activation rules, this method is time-consuming, which makes it difficult to use for large sets of graphs. Moreover, these rules are not intelligible in themselves and it is important to know which parts of the graphs they capture. These are the two limits that we address in the following.

3 Computing Activation Rules

We propose and study three approaches to compute iteratively the activation rule $R = A^\ell \to c$ with the largest SI_SG value and to integrate it in the background distribution P to take into account the knowledge provided by the rule. The first method is an exact algorithm, the two others are approximation methods. In the two last approaches, we are able to consider activated components (indices k such that $(\mathbf{h}_v^\ell)_k > 0$) and non-activated components (when $(\mathbf{h}_v^\ell)_k \leq 0$).

3.1 Using an Exhaustive Search

This enumerate-and-rank approach starts with the empty rule $\emptyset \to c$ and recursively add components to A. We use a branch and bound approach, updating the current best SI_SG value found so far, using the following upper bound:

$$
UB\_SI(R) = \frac{w_c}{\alpha(|A|) + \nu} \times \sum_{g_i \in \mathbf{Supp}(R, \mathcal{G}^c)} \min_{\substack{v \in V_i, \\ \mathbf{Act}(R, v)}} \sum_{(A\&D)_k = 1} \log(P(H^\ell[v, k] = 1))
$$

$$
- \frac{w_{1-c}}{\alpha(|A\&D|) + \nu} \times \sum_{g \in \mathbf{Supp}(A\&D, \mathcal{G}^{1-c})} \min_{\substack{v \in V_i, \\ \mathbf{Act}(R, v)}} \sum_{(A)_k = 1} \log(P(H^\ell[v, k] = 1))
$$

with D a vector whose one's values represent the activated components that can be further added to A during the enumeration process, and $A\&D$ the bitwise **and** operation between vectors A and D. $|A|$ is the L1 norm of A. UB_SI makes the recursion stop if its value is less that the one of the current best rule found.

3.2 Using Beam Search

This algorithm is a tree search algorithm pretty similar to the breadth-first search with the difference that in each stage it only keeps a fixed number of descendants. A selector, an atomic proposition of the form $X == Y$, where X is a component and $Y \in \{True, False\}$, describes the status of a component. A conjunction D of selectors forms a description. For a description D, the length of the description is the number of its selectors. A graph g is in the support of D, if D is true for at least one node of g from logical point of view. Therefore, we can have a mapping between a rule and a description and thanks to this mapping we can define subjective interestingness (SI_SG) for a description. To this ends, the SI_SG of a description is the subjective interestingness SI_SG of its mapped rule. Each node of the beam search tree corresponds to a description and its children are those descriptions by adding one new selector to the corresponding description. The root of the tree is the description with length 0. Thus, nodes in the $depth = 1$ are selectors. At each stage of the algorithm we use a beam-width (bw) parameter that indicates the number of nodes that at the end of the stage would be kept. Those with the highest SI_SG values are kept. Besides discovering the new nodes, we save the node with the best SI_SG that so far we have found. As the depth of the tree can be too high and regarding the fact that we are interested in simple rules, we limit the exploration up to a certain depth. In our task, $bw = 20$ and the maximum depth is 9. After each run, we get one rule in return. Then we update the model with respect to the rule. We use PySubgroup framework [8] for this task.

3.3   Using Monte Carlo Tree Search

MCTS partially explores the tree of possible rules where each node v represents a partial rule as a tuple $(free, fixed)$: the components of the embedding vector are either in the $free$ or the $fixed$ set of the tuple. The $free$ set contains the components that have not been treated yet, and $fixed$ is a set of couples (x, y) that indicates that component x has the state y, y being either $activated$, $non - activated$ or $loose$ meaning that x is activated, non-activated or there is no constraint on it. A partial rule with $free = \emptyset$ is called a rule.

MCTS focuses on analyzing the most promising partial rules, expanding the search tree based on random sampling of the search space. Monte Carlo tree search is based on many roll-outs. In each playout, a rule is constructed by selecting component values at random until $free = \emptyset$. The value of SI_SG from the obtained rule is then used to weight the nodes in the tree so that the best nodes are more likely to be chosen in future roll-outs. To that end, v_1 and v_2 are two numerical values also associated to each node v, with v_1 is the subjective interestingness value of the rule $fixed \cup \{(x, loose) : x \in free\}$, and v_2 value is defined in the roll-out and propagation step of the algorithm. Each round of Monte Carlo tree search consists of four steps:

- **Selection**: Starting from the root node, it selects successive child nodes until a leaf node is reached. A leaf is any node that has a potential child and from which no simulation (roll-out) has yet been done. The section of child nodes is biased so that the tree expand towards the most promising rules, which is the essence of Monte Carlo tree search. A child v is selected if it satisfies $SI\_UB(v) \geq SI\_SG(best\_rule)$ and maximizes the value: $v_1 + \frac{v_2}{n_v} + \kappa \sqrt{\frac{n*\log(N_v)}{n_v}}$. N_v is the number of times the parent of v has been visited, n_v

is the number of times v has been visited, and $n = |fixed|$. Note that in case $n_v = 0$, this function equals to ∞. κ is set to 100.

- **Roll-out and Propagation**: From a leaf-node, if this node is not terminal (i.e. $free \neq \emptyset$), we randomly assign values to the components in $free$ to reach a rule. Then the subjective interestingness of this rule is computed and added in v_2 variables of all the nodes in the path from this node to the root (propagation). In case that SI_SG of this node is the best value found so far, we store it as the $best\_rule$. To avoid visiting already visited terminal nodes, we add to each ith node of the path the value $(-1)^i \frac{x}{2^i}$ to v_2, where $x = SI\_SG$.

- **Expand Children**: Once a node has been visited, we expand all its children and we pursue with the first child u such that $SI\_UB(u) \geq SI\_SG(best\_rule)$. The expand consists in building $2 \times |free|$ children by taking a component in $free$ and assigning values *activated*, *desactivated*, or *loose*.

Each run of the algorithm finds one rule and consists of 100,000 iterations of the above steps. There is another termination condition for a run: if there is a node v, with $n_v > 500$, the run terminates. After finding a rule, we update the model the same as the exact method. We run the MCTS until either we reach 10 rules, or reach a rule with $SI\_SG < 10$ or there would be at least one rule r for each component c in which c has a non-free state.

4 Transforming Rules into Subgraphs

The activation rules make it possible to isolate the characteristics of the graphs useful to the task of classification. However, although we know that the graphs supporting the rule have common characteristics, we do not know which ones it is. We then propose to search for these properties that the graphs supporting the rule have in common by searching for the median graph of this set. This approach makes it possible to summarize the whole set of supporting graphs by a single realistic graph. As we would like to calculate a median for a set of graphs, we need to define a distance between two graphs. Being able to leverage both features and structural information from graphs to calculate their distance can be time consuming, requiring the combination of these two pieces of information in a way that makes it possible to capture the similarity between graphs. We opt for the use of a distance based on Optimal Transport known to unveil the geometric nature of attributed graphs. Wasserstein or Gromov-Wasserstein metrics focus only on features or structure respectively. However, in [17] authors introduced the distance Fused Gromov-Wasserstein (FGW) that exploits jointly both information.

4.1 Optimal Transport

Optimal Transport (OT) defines a distance between two probability distributions. It already prove its utility in a lot of fields, this is not yet very developed for graphs. Features can be compared using a standard metric, such as l_2. At the same time, structural comparison should be done via an isometric invariant metric. Gromov-Wasserstein distance has been introduced in [10] to compare two distance metrics.

In [17], authors introduce the Fused Gromov-Wasserstein (FGW) using OT which uses Gromov-Wasserstein distance on structure and Wasserstein distance on features. At each graph, vertices will be mapped into two metric spaces. One to capture the features (with metric d) and one to capture the structure of the graph (with metric C).

The FGW distance looks for the coupling π between the vertices of the graph that minimizes a cost function which is a linear combination of a cost $d(a_i, b_j)$ of feature transportation between the vertices of the two graphs and a cost $|C_1(i, k) - C_2(j, l)|$ of structure transportation, where C_1 and C_2 are the structure matrix of the two graphs which are compared. FGW is null iff graphs have the same number of vertices and if there exists a one to one mapping between the vertices of the graphs which respect both shortest-paths and the features. The complexity is in $O(n^2m + nm^2)$ and FGW defines a semi-metric.

4.2   Barycenter

A notion of barycenter is also introduced in [17] based on FGW distance. It looks for the graph that minimizes the sum of (weighted) FGW distances within a given set of structured data associated with structure matrices, features and base histograms. We cannot use directly the barycenter in our method for the following reasons: (1) To compute the barycenter of a set of graphs, we need to specify the parameter n that defines the number of vertices in the generated graph; (2) Graphs that are generated are not guaranteed to be realistic; (3) It cannot work on graphs labeled with discrete values. This justifies our following proposal for computing median graphs.

4.3   Associating a Graph to a Rule

To generate completely realistic graphs with an embedding close to an activation rule, we propose to calculate the median graph of all the graphs of the support (those that activate the rule), and then to perform a best first enumeration to find the subgraph with the highest score on the activation rule.

Median Graph. Computing a median graph guaranties that the graph is realist as it is an element of the set of graphs. Also, we are sure that this graph activates the rule. The median graph of a set G of graphs is the graph of G whose average FGW distance to other graphs of G is minimal. It requires to compute all distances between every pair of graphs which can be time expansive. Therefore, we propose to compute an approximation of the median. It makes it possible to avoid considering graphs that are close to other ones.

In Algorithm 1, the approximate median of a set of graphs G starts with and empty set of selected graphs S. It first draws a graph g uniformly at random in G and adds it to S. Then, all the distances between g and the graphs of G are computed. A loop starts that consists in drawing at random a new graph g from $G \setminus S$, but this time according to the distances $dist(g, S)$. This graph is added to S. The loop stops when $dist(g, S)$ is small enough.

The further the graph is from the set, the higher its probability of being drawn and added to the set S. When the loop stops, the median graph on the set S is computed and returned.

Algorithm 1. Approximate median graph

Require: G a set of graphs, t a threshold
Ensure: Median graph
1: $S \leftarrow \{\}$
2: $g \leftarrow$ drawn from G
3: $S \leftarrow S \cup \{g\}$
4: **repeat**
5:     draw $g \sim dist(g, S)$
6:     $S \leftarrow S \cup \{g\}$;
7: **until** $(dist(g, S) < t)$
8: **return** median(S)

The approximate median graph procedure only computes $\sum_{i=i}^{q}(n - i)i = q(q + 1)\left(\frac{n}{2} - \frac{2q+1}{6}\right)$ FGW distances, instead of n^2, with n the size of G and q the number of iterations[3]. In practice q is between 10% to 40% of n.

Improving the Median Graph to Better Describe the Rule. The median graph supports the rule but it is potentially not specific to it and may contain additional information not related to the rule. Starting from the median graph, or its approximation, we search for a subgraph whose embedding vector is the closest to the activation rule. This proximity between the embedding vector and the rule is evaluated by the Cosine metric between the vectors as in [19]. To maximize the Cosine value from a graph g, we first compute the Cosine value for g. Then, we enumerate all the subgraphs of g that are obtained by removing a single vertex. The subgraph with the largest Cosine value is taken, and the process iterates until no better graph is found.

5 Experiments

The purpose of the experiments is twofold: the comparative study of the algorithms to extract activation rules in terms of computation time and rule quality, and the study of distances based on the optimal transport to associate the most

---

[3] $\sum_{i=1}^{q}(n - i)\,i = n\sum_{i=1}^{q}i - \sum_{i=1}^{q}i^2 = n\frac{q}{2}(1+q) - \frac{q(q+1)(2q+1)}{6} = q(q+1)\left(\frac{n}{2} - \frac{2q+1}{6}\right)$.

specific graph to each of the rules. For these experiments, we trained a GNN with 3 layers of dimension $K = 20$ for each dataset. We mined at most 10 rules for each layer and class with $SI\_SG > 10$. All the experiments have been written in python and done on a machine with 8 Intel(R) Xeon(R) W-2125 CPU 4.00GHz cores 128GB RAM, and Debian GNU/Linux operating system.

5.1   Datasets

We have used four datasets Aids [12], BBBP [21], Mutagen [12] and BA2 [24]. BA2 is a synthetic dataset in which graphs with the label 0 have a cycle of length 5 and the graphs of opposite class, have "house" motifs. Graphs in the rest of the datasets represent real molecules. Main characteristics of these datasets are given in Table 1 (left).

Table 1. Dataset description: number of graphs, number of graphs with positive and negative labels, and average number of nodes and edges in each dataset (left). Time comparison for MCTS and exhaustive search. Times are in the format of hh:mm (right).

Dataset Name	#Graphs	(#neg, #pos)	Avg. Nodes	Avg. Edges
Aids	2000	(400,1600)	15.69	322
BBBP	1640	(389,1251)	24.08	51.96
Mutagen	4337	(2401, 1936)	30.32	61.54
BA2	1000	(500, 500)	25	50.92

Dataset	MCTS	Exhaustive search
Aids	14:24	11:14
BBBP	05:15	13:29
Mutagen	35:10	69:16
BA2	00:37	02:22

5.2   Computing Rules

We evaluate two approximation methods, beam search and MCTS, in comparison with the exhaustive search method. The main goal of our work is to reduce the running time. However, we should be careful what we lose in price of the time. Therefore, we measure the total interestingness of patterns obtained by each method in comparison to the exhaustive search. To assess how explainable our patterns are, we use fidelity, infidelity, and sparsity measures.

Time Comparison. Among all the methods, beam search has the best time. All the experiments have been done under twenty minutes. In the second place, MCTS has a better time in three datasets (BA2, BBBP and Mutagen) than exhaustive search. However, in the Aids dataset, the process did not complete in less time than the exhaustive search. This problem is due to the computation of rules for the last layer of the GNN. In the Table 1 (right), the time needed by MCTS and exhaustive search methods are compared.

Cumulative Subjective Interestingness (CSI). To evaluate how good is the quality of the rules mined by beam search and MCTS, one factor is cumulative subjective interestingness of them. Figure 1 shows that exhaustive search has the best CSI in non-synthetic datasets, MCTS works better than beam search despite its early termination in the Aids due to the runtime exceeding. Another interesting point is in the BA2 dataset with MCTS. For the last layer and class 0, the first and second rules discovered by exhaustive search have SI_SG of 700 and 261 respectively and for the same class and layer, by MCTS, the first two rules have SI_SG of 674 and 433 respectively which resulted to have a better CSI in MCTS, which is an approximate method than exhaustive search as an exact algorithm. Therefore, although that MCTS in some places can be time-consuming, it can have interesting features to study.

When we consider non-activated components, although we have more general space, we cannot get better results than when we have only activated components, except for BA2 and Aids. In BA2 we obtain results even better than the exhaustive search and in Aids they are better than the approximation methods but not better than the exact one. The main drawback of the MCTS with the mode consisting activated and non-activated components, is the running time. We could not obtain results for the Mutagen dataset due to this problem.

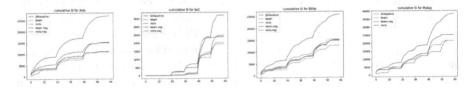

Fig. 1. Cumulative subjective interestingness comparison between the three methods (exhaustive search, MCTS and beam search). In each chart, the horizontal axis is the number of the rules and the vertical axis is SI_SG. The suffix ".neg", represent methods while considering non-activated patterns.

Fidelity, Infidelity, and Sparsity. So far we have rules that are not still human interpretable. To have some human-friendly explanations, in each graph that activates a pattern we build a mask for that pattern. Considering a graph g in the support of the considered rule and $s \subseteq V_g$ is the set of its vertices that activate all the components of the rule. Then the mask for graph g is the induced subgraph by $s \cup N(s)$ where $N(s)$ is the neighbors of s. We expect the mask to be the reason for the decision of the GNN for graph G. To measure how well these masks capture the decision of the GNN, we use three measures fidelity, infidelity, and sparsity [15]. Fidelity measures how the GNN decision changes when removing the mask from the graph. It should be maximized. The infidelity measures the difference in the GNN decision when considering the whole graph and only the mask. It should be minimized. These metrics are not enough to assess a set of masks. As an illustration, assume that $m_i = g_i$ for $1 \leq i \leq n$. In this case, infidelity can be 0. Therefore, we need another metric that is sensitive

Table 2. Assessing the explanations with several metrics. A better explainer achieves higher fidelity, lower infidelity while keeping a sparsity close to 1. The suffix (neg) represent methods while considering activated and non-activated components.

Model	(a) Fidelity				(b) Infidelity				(c) Sparsity			
	Aids	BBBP	Mutagen	BA2	Aids	BBBP	Mutagen	BA2	Aids	BBBP	Mutagen	BA2
Exhaustive	0.179	0.312	0.499	0.343	0.767	0.420	0.305	0.003	0.884	0.916	0.962	0.032
MCTS	0.178	0.624	0.526	0.343	0.767	0.131	0.344	0.004	0.877	0.265	0.939	0.041
BS	0.792	0.522	0.514	0.343	0.074	0.170	0.309	0.002	0.270	0.452	0.938	0.028
MCTS neg.	0.172	0.322	N/A	0.341	0.767	0.385	N/A	0.029	0.901	0.899	N/A	0.105
BS neg.	0.808	0.304	0.417	0.343	0.036	0.352	0.341	0.006	0.132	0.804	0.989	0.058
GnnEx	0.036	0.100	0.177	0.093	0.036	0.099	0.140	0.223	0.501	0.501	0.505	0.804
PGEx	0.032	0.098	0.157	0.004	0.038	0.098	0.157	0.353	0.547	0.534	0.515	0.955
PGM-Ex	0.080	0.212	0.123	0.222	0.766	0.482	0.347	0.296	0.862	0.884	0.900	0.746
SVXEx	0.003	0.008	0.039	0.004	0.771	0.489	0.356	0.341	0.988	0.940	0.931	0.943

to the proportion of a graph used as its mask: $Sparsity(M) = \frac{1}{n}\sum i = 1^n(1 - \frac{|m_i|}{|g_i|})$. So in the case that we have masks identical to their corresponding graphs, which minimizes the fidelity, sparsity will be zero too. Thus, the greater sparsity means the better masks.

Table 2 shows the values of these metrics compared to state of the art methods for explaining GNNs. As it can be seen, on the Aids dataset, MCTS has comparable results in all of the metrics to the exhaustive search. Although beam search has better fidelity and infidelity than MCTS and exhaustive search, it has lower sparsity. It can be interpreted that activation rules obtained by this method cover too many nodes. On the BBBP, both methods in terms of fidelity and infidelity have outperformed the exhaustive search. However, sparsity for both of them is lower than the one of exhaustive search. On the Mutagen and BA2 datasets, metrics are pretty close which means that rules captured by the two approximation methods are as explainable as those captured by the exact method.

These preliminary experiments do not make it possible to conclude on the added-value of the non-activated components. Other rules evaluation measures would be necessary.

5.3 Finding a Representative Graph for a Rule

Our goal is to generate a representative graph for each rule with median approximation and best first enumeration[4]. This experimental study aims to answer the following questions: Is the median approximation good? Is the reduction of the execution time of the approximation significant? How close the median approximation is to the embedding of a targeted rules? How good the best first enumeration improves the score? We compare the generated graph to those generated by DISCERN [19]. For FGW, we set $\alpha = 0.9$, giving more importance to

---

[4] All algorithms are implemented in Python, using the FGW code given by the author https://github.com/ElouanV/optimal_transpor_for_gnn.

the structural information, but in molecule, features and structure information are correlated. We use shortest path as a method for structure matrix of graphs and *sqeuclidean* to compute the cost matrix between the features. In median approximation, we set the threshold $t = 10^{-10}$. In score computation, we use *Cosine* metrics to compute the similarity between an ego-graph and a rule. Most of the experiments are done on two rules of Mutagen datasets (rule 23 and 28) as we know that they are highly correlated to the mutagenicity.

Median Approximation Quality. To study the median approximation quality, the distance between the median of a set and its approximation, we compute at each iteration the distance between the real median and the median of the set S (see Fig. 2). But, in this set of graphs, there are a lot of graphs that are really close to each others, and even some graphs are identical. For example, the real median graph of this set exists in nine copies. The median approximation function uses a threshold to stop when the distance between the newly selected graph and the set S is too small. This distance is monitored over iterations on the same rule and shown in Fig. 2.

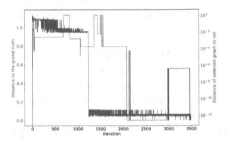

Fig. 2. Distance between the selected graph and the set S at each iteration on a logarithmic scale in red, distance between real median of a set of 3490 graphs supporting rule 23 of Mutagen and the approximation of median over iterations using FGW distance in blue. (Color figure online)

Here, the algorithm stops at iteration 1239 over 3490. It means that we only compute the median on 35% of the graphs of the set. The distance between the median of this set and its approximation is 0.8 which seems to far comparing to all distances between graphs of this set, but it shows that there is a lot of duplicated graphs in the set, and the approximation eliminates them and find a median graph that may better represent the set. On other rules, like the rule 28 of Mutagen, the approximation converges quickly to the same graph as the real median. On the set of graph that are not big enough i.e. less than 200 graphs, the approximation methods is useless since.

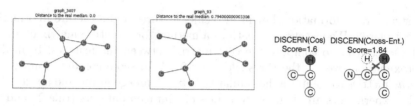

Fig. 3. The real median of the graphs from rule 23 of Mutagen *(left)* and the approximation with $t = 10^{-10}$ *(middle)*. Graphs generated by DISCERN on rule 23, red cross highlights unrealistic bonds or molecules *(right)*. (Color figure online)

On Fig. 3, we compare the median graph of all graphs of the rule 28 of Mutagen and the median approximation of the same set. First of all, they have the same number of vertices. The difference between them comes from the nitrogen atom, which is not present in the median approximation, and the structure also is a bit different, but in both cases, we can identify three part link by an atom of carbon in the middle. Moreover, both graphs have the same number of atoms of carbon. When we compare it to the graph generated by the DISCERN method on the same rule Fig. 3 (right), we find in both of our graphs the three carbon chains, but the nitrogen atom is only present on the real median.

Median Approximation Execution Time. We also want to study the execution time we can win to balance with the loss of accuracy. The execution time reduction depends on each set. On the same rule of Mutagen in Fig. 4 (left), we can observe that the execution time over iterations is almost linear, so by selecting only 35% of the graphs, we highly reduce the execution time by almost 60%. In Fig. 4 (right), we can see the percentage of graphs use to compute the median from a set thanks to the approximation. Among these 60 rules, some of them contain more than 10 000 graphs, which is a lot more than what we have seen in rule 23 of Mutagen. We can see that the percentage of graphs sectioned for the approximation decreases when the number of graphs in the set increases. When there is more than 10 000 graphs, we only select less than 10% of them which allows us to reduce the computation time significantly. When there is less than 1000 graphs, the approximation use almost all the graphs to compute the median, but it is not an issue.

Are the Result Good?. We compute the median approximation on the 60 rules of AIDS dataset, and use the computed median as starting seed for the best first enumeration. In Fig. 5, we focus on the rule 54, and we compare the median approximation to the output of the best enumeration first. The score is increasing from 0.48 to 0.65 thanks to the exploration, and the result is a cycle of 5 atoms.

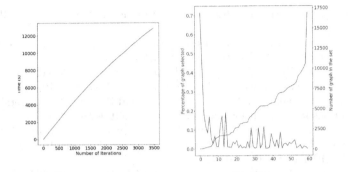

Fig. 4. Computation time over iterations of median approximation (rule 23 of Mutagen) in second (left). Proportion of graphs use from a set in for an approximation for the 60 rules of AIDS dataset in blue (sorted) and number of graphs in each set of graphs in red (right). (Color figure online)

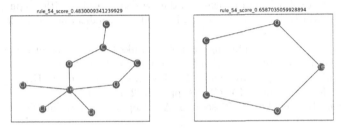

Fig. 5. Median approximation of the rule 54 of AIDS dataset (left) and the subgraph generated by the best first enumeration (right).

6 Conclusion

We have proposed two alternative algorithms for computing activation rules. Experiments showed that beam search reduces the computation time significantly and in terms of fidelity and infidelity has acceptable results. We have also introduced a novel method for explaining internal representations of GNNs. With a median graph computation and a better first enumeration, we associate each rule with a realistic graph that fully embeds in the subspace defined by the activation rule. The study shows that the median approximation makes it possible to reduce the computation time without losing the quality of the generated graphs. In future work, we might try adding vertices and edges to the median graphs to see if this can improve the generated graph, giving the median graph as an exploration seed for MCTS as the method DISCERN did.

References

1. Baldassarre, F., Azizpour, H.: Explainability for GCNs. arXiv:1905.13686 (2019)
2. Burkart, N., Huber, M.F.: A survey on the explainability of supervised machine learning. JAIR **70**, 245–317 (2021)

3. De Bie, T.: An information theoretic framework for data mining. In: SIGKDD, pp. 564–572 (2011)
4. Duval, A., Malliaros, F.D.: Graphsvx: shapley value explanations for graph neural networks. In: ECMLPKDD2021, pp. 302–318 (2021)
5. Fürnkranz, J., Kliegr, T., Paulheim, H.: On cognitive preferences and the plausibility of rule-based models. Mach. Learn. **109**(4), 853–898 (2019)
6. Huang, Q., Yamada, M., Tian, Y., et al.: GraphLIME: local interpretable model explanations for graph neural networks. arXiv:2001.06216 (2020)
7. Kipf, T., Welling, M.: Semi-supervised classification with GCN. In: ICLR (2017)
8. Lemmerich, F., Becker, M.: pysubgroup: easy-to-use subgroup discovery in python. In: ECMLPKDD, pp. 658–662 (2018)
9. Luo, D., et al.: Parameterized explainer for GNN. In: NeurIPS 2020 (2020)
10. Mémoli, F.: Gromov-wasserstein distances and the metric approach to object matching. Found. Comput. Math. **11**(4), 417–487 (2011)
11. Molnar, C.: Interpretable machine learning. Lulu.com (2020)
12. Morris, C., Kriege, N.M., Bause, F., Kersting, K., Mutzel, P., Neumann, M.: Tudataset: a collection of benchmark datasets for learning with graphs (2020)
13. Olah, C., Mordvintsev, A., Schubert, L.: Feature visualization. Distill **2**(11), 46832 (2017)
14. Park, H., Neville, J.: Exploiting interaction links for node classification with deep graph neural networks. In: IJCAI 2019, pp. 3223–3230 (2019)
15. Pope, P.E., Kolouri, S., Rostami, M., Martin, C.E., Hoffmann, H.: Explainability methods for GCN. In: IEEE CVPR, pp. 10772–10781 (2019)
16. Simonyan, K., Vedaldi, A., Zisserman, A.: Deep inside convolutional networks. In: ICLR 2014 (2014)
17. Vayer, T., Courty, N., Tavenard, R., Chapel, L., Flamary, R.: Optimal transport for structured data with application on graphs. In: ICML, pp. 6275–6284 (2019)
18. Veyrin-Forrer, L., Kamal, A., Duffner, S., Plantevit, M., Robardet, C.: On GNN explanability with activation patterns, working paper or preprint (2021)
19. Veyrin-Forrer, L., Kamal, A., Duffner, S., Plantevit, M., Robardet, C.: What does my GNN really capture? IJCAI-ECAI, On the exploration of GNN internal representations. In (2022)
20. Vu, M.N., Thai, M.T.: PGM-Explainer: probabilistic graphical model explanations for graph neural networks. In: NeurIPS 2020 (2020)
21. Wu, Z., et al.: Moleculenet: a benchmark for molecular machine learning. Chem. Sci. **9**, 513–530 (2018)
22. Wu, Z., Pan, S., Chen, F., Long, G., Zhang, C., Philip, S.Y.: A comprehensive survey on GNNs. IEEE Trans. NN and Learn. Syst. **32**(1), 4–24 (2020)
23. Xu, K., Hu, W., Leskovec, J., Jegelka, S.: How powerful are GNN? In: ICLR (2019)
24. Ying, Z., Bourgeois, D., You, J., Zitnik, M., Leskovec, J.: GNNExplainer: generating explanations for graph neural networks. In: NeurIPS, pp. 9240–9251 (2019)
25. Yuan, H., Tang, J., Hu, X., Ji, S.: XGNN: towards model-level explanations of graph neural networks. In: KDD2020, pp. 430–438 (2020)
26. Yuan, H., Yu, H., Gui, S., Ji, S.: Explainability in graph neural networks: a taxonomic survey. arXiv:2012.15445 (2020)
27. Zhang, M., Cui, Z., Neumann, M., Chen, Y.: An end-to-end deep learning architecture for graph classification. In: AAAI-2018, pp. 4438–4445 (2018)

Exposing Racial Dialect Bias
in Abusive Language Detection:
Can Explainability Play a Role?

Marta Marchiori Manerba[1]([✉])(iD) and Virginia Morini[1,2](iD)

[1] Computer Science Department, University of Pisa, Pisa, Italy
{marta.marchiori,virginia.morini}@phd.unipi.it
[2] KDD Laboratory, ISTI, National Research Council, Pisa, Italy

Abstract. Biases can arise and be introduced during each phase of a supervised learning pipeline, eventually leading to harm. Within the task of automatic abusive language detection, this matter becomes particularly severe since unintended bias towards sensitive topics such as gender, sexual orientation, or ethnicity can harm underrepresented groups. The role of the datasets used to train these models is crucial to address these challenges. In this contribution, we investigate whether explainability methods can expose racial dialect bias attested within a popular dataset for abusive language detection. Through preliminary experiments, we found that pure explainability techniques cannot effectively uncover biases within the dataset under analysis: the rooted stereotypes are often more implicit and complex to retrieve.

Keywords: ML · NLP · Explainability · Interpretability · ML Evaluation · Fairness in ML · Algorithmic bias · Bias discovery · Algorithmic auditing · Data awareness · Discrimination

1 Introduction

Biases can arise and be introduced during each phase of a supervised learning pipeline, eventually leading to harm [17,41]. Within the task of automatic abusive language detection, this matter becomes particularly severe since unintended bias towards sensitive topics such as gender, sexual orientation, or ethnicity can harm underrepresented groups. The role of the datasets used to train these models is crucial. There might be multiple reasons why a dataset is biased, e.g., due to skewed sampling strategies or to the prevalence of a particular demographic group disproportionately associated with a class outcome [30], ultimately establishing conditions of privilege and discrimination. Concerning fairness and biases, in [24] is conducted an in-depth discussion on ethical issues and challenges in automatic abusive language detection. Among others, a perspective analyzed is the principle of non-discrimination throughout every stage of supervised machine learning pipelines. Several metrics, generic tools, and libraries such as [8,39] have

© The Author(s), under exclusive license to Springer Nature Switzerland AG 2023
I. Koprinska et al. (Eds.): ECML PKDD 2022 Workshops, CCIS 1752, pp. 483–497, 2023.
https://doi.org/10.1007/978-3-031-23618-1_32

been proposed to investigate fairness in AI applications. Nevertheless, the solutions often remain fragmented, and it is difficult to reach a consensus on which are the standards, as underlined in a recent survey by [9], where the authors criticize the framing of *bias* within Natual Language Processing (NLP) systems, revealing inconsistency, lack of normativity and common rationale in several works.

In addition to fairness, another crucial aspect to consider related to these complex models used on high-dimensional data lies in the opaqueness of their internal behaviour. In fact, if the dynamics leading a model to a certain automatic decision are not clear nor accountable, significant problems of trust for the reliability of outputs could emerge, especially in sensitive real-world contexts where high-stakes choices are made. Inspecting non-discrimination of decisions and assessing that the knowledge autonomously learned conforms to human values also constitutes a real challenge. Indeed, in recent years working towards transparency and interpretability of black-box models has become a priority [11,21]. We refer the reader to the introduction conducted in [23], where authors cover selected explainability methods, offering an overall description of the state-of-the-art in this area.

Few approaches in the literature are at the intersection of fairness and explainability. In [1], through a user study, authors investigate the effects of explanations and fairness on human trust, finding that it increased when users were shown explanations of AI decisions. [6] develops a framework that evaluates systems' fairness through LIME [34] explanations and renders the models less discriminating, having identified and removed the sensitive attributes unfairly employed for classification. A model-agnostic strategy is proposed in [45]: from a biased black-box it aims at building a *fair surrogate* in the form of decision rules, guaranteeing fairness while maintaining performance. In [4] is described a Python package that allows for model investigation and development following a responsible ML pipeline, also performing bias auditing. We refer the reader to the review conducted in [2], where authors collect works that propose strategies to tackle fairness of NLP models through explainability techniques. Generally, authors found that, although one of the main reasons for applying explainability to NLP resides in bias detection, contributions at the intersection of these ethical AI principles are very few and often limited in the scope, e.g., w.r.t. biases and tasks addressed.

Given these evident socio-technical challenges, significant trust problems emerge, mainly regarding the robustness and quality of datasets and the related trustworthiness of models trained on these collections and their automated decisions. This work aims to investigate whether explainability methods can expose racial dialect bias attested within specific abusive language detection datasets. Racial dialect bias is described in [14] as the phenomenon whereby a comment belonging to African-American English (AAE) is more often classified as offensive than a text that aligns with White English (WE). For example, in [38], it is shown that annotators tend to label as offensive messages in Afro-American English more frequently than when annotating other messages, which could lead to the training of a system reproducing the same kind of bias. Paradoxically, the systems learn to discriminate against the very demographic minorities they are supposed to protect against online hate, for whom it should help in creating a safe and inclusive digital environment.

To explore this issue, we chose the collection presented in [19] that gathers social media comments from Twitter manually annotated through crowdsourcing. The advantage of having data labelled by humans resides in the annotation's precision. However, it is a task that requires domain knowledge and can be very subjective [5] and time-consuming. We chose this dataset since it has been shown to contain racial dialect bias, introduced by the human annotator, who demonstrates a disparate treatment against certain dialect words [14]. For example, suppose terms belonging to the African-American language variant are used in the social media post. The instance is often more likely to be classified as abusive, even when, in fact, the content expressed is neutral, endorsing the importance of specific word variants rather than the offensive charge of the sentences. The focus of this work thus lies also in the impact on human annotation data, which can introduce different problems into the information formalized from the texts. As a result, the emerging biases propagate to the models drawn from these skewed collections. The quality of the annotation, and thus the models learned on these data, are significantly affected.

In this work, we adopt a qualitative definition of bias strongly contextual to abusive language detection and the type of unfairness we are investigating. We define as *bias* the sensitivity of an abusive language detection classifier concerning the presence in the record to be classified of terms belonging to the AAE dialect. Specifically, a classifier is considered biased or unfair if it tends to misclassify as abusive AAE records more often than those characterized by a white alignemnt linguistic variant. To understand whether these biases affect a model's outputs, we rely on explainability techniques, checking which aspects are relevant for the classification according to the model and the data on which it was trained. Suppose the explanation techniques give importance to misleading terms, not semantically or emotionally relevant. In that case, the explanation methods are effective for this debugging since they highlight how the knowledge learned from the model is neither reliable nor robust, revealing imbalances, possibly resulting from skewed and unrepresentative training data. Therefore, the question we try to answer is focused on testing if purely explanation techniques can identify biases in models' predictions inherited from problematic datasets. Specifically, according to our hypotheses, we would like to highlight those models demonstrate biases based on latent textual features, such as lexical and stylistic aspects, and not on the actual semantics or emotion of the text.

The rest of the paper is organized as follows. In Sect. 2 we briefly present necessary background knowledge. In Sect. 3, we conduct preliminary experiments to assess the effectiveness of explainability techniques application for evaluation and bias elicitation purposes. Finally, Sect. 4 discusses the limitations of our approach and indicates future research directions.

2   Setting the Stage

The following section reports the main methods and techniques leveraged in this contribution. We start by describing the AI-based text classifiers predicting the abusiveness, and then we proceed to the explanations algorithms used to interpret model outputs.

2.1   Text Classifiers

The task of detecting and predicting different kinds of abusive online content in written texts is typically formulated as a text-classification problem, where the textual content of a comment is encoded into a vector representation that is used to train a classifier to predict one of C classes.

Of course, when dealing with textual data, it is of utmost importance to consider both the suitable type of word representation and the proper type of classifier. Since traditional word representation (i.e., bag-of-words model) encode terms as discrete symbols not directly comparable to others [25], they are not fully able to model semantic relations between words. Instead, word embeddings like Word2vec [29], BERT Embeddings [16] and Glove [32] mapping words to a continuously valued low dimensional space, can capture their semantic and syntactic features. Also, their structure makes them suitable for deployment with Deep Learning models, fruitfully used to address NLP-related classification tasks. Among the available NLP classifiers (e.g., Recurrent Neural Networks like LSTM [22]), recently, in the literature have been introduced the so-called Transformer models that, differently from the previous ones, can process each word in a sentence simultaneously via the attention mechanism [44]. In particular, autoencoding transformer models such as Bidirectional Encoder Representations from Transformers (BERT) [16] and the many BERT-based models spawning from it (e.g., RoBERTa [26], DistilBERT [37]), has proven that leveraging a bidirectional multi-head self-attention scheme yields state-of-the-art performances when dealing with sentence-level classification.

Abusive Language Detection. Automatic abusive language detection is a task that emerged with the widespread use of social media [24]. Online discourse often assumes abusive and offensive connotations, especially towards sensitive minorities and young people. The exposition to these violent opinions can trigger polarization, isolation, depression, and other psychological trauma [24]. Therefore, online platforms have started to assume the role of examining and removing hateful posts. Since the large amount of data that flows across social media, hatred is typically flagged through automatic methods alongside human monitoring. Several approaches have been proposed to perform both coarse-grained, i.e., binary, and fine-grained classification. As noted, pre-trained embeddings such as contextualized Transformers [43], and ELMo [33] embeddings are among the most popular techniques [47]. For this reason, we adopt BERT in the experiments presented in the following sections.

2.2 Post-hoc Explanation Methods

Following recent surveys on Explainable AI [11,18,20,21,27,31,36], we briefly define the field to which the explainers we use in this contribution belong, i.e., post-hoc explainability methods. This branch pertains to the black-box explanation methods. The aim is to build explanations for a black-box model, i.e., a model that is not interpretable or transparent regarding the automatic decision process due to the complexity of its internal dynamics. Post-hoc strategies can be *global* if they target explaining the whole model, or *local* if they aim to explain a specific decision for a particular record. The validity of the local explanation depends on the particular instance chosen, and often the findings are not generalizable to describe the overall model logic. In addition, the explanation technique can be *(i) model-agnostic*, i.e., independent w.r.t. the type of black-box to be inspected (e.g., tree ensemble, neural networks, etc.), or *(ii) model-specific*, involving a strategy that has particular requirements and works only with precise types of models. Thus, given a black-box b and a dataset X, a local post-hoc explanation method ϵ takes as input b and X and returns an explanation e for each record $x \in X$. Returning to the general definition of post-hoc explainability, we now introduce more formally the objective of these methods. Given a black-box model b and an interpretable model g, post-hoc methods aim to approximate the local or global behaviour of b through g. In this sense, g becomes the transparent surrogate of b, which can mimic and account for its complex dynamics more intelligibly to humans. The approaches proposed in the literature differ in terms of the input data handled by b (textual, tabular); the type of b the interpretable technique can explain; the type of explanator g adopted (decision tree, saliency maps).

In the following, we briefly present the explanation techniques we chose to adopt. Specifically, Integrated Gradients and SHAP are used locally and globally, as described in Sect. 3.4.

Integrated Gradients. Integrated Gradients (IG) [40] is a post-hoc, model-specific explainability method for deep neural networks that attributes a model's prediction to its input features. In other words, it can compute how relevant a given input feature is for the output prediction. Differently from mostly attribution methods [7,42], IG satisfies both the attribution axioms *Sensitivity* (i.e., relevant features have not-zero attributions) and *Implementation Variance* (i.e. the attributions for two functionally equivalents models are identical). Indeed, IG aggregates the gradients of the input by interpolating in small steps along the straight line between a baseline and the input. Accordingly, a large positive or negative IG score indicates that the feature strongly increases or decreases the model output. In contrast, a score close to zero indicates that the feature is irrelevant to the output prediction. IG can be applied to any differentiable model and thus handle different kinds of data like images, texts, or tabular ones. Further, it is adopted for a wide range of goals like: *i)* understanding feature importance by extracting rules from the network; *ii)* debugging deep learning models performance and *iii)* identifying data skew by understanding the important features contributing to the prediction.

SHAP. SHAP [28] is among the most widely adopted local post-hoc model-agnostic approaches [11]. It outputs *additive feature attribution methods*, a form of feature importance, exploiting the computation of Shapley values for its explanation process. High values indicate a stronger contribution to the classification outcome, while values close to or above zero indicate negligible or negative contribution. The importance is retrieved by unmasking each term and assessing the prediction change between the score when the whole input is masked versus the actual prediction for the original input. SHAP can also compute a global explanation over multiple instances and provides, in addition to the agnostic explanation model, the choice among different kernels, according to the specifics of the ML system under analysis.

3   Preliminary Experiments

In this section, we present the experiments[1] conducted to assess the effectiveness of explainability techniques application for evaluation and bias elicitation purposes.

3.1   Dataset Description

As dataset, we leverage the corpus proposed in [19], which collects posts from Twitter. The collection includes around 100K tweets annotated with four labels: HATEFUL, ABUSIVE, SPAM or NONE. Differently from the other datasets, it was not created starting from a set of predefined offensive terms or hashtags to reduce bias, which is a main issue in abusive language datasets [46]. This choice should make this dataset more challenging for classification. The strategy consisted of a bootstrapping approach to sampling tweets labelled by several crowd-source workers and then validated them. Specifically, the dataset was constructed through multiple rounds of annotations to assess raters' behavior and usage of the various labels. The authors then analyzed these preliminary annotations to understand which labels were most similar, i.e., related and co-occurring. The result consists of the labels to retain, i.e., the ones most representative and those to eliminate since they were redundant. From the derived annotation schema, labelling was conducted on the entire collection. For our experiments, we have used a preprocessed data version: retweets have been deleted, so the collection contains no duplicates; urls and mentions are replaced by '@USER' and 'URL,' and the order is randomised. We also removed the spam class, and we mapped both hateful and abusive tweets to the abusive class, based on the assumption that hateful messages are the most severe form of abusive language and that the

---

[1] The results of the experiments are available at https://github.com/MartaMarchiori/
Exposing-Racial-Dialect-Bias.

term 'abusive' is more appropriate to cover the cases of interest for our study [12]. The dataset thus organized contains 49430 non-abusive instances and 23764 abusive ones. The number of abusive records is high since it results from the union of hateful and abusive tweets, as reported above. Besides, the class imbalance is typical of abusive language detection datasets: it reflects the dynamics of online discourse, where most content is not hateful. We do not introduce any other alterations to the dataset as the intention is precisely to examine the presence of bias in the collection as conceived and published by the data collectors.

We chose this dataset since in [3] is identified as a relevant source of racial dialect bias. As [3] claim, although this kind of bias is present in all of the collections investigated in their work, it is far more robust in the *Founta* dataset [19]. The authors trace this problem by making several assumptions. One reason may lie in the annotations not being conducted by domain experts. In addition, the platform used to collect and curate the collection may have had a significant impact. Therefore, a text classifier trained on this data will surely manifest a kind of racial bias, as the set is neither representative nor fair. Following such reasoning, the goal of this contribution focused on this collection is to assess via explanation methods if the trained model can correctly detect the comment's abusiveness or if it is predicting the grade of offensiveness based on dialect terms, i.e., manifesting an evident racial bias.

3.2 Methods Overview

Following the rationale in Sect. 2.1, we rely on a BERT-based model to predict the abusiveness. In the following paragraph, we explain the experimental setup and evaluation steps.

The dataset is split into $\sim 59,000$ records for training and $\sim 15,000$ for testing. As for the classifier architecture, we used the pre-trained implementation of BERT [15], i.e., BERT-BASE-UNCASED, available through the library Transformers[2]. We varied the learning rate between $[2e^{-5}, 3e^{-5}, 5e^{-5}]$. We trained the model for 5 epochs, finding that the best configuration was derived from the second iteration, reaching a weighted F1-score of 94.1% on the validation set. The performance achieved on the test set was also high (93.6% weighted F1-score).

Regarding the XAI techniques, IG's SEQUENCE CLASSIFICATION EXPLAINER was exploited, while for SHAP the LOGIT one, both with default parameters. Details on the subsets of instances for which explanations were calculated are provided in Sect. 3.4.

3.3 Local to Global Explanations Scaling

Before presenting the preliminary results, we briefly explain how we scale to a global explanation from the local ones for IG, attempting to represent the whole model. A straightforward way to accomplish this task consists of obtaining local predictions for many items and then averaging the scores assigned to each feature

---

[2] https://huggingface.co/bert-base-uncased.

across all the local explanations to produce a global one. Accordingly, for each record in the dataset, we store the local explanation, consisting of a key, i.e., the word present in the phrase, and a value, i.e., the feature importance. Then we average the obtained scores for each word. This process is repeated for each class predicted by the model in such a way to find what are the words that led the model to output a specific class.

3.4 Results

This section reports the experiments' results to test our hypotheses. We focus the analysis on the BERT-based abusive language detection classifier, adopting IG and SHAP as explanation techniques.

Global Explanations. We begin the analysis by illustrating the outcomes obtained by IG: the results are reported in Fig. 1 (a) as WordClouds. Among the most influential words for the predicted non-abusive class, we find *portrait* and *creativity*, followed by terms that belong to holidays, such as *passport, christmas*, and to a positive semantic sphere (*excitedly*). Interesting to note that the third most relevant non-abusive word is *bitch*. This behavior could be motivated by the fact that IG gives importance to this term in phrases that the classifier gets wrong, i.e., that it considers non-abusive when, in fact, they are. Another possible explanation could be found in the frequent use of this word informally with a friendly connotation in the African-American dialect, stripping this term of its derogatory meaning in specific linguistic contexts. As we would expect, among the most relevant terms for the predicted abusive class, we encounter insults, swear words, and imprecations, such as *fucked, shit, idiots, bastard, bitch, goddamn, crap, bullshit*. To note the presence of neutral words in this setting, which acquire a negative connotation in sentences with a strong toxic charge, such as *streets, clown, pigs, ska* (African-Jamaican folk music) and demographic groups like *homosexual, gay, lesbian, queer, jew*.

Sub-global Explanations. Although the most relevant patterns are primarily consistent with the related sentiment, e.g., toxic words for the abusive class, from this global overview, terms belonging to the African-American dialect did not clearly emerge. We, therefore, isolated from the test set the comments highly characterized by this slang, using a classifier[3] specifically trained to recognize texts belonging to the African-American English dialect [10]. The classifier works as follows: taking in input a text, such as *Wussup niggas*, it emits the probability that the instance belongs to AAE (0.87). Although authors suggest trusting the classifier prediction when the score is equal to or above 0.80, we relax this constraint by imposing 0.70 as bound to have a sufficiently populous subset to conduct preliminary sub-global analysis. We identified a cluster of only 74 AAE records, 65 abusive, and 9 non-abusive.

---

[3] https://github.com/slanglab/twitteraae

(a) Whole test set.

(b) AAE subset.

Fig. 1. For each predicted class is shown a WordCloud representing the terms that obtained the higher global scores by IG for the whole test set and for the AAE subset respectively.

The results for IG, reported in 1 (b), are not remarkable, except for the importance of *ho* in the predicted non-abusive class. The hypothesis could be the same as that underlying the importance of *bitch*: *ho* is used informally in this slang. Among the words of lesser importance (with a score between 0.28 and 0.26) for the predicted abusive class, we find *em* and *gotta*, non-standard variants but not highly relevant to our bias detection. For comparison, we employ SHAP as additional explainer[4] (Fig. 2). SHAP already offers the possibility to compute explanations for multiple records; therefore, we do not have to perform the same local to global scaling applied to IG. For this predominantly abusive subset, the most important words identified by the logit explainer SHAP are *fucked, damn, fuck, bitch, fucking, dirty, shit, dick, ass*.

Since the findings concerning the evidence of racial dialect bias in this corpus are not as observable as we might have expected, we decide to narrow the investigation by focusing on local instances belonging to this subset to assess the classifier further.

---

[4] SHAP was not used on the entire test set (i.e., within the Global Explanations Section) due to the high computational costs of this explainability method. It was therefore preferred to apply it when analysing a narrower subset, i.e., in the subglobal setting.

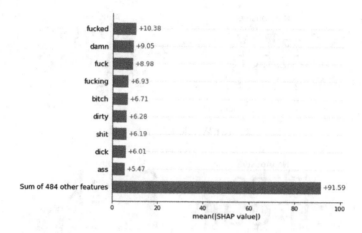

Fig. 2. Explanation for the AAE subset returned by the SHAP logit explainer, consisting of the average impact of each term for the abusive class.

Local Explanations. To further investigate possible racial dialect bias, we inspect local instances. Specifically, we focus the analysis on sentences belonging to the AAE subset according to different scenarios.

As a first exploration, we calculate the explanation for the three non-abusive instances misidentified as abusive by the classifier (specifically, with a probability > 0.5) precisely to assess whether there are AAE terms among the crucial words misleading the prediction. In Fig. 3, both IG and SHAP agree in finding *ass* as an important term, although in these contexts it is used with a neutral connotation, as is *hoes*, broken in both cases in *ho* and *es*. SHAP also gives importance to the contract negative form *ain'*, typically belonging to AAE writers.

Another aspect that we preliminarily investigate is the predicted abusive instances containing the most salient words (identified by the global IG scores). From both explanation methods, the locally most salient words in Figs. 4 and 5 turn out to be *ass, stupid ass, fuck, bitch*. Interestingly, both methods give importance to *nigga*, often split as *ni gga*. This kind of importance could be misleading if this term is used with a friendly informal connotation.

Summarizing, as first insights, we can easily assess that the global explanations highlight informative patterns, i.e., toxic terms for the predicted abusive class. By preliminary assessing certain local instances, we can gather additional findings regarding the influence of specific terms belonging to the AAE variant. Except in these isolated cases, the explainers, and therefore the classifier, do not seem to give importance to terms belonging to the AAE dialect. We can conclude that, in this setting, the pure explanation techniques cannot effectively highlight the racial bias instilled by the crowd-sourcing process, which, for this particular

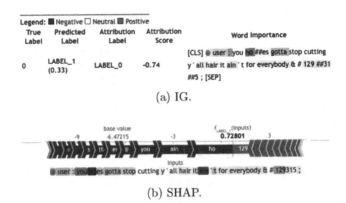

(a) IG.

(b) SHAP.

Fig. 3. Local explanation for the instance: *@USER: You hoes gotta stop cutting y'all hair it ain't for everybody&#129315.*

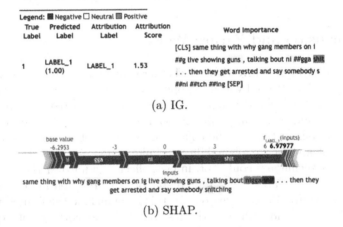

(a) IG.

(b) SHAP.

Fig. 4. Local explanation for the instance: *Same thing with why gang members on IG live showing guns, talking bout nigga shit...then they get arrested and say somebody snitching.*

dataset, is instead well documented in several works [3,38]. Since this stereotype is highly implicit, more specific and sophisticated bias checking techniques are needed to uncover it. Further, we see that the number of records belonging to the AAE variant in the test set is low. Further attempts by averaging the results from different subsets from cross-validation might yield more robust insights. Therefore, further experiments are needed to explore these preliminary hypotheses, involving individuals who speak AAE in everyday conversations and domain experts like linguists.

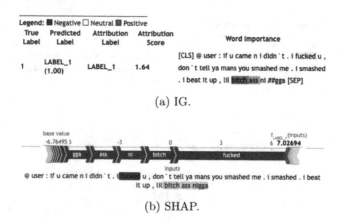

(a) IG.

(b) SHAP.

Fig. 5. Local explanation for the instance: *@USER: If u came n I didn't. I fucked u, don't tell ya mans you smashed me. I smashed. I beat it up, lil bitch ass nigga.*

4 Conclusion and Future Work

In this contribution, we investigated whether explainability methods can expose racial dialect bias attested within a popular dataset for abusive language detection, published in [19]. Although the experiment conducted is restricted to a single dataset and thus cannot directly lead to generalisable inferences, insights from the analysis of this specific collection are relevant to start discussing the limitations of applying explainability techniques for bias detection. The pure explainability techniques could not, in fact, effectively uncover the biases occurring in the *Founta* dataset: the rooted stereotypes are often more implicit and complex to retrieve. Possible reasons for this issue include the limited frequency of the AAE dialect identified in the test set and the shortages of explanation methods applicable to text but mainly developed for tabular data. In agreement with as pointed out in [2], current explainability methods applied to fairness detection within NLP suffer several limitations, such as relying on specific local explanations could foster misinterpretations, and it is challenging to combine them for scaling toward a global, more general level.

For future experiments, first, we want to explore other explanation techniques in addition to IG and SHAP, to compare whether other methods succeed bias discovery, e.g., testing Anchor[5] [35] and NeuroX[6] [13]. It would also be interesting to evaluate other transformer-based models to assess the impact of different pretraining techniques on bias elicitation.

Overall, labels gathered from crowd-sourced annotations can introduce noise signals from the annotators' human bias. Moreover, it is clear that when the labelling is performed on subjective tasks, such as online toxicity detection, it becomes even more relevant to explore agreement reports and preserve indi-

---

[5] https://github.com/marcotcr/anchor.
[6] https://github.com/fdalvi/NeuroX.

vidual and divergent opinions, as well as investigate the impact of annotators' social and cultural backgrounds on the produced labelled data. Having access to the disaggregated data annotations and being aware of the dataset's intended use can inform both models' outcome assessment and comprehension, including facilitating bias detection [41].

Acknowledgements. This work has been partially supported by the European Community Horizon 2020 programme under the funding schemes: H2020-INFRAIA-2019-1: Research Infrastructure G.A. 871042 *SoBigData++*, G.A. 952026 *HumanE AI Net*, ERC-2018-ADG G.A. 834756 *XAI: Science and technology for the eXplanation of AI decision making*), G.A. 952215 *TAILOR*.

References

1. Angerschmid, A., Zhou, J., Theuermann, K., Chen, F., Holzinger, A.: Fairness and explanation in AI-informed decision making. Mach. Learn. Knowl. Extraction **4**(2), 556–579 (2022)
2. Balkir, E., Kiritchenko, S., Nejadgholi, I., Fraser, K.C.: Challenges in applying explainability methods to improve the fairness of NLP models. arXiv preprint arXiv:2206.03945 (2022)
3. Ball-Burack, A., Lee, M.S.A., Cobbe, J., Singh, J.: Differential tweetment: mitigating racial dialect bias in harmful tweet detection. In: FAccT, pp. 116–128. ACM (2021)
4. Baniecki, H., Kretowicz, W., Piatyszek, P., Wisniewski, J., Biecek, P.: dalex: responsible machine learning with interactive explainability and fairness in python. arXiv preprint arXiv:2012.14406 (2020)
5. Basile, V., Cabitza, F., Campagner, A., Fell, M.: Toward a perspectivist turn in ground truthing for predictive computing. arXiv preprint arXiv:2109.04270 (2021)
6. Bhargava, V., Couceiro, M., Napoli, A.: LimeOut: an ensemble approach to improve process fairness. In: Koprinska, I., et al. (eds.) ECML PKDD 2020. CCIS, vol. 1323, pp. 475–491. Springer, Cham (2020). https://doi.org/10.1007/978-3-030-65965-3_32
7. Binder, A., Montavon, G., Lapuschkin, S., Müller, K.-R., Samek, W.: Layer-wise relevance propagation for neural networks with local renormalization layers. In: Villa, A.E.P., Masulli, P., Pons Rivero, A.J. (eds.) ICANN 2016. LNCS, vol. 9887, pp. 63–71. Springer, Cham (2016). https://doi.org/10.1007/978-3-319-44781-0_8
8. Bird, S., et al.: Fairlearn: a toolkit for assessing and improving fairness in AI. Tech. Rep. MSR-TR-2020-32, Microsoft (2020)
9. Blodgett, S.L., Barocas, S., Daumé III, H., Wallach, H.: Language (technology) is power: a critical survey of "bias" in NLP. In: Proceedings of the 58th Annual Meeting of the Association for Computational Linguistics, pp. 5454–5476 (2020)
10. Blodgett, S.L., Green, L., O'Connor, B.: Demographic dialectal variation in social media: a case study of african-american english. In: Proceedings of EMNLP (2016)
11. Bodria, F., Giannotti, F., Guidotti, R., Naretto, F., Pedreschi, D., Rinzivillo, S.: Benchmarking and survey of explanation methods for black box models. CoRR abs/2102.13076 (2021)

12. Caselli, T., Basile, V., Mitrović, J., Kartoziya, I., Granitzer, M.: I feel offended, don't be abusive! implicit/explicit messages in offensive and abusive language. In: Proceedings of the 12th Language Resources and Evaluation Conference, pp. 6193–6202. European Language Resources Association, Marseille, France (2020). https://www.aclweb.org/anthology/2020.lrec-1.760

13. Dalvi, F., et al.: Neurox: a toolkit for analyzing individual neurons in neural networks. In: Proceedings of the AAAI Conference on Artificial Intelligence (AAAI) (2019)

14. Davidson, T., Bhattacharya, D., Weber, I.: Racial bias in hate speech and abusive language detection datasets. arXiv preprint arXiv:1905.12516 (2019)

15. Devlin, J., Chang, M.W., Lee, K., Toutanova, K.: Bert: pre-training of deep bidirectional transformers for language understanding. arXiv preprint arXiv:1810.04805 (2018)

16. Devlin, J., Chang, M.W., Lee, K., Toutanova, K.: BERT: pre-training of deep bidirectional transformers for language understanding. In: Proceedings of the 2019 Conference of the North American Chapter of the Association for Computational Linguistics: Human Language Technologies, Volume 1 (Long and Short Papers), pp. 4171–4186. Association for Computational Linguistics (2019)

17. Dixon, L., Li, J., Sorensen, J., Thain, N., Vasserman, L.: Measuring and mitigating unintended bias in text classification. In: AIES, pp. 67–73. ACM (2018)

18. Doshi-Velez, F., Kim, B.: Towards a rigorous science of interpretable machine learning. arXiv preprint arXiv:1702.08608 (2017)

19. Founta, A., et al.: Large scale crowdsourcing and characterization of twitter abusive behavior. In: ICWSM, pp. 491–500. AAAI Press (2018)

20. Freitas, A.A.: Comprehensible classification models: a position paper. SIGKDD Explor. **15**(1), 1–10 (2013)

21. Guidotti, R., Monreale, A., Ruggieri, S., Turini, F., Giannotti, F., Pedreschi, D.: A survey of methods for explaining black box models. ACM Comput. Surv. **51**(5), 1–42 (2019)

22. Hochreiter, S., Schmidhuber, J.: Long short-term memory. Neural Comput. **9**(8), 1735–1780 (1997)

23. Holzinger, A., Saranti, A., Molnar, C., Biecek, P., Samek, W.: Explainable AI methods-a brief overview. In: Holzinger, A., Goebel, R., Fong, R., Moon, T., Müller, K.R., Samek, W. (eds.) xxAI - Beyond Explainable AI. xxAI 2020. LNCS, vol. 13200, pp. 13–38. Springer, Cham (2022). https://doi.org/10.1007/978-3-031-04083-2_2

24. Kiritchenko, S., Nejadgholi, I., Fraser, K.C.: Confronting abusive language online: a survey from the ethical and human rights perspective. J. Artif. Intell. Res. **71**, 431–478 (2021)

25. Kowsari, K., Jafari Meimandi, K., Heidarysafa, M., Mendu, S., Barnes, L., Brown, D.: Text classification algorithms: a survey. Information **10**(4), 150 (2019)

26. Liu, Y., et al.: Roberta: a robustly optimized bert pretraining approach. arXiv preprint arXiv:1907.11692 (2019)

27. Longo, L., Goebel, R., Lecue, F., Kieseberg, P., Holzinger, A.: Explainable artificial intelligence: concepts, applications, research challenges and visions. In: Holzinger, A., Kieseberg, P., Tjoa, A.M., Weippl, E. (eds.) CD-MAKE 2020. LNCS, vol. 12279, pp. 1–16. Springer, Cham (2020). https://doi.org/10.1007/978-3-030-57321-8_1

28. Lundberg, S.M., Lee, S.: A unified approach to interpreting model predictions. In: NIPS, pp. 4765–4774 (2017)

29. Mikolov, T., Chen, K., Corrado, G., Dean, J.: Efficient estimation of word representations in vector space. In: 1st International Conference on Learning Representations, ICLR 2013, Scottsdale, Arizona, USA, 2–4 May 2013, Workshop Track Proceedings (2013)

30. Ntoutsi, E., et al.: Bias in data-driven artificial intelligence systems - an introductory survey. Wiley Interdiscip. Rev. Data Min. Knowl. Discov. **10**(3), e1356 (2020)

31. Pedreschi, D., et al.: Open the black box data-driven explanation of black box decision systems. CoRR abs/1806.09936 (2018)

32. Pennington, J., Socher, R., Manning, C.D.: Glove: Global vectors for word representation. In: Empirical methods in natural language processing (EMNLP), pp. 1532–1543 (2014)

33. Peters, M.E., et al.: Deep contextualized word representations. In: NAACL-HLT, pp. 2227–2237. Association for Computational Linguistics (2018)

34. Ribeiro, M.T., Singh, S., Guestrin, C.: why should I trust you?: explaining the predictions of any classifier. In: KDD, pp. 1135–1144. ACM (2016)

35. Ribeiro, M.T., Singh, S., Guestrin, C.: Anchors: High-precision model-agnostic explanations. In: AAAI, pp. 1527–1535. AAAI Press (2018)

36. Samek, W., Montavon, G., Lapuschkin, S., Anders, C.J., Müller, K.: Toward interpretable machine learning: transparent deep neural networks and beyond. CoRR abs/2003.07631 (2020)

37. Sanh, V., Debut, L., Chaumond, J., Wolf, T.: Distilbert, a distilled version of Bert: smaller, faster, cheaper and lighter. arXiv preprint arXiv:1910.01108 (2019)

38. Sap, M., Card, D., Gabriel, S., Choi, Y., Smith, N.A.: The risk of racial bias in hate speech detection. In: ACL (1), pp. 1668–1678. Association for Computational Linguistics (2019)

39. Sokol, K., Hepburn, A., Poyiadzi, R., Clifford, M., Santos-Rodriguez, R., Flach, P.: FAT forensics: a python toolbox for implementing and deploying fairness, accountability and transparency algorithms in predictive systems. J. Open Source Softw. **5**(49), 1904 (2020)

40. Sundararajan, M., Taly, A., Yan, Q.: Axiomatic attribution for deep networks. In: International Conference on Machine Learning, pp. 3319–3328. PMLR (2017)

41. Suresh, H., Guttag, J.V.: A framework for understanding unintended consequences of machine learning. CoRR abs/1901.10002 (2019)

42. Vashishth, S., Upadhyay, S., Tomar, G.S., Faruqui, M.: Attention interpretability across NLP tasks. arXiv preprint arXiv:1909.11218 (2019)

43. Vaswani, A., et al.: Attention is all you need. In: NIPS, pp. 5998–6008 (2017)

44. Vaswani, A., et al.: Attention is all you need. In: Proceedings of the 31st International Conference on Neural Information Processing Systems, pp. 6000–6010. NIPS2017, Curran Associates Inc., Red Hook, NY, USA (2017)

45. Wang, T., Saar-Tsechansky, M.: Augmented fairness: an interpretable model augmenting decision-makers' fairness. arXiv preprint arXiv:2011.08398 (2020)

46. Wiegand, M., Ruppenhofer, J., Kleinbauer, T.: Detection of abusive language: the problem of biased datasets. In: Proceedings of the 2019 Conference of the North American Chapter of the Association for Computational Linguistics: Human Language Technologies, pp. 602–608 (2019)

47. Zampieri, M., et al.: Semeval-2020 task 12: multilingual offensive language identification in social media (offenseval 2020). In: SemEval@COLING, pp. 1425–1447. International Committee for Computational Linguistics (2020)

On the Granularity of Explanations in Model Agnostic NLP Interpretability

Yves Rychener[1]([✉]), Xavier Renard[2], Djamé Seddah[3], Pascal Frossard[1],
and Marcin Detyniecki[2,4,5]

[1] EPFL, Lausanne, Switzerland
yves.rychener@epfl.ch
[2] AXA, Paris, France
[3] Inria, Paris, France
[4] Sorbonne Université, Paris, France
[5] Polish Academy of Science, Warsaw, Poland

Abstract. Current methods for Black-Box NLP interpretability, like LIME or SHAP, are based on altering the text to interpret by removing words and modeling the Black-Box response. In this paper, we outline limitations of this approach when using complex BERT-based classifiers: The word-based sampling produces texts that are out-of-distribution for the classifier and further gives rise to a high-dimensional search space, which can't be sufficiently explored when time or computation power is limited. Both of these challenges can be addressed by using segments as elementary building blocks for NLP interpretability. As illustration, we show that the simple choice of sentences greatly improves on both of these challenges. As a consequence, the resulting explainer attains much better fidelity on a benchmark classification task.

1 Introduction and Related Work

Interpretability of Natural Language Processing (NLP) models can be addressed by developing inherently interpretable classification models [5,10,14] or with Post-Hoc interpretability that can be applied to already trained models. With the latter, neural network architectures can be interpreted by white box approaches, which need access to model internals like gradients and activations [2,8]. Patterns in attention layers are also used, but the validity of this practice has been under heavy discussion, see [3] for an overview of recent literature in this domain. However, when model access is not possible or preprocessing methods hinder gradient flow, a Black-Box approach without model access is more suitable. Models like LIME [24] and SHAP [17] are examples of Black-Box interpreters which can be applied to texts. They create an interpretation for a text sample, called *local* interpretation. To this end, a dataset of similar texts, called the neighborhood, is sampled by repeatedly removing words from the original text and observing the change in output. The local behaviour of the model is then approximated using a regression on the presence of words, whose weights are interpreted as local effects of the word presence on the prediction. While LIME and SHAP perform the sampling of the neighborhood directly in the text domain, other approaches use for

© The Author(s), under exclusive license to Springer Nature Switzerland AG 2023
I. Koprinska et al. (Eds.): ECML PKDD 2022 Workshops, CCIS 1752, pp. 498–512, 2023.
https://doi.org/10.1007/978-3-031-23618-1_33

example auto-encoders to generate neighboring texts [11]. While such approaches are promising, their performance heavily depends on the performance of the text generation model. Since in practice, resampling in the text domain is still the most prevelant, we will consider this approach in this work.

We explore the limits of the approach of using words when it comes to complex language models like BERT [7]. In concurrent work, Zafar et al. [27] also investigate if sentences are more suitable for NLP interpretability. They find that sentence interpretations are more robust than word based interpretations and lead to lower variability when using approximation techniques. We hypothesize that these two results may be direct consequences of the results in Sects. 2.1 and 2.2 respectively. Our work can thus be seen as complementary to [27], as it confirms the results independently and gives interpretation for the source of the better performance of sentence-based methods. Our main contributions are the identification of the granularity (words/sentences/paragraphs) as a crucial, often overlooked hyper-parameter in black-box NLP interpretability. In addition to displaying the problems arising from this negligence, we show that an interpreter using sentences as elementary units is able to greatly address the identified problems. Finally, we achieve substantially higher performance in the benchmark problem used for assessing fidelity to the underlying classifier. With this work, we hope to spark a discussion in the literature about the importance of granularity for NLP interpretability.

2 Limits of Word-Based Black-Box Interpretability

While removing words to interpret a model is suitable for Bag-Of-Words (BOW) models without n-grams, the use of models like BERT [7], which try to model word interactions using the attention mechanism, warrants a discussion if this is the appropriate sampling mechanism for such models: Removing random words from a text can make it unreadable for humans, since key interactions, like verb-subject, are broken. Is this also observed with BERT? What are other consequences of word-based sampling? We compare the commonly used word based sampling to sentence-based sampling. We argue it is a more natural choice for interpretability, since sentences represent syntactically closed units and can greatly reduce the dimensionality of the neighborhood to explore.

2.1 Distributional Shift

Sampling the neighborhood is done by altering the text. The sampling mechanism thus has an effect on the embedding of the altered text. For neural networks, it is well studied that the Out-Of-Distribution (OOD, different distribution than training distribution) performance can be significantly worse than In-Distribution (ID, same distribution as training data) performance [1,9,15,19,20], with sometimes dramatic errors known as adversarial attacks. In order for the explanation, which is based on the altered texts, to be truthful, downstream classifier accuracy must be maintained for those altered texts. This can only be guaranteed if texts remain in-distribution after alteration, which we will show is not the case with word-based sampling.

Consider a simple example: Assume a perfect classifier which is able to correctly identify the sentiment of any natural text. However, if the text does not contain a verb, it predicts the opposite sentiment. Consider now the text "The food was nice.". Any text alteration method, which removes the verb, produces an adversarial text for which the model makes an incorrect prediction. An explanation based on such an alteration method does not reflect the behaviour of the classifier on natural (ID) text. Inspired by [13] where hidden activations were used to detect OOD samples for images, we use the text embedding produced by language models ([CLS]-Token) to detect distributional shift in two experiments. This is because in many approaches, the [CLS]-Token is used as an input for downstream models, which may receive an OOD input.

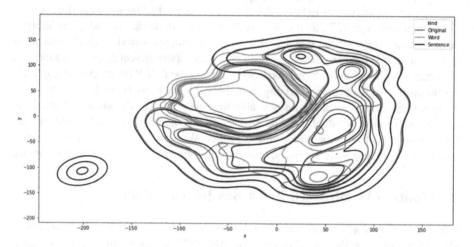

Fig. 1. t-SNE of distributional shift with 10,000 samples. $W_1(words) = 8.6$, $W_1(sentence) = 4.1$ (Color figure online)

Visualizing Distributional Shift. In the first experiment, we compare the distribution of the embeddings of the original text, after removing a random sentence and after randomly removing the same number of words. We compute the embeddings for 10,000 randomly selected Wikipedia snippets from the SQuAD dataset [23] using BERT [7]. On a t-SNE visualisation (Fig. 1) of the distributions of the embeddings (original text, sentence removed, words removed) one can observe that the distribution obtained by removing randomly selected words (orange) is significantly different from the original one (blue), while no big difference is observed with removing sentences (green). To quantify this effect, we consider the *Wasserstein Distance*. Given two distributions $\mathbb{P}$ and $\mathbb{Q}$, it is defined as

$$W_1(\mathbb{P}, \mathbb{Q}) = \min_{\pi \in \Pi(\mathbb{P}, \mathbb{Q})} \mathbb{E}_{(x,y) \sim \pi}[\|x - y\|],$$

where $\Pi(\mathbb{P}, \mathbb{Q})$ is the set of all couplings between $\mathbb{P}$ and $\mathbb{Q}$. The Wasserstein Distance or "earth mover distance" measures the minimum cost (probability mass multiplied by distance moved) to turn one probability distribution into another. We now consider by $\mathbb{Q}$

the empirical distribution of the embeddings of original text, $\mathbb{P}_s$ the empirical distribution of the embeddings of texts with a sentence removed and $\mathbb{P}_w$ the empirical distribution of the embeddings of texts with words removed. We obtain $W_1(\mathbb{P}_w, \mathbb{Q}) = 8.6$ and $W_1(\mathbb{P}_s, \mathbb{Q}) = 4.1$, which confirms that texts with sentences removed are closer to standard text than texts with words removed. Since the classifier is trained on normal texts, its accuracy on the texts obtained by word-sampling, as used by current state of the art model-agnostic interpretability methods, is questionable, since they are OOD. However, sentence sampling produces ID texts, for which normal accuracy can be expected.

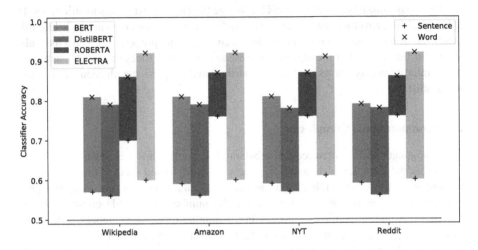

Fig. 2. Comparing distributional shift classifier accuracy

Evaluating Distributional Shift with Classifier Accuracy. One may wonder if the distributional shift observed in the previous experiment is only because a relatively high number of words was removed, reflecting a strong alteration of the text. We perform a second experiment, by framing the detection of distributional shift as a classification problem: The classifier is given text embeddings and tasked with distinguishing between altered and unaltered texts. We compare the embeddings of the original texts, with 5 words removed and with 1 sentence removed. In order to further study if the distributional shift effect is present across different pretraining schemes and prevails after distillation, we use a range of language models other than BERT [7], namely DistilBERT [26], ROBERTA [16] and ELECTRA [6], where DistilBERT is a distilled version of BERT, while ROBERTA and ELECTRA use different pretraining tasks, notably loosing next sentence prediction. We employ a variety of different text domains by using context from SQuAD 2.0 [22] and SQuADShifts [18]. While SQuAD 2.0 contains texts from Wikipedia, SQuADShifts contains texts from other domains, which are often encountered in practice. These include *user generated text* (from Amazon reviews and Reddit comments) and *newspaper articles* (New York Times). For each binary classifications (Original-Word and Original-Sentence for all datasets and transformer models), we train a Random Forest Classifier on the embeddings and observe its performance on a randomly selected, held-out test set. The results are given in Fig. 2. Since the binary classifications are balanced, random predictions would yield a classification accuracy of 0.5. We observe that for all datasets and Language Models, the classification accuracy for sentence-removal is much lower compared to word-removal, almost down to random prediction. This suggests that the distributional shift with sentence-removal is much lower, confirming the results from Sect. 2.1. The fact that the result is not only observed on the Wikipedia subset, but also Amazon, New York Times and Reddit, suggests that distributional shift is a problem across text domains and transformer-based Language Models. Further, using sentences seems to successfully address the issue for most language models except ROBERTA, where the altered text seems to still be OOD, although an improvement can be observed, indicated by the lower accuracy. While this behaviour of the different language models is an interesting property, we leave its analysis for further works. For the arguments presented here, it suffices to note that sentence based interpretability shows preferable distributional properties with reduced distributional shift.

2.2   Computational Complexity

Since language models often require substantial computation power, even in inference, computational complexity is another issue with word based methods. We can view the sampling from the neighborhood as sampling binary vectors, encoding the presence/absence of words or sentences, where the number of possible choices, i.e. the size of the neighborhood is exponential in the number of words/sentences. Taking the SQuAD 2.0 [22] dataset for illustration, the texts contain on average 137.7 words in 5.1 sentences. The number of elements in the neighborhood are thus $2^{137.7} = 2.8 * 10^{41}$ for word-based alteration and $2^{5.1} = 34.3$ for sentence-based alteration. Since in practical applications, computation time is often constrained, only a limited number of samples from the neighborhood can be evaluated. Since the neighborhood resulting from sentence-based alteration is much smaller, a higher portion of it can be explored. If for example time permits only exploring 20 samples, then 58% of the sentence-based neighborhood can be explored. However, of the word based neighborhood, less than $10^{-39}\%$ can be explored. This results in a better estimation of the model's decision surface with sentence-based methods when computation power is limited.

3   Sentence-Based Interpretability

To explain a sample, standard post-hoc model-agnostic interpretability approaches create a dataset of the local neighborhood by repeatedly perturbing parts of the input. The created dataset is then used to train an interpretable surrogate model, for example a linear regression, on the model predictions.

Based on the insights from Sect. 2, we propose to use sentences as atomic units for explanations. In addition to sentence-based alteration, we use a different methodology to select which parts to alter. For tabular data, [12] conclude that defining locality is a crucial issue for local Black-Box interpretability. We hypothesize that the same holds for text classification: Texts should be sampled such that small changes are more frequent than large changes. This is why we use the most *local* neighborhood possible: we enumerate the alterations with the fewest sentences removed. Since the dataset of the neighborhood is well localized, using a weighted regression like in LIME or SHAP is not necessary.

We propose the GUTEK[1] approach in three steps: We first split the text into sentences (**Segmentation**). We then repeatedly remove some sentences in order to create a dataset reflecting the local neighborhood of the sample to explain (**Local Sampling**). This dataset is then used to fit a linear regression on the presence/absence of sentences (**Surrogate Training**). The weights of the regression can be interpreted as the local effect of the presence of sentences on the prediction.

4 Fidelity Experiment

In Sect. 2 we point out the main reasons for proposing sentence-based interpretability: computational complexity and distributional shift. While we give theoretical arguments why these are important drawbacks of word-based methods, we ultimately want to give *better* explanations. Defining what is a *good* explanation is still an open question in interpretability research, but we identify **fidelity** as a desirable property. This means that the given explanation well reflects the reasoning of the underlying classifier.

In order to assess if GUTEK correctly explains the classifier's reasoning, we test if it is able to detect which parts of the text were important for the prediction. We use the QUACKIE [25] benchmark. QUACKIE aims to address the human bias in the ground-truth generation for NLP interpretability tasks. This is done by, instead of human annotating ground truth labels for existing classification tasks, constructing a specific classification task for which the ground-truth labels arise directly from the underlying dataset. That is, for a given question-context pair in Question-Answering datasets, the classification models are tasked with determining if the question can be answered with the context. The sentence containing the answer in the context is then used as ground-truth interpretability label. QUACKIE comprises three performance metrics, namely IOU, calculated as the intersection-over union in terms of sentences and measuring how well the ground truth has been found, HPD, computing inverse rank of the ground truth sentence and SNR, computing the square of the score of the important sentence divided by the variance of the scores of unimportant sentences.

We compare our approach to LIME with *sum* aggregation of token scores for each sentence, which represents the current best-performing Black-Box method in the benchmark in the primary metrics IoU and HPD, representing performance of *correctly identifying the important sentence* and *highly ranking the important sentence* respectively. We report the results for the SQuAD 2.0 dataset in Table 1, results from other domains, such as Reddit posts or New York times Articles, are given in Appendix D and show the same behaviour. We outperform the previous method by a substantial margin in both IoU and HPD for both classifiers. Notably in IoU, our approaches scores are more than double LIME's scores with the same number of samples, which implies that we find

---

[1] GUTEK, "Gutenberg" in Polish, for **G**enerating **U**nderstandable **T**ext **E**xplanations based on **K**ey segments.

Table 1. Results on QUACKIE (SQuAD)

Method	Classif			QA		
	IoU	HPD	SNR	IoU	HPD	SNR
GUTEK 10	**88.55**	**90.75**	**39.48**	**90.53**	**92.37**	37.37
LIME 10	37.70	50.29	39.23	38.47	50.83	38.20
LIME 100	58.04	66.50	39.30	69.90	75.98	**40.91**

the most important sentence twice as often as the word-based approach. When allowing LIME 10 times as many samples as our approach (100 samples vs. 10 samples for GUTEK) it gets closer to our performance in IoU and HPD without matching it.[2] Obviously, drawing 10 times as many samples also results in roughly a 10 fold increase in required computation power and thus a roughly 10 fold increase in computation time. Using 100 samples with the sentence-based approach results in a minor improvement of about 3% points in the primary metrics IoU and HPD, suggesting that the neighborhood is already sufficiently well explored with 10 samples. In the SNR metric, measuring *how much higher the score for the important sentence is compared to the unimportant ones*, LIME is performing better than GUTEK, possibly due to the use of LASSO regression, which was pointed out by the benchmark authors as a possible attack to improve the SNR score. Overall, the explanations from the sentence-based approach thus better represent the model's reasoning. We hypothesize that the improvement in fidelity is due to the reduced distributional shift (Sect. 2.1) and much reduced search space (Sect. 2.2). This is in line with the observation that LIME is able to improve its performance when using more samples.

5   Discussion

We have shown that word-based sampling mechanisms which alter the text by removing words create a distributional shift in the input texts. This may lead to OOD inputs to the underlying model when the neighbourhood is explored. We further showed that the neighborhood created by word-based methods is very big and can not be well explored with a limited number of samples. While using an iterative approach, first finding the important sentences in a text, then the important words in the important sentences would address the second problem, the first would prevail.

While in this work, we used sentences as elementary building blocks for NLP interpretability, this is not the best choice in all applications. For example, in short texts like tweets, where less interdependence between words is present, word-based approaches may be preferable. Similarly, for very long texts where there is a strong interdependence between sentences, even bigger segments, such as paragraphs, may be used. Finally, also parts of sentences may be used. However, this raises the problem of text segmentation, which is beyond the scope of this paper.

---

[2] The scores are also better than the ones obtained for LIME on a random subset of samples using a neighborhood of 1000 samples.

While we have illustrated the importance of the granularity hyperparameter in terms of distributional shift, computational complexity and fidelity, the explanations created by different choices of granularity are also inherently different. For example, the sentence-based interpretations give context, while the word-based methods are easier to understand at a glance. In Fig. 3, we show the interpretations by GUTEK and LIME for a negative movie review given. (TF-IDF based Random-Forest Classifier is used, further examples are given in Appendix C) We can see that both approaches correctly identify *worst* as a key driver for negative prediction. However, since the sentence also contains the context, giving it as explanation also provides the information that it was in fact the *worst villain* and not the *worst screenplay* or *worst story-line*. A similar effect is observed with *poorly*. Which interpretation is easier to understand may be domain and application specific. Nonetheless, this effect should also be considered when choosing the granularity of NLP interpretability applications.

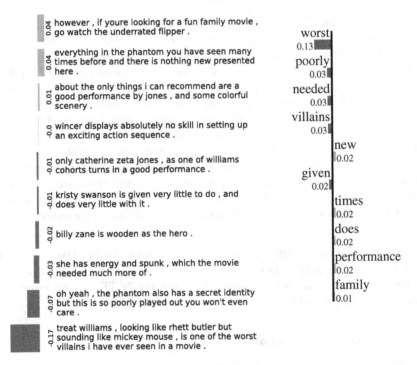

Fig. 3. Comparison of explanations for TFIDF movie sentiment classifier, GUTEK (left) vs LIME (right) (negative sample id 875)

6   Conclusion

In this work, we illustrated limits of current state-of-the-art model-agnostic interpretability methods based on word sampling (*e.g.* LIME, SHAP), prone to out-of-distribution sampling when it comes to complex NLP classifiers like BERT and questioning the truthfulness of the explanations. Word-based sampling also suffers from high computational complexity, limiting the exploration of the neighborhood of the text whose prediction is to explain. These limitations are addressed with a sentence-based approach resulting in better fidelity. The main take-aways thus are (1) the challenges arising with word-based approaches (distributional shift, computational complexity and human interpretability) and (2) the illustration that a simple sentence based model (GUTEK) attains improved performance compared to word-based methods.

A   Reproducibility

To ensure reproducibility, we give the implementation details of our experiments. Direct implementations can also be found directly on our Github[3].

A.1   The Case Against Word-Based Black-Box Interpretability

Distributional Shift. We use the last embedding of the classification token as representation of the whole text. We use base uncased BERT [7]. For the visualisation experiment, we directly use this embedding to calculate Wasserstein distance. To visualize, we use t-SNE on the combined dataset (word removed + sentence removed + original) with PCA initialisation and a perplexity of 100. The algorithm is given a maximum of 5000 iterations, for other parameters we used SKLearn [21] defaults.

For evaluating distributional shift with classifier accuracy, we use base uncased BERT [7], base RoBERTa [16], base uncased DistilBERT [26] and the small ELECTRA [6] discriminator. The text embeddings are pairwise used to create a classification problem, which uses a random 75–25 train test split. We train a Random Forest Classifier using default SKLearn parameters, controlling for complexity using the maximum depth with options 2, 5, 7, 10, 15 and 20. The best choice is selected using out-of-bag accuracy. Results in Fig. 2 and Table 2 represents performance on the test-set.

Computational Complexity. In order to have normal flowing text, we use text from Wikipedia, notably contexts from SQuAD 2.0 [22]. We compare the number of sentences and the number of words, obtained using NLTK [4] *sent_tokenize* and *word_tokenize* respectively.

A.2   Experiments and Analysis

Fidelity Evaluation with QUACKIE. We use code provided with QUACKIE [25] to test GUTEK. In our implementation of GUTEK, we use NLTK *sent_tokenize* to split the text into sentences and use the SKLearn implementation of the Linear Regression as surrogate. The coefficients of the linear regression are used as sentence scores.

---

[3] https://github.com/axa-rev-research/gutek.

B Tabular Results for OOD Classification

In addition to plotting, we give the results from Fig. 2 in Table 2.

C Qualitative Evaluation

In Figs. 4 and 5, we give some more illustrations of the different explanations, similarly to Fig. 3

Table 2. OOD Classification Accuracy in Tabular Form

Dataset	lm	Word	Sentence
Wikipedia	BERT	0.81	0.57
	DistilBERT	0.79	0.56
	ROBERTA	0.86	0.70
	ELECTRA	0.92	0.60
Amazon	BERT	0.81	0.59
	DistilBERT	0.79	0.56
	ROBERTA	0.87	0.76
	ELECTRA	0.92	0.60
NYT	BERT	0.81	0.59
	DistilBERT	0.78	0.57
	ROBERTA	0.87	0.76
	ELECTRA	0.91	0.61
Reddit	BERT	0.79	0.59
	DistilBERT	0.78	0.56
	ROBERTA	0.86	0.76
	ELECTRA	0.92	0.60

D Complete QUACKIE Results

We also give results for all datasets in QUACKIE and report the scores for all other methods currently in QUACKIE in Tables 3, 4 and 5.

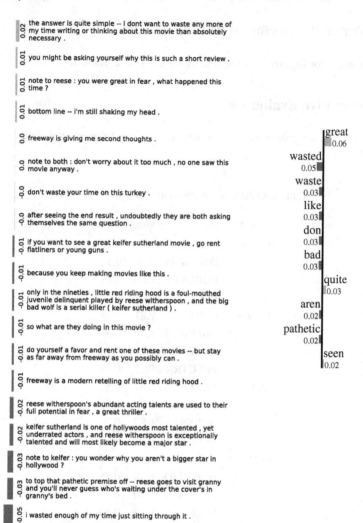

Fig. 4. Comparison of explanations for TFIDF movie sentiment classifier, GUTEK (left) vs LIME (right) (sample id 370)

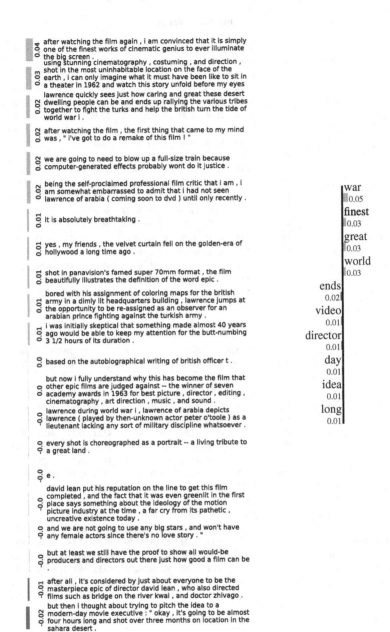

Fig. 5. Comparison of explanations for TFIDF movie sentiment classifier, GUTEK (left) vs LIME (right) (sample id 70)

Table 3. IoU results

Interpreter	Aggregation	Samples	SQuAD		New Wiki		NYT		Reddit		Amazon	
			Classif	QA	Classif	QA	Classif	QA	Classif	QA	Classif	QA
GUTEK	–	10	88.55	90.53	87.7	89.54	87.66	88.04	71.62	76.86	79.09	78.95
		100	91.38	90.53	90.83	90.53	91.56	91.84	80.62	86.98	84.77	86.14
LIME[†]	sum	10	37.70	38.47	40.72	41.40	40.22	41.98	31.35	35.34	32.69	35.27
		100	58.04	69.90	60.74	70.82	62.02	73.50	50.33	69.02	53.57	67.58
	max	10	34.06	35.36	36.98	37.77	36.19	36.43	26.52	28.89	29.80	32.12
		100	57.86	68.30	59.65	68.43	61.57	72.00	48.22	65.23	53.09	66.24
SHAP[†]	sum	10	30.48	32.90	31.66	32.84	29.26	31.03	22.13	23.75	24.59	25.43
		100	54.85	65.92	57.53	65.79	56.38	67.70	49.35	65.02	54.03	67.68
	max	10	29.69	30.81	30.72	31.68	28.32	30.00	21.17	22.58	22.72	23.84
		100	52.45	62.34	54.56	63.18	53.19	64.78	45.79	60.03	49.54	63.35
Saliency	sum	–	74.74	91.12	72.19	91.18	68.87	88.46	57.57	85.26	64.82	85.91
	max	–	66.27	80.79	65.04	80.78	58.95	76.07	48.41	77.33	59.52	79.70
Integrated Gradients	sum	50	66.73	85.93	65.00	85.93	65.44	85.20	51.62	79.73	51.96	78.21
	max	50	62.73	87.05	60.70	86.73	61.63	85.92	50.24	82.35	49.09	82.45
SmoothGrad	sum	5	60.98	91.28	60.29	90.56	60.25	88.29	50.32	84.51	52.34	84.40
	max	5	59.48	82.16	61.45	82.38	56.93	78.33	45.95	77.72	53.03	78.26
Random	–	–	24.64	25.38	26.86	27.39	24.53	24.36	16.51	16.09	18.71	19.17

Table 4. HPD results

Interpreter	Aggregation	Samples	SQuAD		New Wiki		NYT		Reddit		Amazon	
			Classif	QA	Classif	QA	Classif	QA	Classif	QA	Classif	QA
GUTEK	–	10	90.75	92.37	90.17	91.68	89.64	90.02	74.93	79.5	81.76	81.71
		100	93.02	92.37	92.72	92.37	93.02	93.36	83.04	88.66	86.84	88.17
LIME[†]	sum	10	50.29	50.83	53.32	53.76	51.62	53.12	39.99	43.56	42.31	44.64
		100	66.50	75.98	68.93	76.93	69.17	78.58	56.60	72.97	60.12	72.25
	max	10	45.12	46.19	47.85	48.62	46.60	47.11	34.47	36.74	38.43	40.63
		100	63.74	71.33	65.47	71.89	67.28	75.25	53.23	67.65	58.41	69.21
SHAP[†]	sum	10	41.22	44.09	42.87	44.57	39.06	41.38	28.94	31.26	32.97	34.63
		100	63.93	72.75	66.18	72.91	64.39	73.74	55.59	69.44	60.48	72.29
	max	10	37.74	39.28	39.29	40.68	36.40	38.54	27.30	29.13	30.24	32.05
		100	59.85	67.47	61.80	68.35	60.80	69.98	51.19	63.41	55.32	66.86
Saliency	sum	–	79.91	93.01	78.20	93.06	74.97	90.71	63.05	87.21	69.96	88.01
	max	–	72.99	84.83	72.40	84.81	66.86	80.94	55.10	80.32	65.31	82.74
Integrated Gradients	sum	50	73.52	88.85	72.39	88.93	71.99	88.00	57.84	82.46	58.93	81.56
	max	50	70.15	89.67	68.93	89.48	68.73	88.52	56.51	84.70	56.35	85.10
SmoothGrad	sum	5	69.03	93.08	68.92	92.59	68.05	90.52	56.77	86.58	59.36	86.72
	max	5	67.83	85.77	69.64	86.12	65.32	82.65	53.00	80.64	59.84	81.43
Random	–	–	40.28	40.71	42.66	42.92	39.23	39.18	27.41	27.17	30.79	31.34

Table 5. SNR results (Examples for which noise cannot be estimated are omitted)

Interpreter	Aggregation	Samples	SQuAD Classif	QA	New Wiki Classif	QA	NYT Classif	QA	Reddit Classif	QA	Amazon Classif	QA
GUTEK	–	10	39.48	37.37	42.63	37.86	32.21	30.68	19.12	17.69	26.11	22.22
		100	35.49	37.37	39.5	37.37	30.38	33.13	18.22	19.48	20.9	22.92
LIME	sum	10	39.23	38.20	41.82	40.66	36.98	37.26	25.89	22.84	27.87	27.08
		100	39.30	40.91	42.30	43.96	39.41	39.38	32.90	46.71	27.42	32.52
	max	10	91.76	91.54	94.38	88.83	93.24	85.01	107.89	110.55	93.77	95.83
		100	125.98	176.07	124.96	162.51	133.54	184.66	171.42	305.21	151.52	232.94
SHAP	sum	10	73.24	67.24	74.17	67.85	71.42	68.34	91.28	83.95	68.02	60.68
		100	42.27	42.09	44.80	45.60	37.31	43.69	34.30	40.05	28.76	34.64
	max	10	99.16	102.31	97.42	101.44	97.10	92.66	130.98	127.01	99.87	102.16
		100	107.51	137.77	102.01	132.57	94.43	132.64	149.95	240.47	135.62	207.62
Saliency	sum	–	37.29	39.92	40.88	40.14	35.14	34.23	19.10	19.77	22.90	23.34
	max	–	35.58	38.20	39.75	39.81	34.08	36.35	19.15	20.04	22.17	23.78
Integrated Gradients	sum	50	37.28	37.32	39.16	40.19	33.30	33.04	18.96	20.60	22.50	24.60
	max	50	35.71	34.99	38.74	38.09	32.55	32.80	18.41	20.57	21.80	23.69
SmoothGrad	sum	5	38.13	37.22	41.29	40.15	35.16	33.04	19.40	20.33	23.34	23.11
	max	5	37.55	36.61	40.29	40.04	34.85	35.98	19.23	19.62	22.45	22.69
Random	–	–	37.70	37.34	40.63	40.52	34.87	35.06	19.24	19.79	23.21	23.70

References

1. Amodei, D., Olah, C., Steinhardt, J., Christiano, P., Schulman, J., Mané, D.: Concrete problems in AI safety. arXiv preprint arXiv:1606.06565 (2016)
2. Arras, L., Horn, F., Montavon, G.: Explaining predictions of non-linear classifiers in NLP. ACL **2016**, 1 (2016)
3. Bibal, A., et al.: Is attention explanation? an introduction to the debate. In: Proceedings of the 60th Annual Meeting of the Association for Computational Linguistics (Volume 1: Long Papers), pp. 3889–3900 (2022)
4. Bird, S., Klein, E., Loper, E.: Natural language processing with Python: analyzing text with the natural language toolkit. O'Reilly Media, Inc. (2009)
5. Chang, S., Zhang, Y., Yu, M., Jaakkola, T.: A game theoretic approach to class-wise selective rationalization. In: Advances in Neural Information Processing Systems, pp. 10055–10065 (2019)
6. Clark, K., Luong, M.T., Le, Q.V., Manning, C.D.: Electra: Pre-training text encoders as discriminators rather than generators. arXiv preprint arXiv:2003.10555 (2020)
7. Devlin, J., Chang, M.W., Lee, K., Toutanova, K.: Bert: pre-training of deep bidirectional transformers for language understanding. In: Proceedings of the 2019 Conference of the North American Chapter of the Association for Computational Linguistics: Human Language Technologies, Volume 1 (Long and Short Papers), pp. 4171–4186 (2019)
8. Dimopoulos, Y., Bourret, P., Lek, S.: Use of some sensitivity criteria for choosing networks with good generalization ability. Neural Process. Lett. **2**(6), 1–4 (1995)
9. Hendrycks, D., Gimpel, K.: A baseline for detecting misclassified and out-of-distribution examples in neural networks. arXiv preprint arXiv:1610.02136 (2016)
10. Jain, S., Wiegreffe, S., Pinter, Y., Wallace, B.C.: Learning to faithfully rationalize by construction. arXiv preprint arXiv:2005.00115 (2020)
11. Lampridis, O., Guidotti, R., Ruggieri, S.: Explaining sentiment classification with synthetic exemplars and counter-exemplars. In: Appice, A., Tsoumakas, G., Manolopoulos, Y., Matwin, S. (eds.) DS 2020. LNCS (LNAI), vol. 12323, pp. 357–373. Springer, Cham (2020). https://doi.org/10.1007/978-3-030-61527-7_24

12. Laugel, T., Renard, X., Lesot, M.J., Marsala, C., Detyniecki, M.: Defining locality for surrogates in post-hoc interpretablity. arXiv preprint arXiv:1806.07498 (2018)
13. Lee, K., Lee, K., Lee, H., Shin, J.: A simple unified framework for detecting out-of-distribution samples and adversarial attacks. In: Advances in Neural Information Processing Systems, pp. 7167–7177 (2018)
14. Lei, T., Barzilay, R., Jaakkola, T.: Rationalizing neural predictions. In: Proceedings of the 2016 Conference on Empirical Methods in Natural Language Processing, pp. 107–117 (2016)
15. Liang, S., Li, Y., Srikant, R.: Enhancing the reliability of out-of-distribution image detection in neural networks. arXiv preprint arXiv:1706.02690 (2017)
16. Liu, Y., et al.: Roberta: a robustly optimized bert pretraining approach. arXiv preprint arXiv:1907.11692 (2019)
17. Lundberg, S.M., Lee, S.I.: A unified approach to interpreting model predictions. In: Advances in neural information processing systems, pp. 4765–4774 (2017)
18. Miller, J., Krauth, K., Recht, B., Schmidt, L.: The effect of natural distribution shift on question answering models. arXiv preprint arXiv:2004.14444 (2020)
19. Moosavi-Dezfooli, S.M., Fawzi, A., Fawzi, O., Frossard, P.: Universal adversarial perturbations. In: Proceedings of the IEEE Conference on Computer Vision and Pattern Recognition, pp. 1765–1773 (2017)
20. Nguyen, A., Yosinski, J., Clune, J.: Deep neural networks are easily fooled: high confidence predictions for unrecognizable images. In: Proceedings of the IEEE Conference on Computer Vision and Pattern Recognition, pp. 427–436 (2015)
21. Pedregosa, F., et al.: Scikit-learn: machine learning in Python. J. Mach. Learn. Res. **12**, 2825–2830 (2011)
22. Rajpurkar, P., Jia, R., Liang, P.: Know what you don't know: unanswerable questions for squad. In: Proceedings of the 56th Annual Meeting of the Association for Computational Linguistics (Volume 2: Short Papers), pp. 784–789 (2018)
23. Rajpurkar, P., Zhang, J., Lopyrev, K., Liang, P.: Squad: 100,000+ questions for machine comprehension of text. In: Proceedings of the 2016 Conference on Empirical Methods in Natural Language Processing, pp. 2383–2392 (2016)
24. Ribeiro, M.T., Singh, S., Guestrin, C.: why should i trust you? explaining the predictions of any classifier. In: Proceedings of the 22nd ACM SIGKDD International Conference on Knowledge Discovery and Data Mining, pp. 1135–1144 (2016)
25. Rychener, Y., Renard, X., Seddah, D., Frossard, P., Detyniecki, M.: Quackie: A NLP classification task with ground truth explanations. arXiv preprint arXiv:2012.13190 (2020)
26. Sanh, V., Debut, L., Chaumond, J., Wolf, T.: Distilbert, a distilled version of bert: smaller, faster, cheaper and lighter. arXiv preprint arXiv:1910.01108 (2019)
27. Zafar, M.B., et al.: More than words: towards better quality interpretations of text classifiers. arXiv preprint arXiv:2112.12444 (2021)

Workshop on Uplift Modeling (UMOD 2022)

Uplift Modeling Tutorial and Workshop (UMOD 2022)

Uplift modeling concerns the data-driven estimation of individual treatment effects for optimizing or customizing decision-making in business. Uplift modeling is receiving growing interest, both in academia and industry, with an increasing number of applications in marketing, pricing, learning analytics, operations management, etc. Uplift modeling draws from both the field of causal inference and the field of machine learning, and is closely related to causal effect estimation (heterogeneous treatment effect estimation and individual treatment effect estimation) but is strongly application oriented. For example, unlike most research on causal discovery, uplift modeling puts emphasis on randomized trials which are widely available in the industry (e.g,. A/B testing), ranking-based performance measures, and taking into account costs. The motivation behind the workshop was a belief that a large number of open research questions are still to be addressed and that the domain would benefit from tighter integration of its community.

The Uplift Modeling Tutorial and Workshop at ECML-PKDD 2022 attracted a significant number of uplift modeling researchers and brought together experts from both academia and industry. The tutorial part, presented by the organizers, provided a broad but concise overview of the state of the art in uplift modeling and highlighted challenges and directions for future research.

An invited talk by Eustache Diemert, Senior Staff Research Lead at Criteo AI Lab in Grenoble, on "Uplift Modeling for Online Advertising" provided an industry perspective. Eustache discussed how uplift modeling is used at Criteo, presented many practical problems encountered in real life, and discussed open issues faced by the online advertising industry.

The workshop part included presentations of new results by researchers from both academic and business environments. Several interesting results were presented related to uplift model estimation and evaluation, as well as business application scenarios. Interesting problems such as out-of-distribution generalization were also discussed.

We believe that the event provided an opportunity for researchers and developers to present new uplift modeling approaches and novel business applications, and to discuss open issues and connections with related research fields.

September 2022

Szymon Jaroszewicz
Wouter Verbeke

Organization

UMOD 2022 Chairs

Szymon Jaroszewicz — Institute of Computer Science, Polish Academy of Sciences, and Warsaw University of Technology, Poland

Wouter Verbeke — KU Leuven, Belgium

Program Committee

Mouloud Belbahri	TD Bank Group, Canada
Artem Betlei	Criteo, France
Jeroen Berrevoets	University of Cambridge, UK
Kristof Coussement	IESEG School of Management, France
Eustache Diemert	Criteo AI Lab, France
Robin Gubela	Humboldt University of Berlin, Germany
Leo Guelman	Royal Bank of Canada, Canada
Stefan Lessman	Humboldt University of Berlin, Germany
Diego Olaya	ACA Group, Belgium
Krzysztof Rudaś	Polish Academy of Sciences, Poland
Piotr Rzepakowski	Warsaw University of Technology, Poland
Sam Verboven	Vrije Universiteit Brussel, Belgium

Estimating the Impact of Coupon Non-usage

Deddy Jobson[✉]

Mercari Inc., Tokyo, Japan
deddy@mercari.com

Abstract. Coupon incentives are a common tool used by marketers to persuade customers to make purchases in the ecommerce marketplace. While not all coupons are redeemed by users, for the most part due to lack of interest or need, we find a number of users not using coupons at their disposal even when they do make a purchase. In this paper, we do not investigate the causes for such a phenomenon. Instead, we measure the business implication of such a phenomenon. We do so by introducing a partially observable variable U that indicates whether or not a user is able to use a coupon. We then estimate how users are affected by comparing with counterfactual scenarios where the coupons delivered would have been usable to all users. With the help of the estimated impact on users, we then prescribe next actions for the business to follow to improve the effectiveness of coupon campaigns.

Keywords: e-commerce · Causal inference · Coupon redemption

1 Introduction

In online marketplaces, coupons are often used to persuade customers to make purchases. While it is expected that not all coupons get redeemed, it is with great intrigue that we notice a considerable number of users make purchases without using a coupon in spite of possessing one. We observe this phenomenon in our company, a large e-commerce platform with millions of monthly active users, in multiple campaigns across multiple countries and so believe this phenomenon to be highly prevalent in the industry.

At a glance, this may appear to be a favorable phenomenon from a business perspective. After all, if the target users of a buying campaign buy items without using coupons, then the campaign meets its business objective without incurring extra costs. It could after all be the case that users were motivated to make the purchase solely because of the notification message that accompanied the coupon incentives and not the incentive itself. However, one can also reason that if there are users who buy items without coupons even though they received coupons, there may be even more users who don't buy items because they didn't know they could use coupons. Since we don't know which of the above cases are true and to what extent they are true, we need to estimate the business impact of the

I. Koprinska et al. (Eds.): ECML PKDD 2022 Workshops, CCIS 1752, pp. 517–523, 2023.
https://doi.org/10.1007/978-3-031-23618-1_34

existence of users buying items without coupons. The following is the summary of our contributions:

- We use causal inference to formally define the problem of coupon non-usage in marketing campaigns.
- We define segments of users based on how they respond to coupons taking into account whether or not they were able to use the coupon.
- We show how to estimate the size of the newly defined user segments using Bayesian models and also show how the estimations can be used to make data-driven decisions.

The rest of the paper is structured as follows. We first describe the above scenario in the language of causal inference in Sect. 2. We then define the problem statement with the help of the user segments generated from a causal diagram. We model the user response in Sect. 3 and then train a Bayesian model to fit the model to the data. We explain our results in Sect. 4. We consider related methods in Sect. 5 and finally conclude in Sect. 6.

2   Background and the Causal Model

We perform experiments using data obtained from Mercari, a large online CtoC marketplace where one can buy and sell items. Mercari conducts a number of marketing campaigns for the acquisition, onboarding, and retention of buyers (and sellers). When we run marketing campaigns at Mercari, we perform AB tests to measure their impact, randomly dividing the target population into a treatment and control group. In all campaigns, we observe a strange phenomenon wherein a substantial number of users in the treatment group make purchases in the campaign period without using the coupon they were offered. The above scenario can be depicted by the causal diagram as shown in Fig. 1.

According to the causal diagram, treatment (T) can cause a purchase (Y) in two ways. The first way is through the incentive itself; in this case, treatment can only cause the purchase if the incentive is usable (U) for that particular customer. For the second way, we draw an arrow directly between T and Y to allow for the possibility of the incentive causing a purchase without the coupon being redeemed; a customer can have after all been induced to make a purchase just from the notification message through which the coupon was delivered. X consists of measurable confounders such as coupon usage history, prior purchase activity, etc. that can potentially affect both usability (U) and purchase (Y). We control for X to get a better estimate of the causal effect of U on Y. By using the causal diagram, we assume that unobservable confounders such as education level, IQ, etc. don't bias the estimations strongly.

Once the causal diagram has been established, we divide the users into segments based on the usability of the coupon and resulting response of each user to coupons. The segments created are similar to those created for the uplift modeling [2] and we build on the terminology to label our segments. Since we are interested in the user's binary response (Y) for three specific cases:

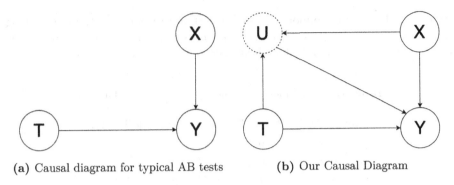

(a) Causal diagram for typical AB tests   (b) Our Causal Diagram

Fig. 1. The causal diagram depicting users who buy items without coupons.
X: user attributes
Y: purchase during the campaign period (yes/no)
T: campaign segment (treatment/control)
U: usability of the coupon (yes/no)

- User is in the control group (T = 0)
- User is in the treatment group (T = 1)
- User is in the treatment group (T = 0) and the coupon is made usable (do(U = 1))

we have $2^3 = 8$ segments to start with. To simplify the analysis, we make an assumption to prune the segments. We assume that treatment on a user who can use the coupon can't have a negative effect on the future purchase propensity. Our assumption can be formulated using the language of do-calculus [1] as follows:

$$Y(T, U = 0) <= Y(do(T = 1), do(U = 1))$$

Eliminating segments that violate the above assumption, we end up with five segments as shown in Table 1.

In order to measure the potential gain in business impact by raising the usability of coupons, we need to estimate the number of users in each of the groups A to E. Of all the groups, group C and E are the most desirable segments under the current scenario and if only such users existed, then leaving things unchanged would be the best course of action from a business perspective. We can call these users "persuadable anyway" and "organic anyway" users respectively. Making the coupons more usable will not change the outcome for these users but will result in the redemption of the coupons and therefore an increase in campaign costs.

However, there are two other segments of users who are negatively affected by the current situation: groups B and D. B users are users who don't make an uplift-contributing purchase because they can't use the coupon while D users don't make an organic purchase because they had a bad experience not being able to use the coupon. We can consider these users to be "persuadable if usable" and "organic if usable" users respectively. In both cases, we miss out on purchases from users because of coupons lacking in usability rather than the user lacking in motivation. Making the coupons more usable in this case will improve the outcome for these users albeit with an increase in campaign costs.

Table 1. User segments obtained from the causal diagram

Group	Y (T = 0)	Y (T = 1)	Y (T = 1, do(U =1))
A	0	0	0
B	0	0	1
C	0	1	1
D	1	0	1
E	1	1	1

3   Modeling the User Response to Coupons

There are many ways to go about modeling the causal graph. Machine learning algorithms like Gradient Boosted Trees [5], Support Vector Machines [10], etc. can be used to estimate different parts of the graph. While we can expect good results with all of the above methods, we find it more convenient to use machine learning algorithms more suited to graphs, so that a single model can make all the inferences we need. Neural networks have shown great promise with various data forms, including graphs [11], though they have only been recently used in tandem with causal graphs [15]. In our case, however, we require a more interpretable model in order to get useful insights. We use a Bayesian model [12] to simulate the causal diagram in Fig. 1 with the following formulation:

$$ln\left(\frac{p_U}{1-p_U}\right) = f_U(X) \tag{1}$$

$$U \sim Bernoulli(p_U) \tag{2}$$

$$ln\left(\frac{p_Y}{1-p_Y}\right) = f_{baseline}(X)$$
$$+ 1_{T=treatment} * f_{treatment}(X)$$
$$+ 1_{T=treatment} * U * f_{coupon}(X) \tag{3}$$
$$Y \sim Bernoulli(p_Y) \tag{4}$$

Note that f_U, $f_{baseline}$, $f_{treatment}$ and f_{coupon} are all affine functions and $1_{T=treatment}$ is an indicator function that indicates whether or not a user belonged to the treatment group. X is a vector of user attributes.

U indicates whether or not the coupon was usable. It is a partially observable variable whose value can be observed only for buyers in the treatment group. It equals 1 when the coupon was used to make a purchase and 0 when a coupon wasn't used to make a purchase. If the user is in the control group, or if they did not make a purchase, then the value of U is unknown. We use our Bayesian model to extrapolate from the users whose U values are known and estimate the value of U for the other users.

We use a Monte Carlo Markov Chain to fit the data to the model and obtain estimates of p_U, $f_{baseline}(X)$, $f_{treatment}(X)$, and $f_{coupon}(X)$ for each user. With the help of the estimates, we use Eqs. 3 and 4 to estimate the counterfactual responses of each user for different interventions on U and T. More concretely, for each user, we sample Y for three different cases:

- $T = 0$
- $T = 1$
- $T = 1$ and $U = 1$

Based on the values of Y sampled, we assign the user to one of Groups A to E. We repeat the sampling procedure multiple times for each user to ensure steady results. With each user assigned to segments, we estimate the fraction of users residing in each of the segments of Table 1.

4   Observed Estimates from Real World Data

With the help of the Bayesian model and by following the process outlined in the previous section, we estimate the relative sizes of the segments of the users of a campaign as shown in Table 2. We use AB test data from a buyer campaign targeting hundreds of thousands of users with discount coupons. We leave out the intermediate treatment effects estimated to focus on the main output which is the estimated segment sizes. We also leave the estimation of error estimates and confidence intervals to future work.

The largest segment of users is group A (lost cause) which is to be expected; a large majority of users don't respond at all to coupon campaigns. The next greatest majority of users reside in group B: users who would have converted if the coupon was made usable ($do(U = 1)$). This suggests that in this particular case, making the coupons more usable can greatly improve the business impact achieved by the coupon campaign.

Table 2. Estimates of the sizes of the user segments

Group	Fraction of users
A	53%
B	36%
C	04%
D	06%
E	01%

We also see a significant number of users in group D (6%), suggesting that a considerable number of users give up on making a purchase because they originally wanted to make, perhaps because they had trouble using the coupons offered to them. About 4% of users reside in group C. While the model suggests that it may be good from a business perspective to allow the usability of the coupon to stay as it is for such users, it may not be a good strategy for those users too in the long term. Lastly, we see around 1% of users are organic users who make a purchase irrespective of the usability of the coupon.

Overall, we see that the number of users whose behavior will be positively affected by improving the usability of the coupon is far greater than the number of users who will use the (now usable) coupon without further contributing to the uplift in purchases. For this buyer coupon campaign, we therefore recommend identifying the cause of the lack of usability of the coupon and resolving it. Potential causes could be lack of awareness of the existence of coupons, uncertainty as to whether the coupon was actually applied or not, etc.

5   Related Work

Causal inference is a versatile tool commonly used to estimate unbiased treatment effects [13]. Statistical models [3], tree-based models [6] and neural networks [14] have been applied to model causality. Causal graphs help depict causal relations between multiple independent and dependent variables. It can be used to embody both causal and probabilistic assumptions [9], analyse missing data due to partially observed outcomes [7], and help recover from selection bias [1].

Many have applied causal graph to model the causality between variables. Nair et al. [8] use causal graphs to incorporate additional information when modeling a stochastic multi-armed bandit problem. They model the causality between item exposure, user interaction and purchase with the help of a causal graph, though they didn't use a Bayesian model. Gu et al. [4] aim to identify the groups of users that are truly affected by advertisements. They plot a causal diagram to model the user response to advertisement exposure and propose an algorithm to predict the counterfactual behavior of users. We use a similar causal diagram in our experiments, though we allow for the possibility of the case where a coupon (our treatment variable) can cause a purchase even if not used.

6   Conclusion

In this paper, we consider the phenomenon of buyers in an ecommerce marketplace not using coupons they could have used when making a purchase. We model the scenario with a causal graph and apply a Bayesian model to estimate the effect of this lack of usability of coupons. Contrary to our expectations, we find that the phenomenon has a strong negative effect on the performance of the campaign and therefore stress the need to identify and resolve the root cause of the lack of usability of the coupons.

Acknowledgements. We would like to thank the reviewers for their many helpful comments that greatly helped improve the quality of the work. We would also like to thank Mercari Inc. for their unbridled support for the research.

References

1. Bareinboim, E., Tian, J., Pearl, J.: Recovering from selection bias in causal and statistical inference. In: Proceedings of the AAAI Conference on Artificial Intelligence. vol. 28 (2014)
2. Devriendt, F., Berrevoets, J., Verbeke, W.: Why you should stop predicting customer churn and start using uplift models. Inf. Sci. **548**, 497–515 (2021). https://doi.org/10.1016/j.ins.2019.12.075, https://www.sciencedirect.com/science/article/pii/S0020025519312022
3. Freedman, D.A.: Statistical models for causation: what inferential leverage do they provide? Eval. Rev. **30**(6), 691–713 (2006)
4. Gu, T., et al.: Estimating True Post-Click Conversion via Group-stratified Counterfactual Inference, p. 6. ADKDD (2021)
5. Ke, G., et al.: LightGBM: a Highly efficient gradient boosting decision tree. In: Advances in Neural Information Processing Systems. vol. 30. Curran Associates, Inc. (2017). https://proceedings.neurips.cc/paper/2017/hash/6449f44a102fde848669bdd9eb6b76fa-Abstract.html
6. Li, J., Ma, S., Le, T., Liu, L., Liu, J.: Causal decision trees. IEEE Trans. Knowl. Data Eng. **29**(2), 257–271 (2016)
7. Mohan, K., Pearl, J., Tian, J.: Graphical models for inference with missing data. In: 26th Proceedings of the Conference on Advances in Neural Information Processing Systems (2013)
8. Nair, V., Patil, V., Sinha, G.: Budgeted and non-budgeted causal bandits. In: International Conference on Artificial Intelligence and Statistics, pp. 2017–2025. PMLR (2021)
9. Pearl, J., et al.: Models, Reasoning and Inference. Cambridge University Press, Cambridge, vol. 19 (2000)
10. Pisner, D.A., Schnyer, D.M.: Chapter 6 - Support vector machine. In: Mechelli, A., Vieira, S. (eds.) Machine Learning, pp. 101–121. Academic Press, January 2020. https://doi.org/10.1016/B978-0-12-815739-8.00006-7, https://www.sciencedirect.com/science/article/pii/B9780128157398000067
11. Scarselli, F., Gori, M., Tsoi, A.C., Hagenbuchner, M., Monfardini, G.: The graph neural network model. IEEE Trans. Neural Netw. **20**(1), 61–80 (2009). https://doi.org/10.1109/TNN.2008.2005605, conference Name: IEEE Transactions on Neural Networks
12. Stephenson, T.A. (ed.): An Introduction to Bayesian Network Theory and Usage. IDIAP, Martigny (2000)
13. Varian, H.R.: Causal inference in economics and marketing. Proc. Natl. Acad. Sci. **113**(27), 7310–7315 (2016). https://doi.org/10.1073/pnas.1510479113, https://www.pnas.org/doi/abs/10.1073/pnas.1510479113, publisher: Proceedings of the National Academy of Sciences
14. Yuan, Y., Ding, X., Bar-Joseph, Z.: Causal inference using deep neural networks. arXiv preprint arXiv:2011.12508 (2020)
15. Zečević, M., Dhami, D.S., Veličković, P., Kersting, K.: Relating graph neural networks to structural causal models, September 2021. 10.48550/arXiv. 2109.04173, https://arxiv.org/abs/2109.04173v3

Shrinkage Estimators for Uplift Regression

Magdalena Grabarczyk[1] and Krzysztof Rudaś[2]([✉])[iD]

[1] Warsaw University of Technology, Warsaw, Poland
[2] Institute of Computer Science, Polish Academy of Sciences, Warsaw, Poland
krzysztof.rudas@ipipan.waw.pl

1 Introduction

Uplift modeling is an approach using a set of statistical and machine learning methods to solve the problem of selecting observations that should be targets of an action (i.e. marketing campaign, medical treatment). To clarify the problem, let us introduce a motivational example. Suppose that we are the owner of the shop. To increase the sale of the given product, we send a discount to the population of our potential customers. Some customers may decide to spend more money because they obtain a discount (i.e. someone who will never buy when a discount is not sent to him, but after obtaining it he decides to buy some of them). The second group of customers are those who spend the same sum of money (i.e. they will never buy independently of obtaining a discount). The last group is those who spend less money (they buy a certain number of products independently of obtaining a discount). Our goal is to find observations from the first group. We should compare the response of observation when action is taken on it and when it is not. Unfortunately, we do not have these two responses at the same time. It is known as *Fundamental Problem of Causal Inference* [3].

To solve this problem, we divide our population into two groups: control (observations on which action is not taken) and treatment (observations on which action is taken). We assume that responses in both groups are linear:

$$y^C = X^C \beta^C + \varepsilon^C, \tag{1}$$

$$y^T = X^T \beta^T + \varepsilon^T = X^T \beta^C + X^T \beta^U + \varepsilon^T, \tag{2}$$

where y^C and y^T are n^T and n^C-dimensional responses in the control and treatment groups. ε^T and ε^C are independent normal error vectors with standard error σ^T and σ^C respectively. We assume that matrix X^T has n^T rows and p columns. Similarly X^C is $n^C \times p$ dimensional matrix. We denote $n = n^T + n^C$. $X^T \beta^U$ is an additional effect observed only in the treatment group which can be identified as an effect of our action assuming the random assignment of observations to the treatment and control groups.

The goal of our article is to find a good estimator of β^U. As a measure of goodness of fitting we assume the mean squared error:

$$MSE(\hat{\beta}^U) = \mathrm{E}(X\hat{\beta}^U - X\beta^U)'(X\hat{\beta}^U - X\beta^U),$$

I. Koprinska et al. (Eds.): ECML PKDD 2022 Workshops, CCIS 1752, pp. 524–537, 2023.
https://doi.org/10.1007/978-3-031-23618-1_35

where $X = \begin{bmatrix} X^T \\ X^C \end{bmatrix}$. In the next chapter, we will describe shrinkage estimators
that existed for ordinary least squares models. Next, we will describe existing
methods of estimating β^U. In the next part, we concentrate on constructing
shrinkage estimators for the best method of estimating β^U described in the previous chapter. We will also describe some theoretical properties of new shrinkage
estimators. Finally, we will discuss the results of experiments on artificial and
real datasets. We will conclude that uplift shrinkage estimators improve the MSE
of their basic versions.

2 Shrinkage Estimators

We now present a short review of shrinkage estimators for classical ordinary least
squares models. The relation between dependent variable y and independent
variable X is given by the formula:

$$y = X\beta + \varepsilon$$

The goal of shrinkage methods is to improve the MSE of the OLS estimator:

$$\hat{\beta} = (X'X)^{-1}X'y.$$

It is a widely known fact that the OLS estimator is unbiased: $E\hat{\beta} = \beta$ and has the
following variance $\text{Var}\hat{\beta} = \sigma^2(X'X)^{-1}$. The idea behind shrinkage methods is to
multiply $\hat{\beta}$ by $\hat{\alpha} < 1$ which may depend on estimators of unknown parameters
of a linear model. Using appropriate forms of $\hat{\alpha}$ we may obtain a small bias of
the new shrinkage estimator but significantly lower variance. Knowing that MSE
depends on bias and variance of the estimator we conclude that the MSE of our
new approach will be lower than the MSE of ordinary least squares estimator.
In the further part of the chapter, we will present the two most typical shrinkage
methods James-Stein estimator and MSE minimizing estimator.

2.1 James-Stein Estimator

The first method of creating a shrinkage estimator for linear models is the James-
Stein estimator, firstly described in [4] for a more general case. The authors
proved that this method allows for obtaining a lower MSE than the maximum
likelihood estimator, which came as a shock to the statistical community. More
precisely consider p-dimensional random variable $Z \sim N(\mu, I)$. Assume that we
construct maximum likelihood estimator $\hat{\mu}$ of mean μ using only one observation.
Obviously $\hat{\mu} = Z$, which is unbiased. However in [4] authors proved that the
estimator:

$$\hat{\mu}_{JS} = \left(1 - \frac{(p-2)}{\hat{\mu}'\hat{\mu}}\right)\hat{\mu}$$

has lower MSE than $\hat{\mu}$:

$$E(\hat{\mu}_{JS} - \mu)'(\hat{\mu}_{JS} - \mu) \leqslant E(\hat{\mu} - \mu)'(\hat{\mu} - \mu).$$

James-Stein estimator for linear regression problem was defined in [1]:

$$\hat{\beta}_{JS} = \left(1 - \frac{p-2}{\hat{\beta}'\left(\text{Var}\hat{\beta}\right)^{-1}\hat{\beta}}\right)\hat{\beta} = \left(1 - \frac{\sigma^2(p-2)}{\hat{\beta}'(X'X)\hat{\beta}}\right)\hat{\beta} \tag{3}$$

If σ^2 is unknown then we replace it with standard estimator: $\hat{\sigma}^2 = \frac{r'r}{n-p}$ where r is a vector of residuals. It can be shown that $\hat{\beta}_{JS}$ has a smaller MSE than the OLS estimator [1].

2.2   MSE Minimizing Estimator

Another method of constructing MSE-reducing shrinkage estimators is finding optimal α which will minimize:

$$MSE(\alpha\hat{\beta}) = \text{E}(X\alpha\hat{\beta} - X\beta)'(X\alpha\hat{\beta} - X\beta)$$

After some calculations α has the following formula:

$$\alpha = \frac{\beta'X'X\beta}{\beta'X'X\beta + \sigma^2 p}$$

After replacing unknown β with $\hat{\beta}$ we obtain the following estimator:

$$\hat{\beta}_{MSE} = \left(\frac{\hat{\beta}'X'X\hat{\beta}}{\hat{\beta}'X'X\hat{\beta} + \sigma^2 p}\right)\hat{\beta}. \tag{4}$$

If σ^2 is unknown we also replace it with $\hat{\sigma}^2 = \frac{r'r}{n-p}$. Similar estimators and their theoretical properties were considered in [6,9].

3   Uplift Estimators

We now introduce some basic methods of estimating $\hat{\beta}^U$. All of them were described in [2,7,8].

3.1   The Double Estimator

The first, basic idea of creating an estimator of β^U is creating two single OLS estimators for treatment and control groups:

$$\hat{\beta}^T = \left(X^{T'}X^T\right)^{-1}X^{T'}y^T$$

$$\hat{\beta}^C = \left(X^{C'}X^C\right)^{-1}X^{C'}y^C$$

Basing on Eqs. 1 and 2 we notice that $\beta^U = \beta^T - \beta^C$, so the double estimator is defined as:

$$\hat{\beta}_d^U = \hat{\beta}^T - \hat{\beta}^C$$

It can be proved that $E\hat{\beta}_d^U = \beta^U$ and $\text{Var}\hat{\beta}_d^U = \sigma^{T2}\left(X^{T'}X^T\right)^{-1} + \sigma^{C2}\left(X^{C'}X^C\right)^{-1}$ [2].

3.2 The Uplift Estimator

An alternate approach for estimating β^U is creating a single estimator on whole data and modified response variable. More precisely, the estimator has the following formula:

$$\hat{\beta}_z^U = (X'X)^{-1}X'\tilde{y} \tag{5}$$

where

$$\tilde{y} = \begin{cases} \frac{n}{n^T}y^T, & \text{if } g_i = T \\ -\frac{n}{n^C}y^C, & \text{if } g_i = C. \end{cases} \tag{6}$$

and n^T and n^C are sizes of treatment and control group respectively. We notice, that we invert the full matrix, which gives us better prediction properties. We also observe that assuming the same size of control and treatment groups and the relation between the number of attributes p and the number of observations n is $n > p > \frac{n}{2}$ then matrix in the uplift estimator is invertible but matrices in the double not. In [2] were proved basic properties of the uplift estimator. Assuming that $\beta^T = -\beta^C$ and $n^T = n^C$:

$$E\hat{\beta}_z^U = \beta^U$$

and

$$\text{Var}\hat{\beta}_z^U = 4\sigma^{T2}(X'X)^{-1}X^{T'}X^T(X'X)^{-1} + 4\sigma^{C2}(X'X)^{-1}X^{C'}X^C(X'X)^{-1}.$$

Unfortunately, the variance of the uplift estimator may be significantly worse than the variance of the double estimator. Intuitively it can be described by Fig. 1 where distributions of the response variable in the double and uplift model when $\beta^T \approx \beta^C$ are presented. We notice that modified response in uplift estimator has bimodal distribution and variance become very large.

3.3 The Corrected Estimator

The last method is based on good properties of the double estimator (small variance) and the uplift estimator (matrix $X'X$ instead of $X^{T'}X^T$ and $X^{C'}X^C$). The main idea is to decrease the distance between two modes of response distribution (Fig. 1). Wherefore we define some β^* and replace β^T and β^C with

$\beta^{T*} = \beta^T - \beta^*$ and $\beta^{C*} = \beta^C - \beta^*$ respectively. The difference between new parameters is still β^U so the value which we want to estimate, but when we take $\beta^* = \frac{n^T}{n}\beta^T + \frac{n^C}{n}\beta^C$, then humps of the response of uplift model constructed on modified parameters are in the same place. Unfortunately β^* is unknown, so firstly we define its estimator:

$$\hat{\beta}^* = (X'X)^{-1}X'y^*$$

where:

$$y_i^* = \begin{cases} \frac{n^C}{n^T}y_i, & \text{if } g_i = T \\ \frac{n^T}{n^C}y_i, & \text{if } g_i = C, \end{cases}$$

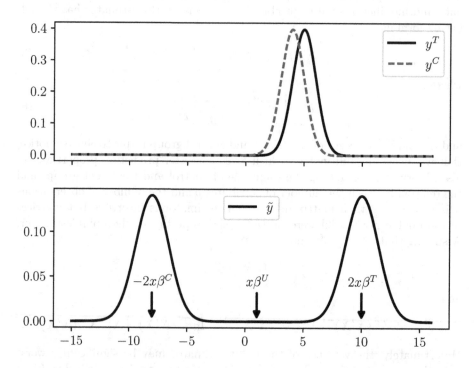

Fig. 1. Distributions of response in the double model (upper plot) and the uplift model (lower plot)

Then we modify the response: $y_c = y - X\hat{\beta}^*$ and create the corrected estimator:

$$\hat{\beta}_c^U = (X'X)^{-1}X'\tilde{y}_c \tag{7}$$

Experiments on artificial data show that this approach has often better properties than previous estimators, especially for $\beta^C \approx \beta^T$ which is a situation often observed in real-life problems. In [2] were presented basic properties of the corrected estimator. Assuming $\beta^T = \beta^C$ and $n^T = n^C$ we obtain:

$$\mathrm{E}\,\hat{\beta}_c^U = \beta^U = 0 \tag{8}$$

and:

$$\mathrm{Var}\,\hat{\beta}_c^U = 16(\sigma^T)^2 (X'X)^{-1} X^{C'} X^C (X'X)^{-1} X^{T'} X^T (X'X)^{-1} X^{C'} X^C (X'X)^{-1}$$
$$+ 16(\sigma^C)^2 (X'X)^{-1} X^{T'} X^T (X'X)^{-1} X^{C'} X^C (X'X)^{-1} X^{T'} X^T (X'X)^{-1}. \tag{9}$$

4   Shrinkage Uplift Estimators

Now we introduce new estimators based on shrinkage modifications of the corrected estimator. We will present results assuming $n^T = n^C$. Under this assumption, we may prove theoretical results. We will present two methods, the first will base on the James-Stein method, second is an adaptation of the MSE minimizing method.

4.1   James-Stein Estimator

Firstly we will define the James-Stein version of the corrected estimator:

$$\hat{\beta}_{cJS}^U = \left(1 - \frac{p-2}{\hat{\beta}_c^{U'} (\mathrm{Var}\hat{\beta}_c^U)^{-1} \hat{\beta}_c^U}\right) \hat{\beta}_c^U, \tag{10}$$

where variance is given by Eq. 9. Now we will show that under some assumptions MSE of $\hat{\beta}_{cJS}^U$ is lower than $\hat{\beta}_c^U$. Firstly, when $\sigma^T = \sigma^C$ we will redefine the variance of the corrected estimator:

$$\mathrm{Var}\,\hat{\beta}_c^U = 16\sigma^2 \left((X'X)^{-1} X^{C'} X^C (X'X)^{-1} X^{T'} X^T (X'X)^{-1} X^{C'} X^C (X'X)^{-1}\right.$$
$$\left. + (X'X)^{-1} X^{T'} X^T (X'X)^{-1} X^{C'} X^C (X'X)^{-1} X^{T'} X^T (X'X)^{-1}\right)$$
$$= 16\sigma^2 W^{-1}$$

We may prove the following theorem:

Theorem 1. *Assume that $n^T = n^C$, $\beta^T = \beta^C$, $\sigma^T = \sigma^C$, $\mathrm{Tr}W^{-1}X'X \geq p > 2$ and $W \geq X'X$. Then:*
$$MSE(\hat{\beta}_{cJS}^U) \leqslant MSE(\hat{\beta}_c^U)$$

The proof of the theorem can be found in the Appendix.

4.2 MSE Minimizing Estimator

To obtain a new shrinkage method we will reformulate the definition of the corrected estimator:

$$\hat{\beta}_c^U = 2(X'X)^{-1}X^{T'}(y^T - X^T(X'X)^{-1}X'y^*)$$
$$- 2(X'X)^{-1}X^{C'}(y^C - X^C(X'X)^{-1}X'y^*)$$

then, we multiply the base estimator by α^T and α^C:

$$\hat{\beta}^U = \alpha^T(X'X)^{-1}X^{T'}(y^T - X^T(X'X)^{-1}X'y^*)$$
$$- \alpha^C(X'X)^{-1}X^{C'}(y^C - X^C(X'X)^{-1}X'y^*)$$

After some calculations we obtain:

$$\hat{\beta}^U = (\alpha^T + \alpha^C)(X'X)^{-1}\left(X^{C'}X^C(X'X)^{-1}X^{T'}y^T - X^{T'}X^T(X'X)^{-1}X^{C'}y^C\right).$$

Noting $\alpha_{TC} = \alpha^T + \alpha^C$, we obtain following formula:

$$\alpha_{TC} = (\beta^{U'}A\beta^U)/(\beta^{U'}A(X'X)^{-1}A\beta^U + \mathrm{Tr}\{(\sigma^T)^2\,A(X'X)^{-1}X^{C'}X^C(X'X)^{-1}$$
$$+ (\sigma^C)^2\,A(X'X)^{-1}X^{T'}X^T(X'X)^{-1}\}),$$

where $A = X^{T'}X^T(X'X)^{-1}X^{C'}X^C$. Replacing β^U with $\hat{\beta}_c^U$ we obtain:

$$\hat{\beta}_{cMSE}^U = \hat{\alpha}_{TC}\hat{\beta}_c^U,$$

where:

$$\hat{\alpha}_{TC} = (\hat{\beta}_c^{U'}A\hat{\beta}_c^U)/(\hat{\beta}_c^{U'}A(X'X)^{-1}A\hat{\beta}_c^U + \mathrm{Tr}\{(\sigma^T)^2\,A(X'X)^{-1}X^{C'}X^C(X'X)^{-1}$$
$$+ (\sigma^C)^2\,A(X'X)^{-1}X^{T'}X^T(X'X)^{-1}\}).$$

If variances σ^T and σ^C are unknown, they may be replaced by their standard estimators based on treatment and control group respectively.

5 Simulations

Now we will check the efficiency of our proposed methods on artificial data. We assume that angle between generated normalized vectors β^T, β^C is $\frac{\pi}{10}$, and rows of matrices X^T and X^C are generated from standard p-dimensional normal distribution $N_p(0, I)$. Vectors ε^T and ε^C are also generated independently from the standard normal distribution. Vectors of responses y^T and y^C are generated using Eqs. 1 and 2.

We will compare different methods of estimation for different n. When n grows, new rows are added to existing matrices X^T and X^C. This procedure is repeated 1000 times. For each iteration, we calculate MSE for each n. Then for each n, we calculate the mean of MSE over repetitions and the standard deviation.

Firstly we will show results for the double, uplift, and corrected estimators (Fig. 2). In situations where the influence of our action is slight, the corrected estimator is the best basic method of estimating $\hat{\beta}^U$.

Now we will compare the basic corrected estimator with their shrinkage methods (Fig. 3). MSE-minimizing estimator is always better than a basic corrected approach. James-Stein estimator obtains the best results from all of the considered estimators.

6   Evaluation on Real Data

6.1   Description of the Data

In this section we will describe results obtained on Lalonde datasets [5]. This dataset describes the effects of a job training program that addressed a population of low-skilled adults. People were divided into the treatment group (people who were invited to take part in the job training program) and the opposite control group. The response variable is their third-year income after assigning them to one of the two groups. Our goal is to find these people who earn more money, because of the job training program.

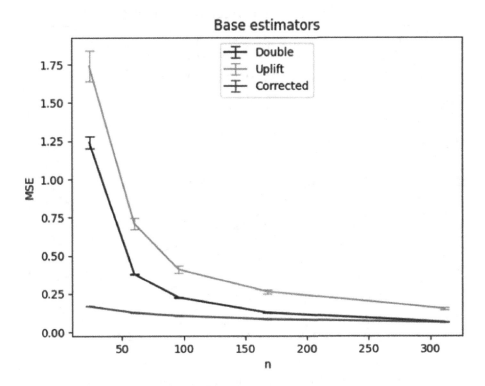

Fig. 2. Comparison of MSE of base estimators

6.2   Evaluation Method

We divide Lalonde dataset into training and testing parts. We construct our estimators on training data and check their efficiency on the test part. Unfortunately, for a given observation, we observe only part of response y^T or y^C, never both of them. As a result, we cannot calculate MSE and we must find another similar measure. In this paper, we will use a measure called Average Treatment Effect on the Treated (ATT), where we compare the mean of the predicted values on the observations from the treated test dataset with the difference in means of true responses in the treated part of the test dataset and the control part. More precisely:

$$ATT_{model}(\hat{\beta}^U) = \frac{1}{n^T} \sum_{i=1}^{n^T} x_{i.}\hat{\beta}^U \quad \text{with} \quad ATT_{means} = \frac{1}{n^T} \sum_{i=1}^{n^T} y_i^T - \frac{1}{n^C} \sum_{i=1}^{n^C} y_i^C.$$

The error of the estimator $\hat{\beta}^U$ is defined as:

$$ErrATT(\hat{\beta}^U) = |ATT_{model}(\hat{\beta}^U) - ATT_{means}|.$$

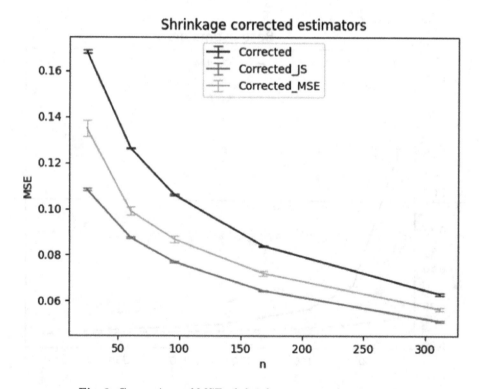

Fig. 3. Comparison of MSE of shrinkage corrected estimators

We repeat this procedure for different partitions for the training and testing part and calculate the mean of $ErrATT(\hat{\beta}^U)$ over repetitions.

6.3   Results

As in the previous chapter, we start with a comparison of the basic methods (Table 1). We observe that results are comparable, but the lowest error is obtained by the corrected estimator. Now we will compare the results for shrinkage methods of the corrected estimator (Table 2). We notice that shrinking the basic estimator gives slightly better results.

Table 1. Comparison of the basic uplift estimators

Estimator	Mean $ErrATT$
Double	0.138635
Uplift	0.139411
Corrected	0.136275

Table 2. Comparison of the shrinkage corrected estimators

Estimator	Mean $ErrATT$
Corrected	0.136275
Corrected JS	0.135449
Corrected MSE	0.132260

7   Conclusions

In this paper, we present methods of constructing shrinkage estimators for the corrected uplift estimator, which is usually the best method for the small influence of the uplift. For James-Stein corrected estimator, we present theoretical results which show that its MSE is lower than the MSE of the basic corrected estimator. For the shrinkage corrected estimators we conclude, based on numerical experiments, that they will work better than the basic version of an estimator. We recommend using new shrinkage methods for real-life uplift problems.

A   Proof of Theorem 1

Proof. Notice that inequality in the thesis can be presented as:

$$\mathrm{E}\left[(\beta^U - \hat{\beta}^U_{cJS})'X'X(\beta^U - \hat{\beta}^U_{cJS})\right] \leq \mathrm{E}\left[(\beta^U - \hat{\beta}^U_c)'X'X(\beta^U - \hat{\beta}^U_c)\right].$$

Assuming that, $\beta^T = \beta^C$, we obtain that $\beta^U = 0$. Then, we may reduce following expression to the following form:

$$\mathrm{E}\left[\hat{\beta}_{\mathrm{cJS}}^{U}{}' X'X\, \hat{\beta}_{\mathrm{cJS}}^{U}\right] \le \mathrm{E}\left[\hat{\beta}_{\mathrm{c}}^{U}{}' X'X\, \hat{\beta}_{\mathrm{c}}^{U}\right].$$

We structure the proof as follows:

- we will show: $\mathrm{E}\left[\hat{\beta}_{\mathrm{cJS}}^{U}{}' X'X\, \hat{\beta}_{\mathrm{cJS}}^{U}\right] \le \mathrm{E}\left[\hat{\beta}_{\mathrm{cJS}}^{U}{}' W\, \hat{\beta}_{\mathrm{cJS}}^{U}\right]$
- we will show: $\mathrm{E}\left[\hat{\beta}_{\mathrm{cJS}}^{U}{}' W\, \hat{\beta}_{\mathrm{cJS}}^{U}\right] \le 4\sigma^2 p$
- we will show: $\mathrm{E}\left[\hat{\beta}_{\mathrm{c}}^{U}{}' X'X\, \hat{\beta}_{\mathrm{c}}^{U}\right] \ge 4\sigma^2 p$. This will finish the proof.

Consider left side of inequality. Assuming $W \ge X'X$ we obtain $\mathrm{E}\left[\hat{\beta}_{\mathrm{cJS}}^{U}{}' X'X\, \hat{\beta}_{\mathrm{cJS}}^{U}\right] \le \mathrm{E}\left[\hat{\beta}_{\mathrm{cJS}}^{U}{}' W\, \hat{\beta}_{\mathrm{cJS}}^{U}\right]$.

Now we will consider expression $\mathrm{E}\left[\hat{\beta}_{\mathrm{cJS}}^{U}{}' W\, \hat{\beta}_{\mathrm{cJS}}^{U}\right]$. We will show that:

$$\mathrm{E}\left[\hat{\beta}_{\mathrm{cJS}}^{U}{}' W\, \hat{\beta}_{\mathrm{cJS}}^{U}\right] = \underbrace{\mathrm{E}\left[(\hat{\beta}_{\mathrm{cJS}}^{U} - \hat{\beta}_{\mathrm{c}}^{U})' W(\hat{\beta}_{\mathrm{cJS}}^{U} - \hat{\beta}_{\mathrm{c}}^{U})\right]}_{①}$$
$$- \underbrace{\mathrm{E}\left[\hat{\beta}_{\mathrm{c}}^{U}{}' W\, \hat{\beta}_{\mathrm{c}}^{U}\right]}_{②} + 2\underbrace{\mathrm{E}\left[\hat{\beta}_{\mathrm{cJS}}^{U}{}' W\, \hat{\beta}_{\mathrm{c}}^{U}\right]}_{③}. \qquad (11)$$

Starting from the right side of the equation:

$$\mathrm{E}\left[(\hat{\beta}_{\mathrm{cJS}}^{U} - \hat{\beta}_{\mathrm{c}}^{U})' W(\hat{\beta}_{\mathrm{cJS}}^{U} - \hat{\beta}_{\mathrm{c}}^{U})\right] - \mathrm{E}\left[\hat{\beta}_{\mathrm{c}}^{U}{}' W\, \hat{\beta}_{\mathrm{c}}^{U}\right] + 2\mathrm{E}\left[\hat{\beta}_{\mathrm{cJS}}^{U}{}' W\, \hat{\beta}_{\mathrm{c}}^{U}\right]$$
$$= \mathrm{E}\left[\hat{\beta}_{\mathrm{cJS}}^{U}{}' W\, \hat{\beta}_{\mathrm{cJS}}^{U} - 2\,\hat{\beta}_{\mathrm{c}}^{U}{}' W\, \hat{\beta}_{\mathrm{cJS}}^{U} + \hat{\beta}_{\mathrm{c}}^{U}{}' W\, \hat{\beta}_{\mathrm{c}}^{U} - \hat{\beta}_{\mathrm{c}}^{U}{}' W\, \hat{\beta}_{\mathrm{c}}^{U} + 2\,\hat{\beta}_{\mathrm{cJS}}^{U}{}' W\, \hat{\beta}_{\mathrm{c}}^{U}\right]$$
$$= \mathrm{E}\left[\hat{\beta}_{\mathrm{cJS}}^{U}{}' W\, \hat{\beta}_{\mathrm{cJS}}^{U}\right]$$

We show that Eq. (11) is correct. Now we will consider parts ①, ② and ③ separately. We start with $(\hat{\beta}_{\mathrm{cJS}}^{U} - \hat{\beta}_{\mathrm{c}}^{U})$ from ①.

$$\hat{\beta}_{\mathrm{cJS}}^{U} - \hat{\beta}_{\mathrm{c}}^{U} = \left(1 - \frac{p-2}{\hat{\beta}_{\mathrm{c}}^{U}{}'(\mathrm{Var}\,\hat{\beta}_{\mathrm{c}}^{U})^{-1}\hat{\beta}_{\mathrm{c}}^{U}}\right)\hat{\beta}_{\mathrm{c}}^{U} - \hat{\beta}_{\mathrm{c}}^{U} = \frac{p-2}{\hat{\beta}_{\mathrm{c}}^{U}{}'(\mathrm{Var}\,\hat{\beta}_{\mathrm{c}}^{U})^{-1}\hat{\beta}_{\mathrm{c}}^{U}}\hat{\beta}_{\mathrm{c}}^{U}$$

Using the fact that $\operatorname{Var} \hat{\beta}_{\mathrm{c}}^{\mathrm{U}} = 4\sigma^2 W^{-1}$, we may write ① as:

$$\mathrm{E}\left[\left(\frac{p-2}{\hat{\beta}_{\mathrm{c}}^{\mathrm{U}'}(\operatorname{Var}\hat{\beta}_{\mathrm{c}}^{\mathrm{U}})^{-1}\hat{\beta}_{\mathrm{c}}^{\mathrm{U}}}\,\hat{\beta}_{\mathrm{c}}^{\mathrm{U}}\right)' W \left(\frac{p-2}{\hat{\beta}_{\mathrm{c}}^{\mathrm{U}'}(\operatorname{Var}\hat{\beta}_{\mathrm{c}}^{\mathrm{U}})^{-1}\hat{\beta}_{\mathrm{c}}^{\mathrm{U}}}\,\hat{\beta}_{\mathrm{c}}^{\mathrm{U}}\right)\right]$$

$$= \mathrm{E}\left[\left(\frac{p-2}{\hat{\beta}_{\mathrm{c}}^{\mathrm{U}'}(\operatorname{Var}\hat{\beta}_{\mathrm{c}}^{\mathrm{U}})^{-1}\hat{\beta}_{\mathrm{c}}^{\mathrm{U}}}\right)^2 \hat{\beta}_{\mathrm{c}}^{\mathrm{U}'} W \hat{\beta}_{\mathrm{c}}^{\mathrm{U}}\right]$$

$$= \mathrm{E}\left[\left(\frac{(p-2)4\sigma^2}{\hat{\beta}_{\mathrm{c}}^{\mathrm{U}'} W \hat{\beta}_{\mathrm{c}}^{\mathrm{U}}}\right)^2 \hat{\beta}_{\mathrm{c}}^{\mathrm{U}'} W \hat{\beta}_{\mathrm{c}}^{\mathrm{U}}\right] = \mathrm{E}\left[\frac{(p-2)^2 4^2\sigma^4}{\hat{\beta}_{\mathrm{c}}^{\mathrm{U}'} W \hat{\beta}_{\mathrm{c}}^{\mathrm{U}}}\right]$$

Now we will consider ②. Notice that this is a one-dimensional expression. Using the trace operator we obtain:

$$\mathrm{E}\left[\hat{\beta}_{\mathrm{c}}^{\mathrm{U}'} W \hat{\beta}_{\mathrm{c}}^{\mathrm{U}}\right] = \operatorname{Tr}\left\{\mathrm{E}\left[\hat{\beta}_{\mathrm{c}}^{\mathrm{U}'} W \hat{\beta}_{\mathrm{c}}^{\mathrm{U}}\right]\right\} = \mathrm{E}\left[\operatorname{Tr}\left\{\hat{\beta}_{\mathrm{c}}^{\mathrm{U}'} W \hat{\beta}_{\mathrm{c}}^{\mathrm{U}}\right\}\right]$$

$$= \mathrm{E}\left[\operatorname{Tr}\left\{\hat{\beta}_{\mathrm{c}}^{\mathrm{U}} \hat{\beta}_{\mathrm{c}}^{\mathrm{U}'} W\right\}\right] = \operatorname{Tr}\left\{\mathrm{E}\left[\hat{\beta}_{\mathrm{c}}^{\mathrm{U}} \hat{\beta}_{\mathrm{c}}^{\mathrm{U}'} W\right]\right\} = \operatorname{Tr}\left\{\mathrm{E}\left[\hat{\beta}_{\mathrm{c}}^{\mathrm{U}} \hat{\beta}_{\mathrm{c}}^{\mathrm{U}'}\right] W\right\}$$

When $\beta^T = \beta^C$ we have $\mathrm{E}\,\hat{\beta}_{\mathrm{c}}^{\mathrm{U}} = \beta^U = 0$. So we may write ② as:

$$\operatorname{Tr}\left\{\mathrm{E}\left[\hat{\beta}_{\mathrm{c}}^{\mathrm{U}} \hat{\beta}_{\mathrm{c}}^{\mathrm{U}'}\right] W\right\} = \operatorname{Tr}\left\{\mathrm{E}\left[(\hat{\beta}_{\mathrm{c}}^{\mathrm{U}} - \mathrm{E}\,\hat{\beta}_{\mathrm{c}}^{\mathrm{U}})(\hat{\beta}_{\mathrm{c}}^{\mathrm{U}} - \mathrm{E}\,\hat{\beta}_{\mathrm{c}}^{\mathrm{U}})'\right] W\right\} = \operatorname{Tr}\left\{\operatorname{Var}\hat{\beta}_{\mathrm{c}}^{\mathrm{U}} W\right\}$$

$$= \operatorname{Tr}\left\{4\sigma^2 W^{-1}W\right\} = \operatorname{Tr}\left\{4\sigma^2 I_p\right\} = 4\sigma^2 p$$

Now we will consider ③.

$$\mathrm{E}\left[\hat{\beta}_{\mathrm{cJS}}^{\mathrm{U}}{}' W \hat{\beta}_{\mathrm{c}}^{\mathrm{U}}\right] = \mathrm{E}\left[\sum_{i=1}^{p}(\hat{\beta}_{\mathrm{cJS}}^{\mathrm{U}})_i [W \hat{\beta}_{\mathrm{c}}^{\mathrm{U}}]_i\right] = \sum_{i=1}^{p}\mathrm{E}\left[(\hat{\beta}_{\mathrm{cJS}}^{\mathrm{U}})_i (W)_{i\cdot} \hat{\beta}_{\mathrm{c}}^{\mathrm{U}}\right]$$

Firstly we need the density formula for $\hat{\beta}_{\mathrm{c}}^{\mathrm{U}}$. We notice that $\hat{\beta}_{\mathrm{c}}^{\mathrm{U}}$ has a normal distribution with 0 mean and variance equal to $4\sigma^2 W^{-1}$. Then density of $\hat{\beta}_{\mathrm{c}}^{\mathrm{U}}$ is given by the formula:

$$f(\hat{\beta}_{\mathrm{c}}^{\mathrm{U}}) = \frac{1}{(2\pi)^{p/2}|4\sigma^2 W^{-1}|^{1/2}}\exp\left\{-\frac{1}{2}\,\hat{\beta}_{\mathrm{c}}^{\mathrm{U}'}\frac{1}{4\sigma^2}W\,\hat{\beta}_{\mathrm{c}}^{\mathrm{U}}\right\}.$$

Now we will transform ③ using integration by parts.

$$\sum_{i=1}^{p}\mathrm{E}\left[(\hat{\beta}_{\mathrm{cJS}}^{\mathrm{U}})_i (W)_{i\cdot} \hat{\beta}_{\mathrm{c}}^{\mathrm{U}}\right] = \sum_{i=1}^{p}\int\cdots\int (\hat{\beta}_{\mathrm{cJS}}^{\mathrm{U}})_i (W)_{i\cdot} \hat{\beta}_{\mathrm{c}}^{\mathrm{U}} f(\hat{\beta}_{\mathrm{c}}^{\mathrm{U}}) d\hat{\beta}_{\mathrm{c}\ i}^{\mathrm{U}} d\hat{\beta}_{\mathrm{c}\ 1}^{\mathrm{U}}\dots d\hat{\beta}_{\mathrm{c}\ p}^{\mathrm{U}}$$

$$= \begin{bmatrix} f = (\hat{\beta}_{\mathrm{cJS}}^{\mathrm{U}})_i & dg = (W)_{i\cdot}\,\hat{\beta}_{\mathrm{c}}^{\mathrm{U}} f(\hat{\beta}_{\mathrm{c}}^{\mathrm{U}}) \\[2mm] df = \dfrac{d}{d\hat{\beta}_{\mathrm{c}\ i}^{\mathrm{U}}}(\hat{\beta}_{\mathrm{cJS}}^{\mathrm{U}})_i & g = -4\sigma^2 f(\hat{\beta}_{\mathrm{c}}^{\mathrm{U}}) \end{bmatrix}$$

$$= \sum_{i=1}^{p}\left(\left[\int\cdots\int -4\sigma^2(\hat{\beta}_{\mathrm{cJS}}^{\mathrm{U}})_i f(\hat{\beta}_{\mathrm{c}}^{\mathrm{U}})\right]_{-\infty}^{\infty}\right.$$

$$\left. + \int\cdots\int 4\sigma^2\frac{d}{d\hat{\beta}_{\mathrm{c}\ i}^{\mathrm{U}}}(\hat{\beta}_{\mathrm{cJS}}^{\mathrm{U}})_i f(\hat{\beta}_{\mathrm{c}}^{\mathrm{U}}) d\hat{\beta}_{\mathrm{c}\ i}^{\mathrm{U}} d\hat{\beta}_{\mathrm{c}\ 1}^{\mathrm{U}}\dots d\hat{\beta}_{\mathrm{c}\ p}^{\mathrm{U}}\right)$$

The first part is 0 because of the exponential decay of the density function of normal distribution. Now we will transform the second part. We will use the $\hat{\beta}_{cJS}^{U}$ formula and calculate the derivative of multiplication.

$$\sum_{i=1}^{p} \int \cdots \int 4\sigma^2 \frac{d}{d\,\hat{\beta}_{c\,i}^{U}} (\hat{\beta}_{cJS}^{U})_i f(\hat{\beta}_c^{U}) d\,\hat{\beta}_{c\,i}^{U} d\,\hat{\beta}_{c\,1}^{U} \ldots d\,\hat{\beta}_{c\,p}^{U}$$

$$= \sum_{i=1}^{p} \mathrm{E} 4\sigma^2 \frac{d}{d\,\hat{\beta}_{c\,i}^{U}} (\hat{\beta}_{cJS}^{U})_i = \sum_{i=1}^{p} \mathrm{E} 4\sigma^2 \frac{d}{d\,\hat{\beta}_{c\,i}^{U}} \left(1 - \frac{(p-2)4\sigma^2}{\hat{\beta}_c^{U'} W \hat{\beta}_c^{U}} \right) (\hat{\beta}_c^{U})_i$$

$$= \sum_{i=1}^{p} \left(4\sigma^2 \mathrm{E} \left(1 - \frac{(p-2)4\sigma^2}{\hat{\beta}_c^{U'} W \hat{\beta}_c^{U}} \right) + \mathrm{E} \left[4\sigma^2 \left(\frac{(p-2)4\sigma^2}{(\hat{\beta}_c^{U'} W \hat{\beta}_c^{U})^2} \right) 2(W)_{i\cdot}\, \hat{\beta}_c^{U} (\hat{\beta}_c^{U})_i \right] \right)$$

$$= 4\sigma^2 p - \mathrm{E} \left(\frac{p(p-2)4^2\sigma^4}{\hat{\beta}_c^{U'} W \hat{\beta}_c^{U}} \right) + \mathrm{E} \left[4\sigma^2 \left(\frac{(p-2)4\sigma^2}{(\hat{\beta}_c^{U'} W \hat{\beta}_c^{U})^2} \right) 2 \hat{\beta}_c^{U'} W \hat{\beta}_c^{U} \right]$$

$$= 4\sigma^2 p - \mathrm{E} \left(\frac{p(p-2)4^2\sigma^4}{\hat{\beta}_c^{U'} W \hat{\beta}_c^{U}} \right) + \mathrm{E} \left(\frac{2(p-2)4^2\sigma^4}{\hat{\beta}_c^{U'} W \hat{\beta}_c^{U}} \right)$$

$$= 4\sigma^2 p - \mathrm{E} \left(\frac{p(p-2)4^2\sigma^4 - 2(p-2)4^2\sigma^4}{\hat{\beta}_c^{U'} W \hat{\beta}_c^{U}} \right) = 4\sigma^2 p - \mathrm{E} \left(\frac{(p-2)^2 4^2 \sigma^4}{\hat{\beta}_c^{U'} W \hat{\beta}_c^{U}} \right)$$

Now we back to (11) and substitute obtained results of ①, ② i ③.

$$\mathrm{E}\left[(\beta - \hat{\beta}_{cJS}^{U})' W (\beta - \hat{\beta}_{cJS}^{U}) \right] = \underbrace{\mathrm{E}\left[(\hat{\beta}_{cJS}^{U} - \hat{\beta}_c^{U})' W (\hat{\beta}_{cJS}^{U} - \hat{\beta}_c^{U}) \right]}_{①}$$

$$- \underbrace{\mathrm{E}\left[(\hat{\beta}_c^{U} - \beta)' W (\hat{\beta}_c^{U} - \beta) \right]}_{②} + \underbrace{2\,\mathrm{E}\left[(\hat{\beta}_{cJS}^{U} - \beta)' W (\hat{\beta}_c^{U} - \beta) \right]}_{③}$$

$$= \mathrm{E}\left[\frac{(p-2)^2 4^2 \sigma^4}{\hat{\beta}_c^{U'} W \hat{\beta}_c^{U}} \right] - 4\sigma^2 p + 2\left(4\sigma^2 p - \mathrm{E}\left(\frac{(p-2)^2 4^2 \sigma^4}{\hat{\beta}_c^{U'} W \hat{\beta}_c^{U}} \right) \right)$$

$$= 4\sigma^2 p - \mathrm{E}\left[\frac{(p-2)^2 4^2 \sigma^4}{\hat{\beta}_c^{U'} W \hat{\beta}_c^{U}} \right] \leq 4\sigma^2 p$$

The last inequality results from the fact that matrix W is positive semi-definite. Now we will prove the last thing:

$$\mathrm{E}\left[(\beta - \hat{\beta}_c^{U})' X' X (\beta - \hat{\beta}_c^{U}) \right] \geq 4\sigma^2 p.$$

Using the same line of reasoning as in ② and assuming that $\mathrm{Tr}\{W^{-1} X' X\} \geq p$ we obtain:

$$\mathrm{E}\left[(\beta - \hat{\beta}_c^{U})' X' X (\beta - \hat{\beta}_c^{U}) \right] = \mathrm{Tr}\left\{ 4\sigma^2 W^{-1} X' X \right\} \geq 4\sigma^2 p,$$

which ends the proof.

References

1. Efron, B., Hastie, T.: Computer Age Statistical Inference: Algorithms, Evidence, and Data Science, 1st edn. Cambridge University Press, New York (2016)
2. Grabarczyk, M.: Estymatory ściągające w modelowaniu przyczynowym. Ph.D., M.Sc. thesis, Warsaw University of Technology (2022)
3. Holland, P.W.: Statistics and causal inference. J. Am. Stat. Assoc. **81**(396), 945–960 (1986)
4. James, W., Stein, C.: Estimation with quadratic loss. In: Fourth Berkeley Symposium on Mathematical Statistics and Probability, vol. 1, pp. 361–379 (1961).
5. Lalonde, R.: Evaluating the econometric evaluations of training programs. Am. Econ. Rev. **76**, 604–620 (1986)
6. Ohtani, K.: Exact small sample properties of an operational variant of the minimum mean squared error estimator. Commun. Stat. Theory Methods **25**(6), 1223–1231 (1996)
7. Rudaś, K.: Linear regression for uplift modeling. Ph.D. thesis, Warsaw University of Technology (2021)
8. Rudaś, K., Jaroszewicz, S.: Linear regression for uplift modeling. Data Min. Knowl. Disc. **32**(5), 1275–1305 (2018). https://doi.org/10.1007/s10618-018-0576-8
9. Theil, H.: Principles of Econometrics. John Wiley, New York (1971)

Workshop on IoT, Edge and Mobile for Embedded Machine Learning (ITEM 2022)

Third International Workshop on IoT, Edge, and Mobile for Embedded Machine Learning (ITEM 2022)

Machine learning (ML) is still among the most promising approaches to address learning and reasoning under uncertainty. While today's deep learning algorithms continue to advance state-of-the-art performance, notable trends include a shift to more "complex-connected" network architectures as well as large ensembles. While for image processing peak performance is already achieved for simple classification tasks, more complex tasks such as segmentation of natural language processing remain challenges. On the contrary, due to a staggering Moore's law and technology scaling, even simple classification tasks usually face limited hardware capabilities when mapped to IoT, edge, or mobile devices. For more complex tasks, deployment on such devices is often impossible.

On-device processing is of paramount importance though, not only for privacy constraints when avoiding cloud-based services, but also when moving ML "to the wild" as solutions have to face real-time constraints, limited availability of cloud services and connectivity issues. In this setting, the tasks are often complicated by incomplete and/or noisy data, resulting in network architectures that are substantially more complex than their plain counterparts.

As a result, we observe a strong need for new ML methods to address the requirements of emerging workloads deployed in the real-world, such as uncertainty, robustness, and limited data. In order to not hinder the deployment of such methods on various computing devices, and to address the gap between application and computer hardware, we furthermore need a variety of tools. As such, this workshop aims to gather new ideas and concepts on ML methods for real-world deployment, methods for compression and related complexity reduction tools, dedicated hardware for emerging ML tasks, and associated tooling like compilers and mappers. Furthermore, the workshop also serves as a platform that gathers experts from ML and systems for joint tackling of these problems, creating an atmosphere of open discussions and other interactions.

The third edition of ITEM took place in September 2022 in Grenoble, France, and actually was the first edition to be held in-person. Due to substantial space and time constraints, this edition was notably selective, and to accommodate more contributed articles, the organizers opted to not include a keynote presentation. As a result, the workshop's program was two-fold: while the first session focused on tools, the second session put a focus on methods.

Contributed talks included authors from the Netherlands, Germany, Romania, Belgium, Italy, France, the UK, and China, representing from industry and academia. Topics of concern with regard to tools covered design space explorations, automated partitioning, deep convolutional neural networks, and predictive modeling. Topics on model architectures included recurrent neural networks, cell optimization, and quantization, while discussed applications covered document localization, speech enhancement, fault diagnosis, denoising, and image processing.

Early take-aways and insights include the increasing trend towards edge computing as well as heterogeneity resulting in more interest in model partitioning, with the main objective to find a good balance between wimpy and brawny processors. Similarly, the complexity associated with distributing processing over edge and cloud, and other examples of heterogeneity, sparked research interest in automated searches to diminish the complexity implication on users, as well as predictive performance modeling to improve reasoning about partitioning decisions. Beyond that, recurrent neural networks as well as convolutional network architectures were again in the focus of acceleration. Quantization is still a major method in model compression, and while quantization-aware training is state of the art, work was presented that proposed a method without a need to involve costly training when quantizing a model. Discussions showed a community-wide interest in benchmarking and performance evaluation, in particular with regard to energy.

October 2022

Holger Fröning
Gregor Schiele
Franz Pernkopf
Michaela Blott
Kazem Shekofteh

Organization

Workshop Co-organizers

Holger Fröning   Heidelberg University, Germany
Gregor Schiele   University of Duisburg-Essen, Germany
Franz Pernkopf   Graz University of Technology, Austria
Michaela Blott   AMD Research, Ireland

Program Chair

Kazem Shekofteh   Heidelberg University, Germany

Technical Program Committee

Jürgen Becker   KIT, Germany
Costas Bekas   Citadel Securities, Switzerland
Herman Engelbrecht   University of Stellenbosch, South Africa
Domenik Helms   DLR, Germany
Michael Kamps   Ruhr-University Bochum, Germany
David King   Air Force Institute of Technology, USA
Benjamin Klenk   NVIDIA, USA
Manfred Mücke   Materials Center Leoben, Austria
Marco Platzner   University of Paderborn, Germany
Sébastien Rumley   HES-SO Fribourg, Switzerland
Dolly Sapra   University of Amsterdam, The Netherlands
Günther Schindler   SAP SE, Germany
Wei Shao   RMIT University, Australia
Yannik Stradmann   Heidelberg University, Germany
Jürgen Teich   Friedrich-Alexander-Universität
     Erlangen-Nuremberg, Germany
Ola Torudbakken   Graphcore, Norway
Nicolas Weber   NEC Laboratories Europe, Germany

It is planned to continue ITEM, so any interested researcher or scientist is invited to contribute to future editions. Also, while ITEM's main focus is to be an academic platform with peer-reviewed contributions, there is also a more informal counterpart called the Workshop on Embedded Machine Learning (WEML), which is annually held at Heidelberg University. WEML distinguishes itself from ITEM by being a platform that only includes invited presentations from the community for mutual updates on recent insights and trends, but without the vigorous demands of scientific peer-review. For more information about these two workshops, please refer to:

https://www.item-workshop.org
https://www.deepchip.org

Last, the co-organizers of ITEM would like to acknowledge the commitment of the ECML PKDD's Workshop Co-chairs, Bruno Crémilleux and Charlotte Laclau, who did an excellent job managing and orchestrating the vast amount of information exchange required to organize such a large event. Similar acknowledgements go to the time and effort spent by our Program Committee, and, last but not least, to the strong commitment of our authors. Ultimate acknowledgements go to Springer for publishing the workshop's proceedings.

Hierarchical Design Space Exploration for Distributed CNN Inference at the Edge

Xiaotian Guo[1,2]([✉]) [iD], Andy D. Pimentel[1] [iD], and Todor Stefanov[2] [iD]

[1] University of Amsterdam, Amsterdam, The Netherlands
{x.guo3,a.d.pimentel}@uva.nl
[2] Leiden University, Leiden, The Netherlands
t.p.stefanov@liacs.leidenuniv.nl

Abstract. Convolutional Neural Network (CNN) models for modern applications are becoming increasingly deep and complex. Thus, the number of different CNN mapping possibilities when deploying a CNN model on multiple edge devices is vast. Design Space Exploration (DSE) methods are therefore essential to find a set of optimal CNN mappings subject to one or more design requirements. In this paper, we present an efficient DSE methodology to find (near-)optimal CNN mappings for distributed inference at the edge. To deal with the vast design space of different CNN mappings, we accelerate the searching process by proposing and utilizing a multi-stage hierarchical DSE approach together with a tailored Genetic Algorithm as the underlying search engine.

1 Introduction

Convolutional Neural Networks (CNNs) have been intensively researched and widely used in many domains, including audio recognition, computer vision, and natural language processing. Since CNNs became the state-of-the-art in large-scale visual recognition and classification, countless advancements in improving CNN models have been made to solve traditionally challenging problems such as image recognition, classification, etc. Deploying these modern CNN models and performing the inference directly on an edge device is typically not possible because of limited resources in terms of memory capacity, computation capacity, and power budget of the edge device. Therefore, to perform CNN inference on edge devices, users typically need to rely on additional compute resources provided as service by the cloud. Realizing CNN inference on edge devices using such cloud services requires users to communicate a substantial amount of data between an edge device and a cloud server. Such data communication may cause data privacy concerns as well as low device responsiveness due to data transmission delays or temporal unavailability of the cloud services.

One approach to address the above problems and achieve CNN inference on an edge device without cloud services, is to perform CNN model compression, such as pruning, quantization, or knowledge distillation [6] that will allow to deploy the entire CNN model on the device. However, such an approach sacrifices the accuracy of the model to some extent, especially when high model

I. Koprinska et al. (Eds.): ECML PKDD 2022 Workshops, CCIS 1752, pp. 545–556, 2023.
https://doi.org/10.1007/978-3-031-23618-1_36

compression rates are required. Another approach is to deploy only a part of the CNN model on the edge device and the rest of the model in the cloud. Such an approach [10], however, still suffers from data privacy and cloud communication latency concerns. A third approach, which solves the aforementioned issues of the other two approaches, is to partition the CNN model and distribute the partitions across multiple edge devices to collaboratively perform the CNN inference. A general direction is to utilize model and data parallelism methods [7] to divide CNN computations over a number of edge devices. Such distributed execution of the CNN model inference often needs to take multiple requirements into account, like latency, throughput, resource usage, power/energy consumption, etc. Here, the way how the different CNN layers are distributed and mapped onto the edge devices plays a key role in optimizing/satisfying these requirements. For example, using model-parallelism techniques and mapping CNN layers in a balanced way may reduce the maximum per-device memory footprint or energy consumption. Or, some CNN mappings may generate a balanced data processing pipeline, thereby improving the overall throughput. As CNN models for modern applications are becoming increasingly deep and complex, the number of different CNN mapping possibilities when deploying multiple edge devices, and the various compute resources in each of them, is vast. Efficient Design Space Exploration (DSE) methods are therefore essential to find a set of (near-)optimal CNN mappings subject to one or more design requirements (i.e., objectives).

In this paper, we present an efficient DSE methodology to find optimal CNN mappings for distributed inference at the edge. To this end, we leverage our AutoDiCE framework [1] to assess the quality (in terms of inference throughput, memory footprint, and energy consumption) of a particular CNN mapping. AutoDiCE is a fully automated framework for distributed CNN inference over multiple edge devices. To deal with the vast design space of different CNN mappings, we accelerate the searching process by using a multi-stage hierarchical DSE approach together with a tailored Genetic Algorithm (GA) as the underlying search engine. At every stage, we perform DSE at two hierarchical levels. In the first level, we use analytical models inside a GA to approximate each objective function (i.e., throughput, memory, and energy consumption) to avoid relatively long evaluation times through real on-device (i.e., on-board) measurements using our AutoDiCE framework. The near-optimal solutions found in the first level together with Pareto-optimal solutions from a previous DSE stage are utilized as the parents for the second level DSE. In this second level, we evaluate each design point using real measurements taken from AutoDiCE-generated CNN inference implementations to determine the Pareto front for a next DSE stage. The output of the last DSE stage provides the final Pareto-optimal solutions. Our contributions can be summarized as follows:

- enhance the DSE process by creating analytical models to approximate each objective function in order to reduce the on-board evaluation cost during the DSE process;
- accelerate the DSE convergence by performing the DSE process in multiple stages where, at each DSE stage, we consider only specific part of the design

space and use as input Pareto-optimal solutions from the previous DSE stage in order to find Pareto-optimal solutions for the next DSE stage;
- improve the searching efficiency with a tailored chromosome encoding method, thereby scaling down the search space.

2 Related Work

Today's prevalent CNN models for computer vision tasks are becoming increasingly large. Their execution, i.e. model inference, requires increasing amounts of memory and compute resources, putting a large burden on the cloud infrastructure. Offloading parts of a single CNN model to the edge has gained the attention of researchers to relieve the pressure on the cloud. For example, Neurosurgeon [10] vertically partitions a CNN model between a single edge device and the cloud. DDNN [17] also tries to partition a model between the cloud and edge devices, but model retraining is needed for each early-exit branch. However, the methods in [10,17] execute only the first few layers of a CNN model at the edge, after which the rest of the computation is still offloaded to the cloud. The unpredictable low responsiveness and data privacy issues are still present in such partitioned CNN inference due to the partial involvement of the cloud [5]. To perform CNN inference on a fully distributed system at the edge, without any cloud involvement, data partitioning or CNN model partitioning is often required. For example, in [19], a data partitioning strategy is used in an object detection CNN-based application to split input data frames. Alternatively, CNN model partitioning splits CNN layers and/or connections of a large CNN model, thereby creating several smaller sub-models (partitioned models) where each sub-model is executed on a different edge device [16]. For instance, Hadidi *et al.* [7] exploits model-partition methods to perform single-batch inference over several collaborative and resource-constrained edge devices and utilizes their aggregated computing power via a local network. In addition to using data and CNN model partitioning to map large CNNs on resource-constrained edge devices, researchers try to optimize the CNN mapping to improve the inference performance. For example, the methodologies in [9,18,20] propose efficient algorithms to determine partitioning policies that generate efficient CNN mappings in order to improve the performance of cooperative inference over multiple edge devices. However, these methodologies optimize and evaluate CNN mappings based on analytical models only and consider limited number of objectives. In contrast, our DSE methodology optimizes more objectives, and besides analytical models, it uses AutoDiCE to evaluate mappings by real on-device measurements.

Distributed inference of large CNN models typically needs to consider a range of different design requirements, such as latency, throughput, resource usage, power/energy consumption, etc. These requirements/objectives can be conflicting, implying that there usually does not exist a single optimal CNN mapping that satisfies all requirements. Typically multiple solutions, so-called Pareto optimal solutions, co-exist and the set of all optimal solutions is called the Pareto front. Finding these Pareto-optimal CNN mappings for a given number of edge devices to perform distributed CNN inference under several requirements is the topic of study in this paper. A popular approach to perform such a search for Pareto-optimal solutions is by using multi-objective evolutionary algorithms [4]. More specifically, in the domain of DSE, multi-objective Genetic Algorithms (GAs), such as the Non-dominated Sorting Genetic Algorithm (NSGA-II) [3], are widely used and have demonstrated to produce good results [15]. For instance, [11,12] use the NSGA-II GA to explore the design space to find improved neural network architectures for CNN-based applications. Our DSE methodology also employs NSGA-II to explore the Pareto-optimal CNN mapping solutions with respect to throughput, maximum memory usage per device, and maximum energy consumption per device. However, NSGA-II can easily get stuck in so-called dominance resistant solutions [14], that are far away from the true Pareto front. How to search the optimal CNN mappings for distributed inference using NSGA-II, and efficiently find the Pareto front in the huge search space, are the main challenges we try to tackle in this paper.

3   Evaluation Methods

In this section, we discuss two different methods to evaluate the three objectives at every stage in our two-level DSE. The first level DSE applies analytical models to approximate the objectives, and the second level uses our AutoDiCE framework to evaluate the objectives of distributed CNN inference by real implementations and measurements on hardware boards.

3.1   Analytical Models

In the first level, we adopt analytical models to approximate the system throughput, memory usage, and energy consumption for each CNN mapping. We use t_{l_j}, M_{l_j}, E_{l_j} to represent the execution time, the memory usage, and the energy consumption of layer l_j in a CNN model, respectively. A CNN mapping $\mathbf{x}$ is denoted as $\mathbf{x} = [x_1, x_2, \cdots, x_L]$, where L is the number of layers in the CNN model and $x_j = PE_i$ means that layer l_j is mapped on processing element PE_i, which could, e.g., be a CPU or GPU inside an edge device. For a given mapping $\mathbf{x}$, the three objectives of the distributed system can be computed as follows.

Throughput. The overall system throughput T_{system} is defined as the images processed per second (IPS) over multiple PEs:

$$T_{system} = \frac{1}{\max_{1 \le i \le N} (t^i)} ; \qquad t^i = \sum_{\forall j : 1 \le j \le L \wedge x_j = PE_i} t_{l_j} + t_{comm}$$

where t^i is the time to process one image on PE_i, N is the total number of deployed PEs in the distributed system, and t_{comm} is the time needed for data communication related to PE_i. We assume that the size of input images are already determined as well as the input and output tensors of every CNN layer are also fixed. Then, we can estimate the total number of operations in every layer and the total size of communicated data related to PE_i. The execution time t_{l_j} is estimated through the number of multiply-accumulate operations (MACs). A proper approximation for communication time t_{comm} depends on data movements, and involves intra-node shared memory communication, intra-node communication between CPU and GPU, or inter-node communication over the network.

Memory. Every PE_i allocates memory M^i which consists of three parts: memory for CNN coefficients (i.e. weights, bias, and parameters), memory for output buffers to store intermediate results of layers, and memory for input buffers of some layers to receive data from other PEs:

$$M^i = \sum_{\forall j:1 \leq j \leq L \wedge x_j = PE_i} (M^j_{coeffs} + M^j_{outbuffs} + M^j_{inbuffs})$$

where M^j_{coeffs}, $M^j_{outbuffs}$, and $M^j_{inbuffs}$ denote the sizes of the aforementioned memory parts associated with layer l_j mapped on PE_i. These sizes (in number of elements) are approximated based on the type of CNN layer l_j. For example, given a convolutional layer l_j, the memory sizes are calculated as follows:

$$M^j_{coeffs} = w_k * h_k * C_{in} * C_{out} + C_{out}$$

$$M^j_{outbuffs} = w_{out} * h_{out} * C_{out} \qquad M^j_{inbuffs} = w_{in} * h_{in} * C_{in}$$

where w_k and h_k are the width and height of the convolution kernel, C_{in} and C_{out} are the number of input and output channels of layer l_j, and w_{in}, h_{in}, w_{out}, h_{out} are the width and height of the input and output tensors of layer l_j. If layer l_j mapped on PE_i does not receive data from layers that are mapped on other PEs then $M^j_{inbuffs} = 0$.

Energy. Every PE_i consumes energy E^i to execute the CNN layers mapped on PE_i. In our energy consumption analytical model, E^i includes the energy consumed for inference computation and data communication with other PEs:

$$E^i = \sum_{\forall j:1 \leq j \leq L \wedge x_j = PE_i} E^j_{comp} + \sum_{\forall j:1 \leq j \leq L \wedge x_j = PE_i} E^j_{comm}$$

where E^j_{comp} and E^j_{comm} denote the computation and communication energy consumption for layer l_j, respectively. Here, E^j_{comm} is non-zero only when layer l_j actually communicates with another PE. We calculate E^j_{comp} and E^j_{comm} as follows:

$$E^j_{comp} = \int_0^{t^j_{comp}} P^j_{comp}(t)\, dt; \qquad E^j_{comm} = \int_0^{t^j_{comm}} P^j_{comm}(t)\, dt$$

where $P^j_{comp}(t)$ is the power consumption during the execution of layer l_j, and $P^j_{comm}(t)$ is the power consumption during data communication of layer l_j with another PE. $P^j_{comp}(t)$ and $P^j_{comm}(t)$ can be acquired by measurements during CNN layer profiling on an edge device.

3.2   AutoDiCE Framework

As explained in Sect. 1, in the second level we use our AutoDiCE framework [1] to evaluate the fitness (i.e., the quality) of a given CNN mapping in terms of the following objectives: CNN inference throughput, maximum memory usage per device, and maximum energy consumption per device. AutoDiCE enables us to evaluate the quality of a CNN mapping through actual on-device measurements. AutoDiCE is a fully automated framework for distributed CNN inference over multiple edge devices. Given a specific input CNN model and specifications of the model partitioning and mapping of the partitions to (various resources within) multiple edge devices, AutoDiCE automates the actual model partitioning, code generation, and deployment of the CNN partitions on the edge devices.

Figure 1 shows the user interface and design flow of AutoDiCE, where the main steps in the flow are divided into two modules: front-end and back-end. The interface is composed of three specifications, namely a Pre-trained CNN Model (provided as an .onnx file), Mapping Specification (a .json file), and Platform Specification (a .txt file). The Pre-trained CNN Model specification includes the CNN topology description with all layers and connections among layers as well as the weights/biases that are associated with the layers and obtained by training on a specific dataset using deep learning frameworks like PyTorch, TensorFlow, etc. Many such CNN model specifications in ONNX format [2] are readily available in open-access libraries and can be directly used as an input to the framework. The Platform Specification lists all available edge devices together with their computational hardware resources and specific software libraries associated with these resources. The Mapping Specification is a list of key-value pairs that explicitly specifies how all layers described in the Pre-trained CNN Model specification are mapped onto the computational hardware resources listed in the Platform Specification. Every unique key corresponds to an edge device with a selection of its hardware resources, like CPUs or GPU, to be used for computation. Every value corresponds to a set of CNN layers to be deployed and executed on the edge device resources. Such Mapping Specification can be provided manually by the user or, like in this paper, generated by an external mapping DSE tool.

The three aforementioned specifications are given as an input to the front-end module as shown in Fig. 1, which then performs two main steps: *Model Splitting* and *Config & Communication Generation*. The Model Splitting takes as an input the Pre-trained CNN Model and Mapping specifications, splits the input CNN model into multiple sub-models, and generates these sub-models in ONNX format. The number of generated sub-models is equal to the number of unique key-value pairs in the Mapping Specification. The Config & Communication Generation step takes all three input specification files and generates specific tables in JSON format containing information needed to realize proper communication and synchronization among the sub-models using the well-known MPI interface. In addition, a configuration text file (MPI rankfile) is generated to initialize and run the sub-models as different MPI processes.

The back-end module subsequently uses the output from the front-end for code and deployment package generation. During the *Code Generation* step, effi-

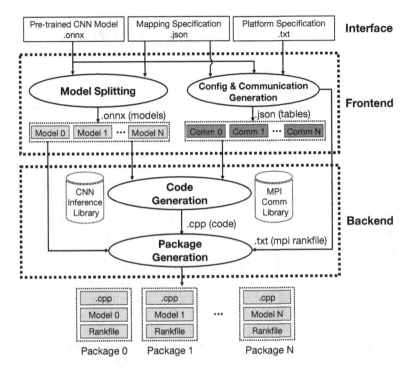

Fig. 1. The AutoDiCE design flow and its user interface

cient C++ code is generated for every edge device based on the input sub-models and tables. In the generated code, primitives from the standard MPI library are used for data communication and synchronization among sub-models as well as primitives from a custom CNN Inference Library are used for implementation of the CNN layers belonging to every sub-model. This CNN Inference Library also integrates OpenMP support. This means that if a CNN layer is mapped onto multiple CPU cores in an edge device, the actual execution of such layer will be multi-threaded using OpenMP to efficiently utilize the multiple CPU cores by exploiting data parallelism available within the layer. Finally, the *Package Generation* step packs the generated C++ code, the MPI rankfile, and a sub-model together to generate a specific deployment package for every edge device.

4   Multi-stage Hierarchical Design Space Exploration

Our DSE methodology utilizes a Genetic Algorithm (GA), namely the NSGA-II algorithm [3], to search for optimal mappings of (complete) CNN layers to different, distributed edge devices. We assume that each edge device contains a number of internal compute resources (i.e. PEs), like a CPU and GPU, and we map CNN layers directly to these specific PEs within an edge device.

Given a trained CNN model with L layers, a layer l_j performs a computation operation in the CNN model such as a convolution (Conv), a matrix

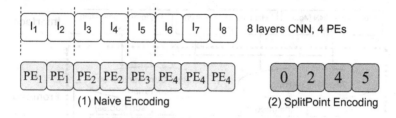

Fig. 2. Two chromosome encoding methods

multiplication (FC), etc. As mentioned in Sect. 3.1, a mapping $\mathbf{x}$ of the CNN layers onto a total of N PEs is denoted as $\mathbf{x} = [x_1, x_2, \cdots, x_L]$. Such mapping notation $\mathbf{x}$ is typically encoded with the GA's chromosome where $PE_i, i \in [1..N]$ define the gene types in the chromosome. An example of such encoding, called Naive Encoding (NE), is shown in Fig. 2. The GA chromosome $[PE_1, PE_1, PE_2, PE_2, PE_3, PE_4, PE_4, PE_4]$ encodes an 8-layer CNN ($L = 8$) mapped onto four PEs ($N = 4$), where layers l_1 and l_2 are mapped on PE_1, l_3 and l_4 on PE_2, l_5 on PE_3, and l_6, l_7, l_8 on PE_4. Such naive encoding for CNN mappings is simple and intuitive but it may require exploration of a huge design space because the space size depends exponentially on the number of layers L in a CNN model and L is typically large. Therefore, in our DSE methodology, we propose and utilize a tailored chromosome encoding method, called Split Point Encoding (SPE). It encodes points in a CNN model that partition the model into N groups of CNN layers, where each group consists of consecutive layers and is mapped on one PE. In Fig. 2, the Split Point Encoding example encodes the same mapping as the Naive Encoding example. It can be seen that the 8-layer CNN has four split points, visualized with the vertical dashed lines, at positions 0, 2, 4, and 5 determined by the layer index j. Therefore, the GA chromosome using our SPE method is [0, 2, 4, 5] and it encodes four groups of layers each mapped on one PE as follows: 1) for $j \in (0..2]$, l_j mapped on PE_1; 2) for $j \in (2..4]$, l_j mapped on PE_2; 3) for $j \in (4..5]$, l_j mapped on PE_3; 4) for $j > 5$, l_j mapped on PE_4. The length of our SPE chromosome is equal to the number of PEs which is N, thus SPE requires exploration of a design space which size depends exponentially on N. Since N is typically much smaller than the number of CNN layers L, our SPE method largely scales down the design space and improves the search efficiency compared to the NE method.

Given a trained CNN model and all edge devices with in total N PEs, our DSE methodology searches for Pareto CNN mappings to optimize the three objectives, mentioned in Sect. 3. In Fig. 3, we present the general structure of our multi-stage hierarchical DSE methodology. On the left, the K stages in our DSE workflow are depicted, and on the right a zoomed-in view of each stage is provided with the two rectangular boxes showing the two hierarchical levels per stage. We accelerate our DSE process by splitting it into K different stages, where K is the ceiling value of $log_2(N)$. At each stage, we perform a two-level DSE. In both levels, the NSGA-II GA is deployed to evolve a population of CNN

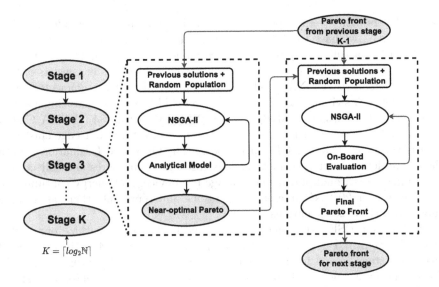

Fig. 3. The DSE methodology workflow

mappings over multiple generations to search for a Pareto front in terms of the targeted objectives. In the first DSE level, we use the analytical models, introduced in Sect. 3, inside the GA to approximate each objective function. In the second DSE level, we use real distributed CNN inference implementations generated by AutoDiCE (see Fig. 1) for evaluation, thereby producing more accurate Pareto solutions as they are based on real (on-board) measurements.

At every DSE stage $k \in [1, \cdots, K-1]$, we search for optimal CNN mappings on 2^k target PEs. Figure 3 shows that to initialize the GA population at stage k, with $k > 1$, the Pareto optimal results found by the previous stage $k - 1$ are used. By doing so, we can retain the information of Pareto CNN mappings in previous stages to improve the DSE convergence. Moreover, the second level DSE at each stage also uses the results from the first level of DSE to initialize its population. Finally, the output of the last DSE stage ($k = K$) provides the final Pareto-optimal solutions for N PEs.

5 Experimental Evaluation

In this section, we evaluate the search efficiency of our multi-stage hierarchical DSE methodology by conducting three DSE experiments and comparing the obtained experimental results in terms of the quality of the found solutions and how this quality changes over time during the DSE process (i.e., the search).

5.1 Experimental Setup

In our three DSE experiments, we search for Pareto-optimal mappings of the popular ResNet-101 [8] CNN model onto a cluster of four edge devices. ResNet-101 has 344 layers with diverse types leading to an immense number of different CNN mappings, i.e., we have to perform the search in a vast design space. Therefore, ResNet-101 is a sufficiently representative model to apply our DSE methodology on and to demonstrate its merits. Our 4-device edge cluster consists of four NVIDIA Jetson Xavier NX development boards [13] that are connected via a Gigabit network switch. Each board has an embedded MPSoC featuring a 6-core CPU (NVIDIA Carmel ARMv8) and a GPU (Volta with 384 NVIDIA CUDA cores and 48 Tensor cores). Thus, we have 8 PEs in total in our edge cluster (4 boards with 1 CPU and 1 GPU per board). The On-Board Evaluation step in the second level of our DSE methodology (see Fig. 3) measures and collects the CNN inference throughput, memory usage per device, and energy consumption per device over 20 CNN inference executions and represents them as average values over these 20 executions.

In the first DSE experiment, referred as 3s-2l-SPE, we utilize our multi-stage hierarchical DSE methodology as presented in Sect. 4 with 3 stages, 2 levels per stage, and the chromosome is encoded using our SPE method. In the second experiment, referred as 1s-non-SPE, we utilize a classical 1-stage, non-hierarchical DSE methodology based on the NSGA-II algorithm with our On-Board Evaluation as the fitness function and our SPE as the chromosome encoding method. In the third experiment, referred as 1s-non-NE, we utilize the same DSE methodology as in the second experiment but we replace SPE with the NE method mentioned in Sect. 4. In all experiments, every CNN layer can be mapped either onto a 6-core CPU or a GPU present in any of the aforementioned four board. The NSGA-II algorithm is executed with a population size of 100 individuals, a mutation probability of 0.2, and a crossover probability of 0.5. In each DSE experiment, we run the search for optimal mappings for 70 h and compare the quality of solutions found within these 70 h.

5.2   Experimental Results

Figure 4 shows how the quality of the found mappings in terms of the three objectives, discussed in Sect. 3, improves during the search in the three DSE experiments. The results for each objective are plotted in a separate chart where the X-axis represents the search time in hours and the Y-axis represents the objective value in images per second (IPS) for the CNN inference throughput, in mega bytes (MB) for the maximum memory usage per edge device, and in joules per image (J/img) for the maximum energy consumption per edge device. Every point in a chart represents the best found mapping with respect to the objective at a given point in time.

The results in Fig. 4 clearly indicate that the 1s-non-NE DSE gets easily stuck in dominance resistant solutions, which means that such DSE cannot find high-quality mappings even after hundreds of generations. In contrast, by replacing the common NE encoding method with our tailored SPE method, the search efficiency is significantly improved as shown in Fig. 4 where the 1s-non-SPE DSE delivers high-quality mappings for the three objectives after 20 h. This is because our SPE method ensures that only consecutive CNN layers will be mapped on

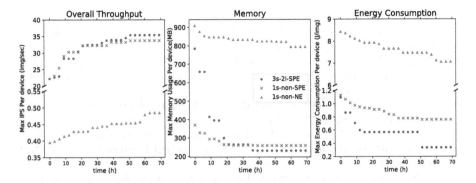

Fig. 4. Quality of found mappings during the three DSE experiments

a PE, thereby scaling down significantly the design space and allowing only exploration of mappings with reduced data communication among PEs. Such mappings are better than less restricted mappings allowed by the NE method.

Finally, comparing the 1s-non-SPE and 3s-2l-SPE results shown in Fig. 4, we see that by introducing multiple stages and hierarchy in the DSE process, it is accelerate further in finding high-quality mappings. For example, after 40 h of search time, our 3s-2l-SPE DSE delivers better mappings for the three objectives than the 1s-non-SPE DSE.

6   Conclusion

We have presented a novel multi-stage hierarchical DSE methodology for distributed CNN inference at the edge. To accelerate the DSE process and improve its efficiency, our DSE methodology combines analytical models with real on-board measurements to speedup the evaluations of individual design points and utilizes a tailored chromosome encoding method to effectively scale down the explored design space. The methodology has been experimentally evaluated by searching for optimal distributed mappings of the ResNet-101 CNN model onto an edge cluster of four NVIDIA Jetson Xavier boards. The experimental results show that our multi-stage hierarchical DSE methodology has significantly improved search efficiency in comparison to a classical one-stage, non-hierarchical DSE methodology which employs the commonly used, naive chromosome encoding method.

References

1. AutoDiCE: https://github.com/parrotsky/autodice
2. Bai, J., et al.: ONNX: open neural network exchange (2019). https://github.com/onnx/onnx
3. Deb, K., Pratap, A., Agarwal, S., Meyarivan, T.: A fast and elitist multiobjective genetic algorithm: NSGA-II. IEEE Trans. Evol. Comput. **6**(2), 182–197 (2002). https://doi.org/10.1109/4235.996017

4. Deb, K.: Multi-objective evolutionary algorithms. In: Kacprzyk, J., Pedrycz, W. (eds.) Springer Handbook of Computational Intelligence, pp. 995–1015. Springer, Heidelberg (2015). https://doi.org/10.1007/978-3-662-43505-2_49

5. Dillon, T., Wu, C., Chang, E.: Cloud computing: Issues and challenges. In: 24th IEEE International Conference on Advanced Information Networking and Applications, pp. 27–33 (2010)

6. Guo, Y.: A survey on methods and theories of quantized neural networks. arXiv preprint arXiv:1808.04752 (2018)

7. Hadidi, R., Cao, J., Ryoo, M.S., Kim, H.: Toward collaborative inferencing of deep neural networks on Internet-of-Things devices. IEEE Internet Things J. 7(6), 4950–4960 (2020)

8. He, K., Zhang, X., Ren, S., Sun, J.: Deep residual learning for image recognition. In: Conference on Computer Vision and Pattern Recognition, pp. 770–778 (2016)

9. Hou, X., Guan, Y., Han, T., Zhang, N.: Distredge: speeding up convolutional neural network inference on distributed edge devices. ArXiv abs/2202.01699 (2022)

10. Kang, et al.: Neurosurgeon: collaborative intelligence between the cloud and mobile edge. ACM SIGARCH Comput. Archit. News 45(1), 615–629 (2017)

11. Loni, M., Sinaei, S., Zoljodi, A., Daneshtalab, M., Sjödin, M.: Deepmaker: a multiobjective optimization framework for deep neural networks in embedded systems. Microprocess. Microsyst. 73, 102989 (2020)

12. Minakova, S., Sapra, D., Stefanov, T., Pimentel, A.D.: Scenario based run-time switching for adaptive CNN-based applications at the edge. ACM Trans. Embed. Comput. Syst. 21(2), 1–33 (2022)

13. NVIDIA: Jetson Xavier NX (2020). https://developer.nvidia.com/embedded/jetson-xavier-nx

14. Pang, L.M., Ishibuchi, H., Shang, K.: NSGA-II with simple modification works well on a wide variety of many-objective problems. IEEE Access 8 (2020)

15. Pimentel, A.: Exploring exploration: a tutorial introduction to embedded systems design space exploration. IEEE Design Test 34(1), 77–90 (2 2017)

16. Stahl, R., Zhao, Z., Mueller-Gritschneder, D., Gerstlauer, A., Schlichtmann, U.: Fully distributed deep learning inference on resource-constrained edge devices. In: International Conference on Embedded Computer Systems, pp. 77–90 (2019)

17. Teerapittayanon, S., McDanel, B., Kung, H.T.: Distributed deep neural networks over the cloud, the edge and end devices. In: 2017 IEEE 37th International Conference on Distributed Computing Systems (ICDCS), pp. 328–339. IEEE (2017)

18. Zeng, L., et al.: CoEdge: cooperative DNN inference with adaptive workload partitioning over heterogeneous edge devices. IEEE/ACM Trans. Netw. 29(2), 595–608 (2020)

19. Zhao, Z., Barijough, K.M., Gerstlauer, A.: DeepThings: distributed adaptive deep learning inference on resource-constrained IoT edge clusters. IEEE Trans. Comput. Aided Design Integr. Circ. Syst. 37(11), 2348–2359 (2018)

20. Zhou, L., et al.: Adaptive parallel execution of deep neural networks on heterogeneous edge devices. In: 4th ACM/IEEE Symposium on Edge Computing, pp. 195–208 (2019)

Automated Search for Deep Neural Network Inference Partitioning on Embedded FPGA

Fabian Kreß$^{(\boxtimes)}$ [ID], Julian Hoefer, Tim Hotfilter [ID], Iris Walter [ID],
El Mahdi El Annabi, Tanja Harbaum, and Jürgen Becker

Karlsruhe Institute of Technology, Karlsruhe, Germany
{fabian.kress,julian.hoefer,hotfilter,iris.walter,
harbaum,becker}@kit.edu

Abstract. Deep Neural Networks (DNNs) are currently making their way into a broad range of applications. While until recently they were mainly executed on high-performance computers, they are now also increasingly found in hardware platforms of edge applications. In order to meet the constantly changing demands, deployment of embedded Field Programmable Gate Arrays (FPGAs) is particularly suitable. Despite the tremendous advantage of high flexibility, embedded FPGAs are usually resource-constrained as they require more area than comparable Application-Specific Integrated Circuits (ASICs). Consequently, co-execution of a DNN on multiple platforms with dedicated partitioning is beneficial. Typical systems consist of FPGAs and Graphics Processing Units (GPUs). Combining the advantages of these platforms while keeping the communication overhead low is a promising way to meet the increasing requirements.

In this paper, we present an automated approach to efficiently partition DNN inference between an embedded FPGA and a GPU-based central compute platform. Our toolchain focuses on the limited hardware resources available on the embedded FPGA and the link bandwidth required to send intermediate results to the GPU. Thereby, it automatically searches for an optimal partitioning point which maximizes the hardware utilization while ensuring low bus load.

For a low-complexity DNN, we are able to identify optimal partitioning points for three different prototyping platforms. On a Xilinx ZCU104, we achieve a 50% reduction of the required link bandwidth between the FPGA and GPU compared to maximizing the number of layers executed on the embedded FPGA, while hardware utilization on the FPGA is only reduced by 7.88% and 6.38%, respectively, depending on the use of DSPs and BRAMs on the FPGA.

Keywords: Distributed sensor systems · Neural network inference partitioning · Design space exploration · Embedded FPGA

I. Koprinska et al. (Eds.): ECML PKDD 2022 Workshops, CCIS 1752, pp. 557–568, 2023.
https://doi.org/10.1007/978-3-031-23618-1_37

1   Introduction

In the recent decade, Deep Neural Networks (DNNs) became the preferred algorithm for evaluating complex data, like images or radar information. These algorithms show great performance and accuracy, while they usually can be deployed readily. However, DNN inference for complex data can cause high computational complexity, resulting in extensive power consumption. This especially becomes an issue when DNN are used in energy-constrained or safety-critical environments like embedded low-power systems. Hence, the execution of DNN moved from traditional computing devices such as Central Processing Units (CPUs) and Graphics Processing Units (GPUs), further into hardware accelerators designed for fast or energy-efficient DNN execution. These are either implemented in an Application-Specific Integrated Circuit (ASIC) or an embedded Field-Programmable Gate Array (FPGA). The latter provides flexibility regarding runtime reconfiguration or future architecture updates and provides significantly reduced development time. Dedicated accelerators for a given DNN offer a great trade-off between power consumption and performance, but they often lack flexibility to model different kinds of DNNs.

Accelerators for DNNs in autonomous driving or assistive robotics are especially demanding as resource and real-time requirements in those multisensory systems are high. These platforms, such as the humanoid assistive robot ARMAR-6 [2], are usually based on a system architecture as shown in Fig. 1. For visual perception, ARMAR-6 is equipped with a stereo camera and an RGB-D camera. As the bus is highly occupied, images are directly streamed to the compute platform consisting of three PCs, a GPU and an FPGA. The actual data processing not only consists of image processing, e.g., person recognition, human pose estimation, object detection and localization, but speech recognition, force control, task planning, etc. as well. These tasks are distributed among the different devices of the compute platform, realizing DNN-based tasks on the GPU and FPGA, respectively. Time-sensitive applications, e.g., face and gesture recognition, are accelerated on the FPGA [17]. However, acceleration of the whole DNN within the FPGA as dataflow is not feasible for each model. Therefore, we propose the co-execution of DNNs in the distributed system of GPU and FPGA.

The example above shows that there is a need for highly efficient and performant DNN accelerators, which also offer a great flexibility for many different DNN workloads. Over the past years, different optimization strategies for DNN have evolved to make the underlying operations more efficient, such as quantization [8] or pruning [5]. A more recent optimization scheme considers DNNs that are executed on complex System-on-Chips (SoCs) with multiple different domains like CPUs, GPUs or FPGAs. Those systems allow combining the advantages of the various system components to achieve a high overall performance. However, efficient partitioning between the different domains is an emerging challenge. Therefore, we present in this paper our approach to automatically partition a DNN workload between FPGAs and GPUs, which are common domains in novel SoC-architectures. Our toolflow takes a model description from PyTorch and interacts with the FPGA design tools to generate different bitstreams and

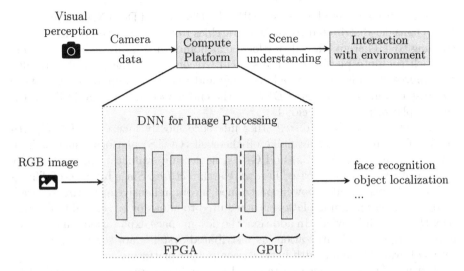

Fig. 1. Conceptual overview. Camera images are captured from the environment and forwarded to the computing platform, which executes a DNN. The scene perception obtained is then used to interact with the environment. Thereby, the DNN inference takes place either on the FPGA, the GPU, or both. For distributed processing, our toolflow determines the optimal partitioning point.

their resource utilization. These are then evaluated considering the given user and FPGA design constraints. Our approach also takes the communication link between the FPGA and the GPU into account, which can be an on-chip solution but also a link between two physically separated platforms. Finally, our tool returns a partitioning point for the DNN that maximizes energy efficiency and performance based on the evaluation results collected before. In summary, our paper makes the following contributions:

- We present our toolflow for determining an optimal partitioning point regarding hardware resource usage and required link bandwidth.
- We apply the toolflow to estimate bandwidth and hardware utilization of quantized DNNs.
- We exemplary show beneficial partitioning points of quantized MobileNet V1 for different FPGA architectures.

2   Related Work

Distributing DNN inference over multiple compute platforms has been a widely studied topic in recent years. Several publications showed that DNN partitioning is a beneficial approach for edge platforms in terms of latency, memory consumption and link bandwidth utilization [7,10,11,14]. Some of these studies use an adaptive approach to further improve efficiency of the distributed systems by dynamically allocating computational resources depending on the overall system utilization.

Teerapittayanon et al. proposed DDNNs (Distributed Deep Neural Networks) which consider distributed compute hierarchies from cloud to end devices during training [16]. Thereby, they define local exit points within the DNN architecture for each compute platform in the system. According to the presented results, this approach leads to improved accuracy and reduced communication costs in contrast to combining a small DNN on the end device and a large DNN on the central platform or in the cloud.

However, research on distributing inference mostly focuses on DNN partitioning for commercially available off-the-shelf (COTS) platforms such as Tensor Processing Units (TPUs) and GPUs, neglecting evaluation of more energy efficient ASICs or FPGA-based hardware architectures. Since Internet-of-Things (IoT) platforms are often power constrained, a comprehensive hardware/software co-design across multiple platforms is required to allow for larger and more complex DNNs in end devices. In addition, the design space exploration must include an evaluation of link utilization, as distributed systems are severely limited in terms of available bandwidth between computing platforms.

Efficient DNN inference on multi-FPGA architectures has been studied by some works recently [4,9,12,13]. As an example, Zhang et al. propose a mapping approach for large-scale DNNs on asymmetric multi-FPGA platforms considering the required link bandwidth in the system as well as resource allocation to achieve increased performance [18]. The presented mapping problem is solved by dynamic programming for DNN partitioning. Alonso et al. presented Elastic-DF, a framework for resource partitioning in multi-FPGA systems including dynamic mapping of applications to an available accelerator in the FPGA cluster [1]. Thereby, the tool can automatically optimize the performance of a pipelined dataflow DNN inference based on the available hardware resources of each individual FPGA. Although both approaches apply resource- and bandwidth-aware DNN partitioning to increase performance, these target datacenter inference and do not provide any investigation on low-power platforms used in IoT applications.

3   Partitioning Toolflow

Distributed sensor platforms, as found in many applications such as autonomous driving or assistive robotics, often face the problem of limited available bandwidth and limited compute resources in the central computing platform. Especially in safety-critical use cases, minimum latency must be guaranteed. In addition, since DNN topologies are still a major research topic, the hardware architectures also have to provide certain flexibility to cope with varying requirements. Hence, we propose a bandwidth- and resource-aware toolflow for pipelined DNN inference partitioning as shown in Fig. 2. In contrast to state of the art, this approach takes limited resources on the embedded FPGA as well as the limited bandwidth to the central compute platform in low-power embedded systems into account. Thereby, to achieve low latency and high throughput, the hardware implementation on the FPGA is designed in a pipelined manner, i.e. each layer

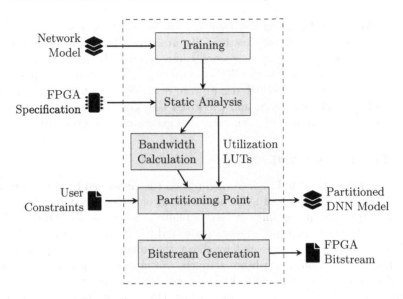

Fig. 2. Overview of our toolflow. As input, we take any given DNN workload, an FPGA specification and user constraints, e.g. available link bandwidth, to determine an optimal partitioning point. The toolflow outputs the partitioned DNN model and generates a bitstream fulfilling the system requirements.

is mapped to a dedicated accelerator. These are not shared between multiple layers of the DNN. Consequently, full hardware implementation on an embedded FPGA would consume a lot of space on the SoC.

3.1 Overview

Our approach offers a toolflow that evaluates any given DNN workload. The DNN is partitioned between an embedded FPGA and a GPU to maximize the performance, while also considering the communication link. Along with the network model, our toolflow also requires an embedded FPGA specification and user constraints as input to distinguish an optimal partitioning point of the DNN regarding resource utilization and required link bandwidth. Especially, the used link bandwidth is an important metric in multi-sensor systems as they can be found in assistive robotics or autonomous driving. In such use cases, the available bandwidth is severely limited by the large amount of data being sent from different nodes on the bus. Hence, the user can set maximum available link utilization to account for other traffic on the bus. Embedded FPGAs on the other hand are often limited in area and thus in available hardware resources. These constraints also have to be taken into account to find an optimal partitioning point of a DNN.

As a whole, our toolflow first optimizes the given DNN by quantizing weights and layer outputs during training to reduce computational complexity and memory footprint. Based on the resulting quantized DNN, a static analysis is performed taking FPGA specifications like available Block RAM (BRAM) and Digital Signal Processor (DSP) resources into account. In addition, finding an optimal partitioning point of the DNN requires calculation of the required bandwidth. Finally, with the estimated hardware resource utilization, the calculated link bandwidth of each layer, and the given user constraints, our tooflow can determine an optimal partitioning point and generate an appropriate bitstream.

3.2   Training and Static Analysis

Achieving low latency and high throughput on the embedded FPGA is a crucial part which enables usage of such platforms in embedded systems. Hence, we need to automatically optimize a DNN architecture and analyze the resulting model to efficiently map the layers to dedicated hardware accelerators.

Various works in recent years have shown that quantization and pruning lead to a drastic reduction in hardware resource consumption, with only a minimal loss of accuracy [17]. Therefore, in use cases such as assistive robotics which require low power consumption, optimizing DNN is inevitable. Our toolflow makes use of Brevitas [15] to achieve this goal during training. It is based on PyTorch and supports quantization-aware training of DNNs through evaluating reduced precision hardware building blocks at different levels. The resulting optimized DNN is then exported to ONNX file containing custom node types.

Since our approach targets Xilinx FPGAs as test platform, we implement FINN framework as one of the central components our toolflow interacts with for static analysis [3]. The FINN framework provides an end-to-end workflow covering design space exploration based on resource cost estimations and performance predictions, as well as automated code generation for High-level Synthesis (HLS). It takes the ONNX file generated by Brevitas of the DNN as input and provides estimates of hardware resource consumption and performance, among others. In addition, FINN can generate a bitstream for the given FPGA based on Vivado HLS.

3.3   DNN Partitioning

Even though the FINN framework tries to find an optimal implementation of the DNN taking multiple constraints into account, the size of the FPGA is not considered during design space exploration. Hence, if the network model requires more hardware resources than available on the given FPGA, the implementation will fail. Our approach addresses this problem by searching for an optimal partitioning point regarding FPGA usage and required link bandwidth.

To estimate the resources per layer, we use the predictions of the FINN framework, which are automatically generated during HLS. FINN offers different ways to estimate the required hardware resources per layer, before and after IP block generation and also after out-of-context synthesis including hardware optimizations. The latter thereby allows for precise resource estimates at the expense of runtime. Since we aim to find an optimal partitioning point for a

---

Algorithm 1: Search algorithm to determine an optimal partitioning point, considering hardware resource usage and required link bandwidth.

---

1 **function** GetOptimalSplitNode;
   Input : hardware resources per layer, layer output size
   Output: Partitioning Point
2 max_layer ← last DNN layer fitting on hardware;
3 part_pnt ← max_layer;
4 **for** *each layer in* [*max_layer*, *first_layer*] **do**
5   bw_ratio ← bandwidth[part_pnt] / bandwidth[layer];
6   hw_ratio ← hw_resources[part_pnt] / hw_resources[layer];
7   **if** *bw_ratio > 1* **and** *bw_ratio/hw_ratio > threshold_ratio* **then**
8 | part_pnt ← layer;
9   **end**
10   **if** *stop condition fulfilled* **then**
11 | **break**;
12   **end**
13 **end**
14 **return** part_pnt;

---

given DNN and thus runtime is not critical, our toolchain takes resource estimates of FINN generated after IP block generation. The link bandwidth can be calculated according to the output feature size of the intermediate layers and the corresponding data bit width. Consequently, this analysis can be neglected with respect to the runtime of the toolflow.

Besides estimating FPGA hardware resources and calculating required link bandwidth, distinguishing an optimal partitioning point of the DNN involves the input of constraints by the designer. This includes the embedded FPGA specifications regarding number of available basic building blocks, the targeted hardware utilization, and the available link bandwidth. Based on these inputs, our approach searches for a suitable partitioning of the DNN, which does not violate any of the given constraints such as area or required link bandwidth. Algorithm 1 presents our approach for finding an optimal partitioning point. First, the algorithm determines a partitioning point in the DNN where the hardware utilization is maximized for a given embedded FPGA platform. Afterwards, the algorithm aims at minimizing the communication overhead while still keeping the hardware utilization as high as possible. To achieve this goal, we set two parameters in advance: The first parameter defines the minimum allowed hardware utilization, which is used as a *stop condition* and should not be undercut. The second parameter defines a *threshold* for the maximum acceptable ratio between optimization of communication overhead and deterioration of hardware utilization. Based on this, the algorithm iterates through the layers starting from the partitioning point determined in the first step of the algorithm and evaluates link bandwidth utilization and hardware resource utilization. Subsequently, these are compared with the current best partitioning point. Only if the bandwidth can be reduced and the threshold value is exceeded, the layer is set as the new

Table 1. Available hardware resources on the evaluated SoC.

Platform	LUTs	FFs	BRAM blocks	DSP slices
ZedBoard	53,200	106,400	280	220
Ultra96-V2	70,560	141,120	432	360
ZCU104	230,400	460,800	624	1,728

partitioning point. Finally, when the stop condition is reached, the algorithm returns the partitioning point with the best ratio.

In summary, our toolflow optimizes the system towards high resource utilization of the embedded FPGA and low link bandwidth. After the partitioning point of the DNN is set, our toolflow splits the DNN model into two sub-models accordingly. Thereby, both are exported to ONNX format based file, which ensures machine learning interoperability. For the embedded FPGA, our toolflow finally generates the bitstream using Xilinx Vivado HLS and Vivado.

4   Evaluation

In this section, we evaluate our toolchain for a DNN on embedded FPGAs. Since we use FINN framework as one of the central components, we exemplary show the results of inference partitioning for three different Xilinx FPGAs. In order to address the various possible sizes of embedded FPGAs, we evaluate DNN partitioning using the following platforms: ZedBoard, Avnet Ultra96-V2 and Xilinx Zynq UltraScale+ MPSoC ZCU104. The available hardware resources on each SoC are listed in Table 1.

The system we use for the evaluation of our toolflow consists of an Intel Core i7-8565U, a quad-core SoC, running Ubuntu 18.04. To ensure the correct functioning of the FINN framework, we use a Docker container generated from the Dockerfile provided by Xilinx for this purpose. Finally, Vivado 2020.1 is used for HLS to determine the required hardware resources.

4.1   Workload

Low-complexity DNNs are required in embedded systems that need to provide low latency and power consumption. Several DNNs architectures have been proposed in recent years fulfilling these properties, such as MobileNet V1 [6]. Therefore, we select it as an exemplary workload and identify optimal partitioning points for a distributed system combining GPUs and embedded FPGAs. To achieve lower hardware resource utilization, we use a pretrained and quantized model with 4-bit weights and activations for the evaluation. The MobileNet V1 was originally proposed in 2017 and achieves an accuracy of 70.6% on the ImageNet dataset while only using 569 million multiply-accumulate operations and 4.2 million trainable parameters. This is achieved by introducing depthwise-separable convolution blocks, where each block consists of a depthwise convolution followed by a convolution with 1×1 kernels. In total, MobileNet V1 uses

13 depthwise-separable convolution blocks, preceded by a standard 3×3 convolution and followed by a fully-connected layer and softmax for classification.

4.2   Results

Executing DNN inference on an FPGA requires to map layers to one or more basic building blocks depending on the layer type. For MobileNet V1, FINN converts the DNN into 86 layers that can be directly translated to the components available in its hardware library. Without considering the runtime for training the DNN, it takes about 81.6 min on our system in dual-core mode from loading the ONNX file in FINN to finishing HLS. As expected, the IP block generation of each building block takes the most time, about 79 min, which is almost 97% of the whole runtime. However, since this step only needs to be performed once for a quantized DNN model and our evaluation was performed on a low-performance SoC, the runtime is still within an acceptable range.

The results of the IP block generation and the output size of each layer are shown in Fig. 3. It can be seen, that the output size tends to decrease towards the last layer. However, the DNN requires large hardware accelerators, especially towards the last layers, which significantly increases the demands on the available resources of the embedded FPGA. Consequently, the identification of an optimal partitioning point depends in particular on the deployed hardware platform and the defined user constraints.

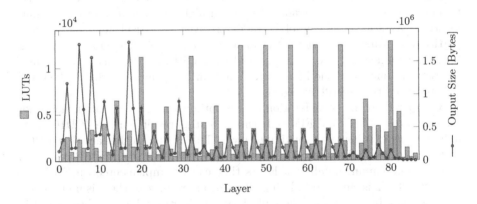

Fig. 3. Resource utilization of each translated MobileNet V1 layer taking LUTs as an example and the corresponding output size in bytes. In this configuration, only LUTs and FFs are used to implement the building blocks in the FPGA.

In the following, we apply our toolflow to find an optimal partitioning point of MobileNet V1 on the three aforementioned exemplary FPGA platforms. Since we want to analyze the impact of DNN inference partitioning independently of the IP cores present on the platforms, we will also evaluate the hardware resource

Table 2. Toolflow evaluation results. Depending on the size of the SoC and whether all resources or only LUTs and FFs are used, the maximum number of layers (max. Layer) that can be implemented on the platform varies. It can be seen that reducing the number of layers executed on the FPGA can significantly reduce the required link bandwidth (BW Red.) since the optimal partitioning point (Part. Point) does not always match the max. layer. Thereby, the hardware utilization reduction (HW Red.) is small.

Platform	Only LUTs/FFs				All resources			
	max Layer	Part Point	BW Red. [%]	HW Red. [%]	max Layer	Part Point	BW Red. [%]	HW Red. [%]
ZedBoard	22	21	6.78	1.19	19	19	0	0
Ultra96-V2	31	25	50	18.73	25	25	0	0
ZCU104	79	73	50	7.88	79	73	50	6.38

consumption of architectures containing only Look-Up Tables (LUTs) and Flip-Flops (FFs). We set the stop condition to 70% minimum hardware resource utilization to allow for low DNN inference latency and the threshold ratio to 1. The results of our exploration are shown in Table 2.

For the ZedBoard, the algorithm finds layer 21 as the optimal partitioning point when only using LUTs and FFs. Even though many hardware resources could be saved when choosing layer 20 instead, this would lead to an increased link bandwidth requirement as can be seen in Fig. 3. Hence, the selected partitioning layer offers a good trade-off between high throughput and low communication overhead. Similarly for Ultra96-V2, layer 25 is identified as an optimal partitioning point since bandwidth can be reduced by 50% in comparison to layer 31 without offloading too many layers to the GPU. In this case, the required hardware resources on the FPGA are significantly reduced by 18.73%, however, the stop condition is still exceeded.

Compared to the consideration of the optimizations for an implementation solely based on LUTs and FFs, only the evaluation results for the ZCU104 show different partitioning than maximum layer. This is due to the fact that FPGA platforms are usually severely limited in terms of BRAM and DSP resources. Since the maximum number of layers that can be implemented on ZedBoard and Ultra96-V2 is small considering all hardware resources, there is no potential to reduce link bandwidth on these platforms. In contrast, link bandwidth can be reduced by 50% on ZCU104, at the cost of a reasonable reduction in hardware utilization.

5   Conclusion and Future Work

DNN inference partitioning can be very advantageous depending on the neural architecture and the deployed hardware. Our results show that it is also beneficial for embedded FPGAs to outsource workload partly from a central compute node to a platform closer to the sensor since this approach reduces the required bandwidth while maximizing the hardware utilization of the embedded FPGA. The latter can thereby result in lower DNN inference latency depending on the hardware deployed on the central compute node. Especially in applications using multiple sensors, our approach can propose a bandwidth-aware partitioning to enable parallel execution of several DNN-based applications in a distributed system. Using our toolflow, we were able to identify several advantageous partitioning points depending on the platform deployed and the type of hardware resources used on the embedded FPGA. In the best case, our approach can reduce the required link bandwidth by 50% compared to implementing the maximum possible number of layers in the FPGA.

In the future, we plan to further investigate DNN inference partitioning by evaluating not only the sensor node and the link but also the central compute platform of the embedded system. Depending on the workload, analyzing latency on both partitions increases the design space but allows to investigate DNN partitioning for even more applications where minimum latency or energy consumption is the main optimization goal.

Acknowledgment. This work has been supported by the project "Stay young with robots" (JuBot). The JuBot project was made possible by funding from the Carl Zeiss Foundation. The responsibility for the content of this publication lies with the authors.

References

1. Alonso, T., et al.: Elastic-DF: scaling performance of DNN inference in FPGA clouds through automatic partitioning. ACM Trans. Reconfigurable Technol. Syst. **15**(2), 1–34 (2021). https://doi.org/10.1145/3470567
2. Asfour, T., et al.: ARMAR-6: a high-performance humanoid for human-robot collaboration in real-world scenarios. IEEE Robot. Autom. Mag. **26**(4), 108–121 (2019). https://doi.org/10.1109/MRA.2019.2941246
3. Blott, M., et al.: FINN-R: an end-to-end deep-learning framework for fast exploration of quantized neural networks. ACM Trans. Reconfigurable Technol. Syst. **11**(3), 1–23 (2018). https://doi.org/10.1145/3242897
4. Cheng, Q., Wen, M., Shen, J., Wang, D., Zhang, C.: Towards a deep-pipelined architecture for accelerating deep GCN on a Multi-FPGA platform. In: Qiu, M. (ed.) ICA3PP 2020. LNCS, vol. 12452, pp. 528–547. Springer, Cham (2020). https://doi.org/10.1007/978-3-030-60245-1_36
5. Han, S., Pool, J., Tran, J., Dally, W.J.: Learning both weights and connections for efficient neural networks. arXiv:1506.02626 [cs], October 2015
6. Howard, A.G., et al.: MobileNets: efficient convolutional neural networks for mobile vision applications (2017). https://doi.org/10.48550/ARXIV.1704.04861, https://arxiv.org/abs/1704.04861
7. Hu, C., Bao, W., Wang, D., Liu, F.: Dynamic adaptive DNN surgery for inference acceleration on the edge. In: IEEE INFOCOM 2019 - IEEE Conference on Computer Communications, pp. 1423–1431 (2019). https://doi.org/10.1109/INFOCOM.2019.8737614
8. Hubara, I., Courbariaux, M., Soudry, D., El-Yaniv, R., Bengio, Y.: Quantized neural networks: training neural networks with low precision weights and activations. arXiv:1609.07061 [cs], September 2016

9. Jiang, W., et al.: Achieving super-linear speedup across multi-FPGA for real-time DNN inference. ACM Trans. Embed. Comput. Syst. **18**(5s), 1–23 (2019). https://doi.org/10.1145/3358192

10. Ko, J.H., Na, T., Amir, M.F., Mukhopadhyay, S.: Edge-host partitioning of deep neural networks with feature space encoding for resource-constrained internet-of-things platforms. In: 2018 15th IEEE International Conference on Advanced Video and Signal Based Surveillance (AVSS), pp. 1–6 (2018). https://doi.org/10.1109/AVSS.2018.8639121

11. Kreß, F., et al.: Hardware-aware partitioning of convolutional neural network inference for embedded AI applications. In: 2022 18th International Conference on Distributed Computing in Sensor Systems (DCOSS), pp. 133–140 (2022). https://doi.org/10.1109/DCOSS54816.2022.00034

12. Kwon, D., Hur, S., Jang, H., Nurvitadhi, E., Kim, J.: Scalable multi-FPGA acceleration for large RNNs with full parallelism levels. In: 2020 57th ACM/IEEE Design Automation Conference (DAC), pp. 1–6 (2020). https://doi.org/10.1109/DAC18072.2020.9218528

13. Mittal, S.: A survey of FPGA-based accelerators for convolutional neural networks. Neural Comput. Appl. **32**(4), 1109–1139 (2020). https://doi.org/10.1007/s00521-018-3761-1

14. Mohammed, T., Joe-Wong, C., Babbar, R., Francesco, M.D.: Distributed inference acceleration with adaptive DNN partitioning and offloading. In: IEEE INFOCOM 2020 - IEEE Conference on Computer Communications, pp. 854–863 (2020). https://doi.org/10.1109/INFOCOM41043.2020.9155237

15. Pappalardo, A.: Xilinx/brevitas (2021). https://doi.org/10.5281/zenodo.3333552

16. Teerapittayanon, S., McDanel, B., Kung, H.: Distributed deep neural networks over the cloud, the edge and end devices. In: 2017 IEEE 37th International Conference on Distributed Computing Systems (ICDCS), pp. 328–339 (2017). https://doi.org/10.1109/ICDCS.2017.226

17. Walter, I., et al.: Embedded face recognition for personalized services in the assistive robotics. In: Machine Learning and Principles and Practice of Knowledge Discovery in Databases, ECML PKDD 2021. CCIS, vol. 1524, pp. 339–350. Springer, Cham (2021). https://doi.org/10.1007/978-3-030-93736-2_26

18. Zhang, W., Zhang, J., Shen, M., Luo, G., Xiao, N.: An efficient mapping approach to large-scale DNNs on multi-FPGA architectures. In: 2019 Design, Automation & Test in Europe Conference & Exhibition (DATE), pp. 1241–1244 (2019). https://doi.org/10.23919/DATE.2019.8715174

Framework to Evaluate Deep Learning Algorithms for Edge Inference and Training

Tiberius-George Sorescu[1], Chandrakanth R. Kancharla[2,3],
Jeroen Boydens[2], Hans Hallez[2,3], and Mathias Verbeke[2,3,4]($\boxtimes$)

[1] Electronics, Telecommunications and Information Technology Faculty,
Gheorghe Asachi Technical University, 700050 Iasi, Romania
[2] Department of Computer Science, Research Unit M-Group,
KU Leuven Bruges Campus, 8200 Bruges, Belgium
`{chandu.kancharla,jeroen.boydens,hans.hallez}@kuleuven.be`
[3] Leuven.AI - KU Leuven Institute for AI, 3000 Leuven, Belgium
`mathias.verbeke@kuleuven.be`
[4] Core Lab DTAI-FET, Flanders Make, Lommel, Belgium

Abstract. Edge computing is a paradigm in which data is intelligently processed close to its source. Along with advancements in deep learning, there is a growing interest in using deep neural networks at the edge for predictive analytics. Given the realistic constraints in computational resources of edge devices, this combination is challenging. In order to bridge the gap between deep learning models and efficient edge analytics, a container-based framework is presented that evaluates user-specified deep learning models for efficiency on the edge. The proposed framework is validated on a rotating machinery fault diagnosis use case. Conclusions on efficient state-of-the-art models for rotating machine fault diagnosis were drawn and appropriately reported.

Keywords: Deep learning · Constrained edge devices · Machine fault diagnosis · Model benchmarking

1 Introduction

Internet of Things (IoT) refers to devices (or groups thereof) that are equipped with firmware, a limited amount of processing power and memory, and other technologies that enable communication between and within networks. This communication is possible between nearby devices or services that are linked remotely. IoT is a fairly broad concept with several possible uses. The amount of linked IoT devices is growing at a pace of 22% annually, in contrast to a modest annual growth rate of roughly 2% for traditional IT devices [4]. By 2025, there will be close to 150 billion devices, producing an estimated 180 Zettabytes of data, based on current trends and needs [7]. At the same time, the advancements in the domain of Artificial Intelligence and Deep Learning (DL) enables to analyse ever larger amounts of data. Analysing this data on cloud-based server

© The Author(s), under exclusive license to Springer Nature Switzerland AG 2023
I. Koprinska et al. (Eds.): ECML PKDD 2022 Workshops, CCIS 1752, pp. 569–581, 2023.
https://doi.org/10.1007/978-3-031-23618-1_38

infrastructure given these resources can easily be scaled to match the computing requirements. However, at the same time this also requires the exchange of data between the edge devices and the cloud, which is increasingly leading to bottlenecks due to the limitations of the current network infrastructure. Therefore, to reduce the amount of bandwidth needed for IoT data communication and to improve reaction times, the edge computing paradigm has emerged as a solution. In this paradigm, the edge infrastructure is supposed to serve as a middleman, strengthening and sustaining the link between widespread endpoints and the cloud.

The combination of edge computing and Artificial Intelligence has boosted a wide spectrum of applications, spanning from real-time video analytics, cognitive assistance, precision agriculture, smart home, and Industrial Internet of Things (IIoT) [13]. Although performing analytics at the edge eliminates the issue of network congestion, it also creates a number of novel challenges, imposed by the edge devices' computing capabilities that form one of the main constraints for such intelligent application deployment. It is impossible to sidestep the difficulty of edge computing given the limitations on processing power. Therefore, the amount of information that can be processed at the edge is increasingly being studied. This question becomes ever more relevant as deep learning becomes the predominant approach to obtain state-of-the-art accuracy in different application domains.

Despite the fact that there has been a lot of research on intelligent data processing using DL models and optimizing the same for particular edge platforms, to the best of the author's knowledge there is no framework or tool to assess the viability of those models under a set of computational constraints. Therefore, in order to close this gap, as a first contribution, an open-source framework is proposed that can evaluate and compare user-provided models and datasets, in order to gain more detailed insights into the training and inference efficiency of these models when performed on the edge. The aim is to simplify and improve the model selection for constrained edge applications. Second, the framework is validated on the use case of industrial fault diagnosis. Implementation of DL models at the edge is challenging for this problem because of the stringent limits on efficiency, latency, and energy. At the same time, high-frequency data processing and analysis (e.g., from vibration or acoustic measurements) is required to perform accurate and proactive fault diagnosis. Next to a validation of the functionality of the framework, the results provide initial insights into the existing tradeoffs between model accuracy and used runtime parameters in constrained settings.

This paper is organised as follows. The next section reviews related work from the perspective of the use case. Section 3 summarizes the contribution and formulates the respective research questions. Section 4 details the proposed framework, whereas Sect. 5 introduces the aforementioned case study used to evaluate the framework. Finally, the article is concluded with a detailed discussion of the results and resulting insights into current machine fault diagnosis models for the constrained edge setting.

2   Related Work

Despite the promise of DL models in enabling edge-based applications, there are significant barriers to effective deployment [13]. While some research focuses on enhancing the efficacy of a model given particular hardware restrictions, other works focus on more advanced models to accomplish more accurate results. In particular, it is crucial yet difficult to select suitable models while taking computational constraints into account.

To illustrate that, rotating machinery diagnosis will be considered as a use case in the industrial machine monitoring and prognostics domain. There are several deep learning models in the literature that differ depending on the task to be performed. While there are generic models such as Multilayer Perceptrons (MLP), Convolutional Neural Networks or Auto-Encoders, there is also a plethora of more advanced models such as LiftingNet, Deep Belief Networks, Long Short-Term Memory Networks, Generative Adversarial Networks, or Capsule Networks that have been proposed for various fault prognosis use cases [10].

Tang et al. investigated DL models encompassing diverse application scenarios within rotating equipment fault diagnosis while emphasizing the need for generalizable models. The authors evaluated the models based on their performance (prediction accuracy) [8]. In contrast, Zhang et al. analyzed and compared state-of-the-art DL models for the specific use case of rotating machine defects, namely bearing fault diagnosis [10]. Although remarkable results of up to 99% accuracy were reported with various DL models, they reveal a gap in the models' generalizability across conditions. Similarly, Lei et al. conducted a comprehensive evaluation of machine fault diagnostics, including an extensive discussion of several DL models for Intelligent Fault Diagnosis. Furthermore, the history, present, and future challenges within this domain have been discussed, along with a proposed roadmap [3]. Surprisingly, the suggested roadmap emphasizes model transparency and transferability while making no mention of edge-based implementability. Khan et al. released a survey paper for DL-based system health management. While detailing the development of DL for system health management, they also point out the absence of suitable benchmark results [2]. Zhao et al. [12] benchmarked a number of cutting-edge DL models for rotating equipment fault diagnosis, but they only compared the models' diagnostic accuracy.

Summarizing the literature for different fault diagnosis applications, we can state with confidence that most comparisons are limited to classification or detection performance and are highly customized for a specific use case. Although many of these recent surveys talk about cutting-edge DL models and their future challenges, almost all of them ignore or fail to take into account the issue of their implementability on the edge. While many of the reviewed DL models perform well (in terms of prediction metrics) for certain applications, specific use cases or specific datasets, none of them are ubiquitous. This presents a challenge in practice because the computing limitations of the edge system are currently not taken into account when choosing an effective model.

3   Overall Description of the Framework

This paper proposes a open-source framework[1] to address the issue of effective model selection. The aim of the developed framework is to enable empirical comparison of user-specified DL models in terms of their overall performance, time and spatial complexity for a practical implementation on edge devices.

More specifically, the aim of the framework is to provide insights to the following questions:

- Which of the user-provided DL models are most efficient in terms of prediction metrics (e.g., accuracy, F1-score) at a constant system setting?
- Which of those models can efficiently be trained or used for inference at test time given the reduced hardware capabilities?
- What are the tradeoffs between the imposed hardware limitations and the performance of the models, and can particular critical thresholds in terms of resource limitations be identified?

This proposed framework allows to change different system characteristics effortlessly.

One possible approach to achieve this ability of systematically reducing the machine characteristics and benchmark DL models for various resource constraints, is using virtual machines (VM) that can successfully simulate machine hardware. VMs have been a tested and proven technology for dynamic resource allocation, substantiated by the research in the domain of Dynamic Virtual Machine Placement. Various computing platform parameters, such as RAM, CPU, energy use, etc. are monitored, and modified VMs with lower or higher resources are deployed in accordance with the specified awareness scheme [5,11].

Another approach is based on container technology, i.e., OS-level virtualization to provide software in packages called containers. One important difference between the containers and VMs is the application-only virtualization. Containers only consist of the code and all the dependencies that are necessary to run a particular application. This leads to a minimal weight of containerized application compared to that of VMs. In addition, container technology also satisfies a more important requirement of our framework, namely the replication and customization properties of these virtualization tools for systematic resource modification. In this respect, containerized virtualization scores higher compared to VMs [9]. Consequently, containerized applications were considered as platform virtualization tool and form the basis for the proposed framework.

4   Framework Implementation and Experimental Setup

This section details the implemented framework. As explained previously, the systematic virtualization of the hardware to emulate constrained edge devices

---

[1] The source code of the framework as well as the associated scripts to reproduce the performed experiments on the fault diagnosis use case are available via https://gitlab.com/Chandu1007/edge-benchmarking-framework.

is performed using containerized applications, for which Docker[2] is employed. Docker is one of the main container technology frameworks that eases the development of containerized applications. The ability to alter the container runtime parameters is a significant feature of this tool as, despite being a virtualized app, containers cannot restrict the utilized resources by themselves. Theoretically, they may utilize the resources as required to operate the application. During runtime Docker can manage the progressive reduction in the resources consumed by the container.

Data: Framework Image
Result: Run time Logs
1. User selects task (train/evaluate) and parameter to monitor (CPU/RAM);
2. User selects dataset/model combination;
3. User selects top and bottom limits + step;
current limit = top limit;
while *current limit > bottom limit* **do**
    run benchmark;
    if *run successful* **then**
        current limit = current limit-step;
    else
        report error;
    end
end

Algorithm 1: Pseudo-code of the experimental framework

As shown in Algorithm 1, first, the runtime results given certain control value parameters must be obtained. Subsequently, these results are plotted in order to obtain a visual representation of the data. The *Framework Image* referred to in Algorithm 1 is a containerized application image created using Docker.

More specifically, as a first step, the datasets and models intended for evaluation have to be configured on the host machine. Once the configuration is in place, we build a Docker image including the datasets, the models and the Python scripts that implement training and inference cycles. The built image provides the environment for the application containers. After the *Framework Image* has been built using the Docker daemon, the input limits for either CPU or RAM are provided as arguments. These limits and the arguments specific to models and datasets are further considered by a shell script to automate the container deployment and to orderly modify the runtime parameters of the containerised application.

Python is used to run the models within the containerized application instance. The input arguments to the Python script define the combination of models and datasets as well as the implemented routines (inference or training). While the application is running, logs are created according to the model

---

[2] https://www.docker.com.

and dataset in use, and are saved in a shared workspace as a CSV file. These logs include the time incurred for tasks like argument parsing, setup, evaluation (training or inference), etc. This process of new container creation by a shell script and the evaluation of a particular model/dataset combination continues till the specified limits are reached. The runtime parameters referred here are RAM and percentage of CPU core used. While the RAM is measured in Megabytes, CPU core is measured as the percentage of time the core is used per second by the application. Finally, the logged data is plotted to visually represent the evaluation results. A flow diagram of the developed framework is presented in Fig. 1.

An Advantech UNO-2272G, a palm-sized embedded computer has been used to implement the proposed framework [1]. It is a rugged embedded system that can run embedded operating systems like Linux-Embedded. With 2 GB of RAM and quadcore Intel® Atom N2800/J1900 2 GHz processors, it came across to be a suitable platform for verifying our framework.

Benchmark Flow Diagram

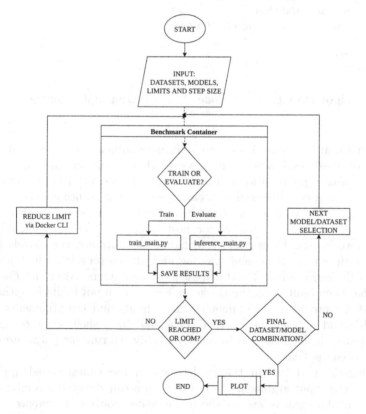

Fig. 1. Flow diagram of the proposed benchmarking framework.

5   Case Study: Fault Diagnosis for Rotating Machinery

To validate the framework, fault diagnosis for rotating machinery on embedded devices has been chosen as a case study. This is motivated by the fact that real-world deployments in this domain often necessitate the implementation of analytics at the edge. Hence, gaining insights into the efficiency of these algorithms in terms of both performance and resource constraints can drastically speed up the selection of the appropriate model for embedded deployment. In addition, this can allow one to gain a better understanding regarding possible methodological improvements.

For this validation, various DL models along with benchmark datasets for fault diagnosis in rotating machinery are used. Both the models and datasets were selected based on the benchmark study of Zhao et al. [12]. In their extensive benchmark study they evaluated the efficacy of DL models for intelligent fault diagnosis of rotating machinery while considering various publicly-available datasets. Also the respective source code is publicly available for research reproducability. The following subsections discuss the selected models and datasets that were used for validation in more detail.

5.1   Models

Out of the 9 models evaluated by Zhao et al., a selection of 6 models was made for this evaluation. The choice of the models is of secondary importance, as the objective of the experimental validation is to test the feasibility of the framework rather than performing a general comparison regarding the fault diagnosis performance of these models. The considered models are the Multi-Layer Perceptron (MLP), AlexNet-1D, Convolutional Neural Network-1D (CNN-1D), ResNet-1D, LeNet-1D and BiLSTM-1D. All the models used in this study are one-dimensional as the provided inputs are single channel time domain signals. A detailed description of each of the models can be found in [12].

5.2   Datasets

A total of 7 datasets are evaluated in the benchmark study, of which 6 are bearing fault datasets and 1 is a gearbox fault dataset. To facilitate a certain variation in the analyzed datasets, one from each category is chosen for final evaluation, i.e., the MFPT bearing set for bearing fault diagnosis and the SEU dataset for gearbox fault diagnosis. Given the impact of the data characteristics on the training and inference performance, each of these datasets will be briefly discussed in more detail.

MFPT Bearing Dataset. The Machinery Failure Prevention Technology (MFPT) dataset is proposed by the Society for Machinery Failure Prevention Technology. It consists of three subsets of data: 1) a baseline dataset, 2) seven outer ring fault datasets, and 3) seven inner ring fault datasets. Taken together, the dataset contains data from 15 classes (1 non-faulty and 14 faulty). Each observation from these 15 classes has a length of 1024 timestamps. Overall, the dataset contains 2059 observations for training and 515 observations for testing. These will be the inputs with which the multi-class classification models will be trained and tested for categorizing the fault classes.

SEU Gearbox Dataset. The Southeast University (SEU) gearbox dataset contains two subsets, including a bearing fault dataset and a gearbox fault dataset, which were both acquired on a dynamic drivetrain simulator. For the evaluation, only the gearbox faults were considered. It contains a total number of 5 classes, i.e., 4 fault states and 1 normal operating state. Within each original data file, there were eight rows of vibration signals, and we used the X-axis signals of the planetary gearbox mentioned in the experimental setup [6]. Similar to the previous dataset, a window of 1024 timestamps was used to create observations from the original data files. In total, there are 1640 observations for training and 420 observations for testing the model performance.

Thus, the experimental validation of the developed framework was set up using 6 models and 2 datasets, which is considered a solid benchmark.

6   Results and Discussion

The results upon running the framework with these model/dataset combinations are multifold and are discussed in this section.

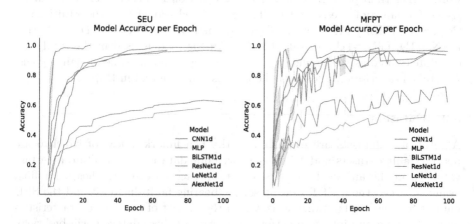

Fig. 2. Accuracy versus the number of training epochs for SEU and MFPT datasets.

6.1 General Results

The framework's first set of outputs is a comparison of the generic implementation of selected models with the datasets of choice. The generic implementation here implies that the models are trained and evaluated on the selected edge platform without any resource limits. According to the findings shown in Fig. 2 for the MFPT and SEU datasets, ResNet-1D appears to be converging to a solution in fewer epochs than the other models. This phenomenon is consistent across the datasets and in line with the conclusions from Zhao et al. [12]. Based on this, it can be concluded that the top performing models in order are ResNet-1D, CNN-1D, BiLSTM-1D, AlexNet-1D, LeNet-1D, and MLP. This order of performance is as expected according to the benchmark study of Zhao at al., at least for the datasets under discussion here.

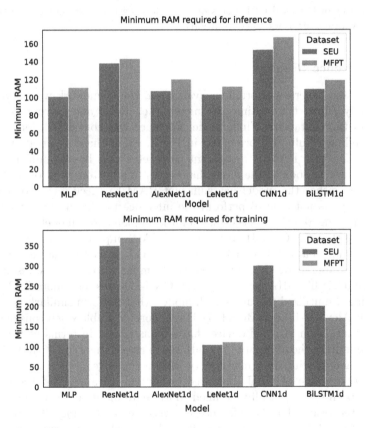

Fig. 3. Minimum RAM (in MB) required for inference and training various models. The plots are the output of the framework ran till it reaches the out-of-memory point.

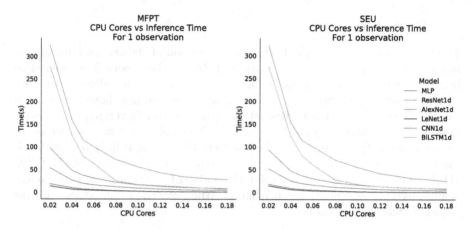

Fig. 4. Effect of the used CPU cores on the inference time. Presented results are for one observation over 5 inference iterations.

6.2   Inference Results

Following the general performance evaluation, the framework was used to systematically adjust the runtime parameters, i.e., RAM and percentage of CPU in use, of the containers. First, model inference was considered, for which the corresponding results are presented in Fig. 3. From these observations, it can be concluded that RAM is a constant parameter that has no influence on the inference time as soon as the model has access to a bottom limit of RAM. More specifically, either the model has sufficient RAM to execute the computation, or the model is not able to perform the inference task as it runs out of memory. Comparing the RAM necessary for the implemented models, it is evident from Fig. 3 that the CNN-1D needs more RAM compared to the other models. This amounts to a factor of at least 13% when compared to the second highest RAM-consuming model, being ResNet-1D. Compared to the lowest resource consuming models like MLP and LeNet-1D, CNN-1D uses 60% more RAM. When comparing the utilized resources with models that perform similarly in terms of accuracy, AlexNet-1D and BiLSTM-1D are more desirable when considering the implementation on an edge device that is constrained in terms of RAM. This result underlines the ability of the platform to assess this type of tradeoffs when considering deploying deep neural networks on the edge.

The percentage of CPU core used is another parameter of the container that has been systematically modified to evaluate model performance. Figure 4 presents the results for the inference analysis when changing CPU core values from 0.2 to 0.01% with a step size of 0.01. As expected, the percentage of cores used has a great influence on the inference time. The computation latency of the MLP and LeNet models are growing from 1 s to approximately 46 s over 0.2 to 0.01% of the CPU cores. Meanwhile, BiLSTM and ResNet demonstrate very high inference times, up to 500 s at the lower limit and approximately 40 s at

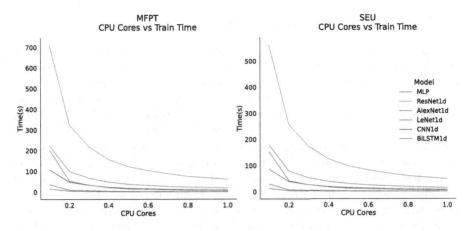

Fig. 5. Effect of the used CPU cores on the training time.

the highest. Overall, the results indicate that AlexNet and CNN are the optimal models to be used for edge-based inference in fault diagnosis systems.

6.3 Training Results

When it comes to real-world applications, next to inference also on-device training is crucial. With respect to the case study under consideration, most state-of-the-art DL models are neither resilient nor generalizable across conditions [12]. This necessitates the (continuous or periodic) re-training for some or most of the layers of a DL model using the newly incoming data. As a result, training near or on the edge is critical for cross-conditional robustness. Using the developed framework, the models can be analyzed against the datasets for training and their performance evaluated for the considered runtime parameters, i.e., RAM and CPU core usage.

The results presented in Fig. 3 show that training the ResNet-1D model takes twice as much RAM than during inference. This is in contrast to CNN-1D's usage, which goes up by about 30%. This is comparatively low to that of ResNet-1D's training. Out of the best performing models, BiLSTM-1d was consuming the lowest resources and for one of the datasets it was similar to that of AlexNet-1D.

As can be observed from Fig. 5, overall the results for the model training with changing CPU cores are rather consistent with the results provided for the inference time. The main difference is that AlexNet-1D and BiLSTM-1D switched positions. AlexNet-1D takes more time for training than BiLSTM-1D, while the reverse was true in terms of inference time.

7   Conclusion and Future Work

This paper presented a container-based framework to compare deep learning models for resource-constrained applications on the edge. It facilitates the systematic restriction of runtime parameters such as RAM and percentage of CPU cores used to emulate the edge hardware. Moreover, it is application-independent and allows to test any set of datasets and models to assess how well they function on hardware platforms with limited resources. This analysis can be performed both for inference and training. Additionally, the framework has been validated using a case study on rotating machinery fault diagnosis. Next to an illustration of the framework's capabilities, based on the results, also a number of initial conclusions could be drawn regarding the performance of the different models in resource-constrained circumstances, as well as on the possible tradeoffs that could influence the model choice. AlexNet-1D clearly comes out as the best solution for an edge-based intelligent fault diagnostic application, as it provides competitive multiclass predictive accuracy while being resource-efficient during both inference and training.

In future work, the runtime parameter limits that are currently specified manually could be complemented with a list of predefined hardware constraints for commonly-used (industrial) IoT edge devices. Other ideas include extending the list of resource constraints that can be imposed. Next to constraining RAM and CPU usage, one could consider to also constrain GPU usage, or to limit the capabilities of the processing unit to test for specific microcontrollers (e.g., FPGAs with only integer computation capabilities). Furthermore, the aim is also to validate the framework for additional use cases by means of other model and dataset benchmarks, in order to gain additional insights in possible tradeoffs between runtime constraints and accuracy on different tasks (e.g., classification, regression) and model types (e.g., models tailored for computer vision).

References

1. ADVANTECH: Advantech UNO-2272g (2022). https://www.advantech.com/products/1-2mlj9a/uno-2272g/mod_2f889619-f9ba-4735-a432-7ac7a08669c4
2. Khan, S., Yairi, T.: A review on the application of deep learning in system health management. Mech. Syst. Signal Process. **107**, 241–265 (2018) https://doi.org/10.1016/j.ymssp.2017.11.024, https://www.sciencedirect.com/science/article/pii/S0888327017306064
3. Lei, Y., Yang, B., Jiang, X., Jia, F., Li, N., Nandi, A.K.: Applications of machine learning to machine fault diagnosis: a review and roadmap. Mech. Syst. Signal Process. **138**, 106587 (2020). https://doi.org/10.1016/j.ymssp.2019.106587, https://www.sciencedirect.com/science/article/pii/S0888327019308088
4. McKinsey: Growing opportunities in the Internet of Things (2019). https://www.mckinsey.com/industries/private-equity-and-principal-investors/our-insights/growing-opportunities-in-the-internet-of-things
5. Mosa, A., Sakellariou, R.: Dynamic virtual machine placement considering CPU and memory resource requirements. In: 2019 IEEE 12th International Conference on Cloud Computing (CLOUD), pp. 196–198 (2019). https://doi.org/10.1109/CLOUD.2019.00042

6. Shao, S.: SEU gearbox dataset. https://github.com/cathysiyu/Mechanical-datasets. Accessed Aug. 2022

7. Shi, W., Pallis, G., Xu, Z.: Edge computing. Proc. IEEE **107**(8), 1474–1481 (2019). https://doi.org/10.1109/JPROC.2019.2928287

8. Tang, S., Yuan, S., Zhu, Y.: Deep learning-based intelligent fault diagnosis methods toward rotating machinery. IEEE Access **8**, 9335–9346 (2020). https://doi.org/10.1109/ACCESS.2019.2963092

9. Yadav, A.K., Garg, M.L., Ritika: Docker containers versus virtual machine-based virtualization. In: Abraham, A., Dutta, P., Mandal, J.K., Bhattacharya, A., Dutta, S. (eds.) Emerging Technologies in Data Mining and Information Security, pp. 141–150. Springer, Singapore (2019). https://doi.org/10.1007/978-981-13-1501-5_12

10. Zhang, S., Zhang, S., Wang, B., Habetler, T.G.: Deep learning algorithms for bearing fault diagnostics - a comprehensive review. IEEE Access **8**, 29857–29881 (2020). https://doi.org/10.1109/ACCESS.2020.2972859

11. Zhao, D.M., Zhou, J.T., Li, K.: An energy-aware algorithm for virtual machine placement in cloud computing. IEEE Access **7**, 55659–55668 (2019). https://doi.org/10.1109/ACCESS.2019.2913175

12. Zhao, Z., et al.: Deep learning algorithms for rotating machinery intelligent diagnosis: an open source benchmark study. ISA Trans. **107**, 224–255 (2020). https://doi.org/10.1016/j.isatra.2020.08.010, https://www.sciencedirect.com/science/article/pii/S0019057820303335

13. Zhou, Z., Chen, X., Li, E., Zeng, L., Luo, K., Zhang, J.: Edge intelligence: paving the last mile of artificial intelligence with edge computing. Proc. IEEE **107**(8), 1738–1762 (2019). https://doi.org/10.1109/JPROC.2019.2918951

Hardware Execution Time Prediction
for Neural Network Layers

Adrian Osterwind[1]([✉]) [iD], Julian Droste-Rehling[2], Manoj-Rohit Vemparala[3],
and Domenik Helms[1] [iD]

[1] German Aerospace Center (DLR), Institute of Systems Engineering for Future
Mobility, Oldenburg, Germany
{adrian.osterwind,domenik.helms}@dlr.de
[2] Siemens AG (Bremen), Bremen, Germany
julian.droste-rehling@siemens.com
[3] BMW Autonomous Driving, Munich, Germany
manoj-rohit.vemparala@bmw.com
https://www.dlr.de/se/

Abstract. We present an estimation methodology, accurately predicting the execution time for a given embedded Artificial Intelligence (AI)
accelerator and a neural network (NN) under analysis. The timing prediction is implemented as a python library called (MONNET) and is
able to perform its predictions analyzing the Keras description of an
NN under test within milliseconds. This enables several techniques to
design NNs for embedded hardware. Designers can avoid training networks which could be functionally sufficient but will likely fail the timing
requirements. The technique can also be included into automated network architecture search algorithms, enabling exact hardware execution
times to become one contributor to the search's target function.

In order to perform precise estimations for a target hardware, each
new hardware needs to undergo an initial automatic characterization process, using tens of thousands of different small NNs. This process may
need several days, depending on the hardware.

We tested our methodology for the Intel Neural Compute Stick 2,
where we could achieve an (RMSPE) below 21% for a large range of
industry relevant NNs from vision processing.

Keywords: Execution time · Prediction · Neural networks ·
Analytical model

1 Introduction

With the constant rise of (AIs) and (NNs) in the industry it becomes important
to obtain definitive data about execution constraints of these algorithms. An
algorithm must be verified to be able to work within a certain set of hardware
and application constraints. As an example the execution time may not exceed a

I. Koprinska et al. (Eds.): ECML PKDD 2022 Workshops, CCIS 1752, pp. 582–593, 2023.
https://doi.org/10.1007/978-3-031-23618-1_39

certain threshold in an autonomous vehicle, so that it is still capable of reacting to the input within safety limits.

The best way to determine this execution time is to measure it on the target hardware. For complex neural networks and difficult to obtain hardware this is not always feasible, for example in an automated network architecture search (NAS). One way of performing hardware execution time aware NAS is to rely on readily available metrics such as MAC count or number of parameters, which leads to suboptimal results [9]. Another is to obtain the execution metrics through hardware in the loop measurements, where feasible [3]. An alternative is to estimate the execution time of the neural network.

The goal of this work is to develop a gray box modeling methodology, which is capable of estimating the latency of a given NN, when running on a specific hardware. This library will be called Model of Neural Network Execution Time (MONNET). After an initial time intensive analysis (characterization) of the hardware, the estimator has to be able to run independently of the hardware itself and within an execution time, small enough to allow comparing different solutions in a design space exploration or network architecture search conveniently.

The only input parameters of the final timing estimator have to be the topology of the NN graph and the characterization data for the target hardware. Thus, it will be possible to apply the estimator directly after specification, avoiding time expensive training of solutions, which do not meet given constraints.

Another design constraint is the reduction of hardware knowledge needed to port the estimator to a different target platform. It should be possible to define a model of a layer type and use it on multiple hardware types. The only hardware related knowledge required should be how to deploy and benchmark a neural network on the target hardware.

The rest of this work is organized as follows. In Sect. 2 similar and flanking work is discussed. This results in a new approach to execution time estimation in Sect. 3. The timing model is leveraged to estimate the execution time in Sect. 4. Experimental results of the approach and an evaluation of memory modeling are discussed in Sect. 5. Section 6 summarizes the work and lays out some future directions, where this work can be taken.

2   Related Work

Execution time and power consumption modeling is a topic of much research in literature. NVIDIA uses performance and energy consumption estimation to inform design decisions in the development of deep NN accelerator hardware [4].

For traditional algorithmic software, there are multiple approaches in literature. In the area of power measurement different levels of abstraction are used to represent the modeled process. These are in order from least to most abstracted gate-, register-transfer-, transaction- and function level modeling [7].

The advantage of lower abstraction levels is higher accuracy in the estimations. Function level and higher abstracted models on the other hand need less in depth knowledge about the exact behaviour of the underlying hardware. This allows for easier portability of the model to different platforms [7].

A useful aspect for time and power modeling is knowledge about the memory utilization and caching strategies utilized. This allows integration of memory latency into the estimation. In general purpose Central Processing Units (CPUs) there are different strategies to manage caching. Direct mapped caches allow writing of memory blocks to predefined locations in the cache. Increasing the associativity of the cache allows distribution of the cached content to different places [5].

NN accelerators such as the herein used Neural Compute Stick 2 (NCS2) use application specific caching strategies. [6] describes some common memory caching strategies. Different approaches use different amounts of cache for the same NN layers, since they change the hierarchy of caching. This would lead to different amounts of cache accesses in each scheme.

Runtime optimization and complexity estimation of NNs is often done by comparing either the number of parameters or the number of floating point operations (FLOPs) for a given NNs. This does not accurately match the execution time of the NN as shown in [9]. A better approach is shown in [8]. Here the authors use an interpolation driven approach to capture the timing behaviour of various NN layers. It uses little hardware knowledge to estimate layer timing.

The contribution of this paper uses a similar approach to the one in [8]. It simplifies the estimator at the cost of a need for a higher amount of samples to create the model compared to [8]. This should allow for easier use in NAS approaches [1].

[1] shows several hardware aware NAS-systems. These utilize different metrics to determine hardware timing. The simplest method is the integration of hardware in the loop measurements. Others use models to estimate execution time ranging from lookup tables to meta-AIs, which learn the timing behaviour of the hardware.

MONNET, which is presented in this work, leads to better abstraction from hardware and framework artefacts. This in turn leads to overall higher accuracy and better transferability to other hardware accelerators and thus simpler application in dependant applications such as NAS.

3   Characterization and Model Building

The timing modeling approach can be separated into two general steps. At first the model needs to be created and characterized, which is discussed in this section. A model needs to be defined once for each neural network layer type to be supported. The characterization needs to be done once per target hardware.

3.1   Model Creation

The general model used in this approach is shown in Eq. 1.

$$t_l = t_{\text{op}_l} \cdot n_{\text{op}_l} \tag{1}$$

Here the execution time per layer t_l is modeled as the number of operations in one layer n_{op_l} (the layer complexity) multiplied by the time required per operation t_{op_l} (the efficiency). The number of mathematical operations in a layer, which is the same for each hardware, is separated from the actual hardware-specific execution time. This way only the t_{op_l} needs to be heuristically determined (i.e. measured on the target hardware), with n_{op_l} being mathematically derived from the layer parameters.

The efficiency t_{op_l} is not a constant, but depends on the actual layer configuration. t_{op_l}, as a function of the input parameters, is thus depending on and reflecting the influence of the hardware itself as well as configuration and artifacts of the neural network library and hardware deployment frameworks. Due to this, it has to be sampled over a large range of parameters for each layer type.

Applying this to one of the most time-consuming and most used layers in a convolutional neural network, the Convolutional 2D (Conv2D) layer, the complexity can be calculated as follows:

$$n_{\text{op}_l} = k_x \cdot k_y \cdot c \cdot x' \cdot y' \cdot f \tag{2}$$

The number of operations for each filter is the number of outputs as $x' \cdot y'$ multiplied by the kernel size $k_x \cdot k_y$ and the number of input channels as c. Multiplying this by the number of filters f results in the number of operations for each layer.

x' and y' themselves are functions of the input size x and y, the stride and if no padding is applied the kernel size. They are calculated as shown in Eq. 3, with y' being calculated similarly.

$$x' = \begin{cases} \lfloor \frac{x-k_x}{s_x} + 1 \rfloor, & \text{if padding} = 0(valid) \\ \lfloor \frac{x-1}{s_x} + 1 \rfloor, & \text{if padding} = \lfloor \frac{k_x}{2} \rfloor(same) \end{cases} \tag{3}$$

To estimate the hardware and deployment framework dependent efficiency for a given layer, a dataset needs to be collected, containing samples at different complexities in different configurations. At the time of writing, the sample locations are determined using manual testing to detect the limits of the hardware and use case fitting, through evaluation of the test networks and determining the upper bounds of the network sizes.

For characterization and timing estimation, Eqs. 1–3 are used. For each layer the execution time t_l can thus be inferred using the base cost per operation t_{op_l} and the complexity n_{op_l}.

The modeling methodology generally relies on the fact, that the inference time of an entire neural network is the sum of the inference times of all its layers. This is an assumption which is in general valid and was already introduced by [4].

During initial measurements it turned out, that separating single NN layers for a characterization can nevertheless have a significant impact on the timing, measured in hardware. E.g. a Conv2D layer with a 3×3 kernel and 32 filters

Table 1. Result of per layer measurement in the MONNET-tool. Full HW measurement refers to the measurement of the per layer timing, if the layer is still executed in sequence with all other layers (here in the DenseNet121). Isolation mode 0 is the measurement of the same layer with identical parameters, but isolated and running standalone. This huge difference is typical and would render all layer wise modeling impossible. Thus better isolation techniques, mode 1 and mode 2 (see Fig. 2) with better per layer isolation had to be developed.

Measurement type	Execution time in mS
Full HW measurement	23 ± 0
Isolation mode 0	45.2 ± 1.46
Isolation mode 1	26.1 ± 0.696
Isolation mode 2	24.8 ± 0.533

working on $7 \times 7 \times 128$ input data has an execution time of 23.0 ± 0.0 ms (see Table 1), when measured within a DenseNet121. Cutting out this layer and synthesizing it standalone on hardware will increase the execution time to 45.2 ± 1.46 ms. A characterization has to be independent of a specific NN, so that the approach can be transferred. To eliminate this separation effect, the layers need to be embedded in a representative testing NN.

In order to gather enough data for a characterization of the estimation model, an automated synthesis flow is used. The flow starts with the host system, specifying a benchmark or characterization NN for the given layer configuration. Then it synthesizes the NN for the target hardware, after which it is executed and measured. Keras was used in order to generate a protobuf description and followed by the OpenVINO^{TM}[2] toolchain to convert this into a hardware-agnostic, yet runtime optimized intermediate XML representation. From there, the NN could be compiled and flashed onto the hardware, using the OpenVINO inference engine. This toolchain is shown in Fig. 1.

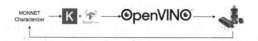

Fig. 1. MONNET toolchain

In order to prevent the layer isolation issue presented in Fig. 1, several methods were developed and tested to properly embed the layer under test. The embedding mode, which was determined to be the best, is to have a feeding layer and a consuming layer, both of type Conv2D with a standardized configuration and to measure only the timing of the middle layer under test, seen in Fig. 2.

From Eqs. 2 and 3 the following parameters of a layer, which can be directly influenced can be extracted: x, y, c, k_x, k_y, f, s_x, s_y and the padding. To decrease

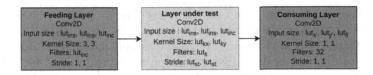

Fig. 2. When measuring a single neural network layer in isolation, the timing may significantly differ from a measurement of the same layer inside a larger neural network. In order to measure each layer independently, but in a typical environment, in characterization, the layer under test is embedded between a feeding layer (mode 1 and 2) and a consuming layer (mode 2)

the amount of measurements needed, the following assumptions are made for the characterization of the efficiency term: $x = y =: i$, and $s_x = s_y =: s$. In the model application, independent input sizes and strides can be described via the complexity term. This focuses on the most prevalent networks, which are benchmarked. In those the inputs of the layer are mostly square. Furthermore, the padding was so far set to same, meaning, that k_x and k_y have no influence on the output size as seen in Eq. 3. This omission is automatically accounted for by the complexity term, which calculates the amount of mathematical operations based on the output size. As a result the characterization space for Conv2D layers can be described as a hypercube with six dimensions. The characterization space is the same for (SepConv2D) layers.

To ensure reliable data for the characterization, each measurement is repeated until a likelihood of above 95% of being within the 95% confidence interval of the unknown real mean value is reached. Numpy's build in statistic tools are used to compute the probabilities after the fifth measurement first and then again after each further measurement until measurements converge.

The open source code from OpenVINO was adapted to allow for a repeated measurement and a stopping condition. As a result of this, the metric to determine the convergence of the execution time could be tightly integrated into the measurement process. Before a reflashing of the device was necessary for every measurement. This step can now be removed, speeding up the characterization process.

The multilinear interpolation, which is used for the estimation and, which will be explained in Sect. 4 requires the sampling points to be on a regular grid in a hypercube. For hardware related reasons not every parameter combination can be synthesized or executed. If for example the layers are too large and have atypical parameter combinations such as highest values of input size, channels and filters at the same time, the hardware might not have enough memory to execute a layer. In other cases the synthetization requires too much memory on the host platform. This results in missing sample points.

To mitigate their impact those are automatically determined by interpolation after hardware characterization. For this a slightly different approach is taken than is used in the final interpolation for end use. If neighboring values were validly sampled, the value is in one axis interpolated. Otherwise, it is set to a default value, which is determined by the lowest value yet seen in the dataset.

Even though this might seem arbitrary, it is well-chosen and leading to the best final estimation results. Missing data points typically exist for large and untypical parameter combinations such as input sizes, channels and filters all in the several thousands. For large regular tensors, the efficiency of the hardware tends to flatten out towards the maximum hypothetical efficiency as defined by the memory bandwidth and/or FLOPs rating.

An attempt was made to replicate the memory modeling from [8], which is integrated in their approach. Some studies were performed to determine the viability of automating this on a hardware-agnostic level. Attempts were made to map the memory models in [6] to our hardware. This led to no usable results as will be shown in Sect. 5.

4   Timing Prediction

Section 3 discussed the creation of the model. To predict an execution time, which is not within the characterization dataset, a multilinear interpolation is used.

In this approach the sample space is viewed as an n-dimensional hypercube. For the Conv2D and SepConv2D layers it has six dimensions as discussed in Sect. 3. Two-dimensional activation layers can be reduced to a three-dimensional characterization space, with the dimensions being in_s, in_c and activation function.

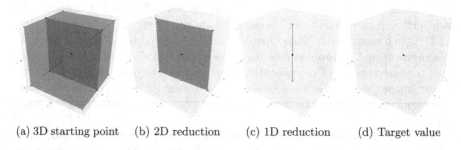

(a) 3D starting point   (b) 2D reduction   (c) 1D reduction   (d) Target value

Fig. 3. A multidimensional linear interpolation can be performed for any dimensionality of the to be evaluated layer model by recursively doing linear interpolations for pairs of neighbouring points along one of the dimensions, reducing the problem dimensions by one.

The interpolation is done stepwise as shown in Fig. 3. At each step the dimensionality of the hypercube is reduced by one. This is done by interpolating the missing value along the axis linearly. As soon as it reaches a 0-dimensional state, the value left is the scalar corresponding to t_{op_l}. Obtaining the execution time of the layer requires calculation of the layer complexity and multiplication of this by t_{op_l}.

This approach assumes that t_{opt} changes at a local level nearly linearly, meaning the characterization in Sect. 3 needs to be granular enough to ensure this. Another approach could be to interpolate the dataset using a piece-wise defined polynomial, which passes through all sample points. Using this a slope in the data could be easily modeled. This was attempted but resulted in the following problem. An erratic behavior was observed if the sample points are too close together while having a high deviation. This can occur if the data is not continuous but as observed stepwise. For this see Sect. 5. This resulted in a worse performance than the linear approximation, which is only influenced by two sample points and only affects values in between.

5   Evaluation

For the evaluation of the timing estimation common NN architectures are used. These can show the strengths and weaknesses of the current model. Specifically the networks from Table 2 were used.

Table 2. Benchmarking networks

Network name	Number of layers	Number of parameters
AlexNet	34	25730506
DenseNet121	429	8062504
DenseNet169	597	14307880
DenseNet201	709	20242984
InceptionResNetV2	782	55873736
InceptionV3	313	23851784
MobileNet	91	4253864
NASNetLarge	1041	88949818
NASNetMobile	771	5326716
ResNet101	347	44707176
ResNet152	517	60419944
ResNet50	177	25636712
VGG16	23	138357544
VGG19	26	143667240
Xception	134	22910480

The characterization and testing is performed on the NCS2, which is a NN hardware accelerator developed by Intel®. It uses the Intel Movidius™ Myriad™ X architecture, serving as a Vision Processing Unit. Due to the usage of the OpenVINO toolchain, multiple NN libraries can be used. In this work the decision was made to use the TensorFlow Keras libraries, which allows usage of the predefined models in the Keras applications.

Table 3. Search space for Conv2D-characterization

Input size	1, 2, 4, 7, 14, 28, 56, 112, 224
Input channels	2, 4, 8, 16, 32, 64, 128, 256, 512, 768, 1024, 2048, 4096
Kernel x	1, 3, 5, 7, 11
Kernel y	1, 3, 5, 7, 11
Filters	2, 4, 8, 16, 32, 64, 128, 256, 512, 768, 1024, 1536
Stride	1, 2

Table 4. Search space for SepConv2D-characterization

Input size	1, 2, 4, 7, 14, 21, 28, 42, 56, 112, 168
Input channels	2, 4, 8, 16, 32, 64, 128, 256, 512, 513, 768, 1024, 1280, 1536
Kernel x	3, 5
Kernel y	3, 5
Filters	2, 4, 8, 16, 32, 64, 128, 192, 256, 512, 513, 768, 1024, 1536, 2048
Stride	1, 2

The comparison focuses primarily on the measured execution time of the modeled layers compared to the estimated execution time. As of the writing of this work the only modeled layers are of type Conv2D and SepConv2D. Other layers such as Activation layers and Pooling layers are being worked on, but the isolation of the layer still needs work, since the measured timings of layers from real NNs strongly deviate from the extracted versions.

In most convolutional neural networks (CNNs) the Conv2D-layers require the highest amount of time to execute. Yet depending on the target application other layer-types need to be modeled as well, to estimate the timing accurately.

For evaluation purposes a characterization with the parameters in Tables 3 and 4 was performed for Conv2D and SepConv2D layers respectively.

This results in 70,200 measurements taken for the Conv2d-layers, which is around twice as much as in [8] and 18,480 for the SepConv2D. This is seen as a reasonable tradeoff, since the measurements need to be taken only once. The search space is adapted to the target application, to increase the relevance of the measurements taken, but could be expanded upon in different target applications. Networks from the Tensorflow Keras Applications library were used for benchmarking the timing estimation approach (see Table 2).

Using this characterization the results for the benchmarking networks are shown in Fig. 4. Blue shows the (MAPE) for the benchmark networks. Red is the deviation of the estimated execution time from the real execution times of the layers under test. This results in a root mean squared percentage error (RMSPE) of 19.02% for all Conv2D- and 26.38% and for all SepConv2D-layers. [8] in comparison achieves 42.6% RMSPE for all Conv2D-layers on a different set of evaluation networks on the same hardware.

Most of the network estimations stay within a 20% error margin. The exceptions are Xception and DenseNet201. In the case of Xception the fault is within the estimation of the SepConv2D layers. This could be mitigated by a larger characterization space for SepConv2D. The DenseNet201 total deviation seems to occur, since it has many repeating layers. Some of these repeating layers are not well estimable by MONNET. This results in an accumulation of errors over the entire network. By including these within the measurement space, the error could be mitigated. This shows the need for automated selection of the sampling points.

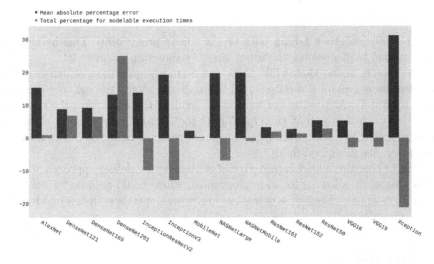

Fig. 4. Benchmark results showing the MAPE for all Conv2D and SepConv2D layers(blue). These stay mostly under 20% with the notable exception of the Xception network which has numerous SepConv2D layers (34 SepConv2D to the 6 Conv2D layers). The red bars show the total deviation from the estimable execution time. Here DenseNet 201 stands out, as it has several repeating layers, on which the estimation performs poorly. (Color figure online)

To evaluate the viability of independent memory modeling several measurement sweeps were performed. Figure 5 shows sweeps varying the input size in y direction, the kernel size in x and y and the amount of input channels.

All measurements show a general linear rise according to the increase in complexity. However, at certain parameter values, the execution time jumps (e.g., for 1024 channels on a (17, 25) input at a (1, 1) kernel [blue curve]). These jumps are not separable per dimension, but depend on all other parameters, too. With just one less row of the input size in y direction [green curve], the step size is significantly reduced from 201% to 42%.

Increasing the kernel size from (1, 1) to (3, 3), the curve shows a completely counterintuitive behavior between 670 and 800 channels, rising in timing by

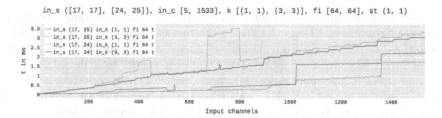

Fig. 5. Execution time as a function of number of input channels for various parameter combinations. A similar behavior can be observed, when measuring over the input size of the filter count. (Color figure online)

almost 140% and then falling back to the linear progression. This behavior is counteracted by decreasing the input size in y direction again to 24.

The results show, that while there are certain regularities, which could be modeled, large amounts of data would be needed to model the memory behavior more accurately. At the time of writing the leading theory is, that the system is layered in such a way, that the OpenVINO toolkit performs different optimizations on different levels, adding to the size dependent behavior of the memory. The latter was described in [6].

Due to this the added complexity of a memory modeling approach was left out of this work, allowing for a simpler model, which could be used for hardware aware NAS-approaches, while being less hardware dependent than a handcrafted memory model.

6   Conclusion

In this work MONNET, a timing estimation approach, was presented, which does not create the need for regarding programming artifacts of the synthesis flow and/or hardware artifacts of the embedded AI accelerator. Instead, the model averages over such artifacts, leading to an unavoidable average error for a concrete evaluation, but on the other hand leading to a much more steady (and differentiable) description of the general behaviour of the hardware, which can be used to control manual or automatical architecture searches. The deviation in the range of 20% can be corrected by a single hardware measurement after the neural networks' topology was defined, and the network was trained. This work thus introduces a significant improvement over the designer's best guess or a MAC and parameter count based timing optimization.

Future work will entail usage of the modeling approach in a hardware aware NAS loop as shown in [1]. Furthermore, the approach needs to be validated on other hardware types such as Graphics Processing Units and Field Programmable Gate Arrays. In the future a system could be created, which automatically determines the upper limits of the hardware capabilities.

To circumvent problems regarding inter-layer optimizations which could be performed by the NN compiler, future work could focus on modeling these optimizations. This would work similarly to [8], modeling whether a layer is optimized out or by mapping the higher level operations to lower level hardware operations.

Acknowledgment. This publication was created as part of the research project KI Delta Learning (project number: 19A19013K) funded by the Federal Ministry for Economic Affairs and Energy (BMWi) on the basis of a decision by the German Bundestag.

References

1. Benmeziane, H., Maghraoui, K.E., Ouarnoughi, H., Niar, S., Wistuba, M., Wang, N.: A comprehensive survey on hardware-aware neural architecture search (2021). https://doi.org/10.48550/ARXIV.2101.09336, https://arxiv.org/abs/2101.09336
2. Intel®: Openvino™. https://docs.openvino.ai/latest/get_started.html
3. Mori, P., et al.: Accelerating and pruning CNNs for semantic segmentation on FPGA. In: Design Automation Conference (DAC) (2022)
4. Parashar, A., et al.: Timeloop: a systematic approach to DNN accelerator evaluation, pp. 304–315, March 2019. https://doi.org/10.1109/ISPASS.2019.00042
5. Patterson, D.A., Hennessy, J.L.: Computer Organization and Design: The Hardware/Software Interface, 5th edn. (2013)
6. Siu, K., Stuart, D.M., Mahmoud, M., Moshovos, A.: Memory requirements for convolutional neural network hardware accelerators. In: 2018 IEEE International Symposium on Workload Characterization (IISWC), pp. 111–121 (2018). https://doi.org/10.1109/IISWC.2018.8573527
7. Sotiriou-Xanthopoulos, E., Percy Delicia, G.S., Figuli, P., Siozios, K., Economakos, G., Becker, J.: A power estimation technique for cycle-accurate higher-abstraction SystemC-based CPU models. In: 2015 International Conference on Embedded Computer Systems: Architectures, Modeling, and Simulation (SAMOS), pp. 70–77 (2015). https://doi.org/10.1109/SAMOS.2015.7363661
8. Wess, M., Ivanov, M., Unger, C., Nookala, A., Wendt, A., Jantsch, A.: Annette: accurate neural network execution time estimation with stacked models. IEEE Access **9**, 3545–3556, December 2020. https://doi.org/10.1109/ACCESS.2020.3047259
9. Yao, S., et al.: FastDeepIoT: towards understanding and optimizing neural network execution time on mobile and embedded devices. In: Proceedings of the 16th ACM Conference on Embedded Networked Sensor Systems. ACM, November 2018. https://doi.org/10.1145/3274783.3274840

Enhancing Energy-Efficiency by Solving the Throughput Bottleneck of LSTM Cells for Embedded FPGAs

Chao Qian[✉], Tianheng Ling, and Gregor Schiele

University of Duisburg-Essen, Duisburg, Germany
{chao.qian,gregor.schiele}@uni-due.de, tianheng.ling@stud.uni-due.de

Abstract. To process sensor data in the Internet of Things (IoTs), embedded deep learning for 1-dimensional data is an important technique. In the past, CNNs were frequently used because they are simple to optimise for special embedded hardware such as FPGAs. This work proposes a novel LSTM cell optimisation aimed at energy-efficient inference on end devices. Using the traffic speed prediction as a case study, a vanilla LSTM model with the optimised LSTM cell achieves 17534 inferences per second while consuming only 3.8 μJ per inference on the FPGA *XC7S15* from *Spartan-7* family. It achieves at least 5.4× faster throughput and 1.37× more energy efficient than existing approaches.

Keywords: IoT · LSTM cell · Energy-efficiency · Embedded FPGA

1 Introduction

Time-series analysis is a crucial topic in *Machine Learning*. The introduction of the *Long Short-Term Memory* (LSTM) model has significantly enhanced the accuracy of time-series analysis. In IoT-related application scenarios, such as temperature forecast and traffic speed prediction, end devices often send data to the Cloud, where data is analysed using the LSTM model. However, once the Internet connection to the Cloud is broken, end devices can no longer analyse. Additionally, the data transmission consumes energy. For these reasons, on-device intelligence, i.e., performing the LSTM model on the end devices, is preferable.

However, IoT devices' microprocessors (MCUs) are often designed with limited memory and processing power to meet constraint power and energy budgets. Performing LSTM model inference on MCUs is therefore a challenge. Our approach is to add a Field Programmable Gate Array (FPGA) as additional computational power to create energy-efficient LSTM accelerators on it. Our paper's contributions are summarised below:

- We propose a novel optimised LSTM cell for embedded FPGAs. It is implemented with VHDL, with a combination of optimisation methods. By solving the throughput bottleneck of the LSTM cell, we maximise its performance while improving the energy efficiency of FPGAs.

I. Koprinska et al. (Eds.): ECML PKDD 2022 Workshops, CCIS 1752, pp. 594–605, 2023.
https://doi.org/10.1007/978-3-031-23618-1_40

- We apply the optimised LSTM cell in the vanilla LSTM model for traffic speed prediction and verify its performance in real-world applications. The optimised LSTM cell is also applicable to other time series analysis tasks in IoT application scenarios.
- We integrate the optimised LSTM cell into a PyTorch-based code generation tool, the *elastic-ai.creator*[1], enabling developers to easily use our approach to develop their accelerators for FPGAs.

We present our work by first discussing some related work in Sect. 2, followed by background of the LSTM model (especially the LSTM cell in it) in Sect. 3. After explaining the optimisations of the LSTM cell in Sect. 4, we give an evaluation of this work in Sect. 5. Finally, we conclude this paper and plan our future work in Sect. 6.

2   Related Work

Previous research applied FPGAs as accelerators to assist LSTM model inference on the Cloud. For example, Cao et al. [3] focused on improving inference speed. However, their approach consumes up to 19 W power and is therefore unsuitable for energy-sensitive IoT application scenarios. With the increased demand for near-end computing, Azari et al. [1] proposed a more energy-efficient FPGA-based LSTM accelerator. Although they optimised the power consumption of the FPGA to 1.19 W, their approach is still too expensive for long-term monitoring with battery power.

Recently, researchers have started considering the energy efficiency of on-device FPGA accelerators. In 2020, Hasib-Al-Rashid et al. [6] proposed a LSTM processor for FPGA *XC7A100T* from *Artix-7* family. Their design only utilises 1% of LUTs, 9% of BRAM and 1.67% of DSP slices of this FPGA by extremely reusing the hardware resources, such as only implementing two multiplication and accumulation (MAC) units in the LSTM cell. It only consumes 17 mW dynamic power and performs 0.055 GOP/s. However, idling the hardware resources of the FPGA does not reduce the static power consumption of the FPGA, which was estimated as 92 mW. The high portion of static power leads to poor overall energy efficiency (0.5 GOP/J).

Noticing this problem, Chen et al. [4] implemented a similar accelerator on a much smaller FPGA *iCE40 UP5K* in 2021. Thanks to the ultra-low static power (at μW scale) of this FPGA, the overall power consumption during inference is approximately equal to the dynamic power of the FPGA, which is 17 mW. The energy efficiency is increased to 3.9 GOP/J, while the throughput is slightly improved to 0.067 GOP/s due to the same parallelism strategy they applied as in [6].

In both works [4,6], researchers applied fixed-point logic to simplify the design and reduce the loss of precision compared to aggressive quantisation. The activation functions $tanh()$ and $sigmoid()$ were replaced with $hard\_tanh()$

---

[1] https://github.com/es-ude/elastic-ai.creator.

and *hard_sigmoid*() respectively, which simplifies the computations but leads to a large reduction of precision [10]. Namin et al. and Meher et al. used lookup tables to implement activation functions for higher speed and precision [7,8].

Inspired by this previous work, we chose a slightly larger FPGA than the *iCE40 UP5K*, the *XC7S15*, which has about 2.5 times LUTs, 10 times BRAM and 2.5 times DSP. Therefore, it can afford higher parallelism and deeper lookup tables with wider fixed-point data for higher precision. As it has around 10% of resources of the *XC7A100T*, it still consumes relatively low static power.

3   LSTM Background and Analysis

Before presenting our optimisations, we first introduce the basic concepts of LSTM models, layers and cells. We then analyse the timing complexity of a single LSTM cell to determine the optimisation potential.

3.1   LSTM Model vs Layer vs Cell

The most conventional and simplistic LSTM model is constructed with one LSTM layer followed by a dense layer. By setting an activation function in the dense layer, the LSTM model can perform regression or classification tasks. We use an LSTM model (see Fig. 1) taken from [5], to predict traffic speed. It takes 6 historical data points as inputs $(x_{t-5}, ..., x_{t-1}, x_t)$, and predicts the next data point (x'_{t+1}) as its output.

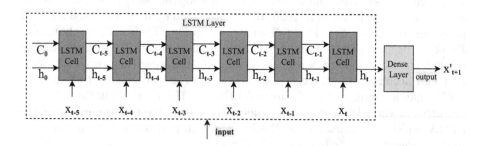

Fig. 1. The unfolded architecture of the LSTM model in the time dimension

Inside the LSTM layer, a single LSTM cell processes the 6 input data points recurrently to perform the long and short-term memory logic, which is visualized as 6 recurrent steps in the time dimension in Fig. 1.

In the LSTM cell (see Fig. 2) the information is carried through the sequence chain in the cell state C_t and the hidden state h_t. Internally, the cell contains three so-called gates, the input gate i_t, the output gate o_t and the forget gate f_t to control which information to retain or discard. All computations that happen in the LSTM cell can be described by Eqs. 3.1 to 3.6, which are explained in detail in [9]. We use $*$ to denote the Hadamard product, $[\cdot, \cdot]$ to denote the concatenation of two vectors. Weight matrices are denoted by W.

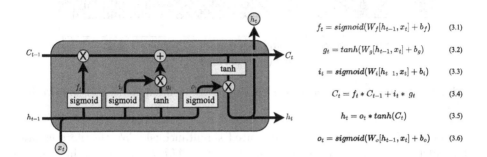

$$f_t = sigmoid(W_f[h_{t-1}, x_t] + b_f) \tag{3.1}$$

$$g_t = tanh(W_g[h_{t-1}, x_t] + b_g) \tag{3.2}$$

$$i_t = sigmoid(W_i[h_{t-1}, x_t] + b_i) \tag{3.3}$$

$$C_t = f_t * C_{t-1} + i_t * g_t \tag{3.4}$$

$$h_t = o_t * tanh(C_t) \tag{3.5}$$

$$o_t = sigmoid(W_o[h_{t-1}, x_t] + b_o) \tag{3.6}$$

Fig. 2. The structure of an LSTM cell

An important factor affecting the model performance is the size of the hidden state, i.e. how many neurons are necessary to represent it. Commonly used hidden sizes include 1 [5], 12 [6], 32 to 256 [13]. In our application case we use a hidden size of 20. The resulting model has a high accuracy on the test set, while being small enough to fit our target FPGA.

3.2 Timing

As Fig. 1 shows, the computation of each recursion depends on the result of the previous recursion, so increasing the number of LSTM cells in the LSTM layer cannot help to improve throughput. A possible way to increase the throughput of the LSTM model is to reduce the time spent processing an LSTM cell. Based on the timing model of the sequentially executed LSTM model in [11], we plotted the timing decomposition of a sequentially processed LSTM cell whose input_size is 1 and hidden_size is 20. Figure 3 shows that the processing of Eq. 3.1, 3.2, 3.3 and 3.6 take up 97.1% of the time to process the whole cell, indicating that the throughput bottleneck of the LSTM cell lies in the computations of these four equations. In contrast, the operations in the dense layer only consume 0.6% of the time.

4 Optimised LSTM Cell Design

This section begins with a description of the parallelisation optimisation in the LSTM cell. Then, we will discuss memory optimisation.

4.1 Parallelising the LSTM Cell

To solve the mentioned performance bottleneck, we analysed the dependencies of Eqs. 3.1, 3.2, 3.3 and 3.6. They take the same data (x_t, h_{t-1}) and process it

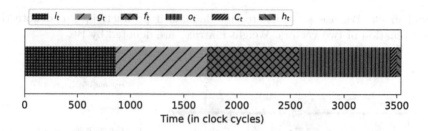

Fig. 3. Time breakdown of a single recursion in a sequentially processed LSTM cell

independently, i.e., they can be computed simultaneously. We therefore create four identical ALU modules (see *ALU1*, *ALU2*, *ALU3*, and *ALU4* in Fig. 4). Each of them consumes 1 DSP slice. These ALU modules are used to execute multiply-accumulate operations of these equations concurrently. By quadrupling the number of ALU modules, the computation speed of gates in the LSTM cell is increased by a factor of four, making the increase in throughput possible. Note that previous work used two DSP slides, one for calculating $W_i x_t$, another one for $W_h h_{t-1}$ [4,6]. Due to the different complexity of x_t and h_{t-1}, this leads to bad utilisation of the DSPs. Our assignment avoids this problem.

Our ALU modules do not include activation functions. Instead, we instantiate a lookup table for each kind of activation function (see the *sigmoid LUT* module and the *tanh LUT* module in Fig. 4). It is well known that the greater the depth of the lookup table, the smaller the degradation in the accuracy of the model inference. By placing the lookup tables once and sharing them on demand, the optimised LSTM cell can save more hardware resources, which can be used to implement larger lookup tables, helping to improve the precision of the activation function. However, even with four ALU modules running concurrently, waiting for the whole matrix multiplication (e.g., $W_f[h_{t-1}, x_t]$) to finish before updating C_t and h_t still takes unacceptable time. Thus, the longest stage of our pipeline is only for computing one row of the matrix multiplication. Once new elements with index n ($f_t[n]$, $i_t[n]$, $g_t[n]$, $o_t[n]$) are computed, the computation for $C_t[n]$, $h_t[n]$ can start.

As shown in Fig. 4, we add another ALU module (*ALU5*) to execute the multiply-accumulate operations in Eqs. 3.4 and 3.5. Since these operations are less complex than the others, it is possible to reuse a single ALU module for both of them without reducing the overall performance. However, this is only true for cells with a larger hidden size. Since we had free DSPs available, we decided to implement *ALU5* with three DSPs. This makes our design suitable for cells with smaller hidden sizes (down to 3).

Figure 5 shows the time breakdown when the above-mentioned parallel computing is applied in an LSTM cell. Although the processing time of each ALU for its corresponding equation has not improved, the overall time consumption of the entire recursion is squeezed to 860 clock cycles, which would give us a 4.1-fold improvement in throughput compared to sequential computing.

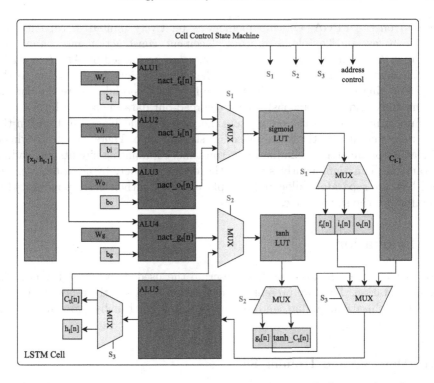

Fig. 4. Architecture of our LSTM cell on an FPGA. $nact\_f_t$ denotes that f_t is not activated, others have similar meaning.

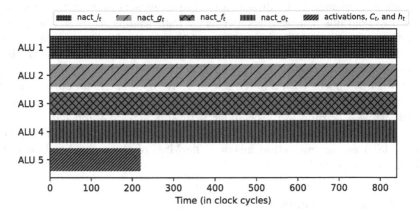

Fig. 5. Time breakdown of a single recursion in a parallelly processed LSTM cell

4.2 Memory Management

Our approach uses only on-chip memory, so-called Block- and Distributed-RAM (BRAM and LUTRAM), to store data (including parameters and intermediate results) on the FPGA. On-chip memory is relatively limited in capacity but extremely fast and flexible in terms of placement, construction and connection.

Since the inputs required for the computation performed by *ALU1* to *ALU4* are the same, we store x_t and h_{t-1} in the same memory module. Due to the flexible wiring feature of the FPGA, these four ALU modules share the data in the memory and simultaneously share the read-out data via a data bus.

Furthermore, the static parameters (i.e., weights and bias) are stored in the bitstream and automatically initialised at startup-time. Therefore, the overhead of loading parameters is eliminated at run-time. Eliminating circuits for loading parameters can significantly simplify the design further. In addition, weights and bias are separately allocated and placed close to their corresponding ALU to minimise the signal delay.

5   Evaluation

To discuss our evaluation, we first describe the used data set and our model implementation. Then we present our evaluation results with respect to FPGA resource utilisation, timing, and power consumption. Finally, we compare our results to other approaches.

5.1   Data Set and Training Settings

For our experiments, we aimed to predict traffic speed. We used the publicly available data set **PeMS-4W**[2], which contains 11,160 time series corresponding to sensor measurements at different locations of sensors over four weeks. Each time series contains a measurement every 5 min, leading to 8064 time points. From these, we randomly selected one time series to form our data set. We divided it into a training set and a test set in a ratio of 3:1. Our full-precision (double-precision floating-point) LSTM model was trained on the selected training set with 30 epochs with a batch size of 1. We used an *Adam* optimiser with $beta_1 = 0.9$, $beta_2 = 0.98$ and $epsilon = 10^{-9}$. The initial learning rate was set to 0.01, while a learning rate scheduler with $step\_size = 3$ and $gamma = 0.5$ was used. Mean-Squared Loss was used as the loss function, and Mean Squared Error (MSE) as the evaluation metric. The MSE of the trained full precision LSTM model is 0.1663.

5.2   Model Implementation

We implemented our optimised LSTM cell using our *elastic-ai.creator* tool. Given a trained PyTorch model, the *elastic-ai.creator* can automatically transform a full precision model into an optimised model and translate it into VHDL code for an FPGA. The *elastic-ai.creator* includes implementations for different layers. Most importantly for us, it contains a built-in optimised dense layer that

---

[2] https://doi.org/10.5281/zenodo.3939793.

uses only 1 DSP slice (see [2]). We used this for our model and extended the tool with an implementation of our LSTM cell design.

We performed post-training quantisation to fixed-point representations on the LSTM model. We describe this representation with a notation of (x, y), where x is the number of fractional bits (representing numbers < 1) and y is the total width in bits [2].

To evaluate the effect of the fractional digit x on the model inference, we varied it from 4 to 12 while utilizing 8 bits for the integer part. We performed this on a custom Python simulator with all parameters and variables at the corresponding fixed-point width. We kept the activation function in full precision. Figure 6 shows that the MSE (0.1722) on the test set no longer drops significantly when x is greater than 8. Therefore, our experiments below are conducted with a fixed-point configuration of (8, 16). Clearly, this can be optimised further in the future. Our design supports scalable bit-width for fixed-point data so that AI developers can choose other settings based on the output of the Python simulator.

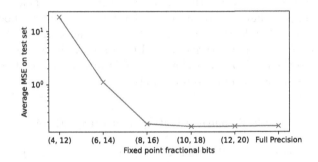

Fig. 6. The MSE of the quantised LSTM model on test set with various fractional bits

Furthermore, we replaced all full precision activation functions with lookup tables of depth 256. We conducted experiments with different lookup table depths both in our simulator and on an *XC7S6* FPGA. The results differ slightly, which may be due to their different rounding mechanisms. As shown in Table 1, the MSE on the test set decreases as the depth of the lookup table increases. Note that the depth of the lookup tables is the same for different activation functions. At depth 256, the MSE (0.1821) is close enough to the MSE with full precision activation functions (0.1722). Since we instantiate only one lookup table for each type of activation function and share it over time, even such lookup tables with larger depths can be used on embedded FPGAs.

5.3   Resource Utilisation on FPGA

Using a fixed-point configuration (8, 16) and lookup tables of depth 256, we analysed the resource consumption using a synthesis tool integrated into the

Table 1. The MSE of the test set when using lookup tables of different depths

Depth of lookup table	MSE on python simulator	MSE on FPGA
64	0.6920	0.6833
128	0.2485	0.2491
256	0.1821	0.1659

Vivado IDE from *Xilinx*. We synthesised our design into three target FPGAs of the *Spartan-7* family with different on-chip resources.

As shown in Table 2, our design can fit the *XC7S6* which is the smallest FPGA of the *Spartan-7* family. Although 80% of the DSP slices (the most critical resource) are used, we still have a considerable amount of other available resources to make the design more accurate. Our optimised LSTM cell requires seven DSP slices, while the dense layer consumes one DSP slice, so we could, e.g., add two more dense layers to the model and still fit onto the *XC7S6*.

Furthermore, the resource utilisation on the *XC7S15* is below 50% for all types, which means that we can either deploy two such LSTM models on this device or at least double the number of layers of the current LSTM model. The *XC7S25* FPGA has 1.8 times more LUTs and 4 times more DSPs than the *XC7S15*, so there is no doubt that the *XC7S25* can be the choice for more complex models using our optimisation method.

Table 2. Resource utilisation on Spartan-7 FPGAs

Resource	Estimation	Utilisation on FPGAs (in %)		
		XC7S6	XC7S15	XC7S25
LUT	1435	38.3	17.9	9.8
LUTRAM	60	2.5	2.5	1.2
BRAM	2	40.0	20.0	4.4
DSP	8	80.0	40.0	10.0

5.4 Processing Time

Our design does not follow the usual CPU-based sequential computing nor a large FPGA-based parallel computing. Therefore, we proposed a timing model to estimate the system throughput.

By calculating the required number of operations n_{total}, we can estimate the processing time of the LSTM model. The simplified timing model we have designed is defined by Eq. 5.1, where t_{clock} is the reference clock period of the FPGA, n_{ll} and n_{dense} are the clock cycles of the LSTM layer and the dense layer respectively.

$$t_{model} = t_{clock} * n_{total} = t_{clock} * (n_{ll} + n_{dense}) \tag{5.1}$$

$$n_{ll} = n_{seq} * n_{lc} = n_{step} * (n_i + n_h) * 2 * (n_h + 1) \tag{5.2}$$

$$n_{dense} = n_f * n_o * 2 \tag{5.3}$$

n_{ll} can be further represented by Eq. 5.2, where n_{seq} represents the length of input sequences, n_i and n_h are the *input_size* and *hidden_size* of the LSTM cell respectively. Furthermore, the factor 2 indicates that our ALU module requires 2 clock cycles to produce an output. Similarly, n_{dense} can be defined by Eq. 5.3, where n_f and n_o represent the number of input and output features of the dense layer. For our model structure, n_f is always equal to n_h since only the latest hidden state is fed into the dense layer.

These equations allow the processing time of our LSTM model to be estimated. The total number of clock cycles n_{total} is 5332. Assuming that we deploy the LSTM model on the *XC7S15* with a clock frequency of 100 MHz, the estimated processing time is 53.32 μs. Our design can then process up to 18754 samples per second.

We validated the timing of the LSTM model on the actual *XC7S15*. The processing time measured in hardware with a 100 MHz clock is 57.25 μs, which is 3.93 μs more than the estimated processing time. Although there is still some discrepancy, it proves that our timing model is valid.

5.5 Inference Power

Using the XPE software, we estimated the power consumption during the inference of the LSTM model for the target FPGAs. We also applied the calibration process according to the guidelines provided by *Xilinx* [12] to improve the confidence of the estimation. The estimated power can be divided into static and dynamic power.

The static power consumption of the FPGAs is characterised by the chip design and independent of switching activity. As Fig. 7 shows, the static power of the *XC7S6* and *XC7S15* is identical (32 mW), while the static power of the *XC7S25* is much higher (87 mW). We infer that the *XC7S6* and *XC7S15* use the same chip (with some resources on the *XC7S6* not being available to users).

The dynamic power is modelled based on the switching activity during inference. The dynamic power of both *XC7S6* and *XC7S15* is 38 mW. In comparison, the dynamic power of the *XC7S25* is 43 mW.

Based on the estimated power consumption and the processing time on the *XC7S15*, the estimated energy per inference is 3.7 μJ. On the actual *XC7S15* hardware, the measured energy per inference is 4.1 μJ.

5.6 Comparison with the State-of-the-Art

As a final evaluation step, we computed the throughput and energy efficiency of our LSTM model on real hardware (see Table 3). Our model is 5.4 times faster than [4] and 6.6 times faster than [6]. The energy efficiency of our model is 10.66 times higher than [6]. Although the *XC7S15* in our work consumes more static power than the *iCE40 UP5K* in [4], due to the improved throughput, the energy efficiency of our model is still 1.37 times higher than theirs.

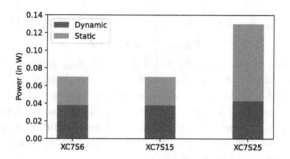

Fig. 7. Power estimation for inference on different FPGAs

Table 3. Compare throughput and energy efficiency with the state-of-the-art

Platform	This work	[4]	[6]
	XC7S15	*iCE40 UP5K*	*XC7A100T*
Clock (MHz)	**100**	17	52.6
Power (mW)	**71**	17	109
Throughput (GOP/s)	**0.363**	0.067	0.055
Energy efficiency (GOP/J)	**5.33**	3.9	0.5

6   Conclusion and Outlook

Energy-efficient artificial intelligence on end devices enables interesting IoT applications. It offers the opportunity to ensure the quality of IoT services without relying on the Internet connection.

Our approach improves the energy efficiency of the LSTM cell by solving its throughput bottleneck. The model with optimised LSTM cell achieves 17534 inferences per second with only 71 mW power consumption. Its super high energy efficiency (5.33 GOP/J) can promise longer battery life for continuous analysis of time series data on the device.

In the future, we plan to increase throughput by achieving lower bit quantisation through quantisation-aware training. In addition, we will validate our approach on further time-series classification tasks, enabling users to solve more targeted applications.

Acknowledgements. The authors acknowledge the financial support by the Federal Ministry of Education and Research of Germany in the KI-LiveS project.

References

1. Azari, E., Vrudhula, S.: An energy-efficient reconfigurable LSTM accelerator for natural language processing. In: 2019 IEEE International Conference on Big Data (Big Data), pp. 4450–4459. IEEE (2019)

2. Burger, A., Qian, C., Schiele, G., Helms, D.: An embedded CNN implementation for on-device ECG analysis. In: 2020 IEEE International Conference on Pervasive Computing and Communications Workshops (PerCom Workshops), pp. 1–6. IEEE (2020)
3. Cao, S., et al.: Efficient and effective sparse LSTM on FPGA with bank-balanced sparsity. In: Proceedings of the 2019 ACM/SIGDA International Symposium on Field-Programmable Gate Arrays, pp. 63–72 (2019)
4. Chen, J., Hong, S., He, W., Moon, J., Jun, S.W.: Eciton: very low-power LSTM neural network accelerator for predictive maintenance at the edge. In: 2021 31st International Conference on Field-Programmable Logic and Applications (FPL), pp. 1–8. IEEE (2021)
5. Fu, R., Zhang, Z., Li, L.: Using LSTM and GRU neural network methods for traffic flow prediction. In: 2016 31st Youth Academic Annual Conference of Chinese Association of Automation (YAC), pp. 324–328. IEEE (2016)
6. Manjunath, N.K., Paneliya, H., Hosseini, M., Hairston, W.D., Mohsenin, T., et al.: A low-power LSTM processor for multi-channel brain EEG artifact detection. In: 2020 21st International Symposium on Quality Electronic Design (ISQED), pp. 105–110. IEEE (2020)
7. Meher, P.K.: An optimized lookup-table for the evaluation of sigmoid function for artificial neural networks. In: 2010 18th IEEE/IFIP International Conference on VLSI and System-on-Chip, pp. 91–95. IEEE (2010)
8. Namin, A.H., Leboeuf, K., Wu, H., Ahmadi, M.: Artificial neural networks activation function HDL coder. In: 2009 IEEE International Conference on Electro/Information Technology, pp. 389–392. IEEE (2009)
9. Olah, C.: Understanding LSTM Networks [EB/OL]. https://colah.github.io/posts/2015-08-Understanding-LSTMs/. Accessed 27 Aug 2015
10. Otte, S., Liwicki, M., Zell, A.: Dynamic cortex memory: enhancing recurrent neural networks for gradient-based sequence learning. In: Wermter, S., et al. (eds.) ICANN 2014. LNCS, vol. 8681, pp. 1–8. Springer, Cham (2014). https://doi.org/10.1007/978-3-319-11179-7_1
11. Sun, Z., et al.: FPGA acceleration of LSTM based on data for test flight. In: 2018 IEEE International Conference on Smart Cloud (SmartCloud), pp. 1–6. IEEE (2018)
12. Xilinx: Power Analysis and Optimization, rev. 2, January 2021
13. Zhang, Y., et al.: A power-efficient accelerator based on FPGAs for LSTM network. In: 2017 IEEE International Conference on Cluster Computing (CLUSTER), pp. 629–630. IEEE (2017)

Accelerating RNN-Based Speech Enhancement on a Multi-core MCU with Mixed FP16-INT8 Post-training Quantization

Manuele Rusci[1,2(✉)], Marco Fariselli[2], Martin Croome[2], Francesco Paci[2], and Eric Flamand[2]

[1] Universita' di Bologna, Bologna, Italy
`manuele.rusci@unibo.it`
[2] Greenwaves Technologies, Grenoble, France
{`marco.fariselli,martin.croome,francesco.paci,`
`eric.flamand`}`@greenwaves-technologies.com`

Abstract. This paper presents an optimized methodology to design and deploy Speech Enhancement (SE) algorithms based on Recurrent Neural Networks (RNNs) on a state-of-the-art MicroController Unit (MCU), with 1+8 general-purpose RISC-V cores. To achieve low-latency execution, we propose an optimized software pipeline interleaving parallel computation of LSTM or GRU recurrent blocks, featuring vectorized 8-bit integer (INT8) and 16-bit floating-point (FP16) compute units, with manually-managed memory transfers of model parameters. To ensure minimal accuracy degradation with respect to the full-precision models, we propose a novel FP16-INT8 Mixed-Precision Post-Training Quantization (PTQ) scheme that compresses the recurrent layers to 8-bit while the bit precision of remaining layers is kept to FP16. Experiments are conducted on multiple LSTM and GRU based SE models trained on the Valentini dataset, featuring up to 1.24M parameters. Thanks to the proposed approaches, we speed-up the computation by up to 4× with respect to the lossless FP16 baselines. Differently from a uniform 8-bit quantization that degrades the PESQ score by 0.3 on average, the Mixed-Precision PTQ scheme leads to a low-degradation of only 0.06, while achieving a 1.4–1.7× memory saving. Thanks to this compression, we cut the power cost of the external memory by fitting the large models on the limited on-chip non-volatile memory and we gain a MCU power saving of up to 2.5× by reducing the supply voltage from 0.8 V to 0.65 V while still matching the real-time constraints. Our design results >10× more energy efficient than state-of-the-art SE solutions deployed on single-core MCUs that make use of smaller models and quantization-aware training.

Keywords: MCU · Speech Enhancement · RNNs · Mixed-Precision

© The Author(s), under exclusive license to Springer Nature Switzerland AG 2023
I. Koprinska et al. (Eds.): ECML PKDD 2022 Workshops, CCIS 1752, pp. 606–617, 2023.
https://doi.org/10.1007/978-3-031-23618-1_41

1   Introduction

Novel speech-centric devices, e.g. miniaturized Hearing Aids, make use of AI-based methods to process audio data in real-time for improving the signal intelligibility. Given the small sizes, these devices present a limited energy budget: a lifetime of up to 20 h can be achieved with a small 60 mAh battery if the average power consumption is 10 mW, considering sensing, computation and actuation costs. Because of the severe energy constraints, low-power Micro-Controller Units (MCUs) are typically chosen as Digital Processing Units to handle control and processing tasks. These processing units feature a limited computational power (single core CPU) and up to few MB of on-chip memory, making the integration process of complex AI speech processing pipelines extremely challenging.

Speech Enhancement (SE), the ability of removing background noises from a (noisy) audio signal, is getting popular among the AI capabilities of speech sensors. While in the past SE methods relied on digital signal processing filters [1,2], recent approaches integrate Deep Learning (DL) strategies, which have demonstrated a superior effectiveness to deal with non-stationary noises [10]. To cancel out noise components, DL based approaches learn in a supervised fashion to estimate spectral suppression masks from a set of features extracted from the noisy speech. Among the causal models tailored for real-time computation, Recurrent Neural Networks have shown promising results [6,8,15,16]. These approaches encode the input signal, typically in the frequency domain (e.g. STFT or Mel spectrograms), into an embedding vector that feeds one or multiple recurrent layers, i.e. GRU or LSTM, acting also as memory components of the RNN based SE filter. The cleaned audio signal is reconstructed by decoding the outputs of the recurrent layers in a frame-by-frame streaming fashion.

Unfortunately, current DL methods target real time execution on high-end devices [11] and are not fully-optimized for MCUs. Only [9] and [4] described design methodologies of RNN based SE models, with less than 0.5M parameters, for single-core MCUs. More in details, the *NNoM* framework was used to deploy the RNNoise model [14] on a single-core ARM Cortex-M MCU [9]. The RNNoise algorithm includes small GRU layers with constrained activation ranges, leading to an effective 8-bit quantization. On the other side, TinyLSTM [4] made use of Quantization-Aware Training (QAT) [7] to compress an LSTM based model to 8 bit without accuracy degradation. Despite its effectiveness, the QAT technique is not always applicable because of the additional compute and data resources needed to simulate the non-linear quantization error at (re-)training time [5]. Hardware-specific fine-tuning such as Block Pruning has been also developed to efficiently map SE RNNs on MicroNPU accelerators [12] Differently from these solutions, *(i)* we aim at a lossless and low-cost Post-Training Quantization methodology for scalable RNN-based SE algorithms and *(ii)* we investigate an optimized deployment flow for general-purpose multi-core MCUs, to achieve a final design more energy-efficient than state-of-the-art solutions.

To this aim, we combine multiple strategies. Firstly, we target a multi-core compute platform with 1+8 RISC-V CPUs, featuring 8-bit integer (INT8) and 16-bit floating-point (FP16) MAC vector units. Secondly, we design an optimized software pipeline, in charge of scheduling at runtime parallel compute calls with

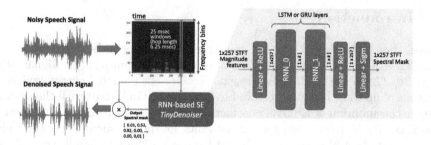

Fig. 1. TinyDenoiser models for Speech Enhancement on MCUs.

Table 1. Characteristics of the RNN-based TinyDenoiser variants.

	LSTM256	GRU256	LSTM128	GRU128
k	256	256	128	128
RNN_0 layer	LSTM (257, 256)	GRU (257, 256)	LSTM (257, 128)	GRU (257, 128)
RNN_1 layer	LSTM (257, 256)	GRU (257, 256)	LSTM (128, 128)	GRU (128, 128)
Params	1.24 M	0.985 M	0.493 M	0.411 M
% rnn params	84%	80%	66.50%	59.80%

manually-managed memory transfers, also from external L3 memories. To gain an almost lossless compression, we also propose a novel Mixed-Precision FP16-INT8 (MixFP16-INT8) Post-Training Quantization scheme, which quantizes only the RNN parameters and activations to INT8 while keeping the bit precision of other tensors to FP16. This paper makes the following contributions:

- We present an optimized HW/SW design for LSTM and GRU based SE models for multi-core MCU systems with limited memory space.
- We propose an almost lossless Mixed-Precision FP16-INT8 Post-Training Quantization scheme to accelerate RNN-based SE on MCUs.
- We provide a detailed analysis of latency and HW/SW efficiency on a 22-nm RISC-V 1+8-core MCU.

Our work demonstrates, for the first time, an optimized design for RNN-based SE models relying only on PTQ, without any need for expensive QAT, with Mixed-Precision FP16-INT8. When benchmarked on the Valentini dataset, the RNN trained models show an average reduction of the PESQ and STOI scores of only 0.06 and 0.007. The proposed HW/SW design results >10× more energy efficient than state-of-the-art solutions deployed on single-core MCUs.

2   RNN Based Speech Enhancement on Multi-core MCUs

This Section firstly describes the scalable RNN-based SE model family, denoted as *TinyDenoiser*, that we consider for this study. Second, we detail the target HW platform and the mapping of the proposed software pipeline. Lastly, we present our novel Mixed-Precision FP16-INT8 PTQ method.

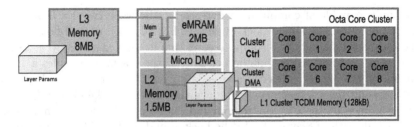

Fig. 2. Micro-architecture of the target platform. The cluster on the right includes 1+8 cores. An external memory or an on-chip non-volatile memory can be used to permanently store the model parameters.

2.1 TinyDenoiser Models

Figure 1 shows the *TinyDenoiser* pipeline. The model takes as input the STFT frequency map of a noisy speech signal and predicts a spectral gain mask, whose values are in the range $[0, 1]$. In more detail, the audio input is sampled at 16 kHz and the STFT frequency features are computed over a 25 ms audio frame, after Hanning windowing. For every audio frame, a total of 257 STFT magnitude values are fed into the model and 257 gain values are returned as output. The hop size is 6.25 ms (25% of the window length), which determines the real-time constraint of the inference task. The filtered frequency spectrum of the audio frame, computed by masking the noisy spectrum, is converted back to the time domain using an inverse STFT transform. In a real-time streaming processing scenario, the denoised speech signal is obtained by overlap-and-add operations of the cleaned audio frames.

Drawing inspiration from TinyLSTM [4], the TinyDenoiser includes two RNN layers with a parametric output size of length k, a Fully-Connected (FC) input layer producing 257 features and two final FC layers both producing 257 features. With the exception of the last layer, which features a Sigmoid activation to estimate the frequency gains, the other FC layers are followed by a batchnorm and a ReLU activation. Concerning the RNN layers, we experiment with both LSTM and GRU layers with an output size of $k = \{128, 256\}$, originating multiple variants of the TinyDenoiser denoted as *LSTM256*, *GRU256*, *LSTM128* and *GRU128*. As reported in Table 1, these variants feature a number of parameters ranging from 0.4M and 1.24M. Note that the majority of the parameters (and the operations) are due to the RNN layers (up to 84% for *LSTM256*).

2.2 Memory Management for RNN Deployment on the Target HW

Figure 2 depicts the architecture of the MCU platform targeted for the deployment of the RNN-based SE model. Internally, the system includes a cluster with 8 RISC-V CPUs tailored for computation and 1 core for control operation, denoted as the Cluster Controller (CC). The 1+8 cores can load data from a 128 kB Tightly Coupled Data Memory, namely the L1 memory, in a single clock-cycle. Note that the L1 memory is not a data cache. Every core has a 8-bit MAC vector unit, capable of computing a dot-product between two 4×8-bit vectors and accumulation in a single clock-cycle (i.e. 4 MAC/clk), while 4 floating point units are shared among the 8 compute cores, implementing single-cycle $2 \times$FP16 vector MAC (2 MAC/clk). Outside the cluster, the platform includes a 1.5 MB L2 memory; the cluster cores can access data from the L2 memory $\sim 10\times$ slower than accessing the L1 memory. To reduce this overhead, the cluster DMA can be programmed by the CC core to copy data between L2 and L1 memories with a peak bandwidth of 8Byte/clk. In the background of the DMA operations, the Control Core dispatches and synchronizes parallel tasks on the 8 compute cores.

To deploy the RNN-based TinyDenoiser on the HW target platform, the layer parameters are permanently stored into a non-volatile memory. Because the storage requirements can grow up to several MBs, we use an off-chip FLASH memory (*ExtFLASH*), also denoted as L3 memory, with a capacity of 8 MB and connected to the MCU via OctoSPI. Data can be copied from L3 to L2 memories in the background of other operations by programming the MicroDMA module. Note that the IO memory interface reaches a max bandwidth of 1Byte/clk, 8× slower than the L2 peak bandwidth. Alternatively, the on-chip *eMRAM* non-volatile memory can be used for permanent storage, gaining a lower power consumption and a higher bandwidth but the total capacity reduces to 2 MB.

At runtime, but before entering the infinite inference loop, layer-wise network parameters can be copied from L3 (either *ExtFLASH* or *eMRAM*) to L2, based on the available space. Thanks to this process, named *tensor promotion*, the time to copy parameters to the L1 memory during inference decreases linearly with respect to the amount of promoted tensors. If a parameter tensor does not fit the available L2 parameter buffer space, it is partitioned in sub-tensors that are sequentially loaded from L3 to L2. Besides storing the promoted parameters, the L2 memory must reserve space to store an activation buffer, for temporarily keeping the activation feature maps, and a parameter buffer, serving the dynamic load of not-promoted parameters from L3 to L2.

During the inference task, the L1 memory inside the cluster acts as the working memory because of the fast access time from the compute cores: parameters and activation features are copied to this memory and then fetched concurrently by the cores. Because of the small size, the L1 memory is kept free from static tensor allocation. Activation or parameter tensors or sub-tensors are rather loaded from L2 to L1 at inference time using the Cluster DMA, as depicted in Fig. 2.

2.3   SW Computation Model

The CC core runs the RNN-based SE inference SW code, which includes a sequence of layer-wise processing calls. Figure 3 shows the pseudo C-code for a RNN layer processing task; the same software architecture applies for FC layer processing. The input and output activation tensor arguments, including the RNN states, are L2 memory arrays. On the contrary, the RNN parameter array (*Weights*) can be stored in L2 or L3 memory, depending if any promotion occurred as discussed before.

Every layer-wise function interleaves data copies from L3 and L2 memories to the L1 memory and calls to the compute tasks. These latter are dispatched

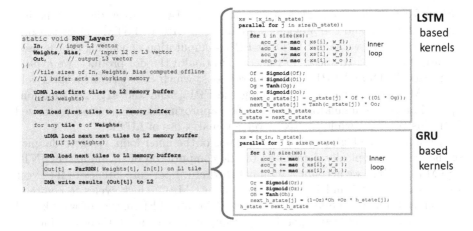

Fig. 3. Pseudo C code of layer-wise RNN processing. The CC core runs the code on the left. The parallel GRU and LSTM basic kernels dispatched on the compute cores are on the right. Biases are omitted for simplicity.

and parallelized over the 8 compute cores of the cluster. To be more specific, the CC core programs the MicroDMA and Cluster DMA modules to operate, respectively, asynchronous data copies from L3 to L2 and from L2 to L1. Note that L3 transfers occurs only if layer parameters are not promoted to L2; in this case the MicroDMA is not programmed.

Typically, input, weight and output tensors of a layer cannot entirely fit the L1 memory (limited to 128 kB). For this reason, large tensors are sliced in sub-tensors, also referred as tiles, during the code generation process. The size of the tiles are computed such as to maximize the memory occupation of the available L1 memory. Therefore the layer-wise software routine implements a `for` loop to sequentially loads (with the DMAs) the tensor slices in the background of the computation that applies on the previously copied data (Fig. 3 on the left). To realize this mechanism, we double the memory requirement of the tensor slices to account both the L1 memory needed by the compute cores and the memory buffer used by the DMA.

Based on the proposed execution model, the minimal theoretical latency $\tilde{t}_{layer}$ to process a layer can be estimated as:

$$\tilde{t}_{layer} = N_{tiles} \cdot \max(t_{dma}^{L3-L2}, t_{dma}^{L2-L1}, t_{core}) \qquad (1)$$

where N_{tiles} is the number of tiles, t_{dma}^{L2-L1} and t_{dma}^{L3-L2} are the latencies required by, respectively, the Cluster DMA and the MicroDMA to copy a single data tile from L2 to L1 and L3 to L2 and t_{core} is the compute time due to the parallel task. Based on HW architecture described in Sect. 2.2, $t_{dma}^{L3-L2} \approx 8 \times t_{dma}^{L2-L1}$ if considering an external SPI flash. t_{dma}^{L3-L2} decreases when using instead the on-chip non-volatile memory (up to 2.6× for eMRAM).

Figure 3 shows on the right more in details the parallel SW kernels for LSTM and GRU computation. Both kernels consists of a 2 nested loops. The outer loop, which is parallelized over the available compute cores, iterates over the size of the output feature tile. The inner loop computes the MAC between the combination of input features and the previous state and the GRU or LSTM weight tensors. More specifically, we target INT8 or FP16 computation depending on the used quantization type. To speed-up the computation of the dot-product, we exploit vectorized INT8 and FP16 MAC instructions, which can perform respectively 4 or 2 MAC/cyc per core. Concerning the FP16 `tanh` and `sigmoid` functions applied on the accumulators, we use a fast approximation exploiting vectorized FP16 instructions, while the INT8 version makes use of LUTs.

Because of the high number of iterations of the inner loop, the total latency of the kernel is typically dominated by the computation of this loop. For INT8 LSTM and GRU, we account a minimal theoretical per-core latency of 9 (5 vect LD + 4 vect MAC) and 7 (4 vect LD + 3 vect MAC) clock cycles to compute 4×4 and 3×4 MAC operations, respectively. In case of FP16, the software kernel computes half of the MAC operations during the same period, if not considering the stalls occurring while accessing concurrently the shared floating-point units.

Note that the peak computation power scales linearly with number of compute cores, up to reach the memory bottleneck (see Eq. 1). In fact, as we increase the number of compute cores, the total bandwidth requirement for RNN computation exceeds the capacity of the target platform for both L3 and L2 memories. For instance, a FP16 LSTM layer processing on 8 cores demands for 8 (cores) $\times$ 5 (LD) $\times$ 2 (FP16 datatype) bytes every 9 cycles, which is much higher than the bandwidth from ExtFlash memory (1 byte/clk). In this case, using a lower datatype, e.g. 8-bit, results in faster computation for multiple reasons. Firstly, the memory bandwidth requirements of INT8 kernels is $2\times$ lower than FP16 ones. Secondly, the $2\times$ higher memory saving can lead the model parameters to entirely fit the on-chip non-volatile eMRAM memory. Lastly, a smaller tensor parameters can be promoted permanently to the L2 memory. On the other side, INT8 leads to a higher quantization error with respect to a full-precision model than FP16, potentially affecting the prediction quality of the full model. Our solution to this problem is discussed in the next section.

2.4   Mixed FP16-INT8 Post-training Quantization

TinyDenoiser models are quantized with Post-Training Quantization. We refer to the IEEE 754 standard for the FP16 format and quantization, i.e. a casting. On the other side, we follow [7] for INT8 symmetric quantization. According to this, every full-precision tensor x is approximated as an integer tensor X as:

$$X = \left\lfloor \frac{clamp(x, q_{min}, q_{max})}{S} \right\rceil, \qquad S = \frac{q_{max} - q_{min}}{2^n - 1} \qquad (2)$$

where n is the number of bits, S is the scale factor, which impacts the conversion resolution, and $[q_{min}, q_{max}]$ is the quantization range of an individual tensor. In particular, the PTQ routine estimates the quantization range of activation tensors (Eq. 2) by collecting the intermediate tensor statistics after feeding a trained model with a set of calibration samples. For the parameters, we refer to the min/max values.

Table 2. STOI and PESQ scores and memory footprint of the quantized TinyDenoiser models after Post-Training Quantization using FP16, INT8 or MixFP16-INT8 options.

Quant	Clamp FC	Clamp RNN	LSTM256			GRU256			LSTM128			GRU128		
			pesq	stoi	MB	pesq	stoi	MB	pesq	stoi	MB	pesq	stoi	MB
FP32			**2.78**	**0.942**	4.75	**2.78**	**0.942**	3.76	**2.76**	**0.941**	1.88	**2.69**	**0.940**	1.56
FP16			**2.78**	**0.942**	2.37	**2.78**	**0.942**	1.88	**2.76**	**0.941**	0.94	**2.69**	**0.940**	0.78
INT8	*max*	*max*	2.42	0.922	1.18	2.19	0.932	0.93	2.40	0.922	0.47	2.20	0.925	0.39
	std3	*std3*	2.35	0.885		2.17	0.902		2.51	0.911		2.12	0.892	
	std3	*max*	2.34	0.886		**2.48**	**0.929**		**2.51**	0.910		**2.36**	0.910	
MixFP16-INT8	*std3*	*max*	2.69	0.926	1.37	**2.72**	**0.940**	1.13	2.67	0.925	0.67	**2.63**	0.935	0.55
	max	*max*	**2.73**	**0.930**		2.56	0.941		**2.69**	**0.927**		2.49	**0.937**	

For RNN-based TinyDenoiser models, we observe a degraded quality, measured using objective metrics (see Sect. 3), if using a uniform 8-bit quantization on the whole model. On the contrary, the FP16 quantization works lossless. We hypothesize the INT8 accuracy drop to originate from unbounded tensor ranges, e.g. STFT input or ReLU output, which are clamped after quantization (Eq. 2) or causing a large scale factor S. Quantization error propagates also over time on RNN-based models. However, we noticed that both LSTM layers and GRU layers use constrained activation functions (`tanh` and `sigmoid`), i.e. output features maps features a numerical range limited by design, with the exception of the *LSTM C_state*. This motivates us *to quantize only the RNN layers, which demands the highest memory requirement of the whole model, to INT8 while leaving the rest to FP16*. We named this quantization as **Mixed-Precision FP16-INT8**, also referred in short as MixFP16-INT8. To this aim, we restrict the tensor statistic collection during PTQ to the input, states and output values of the RNN layers. In addition, two extra-layers, computationally inexpensive, are inserted in the inference graph for data type conversion purpose between FP16 and INT8 nodes and viceversa, according to Eq. 2.

3 Experimental Results

Before showing the effectiveness, in terms of memory, latency and energy gains, of our optimized design, we report the accuracy of the trained SE models after quantization. Lastly, we compare our approach with state-of-the-art solutions.

3.1 Accuracy After Mixed-Precision PTQ

We train the TinyDenoiser models on the Valentini dataset [13], which consists of clean and noisy speech audio clips from 28 speakers sampled at 16 kHz. The training environment is taken from [3]: the loss functions is a weighted combination of the L1 loss and the STFT loss and an ADAM optimizer is used with a learning rate of 3e−4. We use a batch size of 64 and set 200 epochs of training. At the end of the training procedure, we select the trained model with the highest score on a validation dataset composed by audio clips of speakers *p286* and *p287*, opportunely removed from the train set. For evaluation purpose, we refer to the PESQ and STOI objective metrics.

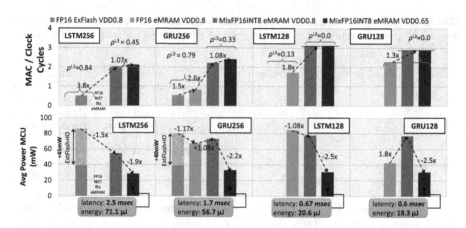

Fig. 4. (Top) Latency, measured in terms of MAC/cyc, and (Bottom) Power Consumption, in mW, of the TinyDenoiser models running on the target HW.

We implement the Post-Training Quantization procedure as a module of the GAP*flow* toolset[1]. The script imports a trained full-precision graph and quantizes it to FP16, INT8 or MixFP16-INT8, before generating the application code for deployment purpose. We use 4 randomly-chosen samples of the validation set (*p286_035*, *p286_166*, *p287_151*, *p287_269*) for the calibration of the quantization ranges. In particular, we consider either the maximum absolute values of the activation parameters x or $q_{max} = \text{mean}(x) + 3 \cdot \text{std\_dev}(x)$, that we denote as *max* and *std3* calibration settings, respectively. Additionally, we make use of a moving average filter in the estimation of the quantization ranges when feeding the models with multiple calibration samples as done in [7].

Table 2 reports the PESQ and STOI scores of the TinyDenoiser models on the Valentini test dataset after PTQ, together with the memory occupation (in MB) of the whole quantized parameters. The FP16 models are lossless with respect to FP32 trained models but gain 2× memory saving. On the contrary, despite the additional 2× memory compression factor, a uniform 8-bit quantization leads to a score degradation of, on average, 0.3 and 0.015 concerning the PESQ and the STOI metrics, respectively. We applied multiple combinations of *max* and *std3* quantization ranges to the RNN layers activations (Clamp RNN in the table) or the FC layers, including the input of the SE model. For INT8, we observed *max* quantization ranges to bring benefits to the RNN layer quantization, therefore we applied this setting also for MixFP16-INT8 quantization. On the contrary, we have not found any experimental evidence to select between *std3* or *max* on other layers. Overall, our proposed Mixed Precision FP16-INT8 PTQ recovers the accuracy degradation of INT8: on average, PESQ and STOI scores result to degrade of only 0.06 and 0.007, respectively. The effectiveness of the approach is also assessed by the 1.4–1.7× less memory to store the model parameters.

---

[1] https://greenwaves-technologies.com/tools-and-software/.

3.2   RNN-Based SE Inference Performance on a Multi-core MCU

We analyze the effectiveness of the proposed software pipeline (Sect. 2.3) and the novel quantization strategy by measuring the TinyDenoiser inference latency and energy consumption on a 22 nm prototype of the target architecture (Sect. 2.2). The chip prototype can be powered at 0.8 V or 0.65 V with a maximum clock frequency of 370 MHz and 240 MHz, respectively. More in details, we deploy *LSTM256*, *GRU256*, *LSTM128*, *GRU128* models after *FP16* and *MixFP16-INT8* quantization. If exceeding 2 MB of storage requirement for model parameters, we make use of an external FLASH memory while, on the contrary, the on-chip eMRAM memory can be used. This latter features a peak BW of 640 MB/s, independently of the voltage supply.

Figure 4 reports on the top the measured inference latencies, expressed in terms MAC/cyc, and the MCU power consumption (in mW) on the bottom. In case of FP16 *LSTM256* and *GRU256* models, the ratio of parameters stored in the L3 memory over the total amount of parameters, denoted as ρ^{L3}, achieves 0.84 and 0.79, thanks to the tensor promotion mechanism. However, the execution is L3 memory-bounded in this scenario. In accordance to the model of Eq. 1, the read time of a FP16 parameter from the ExtFlash takes 2 clock cycles that explains a latency close to 0.5MAC/cyc (every MAC requires one parameter to be loaded). Because of the activity of the external memory, an extra average power cost of 40–45 mW is measured, corresponding to ~50% of the total power.

While FP16 LSTM256 cannot fit the on-chip non-volatile memory, the FP16 GRU256 can cut the extra power cost by storing the FP16 parameters into the eMRAM. The MCU power consumption increases because of the on-chip memory utilization, which was OFF before, and the higher density of operations (higher MAC/cyc) due to the higher eMRAM memory BW than the ExtFlash.

If leveraging MixFP16-INT8 for LSTM256 and GRU256, the ratio ρ^{L3} decreases to 0.45 and 0.33, meaning more tensors are promoted to L2 in contrast to FP16 quantization. Thanks to this and the faster INT8 kernels, the computation efficiency increases up to 1.9 and 2.2 MAC/cyc (one of the two RNN layer is still L3 memory-bound). At the same time, the power cost of the MCU increases because of the higher operation density. Lastly, we obtain a power saving of ~2× by reducing the power supply to 0.65 V. Also note the MAC/cyc improves by up to 8% because the eMRAM bandwidth is independent from the system clock frequency, bringing benefits to the memory-bounded layers.

On the other side, FP16 *LSTM128* and *GRU128* fits the eMRAM memory capacity and show a ρ^{L3} ratio as low as 0.13 and 0.0, meaning that the majority or all the memory parameters are promoted to the L2 memory before the inference. This explains the high FP16 latency efficiency, reaching up to 2.2 MAC/cyc. The MixFP16-INT8 quantization further decreases latency by 1.8× and 1.3×. In case of $LSTM128$ the power consumption of MixFP16-INT8 slightly decreases with respect to FP16 because eMRAM is not used, while $GRU128$ presents a 1.8× higher power, in line with other settings. Scaling down the supply voltage do not contribute to a higher MAC/cyc metric because of the low (or null) L3 memory utilization, while the power consumption is reduced by 2.5×.

Table 3. Comparison with other SE solutions for MCUs.

Model	Mpar	Quant	QAT	Device	Deployment	msec/inf	MAC/cyc	MMAC/W
TinyLSTM [4]	0.33	INT8	Yes	STM32F746VE	N/A	4.26	0.36	0.14
TinyLSTM [4]	0.46					2.39		
RNNoise [9]	0.21	INT8	Yes	STM32L476	NNoM w/CMSIS-NN	3.28	0.45	1.84
LSTM256 [ours]	1.24	MixFP16-INT8	No	8-core RISC-V	GAPFlow	2.50	**2.11**	**17.78**
GRU156 [ours]	0.98					1.70	**2.41**	**17.46**

Figure 4 also reports on the bottom the latency and the energy measures for the inference tasks in the most energy efficient configuration. Even if reducing the clock frequency, the real-time constraints (6.25 ms) are matched. When considering a duty cycled operation with a sleep power much lower than the active power, the average power reduces up to 3 mW for the smallest model.

3.3   Comparison with Other Works

Table 3 compares our solution with state-of-the-art SE solutions on MCUs: TinyLSTM [4], which is benchmarked on a STM32F7 MCU, and RNNoise [14] deployed on a low-power STM32L4 using the NNoM software with CMSIS-NN backend [9]. Both solutions leverage on single-core devices and 8-bit quantization, which results effective thanks to QAT and the model design constraint of using intermediate activation features with limited numerical ranges. Despite our solution being more subject to memory bottleneck issues because of 2.6–6× more parameters and the higher bit precision, we achieve a top latency efficiency, up to 5.3× and 6.7× MAC/cyc higher than RNNoise and TinyLSTM, respectively. This acceleration is obtained thanks to the optimized software pipeline that efficiently exploit the underlying hardware. Additionally, the energy efficiency results up to 9.7× and 123× higher than previous solutions. We also remark that our solution achieves low-degradation with respect to full-precision model without relying on any expensive QAT training procedures.

4   Conclusion

This work proposed a novel design approach to efficiently bring RNN-based SE models on low-power multi-core MCUs. On the one side, we proposed a novel quantization scheme that mixes FP16 and INT8 PTQ to obtain low-accuracy degradation without relying on expensive QAT. On the other side, we designed an optimized software pipeline to efficiently exploit the compute performance of low-power 8-core MCU. Our design demonstrated the fastest RNN-based SE solution for MCUs, featuring > 10× energy-efficiency than previous solutions.

References

1. Boll, S.: Suppression of acoustic noise in speech using spectral subtraction. IEEE Trans. Acoust. Speech Sig. Process. **27**(2), 113–120 (1979)

2. Cohen, I., Berdugo, B.: Speech enhancement for non-stationary noise environments. Sig. Process. **81**(11), 2403–2418 (2001)
3. Defossez, A., Synnaeve, G., Adi, Y.: Real time speech enhancement in the waveform domain. In: Interspeech (2020)
4. Fedorov, I., et al.: TinyLSTMs: efficient neural speech enhancement for hearing aids (2020)
5. Gholami, A., Kim, S., Dong, Z., Yao, Z., Mahoney, M.W., Keutzer, K.: A survey of quantization methods for efficient neural network inference. arXiv preprint arXiv:2103.13630 (2021)
6. Hu, Y., et al.: DCCRN: deep complex convolution recurrent network for phase-aware speech enhancement (2020)
7. Jacob, B., et al.: Quantization and training of neural networks for efficient integer-arithmetic-only inference. In: Proceedings of the IEEE Conference on Computer Vision and Pattern Recognition, pp. 2704–2713 (2018)
8. Liu, J., Zhang, X.: DRC-NET: densely connected recurrent convolutional neural network for speech dereverberation. In: International Conference on Acoustics, Speech and Signal Processing, pp. 166–170. IEEE (2022)
9. Ma, J.: A higher-level Neural Network library on Microcontrollers (NNoM), October 2020. https://doi.org/10.5281/zenodo.4158710
10. Reddy, C.K., Beyrami, E., Pool, J., Cutler, R., Srinivasan, S., Gehrke, J.: A scalable noisy speech dataset and online subjective test framework. In: Proceedings of Interspeech 2019, pp. 1816–1820 (2019)
11. Reddy, C.K., et al.: Interspeech 2021 deep noise suppression challenge. arXiv preprint arXiv:2101.01902 (2021)
12. Stamenovic, M., Westhausen, N.L., Yang, L.C., Jensen, C., Pawlicki, A.: Weight, block or unit? Exploring sparsity tradeoffs for speech enhancement on tiny neural accelerators. arXiv preprint arXiv:2111.02351 (2021)
13. Valentini-Botinhao, C., et al.: Noisy speech database for training speech enhancement algorithms and TTS models (2017)
14. Valin, J.M.: A hybrid DSP/deep learning approach to real-time full-band speech enhancement. In: 2018 IEEE 20th International Workshop on Multimedia Signal Processing (MMSP), pp. 1–5. IEEE (2018)
15. Valin, J.M., Isik, U., Phansalkar, N., Giri, R., Helwani, K., Krishnaswamy, A.: A perceptually-motivated approach for low-complexity, real-time enhancement of fullband speech (2020)
16. Xia, Y., Braun, S., Reddy, C.K., Dubey, H., Cutler, R., Tashev, I.: Weighted speech distortion losses for neural-network-based real-time speech enhancement. In: International Conference on Acoustics, Speech and Signal Processing (ICASSP), pp. 871–875. IEEE (2020)

LDRNet: Enabling Real-Time Document Localization on Mobile Devices

Han Wu[1], Holland Qian[2], Huaming Wu[3(✉)], and Aad van Moorsel[4]

[1] Newcastle University, Newcastle upon Tyne, UK
han.wu@ncl.ac.uk
[2] Tencent, Shenzhen, China
[3] Tianjin University, Tianjin, China
whming@tju.edu.cn
[4] University of Birmingham, Birmingham, UK
aad.vanmoorsel@ncl.ac.uk, a.vanmoorsel@bham.ac.uk

Abstract. Modern online services often require mobile devices to convert paper-based information into its digital counterpart, e.g., passport, ownership documents, etc. This process relies on Document Localization (DL) technology to detect the outline of a document within a photograph. In recent years, increased demand for real-time DL in live video has emerged, especially in financial services. However, existing machine-learning approaches to DL cannot be easily applied due to the large size of the underlying models and the associated long inference time. In this paper, we propose a lightweight DL model, LDRNet, to localize documents in real-time video captured on mobile devices. On the basis of a lightweight backbone neural network, we design three prediction branches for LDRNet: (1) corner points prediction; (2) line borders prediction and (3) document classification. To improve the accuracy, we design novel supplementary targets, the equal-division points, and use a new loss function named Line Loss. We compare the performance of LDRNet with other popular approaches on localization for general documents in a number of datasets. The experimental results show that LDRNet takes significantly less inference time, while still achieving comparable accuracy.

Keywords: Document localization · Real time · Mobile devices

1 Introduction

The integration of paper documents and digital information is an essential procedure in many online services today. An increasing number of users start to use mobile devices (i.e., smartphones) to take photos of the paper documents. The preliminary step to extract digital information from those photos is Document Localization (DL) [3]. DL is a machine learning technology that focuses

---

H. Wu and H. Qian—Equal contribution.

I. Koprinska et al. (Eds.): ECML PKDD 2022 Workshops, CCIS 1752, pp. 618–629, 2023.
https://doi.org/10.1007/978-3-031-23618-1_42

on detecting and segmenting document outlines within image frames. The input is usually a digital photo containing the paper document and the outputs are the predicted quadrilateral (i.e., four-sided polygon) coordinates of the document outline. Accurate DL is crucial for the follow-up process such as Optical Character Recognition (OCR).

In most online services that use DL, photos captured by mobile devices are uploaded to servers for DL processing. Recently, some service providers, for safety purposes, have started to demand users to capture a video of the paper document instead of a static photo [7]. This is because a video is naturally more difficult to counterfeit than a static photo. One concrete example is illustrated in Fig. 1, where the user uses its smartphone to record a video of the identity document. During the video recording, the mobile application (developed by the service provider) requests the user to move the document properly to fit the guidance displayed on the screen (the white borders in the figures). In the previous design using a static photo, an impostor can cheat the system with a scanned copy of the document. However, in this scheme with a live video it needs to hold the actual document to finish the process. Furthermore, the laser security marks on identity documents change dynamically in the recorded video depending on the light environment and camera angle, which provides more comprehensive materials for the verification process.

(1) guidance displayed   (2) user performs action   (3) action approved

Fig. 1. An example of document localization based on video.

The premise to achieve the above video-based process is that the document outline and trajectory can be tracked in real-time during the video recording. A video is actually a series of images, called frames, that are captured at certain frequency, e.g., 30 Frames Per Second (FPS). Thus DL performed on a video can be understood as a series of DL tasks, where each task is performed on one frame. Therefore, real-time DL on a live video means the DL process on each frame needs to be finished within the time interval between two consecutive frames (e.g., 33.3 ms for a 30 FPS video). However, existing DL approaches cannot fulfill these real-time demands due to the long inference time (e.g., over 100 ms even on a PC according to [10]). Furthermore, state-of-the-art DL models are complex and require large storage space, which potentially exhausts the capacity of mobile devices [3,12].

To break through this bottleneck we propose a novel document localization neural network, **LDRNet**, to **L**ocalize **D**ocument in **R**eal-time. Previous works dive into the design of the new network architectures to improve the accuracy, which is time-consuming and diminishes the efficiency. We start from a lightweight Convolutional Neural Network (CNN), MobilenetV2 [15], which is a fundamental feature extractor especially designed for devices with limited memory and resources. Unlike feature pyramid networks [14], we design a feature fusion module that does not enlarge the model size. Existing DL approaches require postprocessing after prediction, which is cumbersome and inefficient. Therefore we design our prediction target to be the coordinates of the quadrilateral corners instead of the contour of the document thus avoiding postprocessing. The orientation of the document also can be obtained from the order of the output coordinates. We propose a novel loss function, Line Loss, to improve the precision. By adding equal-division points between contiguous corner points, LDRNet achieves better formalization of the borderlines.

In summary, the main contributions of this paper include:

- We present LDRNet, a document localization approach with significantly lower computational cost than the state-of-the-art methods. LDRNet paves the way for real-time DL on a live video recorded by mobile devices.
- We design the Line Loss function and equal-division points feature for LDR-Net to guarantee the localization accuracy without undermining its efficiency or enlarging its model size.
- In the experiments, we compare the performance of LDRNet with other popular DL approaches on localizing general document datasets. The results indicate that LDRNet achieves comparable accuracy while outperforming other approaches in terms of efficiency.

2 Related Work

There exist three main kinds of approaches for DL: Mathematical Morphology-based Methods, Segmentation-based Methods and Keypoint-like Methods. Mathematical morphology-based methods are based on mathematical morphology [2]. There are some other hand-designed features used in mathematical morphology-based methods, like the tree-based representation [4]. Along with the popularity of CNN in this field, many CNN-based methods have emerged. Segmentation-based methods regard DL as the segmentation [16] task using the CNN to extract the features. Same as segmentation-based methods, using the features extracted by the CNN, keypoint-like methods [10] predict the four corners of the document directly, considering DL as the keypoint detection task.

Mathematical Morphology-based Methods inherit the ideas which detect the contour of the documents using traditional image processing methods, image gradients calculations [2], Canny border detectors, Line Segment detectors [17] and image contours detectors, etc. Although there are many kinds of different mathematical morphology-based approaches, they are all developed on the basis of the technologies mentioned above, which makes the performance unstable when the datasets change. The accuracy of these methods heavily depends on the environmental conditions in the image. For instance, if the color of the background and the document are difficult to distinguish, or if the image is captured with insufficient lighting, the borders of the document may not be detected. Another weakness of these mathematical morphology-based methods is that they output the four borders or four points disorderly so a necessary step for determining the orientation of the document is the postprocessing, which leads to extra cost.

Segmentation-based Methods regard DL as a segmentation task. Segmentation adapts dense predictions, outputs the heat map for every pixel on the image, and uses classification labels to determine whether the pixels belong to the object or the background. Then by grouping the pixels with the same labels, the document is segmented. By adopting the CNNs to extract the image feature, the segmentors get rid of the impacts from the complex environment conditions. Since every segmentor is a data-driven deep-learning model, it can reach high precision as long as enough data are fed. U-Net [14] and DeepLab [5] are the popular segmentors. However, the large model size and long inference time make these segmentors incompetent for real-time DL. Similar to the mathematical morphology-based methods, postprocessing is inevitable to find the orientation of the document content.

Keypoint-like Methods output the coordinates of the quadrilateral corner points of the document directly. Recent keypoint detection networks do not regress the coordinates of the key points, instead, they produce dense predictions like segmentation networks do. [13] predict heat maps of the keypoints and offsets. [10] predict the points in a sparse-prediction way to locate the four points directly. To improve the precision, it uses CNN recursively to fix the coordinates errors. These key-point models indeed get high precision, but also have the same weakness which segmentation-based methods have, the large model size and the long inference time.

3   Context and Methodology

3.1   Problems and Challenges

In previous online services, DL task is performed on the server while the mobile device only captures and uploads the photo of the document. This structure can not fulfil the real-time DL task on a video due to the transmission cost. Therefore we aim to embed DL module on mobile devices in our work. Tracking the document outline and trajectory in a live video means the DL process for each frame should be completed within the frame interval (33.3 ms for a 30 FPS video). This calls for strict demands on both the accuracy and speed of DL model.

Specifically, the challenges of this study come from four facets: (i) The computational resource on mobile devices is very limited while existing DL approaches require large memory and long inference time. (ii) In addition to the contour of the document, the direction of the content should also be detected to determine the trajectory of the document in a video. (iii) It is complex and time-consuming to calculate the precise angle between the document and the camera to obtain the trajectory. (iv) During the video recording, the corner points of the document may be occluded by the user's fingers, therefore the ability to predict occluded corner points is necessary.

3.2 Task Analysis

To address the challenges listed above, we present a novel neural network model, LDRNet, to Localize Documents in Real-time. Instead of calculating the precise angle between the document and camera, we calculate the distance between each target corner point and the corresponding localized point to track the trajectory of the document. This provides considerable accuracy while consuming less computational resources on mobile devices. As summarized by the following equation, (x_{doc}^i, y_{doc}^i) is the coordinate of the ith corner point of the localized document, while $(x_{target}^i, y_{target}^i)$ represents the coordinate of the ith target corner point. Then we sum the Euclidean distances of the four sets of corresponding points.

$$Distance = \sum_{i=1}^{4} \sqrt{(x_{doc}^i - x_{target}^i)^2 + (y_{doc}^i - y_{target}^i)^2}. \qquad (1)$$

The orientation of the document can be simply inferred from the order of the corner points. Thus our goal is to predict the four quadrilateral coordinates of the document in counter-clockwise order. The order of the four quadrilateral points is determined by the contents of the document instead of the direction that the document is placed. Throughout this paper, we use N to denote the total number of points we predict for each document. In addition to the four corner points, we predict $(N - 4)/4$ equal-division points on each border of the document. These extra $N - 4$ points are used to refine the localization of the document. Moreover, we add a classification head to our network architecture for classifying the document in the input images. Depending on the specific DL task, this classification head is adjustable. The minimum number of classes is two, which represents whether the image contains a document or not, respectively.

3.3 Network Architecture

Fully Convolutional Feature Extractor. As we aim to run DL on mobile devices, we choose a lightweight backbone network, MobilenetV2 [15]. It applies both depth-wise convolution and point-wise convolution operations to achieve faster and lighter extraction. As illustrated in Fig. 2, the last output feature map from the backbone is $F_b \in R^{\frac{H}{32} \times \frac{W}{32} \times 1280}$ with H denoting the height of the input image and W denoting the width. To improve the accuracy, we extract five feature maps with different spatial resolutions from the backbone.

Feature Fusion Module. The low and high-level feature maps are fused together by the feature fusion module. The first step is feature compression, where we use global average pooling to downsample the feature maps, and resize them to the same size. Then we add the five feature maps directly instead of the top-down architecture used in [11].

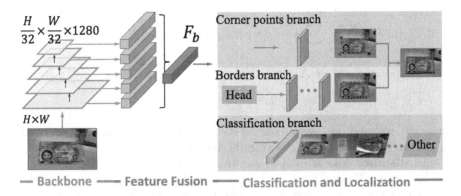

Fig. 2. The network architecture of LDRNet.

Network Output Branches. The outputs of the LDRNet consist of three branches. The first branch is the corner points branch. It outputs in the form of a 4×2 vector, four corners' coordinates (x, y) in order. The second branch is the borders branch, it outputs in the form of an $(N - 4) \times 2$ vector, where $(N - 4)$ is the number of points to be predicted on the four borders. Each border has $(N - 4)/4$ points so there are $N - 4$ coordinates of points in total on the second branch. The third branch outputs the classification label, denoting the type of document in the input image. Unless the size of the classification output is specified, the classification output contains two elements, one denoting the likelihood of having documents in the image, the other one denoting the likelihood that no document is detected in the input image.

Line Loss. Standard Deep Convolutional Neural Network architectures are inherently poor at precise localization and segmentation tasks [9]. This is because the last convolutional layer only contains high-level features of the whole image. While these features are extremely useful for classification and bounding box detection, they lack the information for pixel-level segmentation [10]. In order to improve the precision of DL, we combine the two branches of the LDRNet's outputs (corner points branch and borders branch), we predict the corners in a line-prediction fashion. In addition to the four corner points, we also predict the equal-division points on the lines thus the labels can be generated automatically and no more human effort is required. The proposed **Line Loss** is formulated as $L_{line}(p) = \beta L_{Sim}(p) + \gamma L_{Dis}(p)$, which is a weighted sum of the similarity loss L_{Sim} and the distance loss L_{Dis}. The similarity loss is used to restrict the points from the same border along an identical line, while the distance loss is used to guarantee that along this line the points are equally divided.

To guarantee that the predicted points from each border are on a straight line, we use the **similarity loss** L_{Sim} to calculate the similarity of two vectors of the three successive points on the line. The details of L_{Sim} are shown in Eq. (2), (3), (4).

$$L_{Sim}(p) = [\sum_{k \in l,r,t,b} \sum_{i=0}^{\frac{N}{4}-3} sim(p[k]_i, p[k]_{i+1}, p[k]_{i+2})]/(N-4), \tag{2}$$

$$sim(p[k]_i, p[k]_{i+1}, p[k]_{i+2}) = (\overrightarrow{p[k]}_i^{i+1} \cdot \overrightarrow{p[k]}_{i+1}^{i+2})/(\left|\overrightarrow{p[k]}_i^{i+1}\right| \times \left|\overrightarrow{p[k]}_{i+1}^{i+2}\right|), \tag{3}$$

$$\overrightarrow{p[k]}_i^{i+1} = (p[k]_i^x - p[k]_{i+1}^x, p[k]_i^y - p[k]_{i+1}^y). \tag{4}$$

where $p[l]$, $p[r]$, $p[t]$, $p[b]$ denote the points on the left border, on the right border, on the top border and on the bottom border, respectively.

The **distance loss** is used to constrain the points we predict to be equal-division points. We use Eqs. (5) and (6) to make sure the successive points of each border have the same distance in both x-direction and y-direction.

$$L_{Dis}(p) = [\sum_{k \in l,r,t,d} \sum_{i=0}^{\frac{N}{4}-1} dist(p[k]_i, p[k]_{i+1}, p[k]_{i+2})]/(N-4), \tag{5}$$

$$dist(p[k]_i, p[k]_{i+1}, p[k]_{i+2}) = \left||p[k]_i^x - p[k]_{i+1}^x| - |p[k]_{i+1}^x - p[k]_{i+2}^x|\right| + \left||p[k]_i^y - p[k]_{i+1}^y| - |p[k]_{i+1}^y - p[k]_{i+2}^y|\right|. \tag{6}$$

Furthermore, we use L2 loss for the regression and cross-entropy for the classification. The **regression loss** L_{Reg} is an L2 loss between the predicted points p and the ground truth points g, which can be formulated as:

$$L_{Reg}(p,g) = \frac{1}{N-4} \sum_{i=0}^{N} \sum_{j \in x,y} \sqrt[2]{(\hat{g}_i^j - p_i^j)^2}, \quad (\hat{g}^x = g^x/W, \hat{g}^y = g^y/H). \tag{7}$$

where (g_i^x, g_i^y) denotes the i-th ground truth point of the document. Our regression target is $\hat{g}$, which is the normalization of g by image width (W) in x-coordinate and image height (H) in y-coordinate.

The **classification loss** L_{Cls} is soft-max loss over multiple classes confidences (x), which is calculated as:

$$L_{Cls}(x,c) = \sum_{i=0}^{N_{cls}} -c_i \log \hat{x}_i, \qquad (\hat{x}_i = \frac{\exp(x_i)}{\sum_j \exp(x_j)}). \tag{8}$$

where $c_i \in \{0,1\}$ is an indicator denoting whether the image contains the i-th category document and N_{cls} is the number of the total document categories.

Finally, we define the total loss as the weighted sum of the regression loss L_{Reg}, the classification loss L_{Cls} and the Line Loss L_{Line}:

$$L(x,c,p,g) = L_{Reg}(p,g) + \delta L_{Cls}(x,c) + L_{line}(p). \tag{9}$$

where the weights δ, β and γ are chosen depending on the experimental results, and the values normally range from 0 to 1.

4   Experimental Evaluation

For the comparison experiment, we use the dataset from 'ICDAR 2015 Smart-Doc Challenge 1' [3]. Training and inference setting details are listed in this section. The experimental results are compared to the previous work to show the advantages of our approach. Then we use the ablation study to analyze the contribution of each component of our model. Finally, we test our model on the MIDV-2019 dataset [1] to highlight the characteristic of our model, the ability to predict occluded corner points.

4.1   Training and Inference Details

Unless specified, we use MobilenetV2 with the width multiplier α equal to 0.35 (used to control the width of the network) as our backbone network. We set the number of regression points (N) to 100. Our network is trained with RMSprop optimizer, which uses only one set of hyperparameters (rho is set to 0.9, momentum is set to 0, and epsilon is set to 1e−7). We trained our networks for 1000 epochs, with an initial learning rate of 0.001 and a batch size of 128 images. The learning rate is reduced in a piecewise constant decay way, and is set as 0.0001, 0.00005, 0.00001 at the 250th, 700th and 850 epochs, respectively. Our backbone network weights are initialized with the weights pretrained on ImageNet [6]. We use the Xavier initializer [8] as the final dense layer. The input images are resized to which both the width and the height are 224 pixels. Regarding the Line Loss function parameters, δ is set to 0.32, β and γ are configured as 0.0032.

For the inference, we first forward the input image through the network to obtain the quadrilateral points' coordinates of the documents and the predicted class. Then we multiply the quadrilateral points' coordinates by the width (W) and height (H) of the input image. Note that we only use four quadrilateral points' coordinates instead of the predicted N coordinates, because we found little difference between their performance. Thus we can remove the weights of the final dense layer that are not used for the four quadrilateral coordinates. The size of the input image is the same as we used for training.

4.2   Comparison of Accuracy

To evaluate the accuracy of our DL model, we use the Jaccard Index (JI), which is also adopted in others' work [3,10,12]. First we remove the perspective transform of the ground-truth G and the predicted results S, then obtain the corrected quadrilaterals S' and G'. For each frame f, the JI is computed as $JI(f) = area(G' \cap S')/area(G' \cup S')$. The value of JI range from 0 to 1 and higher JI indicates higher accuracy.

As shown in Table 1, the images in the dataset can be divided into five categories according to different backgrounds. Only backgound05 is complex, with strong occlusions. We compare the accuracy of LDRNet to seven previous DL models. It is observed that our LDRNet outperforms the previous works in terms of background02 and background05 (results in bold). For other backgrounds,

Table 1. Accuracy compared with previous works. The results are listed from top to bottom in the descending order of overall JI.

Method	Background					Overall
	01	02	03	04	05	
HU-PageScan [12]	/	/	/	/	/	**0.9923**
LDRNet-1.4 (ours)	0.9877	**0.9838**	0.9862	0.9802	**0.9858**	0.9849
SEECS-NUST-2 [10]	0.9832	0.9724	0.9830	0.9695	0.9478	0.9743
LRDE [3]	0.9869	0.9775	0.9889	**0.9837**	0.8613	0.9716
SmartEngines [3]	**0.9885**	0.9833	**0.9897**	0.9785	0.6884	0.9548
NetEase [3]	0.9624	0.9552	0.9621	0.9511	0.2218	0.8820
RPPDI-UPE [3]	0.8274	0.9104	0.9697	0.3649	0.2163	0.7408
SEECS-NUST [3]	0.8875	0.8264	0.7832	0.7811	0.0113	0.7393

LDRNet reaches comparable performance with the best ones. The overall JI of LDRNet exceeds the other methods except for HU-PageScan in [12], which does not provide the results of background01 to background05. However, HU-PageScan uses 8,873,889 trainable parameters which is over 21 times the number of parameters in our LDRNet-0.35 (denotes LDRNet with $\alpha = 0.35$). Therefore HU-PageScan requires significant memory and computing time thus can not fulfill the real-time demand. This will be introduced in the next section. Additionally, since HU-PageScan is segmentation-based, it only predicts the contour of the document. Thus the orientation of the document is unknown and requires follow-up process to calculate the document trajectory.

4.3   Comparison of Inference Time

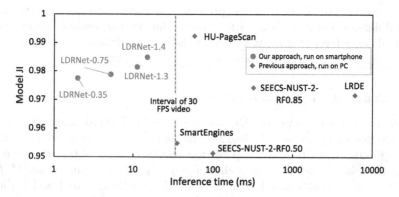

Fig. 3. The inference time comparison between LDRNet and the previous DL methods on the 'ICDAR 2015 SmartDoc Challenge 1' dataset. The horizontal axis is log scaled.

Our Network is tested on iPhone11 using TNN engine. HU-PageScan is tested on a PC equipped with Intel Core i7 8700 processor, 8 GB RAM, and 6 GB

NVIDIA GTX 1060 [12]. In Fig. 3, the vertical axis is the JI of the model while the horizontal axis is the log scaled inference time. We illustrate the result of four settings of LDRNet, all using MobilenetV2 but with different values of α (0.1, 0.35, 0.75, 1.3, 1.4). We observe that higher α leads to higher JI but longer inference time. The JI of HU-PageScan (run on a PC) is 0.0074 (absolute value) higher than LDRNet-1.4 (run on smartphone), whereas the inference time is about 4x longer. The short inference time of LDRNet meets the demand for localizing documents in the image frames in a live video (usually photographed at 30 FPS, represented by the dashed vertical line in Fig. 3). For general usage, LDRNet-1.4 is the best option and its model size is only 10 MB.

4.4   Ablation Study

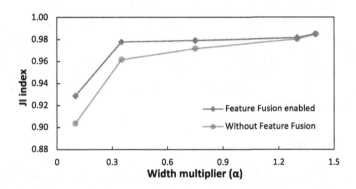

Fig. 4. The JI of LDRNet with different α and with or without feature fusion module. The number of regression points is set to 100. All are trained with Line Loss.

In our experiments using LDRNet, we construct the feature fusion module using *average pooling* and *add* operation. To evaluate the efficiency of this feature fusion module, we run experiments with this module enabled and disabled. Figure 4 compares the JI of these two scenarios with α ranging from 0.1 to 1.4. We can observe that the feature fusion-enabled models outperform those without feature fusion. Since the model complexity grows as we increase α, it is observed that the efficiency of our feature fusion module drops as the model becomes more complex. Thus in the cases that $\alpha > 1.0$, feature fusion is not recommended.

We also evaluate the efficiency of the Line Loss by comparing the JI of models with and without Line Loss. For LDRNet-0.35, enabling Line Loss improves the JI from 0.9643 to 0.9776.

4.5   Predictions of the Occluded Points

Benefiting from the task analysis and the network architecture, LDRNet is able to predict the occluded points, including the points occluded by other objects and the points out of the input image. This characteristic is crucial for video

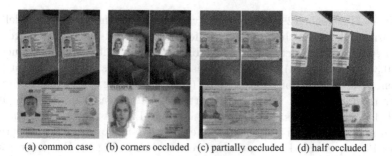

(a) common case   (b) corners occluded   (c) partially occluded   (d) half occluded

Fig. 5. Examples of occluded points prediction. Each case contains three images, namely, the input image (top left), the predicted corners on the input image (top right), the localized document after removing the perspective transformation (bottom).

recording since the document is usually occluded by the user's fingers during the interaction. For evaluation we test our model on the MIDV-2019 dataset, which contains video clips of identity documents captured by smartphones in low light conditions and with higher projective distortions [1]. As depicted in Fig. 5(b), LDRNet can predict the corner occluded by fingers. Even if more than half of the passport is out of the image, as illustrated in Fig. 5(d), our LDRNet predicts the occluded corners correctly.

5   Conclusion

We design LDRNet, a real-time document localization model for mobile devices. LDRNet extracts the image features using neural networks and predicts the coordinates of quadrilateral points directly. We propose the novel loss function, Line Loss, and design the equal-division points feature to guarantee its efficiency and accuracy. The most practical scenario of LDRNet is tracking the trajectory of document in a live video captured on mobile devices. The experimental results show that LDRNet has lower inference time than other methods, while achieving comparable accuracy. Currently, LDRNet is being deployed in the identity verification system of a company that serves about 3.8 million customers. The code is available at: https://github.com/niuwagege/LDRNet. In future work, we will finetune the hyper-parameters more precisely, use low-level and high-level image features fusions like FPN, or a larger backbone, etc.

References

1. Bulatov, K., Matalov, D., Arlazarov, V.V.: MIDV-2019: challenges of the modern mobile-based document OCR. In: Twelfth International Conference on Machine Vision (ICMV 2019), vol. 11433, p. 114332N. International Society for Optics and Photonics (2020)
2. Bulatov, K.B.: A method to reduce errors of string recognition based on combination of several recognition results with per-character alternatives. Bull. South Ural State Univ. **12**(3), 74–88 (2019). Series: Mathematical Modeling and Programming

3. Burie, J.C., et al.: ICDAR 2015 competition on smartphone document capture and OCR (SmartDoc). In: 2015 13th International Conference on Document Analysis and Recognition (ICDAR), pp. 1161–1165. IEEE (2015)

4. Carlinet, E., Géraud, T.: MToS: a tree of shapes for multivariate images. IEEE Trans. Image Process. **24**(12), 5330–5342 (2015)

5. Chen, L.C., Papandreou, G., Kokkinos, I., Murphy, K., Yuille, A.L.: DeepLab: semantic image segmentation with deep convolutional nets, atrous convolution, and fully connected CRFs. IEEE Trans. Pattern Anal. Mach. Intell. **40**(4), 834–848 (2017)

6. Deng, J., Dong, W., Socher, R., Li, L.J., Li, K., Fei-Fei, L.: ImageNet: a large-scale hierarchical image database. In: 2009 IEEE Conference on Computer Vision and Pattern Recognition, pp. 248–255. IEEE (2009)

7. Electronic IDentification: Why is video identification more secure than face-to-face? (2021). https://www.electronicid.eu/en/blog/post/video-identification-vid-secure-face-face-identification/en. Accessed 20 June 2022

8. Glorot, X., Bengio, Y.: Understanding the difficulty of training deep feedforward neural networks. In: Proceedings of the Thirteenth International Conference on Artificial Intelligence and Statistics. JMLR Workshop and Conference Proceedings, pp. 249–256 (2010)

9. Hariharan, B., Arbeláez, P., Girshick, R., Malik, J.: Hypercolumns for object segmentation and fine-grained localization. In: Proceedings of the IEEE Conference on Computer Vision and Pattern Recognition, pp. 447–456 (2015)

10. Javed, K., Shafait, F.: Real-time document localization in natural images by recursive application of a CNN. In: 2017 14th IAPR International Conference on Document Analysis and Recognition (ICDAR), vol. 1, pp. 105–110. IEEE (2017)

11. Lin, T.Y., Dollár, P., Girshick, R., He, K., Hariharan, B., Belongie, S.: Feature pyramid networks for object detection. In: Proceedings of the IEEE Conference on Computer Vision and Pattern Recognition, pp. 2117–2125 (2017)

12. das Neves Junior, R.B., Lima, E., Bezerra, B.L., Zanchettin, C., Toselli, A.H.: HU-PageScan: a fully convolutional neural network for document page crop. IET Image Process. **14**(15), 3890–3898 (2020)

13. Papandreou, G., et al.: Towards accurate multi-person pose estimation in the wild. In: Proceedings of the IEEE Conference on Computer Vision and Pattern Recognition, pp. 4903–4911 (2017)

14. Ronneberger, O., Fischer, P., Brox, T.: U-Net: convolutional networks for biomedical image segmentation. In: Navab, N., Hornegger, J., Wells, W.M., Frangi, A.F. (eds.) MICCAI 2015. LNCS, vol. 9351, pp. 234–241. Springer, Cham (2015). https://doi.org/10.1007/978-3-319-24574-4_28

15. Sandler, M., Howard, A., Zhu, M., Zhmoginov, A., Chen, L.C.: MobileNetV2: inverted residuals and linear bottlenecks. In: Proceedings of the IEEE Conference on Computer Vision and Pattern Recognition, pp. 4510–4520 (2018)

16. Tian, Z., He, T., Shen, C., Yan, Y.: Decoders matter for semantic segmentation: data-dependent decoding enables flexible feature aggregation. In: Proceedings of the IEEE/CVF Conference on Computer Vision and Pattern Recognition, pp. 3126–3135 (2019)

17. Von Gioi, R.G., Jakubowicz, J., Morel, J.M., Randall, G.: LSD: a fast line segment detector with a false detection control. IEEE Trans. Pattern Anal. Mach. Intell. **32**(4), 722–732 (2008)

Author Index

Printed in the United States
by Baker & Taylor Publisher Services